THE RULE OF LAW

Law and Philosophy Library

VOLUME 80

The Rule of Law History, Theory and Criticism

Edited by

PIETRO COSTA
University of Florence, Italy

DANILO ZOLO
University of Florence, Italy

With the cooperation of Emilio Santoro

A C.I.P. Catalogue record for this book is available from the Library of Congress.

ISBN 978-1-4020-5744-1 (HB)
ISBN 978-1-4020-5745-8 (e-book)

Published by Springer,
P.O. Box 17, 3300 AA Dordrecht, The Netherlands.

www.springer.com

Printed on acid-free paper

TABLE OF CONTENTS

Preface ix
Pietro Costa and Danilo Zolo

Part I INTRODUCTORY ESSAYS

1 The Rule of Law: A Critical Reappraisal 3
Danilo Zolo

2 The Rule of Law: A Historical Introduction 73
Pietro Costa

Part II THE RULE OF LAW IN EUROPE AND THE UNITED STATES

3 The Rule of Law and the "Liberties of the English": The Interpretation of Albert Venn Dicey 153
Emilio Santoro

4 Popular Sovereignty, the Rule of Law, and the "Rule of Judges" in the United States 201
Brunella Casalini

5 *Rechtsstaat* and Individual Rights in German Constitutional History 237
Gustavo Gozzi

6 *État de Droit* and National Sovereignty in France 261
Alain Laquièze

7 *Rechtsstaat* and Constitutional Justice in Austria: Hans Kelsen's Contribution 293
Giorgio Bongiovanni

Part III THE CONTEMPORARY DEBATE

8 The Past and the Future of the Rule of Law 323
Luigi Ferrajoli

9 Beyond the Rule of Law: Judges' Tyranny or Lawyers' Anarchy? 353
Pier Paolo Portinaro

10 The Rule of Law and Gender Difference 371
Anna Loretoni

11 Machiavelli, the Republican Tradition, and the Rule of Law . . 387
Luca Baccelli

12 Leoni's and Hayek's Critique of the Rule of Law in Continental Europe 421
Maria Chiara Pievatolo

Part IV THE RULE OF LAW AND COLONIALISM

13 The Rule of Law and the Legal Treatment of Native Americans 443
Bartolomé Clavero

14 The Colonial Model of the Rule of Law in Africa: The Example of Guinea 467
Carlos Petit

Part V THE RULE OF LAW IN ISLAM

15 Is Constitutionalism Compatible with Islam? 515
Raja Bahlul

16 The Rule of Morally Constrained Law: The Case of Contemporary Egypt 543
Baudouin Dupret

PART VI THE RULE OF LAW AND ORIENTAL CULTURES

17 "Asian Values" and the Rule of Law 565
Alice Ehr-Soon Tay

18 The Rule of Law and Indian Society: From Colonialism to Post-Colonialism 587
Ananta Kumar Giri

19 The Chinese Legal Tradition and the European View of the Rule of Law 615
Wu Shu-Chen

20 Modern Constitutionalism in China 633
Lin Feng

21 Human Rights and the Rule of Law in Contemporary China 647
Wang Zhenmin and Li Zhenghui

Select Bibliography 671
Francesco Paolo Vertova

List of Authors 683

Index 689

PREFACE

Pietro Costa and Danilo Zolo

1. Today the expression "rule of law" is remarkably widespread, not only in political and legal literature but, most notably, in newspapers and political language. This expression is by no means a fresh lexical creation: the formula "rule of law" has in fact a long history, deeply affecting its meanings and contemporary popularity. However, it is unclear whether the popularity of the expression reflects its vitality as a theoretical-critical category or the dying splendour of an obsolete notion.

First of all, we need to explain why we assume that our use of the phrase "rule of law" is able to cover the experience of both English-speaking and continental European countries. Of course, we cannot take for granted that expressions such as *Rechtsstaat*, *État de droit*, *Stato di diritto*, and *Estado de derecho* refer to the same phenomenon. The semantic field of these expressions seems to be the same because of their linguistic kinship but the historical and conceptual specificity of the underlying "national traditions" should not be overlooked. Even if we were inclined to minimize differences within continental Europe, the dramatic contrast between civil law and common law systems would prevent us from considering "rule of law" and *Rechtsstaat* (with similar expressions) as simply synonyms. Briefly, it is the *thema probandum* of our research, and not an axiom, that different expressions belong to a basically consistent universe of meaning. However, we will try to get out of our terminological trouble by using the phrase "rule of law" in general, i.e. not only with reference to the English-speaking world. We will use the term *Rechtsstaat* (and such similar expressions) only when we refer to the specific experiences of continental Europe. Of course, the problem cannot be solved by resorting to terminological tricks; our purpose is rather to sketch the historical diagram and multiple meanings of a "semantic field" whose relevance in Western political culture is indisputable.

Nevertheless, we are interested not only in the past, but also in the present of the "rule of law". This book is also intended to contribute to an understanding of the notion of the rule of law within contemporary philosophical, political, and legal debate. We do not propose an accurate classification of its meanings and lexical uses: at the very least, such a task would require complementing our analysis with the bulk of current constitutional and administration sciences. Rather, we intend to find out the problematic area referred to in the present debate about the rule of law.

2. The semantic complexity of the notion of "rule of law" is not a recent phenomenon. It has characterized the whole historical span of a notion that cannot be detached from national cultures where it came to being and was actually used. It is a notion connected with political and legal projects and conflicts; it carries an intrinsic plurality of meanings, and is value-laden and ideologically momentous.

It is precisely the deep historical rootedness of the rule of law that makes historical reconstruction crucial: we cannot but deal with stratified and diverse meanings that, to different extents, still bear upon our present day. However, while in the framework of our book a historical-semantic analysis is necessary, its role is somewhat preparatory: an inquiry into the past of the rule of law is not for us a goal in itself but the starting point for studying the present value and possible fate of this theoretical formulation.

In this perspective, not only does our book include a "historical introduction" (after the general and theoretical introduction that opens the volume), but it devotes its first part to an account of the genesis and historical development of the concept of "rule of law". While the chapters in this part are different in inspiration, they all express a "critical-conceptual" historical approach, paying attention to the theoretical implications of its subject matter and thus functional to clarifying the present debate.

The historical chapters in our book aim to compare the different historical instances of the rule of law, by considering some significant historical and cultural areas. Emilio Santoro reconstructs the meaning of "rule of law" in the British constitutional tradition through a reflection on the work of Albert Venn Dicey, the lawyer who is chiefly responsible for the fortune of the very expression "rule of law". Brunella Casalini studies the problem of the "rule of law" in American constitutional development: while the American system is linked to the English model of "common law", it exhibits remarkably different features, because of a written constitution and a complex system of judicial review of legislation. Gustavo Gozzi portrays the emergence of the rule of law in Germany from the origins of the concept in the early nineteenth century to the "Basic Law" enacted after the Second World War. Giorgio Bongiovanni then focuses on Hans Kelsen, the lawyer who in the early twentieth century made a key contribution to the concept and practice of judicial review of legislation (helping to draft the 1920 Austrian constitution, too). Finally, the development of the idea in France is covered in the chapter by Alain Laquièze: in France the relationship between national sovereignty and personal rights developed after the Revolution, following an original paradigm of its own.

3. Our historical chapters do not claim to provide the reader with a thorough analytical reconstruction of the past of the rule of law. We would rather make a close comparison possible among different, historically laid down images of the rule of law, in order to shed light over some recurring characteristic features of this notion. These features (emphasized in the general introduction to the volume) present themselves as an important standpoint for contemporary debate: on the one hand, the ancient and constantly recurrent ideal of "regulating" power, thus constraining and checking it; on the other hand, the recent demand, ridden with inner tensions, to establish a functional link between power and individuals and making it the basis of a complex apparatus of rights.

Once the rule of law is placed within its genetic and historical context, the problem of the relationship between individuals, rights, and power emerges. These essential "voices" are the focus of the chapters in the second part of our book, devoted to deepening some of the most-debated theoretical implications of the rule of law. Luigi Ferrajoli analyses the opposition between a formalist (liberal) notion of the rule of law and a conception responsive to the demands of political participation and social rights, in a chapter which is both critical-analytical and project-oriented. Anna Loretoni studies the relationship between the normative universalism of law and the gender identity of individuals referring to it. Pier Paolo Portinaro dwells on the tension between the declining power of parliaments and the increasing power of the courts. Luca Baccelli analyses some contemporary definitions of the "rule of law" and suggests reformulating them in the light of the republican tradition. Maria Chiara Pievatolo dwells on the thought of Hayek and Leoni in order to thematize the relationship between freedom and order.

4. The first two parts of our book are not meant to draw a comprehensive picture of the historical developments and theoretical issues hinging upon the rule of law. Rather they offer a selection of themes whose synergy can suggest the sense direction of a historical process and the theoretical implications of present debate. The task of providing a historical and theoretical analysis of the rule of law might now seem to have been accomplished in our pages. However, it is our conviction that a proper understanding of the rule of law today requires referring to a wider problematic horizon.

It seems unavoidable to investigate a field which up to now has been mostly ignored by the analysis of political and legal discourse: the relationship between Europe and the United States, on the one hand, and the "rest" of the world, on the other. Over the past centuries this relationship developed in terms of conquest and colonization, on the widespread view that (European, North American, Western) "civilization" should be opposed as a whole to "barbaric" (static, backward) "others".

In this perspective, then, a new reflection should address the different significance that some "great concepts" of Western culture – the "rule of law" – take on when they get in touch with conditions deeply different from those of their birth and "normal" functioning: for example, when they are used in America, during the process of the violent subjugation and eradication of native peoples, or in Africa, during the colonial expansion of European nations. This is the "pioneer" research direction of the chapters by Bartolomé Clavero and Carlos Petit, collected in the part on "The rule of law and colonialism". Bartolomé Clavero studies the "devices of exclusion" that characterized the whole political-institutional history of America, condemning native populations to a condition of inequality and marginality, whereas Carlos Petit, in his analysis of Spanish domination in equatorial Africa, emphasizes the "domestic" character of the rule of law as opposed to enduring "archaic" structures of domination in the colonial reality.

5. After focusing on the tensions the rule of law undergoes in the "overseas" lands subjected to colonial domination, the analysis of the genesis and meaning of the rule of law may be said to have been virtually accomplished. Today, however, this notion is still rousing a debate that cannot be said to have come to an end. The reason is quite simple: though the origins of the rule of law are in "Western" societies and cultures and, until recently, the West took the lion's share of the debate, today other societies and other cultures take an active and creative part in a sustained philosophical-political debate. Thus this debate cannot concern only the views put forward by the *maîtres à penser* of Western countries: at least for those rejecting a parochial "Eurocentric" bias.

Among the participants in the contemporary theoretical-political debate are those cultures that the colonial attitude *d'antan* used to label as "other", putting together highly complex and dramatically different historical-cultural worlds (e.g. the Arab-Islamic world, India, Far East countries) in a big pot of "backwardness". Departing from entrenched "Eurocentric" habits seems to us, therefore, a plain duty of information when there are at stake themes such as the rule of law that go beyond the formerly impassable borders of Western cultures.

We should, however, expand on the sense of a debate which is allegedly open to members of utterly different traditions and cultures. If this debate is to be effective and instructive, it cannot take place in a nebulous space in which participants lose their historical-cultural identity; nor can it ignore the definitely historical character, and the Western roots, of the idea of the rule of law. Instead, the debate should meet the requirements of an *intercultural dialogue*: it should be an attempt to start a dialogue among original and different cultures, on the assumption that the rule of law is both the stake and the means of the dialogue.

It is therefore obvious that the attitude of Western intellectuals towards the rule of law is different from the attitude raised by non-Western partners, whether they belong to the Arab-Islamic world, the Indian continent, or Chinese society. While Westerners belong to a historically unified tradition (even if it is open to different interpretations and outcomes), non-Westerners look at that tradition "from outside" and compare it to their own cultural forms. They ask, first, whether and how the demands that in the West resulted in the formula of the "rule of law" also emerged in different (Islamic, Confucian, etc.) traditions and, second, about the possibility and usefulness of grafting the rule of law onto the trunk of societies and cultures deeply different from those where it originated.

This is by no means a merely intellectual or academic question: the Arab-Islamic world, India, and China are not faraway planets whose orbits never cross those of the European and American West. On the contrary, in fairly recent times encounters with the expansionist and colonizing violence of the West have been close and traumatic. It is not by accident that the chapters by our Arab, Indian, and Chinese partners dwell on this crucial turning point of our and their history. Moreover, today the process of globalization (or rather "Westernization") of the world intensifies the transactions between different societies and cultures and urges an answer to a key question concerning the rule of law itself: the question of the possibility, the sense, and the limitations of the intercultural "transfers" of institutional arrangements, values, and theoretical schemes bearing the historical marks of their original context.

The answers to all these questions are of course quite different, depending on the original character of the diverse societies and cultures to which the collaborators of our book belong. A fourth part, "The rule of law and Islamic culture", brings together chapters by intellectuals from the Arab-Islamic world. Raja Bahlul investigates the possibility of formulating "constitutionalist" issues within an Arab-Islamic discourse based on *Shari'a* and its different interpretative methods. Baudoin Dupret treats the relationship between a "modern" or "Western" codification, adopted by Egypt since the nineteenth century, and a set of moral principles, which, while lacking formal legal validity, nonetheless determine the actual operation of the legal system.

The following part, "The rule of law and Eastern cultures", begins with a chapter by Alice Ehr-Soon Tay, devoted to a sustained discussion of the category of "Asian values": a category, on the author's view, built by arbitrarily equating "Asian values" with an "authoritarian" reading of

Confucian tradition and a bracketing off of "human rights". India is the subject matter of the chapter by Ananta Kumar Giri, who brings the problems of the rule of law against the background of the ancient Hindu tradition in order to analyse the impact of colonization and the issues raised by present Indian democracy. Legal and constitutional development in China is the subject matter of the chapters by Wu Shuchen and Lin Feng, as well as the joint chapter by Zhenmin Wang and Zhenghui Li. The authors deal with different moments of the long legal and institutional development of China, focusing from different perspectives on the original character of that experience and the differences and similarities emerging from a comparison with Western models.

6. It is not by accident that the volume ends with the chapters on intercultural dialogue: the evident diversity of the voices may be taken to be a key feature of our book. It is not characterized by a mechanical identity of views, style, or judgement among editors and authors. On the contrary, it hosts a plurality of orientations and thematic selections, ruling out the tyranny of a strictly unified "point of view". In particular, it is worth remarking that the two opening chapters do not claim to point to a necessary path or to provide a strict definition of the subject matter; they are only meant to outline a framework for debate. Therefore, it should not be surprising that some contributions – e.g. the chapter by Luigi Ferrajoli – are premised upon epistemological and philosophical-legal assumptions at variance with, but no less legitimate than, those endorsed by the opening theoretical-critical chapter. No more surprising should be the fact that the judgement by Alice Ehr-Soon Tay on the universal nature of human rights differs from that in the chapter by Li Zhenghui and Wang Zhenmin. Our persuasion is precisely that a plurality of perspectives is a value that should prevail over a reassuring but unfruitful unanimity of views.

We do not aim at an "encyclopaedic" picture of the past and present of the rule of law. The chapters on intercultural dialogue are even more alien from any ambition to completeness. They do not have the unsound purpose of summing up all of the views held in "all" non-European societies in a few pages, but they carry some particular, albeit significant, testimonies and are chiefly meant to convey the urgency of a dialogue among different civilizations, a dialogue still not too much practised (in our view) by our cultural institutions.

In sum, our book intends to offer some relevant guidelines for orienting the reader through a political and legal debate where the rule of law (and the doctrine of "human rights") is a concept both controversial and significant at the national and international levels.

PART I

INTRODUCTORY ESSAYS

CHAPTER 1

THE RULE OF LAW: A CRITICAL REAPPRAISAL

Danilo Zolo

1 THE RETURN OF THE RULE OF LAW

The "rule of law" has been one of the most popular formulas employed by Western political and legal thinkers in the last two decades of the twentieth century that followed the long post-war period.[1] Yet, as well as the expression "rule of law" which, though typical of Anglo-Saxon culture, is nonetheless used everywhere, the theoretical lexicon of the European social sciences also includes other, analogous expressions, such as the German *Rechtsstaat*, the French *État de droit*, the Italian *Stato di diritto*, and the Spanish *Estado de derecho*.[2] Although in Europe these expressions – rule of law, on the one hand, *Rechtsstaat* and the other continental expressions, on the other – are used promiscuously, their conceptual equivalence is far from being straightforward. Indeed, their terminological differences, and the ensuing well-known translation problems,[3] epitomize the diversity of cultural contexts and the relative independence of the theories advanced. In fact, the different expressions refer to two clearly distinct political and legal traditions. The "rule of law" is deeply rooted in Great Britain's political and constitutional history, from the Norman conquest to modern times, and has left significant traces upon the constitutional structures of the United States of America and of many other countries influenced by British institutions. The *Rechtsstaat* was first developed by German liberal culture in the second half of the nineteenth century and later spread throughout Europe, especially affecting the public law of both unified Italy and the French Third Republic.

For these reasons, the thesis of the conceptual equivalence of the "rule of law" with the *Rechtsstaat (État de droit, Stato di diritto, Estado de derecho)* – this is one of the main theses of the present essay – needs to be accurately argued for, both on a historical and a conceptual level. However, the renewed value of the "rule of law" formula and its analogous continental expressions corresponds to given political circumstances and cultural beliefs that seem to justify a theoretical approach

P. Costa and D. Zolo (eds.), The Rule of Law: History, Theory and Criticism, 3–71.

uniting Anglo-Saxon and continental notions within the general category of the "rule of law". Following the downfall of "actually existing socialism" and the crisis of representative institutions, the rule of law has been brought back to life in Western culture in close connection with the doctrine of individual rights (or "human rights"): one need only think of authors such as Ronald Dworkin, Ralf Dahrendorf, Jürgen Habermas, Norberto Bobbio, and Luigi Ferrajoli.[4] Thus, the rule of law has been revived as a political and legal theory that gives pre-eminence to the protection of human rights, i.e. rights which have been defined by a great number of nineteenth- and twentieth-century national constitutions and international conventions, in particular the rights to life, personal security, freedom, private property, and contractual autonomy, as well as political rights.

Within such a historical setting, defined by Bobbio as "the age of rights",[5] to support the rule of law means to advocate the protection of individual rights as the primary aim of political institutions and legal bodies. Contrary to recurrent formalistic interpretations of the rule of law, it may be argued that its institutional characteristics are nowadays explicitly revived by Euro-continental and Anglo-Saxon theorists in the light of an "individualistic" political philosophy. Not only does such a philosophy relinquish social organicism, collectivist utilitarianism, and statism, but it also subordinates the public dimension and the general interest to the absolute primacy of individual values and expectations.[6] The current proponents of the rule of law, both in the Anglo-Saxon world and in continental Europe, view the attainment of such values and expectations as the primary source of legitimization of the political system. However, this view does not entail either underestimating the different normative and institutional particularities of the two traditions or overlooking the plurality of political and constitutional developments that have arisen within each of them.

2 A CONSTRUCTIVIST INTERPRETATION

The theoretical lemma "rule of law" is nowadays a prestigious formula of Western political and cultural language. In particular, political writers and journalists increasingly use this phrase and are inclined to present it as an institutional characteristic, which helps define Western civilization and its contrasts with other civilizations, especially Islamic and Chinese-Confucian cultures. Yet the conceptualization of the "rule of law" remains particularly uncertain and controversial.[7] It is widely recognized that specialist literature has so far devoted little attention either to analytically defining the state characterized by the rule of law, from an institutional and normative perspective, or to differentiating it from contiguous notions, such as "legal state", "liberal state", "democratic state", "constitutional state", with which it is often erroneously or purposely identified. In continental Europe, theoretical–political handbooks and encyclopedic dictionaries mostly do not deal with the above matter, while the corresponding Anglo-Saxon texts exclusively refer to English constitutional history and to the specific Anglo-Saxon notion of the rule of law, thus ritually paying homage to Albert Venn Dicey's work.[8]

In this manner, a long tradition of blurred definitions is perpetuated: Carl Schmitt, in the early 1930s, had already argued that the expression *Rechtsstaat* "can stand for as many different things as the word *Recht* [law] itself and for as many different concepts as the many institutional arrangements implied by the word *Staat* [state]". He also sarcastically added that it was understandable "that propagandists and lawyers of all kinds gladly used the word to slander their adversaries for being enemies of the rule of law".[9] Even in Italy, 20 years later, authors such as Fernando Garzoni lamented the conceptual indeterminacy and ambiguity of the notion *Stato di diritto*.[10] Garzoni argued that the long-standing popularity of the notion, like that of "natural law", was due precisely to its pliability and ideological fungibility.[11] Revealingly, even theorists of German National Socialism and Italian Fascism, such as Otto Koellreutter, Heinrich Lange, and Sergio Panunzio, were able to claim the notion *Rechtsstaat* or *Stato di diritto* for their own political models.[12]

Quite obviously, it would be naive to seek a semantically univocal and ideologically neutral definition of the "rule of law". Given the many legal and institutional determinations, which have been – and may be – ascribed to the rule of law, such a "scientistic" approach would end up by *tout court* dismissing the concept and its related expressions.[13] However, it is obvious that, using similar criteria, the entire conceptual apparatus of political and legal theory – even of social sciences in general – could be expunged from scientific communication on the grounds of being deemed imprecise, unascertainable, and contaminated by evaluative judgements.

If, on the contrary, we ground our analysis on epistemological assumptions drawn from cognitive conventionalism and pragmatism, what matters is not the semantic definiteness and ideological neutrality of theories advanced in this respect; rather, it is their communicative clarity and usefulness within enunciative conventional ambits, aimed at understanding and solving problems.[14] By endorsing such a "weak epistemology", social theory is thus entrusted with the task of elaborating "coherent interpretations" – rather than explicative definitions – of the concerned subjects and of providing persuasive grounds for their acceptance. This can be done and, in the writer's opinion, must still be done with respect to the rule of law.

It follows that a coherent theoretical understanding of the rule of law must not merely provide detailed historical and philological evidence of single experiences and their corresponding literature;[15] rather, it must detect the ethical assumptions, legal models, and institutional forms inherent in different experiences which all have – or have been – referred to the rule of law. Such a kind of interpretation is, by nature, "constructivist", i.e. selective and conjectural, and this inevitably leaves the interpreter ample room for discretion: he will be free to decide, at least, which historical experiences are to be included within a "coherent" general interpretation. In our case, for instance, we shall mainly focus on the "external history"[16] of the rule of law, rather than on the developments of its British or German "internal history". Its "external history" is a theoretical development that begins with the process leading to the rise of European modern states and can be properly reconstructed only by referring, in implicit though discriminating terms, to classical liberal thinking, from Locke to Montesquieu, from Kant to Beccaria, and from Humboldt to Constant. Such a historical scenario includes diverse experiences, such as the English eighteenth-century civil wars, the rebellion of Britain's American colonies against their homeland, French revolutionary constitutionalism, the process leading to the German Reich, and the institutions of the French Third Republic.

Such an interpretative approach will pay little attention to the German traditionalist thinking of the first half of the nineteenth century – whose main exponents are Friedrich Julius Stahl, Rudolf von Gneist, Robert von Mohl, and Otto Bähr – though it cannot forget that such philosophical currents did indeed prompt the creation of the continental notion of "rule of law" (*Rechtsstaat*).[17] It will also neglect the (embarrassing) circumstance that the rule of law was established in North America not only within the context of the well-known rebellion against the colonial motherland but also within that of the genocide of American natives, and also that it coexisted for a long time with the slavery of African Americans and, later on, with racial discrimination against them.[18] Moreover, such an approach will overlook the theses propounded by Nazi theorists who, unlike Carl Schmitt and sometimes in contrast with him, whilst not rejecting the rule of law, sought to render it compatible with the kind of totalitarian state they depicted as a *nationaler Rechtsstaat*: they argued that the totalitarian state represented a sort of *Rechtsstaat*, in that it was a 'legal state' (*Gesetzesstaat*), which used law (*Gesetz*) as a "general and abstract" normative instrument, and guaranteed the political independence of the judiciary.[19] Finally, we shall not deal with constitutional doctrines and experiences that have referred to the rule of law without providing any particularly original theoretical contribution: this is the case, for example, for Vittorio Emanuele Orlando's work, which, within the monarchic-parliamentary context of Giolitti's Italy, referred to the state-centred model of the German *Rechtsstaat*.[20]

3 THE HISTORICAL EXPERIENCES OF THE RULE OF LAW

Within such an interpretative framework, four key experiences of the "external history" of the rule of law deserve our full theoretical appraisal: (1) the English rule of law; (2) the North American version of the rule of law; (3) the German *Rechtsstaat*; and (4) the French *État de droit*. We will argue that the theoretical elements drawn from these four historical experiences may be consistently united within a general model. This should provide a solid theoretical identity for the notion of the "rule of law", meant as the normative and institutional structure of a modern state within which the legal system – and not other functional subsystems – is entrusted with the task of guaranteeing individual rights, curbing the natural tendency of political power to expand and act arbitrarily.

3.1 The English rule of law

In 1867, William Edward Hearn wrote that wind and rain could enter the hut of the pauper, yet not the king. Each English citizen, whether a civil servant or a nobleman, was equally subject to law and to the common law courts.[21] Hearn introduced the expression "rule of law", as Albert Venn Dicey acknowledged in the introductory pages of his famous and authoritative treatise, *Introduction to the Study of the Law of the Constitution*.[22]

The constitutional "guiding principles" of the English rule of law include, first of all, individuals' legal equality, irrespective of their status and economic conditions. Notwithstanding individuals' deep social inequality – which is deemed to be obvious – all citizens are subject, with no exceptions, to the general rules of ordinary law, in particular to the ones regarding criminal punishment and patrimonial integrity. Such rules are enforced not by special courts, such as the Privy Council and the Star Chamber – which characterized English history – or as French administrative courts[23] (as claimed by Dicey), rather by ordinary courts.

Hence, individuals' equality before the law implies the rejection of both the granting of personal privileges and the arbitrary or excessively discretionary use of executive power.

The second "guiding principle" is the normative synergy between Parliament and judiciary, through which the settlement of single cases is in England the result of decisions stemming from two sources that are in fact, if not certainly in law, equally sovereign. On the one hand, there is the legislative sovereignty of Parliament, i.e. the Crown, the House of Lords, and the House of Commons, according to the famous "King in Parliament" formula. On the other hand, there is the common law, in the hands of ordinary courts. The former is a formal legal source; the latter is an actual legal source. Ordinary courts are not entitled to question Parliament's acts and cannot pretend to be "guardians of the constitution". Ordinary courts are obliged to apply the law rigorously; yet, they are to do so in a very complex manner, being also bound by legal "precedents", i.e. their own and autonomous jurisprudential tradition. Moreover, common lawyers have the power to interpret the law and such an instrument in their hands can – as they are perfectly aware – render the relationship between legislative acts and sentences quite flexible. In this respect, Dicey writes as follows:

> Parliament is the supreme legislator, but from the moment Parliament has uttered its will as lawgiver, that will become subject to the interpretation put upon it by the judges of the land, and the judges [...] are influenced by the feelings of magistrates no less than by the general spirit of the common law.[24]

The sovereignty of law, whether it stems directly from an act of Parliament (statute law) or from the jurisprudential tradition of common law courts, is thus conceived and essentially used against the discretionary prerogatives of executive power, within an institutional framework that has been emblematically called "the reign of law and judges".

The third and equally fundamental "guiding principle" is the protection of individual rights. Throughout the centuries-old history of English constitutionalism – from the feudal guarantees of the Magna Carta to the procedural rule of habeas corpus, to the list of human rights in the Petition of Rights and in the Bill of Rights – such a protection has more often been provided by common law courts than by Parliament. The extraordinary capacity of the courts to counteract the monarchy's absolutist demands has been crucial in favouring the development of "Englishmen's freedoms". Legislative acts themselves, such as the *Habeas Corpus* Acts of 1679 and 1816, have often been preceded by a long common law elaboration, which Parliament essentially ratified.[25]

Moreover, judicial decisions have safeguarded the rights of liberty and property against the potential arbitrariness of both administrative civil servants (employed by the Crown) and Parliament. Edward Coke – let us just mention the famous *Bonham's* case – already argued that ordinary judges would consider null, and thus would not apply, any act of Parliament deemed to be "against common right and reason".[26] Two centuries later, Dicey underlined that one of the functions actually performed by common law courts was to secure, even before Parliament where necessary, the supremacy of ordinary law as a general rule of the constitution.[27] Common law judges professionally engaged in respecting "precedents", i.e. in practice a number of rules and procedures aimed at safeguarding individual rights, could not but be uncompromising adversaries of any form of arbitrariness. They would inflexibly contrast, for instance, the application of excessive fines or unusual punishments, possibly introduced by Parliament, against the principles of certainty and non-retroactivity of criminal law.

On the whole, the originality of the English constitutional regime, as underlined by William Blackstone, lies in the fact that in England the widespread and differentiated nature of powers is not due to any imperative acts by the state or to the "general will" of a constituent assembly, expressing popular sovereignty. Neither is it due to a written, rigid, and normatively supreme constitutional Charter in line with the political experience of the United States, which had a significant impact on the continental Europe throughout the twentieth century. In England, Parliament can change the constitution at any time, and no political body is entrusted with controlling the constitutionality of legislative acts. The English constitutional structure depends on a long-standing civil tradition rooted in political conflicts, normative acts, customs, usages, and (not strictly legal) precepts, which in some cases date back to centuries before the development of the modern state and liberal philosophy.[28] This largely unwritten normative tradition even claims to be tied to a millenary and immemorial "ancient constitution", whose validity is allegedly derived from its own "antiquity" rather than from mythical or transcendent origins, or from the universal value of its contents. It hinges upon its quite particular quality of being "the law of the land", respected by and handed down from generation to generation, and of being the result of historical struggles.[29] In his essay on *Law and Public Opinion in England*, Dicey writes:

> The Revolution of 1689 was conducted under the guidance of Whig lawyers; they unwittingly laid the foundations of a modern constitutional monarchy, but their intention was to reaffirm in the Bill of Rights and in the Act of Settlement, not the innate rights of man but the inherited and immemorial liberties of Englishmen.[30]

The rule of law is only very indirectly a legal theory of the state; it is not its "juridicalization" or "constitutionalization". It is in striking contrast with the German (and in general continental) "legislative state", where judges are state's officials applying the state's law and where individual rights are "laid down" by Parliament.[31] In this respect, the rule of law, as argued by Dicey, is "a distinctive characteristic of the English constitution".[32]

3.2 The North American version of the rule of law

Dicey argued that the constitutional structure of the United States was a typical example of the rule of law on the mere ground that its founding fathers had drawn inspiration from English traditions. Indeed, the North American attribution to the judiciary, and not only to Parliament, of the task of protecting individual subjects against the executive power's arbitrary acts was undoubtedly influenced by the English model.[33] Similarly, the decision not to draft a Bill of Rights to be included in the text of the Constitution was influenced by the English precedent: the Bill of Rights as known today was introduced (as an open list) by the first ten constitutional amendments only at the end of 1791.

In the institutional development following the Declaration of Independence and the approval of the Constitution, the moderate and liberal approach of republican federalism, supported by Alexander Hamilton and James Madison, prevailed over the democratic philosophy of Thomas Jefferson and Thomas Paine; the latter being closer to French doctrines of popular sovereignty and the primacy of the constituent power. Within the context of a somewhat fundamentalist understanding of freedom and property rights as grounded in natural law, there arose a kind of religious approach to the rule of law, which was alien to the English ideology of the rule of law and would not be shared by the positive law doctrines that inspired the German *Rechtsstaat*.[34] The very idea of sovereignty seemed to crystallize, under a natural law perspective, within the principles of the constitution. The normative primacy of the constitution emerged in direct opposition to the sovereignty of the legislative function of the Federal Parliament, which was viewed as more dangerous for fundamental freedoms and property than administrative power itself.[35]

The constitutional regime of the United States soon displayed a clear penchant for solutions drawing from moderate liberalism, being poorly sensitive to democratic representation, and to the conflictual dynamics of social interests. It paid much more attention to the need, which would later be at the heart of Alexis de Tocqueville's aristocratic liberalism, formally to avoid the threat represented by parliamentary majorities to individual liberties. Against this threat the suggested remedy, besides the tendential inflexibility of the written constitution, was the "judicial review of legislation" and, following Judge Marshall's sentence in *Marbury v. Madison* (1803), the possibility for the Supreme Court to determine the constitutional legality of legislative acts. Hence, the Federal Parliament's power, especially with respect to individual rights, was greatly weakened: this was a radical denial of any potential link between the acknowledgement of rights and normative claims in the name of popular sovereignty deriving from political conflicts.[36] In fact, it was believed that the professionalism and technical expertise of expert judges would ensure, much more effectively than Parliament, a correct interpretation of the constitution, and thus an impartial and meta-political protection of individual rights.[37]

Such institutional solutions, albeit falling within the paradigm of the rule of law, distinguished the American experience from the English one. In England, neither common law courts nor higher judicial bodies ever exercised judicial review on the grounds of the normative superiority and formally unchallengeable authority of the constitution.[38] The protection of "Englishmen's freedoms" relied on a long common law tradition, and not on institutional devices in the hands of high judicial bureaucracies. Moreover, in the continental Europe, throughout the nineteenth century and even later, constitutional charters remained flexible and were at the legislative power's disposal.

3.3 The Rechtsstaat

As far as we know, the expression *Rechtsstaat* was first used in the 1830s by Robert von Mohl, in his treatise *Die Polizeiwissenschaft nach den Grundsätzen des Rechtsstaates*, where individual freedom was, at the time, already viewed as a central aim of the state's action.[39] Yet, the *Rechtsstaat* was actually established in Germany during the Restoration, which followed the 1848 revolts, and epitomized a compromise between liberal doctrine, supported by the bourgeoisie, and the authoritarian ideology supported by conservative forces, above all the monarchy, the rural aristocracy and the high military bureaucracy. During the period including the first and second Empire, the institutional compromise was theoretically supported, through extremely rich and refined doctrinal instruments, by German public law jurists, represented especially by Georg Jellinek, Otto Mayer, and Rudolf von Jhering.[40]

By drawing inspiration from Kant and Humboldt, such a doctrine juxtaposed the *Rechtsstaat* with the absolute state and the police state, and re-elaborated in positive legal terms – in accordance with the "legal method" – key elements of classical liberal thinking, in particular the public protection of human rights and the "separation of powers". The German re-evaluation of such liberal principles led to the formulation of the well-known theory of "subjective public rights" – propounded by Jellinek – and to the primacy of law as a system of impersonal, abstract, general, and non-retroactive rules.

The "subjective public rights" theory undoubtedly represents a statist conception of rights. It is the state's sovereign authority – this balancing between the monarchical principle and Parliament's representative function – that establishes individual rights by being "self-limiting". The source of individual rights is not popular sovereignty, as theorized by the French Revolutionaries: the only original and positive source of law is the law-making power of the nation state, through which the people's spiritual identity is expressed. It is not by chance, as critically underlined by Carl Schmitt, that German constitutional doctrines and practices, following Kant's lead, cancelled the "right of resistance" from the list of individual freedoms.[41] Failing a rigid constitution – which was quite common in nineteenth-century European constitutionalism[42] – it was the legislative power that decided and regulated the granting of individual rights. Rights were at the exclusive disposal of the legislative power by virtue of the "statutory reservation". Such an anticontractualist stance, far closer to English than French constitutionalism, undoubtedly appeased the concerns of moderates and, quite likely, also of conservatives.[43] However, it also expressed a rooted tendency of German constitutional thinking: the need, influenced by Savigny and Puchta's historicist and anti-natural-law thinking, for a rigorous secularization of both the legal system and individual rights. The pre-political origin and religious nature (transcendent, universalist, and natural law–based) of individual freedoms, supported by John Locke's contractualism, was not conceded.[44]

The *Rechtsstaat's* second axiom, i.e. the primacy of law, was reflected in the "principle of legality" (*Gesetzmässigkeit*), according to which the set of rules established by Parliament had to be rigorously respected by the executive and judicial powers in order for their acts to be legitimate. Such a double subordination to the primacy of law was emphatically deemed to be both the most effective defence against any political misuse of powers and the supreme guarantee for the protection of individual rights.

Such a theory of the rule of law failed to take into account the potential arbitrary use of legislative power, since it assumed a perfect correspondence between the state's will, legality, and moral legitimacy; moreover, citizens' trust in such a correspondence was taken for granted. The German *Rechtsstaat* was thus regarded as legalistically vacuous, as a "tautological", procedural, and mere "legal state". The *Rechtsstaat* appeared to be nothing but the "law of the state" (*Staatsrecht*), characterized by a purely technical and formal concept of law (the generality and abstractness of norms). Detached from any reference to ethical values and political content, and not subject to jurisdictional controls on its constitutionality, such a state's law appeared to be paradoxically arbitrary: *sic volo, sic jubeo*. However, Carl Schmitt himself, a severe critic of the *Rechtsstaat*, acknowledged that legislative procedures, with their complicated mechanism of bonds and counterbalances, provided significant guarantees of moderation and protection of individual subjects against any possible misuse of the law.[45] Going beyond any legal formalism and any "religion of statute law", the protection of freedom and property was indeed the "material content" – both on a political and an ideological level – of the German *Rechtsstaat*.[46]

3.4 The État de droit

In France, an explicit theory of the *État de droit* was very belatedly formulated. It was first propounded by Raimond Carré de Malberg during the Third Republic, in the early decades of the twentieth century.[47] Unlike Dicey, who had conceived the idea of the rule of law independently of the notion of *Rechtsstaat*, Carré de Malberg was influenced by the German experience and, in part, by that of the United States. As a matter of fact, it could be argued that, while Dicey had reconstructed England's constitutional tradition claiming its autonomy and excellence, Carré de Malberg seemed concerned about acknowledging the superiority of German and US doctrines over French public law: in substance, he attempted a theoretical synthesis between these two experiences to be applied to French institutions. Moreover, while Dicey and German theorists of the *Rechtsstaat* had advanced their theories on the basis of effective historical experiences of the "rule of law", Carré de Malberg suggested his model of *État de droit* as an alternative to the reality of French constitutionalism, harshly criticizing the institutions of the Third Republic themselves.

Like the German liberal jurists, Carré de Malberg believed that the protection of individual rights against the state's potential arbitrariness was the main aim of the *Etat de droit* which, for this purpose, had to "self-limit" its sovereign power by binding it to respect general and *erga omnes* (towards everybody) valid rules. Yet, Carré de Malberg argued that the protection of rights required a profound reassessment of the

French constitutional tradition, including a critical examination of the Revolution itself. He claimed that French public institutions were dominated by Parliament's omnipotence, which seemed to have inherited a monopolistic entitlement to the state's sovereignty from monarchical absolutism, and this represented the greatest danger to French people's freedom.[48]

In France, the most dynamic expression of the revolutionary theory had been the idea of popular (or national) sovereignty, according to which Parliament was endowed with absolute primacy with respect to other powers of the state, since it was the sole body, which could claim direct popular investiture. "Law" had been conceived of, in line with Rousseau's thinking, as the expression of the nation's general will, whose prescriptions rigorously bound the executive power. As regards the judicial power, in the French Revolution's declarations of rights and constitutional texts judges had been the object of exclusively negative regulations: judges were not to meddle in the exercise of the legislative power and could not suspend the enforcement of laws.[49] Such a mistrust of judges, which was explicable in the light of the role played by the *ancien régime*'s magistrates, rendered the French constitutional system radically different from both British and US models.

Moreover, Rousseau's idea as to the indefeasibility and inalienability of popular sovereignty had led so a prestigious author as Emmanuel-Joseph Sieyès to draw his famous distinction between *pouvoir constituant* and *pouvoirs constitués*.[50] The constituent power was meant as a great collective legislator, defining values and principles, and laying down the rules upon which the political community was grounded. It was a pre-legal power, which was not nevertheless extinguished by the original act leading to the rise of the state and its "constituted powers". Unlike such powers, which were limited powers, the constituent power had an unlimited and inexhaustible strength, free from the normative restraints imposed by the constitution. Article 28 of the 1793 Declaration of Rights, for instance, very explicitly established that the people were always entitled to review, reform, and change their constitution and that no generation was bound by laws created by previous generations.

The normative voluntarism of such a radical-democratic doctrine brought about two significant consequences: firstly, Parliament simultaneously tended to act in the capacity of both constituent power and constituted power, thus assuming sovereign prerogatives. In particular, it claimed the permanent right to review the constitution, as well as an unlimited power of revision, equivalent to that of the constituent power.[51] Secondly, there was a clear constitutional tendency towards sharply rejecting the *gouvernement des juges*, i.e. towards rejecting both constitutional rigidity and judicial control over the constitutional legitimacy of ordinary laws.

Carré de Malberg strongly attacked such a Jacobin tradition and upheld an understanding of the rule of law, which submitted all powers, including the legislative one, to law. Parliament had to be viewed as a merely constituted power – not by any means as a constituent power – whose functions had to be subjected to limits and controls, just as was the case of administrative power. To submit administrative acts to the principle of legality was indeed important, though not sufficient to guarantee the full protection of individual rights: the *Etat légal* was not yet a proper *Etat de droit*. An authentic *État de droit* had to provide individuals with legal means to allow them to oppose the legislator's will whenever its acts violated their fundamental rights.[52] For this purpose, if judicial review of legislation (in force in the United States) was regrettably not feasible in France, as argued by Carré de Malberg, then a clear distinction between the constitution and the ordinary laws was needed. It was necessary to place the former above the latter and compel Parliament to respect all legal limits laid down by the constitution, thus relinquishing any constituent claim.[53]

3.5 The English rule of law: a "founding exception"

The above four historical experiences of the rule of law display both normative and institutional differences. This may be illustrated by resorting to three comparative parameters: the attribution of sovereignty, the constitutional function, and the means for protecting individual rights.

Under the English rule of law sovereignty belongs to Parliament, which exerts its normative primacy almost exclusively with respect to the executive power. Not only is the English constitution unwritten but it is also not a legal act or a legal custom: rather, it is a set of legal traditions, normative acts, social conventions, and practices concurring in limiting and controlling the executive power. The legal determination of individual rights and their protection are, in practice, entrusted to common law ordinary courts.

The American variant of the rule of law further limits, distributes, and differentiates the state's sovereignty. Sovereignty ends up by symbolically coinciding with the normative supremacy of a written and substantially rigid constitution, which limits all of the state's powers, including the legislative power. The determination and protection of individual rights largely depend on the judicial power to construe constitutional principles.

As regards the German *Rechtsstaat*, sovereignty is ascribed to the legislative power, this having an absolute normative primacy over the other powers. The constitution is written, though it is flexible, it is not placed above ordinary laws and is not safeguarded by a constitutional jurisdiction. The protection of individual rights is exclusively entrusted to Parliament, which is their original source and guarantor.

According to Carré del Malberg's model of the *État de droit*, sovereignty coincides with the normative primacy of Parliament, which is meant as the expression of popular sovereignty. Yet, Parliament is not a constituent power: it is merely one of the "constituted powers". It follows that its functions must be subject to limits and controls. This implies a sharp distinction between the constitution and the ordinary laws, the constitution being superior with respect to such laws. In the *État de droit* citizens are provided with legal remedies against legislative acts – not only against administrative ones – whenever these violate their fundamental rights.

It is undeniable that the above political-cultural experiences and legal regimes are very different, both in terms of the sovereignty of their normative authorities and of the constitutional techniques they use to curb the state's powers and differentiate them one from another. Moreover, they adopt different approaches with respect to the foundation of individual rights and their actual protection. A "great divide" within the Western tradition of the rule of law that underpins the three perspectives can be clearly discerned: on the one hand, there is the "founding exception" of the English version of the rule of law and, on the other, albeit with significant internal differences, the North American version and the model of *Rechtsstaat*, together with similar Euro-continental experiences.[54]

As underlined by Carl Schmitt (following Friedrich von Savigny), what renders English constitutionalism both an exceptional and founding phenomenon is its being "a living customary law". Rather than being grounded on theoretical reasoning and conceptual systemization, the English "constitutional law" was nourished by a long tradition of practical adjustments of the law carried out by a juridical "private" and "autonomous" body. Such body was neither the state nor a public corporation or bureaucracy. In fact, English constitutionalism does not use or even know of the notion of "state". Rather, common lawyers tended to interpret political history, social conflicts, civil customs, and people's normative *ethos* by elaborating a socially widespread legal culture.[55]

The very formulation of individual rights does not depend on doctrinal inferences drawn from the principles of a written constitution or code but rather is the result of normative induction and generalization, drawn from specific judicial decisions concerning individual freedom, property, and contracts. The split between "law in books" and "law in action", which American and Scandinavian legal realism would claim to be a constant trait of both legal positivism and normativism, seems to be completely extraneous to the common-law tradition. In England, the constitution is, by nature, pliable and flexible; yet, unlike what happens on the continent, it is rigorously applied by ordinary courts. In the continental Europe, as held by Dicey, solemn and redundant constitutional declarations include mostly abstract enunciations of principle, lacking suitable procedural means and doomed to be largely unenforced.[56] The English constitution is not a set of general principles and rules deriving, as Rousseau would have it, from the constituent will of a political *élite*. The constitution is not the "normative manual" of the new society used by the people's or nation's representatives as a guide in setting up an order perfectly rationalized by law. Quite coherently, the protection of individual rights is not founded on universal values and claimed in their name. Neither is it inferred from the moral or rational "nature" of mankind, deemed therefore to be the heritage of the entire human species. The particularistic and peculiar nature of "Englishmen's freedoms", being rooted in the "law of the land" and thus lacking universalistic ambitions, is, as we have seen, constantly upheld by the common law tradition, from Coke to Blackstone and Dicey.

Quite paradoxically, the particular and localistic English constitution was the generating nucleus of the entire Western experience of the rule of law, thus proving to be the exemplary paradigm of the protection of individual rights. After all, the historical primacy of "Englishmen's freedoms" – from the Magna Carta to the Bill of Rights – was always widely acknowledged both across the Atlantic and in the continental Europe, from American federalists to French revolutionaries and German theorists of "subjective public rights".[57]

At the same time, however, the English rule of law lacked any transitive capacity in terms of constitutional techniques and institutional mechanisms formally guaranteeing individual rights. This was, precisely, what led to the "great divide" in Western constitutionalism: in the United States, just like in Germany, France, Italy, and other liberal democracies, the model of an unwritten and flexible constitution did not gain ground. Neither did the idea that a normative list of rights was unnecessary or even counterproductive. The very idea that fundamental freedoms could be better protected by a body of pragmatic judges and jurists – these stabilizing and socially spreading the standards of a legal culture keen on the rigorous settlement of single cases rather than on a generalizing, formalistic "legal science" – did not take root in continental Europe.

Both in the United States and in continental Europe, albeit with different modes and times, the model of a written constitution prevailed, together with that of an explicit formulation of tendentially "universal' rights". Constitutions and Bills of Rights were seen as sovereign expressions of a social group which organized itself in the form of a nation state, laying down, as foundations of its political life, some inviolable principles. The tendency to hierarchize the legal system, so as to subject ordinary laws to the normative primacy of the constitution and to make constitutional principles and rules inflexible, gained ground. Such a trend developed throughout the twentieth century and gave rise, especially through Hans Kelsen's contribution, to a real "judicial review" of legislation, controlling its constitutional legality, which went well beyond the United States judicial review practice. As from its introduction into the 1920 Austrian Constitution – the well-known *Verfassungsgerichtshof* – the institution of the Constitutional Court gradually spread out through Europe, and was particularly successful in the post–Second World War period in countries freed from authoritarian regimes, especially in Italy, Germany and, later on, Portugal and Spain. The tragic end of the Weimar Republic, which concluded the crisis of parliamentarism during the first German democracy (which had been unable to defend the 1919 Constitution), further supported the setting up of a specific court acting as the "keeper" of the constitution. Such a court was empowered not merely to render a law not applicable in a specific judicial case, as was the case in the United States, but also to declare the invalidity *erga omnes* of a law and thus deem it unconstitutional *tout court*. As we shall see, recent theory advocating a "constitutional democracy" is strictly connected with such important political and constitutional developments.[58]

4 A COHERENT AND UNITARY THEORETICAL FRAMEWORK

As we have seen, legal and institutional differences between the experiences and doctrines of the rule of law hinge upon the attribution of sovereignty, constitutional mechanisms, and the protection of individual rights. Such elements are particularly meaningful with respect to the "great divide" between the English version of the rule of law and other Western experiences. However, as we shall now argue, such diversities are strongly reduced and eventually disappear when their philosophical and political assumptions, as well as their grounding values, are taken into account. This is also the case with respect to a great number of legal institutions and political structures, which in substantially similar ways, characterize all the above experiences. It is on the basis of such assumptions that the complexity of the "external history" of the rule of law may be rightfully reduced on a theoretical level. Our attempt to unify the diversity of historical experiences within a coherent and unitary theoretical framework thus becomes plausible and provides the "rule of law" with a precise conceptual identity.

Under such a perspective, the rule of law is a normative and institutional structure of the European modern state, within which, on the basis of specific philosophical and political assumptions, the legal system is entrusted with the task of protecting individual rights, by constraining the inclination of political power to expand, to act arbitrarily and to abuse its prerogatives. In more analytical terms, it may be argued that the rule of law is a legal and institutional figure resulting from a centuries-old evolutionary process, which leads to the establishment, within the structures of the European modern state, of two fundamental principles: the "distribution of power" and the "differentiation of power".[59]

The "principle of distribution" tends to limit the powers of the state by means of explicit restraints, with the aim of enlarging the scope of individual freedoms. Therefore, it entails a legal definition of public powers and their relationship with respect to the powers of each individual, these also being legally defined.

The "principle of differentiation" stands for the functional differentiation of the political-legal system from other social subsystems, in particular from ethical-religious and economic ones. It stands also for the delimitation, coordination, and legal regulation of the state's distinct functions, summarily corresponding to the enactment (*legis latio*) and enforcement (*legis executio*) of legislation.

4.1 The philosophical and political premises

Let us first examine the philosophical premises and the underlying ethical assumptions shared by the different experiences of the rule of law and their corresponding theories. Norberto Bobbio strongly argues that individualism is the general philosophical and political premise of the rule of law and the doctrine of fundamental rights.[60] Providing an inevitable historiographic simplification, Bobbio claims that the relationship between the state and citizens has been "overturned": in Europe, through the rise of the modern nation state, the priority of individuals' duties towards political (and religious) authorities has been turned into the priority of citizens' rights and into the authorities' duty to acknowledge, protect, and finally promote such rights. In the European modern (sovereign, national, and secular) state, the original deontic figure, i.e. individual duty, gives way to another largely contrasting deontic figure, i.e. individual expectation or claim, which is collectively acknowledged and protected in the shape of "individual right".

On a historical level, the above "overturning of perspectives" clearly occurred during the religious wars, which ended in the middle of the seventeenth century with the Peace of Westphalia. During such wars, the right to resist oppression, i.e. individuals' rights to enjoy some fundamental freedoms, started to gain ground. Such freedoms were deemed to be fundamental because they were metaphysically taken as "natural". Therefore, it may be maintained that the political and legal model of the rule of law took root in Europe and, it is worth underlining, exclusively in Europe, in that, throughout a long political and anthropological evolution, a precise line of thought in contrast to the "Aristotelian" (and Aristotelian-Thomist) model arose and became prevalent.

Having relinquished the organicist conception of social life, according to which an individual's integration in the political group was the very condition for his humanity and rationality, there emerged the natural-law perspective or, as it has been suggested, the perspective of "modern natural law" in contrast with "old natural law".[61] Through very complex events dating back, at least, to the voluntarism of Franciscan theology of the thirteenth and fourteenth centuries and its further development by William of Ockham – without overlooking the conflictualist and democratic-radical traditions, from Machiavelli to Spinoza – the conceptualization of individual rights as "natural rights" became rooted.[62] Natural rights were *jura* in contrast with *leges*, i.e. in contrast with the sovereign's orders and with "objective law" expressed and guaranteed by the sovereign *potestas*. The harmonistic and nomologic conceptions of the natural order declined, together with its hierarchical structure, dating back to classical doctrines (the Greeks' *homonoia* and Cicero's *concordia*) and largely developed by Catholic scholars. In direct contrast with such philosophies, the metaphysical and social primacy of the human being was consolidated and his individual "conscience" emerged as a scope for his moral autonomy and political freedom, even though within a social context to be ordered by reason, ethics, and law.[63] "Old" natural law lost its normative compactness and was fragmented into a plurality of "natural rights" no longer depending on the group's will – not being granted by its political and religious authorities – rather, being acknowledged by the political community as its own foundation, as a condition for its own legitimacy. The preservation of human natural and indefeasible rights became, according to the revolutionary emphasis of the 1789 *Declaration*, "the aim of any political association".[64]

In terms of political philosophy and legal theory, the following two principles are the corollaries of the ontological primacy of the individual subject and the axiological value of his freedom and autonomy: (1) political pessimism, namely the idea of the intrinsic dangerousness of political power; and (2) normative optimism, namely the belief that the dangerousness of political power can be constrained by law, that is by a set of constitutionally guaranteed individual rights and the "juridicalization" of the whole structure of the state.

Pessimism towards political power – which is a classical theory of European liberalism – is grounded on the assumption that power is both functionally necessary and socially dangerous. Although power, especially in its repressive manifestations, is necessary to guarantee political order, cohesion, and stability, it is also dangerous – and as such it is the most serious threat to individual rights – because, by nature, it tends to concentrate, to recursively reproduce itself, and to become arbitrary.

Political pessimism is profoundly extraneous to the Aristotelian-Thomist philosophy, since such philosophy grants political power a "ministerial" function to serve the "common good" and conceives of it as the vicarious projection of ethical and religious authorities, if not even of divine omnipotence. Pessimism towards political power is also extraneous to the political organicism endorsed by Islam and by most Eastern philosophies, especially Confucianism, which believe that the individual, at least in principle, ought loyally to obey political authorities, towards which he cannot oppose any legal claim.

The pessimistic theory is also extraneous both to the revolutionary optimism of Marxism and to the ethical conceptions of the state, which inspired twentieth-century totalitarian regimes, *in primis* German National Socialism. According to Carl Schmitt, the belief that political power can be subject to law, i.e. exerted according to general and neutral legal rules, is a normativistic (Kelsen-based) illusion, since power is "decision" by nature, namely discretion, partiality, particularism, and exception.[65] Political decisions have nothing to do with following rules; rather, they create them *ex novo*, and this is indeed the specific and positive function of political power.

In contrast with the many versions of political optimism – whether they be ethical-religious, revolutionary, or totalitarian – the pessimism inspiring the theorists of the rule of law requires the presence, within the state, of normative apparatuses and institutional bodies entrusted with the task of identifying, contrasting, and repressing the political misuse of power and legal arbitrariness. Moreover, in order to curb power's arbitrariness, the theorists of the rule of law believe that the force of the legal system is a necessary, and somehow sufficient, means. Law – positive law, no longer just natural law – can and must act as an instrument for the ritualization of the exercise of power. In other words, the state's powers (above all executive and judicial powers) must be bound to respect general rules. Being a "general and abstract" normative instrument, "law" must replace the *commissio*, i.e. the monarch's personal orders and his arbitrary *lettres de cachet*. By imposing general forms and procedures – much more effectively than by prescribing specific contents or aims – legislative provisions can drastically reduce political discretion. If power is bound to act in accordance with general rules and preset forms, it is more transparent – or less opaque – and thus more "visible" and open to citizens' control.[66] Therefore, within the European contemporary state, the legal system is required to perform a threefold – problematic and somewhat ambiguous – function: to be an instrument for the social order and have political stability it expresses governmental power, to be a legislative mechanism to ritualize and limit political power and, strictly complementary to this function, to guarantee individual rights.

4.2 The distribution of power

The principle of the "distribution of power" acts as a general legal criterion for the granting of opportunities and powers to individual subjects. Under the rule of law, individuals – together with the institutions and the associations they legitimately give rise to – are holders of a wide range of legitimate claims and micropowers. Such claims and powers, being legally defined, may be legitimately exerted even against governmental institutions, whose scope of action is limited accordingly. The legal system, through its behavioural rules and procedural restraints, concurs in rendering the exercise of political power more "visible" and in contrasting its intrinsic despotic penchant. At the same time, it limits the scope of political power by defining the ambits of political "non-interference" so as to protect individuals' fundamental rights, above all their freedom and property. The legal entitlement to opportunities, claims, and powers that monarchical absolutism had hierarchized and concentrated in the subjects and organs of the state, is therefore socially spread out. Outside the scope of official power, there are no longer mere submitted subjects but, rather, citizens endowed with legally acknowledged powers.

Throughout the different historical experiences of the rule of law, the principle of the distribution of power has been essentially expressed by the following normative or institutional modalities.

4.2.1 Unicity and individuality of the legal subject. Under the rule of law all individuals are subjects of the legal system. Therefore, all members of the political community are granted, in principle, an equal capacity of being holders of rights, and of performing acts bearing legal consequences.[67] By overcoming a millenary tradition, which was still in force in medieval legal systems – suffice it to mention the Edict of Theodoric or the Edict of Rotary, or the Magna Carta itself – the rule of law first applied the principle of the unicity and individuality of the legal subject. "Quite obviously", female inequality still remained within the rule of law, especially with respect to family law and political rights.[68] As for such rights, different criteria for census-based discrimination, theorized by both Sieyès and Kant, were long applied also to male citizens. Yet, apart from such well-known anomalies, under the rule of law any difference pertaining to individual legal status (e.g. among free men, freed men, servants, and slaves) were erased in Europe.[69] Furthermore, cities, corporations, baronies, or episcopates were no longer acknowledged as holders of feudal privileges guaranteed by charters or ad hoc statutes.

4.2.2 The legal equality of individual subjects. All individual subjects are equal before the law. Thanks to the general nature of any legislative act, subjective situations falling within a given abstract legal figure are treated alike, namely in the light of the same normative principles and according to the same rules. Hence, the legal consequences of legally equivalent actions are the same. This does not mean that the rule of law equalizes citizens on the basis of given factual or finalistic standards. Legal equality is not to be mistaken either for "substantial equality" (in Western countries, such a generic expression mostly stands for some kind of equalization of economic and social conditions), or for the effective and equal enjoyment of the rights individuals formally hold. In fact, each individual is able to enjoy the same rights (freedom of speech, teaching, press, association, economic initiative, etc.) in different ways and scopes, and it is only with respect to his actual entitlement to such rights that he is treated equally with respect to other holders of rights. In many legal (not only factual) respects, property-owners are indeed different from the property-less, employees are different from self-employed workers, minors are different from adults, citizens are different from foreigners, and previous offenders are different from citizens without criminal records. Ergo, formal equality stands for the suppression of privileges, these being tantamount to normative discriminations among citizens in legally equivalent factual conditions. Hence, at the same time, formal equality implicitly acknowledges the vast range of factual inequalities – above all, economic and social inequalities, which the rule of law is not expected *qua talis* to reduce or cancel – assumed by the legal system as legitimate premises for different treatments.[70]

4.2.3 The certainty of law. Under the rule of law the state commits itself to guarantee all citizens the possibility to foresee, in principle, the legal consequences of both their behaviour and that of the other social subjects they necessarily interact with. In other words, all citizens – not only members of social elites – must be provided with cognitive means allowing them to foresee what kind of decisions affecting them may be taken in the future by the state's powers – especially by the executive and the judiciary. Under this perspective, the "certainty of law" is a widespread social good, which concurs in strengthening individual expectations and reducing social uncertainty. Employing Niklas Luhmann's systemic terminology, it may be held that, by guaranteeing the certainty of law, the state and its legal system perform a "reduction of complexity", which helps to mitigate citizens' uncertainty towards the risks of the social environment, and thus allows for a more stable, ordered, and functionally economical social interaction.[71] The specific contribution of the certainty of law – this reducing citizens' insecurity towards legal risks – is the possibility for all citizens to confidently take care of their own business and to claim their rights, with good chances of success, with respect to both their social partners and political authorities.

In order for the certainty of law to be implemented, citizens must above all be given the opportunity to know the law in force. They must not be doomed to *ignorantia legis* (ignorance of the law) as a result of the impossibility of knowing in advance and of interpreting with relative certainty the rules concerning them and applied by administrative authorities. Hence, laws must not be secret, and normative propositions must be clearly formulated and must not give rise to possible antinomies. Moreover, laws must not have a retroactive effect, especially in criminal matters, where the *nullum crimen sine lege* (no crime without law) principle must be upheld. Furthermore, since even the most absolute certainty of law may be frustrated by an arbitrary jurisdiction, the principle of the "natural judge" (a judge predetermined by law) must be upheld and, connected with such principle, ad hoc courts must be prohibited.[72] Lastly, as controversially underlined by Leoni and Hayek, the certainty of law requires legislative power itself not to cause normative instability, which may occur if, by means of redundant legislation, parliaments, or governments – especially when not bound by rigid constitutional provisions – frequently and unforeseeably alter the regulation of cases.[73]

4.2.4 The constitutional acknowledgement of individual rights. The rule of law hinges upon the acknowledgement of rights as "original" normative prerogatives of individual subjects or the "positive" granting of such rights to all members of the political community. Going beyond notable differences in terms of philosophical reasoning and modes of legal protection – natural law doctrines versus legal positivism, universalism versus particularism, constitutional rigidity versus constitutional flexibility, and judicial review of legislation versus the absolute primacy of legislative power – different experiences of the rule of law are characterized by the constitutional commitment to guarantee individual rights, granting their holders the power to claim them on a judicial level, even against the state's organs.

If Thomas Marshall's historical and sociological taxonomy is endorsed, individual rights may be divided into three categories: civil rights, political rights, and social rights.[74] In addition to the right to life, civil rights include the "freedom rights": personal freedom, the procedural guarantees of *habeas corpus* against repressive powers, freedom of thought, speech and religion, the inviolability of personal domicile, the confidentiality of personal communications, and so on. Patrimonial rights – firstly the right of property and the freedom of economic initiative – contractual autonomy (i.e. the right to make binding contracts) and the right to apply to the courts are strictly connected with civil rights.

Political rights formally acknowledge citizens' interest in participating in the exercise of political power, either as members of bodies endowed with decisional authority or as electors of them. The general suffrage for the election of Parliament and of other public assemblies is the main expression of this acknowledgement. Lastly, social rights – affecting job, health, home, social assistance, social security, etc. – aim at giving a normative status to citizens' interest in education, well-being and social security, in line with the prevailing standards of a given (industrialized) country.

If the above threefold division of rights is upheld, the rule of law may be said to be essentially concerned with the protection of civil rights, in that these coincide with the range of "negative freedoms".[75] In the second half of the nineteenth century, such a protection was extended – albeit through social tensions, difficulties, and deficiencies – to political rights, whereas "social rights", safeguarded only in part by the twentieth century European Welfare state, remained substantially outside the functional logic of the rule of law. According to such a logic, to be entitled to civil and political rights allows each individual to be freely involved, as an "independent unit", in social interaction. At the same time, this justifies the assumption that all individuals are provided with the legal tools necessary to be socially successful without resorting to the state's paternalistic protection.[76]

4.3 *The differentiation of power*

As mentioned above, the principle of the differentiation of power, being a characteristic element of the rule of law, entails two main aspects: (1) the self-differentiation of the political and legal subsystem from other functional subsystems; (2) the internal differentiation of the political subsystem within a process, which increases its complexity, specialization and efficiency, and gives rise to a plurality of different political structures and ways of waging power. As it is known, such a process has been interpreted and popularized by liberal political theories (from Montesquieu onwards) as a strategy for the "separation of powers" intentionally aimed at guaranteeing balance among the state's organs (the "moderate government") and, ultimately, the protection of individual rights.[77]

As regards the first aspect, the European rule of law is characteristic of a specific kind of political subsystem which stands out, when compared with political forms of the past, for its high functional autonomy with respect to ethical-religious and economic subsystems. It is through this functional autonomy that the individualistic political philosophy was successful within the experience of the rule of law, in contrast with the ancient organicist model. In fact, the conception of individual opportunities, claims, and powers as legal rights (not as mere ethical-religious expectations) refers to the general process of the 'positivization of law' as its necessary functional premise. In other words, the "positive" legal system grounds the normative value of its prescriptions on the "social contract", that is on the will of the members of the political community, thus no longer referring to transcendent deontologies.[78] It is through such an evolutionary conquest that, in Europe, the legal system, freed from its traditional ethical and theological envelopments, also broke with Aristotelian-Thomist organicism and with the monistic conception of what is true and good. As seen, this is particularly the case of the English tradition of the common law and the liberal philosophy that in Germany gave rise to the *Rechtsstaat*. Moreover, it is precisely the high functional autonomy of the legal subsystem that allows for the rule of law to establish the principle of individuals' formal equality, namely an equality, which ignores the different positions that individual subjects hold within other functional subsystems grounded on property, political power, or family relationships. Not surprisingly, it is precisely such a "formalistic" and "atomistic" social structure that was later at the heart of Marx's early communist criticism of "equal law" and "bourgeois freedoms".[79] After all, both the unicity-individuality of legal subjects and their formal equality are, in turn, functional factors concurring in the development of a market economy that is itself freed from organicist premises and ethical-religious aims.[80]

As regards the second aspect – the internal functional differentiation – the rule of law is typical of a highly complex political system. Such complexity is due, first of all, to the division of the political system into two formally separate ambits: on the one hand, the conquest and management of political power through the organization of political parties and electoral rituals; on the other hand, administrative activity, unified by the task of issuing binding decisions through bureaucratic procedures.[81] Unlike in despotic or totalitarian regimes, under the rule of law political parties (just like trade unions) are not organs of the state's bureaucracy and cannot make *erga omnes* binding decisions. In turn, the administrative function is organized on the basis of two sub-functions which, in principle, are performed within distinct institutional settings and with different procedures: on the one hand, the legislative power, primarily conferred upon elective parliaments entitled to enact general and abstract laws; on the other hand, the enforcement of general and abstract laws or, more precisely, the issuing of binding decisions with respect to single actual cases,[82] which is essentially performed by organs that are administrative in strict terms. Lastly, within administration, a further functional autonomization process has been developed: the "judiciary power" has parted from the "executive power", thus freeing itself from being bureaucratically subject to the political government. The judiciary makes decisions on the basis of its members' (disputed) impartiality and political autonomy.

Very schematically, it can thus be asserted that throughout the different historical experiences of the rule of law, the principle of the differentiation of power has been expressed by the following institutional modalities.

4.3.1 The delimitation of the scope of political power and law enforcement. The self-differentiation of the political system, which is fully accomplished under the rule of law, has two symmetrical effects: on the one hand, it tends to exclude the functional interference of ethical-religious and economic subsystems from the ambit of politics and law; on the other hand, it explicitly defines the functional scope of the legal-political subsystem by limiting (or self-limiting) the state's internal sovereignty. The clear-cut boundary line between "the public" and "the private", excludes what in Europe has been called – from Ferguson to Marx and Gramsci – "civil society" (*bürgerliche Gesellschaft, società civile*) from the scope of politics and law. Civil society includes the realm of privacy, i.e. religious beliefs and practices, sexual and family relationships, personal communications and information, the expression of literary and artistic creativity, and so on. It also includes the sphere of contractual autonomy, entrepreneurial initiatives, and patrimonial activities in general.

4.3.2 The separation between legislative institutions and administrative ones. As we have seen, under the rule of law a specialized organ (parliament) is entrusted with the task of enacting general and abstract norms (laws), whereas the executive and the judiciary are given the role of applying the laws, i.e. more precisely of issuing particular and concrete norms (administrative decisions or judgements), and seeing to their enforcement. Although the line between enacting general norms (*legis latio*) and applying them (*legis executio*) is very subtle, it is nonetheless unquestionable that the rule of law provides for a dual system which, at least in principle, separates legislative institutions from administrative ones.

4.3.3 The primacy of the legislative power, the principle of legality, the reserve of legislation. Under the rule of law, organs entitled to enact general norms (laws) are granted functional primacy with respect to organs deciding particular cases by issuing specific norms (executive acts and judgements). Such primacy may be more or less absolute according to the high or low degree of subordination of the legislative power to constitutional principles and according to the how intense is control on constitutional legality by the judiciary. However, the entire normative and institutional functioning of the rule of law is moulded by the "principle of legality", through which each administrative act – whether executive or judicial – must comply with a previous general norm.[83] The same functional logic underpins the principle of "statutory reservation", stating that only the legislative power is entitled to enact norms concerning individual rights, thus excluding executive and judicial powers from such a function.

4.3.4 The obligation of the legislative power to respect individual rights. The limitation of the legislative power is one of the most delicate and controversial problems of the rule of law's experience. However, it can be argued that, albeit in different ways, within all the historical experiences of the rule of law the legislative power appears to be limited by its political commitment or legal obligation to respect constitutionally acknowledged individual rights. Such restraints have an implicit, i.e. political, nature in Great Britain, Germany, and France, whereas they have a mainly legal (judicial) nature in the United States.

4.3.5 The autonomy of the judiciary. Leaving aside the question of public prosecutors – which would require a different and much more complex analysis – under the rule of law all judges are "subject only to law". Among the various administrative activities, the judicial function is notable for its ambition to occupy a "third" or neutral institutional ambit with respect to conflicting political and social interests. Therefore, in the exercise of their decisional powers, judges act independently of any hierarchical subordination, in particular towards the executive high ranks, which by their nature follow the ideological preferences of a given political majority.

5 THE EPISTEMOLOGICAL STATUS OF THE RULE OF LAW, ITS POLITICAL ASSUMPTIONS, AND LIMITS OF VALIDITY

The theoretical synopsis of the previous paragraph should satisfy the double need our essay sprang from, namely to elaborate a theory of the rule of law that could be both acceptable from a historical point of view and, at the same time, useful in cognitive terms, that is, helpful in understanding and solving practical problems.

The above theoretical reconstruction of the rule of law provides a unitary and coherent picture of the philosophical assumptions and the normative-institutional means, which have characterized its most important experiences. Although such a reconstruction is only one of the many possible interpretations of a highly complex phenomenon, it should be persuasive in a historical perspective. However, it endows the notion of rule of law with a rather precise meaning and differentiates it from other notions for which it has often been mistaken within the intricate bundle of concepts, formulas, and postulates in which it has long been submerged. In the light of our interpretation, the rule of law may be defined as *the normative and institutional framework of the European modern state which, on the basis of an individualistic philosophy (with the double corollary of political pessimism and normative optimism) and through processes of distribution and differentiation of power, entrusts the legal system with the primary task of protecting civil and political rights, thus contrasting, for this purpose, political authorities' inclination towards arbitrariness and misuse of their powers.*

We shall now specify the epistemological status of this theory, its philosophical and political implications, as well as the limits of its validity. This will then allow us to assess the cognitive usefulness of the rule of law when set against the range of problems which, within the contemporary processes of increasing social complexity and global integration, must be tackled to protect individual rights and limit political arbitrariness. Quite obviously, such matters nowadays need to be examined by giving ample room to international and transnational experiences, thus going well beyond the political space of the rule of law, i.e. that of the sovereign nation state.[84]

5.1 The epistemological status

As far as the epistemological status of the suggested theory of rule of law is concerned, its evaluative and not formalistic character ought to be underlined. Despite not being a general theory of justice and not drawing from classic ethical and political metaphysics, the theory of the rule of law entails, as we have seen, some specific options as to the aims of politics and law. The hostility towards arbitrary power and the call for the certainty of law – which have been interpreted by some authors as axiologically adiaphorous[85] – themselves entail a clear ethical assumption, in that they favour a rational and foreseeable political order, where law primarily guarantees individuals' freedom and the security of their transactions (thus giving less importance to "communitarian" topics, such as social justice, solidarity, and equality). Though the rule of law is not an ethical and political project for the realization of the "best republic" – neither is it aimed at realizing a "state of justice"[86] – and though it relies on the functionally differentiated instrument of law, it is inconceivable outside the scope of a typically Western anthropology, namely individualistic, rationalistic, and secularized.

Neither can it be held that the theory of the rule of law merely recommends given procedures lacking prescriptive content, i.e. it is a merely procedural conceptualization of the state and the law, and as such is ideologically neutral. It is undeniable that, in many respects, the model of the rule of law is concerned with procedural techniques or institutional devices which, as such, may appear as axiologically indefinite and merely formal. The certainty of law may seem indifferent to the ethical and political contents of law, so much so that it could be argued, for instance, that racist legislation might be compatible with the rule of law as long as its prescriptions were clear, non-contradictory and non-retroactive: *la légalité qui tue*, in other words. By resorting to similar considerations, also the "principle of legality" might be construed in a purely formal way, as claimed by Antonin Scalia, who views the rule of law as the "rule of rules".[87] In fact, the principle of legality does not imply any ethical and political assessment of the contents of a given law, either by the administrator bound to apply it or by the citizens, who are its ultimate recipients.

Yet, such interpretations seem to overlook the circumstances that, according to the theory of the rule of law, formal institutions and procedures are not self-referential and self-grounding. Rather, they pursue the aim of protecting individual rights, by which the legislator himself is bound. They are nothing but the linear means for such an aim, which is after all cogently declared by constitutional texts or traditions. By ignoring such a simple and enlightening axiom, formalistic interpretations of the rule of law – just like similar proceduralist theories of democracy – display the general flaw of all formalistic doctrines on politics and law, not to speak of the linguistic and cognitive formalism they implicitly refer to.[88]

5.2 The rule of law and the theory of individual rights

The doctrine of the rule of law is, quite probably, the most important heritage that, at the beginning of the third millennium, the European political tradition offers the world's political culture. Its exceptional theoretical relevance lies in its (successful) attempt to guarantee the individual's fundamental freedoms within, and by means of, a given organization of political power, i.e. the nation state. In comparison with any other civilization, the European rule of law uniquely combines the need for order and security, which is at the heart of political life, with the demand for civil and political freedoms, which is particularly felt within complex societies. The invention of "subjective rights" as the legal expression of individual freedom is, besides the undoubted effectiveness of the techniques used to differentiate and balance powers, the key to its originality and success. Within a few centuries, such an "invention" has taken hold as a general model both in Europe and in North America. The demise of fascist authoritarianism and Marxist collectivism only confirmed its success in the twentieth century. Nowadays, not only is the model of the rule of law not challenged by other alternatives in the Western world, but it also seems bound to be imposed at an international level as a condition for the rationality, modernity, and progress of the cultures of all continents, including the farthest ones, such as Islamic cultures, American and African autochthonous cultures and, in the Far East, Hinduism, Buddhism, and Confucianism.[89]

However, in order to uphold the universality of the model or support its increasing international expansion, there are at least three theoretical issues concerning its conceptual instrumentation and its institutional implications that need to be assessed and possibly solved. The first issue concerns the relationship between the model of the rule of law and democratic theory; the second issue stems from the conflict between the (democratic) principle of popular sovereignty and the suggestion – advanced by a large number of theorists of the rule of law – to render constitutional Bills of Rights more rigid; the third issue concerns the philosophical foundations and thus the universal value of the theory of individual rights (or, in the international legal lexicon, "human rights").

5.2.1 Rule of law and democracy. The doctrine of the rule of law is clearly different from the idea of democracy (and of a "democratic state"), even in its weakest versions drawing inspiration from Schumpeter's criticism of classical participatory and representative models of democracy.[90]Although authoritative liberal-democratic thinkers, starting with Norberto Bobbio, Ralf Dahrendorf and Jürgen Habermas, deem the protection of individual rights to be a *conditio sine qua non* (an absolute condition) of any possible democratic regime, the institutions of the rule of law are, as such, indifferent to given key points of the – classic and post-classic – democratic conception of the political system. With the exception of a very weak and implicit hint at the representative nature of the legislative power, the theory of the rule of law is not committed to issues, such as popular sovereignty, citizens' actual participation in collective decisions, the procedures and values of political representation, the pluralism of political contenders or governments' accountability, and responsiveness.[91]

In a nutshell, the legal and political framework of the rule of law may be juxtaposed to the classical absolute state, the modern totalitarian state and, in general, the police state. However, it is not in conflict with oligarchic and technocratic regimes, characterized by a mass political apathy and by great economic and social differences. The rule of law seems to be more in line with the liberal political tradition than with a political philosophy grounded on citizens' civil responsibility, on the transparency and diffusion of political communication, and on the vitality of the public sphere. Under the rule of law, the threat to individual freedoms seems to derive exclusively from the arbitrary acts of the state's organs, and not also from the misuse of their powers by subjects belonging to the social and economic world.

It follows that the internationalization of the model of the rule of law may oppose principles and values which are – or, rather, have been – important components of the European democratic experience. In practical terms, this is nowadays true for the process of European integration, as underlined by the undergoing debate on the "democratic deficit" of European institutions, despite their commitment to protecting individual rights (confirmed by the Charter of Fundamental Rights approved at the Nice summit[92]). The risk of dismissing crucial democratic values is also dramatically present on a global scale, as proven by the sharp contrast between, on the one hand, great Western powers and, on the other, many non-Western countries and a great number of non-governmental associations and transnational political movements. Western powers favour the international expansion of the model of the rule of law, together with an uncompromising defence of the universality, interdependence, and indivisibility of "human rights". Other countries, however, are much more sensitive to what they call "collective rights", extended so as to comprise the reduction of economic and social inequalities, the protection of peoples' cultural identity and political autonomy, the fight against poverty and epidemic illnesses, and the freedom of economically backward countries from foreign indebtedness.[93]

5.2.2 Constitution, individual rights, popular sovereignty. As we have seen above when specifically examining US and French constitutionalism – the English "exception" has been separately analysed – two different approaches, here conventionally called "liberal" and "democratic", may be adopted with respect to the constitutional guarantee of individual rights.

5.2.2.1 *The liberal approach.* The liberal approach, which is typical of the United States experience, tends to conceive the Bill of Rights as the source of all principles and rules protecting fundamental freedoms. The normative validity of the rule of law stems from the assumption of rationality and ethical universality of its principles, so that no parliamentary majority – not even the unanimous consent of the members of elective assemblies – can abrogate constitutional provisions regarding, for example, the right to life, the rights of freedom, and the right of property and economic initiative. Any parliamentary decision to abrogate such provisions, even when it complies with the procedures established for constitutional amendments, should be deemed to be constitutionally subversive and thus null and inapplicable.

Such a theoretical stance entails procedurally and institutionally notable corollaries: firstly, the foundations of the rule of law need to be firmly grounded by rendering the constitutional provisions that protect individuals' rights as rigid as possible, that is, by requiring qualified majorities and other procedural hindrances for the parliamentary review of the constitution. Secondly, and most importantly, the legislative power must also be institutionally limited, thus entrusting the judiciary with the task of evaluating (with *erga omnes* efficacy) the constitutionality of laws.

In the second half of the twentieth century, with the persistent exception of Great Britain, the "liberal" approach, initially developed in the United States, prevailed also within the experience of European constitutionalism, especially in Germany and Italy, and thus ended up by being identified *tout court* with the continental doctrine of the rule of law. According to such an approach, the guarantee of fundamental rights depended on mutual checks and balances between "constituted powers", including the legislative power, under the watchful eye of the Constitutional Court, as authoritatively suggested by Hans Kelsen. At the same time, the "democratic" idea, according to which the constituent power is the source of any possible constitutional legitimacy, lost its strength.[94] Accordingly, the idea of the almightiness of the democratic legislator was rejected: democracy could not but be a "constitutional democracy", limited by a liberal constitution within which fundamental rights, as written by Luigi Ferrajoli, were deemed to be inalienable and inviolable and therefore "not susceptible of decision"[95] by any political majority or power, since they were beyond popular sovereignty.

5.2.2.2 *The democratic approach.* According to the "democratic" approach, the protection of individual rights and, more generally, the establishment of the state's organs and the definition of their functions depend on the constituent power and on the permanent initiative of the political community. Such a voluntaristic approach does not identify the constitution with the guarantee of rights and the separation of powers, as advocated by the famous Article 16 of the 1789 Declaration of the Rights of Man and the Citizen.[96] Provided the constitution has been freely desired and democratically established by most members of the political community, it is fully valid, even if it is not inferred from liberal principles. In this case, the model to draw inspiration from is the French revolutionary experience, which preceded the formulation of the theory of the *État de droit* and which Carré de Malberg directly criticized. In the French experience, the establishment of rights was the result of political struggles, which were successful thanks, *inter alia*, to the support of the elective assemblies; it was not the result of a sophisticated and bureaucratic balance between the powers of a "mixed" or "moderate" government. According to this approach, it is believed that the rigid nature of the constitution or the review of legislation by a Constitutional Court is not a crucial means to protect individual rights. What is more important is a watchful public opinion, an open and competent political debate and a permanent popular initiative, leading, if necessary, to the prompt legislative (or referendum-based) updating of constitutions and declarations of rights. Just like any other normative act, the Bill of Rights is doomed to be overcome by social changes, especially because such changes are quickened by the evolutionary rapidity of complex societies. Excessive constitutional inflexibility may lead to social backwardness and may hinder democracy. It may also poorly protect rights since it relies on legal institutions that pretend to neutralize politics.[97]

5.2.2.3 *An ideological-political alternative.* Although the above two approaches are equally concerned with the protection and promotion of individual rights, a theoretical solution that reconciles them in a compromise between normativistic rationalism – typical of the Euro-continental doctrine of the rule of law – and democratic voluntarism is not feasible. Quite obviously, the "democratic" approach may be criticized because the lack (or weakness) of procedural and institutional restraints safeguarding the Bill of Rights may be dangerous, since it leaves both the fate of individual rights and of democracy itself in the hands of temporary parliamentary majorities. In fact, a formal democratic regime is inconceivable without respect for the main freedom rights. Hence, the "liberal" approach is, in truth, a vital guarantee of democracy itself, since it reduces the risk – not a mere scholastic risk, as shown by the downfall of the Weimar Republic – that a democratic regime may be removed and replaced by an authoritarian regime without this requiring any breach of parliamentary procedures.[98] Democracy is thus strengthened, not weakened, by liberal restraints preventing its self-destruction.

However, the "liberal" approach can also be criticized. In rigorous theoretical terms, it is irrelevant whether a constitution is approved or modified by a qualified majority rather than by a simple majority or by an absolute majority. The point is that a constitution – as a single constitutional norm – always expresses the will of a given portion of the "people" (or of the "nation"), no matter how wide it may be, against the will of another portion, just as it happens with ordinary laws, which are usually approved by simple majority. This is particularly the case of complex societies, characterized by the "polytheism" of cultures and moral values. Hence, also constitutional norms concerning individual rights are not the expression of a Rousseau-inspired "general will" but rather of the preferences of a given political majority. Little does it matter whether this majority deems the principles it endorses to be beyond political dispute; on the contrary, such a belief renders its "liberal" stance dogmatic and potentially intolerant.

Its historical and partisan genesis should thus discourage any attribution of rationality, unchangeability, or even sacredness to any constitution, even to one committed to civil liberties and politically inclusion. Contrary to Kelsen's claim that a constitution has no political author, it must be acknowledged that constitutional principles express political ideologies and ethical values that were shared (and or are still shared) only by a greater or smaller majority of citizens and rejected (and/or are still rejected) by a minority. It follows that even a liberal-democratic constitution may be oppressive towards the interests and expectations of minorities that dissent from the constituent majority. In fact, the majority might even be favourable to the death penalty and to war, and/or might be opposed to homosexual family rights, abortion, euthanasia, or to respect for animals and the prohibition against killing them. Therefore, the tendency to fix the range of liberal values at a given moment of their historical development, and to entrust judicial bureaucracies with the task of ensuring that elective assemblies do not introduce illiberal legislative innovations, runs the risk of being paradoxically dogmatic, and despotic. The relevance and originality of the Euro-continental versions of the rule of law within its "external" history in the twentieth century cannot be denied. However, the risk they currently run is a kind of constitutional conservatism, fossilizing the will of their "founding fathers". Such a risk may be worsened by granting high judicial courts the power to interpret the constitution – which is in fact a constituent and legislative power – such as to allow them to mould the constitution, which is nonetheless regarded as "rigid", i.e. untouchable by Parliament.[99] Besides, one might ask advocates of the "liberal" approach which bodies, if not supreme courts, should be entitled to decide which political issues cannot be subject to free public debate and decision – e.g. referendum-based – on the grounds that they are constitutionally not susceptible to political decision.[100]

Therefore, it seems that the "liberal" approach is open to criticism no less than the "democratic" one. In order to remedy such criticism, US and Euro-continental theorists of the rule of law should rigorously isolate the (few or even very few) constitutional principles – regarding, for instance, freedom of thought and its public expression – whose breach prevents free expression of political will, this being an essential condition of the political legitimacy of governments according to both the "liberal" and the "democratic" approach. Only such constitutional principles should be protected by specific procedures – not by metaphysical biases – rendering their abrogation extremely difficult. It should also be recalled that, within politically fragmented societies – this is often the case of differentiated and complex societies – a simple majority in parliamentary decisions is already a threshold beyond which decisional paralysis is likely to occur.

Thus, the choice between the "liberal" and the "democratic" approach appears to be connected with largely questionable empirical considerations and ideological-political preferences. Such a dilemma may be clarified by a theoretical analysis, though it cannot be resolved.[101]

5.2.3 Foundation and universality of individual rights. A third set of unsolved theoretical questions concerns the philosophical foundation and the universality of human rights. Such questions touch upon the issue as to their general coercive applicability, which was dramatically highlighted by the 1999 "humanitarian war" for Kosovo.[102] According to Norberto Bobbio, a philosophical – and thus rational and universal – foundation of the doctrine of human rights is not conceivable. The reason is, in his opinion, that human rights are burdened by deontic antinomies, especially by that opposing freedom and patrimonial rights to social equality, the latter being a value that the establishment of "social rights" should promote and protect.[103]

Other authors (among them Jack Barbalet) juxtapose, within the normative list of freedom rights, "non-acquisitive" to "acquisitive" rights. The former include first of all the protection of "negative freedom", i.e. the limits imposed on the state's (and third parties') intervention within the private domain, as is the case of personal freedom, freedom of thought, and inviolability of personal domicile and private property; non-acquisitive rights also include the "social rights", which attribute simple powers of consumption or enjoyment. Acquisitive rights, including contractual autonomy, freedom of association of press, and economic initiative, have a marked acquisitive capacity since, under given conditions, their exercise brings about political, economic, and communicative power to the benefit of their holders. Since only a minority of individuals is usually provided with the political, economic, and organizational means necessary to take advantage of the acquisitive capacities of such rights, it follows that their exercise leads to a notable restriction of other individuals' freedoms and an increase in social inequalities. Therefore, the widespread idea that human rights provide individuals with legitimate claims spontaneously converging in a peaceful and progressive social interaction should be abandoned and replaced by the agonistic and selective approach of the "struggle for rights".[104]

Along with Bobbio and Barbalet's theories, it must be added that the doctrine of human rights lacks the necessary criteria (as the systemic lexicon would put it) for cognitive self-regulation, in that it lacks theoretical categories rigorously determining and defining individual rights (the taxonomy suggested by Thomas Marshall, albeit very useful, has a historical and sociological imprint, and is moreover directly moulded on the last three centuries of English history). Hence, the "catalogue of rights" is constantly open to inflation by means of anomic accumulation through successive "generations" of rights or normative interpolations arising out of mere factual circumstances.[105] Some Western philosophers and jurists have even suggested that the theory of individual rights should also cover living beings not belonging to the human species, embryos, and even inanimate objects. In other words, despite the 1948 Universal Declaration and apart from a widespread pragmatic consensus on a number of "fundamental" rights, substantially corresponding to Marshall's "civil rights", nowadays there is no theoretically defined and generally shared "catalogue" of individual rights, even in Western countries. This holds true also for the normative implications and practical applications of single rights.

Let us provide some illustrative examples (among the many available) in this respect. If it is true that the right to life is one of the most normatively "certain" individual rights, it is equally true that there is no theoretical consensus as to its incompatibility with the death penalty, which is widely practised in the United States, although the United States is widely recognized as, and considers itself to be, the homeland of individual rights and of the rule of law. Another example is provided by life imprisonment which, even in the brutal, close-to-torture forms often practised in Western countries, is usually believed to be compatible both with the right of freedom and with prisoners' right to physical and psychic integrity; only a few express dissenting opinions on this subject.[106] A further example: the mutilation of female genitals (known as 'infibulation') – a very common practice in many North-Eastern and Central African countries – has coherently been declared by some European countries to infringe women's right to physical and psychical integrity. As regards the mutilation of male genitals ("circumcision"), it is known that this is practised on millions of minors not only in the Islamic and Jewish world but also in the Western world, especially in the United States, –without explicit religious reasons. Such mutilations are not usually considered a violation of minors' personal integrity. Although the ensuing lesion normally bears less serious consequences than female "infibulation", a minority of Western doctors and jurists stress that it nonetheless entails the irreversible mutilation of a healthy organ, carried out without the consent of the concerned individual and for no valid hygienic reason.[107]

In the light of the above considerations, it may be concluded that the elaboration of a rigorous theory of individual (or "human") rights is not very useful and that a practical commitment to the actual application of rights is sufficient. Bobbio himself seems to agree with this pragmatic stance.[108] It is unquestionable that the legitimization of individual rights cannot but be historical and contingent. After all, it is well known that civil and political rights took root in Europe, at a particular time in its history, as a result of long and bloody social struggles. Hence, it would seem that there is no alternative than to admit that any doctrine of individual rights is philosophically unfounded and deontically imperfect. It is a Western historical output, indeed important for Western countries, yet unable to justify either any universalistic claim or any "civilizing" proselytism.

However, it might also be argued that a rigorous theory of the rule of law requires a rigorous elaboration of the doctrine of individual rights. It might also be added that it is precisely the lack of theoretical rigour that nowadays concurs in rendering uncertain the effectiveness of many aspects of the rule of law, as we shall see below. Moreover, what is even worse, such a deficiency favours the propagandistic distortion of the doctrine of "human rights" and its transformation into a kind of aggressive humanitarian universalism – as indeed was the case of the war for Kosovo, led by Western powers against the Federal Republic of Yugoslavia. Although lacking a philosophical foundation and normative universality, and perhaps precisely for this reason – in that it is freed from the hindrance of universal concepts – the doctrine of individual rights may be "universalized" in communicative terms. In order to do so, two conditions should be met: firstly, the doctrine of individual rights should take on a more rigorous physiognomy – in terms of legal and political theory, not of metaphysical justification; secondly, its communicative universalization should be grounded on an intercultural "translation" of the entire deontical lexicon and syntax of the rule of law model.[109] The topicality and relevance of such problems of intercultural communication are confirmed by the debate, mainly involving Singapore, Malaysia, and China, as to the necessity of opposing "Asian values" to the tendency of Western countries to impose their ethical and political values – above all the rule of law, individual rights, and democracy – together with Western technology, industry, and bureaucracy on Eastern cultures.[110]

5.3 The rule of law and international relations

The most serious constraint on the validity of the doctrine of the rule of law is due to its narrow normative scope, which does not extend beyond the political space of the nation state. Such a limit, which contrasts strangely with the universalistic claim of most of its contemporary advocates, is double-faceted.

5.3.1 Interstate relationships. Firstly, the doctrine of the rule of law is not concerned with the relationship between any single state and other states. Rather, it exclusively deals with the "internal sovereignty" of the state and does not cover its international political and legal relations – its "foreign policy" –, these being entirely left to the agreement-based regulation of conventions and treaties. In other words, while significantly restraining the "internal sovereignty" of the nation state, the rule of law leaves its "external sovereignty" intact, including the *jus ad bellum*, which, since the mid seventeenth-century Peace of Westphalia, has been considered a sovereign prerogative of the state.[111] A rigorous internal application of the provisions of the rule of law may sometimes coexist – Great Britain and France are emblematic examples in this respect – with a warlike and imperialist foreign policy, and the enactment of "colonial law".[112]

It is not by chance that, according to Dicey, the greatest theorist of the English rule of law, the international order was not even a real legal order. Following John Austin's lead, Dicey claimed that international rules could be considered, at most, a sort of (legally not binding) "public ethics".[113] According to Georg Jellinek, an equally authoritative theorist of the *Rechtsstaat*, international law was a set of rules not different and separate from the state's legal system. International obligations were, just like constitutional law and administrative law, the output of the "self-limitation" of the sovereignty of the nation state.[114]

The reason why the doctrine of the rule of law lacks a theory of international law and relations is thus clear. Its principles, in particular the principles of the distribution and differentiation of power, have been conceived so as to be applied only to the state's citizens and institutions. Citizens and institutions of foreign countries are given legal relevance only upon explicitly coming in touch with the domestic legal system and, even in such a case, under given conditions – e.g. the reciprocity clause – and with remarkable exceptions (especially for subjects and institutions not belonging to the Western "civilized world"). What is more, since the time of its founding fathers such as Hugo Grotius, Richard Zouche and Emeric de Vattel modern international law – the Westphalian *jus publicum europaeum* – has acknowledged only nation states as the subjects of its system, excluding individuals, whose rights have been deemed to be automatically represented and protected by the states they belong to.

It ought to be added that the principle of non-interference in domestic jurisdiction, namely into the "internal affairs" of sovereign states, which was the pillar of the Westphalian order until at least the 1980s, excluded the relationship between single governments and their citizens from the competence of international law and institutions, thus not allowing the protection of individual rights to have an international relevance. A remarkable exception was represented by the ad hoc international criminal courts, set up in the twentieth century with the formal aim of trying individuals responsible for serious violations of human rights. Yet, the establishment of such courts – from Nuremberg to Tokyo, and from The Hague to Arusha – has so far been disappointing in many respects. In fact, their experience has proven that an international criminal jurisdiction, failing an international order somehow modelled on the rule of law, cannot have a sufficient degree of impartiality and autonomy with respect to the great powers.[115]

5.3.2 The world order. Secondly, the principles of the rule of law, with the partial exception of Kant's pacifism, have never been theoretically connected with world order and peace,[116] even when, in the first half of the twentieth century, the "Westphalian system" – the "anarchical" system of sovereign states – was modified by the rise of centralized supernational institutions, such as the League of Nations and the United Nations. Despite widespread rhetoric about the international rule of law, the doctrine of the rule of law has had no influence on the organization of institutions – in particular the United Nations – aimed at limiting states' sovereignty for the unlikely attainment of a "stable and universal peace". In fact, international peace was dependent on the hegemonic great powers from time to time successfully ending world conflicts. The establishment of international institutions was inspired more by the hierarchical and authoritarian model of the Holy Alliance than by Kantian cosmopolitan pacifism and the connected ideology of universal citizenship and "cosmopolitan law" (*Weltbürgerrecht*).[117] As Hans Morgenthau held, the United Nations structure, in particular, is based on such a model, in that it is centred around the Security Council, which is dominated by the veto power of five great powers and thus contravenes one of the key principles of the rule of law: the formal equality of all legal subjects.[118]

The thesis that the experience of the rule of law has not inspired any theory on international law and institutions might seem overstated. It might be objected that a great number of contemporary Western thinkers – the "Western globalists", as they were ironically called by Hedley Bull – who, following Kant's and Kelsen's lead, advocate the application of the principles and values of the rule of law to the realization of a political and legal "global system". However, globalist thinkers such as Richard Falk and David Held are, above all, interested in divulging some impressive key words – "global civil society", "global constitutionalism", "global democracy", and "cosmopolitan order" – and in globally "pantographing" their liberal-democratic beliefs. At the same time, they seem scantily interested in either normatively or institutionally specifying the project of a possible "global rule of law" or in interacting with non-Western political and legal cultures, which should be involved in their cosmopolitan projects.[119] As for the most authoritative globalist author, Jürgen Habermas, he does not seem to have any doubts as to the evolutionary causal nexus, so to speak, which closely connects "cosmopolitan law" to the rule of law and universal citizenship to democratic citizenship. "Cosmopolitan law – as he sententiously writes – is a consequence of the idea of the rule of law".[120] Habermas maintains that the cosmopolitan expansion of the Western rule of law obeys both the internal logic of democratic institutions and the semantic content – to the intrinsic universalism – of human rights.

All these are typical instances of a strongly ethnocentric usage of the "domestic analogy", this taking for granted the analogy between, on the one hand, the "civil society" that supported the development of the modern European state in the seventeenth and eighteenth centuries and, on the other hand, the current supposed "global civil society". The analogical argument would allow for all principles of democratic representation, separation of powers, and protection of "human rights" to be applied to all world populations – and to the world as a whole.[121] On the basis of such anthropologically dogmatic premises, Habermas stands out, as is well known, for having advanced universalistic claims favouring both the Gulf War of 1991 and North Atlantic Treaty Organization's (NATO) "humanitarian war" against the Federal Republic of Yugoslavia of 1999.[122]

6 THE CRISIS OF THE RULE OF LAW

The theory of the rule of law should help us in understanding new problems, which today, at the beginning of the third millennium, must be tackled in order to promote individual rights and restrain arbitrary power in the context of increasing social complexity and globalization processes. Such problems can be categorized as adding up to a "crisis of the rule of law". The crisis affects both the functioning of the democratic structures of Western states, especially in their post–Second World War versions, and the international protection of human rights. According to reports by the United Nations and non-governmental organizations (NGOs), such as Amnesty International and Human Rights Watch, millions of people are nowadays victims in all continents of unprecedented violations of their fundamental rights.

The extent of this phenomenon is due not only to the despotic or totalitarian nature of many political regimes but also to arbitrary decisions taken by international bodies endowed with great political, economic, or military power, which globalization processes have rendered uncontrollable and that increase the threat of "global terrorism".[123] Wars, the death penalty, torture, the ill-treatment of prisoners, genocides, poverty, epidemics, international trade rules, foreign indebtedness squeezing the poorest countries, the slavery-like exploitation of minors and women, and the racist oppression of marginalized peoples – from Palestinians to Kurds, Tibetans to Indo-Americans, Roma to African and Australian aboriginals – the destruction of the environment, all contribute to this crisis.

The reasons for the crisis of the rule of law may be grouped in two distinct lists: one concerns the increasing social complexity within advanced industrial societies involved in technological and information revolutions; the other regards integration processes both on a regional – the European Union, first of all – and a global scale. Within the first group, the crisis of the governing capacity of the legal system and the decreasing effectiveness of the protection of individual rights are particularly important. Within the second list, the main issue is the erosion of states' sovereignty and the prevalence of transnational powers and organs not subject to the institutional mechanisms for the distribution and differentiation of power.

6.1 The crisis of the governing capacity of law

It certainly cannot be said that the philosophical premises of the rule of law are nowadays undergoing a crisis within complex Western societies. On the contrary, since the collapse of the Soviet empire and the exhaustion of Marxist ideology, individualism seems to have permeated all aspects of social life, from consumer habits to lifestyles, from family to professional experiences and to the meticulous protection of individual privacy by ad hoc bureaucratic institutions. What seems to be undergoing a serious crisis, instead, is the "governing capacity" of the legal system, i.e. the actual enforcement and regulatory efficiency of the legal prescriptions enacted by different organs performing legislative functions. The reasons behind such a functional *impasse*, particularly affecting Euro-continental democracies, have been assessed by the systemic sociology on law in terms of "law inflation" within differentiated and complex societies.[124]

The process of differentiation of social subsystems compels the legal system to react to their rapid development by increasingly producing more specialized and particular provisions. Yet, law is a rigid and slow structure compared with the evolutionary flexibility of subsystems such as, in particular, the scientific-technologic and economic ones, which are endowed with a notable capacity of rapidly self-programming and self-correcting. This brings about "law inflation", which entails normative devaluation, redundancy and instability and, ultimately, law's regulative inability. Not only is the number of legislative acts multiplied but their texts are also increasingly muddy and far too long, more and more loaded with technological expressions and cross references to other normative texts. The fragmentary nature of norms, the reference to "emergency situations", the inclination to "programme" rather than regulate, worsen the tendency of a state's legislation to lose the requirement of generality and abstractness, and to become more and more similar to administrative acts.[125] Quite obviously, the "Code" model, with its rationalistic claim to be clear, systematic, universal, and unchangeable over time, now appears to be a real historical wreck, overwhelmed by the muddled flood of microlegislation.

Along with such phenomena, and especially in European countries directly involved in the political integration process, there is the multiplication of not only domestic normative sources but also of supranational sources. The tendency towards anomie due to normative overload is thus worsened by the difficulty in identifying the "general principles" of the legal system whose definition is given also by many jurisdictional organs – let us just mention the European Court of Justice – which claim to be entitled to construe national, European Community, and international law. This gives rise to a mainly judge-made European law which, by definition, falls outside the schemes of the rule of law.[126]

The weakened governing capacity of law affects both the principle of distribution of power and that of differentiation of power. In particular, the certainty of law and, as a direct consequence, the principle of legality are seriously jeopardized. The hypertrophy of criminal and civil law increases the power of interpreters and judges, so much so that courts hold real normative power, being in fact authorized to selectively redraft legislative texts. Not only is *ignorantia legis* widespread, since citizens are increasingly unable to know which laws are valid and what their normative impact is, but the deliberate ignorance of law is an inevitable judicial practice, even within the highest courts. To tacitly ignore the law, either totally or partially, seems to be a condition required not only to deliver a judgement, but also to carry out ordinary administrative activities. Therefore, within the structures of the rule of law, the areas for autonomous decision-making *ultra legem* and, often, *contra legem*, are multiplied.

It is around such "legislative despotism" of Euro-continental democratic states that the harsh controversy led by authors such as Bruno Leoni and Friedrich von Hayek is centred. Such authors contrast the normative orgies of the democratic *pouvoir législatif* with the very liberal tradition of the Anglo-Saxon rule of law, founded on the common law tradition and relying upon the judiciary – not parliaments – for protecting individual liberties.[127] "Englishmen's freedoms" are incompatible, as argued by Leoni and Hayek, with the authoritarian and illiberal tradition of the continental democratic rule of law. The authors advocate the replacement of parliamentary legislation with a legal order based on customs and general principles, entrusted essentially to the discretionary power of the judiciary. A "law of judges" should be able to guarantee both the certainty of law and the protection of individual rights much more efficiently than the chaotic enactment of specific commands, which are nowadays typical of the legislation of democratic parliaments. Although such a liberal-conservative criticism of the Euro-continental democratic rule of law is very lucid in many respects, it seems to overlook the fact that precisely the inflation and disability of legislative acts and the collapse of the certainty of law are bringing about the decline of Euro-continental parliaments and are strengthening the normative function of the judiciary, i.e. one of the most primitive and sub-differentiated ways of law-making.

6.2 The decreasing effectiveness of the protection of rights

In his essays on citizenship in Europe, Thomas Marshall claimed that the acknowledgement of civil rights – among which, in particular, private property and contractual autonomy – proved to be entirely functional to the early expanding stage of the market economy. Political rights, instead, arising from nineteenth-century class struggles, favoured the entrance of working classes into the elitist institutions of the "liberal state". As regards "social rights", Marshall underlined their radical paradox. Unlike civil rights and most political rights, social rights were in contrast with the market's acquisitive logic, in that social rights were essentially oriented towards equality, whereas the market produced inequality. Despite this circumstance, Marshall believed that British institutions, moulded on the principles of the rule of law, would succeed in subordinating market mechanisms to social justice, thus permanently contaminating the logic of free exchange with the protection of "social rights". Ultimately, economic inequalities and social competition would be greatly reduced.[128]

Although Marshall's analytical scheme has been rightly criticized for its evolutionary reductionism,[129] it nonetheless suggests a useful approach to the relationship between the development of the market economy, the progress of political institutions, and the establishment of individual rights in modern Europe. On the basis of such a scheme, though keeping at a distance from the social-democratic optimism underpinning it, it may be held that the gradual acknowledgement in continental Europe of civil rights, political rights and, finally, the "social rights" has been matched by a gradually more selective, legally imperfect, and politically reversible guarantee of rights. A sort of "law of decreasing effectiveness" as to the protection of individual rights may thus be argued. Such "law" is due to the different relationship, which has gradually been established in Europe between the acknowledgement of rights, on the one hand, and the functional requirements of a political system correlated with the market economy, on the other. Starting with the industrial revolution, the "rule of law" has progressively opened up to the formal acknowledgement of a number of successive "generations" of rights, ultimately taking the shape of the constitutional state[130] and then of the welfare state.

The European Union Charter of Fundamental Rights (December 2000), drafted by the delegations of 15 member states, has further enlarged the list of rights by including "new rights" on privacy, environmental protection, consumer protection, respect for physical integrity, and the prohibition of reproductive cloning.[131] Yet, throughout the history of Euro-continental constitutionalism – and this is precisely the paradox lucidly pointed out by Dicey as early as at the end of the nineteenth century – the formal acknowledgement of citizens' "entitlement" to new categories of rights has not been matched by the parallel effectiveness of their "endowment". If this is the case, we might then expect European "new rights" to be equally doomed.

When compared with civil rights, political rights have always been less rooted in modern Europe's political tradition. As mentioned above, until more than a century after the great bourgeois revolutions, the right to vote was subject to census-based criteria connected with the market. Furthermore, large sections of economically marginalized individuals were excluded from the exercise of political rights until the early decades of the last century. This was in particular the case of workers and farmers, let alone women, whose political exclusion was cancelled only in the mid twentieth century. It was Hans Kelsen who argued that, in the twentieth century "state of political parties", citizens' political rights were nothing more than a "totemic mask", namely the mask of popular sovereignty and representation, these being political institutions no longer entailing any actual participation in the exercise of power.[132] Nowadays, authoritative political scientists such as Giovanni Sartori hold that citizens' political rights have been frustrated by "videocracy", that is the overwhelming power of mass media dominating both the economic market and the political world through substantially equivalent advertising devices.[133]

Even more evidently than political rights, "social rights", ever since their first appearance in the Weimar Constitution, have been weakly effective, being more directly exposed to market contingencies. In order for "social rights" to be effective, they need public services – social security, financial allocations, minimum standards of education, health, well-being, etc. – which consume a large amount of resources. It follows that, given the considerable impact of social rights on the accumulation of wealth and taxation, such rights are particularly precarious. Nowadays, since the global success of the market economy has imposed on Europe the necessity for the "reform" of the welfare state, "social rights" have mostly lost the legal requirements of universality and actionability – suffice it to think of the right to work and, partly, the right to health – and tend to become national assistance services discretionally provided by political power. Leaving aside the question of its economic feasibility and effectiveness, the proposed distribution of a "basic income" or "citizenship income" to all citizens, in line with the above reformist logic, would be subject to the same fragile dependence on discretionary political decision-making.[134] This illustrates the limitations of the idea hopefully advocated by last century's European social-democracy – that the "rule of law" naturally progresses towards not only the protection of "negative freedoms" but also the promotion of "substantial equality". As Bobbio has written:

> [M]ost social rights have not been implemented. Till today it can merely be said that they express ideal aspirations and that calling them 'rights' can only serve the purpose of granting them a noble title. [...] It can only be generically and rhetorically said that we are all equal with respect to the three fundamental social rights – to work, health, education – whilst it can be realistically said that we are all indeed equal in the enjoyment of negative freedoms.[135]

A number of authors, such as Pierre Bourdieu and Loïc Wacquant, argue that globalization processes, by depriving nation states of an important part of their traditional prerogatives, tend to reduce their functions essentially to guaranteeing domestic political order. In this respect, also the European welfare state would be expected to replace its social services with mainly repressive functions. The welfare state is supposedly ceasing to be a guarantor of collective well-being and turning into the policeman of its citizens' individual safety, in line with the US model, which is essentially of a "penally repressing state".[136]

6.3 The erosion of nation states' sovereignty

The downfall of nation states' sovereignty seems by now to be irreversible. Globalization processes have definitively caused the crisis of the Westphalian model of sovereign states, these no longer being able to tackle global issues, such as the reduction of environmental degradation, demographic equilibrium, economic development, peace, the repression of international crime, and the fight against "global terrorism". Alongside nation states, new powerful subjects arise within the international arena, namely multinational corporations, regional unions, political and military alliances, such as the NATO, NGOs, etc. Alongside international treaties and conventions, there arise new international law "sources", such as transnational "law firms", namely large lawyers' offices moulding new forms of *lex mercatoria*, and arbitral courts. At the same time, the judicial function and power tend to expand also on an international level, further eroding states' jurisdictional sovereignty, as proven by the setting up of ad hoc international criminal tribunals and the International Criminal Court (ICC) of The Hague, as polemically pointed out by theorists of the "global expansion of judicial power".[137]

Within a system of international relations largely conditional on the conveniences of economic and financial corporations, the weak governing capacity of states' legal systems is overwhelmed by the dynamic and innovative decisional power of market forces, especially with regard to industrial, fiscal, and social policies. In such fields, international law tends no longer to operate (in a Weberian manner) as a "rational" structure strengthening the expectations of international subjects; rather, it works as a composite and pragmatic means for the management of risks peculiar to highly uncertain interactions.[138]

Such changes in international law are accompanied by a serious crisis of the international legality and the traditional functions of international institutions, in particular the United Nations, which is unable to control the international use of force and to protect, in this respect, "human rights", above all the right to life. Within a general context of erosion of nation states' sovereignty and of international "anarchy", great Western powers deem it necessary to cancel the Westphalian principle imposing the respect of territorial integrity and the political independence of nation states. They claim the right to resort to force on humanitarian grounds against political regimes seriously violating "human rights". In NATO's "humanitarian interventions" in the Balkans in the twentieth century's last decade, force was used in open violation of the United Nations Charter, of general international law and of the constitutions of many European members of the NATO. It was believed that the use of mass destruction weapons (missiles, cluster bombs, depleted uranium projectiles) and the killing of thousands of civilians are in line with the aim of protecting "human rights".[139]

In the light of such exogenous processes, the schemes of the distribution and differentiation of power, which are typical of the rule of law, seem, so to speak, to be functionally and "spatially" out of phase, while the theory of individual rights is compelled to face problems going well beyond the horizon of nation states, and to attempt to "internationalize" itself. However, some authors believe it would be unrealistic both to try to revive the sovereignty of nation states and to devise cosmopolitan projects of political and legal unification of the world. Rather, a general deregulation would be necessary, gradually attributing sovereignty only to global market forces.[140] Other authors believe that, in the light of a possible future "global constitutionalism", a key role can be played by an international criminal jurisdiction acting on the basis of a universal criminal code and supported by an international police force. In this respect, the new ICC is viewed as the main instrument for the future development of a "legal globalism" aimed at protecting individual rights and at repressing power's arbitrary acts on an international level.[141]

7 OPEN QUESTIONS

The above analysis poses such deep-rooted questions as to call the whole experience of rule of law into question. In fact, today there is uncertainty about both the function and fate of all the Western political institutions that, for some centuries, have guaranteed – at least to a certain extent – the protection of individual freedoms and the limitation of the state's power.

The open questions are serious and numerous. For instance, given the crisis of the legal category itself, how can the certainty of law be restored within contemporary complex societies? By the way, it ought not to be forgotten that the concept of "legal certainty" had already been subject to criticism by American and Scandinavian legal realists in the first half of the twentieth century for being tantamount to pure normative idealism. Nowadays it is severely criticized by the exponents of "critical legal studies" and of the economic analysis of law.[142] What can be done to restore the "general and abstract" character of law and stop its current inflationary trend? By what means can the principle of legality regain its effectiveness, given that the scheme of the differentiation of powers is overwhelmed by phenomena, such as the degenerative metamorphosis of political representation, the technical decline of legislation, and the administrative – executive and judicial – nature of the settlement of actual single cases? Furthermore, how is it possible to protect political rights and, above all, the "social rights", given the increasing privatization of social functions, the decay of the "public sphere" and the decline of collective structures of social solidarity? What fate will "new rights" have, in particular the rights of foreigners, especially when tried or detained? What will happen to the protection of the environment and to the "cognitive autonomy" of audiences increasingly subject to the subliminal pressure of mass media?

Analogously, with respect to international law, we may wonder whether it is possible to use legal means to contrast the arbitrariness of large world economic and military powers and their communicative ramifications, and whether it is possible to prevent "global terrorism" from successfully establishing its bloody alternative to law and politics. It is doubtful whether Kelsen's strategy – "peace through law" – can be seen as the most suitable means to promote international peace and to reduce world political and economic imbalances, these being themselves the main hindrance to peace. Moreover, it is equally controversial whether new vigour can be given to states' legal systems, thus enabling them to subject global market forces to legal rules, especially in industrial, financial, and fiscal fields. Furthermore, it is not clear how the European Union can somehow draw inspiration from the model of the rule of law, freeing itself from the hegemony of great economic and financial interests, and from the encroachment of administrative bureaucracies which, in practice, keep the European constitution in their "custody". Equally uncertain is the possibility (and desirability) of creating a planetary rule of law, resulting from the reform of current international institutions and affecting not only the United Nations but also the very controversial Bretton Woods economic institutions. Neither are there being currently envisaged reformist solutions directing international criminal justice to the effective protection of "human rights", and not towards what is strategically convenient for great Western powers. Lastly, it may be wondered how the international protection of human rights can be rescued through legal and non-violent means from its judicial and military neocolonial degeneration.

These are all crucial questions with reference to the concept of rule of law has allowed us to pose with sufficient clarity and realism. However, no relevant answers will be provided in this essay other than the ones implicit in the above analysis. Such questions are thus left "open" to, above all, the further theoretical and historical contributions of the essays in this volume.[143] After all, an analytical elaboration touching all these issues would require an entire volume. This essay can thus be concluded with a simple (and anyway incautious) suggestion of a few general "starting points", which sum up the above theoretical discussion and may hopefully be useful for further and more detailed research. In some respects, however, they correspond to the writer's very explicit political and ethical preferences and thus deserve, at the most, to be recorded and discussed.

7.1 The rule of law as a "minimum political order"

Claiming a rigorous protection of human rights, the rule of law is nowadays brought back to life within an unfavourable global scenario. Such a scenario is marked by rapid social changes taking place in the most industrialized countries and by the increasing polarization of power and wealth on a global scale; both factors lead to social instability and political turbulence. Yet, the present return of the rule of law, so long as it is carried out in a theoretically rigorous and politically responsible manner, may be welcomed as an attempt by Western political culture to recover its most severely tested and precious heritage.

Despite its imperfections, serious limitations, internal tensions, and, most importantly, its current crisis, there does not seem to be any sound alternative in the Western world to the rule of law, either on a theoretical or political level. It is precisely the downfall of last century's main ideologies – together with the crisis of "actually existing socialism" and the videocratic degradation of representative institutions – that seems to recommend the rule of law as a "minimum political order", namely a sufficiently stable political order, characterized by an acceptable level of protection of civil rights. Indeed, the protection of civil rights – the right to life, fundamental freedoms, and private property – appears nowadays to be the primary political aim within complex societies, in which citizens' feelings of insecurity and loneliness are increasing. Even in the most developed countries, a large number of people are afraid for their own physical safety and for the security of their own belongings; they feel threatened by urban criminality and are anxiously looking for a job or are afraid of losing it. Within such a context, which Ulrich Beck has called *Risikogesellschaft* (risk society), the rule of law may be seen as a non-despotic, non-plebiscitary, and non-totalitarian political system, capable of governing collective risks and guaranteeing at the same time ample room for individual freedom and social autonomy. This general issue may be seen as a subject of great topical interest if it is acknowledged that the development of a "world risk society" is very likely, being fostered by globalization processes.[144]

This does not imply – needless to say – that the minimum political order of the rule of law can be taken as a universal minimum, as if it could correspond to a sort of Rawls-inspired "overlapping consensus". The minimum political order of the rule of law may not, in fact, be compatible with non-Western cultures not sharing its individualistic premises, and thus it may be intolerant and oppressive.

7.2 The international inflation of Bills of Rights

According to Norberto Bobbio, the moral progress of mankind may be measured by the succession of international declarations, which define human rights in an increasingly wide manner and specify them in distinct subcategories. At the same time, however, Bobbio does acknowledge the increasing difficulties encountered by the international protection of rights and consequently has even ended up by suggesting we abandon theoretical discussions and adopt a purely pragmatic approach.[145] In fact, it can be said that, along with legislative inflation, the second half of the twentieth century has witnessed the emergence of the same inflationary problem also with respect to Bills of Rights. No matter what their symbolic or moral value might be, they have resulted in a mass of international documents, treaties, and conventions, which are nothing but verbose, repetitive, and ineffective normative compilations. Many governments of the West (or politically connected with the West, such as for instance the last governments of Brazil[146]) have without hesitation subscribed to such documents with the intention of sedating domestic political opposition, and relying on the indulgence of allied (or protective) great powers towards their own systematic violations of human rights. As Bobbio writes, the discourse on rights may have a great practical role, though it "becomes misleading when it overshadows or conceals the difference between claimed rights on the one hand and acknowledged and protected rights on the other".[147]

The inflation of Bills of Rights, together with the widespread international violation of human rights, brings about general problems, which need to be examined at least along the following three theoretical lines.

7.2.1 "Law in books" and "law in action". The international hypertrophy of Bills of Rights should lead to a deep realist mistrust – in terms of political and legal realism – of the "paper-based" tradition that developed in the second half of the last century, and which was especially due to the rhetorical vocation of great international assemblies, above all of the General Assembly of the United Nations. Such a declamatory habit might be contrasted with the sobriety of British tradition. In the homeland of individual rights and the rule of law, the unwritten character of the constitution goes hand in hand with a social widespread consensus as to the protection of "Englishmen's freedoms" and with a largely coherent administrative practice. This takes place in the absence of a rigid constitution, of the judicial control of constitutional legitimacy and of any (Kelsen-inspired) hierarchization of the legal system. It might be argued that, in Great Britain, the entire rule of law is "a living customary law", and thus it is much closer to being "law in action" than "law in books". Within the international context, such an argument could be used against the fervent propounders of global constitutionalism, and also against whoever believes that a rigid constitution is the *conditio sine qua non* for the protection of rights within a unified Europe. It seems more plausible to argue that European citizens suffer, on the contrary, from excessive constitutional rules stemming from both national constitutions and constitutional courts of different countries.[148]

7.2.2 "Rule of men" and "rule of laws". The plethoric expansion of normative texts might be contrasted, as mentioned above, not only with an attempt to rigorously and selectively define the doctrine of the rule of law and of individual rights but also with the setting up of political and legal structures controlling the implementation and effectiveness of legal provisions. It would be a mere rationalistic illusion to think that a given society – especially a contemporary complex and transnational society – meekly accepts legislation and may be easily shaped according to the intrinsic rationality of legal principles. Besides, it would be a normative blunder to believe that the considerable power of legal interpreters – above all judges – is only due to the technical and structural reasons, which have led to the crisis of the certainty of law, namely, that it is only attributable to the inflation of law, to the poor technical quality of legal texts, to their particularistic contents and to the confused plurality of national and international legal sources.

The founding fathers of the American constitution firmly believed in the contraposition between the "rule of men" and the "rule of law": they argued that, thanks to a written constitution, there would only be in the United States a rule of law, not of men. Yet, as warned by legal realism, a "rule of men" always exists within a "rule of law", and it cannot be meant, in a rationalistic way, as the latter's denial. Even in the most perfect "republic of laws", as argued by Carl Schmitt, men – not laws – govern, and interpreters – not legislators – are sovereign.[149] Contrary to Portalis and Bentham's thinking, the discretion of interpreters, especially judges, may be simply checked and reduced, not suppressed, by normative restraints and institutional devices. To suppress the power of interpreters would mean, *tout court*, to suppress public administration and politics. It is emblematic, and paradoxical, that in the practice of the English rule of law, it was precisely the power of interpreters, namely the power of common law judges, to ultimately guarantee the protection of individual rights, even against the letter of Parliament's acts. Therefore, in the English common law tradition, the "principle of legality" has as its main premise not only parliamentary law but, together with it and if necessary against it, the principles of freedom of an unwritten constitution, which mirrors the immemorial traditions and civil culture of a whole people. Hence, also under this perspective, the normativistic emphasis of "legal globalism" and political cosmopolitanism should be replaced by a cautious historicist and pluralist understanding of the development of legal systems.

7.2.3 Legal culture and judges' training. It may be useful to develop a theory on the "rule of men" within the rule of law. This means, by assuming the English "founding exception" as an ideal reference point, that the legal culture of judges and administrators plays a crucial role in the functioning of the rule of law and in the protection of individual rights. Such a role is performed, in a specific manner, by the "normative ideology" of ordinary judges (as Alf Ross puts it).[150] Hence, the effectiveness of the protection of individual rights largely depends not only on the normative and institutional structures of the rule of law, but also, so to speak, on the "prejudices" of ordinary magistrates as to the support of civil liberties. It follows that a "politics of law" committed to the protection of individual rights should be centred around issues, such as the cultural training and recruitment of judges, their social sensitivity, their professional identity and integrity, and their orientation towards the general principles and aims of law, namely the strengthening of social expectations and the protection of individual rights; thus going beyond the formalism of an evanescent "legal method", which is erroneously thought of as "pure" and morally neutral. This is all the more the case of international criminal jurisdictions, whose magistrates are usually uprooted from any local normative tradition and are unaware of the political and social problems underlying the "deviant" behaviour to which they pretend to apply international justice.

7.3 The "struggle for law"

The rule of law may be considered as a "minimum political order", essentially limited to protecting civil rights. This might have two distinct meanings: on the one hand, that the rule of law is a normative and institutional structure *rebus sic stantibus* with no alternatives in the Western world. Trying to demolish or simply to contrast it in the name of anarchic, authoritarian, or totalitarian ideologies would be very risky. On the other hand, it may mean that while the protection of civil rights belongs, so to speak, to the physiological normality of the rule of law, the minimum level might be exceeded only by a conflictual pressure. In other words, only social conflict can restore the effectiveness of political rights, redeeming them from their condition of pure electoral ritual, and satisfy further expectations and claims on a national or international level, starting from the "social rights".

Two possible interpretations of the rule of law thus emerge, these mirroring the above mentioned opposition between the "liberal approach" and the "democratic approach", though in part going beyond it. The first interpretation – which is essentially taken from United States constitutionalism – identifies the protection of individual rights with what has been called "constitutional democracy".[151] The necessary and somewhat sufficient protection of individual rights is guaranteed by the balance and interaction among "all" of the state's powers, assisted by a written and rigid constitution, by a constitutional court (or a court with similar functions) and by a thorough control of the constitutionality of legislative acts. What counts, above all, is to remove "constitutional principles" from the decisional competence of parliamentary majorities and to entrust them to the "impartial" care of the judiciary. Within such a framework of immunity, the judicial practice of the US Supreme Court may be even considered as a "moral reading" of the constitution (as suggested by Ronald Dworkin) or as the "exercise of a sort of self-government" surrogating citizens' self-management (as suggested by Frank Michelman).[152] It follows that such interpretations of the rule of law and democracy are "non-political", paternalistic and non-conflictual, and entrust the future of all political institutions to the "care" of high judicial bureaucracies.

Alternatively to such an interpretation, an activistic and conflictualistic conception of both the protection of individual rights and the functioning of the rule of law might be advanced: rights "exist" and political institutions enforce them in so far as they are activated by the social conflict.[153] Such a realist – Machiavellian – alternative might be called a "struggle for law", to use Rudolph von Jhering's words.[154] Without minimally neglecting the importance of institutions and procedures, Jhering's formula might stand, firstly, for a political commitment to ensure that the legal ritualization submits national and international powers to general rules, thus rendering them somehow controllable. The active forces of "civil society" – among which, in particular, the exponents of the legal world – should avoid delegating to the political organs even the protection of civil rights. In fact, even the right to life is constantly threatened today. Suffice it to mention the series of military interventions in the Balkans and in central Asia, which were decided by European governments and parliaments in open violation of their respective constitutions.[155] Analogously, fundamental freedoms – above all, freedom of thought – are threatened within contemporary societies dominated by mass media corporations.

Secondly, a civil battle would be necessary to ensure the actual enjoyment of political rights and the effective satisfaction – whatever this may mean in formally constitutional terms – of expectations underpinning the "social rights" and "new rights". The rule of law, as such, is not functionally equipped and politically inclined to acknowledge such interests and expectations, apart from the welfare state's services which are, anyway, largely ineffective. If reference may be ideally made to the British common law's courts, only a new "living legal custom" might render the protection of such interests and expectations effective, quite obviously at given general political and economic conditions.

In Western countries, individual rights can be defended and promoted not only within the system of the rule of law but also outside its formalized realm by political, communicative, cultural, educational, and economic means. Quite certainly, nowadays it would be improper to appeal to Rousseau's idea of "popular sovereignty", which is, *inter alia*, not in line with the global dimension of problems, conflicts, and antagonistic forces. It would be equally useless to generically refer to the constituent power as the original and legitimate source of political and legal power. It might rather prove to be more useful to adopt a realist sociological theory on the new "law-making" subjects and on the potential forms of a new "political jurisgenesis", to use Michelman's words.[156] Anyway, it ought not to be forgotten that individual rights, even when they are proclaimed in the most solemn and morally laden way, are mere "opportunities" rewarding the winners of the political struggle, which is often conducted, as underlined by Bobbio, through the use of force.[157] Rights are (extremely precious) social prostheses, which allow citizens to claim, with greater chances of success and without having to resort again to the use of force, the satisfaction of socially shared interests and expectations. Even the reduction of arbitrary power and the institutional protection of individual rights – the two specific functions of the rule of law – are the historical output of a number of "struggles for the defence of new freedoms against old powers":[158] they are the other side of social struggles; they lie in and fall with them.

NOTES

1. Evidence of the widespread usage of this notion, even beyond a strictly scientific ambit, is given by the fact that the European Union's Charter of Fundamental Rights, approved in Nice in December 2000, refers in the first lines of its preamble to the "principles of the rule of law" as a foundation of the Union. Also the "Cairo Declaration" of 3–4 April 2000, drafted upon the conclusion of the summit between Africa and Europe, includes a norm endorsing the "principles of the rule of law" (chap. 4, art. 53).
2. Neil MacCormick translates *Rechtsstaat* with the formula of "state-under-law"; cf. N. MacCormick, "Constitutionalism and Democracy", in R. Bellamy (ed.), *Theories and Concepts of Politics*, Manchester (NY): Manchester University Press, 1993, pp. 125, 128–30; N. MacCormick, "Der Rechtsstaat und die 'rule of law'", *Juristenzeitung*, 39 (1984), pp. 56–70.
3. See M. Barberis, "Presentazione", in A.V. Dicey, *Diritto e opinione pubblica nell'Inghilterra dell'Ottocento*, Bologna: il Mulino, 1997, p. xv.
4. See R. Dworkin, *Taking Rights Seriously*, London: Duckworth, 1977; R. Dworkin, *Law's Empire*, Cambridge (MA): Harvard University Press, 1986; R. Dahrendorf, *Quadrare il cerchio*, Roma-Bari: Laterza, 1995; J. Habermas, *Faktizität und Geltung. Beiträge zur Diskurstheorie des Rechts und des demokratischen Rechtsstaats*, Frankfurt a.M.: Suhrkamp Verlag, 1992; N. Bobbio, *L'età dei diritti*, Torino: Einaudi, 1990, Eng. tr. *The Age of Rights*, Cambridge: Polity Press, 1996; L. Ferrajoli, *Diritto e ragione. Teoria del garantismo penale*, Roma-Bari: Laterza, 1989; L. Ferrajoli, "Diritti fondamentali", *Teoria politica* (1998), 2, pp. 3–33. On the theses

maintained by Ferrajoli in the latter essay, see D. Zolo, "Libertà, proprietà ed eguaglianza nella teoria dei 'diritti fondamentali'", *Teoria politica*, 15 (1999), 1, now also in L. Ferrajoli, *Diritti fondamentali*, Roma-Bari: Laterza, 2001. See also Luigi Ferrajoli's essay in this volume.

5. See N. Bobbio, *L'età dei diritti*, passim.
6. Among the supporters of the formalistic conception of the rule of law, see J. Raz, "The Rule of Law and its Virtue", *The Law Quarterly Review* (1977), 93; J. Raz, "The Rule of Law", in J. Raz, *The Authority of Law*, Oxford: Clarendon Press, 1979; A. Scalia, "The Rule of Law as a Law of Rules: Oliver Wendell Holmes Bicentennial Lecture", *Harvard Law School*, 56 (1989), 4; for the alternative option between formalistic and antiformalistic (or ethical) conceptions of the rule of law, cf. P.P. Craig, "Formal and Substantive Conceptions of the Rule of Law", *Diritto pubblico*, 1 (1995), 1, pp. 35–54. See also L.L. Fuller, *The Morality of Law*, New Haven (CT): Yale University Press, 1969; D. Lyons, *Ethics and the Rule of Law*, Cambridge: Cambridge University Press, 1984; J. Waldron, "The Rule of Law", in J. Waldron, *The Law*, London/New York: Routledge, 1990; I. Shapiro (ed.), *The Rule of Law*, New York: New York University Press, 1994.
7. Cf. J.N. Shklar, "Political Theory and the Rule of Law", in A.C. Hutchinson and P. Monaham (eds), *The Rule of Law: Ideal or Ideology*, Toronto/Calgary/Vancouver: Carswell, 1987, p. 1.
8. See N. Bobbio, N. Matteucci, and G. Pasquino (eds), *Dizionario di politica*, Torino: Utet, 1983, in which the lemma "rule of law" does not appear. For Great Britain, see, *inter alia*, R. Scruton, *A Dictionary of Political Thought*, London: Pan Books, 1982; D. Miller (ed.), *The Blackwell Encyclopedia of Political Thought*, Oxford: Basil Blackwell, 1987. For German literature, see for instance, M. Stolleis, "Rechtsstaat", in A. Erler and E. Kaufmann, *Handwerterbuch zur deutschen Rechtsgeschichte*, Berlin: Erich Schmidt, 1990.
9. Cf. C. Schmitt, *Legalität und Legitimität* [1932], now in C. Schmitt, *Verfassungsrechtliche Aufsätze aus dem Jahren 1924–1954*, Berlin: Dunker und Humblot, 1932, p. 274; for Schmitt's criticism of the rule of law, cf. C. Galli, *Genealogia della politica. Carl Schmitt e la crisi del pensiero politico moderno*, Bologna: il Mulino, 1996, pp. 513–36; P. Costa, *Civitas. Storia della cittadinanza in Europa*, vol. 4, *L'età dei totalitarismi e della democrazia*, Roma-Bari: Laterza, 2001, pp. 328–38.
10. See F. Garzoni, *Die Rechtsstaatsidee im schweizerischen Staatsdenken des 19. Jahrhunderts*, Zürich: Polygraphischer Verlag, 1953.
11. See A. Baratta, "Stato di diritto", in A. Negri (ed.), *Scienze politiche*, Enciclopedia Feltrinelli Fisher, Milano: Feltrinelli, 1970.
12. See O. Koellreutter, *Grundriss der allgemeinen Staatslehre*, Tübingen: Mohr, 1933; H. Lange, *Vom Gesetzesstaat zum Rechtsstaat*, Tübingen: Mohr, 1933; S. Panunzio, *Lo Stato di diritto*, Città di Castello: Il solco, 1922.
13. Ph. Kunig has actually advanced such a suggestion (as recalled by P.P. Portinaro in his essay in this volume) in *Das Rechtsstaatsprinzip*, Tübingen: Mohr Siebeck, 1986; for a careful analysis of the theoretical polysemy of the notion of *Rechtsstaat*, see K. Sobota, *Das Prinzip Rechtsstaat. Verfassungs- und verwaltungsrechtliche Aspekte*, Tübingen: Mohr Siebeck, 1997; C. Margiotta, "Quale Stato di diritto?", *Teoria politica*, 17 (2001), 2, pp. 17–41.

14. For a criticism of the neopositivistic myth claiming the precision of scientific language and, in general, for an epistemological "post-empiricist" approach to social sciences, see D. Zolo, *Reflexive Epistemology*, Boston (MA): Kluwer, 1989.
15. A large historical and theoretical account is provided by Pietro Costa's essay in this volume.
16. Cf. A. Baratta, "Stato di diritto", p. 513.
17. On these authors and in general on the "state-centred" paradigm typical of early nineteenth century German doctrines of public law, cf. P. Costa, *Civitas. Storia della cittadinanza in Europa*, vol. 3, *La civiltà liberale*, Roma-Bari: Laterza, 2001, pp. 137–93.
18. Mario Dogliani underlines such a commonly overlooked issue in *Introduzione al diritto costituzionale*, Bologna: il Mulino, 1994, pp. 191–3. On this matter, see the essay by Bartolomé Clavero in this volume.
19. On this theme, see E.-W. Böckenförde (ed.), *Staatsrecht und Staatsrechtslehre im Dritten Reich*, Heidelberg: Müller, 1985.
20. See V.E. Orlando, *Diritto pubblico generale. Scritti vari coordinati in sistema (1881–1940)*, Milano: Giuffrè, 1940. According to Orlando, the state characterized by the rule of law "imposes upon itself legal norms capable of limiting the activities of public authorities with the aim of acknowledging and respecting its subjects' legitimate interests" (V.E. Orlando, *Primo trattato completo di diritto amministrativo italiano*, vol. 1, Milano: Società Editrice Libraria, 1900, p. 32 ff.). On Orlando's political theory, cf. P. Costa, *Lo Stato immaginario. Metafore e paradigmi nella cultura giuridica italiana fra Ottocento e Novecento*, Milano: Giuffrè, 1986, pp. 124–35 and passim.
21. Cf. W.E. Hearn, *The Government of England: Its Structure and its Development*, London: Longmans, 1867, pp. 89–91; S. Cassese, "Albert Venn Dicey e il diritto amministrativo", *Quaderni fiorentini per la storia del pensiero giuridico moderno*, 19 (1990), pp. 37–8.
22. Cf. A.V. Dicey, *Introduction to the Study of the Law of the Constitution* (1885), London: Macmillan, 1982, pp. cxxxvii–cxxxviii. Dicey sums up the rule of law in the following manner: "In England no man can be made to suffer punishment or to pay damages for any conduct not definitely forbidden by the law; every man's legal rights or liabilities are almost invariably determined by the ordinary Courts of the realm, and each man's individual rights are far less the result of our constitution than the basis on which our constitution is founded" (ibid., p. lv). For the exceptional success of Dicey's work, which was reprinted eight times in 30 years, and is considered a classic of English constitutional law by both juridica legal doctrine and jurisprudence, cf. E. Santoro, Common law *e costituzione nell'Inghilterra moderna*, Torino: Giappichelli, 1999, pp. 5–15. On Dicey's thought see R.A. Cosgrove, *The Rule of Law: Albert Venn Dicey, Victorian Jurist*, London: Macmillan, 1980; T. Ford, *Albert Venn Dicey*, Chicester: Barry Rose, 1985; D. Sugarman, "The Legal Boundaries of Liberty: Dicey, Liberalism and Legal Science", *Modern Law Review*, 46 (1983).
23. Cf. A.V. Dicey, *Introduction to the Study of the Law of the Constitution*, pp. 213–67. For Dicey's famous and controversial criticism of (French) administrative law, cf. S. Cassese, "Albert Venn Dicey e il diritto amministrativo", pp. 6–17; S. Cassese, "La recezione di Dicey in Italia e in Francia", *Materiali per una storia della cultura giuridica*, 25 (1995), 1, pp. 107–31; B. Leoni, *Freedom and the Law*, Princeton (NJ): Van Nostrand, 1961, pp. 59–77.

24. Cf. A.V. Dicey, *Introduction to the Study of the Law of the Constitution*, p. 273.
25. Cf. A.V. Dicey, *Introduction to the Study of the Law of the Constitution*, pp. 117–130 ff.
26. Cf. C.K. Allen, *Law in the Making*, Oxford: Clarendon Press, 1964, pp. 456–7. On Coke and his understanding of common law, cf. J. Beauté, *Un grand juriste anglais: Sir Edward Coke 1552–1634. Ses idées politiques et constitutionnels*, Paris: Presses Universitaires de France, 1975, pp. 72–6; P. Costa, *Civitas. Storia della cittadinanza in Europa*, vol. 1, *Dalla civiltà comunale al Settecento*, Roma-Bari: Laterza, 1999, pp. 188–97.
27. Cf. A.V. Dicey, *Introduction to the Study of the Law of the Constitution*, p. cxlviii. The English constitution, writes Dicey, is "the fruit of contests carried on in the Courts on behalf of the rights of individuals...., is a judge-made constitution, and it bears on its face all the features of judge-made law" (ibid., p. 116).
28. See H. Bracton, *De legibus et consuetudinibus Angliae*, ed. by T. Twiss, Buffalo (NY): Hein, 1990.
29. On the myth of the "ancient constitution" as foundation of the common law, and on the "rationalizing" contributions by William Blackstone (with his famous *Commentaries*) and, later on, by Dicey, cf. E. Santoro, Common law *e costituzione nell'Inghilterra moderna*, pp. 45–56, 109–46; see also J.G.A. Pocock, *The Ancient Constitution and the Feudal Law*, Cambridge: Cambridge University Press, 1987.
30. Cf. A.V. Dicey, *Lectures on the Relation between Law and Public Opinion in England during the Nineteenth Century*, London: Macmillan, 1914, p. 82. Similar theses had been maintained, as it is known, by Edmund Burke, in his *Reflections on the Revolution in France*, in E. Burke, *Works*, vol. 2, London: George Bell, 1790.
31. According to MacCormick, in the UK individual rights are a kind of 'customary rights' (they are neither Bentham-inspired "constitutionally derivative rights", nor Locke-drawn "fundamental rights"); cf. N. MacCormick, "Constitutionalism and Democracy", pp. 124–5, 135.
32. Cf. A.V. Dicey, *Introduction to the Study of the Law of the Constitution*, p. lv.
33. Cf. B. Leoni, *Freedom and the Law*, p. 63.
34. Both Georg Jellinek and Ernst Troeltsch have underlined the religious origins of American democracy (cf. G. Gozzi, *Democrazia e diritti. Germania: dallo Stato di diritto alla democrazia costituzionale*, Roma-Bari: Laterza, 1999, pp. 6–10).
35. Cf. M. Fioravanti, *Costituzione*, Bologna: il Mulino, 1999, pp. 102–9.
36. On this issue, in addition to Brunella Casalini's essay in this volume, see J. Ely, *Democracy and Distrust: A Theory of Judicial Review*, Cambridge (MA): Harvard University Press, 1980; J. Agresto, *The Supreme Court and Constitutional Democracy*, Ithaca (NY): Cornell University Press, 1984; P. Kahn, *The Reign of Law: Marbury v. Madison and the Construction of America*, New Haven (CT): Yale University Press, 1997; E. Lambert, *Le gouvernement des juges et la lutte contre la législation sociale aux Etats-Unis*, Paris: Giard & Cie, 1921. More generally, see B. Ackerman, *We The People. Foundations*, Cambridge (MA): Harvard University Press, 1991; C.R. Sunstein, *The Partial Constitution*, Cambridge (MA): Harvard University Press, 1993; J. Waldron, "A Right-Based Critique of Constitutional Rights", *Oxford Journal of Legal Studies*, 13 (1993), 1; S.M. Griffin, *American Constitutionalism*, Princeton (NJ): Princeton University Press, 1996. For a criticism of US constitutional moralism under the perspective of an economic analysis of law, see the classic R.A. Posner, *Economic Analysis of Law*, Boston (MA): Little, Brown, 1992.

37. See M.V. Tushnet, *Red, White and Blue. A Critical Analysis of Constitutional Law*, Cambridge (MA): Harvard University Press, 1988; R.M. Unger, *Law in Modern Society*, New York: The Free Press, 1976; A. Carrino, "Roberto M. Unger e i 'Critical Legal Studies': scetticismo e diritto", in G. Zanetti (ed.), *Filosofi del diritto contemporanei*, Milano: Cortina, 1999, pp. 171–7; G. Minda, *Postmodern Legal Movements*, New York: New York University Press, 1995.
38. On this issue, see P.P. Craig, *Public Law and Democracy in the United Kingdom and the United States*, Oxford: Clarendon Press, 1990; A.L. Goodhart, "The Rule of Law and Absolute Sovereignty", *University of Pennsylvania Law Review*, 106 (1958) 7, pp. 950–5.
39. See Robert von Mohl, *Die Polizeiwissenschaft nach den Grundsätzen des Rechtsstaates*, Vol. 3, Tübingen: Laupp, 1832–4.
40. See R. von Jhering, *Der Geist des römischen Rechts auf den verschiedenen Stufen seiner Entwicklung*, Leipzig: Breitkopf und Härtel, 1878–88; G. Jellinek, *System der subjektiven öffentlichen Rechte*, Tübingen: Mohr, 1905; O. Mayer, *Deutsches Verwaltungsrecht*, Leipzig: Dunker und Humblot, 1895. See also Gustavo Gozzi's essay in this volume.
41. Cf. C. Schmitt, *Legalität und Legitimität*, pp. 264, 276–7, 279. As it has been suggested, Kant's contribution to the theory of the rule of law is the ethical and metaphysical idea that the "rule of law" is an obligation in the light of the principles of a general moral theory.
42. For the German situation, cf. G. Gozzi, *Democrazia e diritti*, pp. 59–63.
43. Jellinek carefully studies English and German constitutional traditions, which he contrasts with the French Revolutionary contractualistic philosophy; cf. M. Dogliani, *Introduzione al diritto costituzionale*, pp. 162 ff.; M. Fioravanti, "Costituzione e Stato di diritto", *Filosofia politica*, 5 (1991), 2, pp. 336–7.
44. Therefore, it may be held that the rule of law does not necessarily rely on a contractualistic conception, although the fundamental civil rights it protects are the ones that Locke believes are grounded on the *pactum societatis*: life, safety, freedom, and property; cf. N. Luhmann, "Gesellschaftliche und politische Bedingungen des Rechtsstaates", in N. Luhmann, *Politische Planung*, Opladen: Westdeutscher Verlag, 1971, pp. 57–9; G. Gozzi, *Democrazia e diritti*, pp. 31–3.
45. Cf. C. Schmitt, *Legalität und Legitimität*, pp. 274–83.
46. In this respect, cf. P. Costa, *Civitas. Storia della cittadinanza in Europa*, vol. 3, *La civiltà liberale*, pp. 192–3; see also E. Forsthoff, *Rechtsstaat im Wandel*, München: Beck, 1976.
47. See R. Carré de Malberg, *Contribution a la théorie général de l'État*, vol. 2, Paris: Sirey, 1920–2. On the notion of the "rule of law" according to Carré de Malberg, cf. P. Costa, *Civitas. Storia della cittadinanza in Europa*, vol. 4, *L'età dei totalitarismi e della democrazia*, pp. 106–15. More generally, on French doctrines of public law, see M.-J. Redor, *De l'État légal à l'État de droit. L'évolution des conceptions de la doctrine publiciste française 1879–1914*, Paris: Economica, 1992; M. Troper, "Le concept d'État de droit", *Droits*, 5 (1992); on the impact of the German model in France, see J. Chevallier, *L'État de droit*, Paris: Montchrestien, 1999; see also the essay by Alain Laquièze in this volume.
48. Cf. R. Carré de Malberg, *Contribution a la théorie général de l'État*, vol. 1, pp. 140 ff.
49. See art. 3 (chap. 5, title 3) of the 1791 Constitution.

50. Cf. P.P. Portinaro, "Il grande legislatore e il custode della costituzione", in G. Zagrebelsky, P.P. Portinaro, and J. Luther (eds), *Il futuro della costituzione*, Torino: Einaudi, 1996, pp. 18–22.
51. On the relationship between the constituent power and the revision of the constitution in European history, cf. M. Dogliani, "Potere costituente e revisione costituzionale", in G. Zagrebelsky, P.P. Portinaro, and J. Luther (eds), *Il futuro della costituzione*, pp. 253–89; E.-W. Böckenförde, "Il potere costituente del popolo. Un concetto limite del diritto costituzionale", ibid., pp. 231–52.
52. Cf. R. Carré de Malberg, *Contribution a la théorie général de l'État*, vol. 1, pp. 488–92.
53. On the relationship between the US institutions and French constitutional tradition, cf. R. Carré de Malberg, *La Loi, expression de la volonté générale*, Paris: Librairie du Recueil Sirey, 1931, pp. 104–10; on the relationship between written constitutions and constituent power, cf. R. Carré de Malberg, *Contribution a la théorie général de l'État*, vol. 2, pp. 493–500.
54. Cf. N. MacCormick, "Constitutionalism and Democracy", pp. 124–30, 144–5.
55. Cf. C. Schmitt, *Die Lage der europäischen Rechtswissenschaft* (1943–1944), now in C. Schmitt, *Verfassungsrechtliche Aufsätze aus dem Jahren 1924–1954*, Berlin: Duncker und Humblot, 1958, pp. 413–4.
56. Cf. A.V. Dicey, *Introduction to the Study of the Law of the Constitution*, pp. 198 ff.; we shall deal with the issue of the lack of effectiveness of Euro-continental constitutional declarations in sects. 6 and 7.
57. On the relationships between the French and American Revolutions and on the famous debate raised by Georg Jellinek in this respect, cf. N. Bobbio, "La Rivoluzione francese e i diritti dell'uomo", in N. Bobbio, *L'età dei diritti*, pp. 89–120; on the primacy given by Jellinek to the common law in the history of the "legislation of freedom". cf. G. Gozzi, *Democrazia e diritti*, pp. 16–22.
58. "Constitutional democracy" is at the heart of the essay in this volume by G. Gozzi, *Democrazia e diritti*, especially in its second section; cf. also L. Ferrajoli, *Diritti fondamentali*, passim; M. Fioravanti, *Costituzione*, pp. 157–62.
59. For a reinterpretation of the *Rechtsstaat* underlining the aspects of its functional differentiation, cf. N. Luhmann, "Gesellschaftliche und politische Bedingungen des Rechtsstaates", pp. 53–65. In this respect, cf. also: C. Schmitt, *Verfassungslehre* (1928), Berlin: Duncker und Humblot, 1957, pp. 123 ff.; C. Schmitt, "Der bürgerliche Rechtsstaat", *Die Schildgenossen* (1928), 2, pp. 128–33; C. Schmitt, "Nazionalsozialismus und Rechtsstaat", *Juristische Wochenschrift*, 63 (1934), pp. 714–5; C. Schmitt, "Was bedeutet der Streit um den 'Rechtsstaat'?" (1935), in C. Schmitt, *Staat, Grossraum, Nomos. Arbeiten aus den Jahren 1916–1969*, Berlin: Duncker und Humblot, 1995, pp. 124–5.
60. Cf. N. Bobbio, *L'età dei diritti*, pp. ix, 58 ff.
61. See N. Bobbio, *Giusnaturalismo e positivismo giuridico*, Milano: Comunità, 1965; P. Piovani, *Linee di una filosofia del diritto*, Padova: Cedam, 1968; N. Bobbio, "Il modello giusnaturalistico", in N. Bobbio and M. Bovero, *Società e Stato nella filosofia politica moderna*, Milano: Il Saggiatore, 1979; P. Piovani, *Giusnaturalismo ed etica moderna*, Roma-Bari: Laterza, 1961.
62. On the issue, see M. Villey, *La formation de la pensée juridique moderne*, Paris: Montchrestien, 1975; G. Tarello, "Profili giuridici della questione della povertà nel francescanesimo prima di Ockham", in *Scritti in memoria di Antonio Falchi*, Milano:

Giuffrè, 1964; E. Santoro, *Autonomia individuale, libertà e diritti*, Pisa: ETS, 1999, pp. 148–65. For the conflictualistic approach, see for instance J.I. Israel, *Radical Enlightenment: Philosophy and the Making of Modernity 1650–1750*, Oxford: Oxford University Press, 2001; E. Esposito, *Ordine e conflitto. Machiavelli e la letteratura politica del Rinascimento italiano*, Napoli: Liguori, 1984; G. Borrelli, *Ragion di Stato e Leviatano. Conservazione e scambio alle origini della modernità politica*, Bologna: il Mulino 1993.

63. See E. Santoro, *Autonomia individuale, libertà e diritti*, passim.
64. See H. Blumenberg, *Die Legitimität der Neuzeit*, Frankfurt a.M.: Suhrkamp Verlag, 1974.
65. For Schmitt's criticism of Kelsen's normativism, see C. Schmitt, *Politische Theologie. Vier Kapitel zur Lehre der Souveränität*, München/Leipzig: Duncker & Humblot, 1922; C. Galli, *Genealogia della politica*, passim; G. Preterossi, *Carl Schmitt e la tradizione moderna*, Roma-Bari: Laterza, 1996; for Nietzsche's assonant (and inspiring) criticism of the rule of law, cf. P. Costa, *Civitas. Storia della cittadinanza in Europa*, vol. 3, *La civiltà liberale*, in particular pp. 536 ff.
66. Norberto Bobbio's writings on the "visibility/invisibility" of power are a classic: see, above all, *Il futuro della democrazia*, Torino: Einaudi, 1984, Eng. tr. Cambridge: Polity Press, 1987. On the legitimization of power that procedural ritualization is able to promote, see the realistic comments by N. Luhmann, *Legitimation durch Verfahren*, Neuwied, Berlin: Luchterhand, 1969.
67. The explicit declaration of equality before the law is to be found in many documents, from the 1789 "Declaration of the Rights of Man and of the Citizen" to the French Republican Constitution of 1991, and the 1849 *Verfassung des Deutschen Reiches*.
68. On the relationship between the rule of law and the female status, see Anna Loretoni's essay in this volume. In general: A. Phillips, "Citizenship and Feminist Theory", in G. Andrews (ed.), *Citizenship*, London: Lawrence & Wishart, 1991, pp. 76–88; M. Dietz, "Context Is All: Feminism and Theories of Citizenship", in C. Mouffe (ed.), *Dimensions of Radical Democracy*, London: Verso, 1992, pp. 63–85. On the relationship between gender differences and law, see F. Olsen, "Feminism and Critical Legal Theory: An American Perspective", *The American Journal of the Sociology of Law*, 18 (1990), 2; C. Smart, "The Woman of Legal Discourse", *Social and Legal Studies*, 1 (1992), 1; T. Pitch, "Diritto e diritti. Un percorso nel dibattito femminista", *Democrazia e diritto*, 33 (1993), 2, pp. 3–47; L. Ferrajoli, "La differenza sessuale e le garanzie dell'eguaglianza", ibid., pp. 49–73; M. Graziosi, "Infirmitas sexus. La donna nell'immaginario penalistico", ibid., pp. 99–143; A. Facchi, "Il pensiero femminista sul diritto", in G. Zanetti (ed.), *Filosofi del diritto contemporanei*, pp. 129–53; G. Minda, *Postmodern Legal Movements*, passim.
69. This does not mean, as we have mentioned and as emerges from some essays in this volume – in particular the ones by Bartolomé Clavero and Carlos Petit – that, in America, the rule of law has not legitimated the slavery of African Americans and that, throughout the nineteenth century, European institutions have not been imposed on non-European countries in a colonial manner, i.e. in illiberal and discriminatory ways.
70. It is not by chance that in the latter decades of the nineteenth century, it was precisely Albert Venn Dicey who launched an attack at the rising welfare state, accusing it of breaching the fundamental principles of the rule of law as a result of its collectivistic and egalitarian stances: cf. A.V. Dicey, *Lectures on the Relation between Law and*

Public Opinion in England during the Nineteenth Century, pp. 211–302. On the relationship between formal legal equality and substantial equality, see the enlightening work by Alf Ross, *On Law and Justice*, London: Steven & Sons, 1958.

71. On these issues, see N. Luhmann, *Rechtssoziologie*, Reinbek bei Hamburg: Rowohlt, 1972; N. Luhmann, *Macht*, Stuttgart: Enke Verlag, 1975; see also D. Zolo, "Function, Meaning, Complexity. The Epistemological Premisses of Niklas Luhmann's 'Sociological Enlightenment'", *Philosophy of the Social Sciences*, 16 (1986), 2.
72. For a criticism of *ad hoc* courts, cf. A.V. Dicey, *Introduction to the Study of the Law of the Constitution*, pp. 213–67.
73. Cf. B. Leoni, *Freedom and the Law*, pp. 63–77; see also F.A. von Hayek, *Law, Legislation and Liberty*, London: Routledge and Kegan Paul, 1982.
74. See T.H. Marshall, "Citizenship and Social Class", in T.H. Marshall, *Class, Citizenship, and Social Development*, Chicago: The University of Chicago Press, 1964. For a criticism of Marshall's tripartition, cf. L. Ferrajoli, "Dai diritti del cittadino ai diritti della persona", in D. Zolo (ed.), *La cittadinanza. Appartenenza, identità, diritti*, Roma-Bari: Laterza, 1994, pp. 277–83.
75. On the distinction between "negative freedom" and "positive freedom", see the classic essay by Isaiah Berlin, *Two Concepts of Liberty*, now also in I. Berlin, *Four Essays on Liberty*, Oxford: Oxford University Press, 1969; see also G. De Ruggiero, *Storia del liberalismo europeo*, Roma-Bari: Laterza, 1925. On the ensuing debate: R. Young, *Personal Autonomy: Beyond Negative and Positive Liberty*, London: Croom Helm, 1986; D. Parfit, *Reasons and Persons*, Oxford: Clarendon Press, 1984; E. Santoro, *Autonomia individuale, libertà e diritti*, passim.
76. Cf. T.H. Marshall, "Citizenship and Social Class", pp. 95–6.
77. For an analytical discussion of the different functional meanings of the "separation of powers", cf. R. Guastini, *Il diritto come linguaggio*, Torino: Giappichelli, 2001, pp. 73–80.
78. On the "positivization of law" as a precondition for the modern state and, in particular, for the rule of law, cf. N. Luhmann, *Grundrechte als Institution*, Berlin: Duncker und Humblot, 1965, pp. 16 ff., 186–200.
79. Cf. K. Marx, *Zur Judenfrage*, in *Marx-Engels Werke (MEW)*, vol. 1, Berlin: Institut für Marxismus-Leninismus, 1956–69, p. 364. On the issue, cf. G. Lohmann, "La critica fatale di Marx ai diritti umani", *Studi perugini* (1998), 5, pp. 187–99.
80. Cf. N. Luhmann, *Politische Planung*, pp. 35–45, 53–89; on the issue, cf. D. Zolo, *Complessità, potere, democrazia*, now also in D. Zolo, *Complessità e democrazia*, Torino: Giappichelli, 1986, pp. 69–90.
81. Cf. N. Luhmann, *Politische Planung*, pp. 42, 62.
82. According to legal realism, the executive's activity, and in particular the judiciary's, consists in the enactment of ad hoc rules for the settlement of single cases.
83. The meaning of the "conformity" of a single administrative act – either executive or judicial – to a previous general norm is, as it is known, a highly controversial subject; cf. for instance R. Guastini, *Il giudice e la legge*, Torino: Giappichelli, 1995, pp. 35–66.
84. The expression "political space" is used here in the meaning, which has been ascribed to it by Carlo Galli in his collection of essays, *Spazi politici. L'età moderna e l'età globale*, Bologna: il Mulino, 2001.

85. Cf. P.P. Craig, "Formal and Substantive Conceptions of the Rule of Law", pp. 42–5; J. Raz, "The Rule of Law and its Virtue", pp. 195 ff.; J. Raz, "The Rule of Law", passim.
86. On the contraposition between rule of law and 'state of justice' see G. Fassò, "Stato di diritto e Stato di giustizia", in R. Orecchia (ed.), *Atti del VI Congresso nazionale di filosofia del diritto. Pisa, 30 maggio-2 giugno 1963*, Milano: Giuffrè, 1963.
87. See A. Scalia, "The Rule of Law as a Law of Rules: Oliver Wendell Holmes Bicentennial Lecture"; see also Brunella Casalini's essay in this volume.
88. Cf. D. Zolo, *Reflexive Epistemology*, pp. 167–77; D. Zolo, *Democracy and Complexity*, pp. 19–53.
89. On the relationship between the Western tradition of the rule of law and the Islamic legal and political culture, see the essays in this volume by Raja Bahlul, Baudouin Dupret, and Tariq al-Bishri. In general: A. Abu-Sahlieh and A. Sami, *Les Musulmans face aux droits de l'homme: religion, droit, politique*, Bochum: Winkler, 1994; G. Gozzi (ed.), *Islam e democrazia*, Bologna: il Mulino, 1998; further bibliographic notes in M.G. Losano, *I grandi sistemi giuridici*, Roma-Bari: Laterza, 2000, pp. 325–80. On the relationship between the Western doctrine of human rights and the Chinese-Confucian tradition (and on the *vexata quaestio* of the violation of individual rights in China), see the essays in this volume by Alice Ehr-Soon Tay, Wu Shu-chen, Lin Feng, and Wang Zhenmin-Li Zhenghui. In general: J.A. Cohen, *Contemporarey Chinese Law: Research Problems and Perspectives*, Cambridge (MA): Harvard University Press, 1970; E. Dell'Aquila, *Il diritto cinese*, Padova: Cedam, 1981; W. Chenguang and Z. Xianchu (eds), *Introduction to Chinese Law*, Hong Kong/Singapore: Sweet & Maxwell Asia, 1997; J. Tao, "The Chinese Moral Ethos and the Concept of Individual Rights", *Journal of Applied Philosophy*, 7 (1990), 2; A.H.Y. Chen, *Chinese Cultural Tradition and Modern Human Rights*, Amnesty International Annual General Meeting, Hong Kong, 2 December 1997; M.G. Losano, *I grandi sistemi giuridici*, pp. 405–33. More generally: W. Schmale (ed.), *Human Rights and Cultural Diversity: Europe, Islamic World, Africa, China*, Goldbach: Keip, 1993; M. Yasutomo (ed.), *Law in a Changing World: Asian Alternatives*, Archiv für Rechts- und Sozialphilosophie, Beiheft 72, 1998.
90. On this issue, cf. D. Zolo, *Democracy and Complexity*, pp. 54–98.
91. For a "minimal definition" of democracy's rules and values, see N. Bobbio, *Il futuro della democrazia*, pp. 4–7, 10–1, 33–7, 59–62.
92. On the issue in general, there is ample literature: D. Grimm, "Una Costituzione per l'Europa?", in G. Zagrebelsky, P.P. Portinaro, and J. Luther (eds), *Il futuro della Costituzione*, pp. 339–67; J. Habermas, "Una Costituzione per l'Europa? Osservazioni su Dieter Grimm", ibid., pp. 369–75; R. Bellamy, V. Bufacchi, and D. Castiglione (eds), *Democracy and Constitutional Culture in the Union of Europe*, London: Lothian Foundation Press, 1995; R. Bellamy (ed.), *Constitutionalism, Democracy and Sovereignty: American and European Perspectives*, Avebury: Aldershot, 1996.
93. See for instance the "Banjul Charter on Human and People's Rights", ratified in 1981 by the Organization of African Unity, where economic and social rights, viewed as collective rights of all peoples, prevail over individuals' civil and political rights; this is the case also of the "Arab Charter of Human Rights", ratified in El Cairo in September 1994; cf. in general R.J. Vincent, *Human Rights and International Relations*, Cambridge: Cambridge University Press, 1986, pp. 39–44.

94. See Giorgio Bongiovanni's essay in this volume.
95. Cf. L. Ferrajoli, "Democrazia e Costituzione", in G. Zagrebelsky, P.P. Portinaro, and J. Luther (eds), *Il futuro della costituzione*, pp. 323–4; on the issue, see also S. Holmes, "Precommitment and the Paradox of Democracy", in J. Elster and R. Slagstad (eds), *Constitutionalism and Democracy*, Cambridge: Cambridge University Press, 1988; in general UK Preuss, *Zum Begriff der Verfassung. Die Ordnung des Politischen*, Frankfurt: Fischer Verlag, 1994; J.L. Jowell, *The Changing Constitution*, Oxford: Clarendon Press, 1994.
96. "Toute societé dans la quelle la garantie des droits n'est pas assurée, ni la séparation des pouvoirs déterminée, n'a point de constitution".
97. Cf. P.P. Portinaro, *Stato*, Bologna: il Mulino, 1999, pp. 110–12.
98. In this respect, besides the Weimar Republic, reference is made to the "suicide" of the French Second Republic.
99. Cf. P.P. Portinaro, "Il grande legislatore e il custode della Costituzione", pp 22–31; with respect to the "Critical Legal Studies" and Mark Tushnet's criticism of American constitutionalism, cf. A. Carrino, "Roberto M. Unger e i 'Critical Legal Studies': scetticismo e diritto", pp. 171–7.
100. For a criticism in this respect of American constitutional practice, see C.R. Sunstein, *The Partial Constitution*, passim; C.R. Sunstein, *Legal Reasoning and Political Conflict*, Oxford: Oxford University Press, 1996; see also Brunella Casalini's essay in this volume. For Germany, see in particular E.-W. Böckenförde, *Staat, Verfassung, Demokratie*, Frankfurt a.M.: Suhrkamp, 1991.
101. This fully legitimates, for instance, the important "liberal" arguments maintained by Luigi Ferrajoli in his essay in this volume.
102. See D. Zolo, *Invoking Humanity. War, Law and Global Order*, London/New York: Continuum International, 2002.
103. Cf. N. Bobbio, *L'età dei diritti*, pp. 40–44; D. Zolo, "Libertà, proprietà ed eguaglianza nella teoria dei 'diritti fondamentali'", pp. 3–24.
104. See J.M. Barbalet, *Citizenship*, Milton Keynes: Open University Press, 1988; L. Ferrajoli, *Diritti fondamentali*, passim; D. Zolo, "La strategia della cittadinanza", in D. Zolo (ed.), *La cittadinanza*, pp. 33 ff.
105. The expression "generations" has been used by Bobbio, without any specific theoretical claim. P. Barile, in *Diritti dell'uomo e libertà fondamentali*, Bologna: il Mulino, 1984, equally provides a (useful) account of positive constitutional law. Attempts to a theoretical elaboration are to be found in R. Alexy, *Theorie der Grundrechte*, Baden-Baden: Nomos Verlagsgesellschaft, 1985; J. Rawls, "The Basic Liberties and Their Priorities", in S.M. McMurrin (ed.), *The Tanner Lectures on Human Values*, vol. 3, Salt Lake City (UT): University of Utah Press, 1982, pp. 1–87; G. Peces-Barba Martínez, *Curso de derechos fundamentales*, Madrid: Eudema, 1991.
106. Cf. D. Zolo, "Filosofia della pena e istituzioni penitenziarie", *Iride*, 14 (2001), 32, pp. 47–58; A. Cassese, *Umano-disumano. Carceri e commissariati nell'Europa di oggi*, Roma-Bari: Laterza, 1994; T. Mathiesen, *Prison on Trial: A Critical Assessment*, London: Sage Publicatons, 1990; E. Santoro, *Carcere e società liberale*, Torino: Giappichelli, 1997; L. Wacquant, *Les prisons de la misère*, Paris: Raisons d'agir, 1999.
107. Clinical evidence concerns serious pathologies: haemorrhages, infections, urethral fistulas, urine retention, prepuce cysts, and glands necrosis. For such reasons, many

organizations, such as Nocir, Noharm, and Norm, have been set up in the United States to oppose male circumcision. See W.J. Prescott, "Genital Pain versus Genital Pleasure", *The Truth Seeker*, 1 (1989), 3; A. Abu-Sahlieh, "To Mutilate in the Name of Jeowa or Allah: Legitimation of Male and Female Circumcision", *Medical Law*, 13 (1994); A.J. Chessler, "Justifying the Injustifiable", *Buffalo Law Review*, 45 (1997).

108. Cf. N. Bobbio, *L'età dei diritti*, pp. 40–44.
109. See L. Baccelli, *Il particolarismo dei diritti*, Roma: Carocci, 1999, passim.
110. See Alice Ehr-Soon Tay's essay in this volume, where a sharp distinction is drawn between "authentic" Confucian values and their instrumental political usage by the Singapore model's supporters; see also: M.C. Davis (ed.), *Human Rights and Chinese Values. Legal, Philosophical and Political Perspectives*, New York: Columbia University Press, 1995; W.T. de Bary and T. Weiming (eds), *Confucianism and Human Rights*, New York: Columbia University Press, 1998; D.A. Bell, "A Communitarian Critique of Authoritarianism. The case of Singapore", *Political Theory*, 25 (1997), 1; see also the section dedicated to this issue by B. Casalini on the site *Jura Gentium*, at http://www.juragentium.unifi.it.
111. See L. Ferrajoli, *La sovranità nel mondo moderno*, Milano: Anabasi, 1995.
112. With respect to British colonialism in the Indies, see Ananta Kumar Giri's essay in this volume. For Spanish "colonial law" see Carlos Petit's essay in this volume. More generally, with respect to "colonial law", see S. Romano, *Corso di diritto coloniale*, Roma: Athenaeum, 1918; J.M. Cordero Torres, *Tratado elemental de derecho colonial español*, Madrid: Editora Nacional, 1941. On imperialism see, above all, M. Nicholson, *International Relations*, London: Macmillan, 1998; for an updated reinterpretation, see M. Hardt and A. Negri, *Empire*, Cambridge (MA): Harvard University Press, 2000. See also the classic H. Bull and A. Watson, *The Expansion of International Society*, Oxford: Clarendon Press, 1984.
113. Cf. A.V. Dicey, *An Introduction to the Study of the Law of the Constitution*, p. 22; C. Schmitt, *Die Lage der europäischen Rechtswissenschaft*, p. 387.
114. Cf. G. Jellinek, *Die rechtliche Natur der Staatenverträge*, Wien: Hoelder, 1880, p. 27.
115. Cf. D. Zolo, *Invoking Humanity*, pp. 99–132.
116. For a realist critique of Kantian pacifism – from Kelsen to Bobbio and Habermas – see D. Zolo, *I signori della pace. Una critica del globalismo giuridico*, Roma: Carocci, 1998.
117. Cf. P.P. Portinaro, *Il realismo politico*, Roma-Bari: Laterza, 1999, pp. 119–25; P.P. Portinaro, *Stato*, pp. 128–32.
118. See H.J. Morgenthau, *Politics among Nations*, New York: Knopf, 1960; D. Zolo, *Cosmopolis: Prospects for World Order*, Cambridge: Polity Press, 1996.
119. See R. Falk, *Human Rights and State Sovereignty*, New York: Holmes & Meier, 1981; D. Held, *Democracy and the Global Order*, Cambridge: Polity Press, 1995. See also the essays in the volume *Global Democracy: Key Debates*, ed. by B. Holden, London/New York: Routledge, 2000; see in particular, besides the editor's contribution, the essays by D. Held, "The changing contours of political community: rethinking democracy in the context of globalization", pp. 17–31; D. Zolo, "The lords of peace: from the Holy Alliance to the new international criminal tribunals", pp. 73–86; R. Falk, "Global civil society and the democratic prospect", pp. 162–78.
120. "Das Weltbürgerrecht ist eine Konsequenz der Rechtsstaatsidee" (J. Habermas, "Kants Idee des ewigen Friedens – aus dem historischen Abstand von 200 Jahren",

Kritische Justiz, 28, 1995, p. 317, now also in J. Habermas, *Die Einbeziehung des Anderen*, Frankfurt a.M.: Suhrkamp, 1996); see also J. Habermas, *Faktizität und Geltung*. For a realist criticism of Habermas's cosmopolitanism, cf. D. Zolo, "A Cosmopolitan Philosophy of International Law? A Realist Approach", *Ratio Juris*, 12 (1999) 4, pp. 429–44; cf. also Habermas's reply, ibid., pp. 450–3.

121. For a criticism of such approaches, see P. Hirst and G. Thompson, *Globalization in Question*, Cambridge: Polity Press, 1996; P. Hirst and G. Thompson, "Global Myths and National Policies", in B. Holden (ed.), *Global Democracy*, pp. 47–59; on domestic analogy, see the classic monograph: H. Suganami, *The Domestic Analogy and World Order Proposals*, Cambridge: Cambridge University Press, 1989.
122. See J. Habermas, "Bestialität und Humanität. Ein Krieg an der Grenze zwischen Recht und Moral", *Die Zeit* (1999), 18.
123. There is boundless literature on globalization. See for instance: I. Clark, *Globalization and Fragmentation*, Oxford: Oxford University Press, 1997; U. Beck, *Was ist Globalisierung?*, Frankfurt a.M.: Suhrkamp Verlag, 1997; Z. Bauman, *Globalization. The Human Consequences*, Cambridge: Polity Press; Oxford: Blackwell, 1998; P. de Senarclens, *Maîtriser la mondialisation*, Paris: Presses de Sciences Po, 2000; L. Boltanski and E. Chiapello, *Le nouvel esprit du capitalisme*, Paris: Gallimard, 1999; L. Gallino, *Globalizzazione e disuguaglianze*, Roma-Bari: Laterza, 2000; K. Bales, *Disposable People. New Slavery in the Global Economy*, Berkeley (CA): California University Press, 1999. On the global threat of terrorism, cf. D. Zolo, *Invoking Humanity*, pp. 135–6, 171–2.
124. See N. Luhmann, "The Self-Reproduction of the Law and Its Limits", Conference Materials on *Autopoiesis in Law and Society*, Firenze: European University Institute, 1984; N. Luhmann, "The Unity of the Legal System", ibid.; N. Luhmann, "The Sociological Observation of the Theory and Practice of Law", ibid.; G. Teubner and H. Willke, "Kontext und Autonomie: Gesellschaftliche Selbststeuerung durch reflexives Recht", *Zeitschrift für Rechtssoziologie*, 6 (1984), 1, pp. 4–35.
125. There is an extensive literature in this respect: see for instance, in this volume, the reference made to the issue by Luigi Ferrajoli's essay. As early as 1958, Carl Schmitt, in his essay *Die Lage der europäischen Rechtswissenschaft*, pp. 407–8, criticized the "motorization" of law turning it into an administrative measure (*Verordnung*).
126. See, in this volume, the references made to the issue by Alain Laquièze and Luigi Ferrajoli.
127. See F.A. von Hayek, *The Constitution of Liberty*, London: Routledge & Kegan Paul, 1960; F.A. von Hayek, *The Rule of Law*, Menlo Park (CA): Institute for Human Studies, 1975; B. Leoni, *Freedom and the Law*, pp. 59–96. Similar theses are upheld by Nicola Matteucci (*Positivismo giuridico e costituzionalismo*, Bologna: il Mulino, 1996, pp. 108 ff., 113), who supports the idea of a liberal state founded on the judicial power, not on the legislative one. See in this respect the critical commentary to the Italian version of Leoni's book: D. Zolo, "La libertà e la legge", *Quaderni fiorentini per la storia del pensiero giuridico moderno* (1995), 14; and D. Zolo, "A proposito di 'Legge, legislazione e libertà' di Friedrich A. von Hayek", *Diritto privato*, 1 (1996), 2, pp. 767–81. See also Maria Chiara Pievatolo's essay in this volume.
128. Cf. T.H. Marshall, "Citizenship and Social Class", pp. 127–32.

129. Cf. A. Giddens, "Class Division, Class Conflict and Citizenship Rights", in A. Giddens, *Profiles and Critiques in Social Theory*, London: Macmillan, 1982, pp. 171–3, 176; J.M. Barbalet, *Citizenship*, passim; D. Held, "Citizenship and Autonomy", in D. Held, *Political Theory and the Modern State*, Stanford (CA): Stanford University Press, 1989, pp. 189–213; L. Ferrajoli, "Dai diritti del cittadino ai diritti della persona", pp. 272–6.
130. See M. Fioravanti, *Appunti di storia delle Costituzioni moderne*, Torino: Giappichelli, 1990.
131. See the Charter of Fundamental Rights of the European Union, especially arts. 3, 8, 37, 38.
132. Cf. H. Kelsen, *General Theory of Law and State*, Cambridge (MA): Harvard University Press, 1945, pp. 288–9; see also H. Kelsen, *Vom Wesen und Wert der Demokratie*, Tübingen: J.C.B. Mohr, 1929.
133. See G. Sartori, *Homo videns*, Roma-Bari: Laterza, 1997.
134. Even where they are not suppressed, "social rights" are granted in discretionary forms and measures, primarily for reasons of public order and managing critical situations. Not erroneously, therefore, Jacques Barbalet has argued that, rather than "social rights", nowadays we should speak of "social services" (cf. J.M. Barbalet, *Citizenship*, pp. 60–72). On the "basic income" cf. L. Ferrajoli, "Dai diritti del cittadino ai diritti della persona", pp. 277–83 and Ferrajoli's essay in this volume; cf. also Z. Bauman, *In Search of Politics*, Cambridge: Polity Press, 1999, pp. 180–90.
135. Cf. N. Bobbio, *L'età dei diritti*, pp. xx, 72.
136. See P. Bourdieu (ed.), *La misère du monde*, Paris: Seuil, 1993; L.J.D. Wacquant, "La tentation pénale en Europe", *Actes de la recherche en sciences sociales*, 124 (1998); L.J.D. Wacquant, "L'ascension de l'Etat pénal en Amérique", ibid.; L.J.D. Wacquant, *Les prisons de la misère*.
137. See N. Tate and T. Vallinder (eds), *The Global Expansion of Judicial Power*, New York: New York University Press, 1995; G. Zagrebelsky, *Il diritto mite*, Torino: Einaudi, 1992, pp. 213 ff.; A. Pizzorno, *Il potere dei giudici*, Roma-Bari: Laterza, 1998; cf. also D. Zolo, "A proposito dell'espansione globale del potere dei giudici", *Iride*, 11 (1998), 25, pp. 445–53. On the debate concerning the power of German Constitutional Courts, cf. G. Gozzi, *Democrazia e diritti*, pp. 256–60. See also Pier Paolo Portinaro's essay in this volume.
138. See the useful work by M.R. Ferrarese, *Le istituzioni della globalizzazione. Diritto e diritti nella società transnazionale*, Bologna: il Mulino, 2000.
139. Cf. D. Zolo, *Invoking Humanity*, pp. 66–98; see also P. de Senarclens, *L'humanitaire en catastrophe*, Paris: Presses de Sciences Po, 1999.
140. See, *inter alia*, K. Ohmae, *The End of the Nation State. The Rise of Regional Economies*, New York: The Free Press, 1995; J.-J. Roche, *Théories des relations internationales*, Paris: Editions Montchrestien, 1999.
141. See "Statuto di Roma della Corte penale internazionale", *Rivista di studi politici internazionali*, 66 (1999), 1, pp. 25–95; see also G. Vassalli, "Statuto di Roma. Note sull'istituzione di una Corte Penale Internazionale", ibid., pp. 9–24. For a large number of documents in this respect, visit the United Nations' website at http://www.un.org/law/icc. An example of "legal globalism" applied to criminal law is given by O. Höffe, *Gibt es ein interkulturelles Strafrecht? Ein philosophischer Versuch*, Frankfurt a.M.: Suhrkamp Verlag, 1999.

142. See J. Frank, *Law and the Modern Mind*, New York: Coward-McCann, 1949; A. Ross, *On Law and Justice*; R.M. Unger, *Law in Modern Society*; R.A. Posner. *Economic Analysis of Law*; G. Tarello, *Il realismo giuridico americano*, Milano: Giuffrè, 1962.
143. Luigi Ferrajoli's essay in this volume deserves specific reference for its critical and project-oriented approach.
144. See U. Beck, *Risikogesellschaft. Auf dem Weg in eine andere Moderne*, Frankfurt a.M.: Suhrkamp, 1986; Z. Bauman, *In Search of Politics*; A. Dal Lago, "Esistenza e incolumità", *Rassegna italiana di sociologia*, 41 (2000), 1, pp. 131–42; see also U. Beck and D. Zolo, "Dialogo sulla globalizzazione", *Reset* (1999), 55.
145. Cf. N. Bobbio, *L'età dei diritti*, pp. 5–44.
146. See M. Reale, *Crise do capitalismo e crise do estado*, Sao Paulo: Editora Senac, 2000. Apart from having a "long" and advanced constitution, Brazil has signed nearly all international treaties and conventions protecting human rights. Yet, it remains one of the countries in which individual rights are seriously violated; see for instance L. Mariz Maia, *Tortura no Brasil: a banalidade do mal*, on the website *L'altro diritto* at http://www.altrodiritto.unifi.it.
147. Cf. N. Bobbio, *L'età dei diritti*, p. xx.
148. Cf. J.H.H. Weiler, "I rischi dell'integrazione", in A. Loretoni (ed.), *Interviste sull'Europa*, Roma: Carocci, 2000, pp. 72–3; J.H.H. Weiler, *The Constitution of Europe: Do the New Clothes Have an Emperor?*, Cambridge: Cambridge University Press, 1999.
149. Cf. C. Schmitt, *Über die drei Arten des Rechtswissenschaftlichen Denkens*, Hamburg: Hanseatische Verlagsanstalt, 1934, pp. 11–24, 33–4; cf. N. Bobbio, "Governo degli uomini o governo delle leggi?", now also in N. Bobbio, *Il futuro della democrazia*, pp. 169–94.
150. See A. Ross, *On Law and Justice*, passim.
151. Cf. R. Dworkin, *Freedom's Law: The Moral Reading of the American Constitution*, Cambridge (MA): Oxford University Press, 1996, pp. 37 ff.; F.I. Michelman, "The Supreme Court 1985 Term", *Harvard Law Review*, 100 (1986–1987); F.I. Michelman, "Law's Republic", *The Yale Law Journal*, 97 (1988), 8; cf. also M. Fioravanti, *Appunti di storia delle Costituzioni moderne*, pp. 73 ff.; M. Fioravanti, "Costituzione e Stato di diritto", now also in M. Fioravanti, *La scienza del diritto pubblico*, Milano: Giuffrè, 2001, pp. 575–604; G. Gozzi, *Democrazia e diritti*, pp. 256–93; G. Bongiovanni, *Teorie 'costituzionalistiche' del diritto*, Bologna: Clueb, 2000, pp. 209–31.
152. Cf. G. Gozzi, *Democrazia e diritti*, pp. 287–90. Gozzi claims that constitutional courts (for instance, the German Constitutional Court) run the risk of losing prestige by supporting innovative theories (ibid., pp. 254–5).
153. See Luca Baccelli's essay in this volume, linking an activistic understanding of rights with Machiavellian realism; cf. also L. Baccelli, "Diritti senza fondamento", in L. Ferrajoli, *Diritti fondamentali*, pp. 201–16; L. Baccelli, *Il particolarismo dei diritti*, pp. 145–85.
154. See R. von Jhering, *Der Kampf um's Recht*, Wien: Manz, 1874; R. von Jhering, *Der Zweck im Recht*, Leipzig: Breitkopf und Härtel, 1923.
155. Cf. L. Ferrajoli, "Una disfatta del diritto, della morale, della politica", *Critica marxista* (1999), 3, pp. 18–20; U. Villani, "La guerra del Kosovo: una guerra umanitaria o un crimine internazionale?", *Volontari e terzo mondo* (1999), 1–2, pp. 35–7.

156. Cf. F.I. Michelman, "Law's Republic", p. 1514; M.R. Ferrarese, *Le istituzioni della globalizzazione*, pp. 101–58; see Luca Baccelli's essay in this volume.
157. Cf. J.M. Barbalet, *Citizenship*, pp. 44, 97 ff.; N. Bobbio, *L'età dei diritti*, pp. xiii–xiv: "[R]eligious freedom was the result of religious wars, civil liberties were the result of parliaments' struggles against absolute monarchs, political freedom and social freedoms were the result of the birth, growth and maturity of workers' movements, of farmers with little or no land, of poor people asking public powers not only to acknowledge personal freedom and the other 'negative freedoms', but also to protect them against unemployment, and to provide them with the basic means against illiteracy."
158. Cf. N. Bobbio, *L'età dei diritti*, p. xiii.

CHAPTER 2

THE RULE OF LAW: A HISTORICAL INTRODUCTION

Pietro Costa

1 THE HISTORICAL DEVELOPMENT OF THE RULE OF LAW

The expression "rule of law" has become widely popular in the last few years, both in scholarly literature and political journals. The idea of rule of law is invoked for a number of purposes depending on the interests at stake, for example, to oppose individual freedom to totalitarianism, to claim the importance of individual rights, or to propound individual autonomy against bureaucratic intrusiveness.[1] The contemporary discontent towards centralized organizations of power, the crisis of the Welfare state, the extraordinary proliferation of rights, the exhaustion of alternatives to Western democracies have all, albeit in different ways, given new life to the notion of rule of law.

The contemporary value of the notion of rule of law, as well as its analytical, critical, and evaluative utilizations are matters that may be properly dealt with by jurists and philosophers of law and politics; the theoretical essays in this volume aim precisely at providing a contribution in this respect. To write an "historical introduction" – the task I am entrusted with – is indeed an easier and more modest charge: it suffices to go back in time and examine the history (and prehistory) of the concept in order to outline an inevitably schematic and selective map of its several meanings; my aim, quite simply, is to provide a framework or background to the essays in this volume, which focus analytically on some stages of the historical parable of the rule of law.

What is the history of the rule of law about? In order to answer such a question, we ought to examine the various meanings ascribed to the "formula" or compound expression that is known in German as *Rechtsstaat*, in French as *État de droit*, in Italian as *Stato di diritto*, and in English, at least hypothetically speaking, as the "rule of law" (such a translation will be examined and qualified below). Yet, before formulating the above question, a tentative pre-understanding of the concept might be useful to serve as a rudimentary compass guiding our research.

P. Costa and D. Zolo (eds.), The Rule of Law: History, Theory and Criticism, 73–149.

At first sight, the cardinal points of the rule of law seem to be the following: political power (sovereignty, the state), law (objective law, norms), and individuals. More specifically, these three elements are the conditions for the existence and meaning of the rule of law, while the rule of law "as such" is a peculiar relationship between "state" and "law" which is, overall, beneficial to individuals. The rule of law, in other words, appears as a means to achieve a specific aim: it is expected to direct us about how to intervene (through "law") on "power" so as to strengthen individuals' positions. It follows that the problem of the rule of law can be included within the "discourse of citizenship": since the latter focuses on the relationship between the individual and a given political community and determines his or her political and legal identity, the rule of law is one of the potential strategies of such a discourse; for the *raison d'être* of the rule of law is to affect the state–individual relationship by introducing ("legal") curbs on sovereign power to the individual's benefit.[2]

Moreover, the circumstance that the rule of law aims at benefiting the individual suggests that the favourable treatment of the individual is implemented by means of a wide spectrum of rights granted to him. A thematic link between the rule of law and "individual rights" is therefore possible though not necessary, for the rule of law may guarantee beneficial conditions to individuals that may not necessarily stem from the granting of specific rights.[3]

What are the historical periods within which the evolution of the rule of law can be framed?

Viewing the modern state as one organized and limited by law, Blandine Barret-Kriegel believes that the origins of the rule of law are to be found in the early establishment of great national monarchies.[4] Such an understanding is indeed legitimate, but it is equally plausible to ascribe to our problem – which the formula "rule of law" purports to solve – a wider time span substantially coinciding with Western political and intellectual history, which has been constantly concerned with the inevitable tension (and necessary connection) between power and law.

It is nonetheless useful to draw a line between the general problem implicit in the phrase "rule of law" and its recent historically specific meaning, in order to determine the different phases of its evolution.

I suggest, therefore, a "three-stage" division, to be outlined in an order of decreasing proximity with respect to our subject matter. The first stage is the *history* (this being narrowly meant) of the rule of law: it begins with the emergence of the lexical expression in question, i.e. when the large and recurrent problem of the relationship between power, law, and individuals was provided with a particular solution and given a name (the "rule of law", precisely). Yet, our formula also has a *prehistory* concerning contexts and times when, even though the problem did not yet have a name, there nonetheless existed the "thing", namely the specific traits of an approach which would subsequently be explicitly formulated by the "rule of law" theory. The prehistory of the rule of law, i.e. the number of conditions directly giving rise thereto, is therefore the second "stage" of our analysis. Further back in time is our third "stage", when attention given to the power/law relationship depended on a cultural background very different from the preconditions (the "prehistory") of our "formula". The significance of such remote "precedents" should not be reduced to the trivial (and false) "nihil sub sole novi", since the understanding and solutions of our problem radically changed over time; neither should it be grounded on the idea of a linear development, where each new phase draws from the previous one. Rather, these precedents are significant because they provide the history (and prehistory) of the rule of law with a *horizon of meaning*, which still includes its most recent developments.

2 THE HORIZON OF MEANING OF THE RULE OF LAW

Assuming the rule of law to be grounded on the need to curb the overwhelming and unbridled strength of power (a terrible and threatening power, though at the same time necessary for the creation and preservation of order) and that the rule of law expresses individuals' trust in law as a means to prevent or at least regulate the numinous and arcane strength of power, the horizon of meaning of the rule of law is to be found within an extremely wide time span, encompassing both ancient and medieval times.

The awareness of a "great dichotomy" between different kinds of regimes, grounded on the relationship between "government" and "law", is far from being a modern issue. Both Plato and Aristotle (albeit in different ways) examined different forms of government – a fundamental trait also of "Western" political thinking – by focusing on the central role of law.

Plato did not favour the idea of the government being shaped by law: if the government was in the hands of those who, possessing the "art", were capable of delivering justice, laws would not be needed; yet, "as the state is not like a beehive, and has no natural head who is at once recognized to be the superior both in body and in mind", law is inevitably important, so much so that Plato defined the "counterpart" of three kinds of government (monarchy, the rule of the few, and the rule of the multitude), depending on whether the "sole ruler", few rulers, or many rulers govern "observing the laws or not".[5] Similarly, by criticizing democracies Aristotle introduced the sovereignty of law: "Such a democracy is fairly open to the objection that it is not a constitution at all; for where the laws have no authority, there is no constitution. The law ought to be supreme over all, and the magistracies and the government should judge of particulars".[6]

The role of law, the tension between its general character and the inexhaustible variety of individual cases, together with the difficult though necessary compromise between "despotic" decisions and the respect for a binding legal system, were common problems in ancient thinking and have been subsequently inherited and transformed by medieval culture. According to theologians and jurists discovering and creatively reinterpreting Aristotle's *Politics* and the *Corpus Iuris*, power was part of an order that both transcended it and provided its foundations. Power was emblematically expressed in the *iurisdictio*: in a *dicere ius* which embodied power precisely because power presupposed a given order and "declared" it, confirmed it, implemented it; power was inseparable from a legal system within which individual wills were subject to natural hierarchies, these being the supporting structures of cosmos and society. One of the great concerns of medieval culture (though already discussed in ancient times), i.e. tyranny, is explicable only by bearing in mind the constitutive link between government and law, power, and order.

For the sake of didactic comparison, though without straining things too much, it might be argued that the medieval relationship between power and order was a mirror image of the one we are nowadays led to envisage. While, under our perspective, the idea of a (spontaneously) excessive and "disordered" power is commonly perceived, in the medieval culture the idea of a given order within which power, or powers, fell and which controlled and governed them, thus containing them within a precise and ideal hierarchy, was taken for granted.

The rise of a new and "absolutist" idea of sovereignty coincides with the process of political entities (*civitates*, *regna*) slowly but steadily achieving autonomy. While medieval jurists placed them within their ideal hierarchy culminating in the imperial summit, according to Bodin's innovative doctrine, the sovereign, endowed with "absolute" power, was the king of France. A few words ought to be said to dispel an outdated misunderstanding that is, that sixteenth- and seventeenth-century "absolutism" was marked (in theory and practice) by unbridled and unlimited power. In fact, the establishment of a really "sovereign" power was a slow and muddled process; it was opposed by local resistance, centrifugal forces, powers and rights claimed by estates, cities, classes that (in France) only the post-revolutionary state was able to vanquish (but one may wonder whether "particularistic" stances did not resurge from the ashes of the *ancien régime*). Not surprisingly, therefore, the "absolutist" theory of sovereignty itself, despite relevant discontinuities with medieval tradition – Bodin's doctrine is emblematic in this respect – did not heavily rely on power's "boundlessness": the "absolute" nature of power was claimed only to stress its original character; moreover, even though the legislative *potestas* was given prime importance, attention was also paid to the limits of power, which was obliged to abide by divine law and natural law, by the pacts with its subjects ("pacta sunt servanda") and by the reign's *leges fundamentales*.

Far from being endowed with absolute power, the "absolute" sovereign had limited power, since it was compelled to take into account normative systems, institutional structures, and *iura et privilegia* belonging to largely autonomous bodies and cities opposing and constraining it. To employ a provocative expression, it might be said that the "absolute" state was the most successful accomplishment of the rule of law: such a state, in fact, was limited by law (and by rights) and, far from using an unrestrained legislative power, it had to deal with the rules, the rights, and the privileges entailed by a prior social and legal order.

3 THE "PREHISTORY" OF THE RULE OF LAW: BETWEEN ENLIGHTENMENT AND REVOLUTION

The "absolute" state was "limited" by law, by rights, and by the *iura et privilegia* of individuals, ranks, and political bodies: the *ancien régime* was not the realm of arbitrariness which old "liberal" apologists used to oppose to the new "rational" nineteenth-century order. The opposition is not a "metaphysical", absolute one between non-reason and reason, disorder, and order. Simply, radically different approaches and values met and clashed throughout the seventeenth and eighteenth centuries. A new vision of sovereignty, of the individual and of his rights began to develop and a new "citizenship discourse" founded and provided the framework within which the idea of a *Rechtsstaat* came into existence. The solution provided by the rule of law to the relationship between power and law was closely related to the deep change in the political lexicon which took place in Europe during the Enlightenment.

The new idea of sovereignty and law presupposed a new philosophical anthropology: the individual was viewed in his essential and perennial traits (in the "state of nature"); he was conceived independently of his belonging to social and political bodies and seen as a unitary subject with specific needs and rights, determined by freedom and equality. A free individual, however, was not an unbridled individual escaping all boundaries: on the one hand, individual freedom was an ambit protected from others' undue intrusion (as if the ancient *immunitas* had become a quality endemic to human beings "as such") and, on the other hand, it had to come to terms with law, i.e. there developed a space for personal action and personal expansion that was grounded on law, both limited and guaranteed by it.

Law was not in a (Hobbes-inspired) disjunctive relationship with freedom: freedom did not begin where coercion ended. Rather, according to Locke and Montesquieu, law (natural law, civil law) was the indispensable medium for freedom. According to Montesquieu, what prevents despotism – i.e. the degeneration of a politically sound regime – is a strong connection between freedom and law. The individual is free in so far as he acts within the law and law is, in turn, his only protection against arbitrariness. It is the nexus between freedom and law which restrains the sovereign's will and guarantees individual security. Freedom and security (of person and goods) are the key values guaranteed to individuals by law's protection against arbitrariness.

Law was not just an internal aspect of sovereignty. It had a specific functional destination and provided individuals with the framework and the protection of their actions. This led to the principles of lawfulness (*nullum crimen sine lege*) and of legal equality (all individuals are equally bound by law), which were taken for granted by nineteenth-century civilization (at least on an ideal level, since their effective implementation remained uncertain and problematic). In any event, in the age of Enlightenment, trust in law as a means for protecting and strengthening individuals' freedom, property, and rights went hand in hand with an optimistic vision of sovereignty. While at that time sovereignty had a dangerous tendency to become despotic, it could, or rather had to, express and realize a final rational order.

Sovereignty, law, and freedom (property, rights) were seen by eighteenth-century reformers as closely intertwined and such a connection was not overturned by the upheavals caused by the French Revolution, though the latter introduced a new language and practice going far beyond the *philosophes*' forecasts and expectations. Just like the enlightened reformers, revolutionaries believed that sovereignty must protect individual rights (above all freedom and property), which were the keystone and condition for the new order's legitimacy: according to the 1789 Declaration of the Rights of Man and of the Citizen, sovereignty must realize (protect, coordinate) individuals' natural rights through the law. Natural rights were transformed (in a Rousseau-like fashion) into civil rights and, as such, they were strengthened and protected.

Yet, revolutionaries also brought significant innovations affecting both the sovereign and the individual. "Who is the sovereign?" asked Sieyès at the dawn of the Revolution: sovereignty belonged to "20 million French people" who, being equal and immune from the stigma of "privileges", *were* the nation. The nation was sovereign and the individuals were citizens: together with their natural civil rights, they enjoyed political rights and played an active role in the political body.

The optimistic eighteenth-century idea of sovereignty was confirmed by the Revolution's "philosophy": the commonplace of a merry-go-round between sovereignty, law, and freedom was strengthened by the new concept of sovereignty, which no longer belonged to the Enlightened monarch, but rather to the nation, the collective entity or "body". The "corporatist" pathos outlined by Rousseau in his *Social Contract* then became the key element of the relationship between the sovereign and the individual: since the sovereign was the "moi commun", i.e. the collective body, since sovereignty and community coincided, the vision of individuals' relationship with the sovereign was underpinned by the belief that, as Rousseau said, "the body cannot damage its own limbs".

It is on such grounds (the optimistic vision of sovereignty, strengthened by the "corporatist" image of a sovereign nation) that the revolutionary discourse paid little attention to "guarantees", i.e. to all normative and institutional devices capable of implementing solemnly declared freedoms and protecting them from the interference of power. Indeed, there was no need for guarantees since power's despotic temptations were blocked, at their very root, by the nature of the sovereign body.

Although, according to revolutionaries' most widespread thinking, the sovereign nation was the guardian of rights, and sovereignty (being embodied in the nation) was not a threat but rather a means to achieve individual rights, some of the Revolution's most brilliant leaders (Sieyès, Condorcet) did nonetheless envisage the possibility of a "tyrannical" degeneration of political institutions. According to Condorcet, the Declaration of Rights, deemed to be superior to ordinary legislation, may represent the real *rempart des citoyens*, i.e. the best shield against unjust laws possibly enacted by the nation's representatives.[7]

Far from being a harmless and academic issue, the potential "despotic" degeneration of republican institutions was at the centre of the political debates and conflicts that characterized the ensuing radicalization of the revolutionary process. It was within a besieged France and within the context of a threatened revolution that the relationship between sovereignty, law, constitution, government, and rights acquired a new and dramatic meaning. According to Robespierre and Saint-Just, to appeal to the constitution was useless when there was an urgent need to face the enemy and to save the nation: what was needed, instead, was terror and virtue; what was needed was a government ready to react and strike, a government free from legal obstacles and from laws' slowness and abstraction; what mattered was not law but rather the urgency of the situation; the "state of exception" was thus the principle demanding the terroristic defence of republican freedom: it was the "necessity", it was "the saintliest of all laws, the safety of the people" to legitimate a revolutionary government rendering it "terrible towards the bad" and "favourable towards the good".[8] Only Condorcet, once again, refused the "state of necessity" as a "pretext for tyranny",[9] and claimed the need to rigidly determine the boundaries and duration of exceptional measures, i.e. to preserve the essential parameters of common justice and lawfulness.

In the whirling "historical acceleration" caused by the Revolution, the spontaneous harmony that seemed to characterize the relationship between sovereignty, law, and rights – and the belief that law could act as an intermediary between citizens and power by implementing the natural rights of the individual – were overturned and replaced by dramatic alternative beliefs: on the one hand, the perception of power's dangerousness, of the potential discrepancy between the formal lawfulness and substantial despotism of legislative provisions (and the ensuing attempt to make the *Declaration of Rights* an unassailable safeguard); on the other hand, the theorization of a "state of necessity" capable of sweeping away formal lawfulness and individual rights in the name of the fight against darkness, of freedom against despotism, of virtues against corruption.

The expression "rule of law" is not yet to be found within the Revolution's debate and we are therefore still dealing with the "prehistory" of our formula. Yet, during this period numerous expectations and problems arose which are the conditions of the future rule of law. The Revolution's "philosophy" and practices decidedly break with a "regime" – the ancient society of hierarchies and "privileges" – that began to be referred to as *ancien*. A new subject came into play which claimed its right to property, freedom, and political participation, and a new image and "experience" of power was conceived of. As never before, power had been able to manifest its extraordinary energy as well as its reforming and incisive capacity. While the ancient monarch's "absolute" power was bound to come to terms with "objective" realities, giving rise to differentiated and consolidated individual statuses, the sovereign nation's power, instead, was free from any predetermined constraint: the nation, according to Sieyès, is quite simply, whatever it needs to be. It was an absolute constituent power that, by means of its irresistible strength, swept away the ancient regime and created a new order based on freedom and property. Natural rights (freedom, property) existed "as such" and were simply declared by the nation; yet, the very act of declaring and then implementing and coordinating natural rights expressed the nation's capacity to bring a rights order into being. The order was grounded on rights but was founded by the nation. Legislating will and rights were thus closely intertwined and their relationship was mediated by a revolution that was conceived of and legitimated as an act aimed at demolishing the ancient regime and founding a new order.

The revolutionary break has been a specifically French phenomenon. Even though the "French model" had important effects on the rest of Europe, it was not the only possible solution advanced with respect to the relationship between power and law (and rights): even before the Revolution, a great European country, namely Britain, had precociously demonstrated how the sovereign's "absolute" vocation could be combined with restraints limiting arbitrariness and protecting individuals, so much so that the English experience was deemed by many Enlightenment French intellectuals to embody the freedom and tolerance still fiercely opposed in their own country.

Great Britain's political and social structures indeed appeared, to many "Enlightened" intellectuals, to be the best possible approximation to their recommended social model. The idea of society shared by different French and British (especially Scottish) social philosophies had a "dichotomic" character: the key to order lay in individuals' actions and interactions; society was organized spontaneously by some constitutive rules (freedom, property, and contract), whereas political power acted "from outside" as a protective and safeguarding means. Individual freedom (the free satisfaction of personal needs within the "rational" framework of property and contract) was the vital nourishment of an order existing independently of the sovereign's intervention and decisions, while the latter's legitimacy was to be found in his functional link with society. Whether one referred to Locke's ideas of natural law and social contract or to different theories, there was a shared conviction that the law of the sovereign should simply protect and strengthen an autonomous and self-sustaining social order.

Such a scheme – whose essential traits were endorsed, even if differently founded, by Hume, Hutcheson, Smith, and Blackstone – was not a utopian outlook: it was the representation, in the abstract shape of a theory or "model", of a society resulting from a long historical process which had developed in England in the previous centuries.

Until the seventeenth century, the English monarchy – not very different from its continental counterparts (Spain and France) – more or less successfully strove to assume to itself strong, centralized power. It was during the seventeenth century that the histories of these European realms ceased to be similar and that the English "exception", though not rapidly and bloodlessly, came into being. It took a century or little less than that (a century marked by bloody battles, *coups de scène*, a regicide, revolutions, restorations, gallows, and conspiracies) for history to ultimately confirm Coke's stance and deny Hobbes' pessimism: finally a form of divided or shared sovereignty arose, without the collapsing of order and the breaking out of *bellum omnium*.

Coke's assumptions were confirmed, *post-mortem*, since after the "Glorious Revolution" the English political system was based not on the king's autocratic will but on the sharing of sovereignty and the primacy of the common law. The legal order was not determined by the sovereign; rather, it depended on an immemorial tradition, developed over time, autonomously growing and changing, and consisting of a coherent set of rules and principles which could not be disregarded by any political institution.

Common law was, according to the Roman tradition, *ratio scripta*: it was not abstract or natural reason but a reason historically implemented through a consolidated technique passed down from generation to generation of jurists and judges; thus, it was an artificial, technical, and objectified reason, embodied within the legal system: it was a collective reason, i.e. the expression of a community of *sapientes* ameliorating the system throughout generations, refining and suiting it to changing circumstances. Coke, Hale, and Blackstone thus described and legitimized the new English constitutional system as one which guaranteed benefits and individuals' freedoms and rights.

On the one hand, therefore, "a number of conflicts for the control and composition of the state's different bodies"[10] demolished sovereignty's "absolutist" vocation; on the other hand, individual rights and duties were linked to a normative system which was largely independent of one centralized will. The "dichotomic" model (the idea of a legal and social order strengthened "from outside" by governmental intervention), too, was not an academic abstraction, but a plausible translation (into the idiom of social philosophy) of the deep logic of eighteenth-century British arrangements.

It follows that the difference between the English and French contexts was apparent even when the *philosophers* expressed their admiration for the "English model". The English model, evoked by French reformers in order to criticize the French political establishment, was not confined in England to the realm of what was "possible" and "alternative", but seemed to coincide with the existing regime; not surprisingly, Blackstone was able to combine natural law doctrine with common law precisely because he believed that the former (with its wealth of rights, freedoms, property, etc.) was accurately implemented by the existing constitutional system.

According to the French Revolutionaries, the order of rights could be implemented and the sovereign could become the guardian of freedom and property only if a new demiurge, the sovereign nation, crushed the *ancien régime* and implemented rights. In this light, Burke's heated criticism – made as early as at the beginning of the Revolution – of the revolutionary programme makes sense. Even if both countries were concerned with "liberty and property", Burke believed that fundamental rights could not be determined and imposed by an assembly's "instantaneous" act; rather, they were the country's "inheritance", the legacy of an immemorial tradition, the product of a constitution which autonomously grows and develops over time.

Individual rights in revolutionary France were indeed "natural"; yet, they did not affirm themselves on their own and required the sovereign nation's intervention. The law acquired a somewhat constitutive role inasmuch as it turned "natural" rights into "civil" rights. The "voluntaristic" component of the French model, which viewed law (and ultimately rights) as the expression of the sovereign will, was in striking contrast with the (emblematically Burkean) idea of an objective, impersonal, and "unintentional" legal system, on which individual statuses depended.

The framework of the American Federation[11] *in statu nascenti* is yet another model. For the sake of simplification, the American model could be seen as a "third option" that, whilst largely drawing from the English common law, was nonetheless centred around issues and concerns which would later be endemic in the French world. Revolutionary France and the American Federation shared the need to draft a constitution legally acknowledging human and natural rights. Yet, the French and American contexts are very different and so are their "enemies": Great Britain's hostile and mortifying sovereign order, for the Americans; and an entire political and social organization, i.e. a burdensome "feudal" past, for the French people.

In any event, in both cases there arose a constituent process which, both in its dynamics and outcome, was radically different from the English model: it was the constituent power that transformed natural rights (which, otherwise, would remain weak and precarious) in legal rights. The constituent will thus acquired a relevance that was not to be found in Great Britain – and which accounts for the American "success" of Locke's contractualism – though it did not lead to such concepts as the Nation's omnipotence, the law's centrality or, above all, the strong link between law and rights, which would be endorsed by the French assembly.

The American colonies did not fight against feudalism: they fought against the English parliament's sovereignty and against the tyrannical use of sovereignty allegedly exerted thereby.[12] Thus, the potential danger of popular sovereignty was soon and strongly perceived in the American debate: while Jefferson and Paine strove to subject the constitutional structure to the people's "absolute" will, which was always free to "start anew" and redefine the rules of the game, other writers (among whom Adams), although endorsing popular sovereignty as the ultimate foundation, reduced its impact by calling for federalism and power-balancing.

It is undeniable that some French thinkers, such as Condorcet, were concerned with the risks of despotism and perceived the need to curb legislators' omnipotence. Nevertheless, French concerns about the necessity for constitutional "guarantees" led only to dead ends, whereas in the United States they achieved full expression, starting with Judge Marshall's famous judgment, in a legal doctrine and practice that, although grounding the political order on popular sovereignty, deemed constitutional principles to be indestructible and to be protected by judges' control on legislative power.

It follows that freedom and property were the pivotal elements of a social order that both law and the sovereign must respect and protect. In the United States, just like in contemporary France and Great Britain, a widespread social theory conceived of individual freedom and property as the supporting pillars of order and required the sovereign to respect and protect them. If the organization of power was always legitimated by its functional link with individuals and rights, the relationship between power and law, and between law and sovereignty, took different shapes in different countries. In France and the United States it was the sovereign people's will which, at least as an ultimate instance, guaranteed the implementation of individual rights; yet, in the United States and not in France, the people's will was split into two clearly differentiated legal structures – the constitution and legislation – so much so that the former's "voluntaristic" foundation was overlooked; conversely, Great Britain brought rights back within an objective order that did not require a specific founding act of the people's will.

Regardless of the diversities of contexts and outcomes, the relationship between sovereignty, law, and freedom was at the heart of the eighteenth-century representation of the political order. According to Kant, the ultimate conundrum was how to combine sovereign power with individual freedom. Under an ethical perspective, freedom coincided with the subject's inner autonomy; under a legal perspective, focused on "those relationships between one person and another which are both external and practical",[13] freedom was inseparable from human interaction. Law became the legal framework within which individual actions took place and was the condition for their coexistence: the law reconciled an individual being's freedom with that of others; "right is therefore the sum total of these conditions within which the will of one person can be reconciled with the will of another in accordance with a universal law of freedom".[14] The legal system thus coordinated individual wills and, being "extracted from a priori principles", was not contingent, nor subject to variations in time and place or to the sovereign's decisions: it was a "natural" law in that its fundamental characteristics were independent of any given political organization.[15]

However, the coordination of individual freedoms was not guaranteed by the mere existence of a normative system: given that conflicts and prevarications could always arise, law could not simply advocate the coordination of freedoms, but must guarantee its effective implementation. Since law was not grounded on ethical reasons but "depends on the principle of the possibility of an external coercion"[16] allowing for the coexistence of individual "wills", coercion became an integral part of the law.

Coercion, in turn, called for the presence of a sovereign: law implies a force capable of settling conflicts and repressing violations; for such a reason, Kant believed that the shift from the "natural state" to the "civil state" (from a legal system lacking coercive force to a regime where rules are guaranteed by force) was the "postulate of public law" and grounded the political community on the "original contract".

The original contract was not "a fact" but rather an "idea of reason":[17] the old idea of a social contract, that Sieyès had transformed into the reality (and symbol) of the nation's constituent will has been turned by Kant into the regulating idea of the political order, the latter being the "coalition of the wills of all private individuals in a nation to form a common public will".[18]

According to Kant, law was not an expression of the sovereign's will, neither was the sovereign dependent on the creative will of a constitutional process. Nonetheless, law did need a sovereign with coercive power to perform its ordering role; it required the intervention of a "master" controlling each individual's will and forcing him "to obey a universally valid will under which everyone can be free". At this stage of his reasoning, Kant was faced with what he called the most difficult problem humanity needs to tackle: law needed the sovereign's coercive intervention, yet the latter is "an animal who needs a master"; a process of regression ad infinitum begins, which could only be resolved by way of approximation: "Nothing straight can be constructed from such warped wood as that which man is made of".[19]

Kant's solution lay in the implementation of "a perfectly just civil constitution".[20] Individual happiness did not pertain to the latter, since it was left to each individual's free determination. If the government regarded its subjects' happiness as its final goal, not only did it saddle itself with an impossible task (given the variety of ends that individuals may identify happiness with), but it also took the place of individuals' choices, thus severely encroaching upon their freedom: if a constitution "suspends the entire freedom of its subjects", the "paternal government" becomes the "greatest conceivable despotism".[21]

Therefore, far from being engaged in attaining individual happiness, the state was bound to respect the principles of the "just constitution", i.e. freedom, equality before the law, independence, and must coercively ensure their effective realization: the state's *raison d'être* and its constitutional arrangement were legitimated by a specific aim, which had nothing to do with individual well-being or happiness, promised (or even attained) by a despotic regime; rather, the state's aim was to protect "that condition in which the constitution most closely approximates to the principles of right".[22] The sovereign's role was both essential (given the necessary relationship between law and sanctions) and bound by its goal: the sovereign must act to respect and defend the principles of freedom, equality, and independence, which are not laws enacted by the already-constituted state, are not principles of positive law (even of a "higher" level), but are principles of pure reason that guarantee the just constitution of civil society.[23]

Kant's rigorous model thus deemed the sovereign and law to be perfectly distinct though necessarily intertwined. According to Kant, law is a normative scheme that freedom hinges upon, though only the state's coercive intervention can render the latter effective. The sovereign's tasks are thus clearly predetermined: not being entrusted with the "positive" realization of its subjects' happiness, the sovereign aimed at ensuring the "just constitution" of freedom (and thus deserved the ready and absolute obedience of its subjects). The sovereign or the people's will played no role in the foundation of law (and rights). The rational organization of the state, together with the link between its coercive force and the law, provided a solution (by way of approximation) to what Kant lucidly presents as a decisive dilemma: how to combine the "master's" – "absolutely" dominant position with the inflexibility of a rule of which he ought simply to be the guardian.

4 THE RULE OF LAW BETWEEN THE FRENCH REVOLUTION AND 1848

Kant did not use the word *Rechtsstaat* or "rule of law"; yet, as early as 1798, whilst referring to Kant and his followers, J. W. Placidus spoke about the "Schule der Rechts-Staats-Lehre",[24] thus creating an "original" link between Kant and the rule of law which would subsequently be taken for granted; and it was in Germany that, throughout the nineteenth century, the expression "rule of law" abandoned the realm of "prehistory" and officially entered that of "history". It was in Germany that a doctrine developed which would strongly (even though belatedly) affect both Italian and French legal cultures.

Even where the expression "rule of law" made a belated appearance, as in France, the problems highlighted by Kant's dilemma needed nonetheless to be resolved, especially when they were worsened by the French Revolution's decisive but cumbersome legacy. A number of intellectuals who are now depicted as "liberals" – such as Constant, De Staël, Guizot, and Tocqueville – had thus to come to terms with the Revolution; and indeed it was by examining this momentous historical experience that they came to the conclusion that sovereignty, law, and rights needed to be reassessed. Constant's criticism of Rousseau (and, through him, of Jacobinism) focused on the guarantees which had been sidestepped, during the revolutionary debates, by corporatist pathos and by trust in the sovereign nation. Trust in the sovereign and in its natural alliance with the individual collapsed because of the traumatic experience of the Terror and gave way to a "strategy of suspicion" vis-à-vis political power.[25]

Even though the sovereign, according to Constant, was necessary to guarantee order, its presence constitutively entailed the risk of despotism. Therefore, the problem of controlling and restraining the terrible energy of power – which had already marked the "prehistory" of the rule of law – acquired a new impetus and centrality for Constant and other French liberal thinkers of early nineteenth century. The protection of individual rights (freedom and property) was deemed to be an "absolute" need, not open to exceptions or weakening; it required a suitable constitutional organization and a fierce fight against what Constant deemed to be the most serious degeneration of power, i.e. arbitrariness, namely the avoidance of rules in the name of efficiency or necessity. The "state of necessity" relied upon by Jacobins to legitimate the constitution's inapplicability was deemed to be the expedient whereby the unbridled and dreadful strength of power had been exerted. The dramatic epitome of the pathology of power was the Jacobin Terror, which, by postulating unlimited and uncontrolled power of the sovereign over the individual suggested that such tyranny could only be prevented in future by respect for rules, i.e. the observance of formal bonds.

The certainty of rights hinges upon the certainty of legal rules. Constant's critique of Mably's and Filangieri's "Enlightened" interventionism[26] arose from the belief that "speculative laws", i.e. laws affecting social dynamics and pursuing constantly new and unexpected goals, surreptitiously reintroduce (as a result of their being "forward-looking") unpredictability, uncertainty, and arbitrariness, which are precisely what procedures and rules seek to avoid.

The certainty of rights thus presupposes the certainty of legal rules and procedures which, in turn, require the external support of the political system's "closing valve", i.e. public opinion, as propounded by Constant and the entirety of nineteenth-century liberal thinking.[27]

Hence, the system's necessary aims and means, i.e. its "allies" and "enemies", were clearly defined. The aim was to safeguard freedom and property; the means were the network of formal rules and bonds conditioning the sovereign and requiring him (through public opinion's "external" intervention) to perform the indispensable task of safeguarding public order. The difficulty endemic to such a framework – the dilemmatic shift from Kant's "warped piece of wood" to a "straight piece of wood" – is that the (coercive) protection of rights was inevitably in the hands of precisely the same power which most dreadfully threatened rights.

Constant was writing not long after the perturbing period of Terror but nonetheless shows evidence of the expectations and fears endorsed by the French liberalism in the following period, when the fundamental traits of this kind of power, already traced in the brief "Great Revolution", seemed to be conclusively confirmed in the aspirations and convulsions of 1848. Politicians not advocating a "political and social republic", looking at the events of 1789 rather than of 1793 for reference, at the *Declaration of the Rights of Man and of the Citizen* rather than at the Jacobins' Republic, believed that power was a threat historically brought about by the "tyrannical majority": it was the blind and brutal triumph of quantity over quality, the despicable advent of a "no-quality democracy" that, by appealing to some of the most influential symbols of the Revolution – equality, popular sovereignty, and universal suffrage – was dangerously capable of removing all restraints and guarantees. The omnipotent majority reintroduces the primacy of the "popular will", which the theory grounded on "absolute" rights had tried to exorcize by calling for the respect of rules and the strength of public opinion.

Pre-1848 liberalism was perfectly conscious of both the importance of what was at stake and of the fragility of the "remedies" available: what was at stake was freedom and property (the pillars of a legitimate order) and the remedies against tyranny were frail since they were ultimately dependent on the sovereign who, in the name of the primacy of the will of the assembly, of the majority, of the people, could freely get rid of them. Having to deal with such a commonly perceived danger, Antonio Rosmini advanced one of the most accurate and complete suggestions in this respect: on the one hand, rights ought to be provided with a "strong" and metaphysically unobjectionable foundation; on the other hand, a rigidly census-based representative method should be introduced, so that the sovereign could be the faithful image of the proprietary apparatus; lastly – and mostly importantly – a "Supreme Court", a "political tribunal", should be set up in order to realize an effective control of the legislative assembly. The Court would "preserve and safeguard the national constitution", ensuring that rules conformed to "the fundamental law, which stands above them all, and is their touchstone". Rather than enacting a constitution and then leaving it "alone", without envisaging any power "entrusted to safeguard it", a body should be created to protect the constitution from any potential infringement thereof: in this way, the constitution is "no longer a written piece of paper with no voice", and it is "given both a life and a voice".[28]

Besides "constitutional engineering" interventions aimed at curbing the threats of power,[29] the conflict between power and law could not be resolved by simple expedients and formal mechanisms. This was true even where a higher and untouchable constitutional provision was envisaged or where the guaranteeing role of legal provisions and procedures was relied on: such expedients and mechanisms were deemed, on the one hand, to be instruments needed for a specific "absolute" goal (the preservation of individual rights); on the other hand, they were not a self-sufficient remedy: albeit indispensable, they required public opinion's intervention to be properly effective.

While pre-1848 liberalism reintroduced the constitutive elements of Kant's dilemma and attempted to resolve the latter by relying on a double connection (between power and law, and between the legally bound power and individual rights) strengthened by the control of public opinion, in Germany the same thematic tangle was examined by introducing (even before 1848) a specific expression (*Rechtsstaat*) that would become very popular.

Independently of the number of meanings ascribed to such a lemma in nineteenth century Germany, these belonged to a legal doctrine which differed from the "French model" in all respects, i.e. in the state's foundation and role, as well as in the representation of individuals and their rights. German culture was permeated by a "historicist paradigm" which, though interpreted in different manners and employed by conflicting (conservative or liberal) perspectives, was nonetheless anchored to some recurrent assumptions: firstly, the political order was not a "voluntaristic" or built-up system but linked to tradition, to a historically continuous development; secondly, the "subject" of such a development was a collective entity, i.e. the people, that, being historically moulded and endowed with a specific ethical and spiritual identity of its own, was fully realized and expressed within the state;[30] thirdly, an individual's political and legal identity was determined by his belonging to the people-state, so that his rights could be referred not to an abstract natural personality, but rather stem from the vital link between the individual himself and the people-state.

The two main theories on the *Rechtsstaat* propounded in Germany in the first half of the nineteenth century were developed within such a framework: their authors are Friedrich Julius Stahl and Robert von Mohl.[31]

According to Stahl,[32] "the legal subject is the people in its entirety ..., not the individual being as such". Human personality is concretely and historically realized by the individual's belonging to the people.

The relationship between the individual being and the legal order is mediated by this belonging: the individual is subject to law "not as an individual being, as a *homo*", rather as a member of his people, a "component of the whole", a "*civis*".[33] The people, in turn, is transfused and realized within the state, viewed as the "personification of the human community", the union of people under a sovereign authority,[34] an original totality, the objective and necessary expression of the national community, rather than an arrangement dependent on individual beings' will.

Stahl ascribed the expression *Rechtsstaat* to such a state and thoroughly explained its meaning. According to Stahl, a state characterized by the rule of law is not an indifferent ethical reality (a circumstance which, in any event, would be excluded by its historical and spiritual bondage with the people); neither is it the expression of Kant's (or Humboldt's) idea of a sovereign merely engaged in protecting individual rights. The state is not prevented from pursuing its aims and neither is the law's control extended so as to encompass "the aim and content of the state". "Rule of law", *Rechtsstaat*, simply refers to a state acting in a legal form and purporting to "exactly determine and unquestionably establish the lines and boundaries of its actions as well as the free ambits of its citizens in accordance with law (*in der Weise des Rechts*)". Law is the state's formal way of action, its legal format: the state characterized by the rule of law is opposed to the "police state" and to Rousseau's and Robespierre's *Volksstaat* and matches the modern evolutionary trend not so much because it endorses this or that content but because it removes extemporaneousness and arbitrariness from the state's action and makes it regular, legal. The modern state, being grounded on the rule of law, cannot but act (no matter what its actions are) in a legal form.[35]

The rule of law does not consist in a state's being ultimately aimed at protecting individual rights and, for this purpose, constraining power and neutralizing its dangerousness. Stahl did focus on fundamental rights, freedoms, and, equality, with the aim of providing a doctrine free from the French model's "individualistic" abstractions and aware of the need to mediate individual rights with a necessarily unequal and hierarchical order. Yet, what really matters, according to Stahl, is that the *Rechtsstaat* is reflected not in a number of content-based limits respected by the state, but in the formal, legal manners whereby the state's actions are taken.

The circumstance that the *Rechtsstaat* prescribes a given mode of action for the state rather than a law-created connection between the sovereign and its subjects was a coherent consequence not so much (and not only) of Stahl's politically conservative choices but rather of his overall theoretical assumptions, dominated by the centrality of the people-state and by the belief that individual rights were closely connected with the individual's belonging to the political community.

Robert von Mohl's doctrine radically differed from Stahl's. By including the expression *Rechtsstaat* in the title of his extensive work on *Polizeiwissenschaft*,[36] Mohl officially christened, as it were, such an expression.[37] This was certainly not a "Kantian" title; besides, Mohl was dissatisfied with Kant's perspective, which excessively mortified and contracted the state's administrative and "governing" task. It was the sovereign's interventionism (a *topos* of German cameralistic tradition) which, according to Mohl, had to be reassessed in the light of the rule of law's fundamental enunciations, giving primacy to individual freedom whilst, at the same time, overcoming Kant's rigorous "non-interventionism".

Mohl believed that the rule of law was typical of a specific kind of state, namely that which suits itself to a society developing through its members' energies and initiatives. The value of individual and collective resources was enhanced by strengthening individual freedom; this was not a mere "empty domain" free from external intrusions but was substantiated in the individual's positive and expanding actions. Under the rule of law, the state was able to determine the measure and limits of its intervention: it strove not to compromise the autonomy of individual choices and initiatives and was also ready to back the individual by removing hindrances he may not be able to overcome on his own.

Unlike Stahl, Mohl believed that the state's intervention must take in account some content-based restraints: in order for the state to be a *Rechtsstaat*, law must intervene by binding its action to the attainment of a specific goal – individual freedom – which did not coincide with an area protected from interferences of power but rather implied the individual personality's complete development. Thus, even if individual freedom must be guaranteed by law and implemented by a judge, the state's intervention should not be limited to the performance of its jurisdictional role, since a state providing no services other than the administration of justice was not feasible.[38]

The guiding light of Mohl's reasoning was not the state's centrality, but rather individual freedom: freedom (conceived of as *immunitas* and as positive and expanding action) was the goal, the limit, and the criterion for the state's action, which, even when upholding individual action, must respect all laws and customs, must take into account a given people's dispositions and particular inclinations[39] and must, above all, respect property, this being the unavoidable condition for individual development.[40]

Although criticizing a Kant-modelled state concerned merely with safeguarding rights, Mohl underlined the functional link between the state and an individual freely and creatively using his own resources: Stahl's criticism of Mohl's excessive tilt towards "atomism" (the deadly sin, according to the historicist paradigm) is thus not surprising. In fact, even if Mohl thought he escaped Stahl's criticism because he himself believed in the state's active and irreplaceable role and in its vital link with society, the roots of dissent lay in two profoundly different ideas of the state and of the rule of law. Stahl did indeed refer to *Rechtsstaat* and advocated the state's legally "regulated" action: yet, while Stahl believed that the gravitational centre was the people-state and the individual's belonging to the political community (which the implementation of individual rights depended upon), Mohl argued that the legitimacy and boundaries of the state's action were dictated by individual freedom.

Stahl equally believed that the intimate connection between the state and the law, i.e. the legal shape which the state's action (*qua Rechtsstaat*) could not avoid adopting, benefited individuals, in that they could rely on the foreseeable, regular, and regulated character of the state's intervention. However, what was forsaken by Stahl and was central to Mohl's view was the functional destination of the state and its connection with the individual's fundamental rights.

5 THE RULE OF LAW IN GERMAN LEGAL DOCTRINE IN THE SECOND HALF OF THE NINETEENTH CENTURY

While the expression *Rechtsstaat* could be used in the pre-1848 period as a key word underpinning constitutional reforms, in the second half of the century it underwent a depoliticization and technicalization process[41] and stimulated theoretical investigations legitimating institutional innovations in the field of administrative law.

In this respect, we must take into account the changes which affected German jurisprudence and its historicist assumptions in the second half of the nineteenth century. Even if the historicist and organicistic background was still alive, diverging theories started emerging in the 1850s and 1860s: some authors took organicistic suggestions seriously, so that they assumed the association, the *Genossenschaft*, as the matrix of the entire public law and located the state within a network of groups and associations with which it was ontologically connected; others, despite sharing the idea of a genetic link between "people" and "state" (between the nation's historical identity and its institutional realization), deemed the state's sovereignty to be the social order's hinge as well as the specific and exclusive object of legal knowledge.

The "rule of law" formula cannot but be involved in such a complex cultural change.

In the early 1860s, Otto Bähr employed the formula *Rechtsstaat* in the title of a work which would become an important landmark for both German and Italian legal doctrine. Bähr's perspective, shared by others such as Beseler and Gierke, was grounded on the central role of the social group, the *Genossenschaft*. Bähr believed that it was only within such a perspective that Stahl's deficient stance could be overcome. While Stahl had praised the rule of law's virtues, by failing to effectively limit the sovereign's discretion, he had reduced the rule of law to a merely formal bound.[42]

According to Bähr, when the structure of any given social group is examined, the general traits of the legal phenomenon stand out: each association is a microcosm characterized by constitutive rules, control roles, and by a specific distribution of rights and burdens. In other words, the existence of each association hinges upon the combination of governors' decisional supremacy with the protection of its associates' rights.[43] What is true for any association is true also for the state, this merely representing the apex of many groups with different dimensions and levels of complexity.[44] Even the state implies the existence of a "fundamental law", which is not the output of a sudden and voluntaristic "decision", but springs from the actual legal order and determines both each organ's jurisdiction and individuals' rights and duties.

Under Bähr's perspective, the delicate problem faced by the state and not by any other smaller association was the difficulty clearly illustrated by Kant and doomed to become the crucial dilemma of nineteenth-century doctrines on the rule of law: how can an impartial arbitrator of disputes be envisaged when the opposing parties are the subject, on the one hand, and the sovereign, on the other? How can a controller of the controller be plausible when the *sub iudice* action is imputable to the sovereign, i.e. to the same person upon whom the overall order depends?

In this respect, Bähr's solution resulted from the distinction between the state's different functions: before the legislating state and the judging state, citizens' rights were only moral; when, however, the state acted as an administrative power, the control could be entrusted to a judge committed to protecting the individual's legal sphere.[45] This was the conceptual core that would be continuously referred to and further elaborated in the following decades,[46] given the importance of a theory that paved the way for a judicial control of the state's administration and favoured the setting up of the administrative justice bodies that were actually created in the last decades of the nineteenth century, not only in Germany, but also in Italy and France.[47]

However, no matter how popular and brilliant Bähr's solution to Kant's problem of the "warped piece of wood" was, no matter how much it was linked with the relevant implications of administrative justice, it was only a partial solution: it was not the state as such, but rather only one specific expression of it (its administrative action) that was deemed to be legally controllable. Under such a perspective, the rule of law doctrine partly reduced its claims and partly rendered them more specific and attainable: it did not aim at a "global" limit which, in the name of law, could be opposed to the sovereign's free will, but at the same time it went beyond Stahl's "formal" solution (the *Rechtsstaat* as a state acting in the form of law) and highlighted a domain where rules and controls could be clearly founded and embodied in a specific institutional arrangement.

Bähr takes for granted the idea of *Genossenschaft* and the pivotal homogeneity between the social organization and the state and conceptualizes the rule of law on such grounds. The jurist Carl Friedrich Gerber also underlined the importance of the rule of law. However, he distanced himself from the organicist and historicist tradition by making the state–person the exclusive object of legal knowledge.[48]

According to Gerber, the "organic" life of the *Volk* and its ethical and spiritual identity were legally relevant and conceivable only when realized within the state. The state, as a "legal personality", was the "guardian and discloser of the people's forces", "the supreme personality of law",[49] embodying the "ethical power of a self-aware people", the "social expression of humanity": no rival power could limit or encroach upon its sovereignty. Gerber's representation of individuals and their rights stemmed from his uncompromising state-centred idea. Individual rights are the indirect consequence of the state's autonomous decision, this acting unilaterally in pursuing its aims: individual rights are conceived of as "a series of public law effects", as reflections of a legal system centred around the state's will.[50]

It follows that a functional link between the state, law, and individuals was hardly conceivable: when referring to the state as ruled by law, as *Rechtsstaat*, Gerber simply purported to stress the need for the state to implement "its greatest force" acting "within its sphere of legal existence".[51] However, the importance of Gerber's theory in the history of the rule of law is to be found elsewhere, namely in his suggestions about the formula's critical point: how to envisage and realize a state which can be both master and servant of the law.

Gerber's solution is clear-cut: the state is the master and determines, together with the normative system, the individual's rights, which are the former's "reflections". From an exclusively legal viewpoint, no formal limits are placed on the state's sovereignty and the state is the jurist's unitary and exclusive object of investigation. However, Gerber himself believed that the state historically exists in relationship with its people, of which it is the legal realization and embodiment. The state is thus concerned with "interests", "life manifestations and conditions", which belong to the same historical and spiritual process that the state itself stems from: to ignore such interests would be tantamount to "insulting the ethical dignity of a Nation or hindering its free development".[52] The salient features of modern civilization that Gerber examines (freedom of conscience, press, association, expatriation, and judicial independence) were thus deemed to be the historically necessary contents of the state's will, which unilaterally determined the legal system and the individual's rights.

Even though Gerber's reasoning was centred on the state and the rigorous inference of individual rights from the state-determined legal system, it did not escape the postulation of a "double route": the route of history, moulding the "modern state" and endowing it with rights that the collective conscience could not relinquish, and the route of law, granting rights no foundation other than their dependence on the state's objective order.

The idea that rights were a mere indirect effect of the state's will was decisively rejected by Otto von Gierke,[53] the fiercest defendant of the organicistic tradition. With respect to Gerber's "turning point", and in particular to the dogmatic inflexibility of his disciple Paul Laband in adopting and developing Gerber's reasoning, Gierke expressed his strong dissent, both in terms of its methods and contents. As for the method, Gierke claimed that Laband broke the link between history and law, overestimating logics and ignoring that the state's historical and spiritual substratum is an integral part of its "positive" reality; as for the content, Laband applied private law schemes to public law and thus reduced the state to its "dominating will", neglecting the *Gemeinwesen*, i.e. the "communitarian" substratum the state depends on.

According to Gierke, neither the relation of citizenship nor the foundations and scope of individual rights could be understood without considering the state's "organic" and communitarian dimension. On the contrary, the relationship between the individual and the political community can be accounted for only by recognizing the individual's belonging to the social whole (to the state as a political association) and the protection of the individual's legal sphere as complementary. Gierke rejected Gerber's contention that rights were grounded on the state's unilateral will: rights did not mirror the legal system chosen by the state but were rooted in community life. Together with the individual's belonging to the community and his duties of obedience, a number of limits forbidding other entities (including the state) to impinge upon the individual's legal sphere arose within the social organism itself.

According to Gierke, individual rights were not natural, pre-social, pre-state rights, which absolutely and "externally" limited the positive legal order. Rights had no origin other than that of the *Mitgliedschaft*, i.e. the common belonging of "rights-holders" to the organic political community: individuals' duties and rights (both "negative" and "positive") derived from their belonging to the community. The state, the legal order, and the individual's rights must be conceived of as "limbs" of the social-political organism. Far from being the "reflection" of the state's legal system, individual rights were rooted in the community's social framework and, as such, they limited, channelled, and bound the state's action. The difference from Laband and Gerber's rigorous state-centred approach could not be more evident.[54]

However, two aspects need to be stressed. Firstly, Gierke did not believe that rights have an "absolute" value: not only because he submerged them in history and represented them without giving in to natural law nostalgia, but also because he believed that rights were open to being erased by the state, holder of the supreme *potestas*, if it so decided.[55] It is true that such a possibility was abstract, because rights were rooted in the people's historical and spiritual development and as such were imposed on the state. Nonetheless – and this is the second aspect to focus on – Gierke believed that the state's sovereignty was ultimately decisive and that the "final" guarantor of the limits imposed thereon was history, i.e. the strength of a society "dictating" to the state given choices, coherent with the civilization it expresses. Gierke's distance from "formalists" remains undoubtedly significant (with respect to the representation of laws and rights), but Gierke's theory has some common traits (if not with Laband) with Gerber, who similarly tried to detect within history those content-based limits that law "as such" could not oppose to the state.

In other words, a particular *concordia discors* arose around the formula *Rechtsstaat*: on the one hand, formalists and organicists differed on the link between state, law, and rights and suggested conflicting theories; on the other hand, both positions regarded the sovereign (at least ultimately) as an uncontrollable arbitrator and found their last resort in history, i.e. in the substantive bonds which a given civilization imposes on the state.

It was in this context that one of the most brilliant outcomes of German jurisprudence took place: the theory of the state's "self-limitation", first hinted at by Jhering and then thoroughly developed by Jellinek.

Jhering dealt with the main dilemma (how to ensure the coexistence of the state's supreme force with law, limitation, and check) by arguing that force was not to be given up in the name of law. While no coexistence was possible without hierarchy and coercion, even an "unbridled" force could have – at least for short and exceptional periods – an ordering role:[56] the state was "the organization of social coercion", the "regulated and guaranteed" exercise of "social coercive power",[57] whereas "anarchy, namely the impotence of the state's power" was the denial of order and the "decomposition and disintegration of society".[58]

Order being dependent on the sovereign's strength, the problem faced by Jhering was to understand if, up to what extent and by means of which guarantees, it was possible to direct power along legal routes, to unite the sovereign's free will and "absolute" decisional capacity with the supremacy of norms. According to Jhering, legislative power cannot be limited, because law was the expression *par excellence* of sovereignty; a legislative act could be arbitrary only with respect to "law's general principles", though in this case it is deemed "unfair",[59] rather than illegal.

Things are different concerning the relationship between the state and the law: law could be seen as a limit to the state's action, provided that the famous dilemma was resolved or sidestepped: "how can the state's power be subdued to a given entity since there is no power above it?"[60]

According to Jhering, the answer was provided by the "self-limitation" theory: the sovereign was not conditioned by an "external" limit, since no higher power could be the holder of sovereignty beyond the state; on the contrary, the state was restrained by its free decisions. Hence, there arises the problem of guarantees: if free will is restrained by self-limitation, there is nothing preventing the state from getting rid of a restraint created thereby. Jhering's solution centred around the genetic and functional link uniting the state with society: it is in the state's interest to cultivate its own "self-control" and to guarantee the "certainty" of the system which "the spiritual and moral strength of a people"[61] depended on; yet, the real decisive factor was society's pressure on the state, "the sense of law" that modern society deems to be the essence of civilization and imposes on both individuals and the sovereign.

The conceptual components of the state–law link are now clear. Jhering believed that "self-limitation" could reconcile the state's absolute sovereignty with a system of restraints limiting and directing its action. The protection of individuals' legal sphere from undue administrative intrusions was thus grounded. The legislative power instead, which was deemed to be the essence of sovereignty, remained free from restraints and controls.

Although a sovereign state bound by law could be envisaged, the connection between the state and the law was preserved only as long as "external" forces intervened to support the legal mechanism. According to Jhering, the certainty of law "is not grounded on the constitution, which can be interpreted as desired; neither is it possible to conceive of a constitution removing from the state the possibility to encroach upon law". What matters is "the real strength behind law, i.e. people for whom law is a condition of its own existence and for whom an offence against law is like an offence against itself".[62] Consequently, while state and law can coexist within a calm and self-confident world, a "state of necessity" could cause their pathological though inevitable divorce, since the respect of formal rules had to give way in this case to the absolute surplus of sovereign power for the sake of preserving order and the supreme "salus populi".[63]

By abandoning the rigorous legal formalism which had characterized the first stage of his thinking, Jhering entrusted the historical and social development with the task of regulating "from outside" the link between the state and the law. Unlike Jhering, Jellinek's starting point was the "state-centred paradigm" launched by Gerber and his aim was what might appear as "squaring the circle": he tried to preserve the dogma of the state's absolute sovereignty and make rights dependent on the individuals' belonging to the political community, but at the same time he conceived of such rights as true individual prerogatives rather than mere reflections of the state's normative system. The cornerstones of Jellinek's reasoning coincided, in some respects, with the theory of the state's self-limitation,[64] and, in other respects, with the demonstration that the state, albeit pursuing the general interest, often attained it by multiplying rights and thus establishing true legal relationships between the individual and the state. *Rechtsstaat* was therefore a sovereign state which, by limiting itself, appeared as a legal person, a holder of rights and obligations, and was bound to respect both objective law and the rights of the individuals which it entered into a relationship with.[65]

The rule of law thus appeared to be formally complete in that the state established legal relationships with the individuals who have been made holders of rights (in a somewhat paradoxically circular way[66]) by the state itself, i.e. by its sovereign decision to self-limit its power. The rule of law did also coincide with a number of legal relationships in which the state and the individuals, the administration and the subjects, were holders of rights and obligations that were legally established and open to judicial control. Jellinek's difficulty arose, as for every nineteenth-century jurist, when attention was shifted from administration to legislation; once again, the difficulty of limiting the legislative power was resolved or sidestepped by going "beyond" the formal shape of the legal system and by appealing to the maturity and civilization of a people capable of counteracting "the state's formally unassailable acts of will" by relying on slowly modifiable or even constant and untouchable principles.[67]

When synthetically examining the nineteenth-century German debate on the rule of law, it is possible to detect recurrent themes and problems underlying the many different approaches.

Both "formalists" and "organicists" denied the natural law foundation of rights and shared the idea of the individual's dependence on the political community and the dogma of the state's absolute sovereignty. The impossibility of opposing to it *aliunde*-founded elements was the ground of the central dilemma: how to combine an unlimited sovereign power with a legal order regulating it and making its intervention foreseeable. The central features of the theory that was gradually refined throughout the second half of the century and was thoroughly elaborated by Jellinek were the idea of the state's self-limitation (which made sovereign absolutism compatible with the existence of fetters on its power), the existence of legal relationships between the state and individuals, the distinction between the state (as a whole) and its several institutional components, so that this or that organ could be limited whilst the state "as such" could be deemed as the holder of an absolute power.[68]

Thanks to this theory, relationships between the state and individuals could be regulated and the administration could be submitted to judicial control, in order to protect the individual's legal domain; however, the difficulty inherent in imposing precise formal restraints on legislation (assumed as the emblematic embodiment of the state's sovereignty) still remained unresolved.

The nineteenth-century *Rechtsstaat* was realized as a "*sub lege* administration", leading to the setting up of an administrative jurisdiction, in order to compensate a seemingly opposing though in fact complementary phenomenon, namely the growing impact of administration on social dynamics. While, on the one hand, administration was more and more employed as a means for social integration and the settlement of conflicts, as a means for reforms capable of diminishing inequalities without challenging the distribution of power and wealth, on the other hand there was an increasing dread of threats to freedom and property and there was an attempt to devise measures subjecting the state's interventionism to checks and restraints.

The importance attached to the idea of an administration *sub lege* was therefore intelligible in the light of a number of factors: the concern for the state's increasing interventionism, the depoliticization undergone by the rule of law after the 1848 failure (when attention shifted from political rights to individuals' private interests) and the feeling that administration could be subjected to restraints without this amounting to an "offence to sovereignty". Such reasons, which placed administration in the spotlight, also tended to keep the rule of law on the threshold of legislation: legislation appeared (though not for long) as a force which was less aggressive towards freedom and property, these being more closely threatened by administration; moreover, legislation seemed to be the most direct outcome of sovereignty, which by definition could not meet restraints and resistances.

Yet, the theory of the legislating state's almightiness did not imply, even for German "state-centred" jurisprudence, indifference, or silence towards freedom, property, and individual rights. In this respect, nineteenth-century jurisprudence shared a basic conviction: according to Jellinek and Jhering, Gerber and Gierke, and Mohl and Constant, the essential tension between the state and law, the sovereign and norms, found its solution "beyond" itself, in the dynamics of historical forces: in public opinion, which Constant (and the entire liberal tradition) viewed as the "external" safety valve of a system centred on the respect of rules and legal forms; or in the people, whom German jurists deemed to be realized in the state and capable of imposing on it choices mirroring its degree of civilization. The conflict between "formalists" and "organicists" was certainly momentous within German jurisprudence but should not conceal their common heritage, which, on the one hand, included the maximum acknowledgement of the state's sovereignty and, on the other, regarded the people and its history as a "safety valve". According to nineteenth-century legal culture, the circumstance that legislation was not subject to formally cogent constraints was not decisive, not because the problem was deemed irrelevant or nonexistent, but because its solution was offered by history, which dictated the inescapable contents of civilization to the state. The common thread running through all these theories was an optimistic "philosophy" of social progress including the "state", "law", and "freedom and property" within a single network and viewing them as expressions of a "modern" civilization conceived of as the culmination of universal history.

6 *RECHTSSTAAT* AND RULE OF LAW: DICEY'S CONTRIBUTION

The theory of the *Rechtsstaat* advanced by German nineteenth-century legal doctrines led to a peculiar understanding of the power–law link: on the one hand, administrative action was scrutinized with the aim of imposing precise legal bonds and corresponding judicial checks on it; on the other hand, constraints on legislative action were hardly envisaged since the latter was taken to emblematically embody the state's absolute sovereignty.

In any event, the *Rechtsstaat* formula rotated around a specific legal conceptualization of the state which represented one of the most significant outputs of nineteenth-century German culture. We must now ask up to what extent it is possible to extend the idea of *Rechtsstaat* to contexts which, albeit sensitive to the power–law relationship, had not developed a legal theory of the state which was somewhat analogous to that expressed by German culture.

Although both Italy and France developed – partly furthering native traditions, partly assimilating the suggestions of the "German model" – a theory of the state allowing for the similar resurgence of dilemmas and suggestions endemic to the German *Rechtsstaat*, in contexts with radically different constitutional histories and cultures the power/law interplay did not entail the same dilemmas or suggest analogous solutions.

This was the case of Great Britain, where an original theory of sovereignty was fully elaborated by Austin in the nineteenth century without referring to the "continental" idea of state. The key figure was not the "state" seen as the global synthesis of powers and the embodiment of the nation's ethos; rather, it was a polycentric apparatus characterized, on the one hand, by a precocious division of sovereignty and, on the other hand, by a legal system which, throughout its alluvial development, was the main bulwark of "Englishmen's rights".[69]

It was within such a composite political and legal structure that the expression "rule of law" gained ground in Great Britain and soon became not less popular than the German *Rechtsstaat*. Inasmuch as the expression "rule of law" was used to denote a particular way of setting and resolving the power–law–individuals relationship, such a formula was semantically akin to the expression *Rechtsstaat* (*Stato di diritto, État de droit*) and can be used as a translation thereof (or vice versa). Nonetheless, the translation process ought to be taken seriously and not be naively limited to a mechanical tracing any given word to another one, e.g. the fact that the Greek *iatrós* and the English *doctor* have the same meaning depends on "our decision": among all the activities respectively ascribable to the *doctor* and the *iatrós*, we draw a line between those that are "culture-bound" and must be expunged from the "translating" process, and those that are referable to a functional "culture-invariant" core and make equivalence and translation possible.[70]

The circumstance that the "rule of law" is tantamount to (and translatable as) *Rechtsstaat* (*Stato di diritto*, *État de droit*) does not mean that the former can be exactly equivalent to any of the latter; rather, it simply means that different "culture-bound" features nonetheless allow for the (obviously "chosen" and not "objectively indisputable") determination of a shared "culture-invariant" function. We shall not underline the macroscopic differences among the different contexts involved (English and German, and in general European–continental). It is interesting, instead, in order to compare different "national cultures", to focus on a major English work, characterized by a purportedly systematic and "scientific" method: Albert Venn Dicey's[71] *An Introduction to the Study of the Law of the Constitution*, published in 1885 and destined to become very popular for many years to come.[72]

It is not by chance that, precisely at a time when German public law doctrines developed a thorough "theory of the state", Dicey, by purporting to write an authentically legal work – breaking off with the "antiquarianism" of tradition, which simply and "externally" examined constitutional history, and thus aiming at demonstrating the legitimacy and usefulness of theory[73] – drafted an "introduction to the constitution": the reference to the constitution was the "culture-bound" trait, just like the idea of the people-state was for German public law theories; and the point is whether Dicey's "rule of law" and German (and continental) *Rechtsstaat* shared "invariant" traits, both in the conceptualization of and the solution provided to the relationship between power and law (and rights), and whether such traits allow for the two formulae to be (relatively) equivalent.

Dicey did not elaborate an exhaustive "theory of the state", but his "theory of the constitution" was largely a theory of sovereignty: sovereignty was the object of the entire first section of his work, and the main issues he dealt with hinged upon such a concept. Sovereignty was not abstractly examined and was not viewed as the essence of the "state as such", but was referred to the political institutions holding such power:

the Queen, the "House of Lords", the "House of Commons", in other words parliament ("Queen in parliament"). However, rather than describing constitutional institutions and mechanisms, Dicey aimed at accurately demonstrating the absolute nature of sovereign power: since the holder of sovereignty was parliament, sovereignty's absolutism coincided with the non-coercible, irresistible power of parliament's assembly. Being a law-making assembly, parliament was entitled to enact and abrogate all laws, which individuals and bodies were required to abide by.

According to Dicey, De Lolme's popular expression (whereby the English parliament can do everything but make a woman a man, and a man a woman) illustrated a particular tradition which, from Coke to Blackstone, has always celebrated parliament's omnipotence.[74] The "judge-made law" character of the English legal system did not affect the above assumption, not only because Austin himself had already provided an "imperativistic" foundation of the common law, but also because no judge has ever thought of himself as entitled not to apply an act of parliament; acts of parliament, on the contrary, could confidently overrule any consolidated judge-made law.[75]

Parliament's supremacy was thus the "very keystone of the law of the constitution";[76] no legal constraints on parliament's omnipotence could be conceived. The "absolute" sovereignty, that German "state-centred" theory attributed to the state "as such", was transferred by Dicey to parliament, but kept its original feature and was conceived of as a power free from all restraints. However, as promptly specified by Dicey, parliament's omnipotence had to be viewed in its specifically legal meaning: if it had been understood as "effective" omnipotence, it would have been, quite simply, absurd. The sovereign's power (parliament's power) was effectively and politically restrained by internal and external limits: the electoral mechanism itself allowed citizens to exert their influence upon parliament and, whenever such influence was insufficient, disobedience and resistance were always feasible; after all, parliament itself was the expression and interpreter of a specific political and social equilibrium and, precisely for this reason, parliament's will was usually not very different from what it could actually achieve.

It follows that a line must be drawn between two "levels of reality", the legal and the political: when referring to the legal level, sovereign omnipotence stood for the impossibility of imposing legal constraints to the sovereign's law. Once again, given the contextual diversity, Dicey's doctrine, even if not identical, was nonetheless equivalent to the reasoning of many German jurists, who celebrated the state's omnipotence, but postulated at the same time a (historically spontaneous) harmony between the state's will and the people's civilization.

The first assumption was therefore conceived of in a manner which we have already encountered and was centred around the sovereign's omnipotence and the ensuing impossibility of imposing legal limits on the sovereign's actions. Differences arose when the problem of the relationship between sovereignty and law (as a system of limits) was dealt with: while German jurists advanced the state's self-limitation theory as a feasible solution, together with the distinction between the state and its organs and the foundation of an administrative judicial system, Dicey took a different stand, whose fundamental traits were grounded on the role of the constitution and on the nature of the common law.

As for the theory of the constitution, Dicey heavily relied (throughout the several editions of his work) on a famous contribution by James Bryce who, first in his *The American Commonwealth* of 1888 and later in a long essay,[77] drew a distinction between rigid and flexible constitutions, destined to become very popular. Assuming that the constitution, as such, is the bone structure of a political society organized through and according to law, a line must be drawn between two different kinds of constitution: a constitution that develops over time, grows on itself as a result of differently originated inputs, and can be defined as *flexible* because it is open to continuous adjustments and changes introduced without following specific procedures; and a *rigid* constitution which, being enacted uniquely by a given body, determines the state's shape "once and for all" and does not favour changes thereto, by claiming to be unchangeable or by establishing cogent provisions for its own alteration.

Both Bryce and Dicey believed that, while past constitutions were flexible, modern ones were usually rigid, the main exception being the English constitution. By deeming the English constitution to be flexible, Dicey's theory was strengthened: parliament's absolute sovereignty was proven, *inter alia*, by the circumstance that parliament could introduce the most upsetting constitutional changes by simply enacting an ordinary act; there was no constitutionality review: whereas in the United States the presence of a rigid constitution and the distinction between ordinary and constitutional law made the judge a guarantor of the constitution and a controller of the legislator, in Great Britain judicial courts must refrain from interfering with the "machinery of government".[78]

Curbs on parliament's absolute sovereignty were thus not to be found in the constitution: the relationship between law and power heavily tilted in the latter's favour. According to Dicey, the tension between power and law arose when parliament's sovereignty and the "law of the land" were jointly taken into account; and it was precisely in the combination of such two principles "which pervade the whole of the English constitution"[79] that Dicey found the solution to the power–law link, together with the authentic value of the "rule of law".

Dicey detected three key features of the "rule of law". Firstly, the "rule of law" entailed respect for the *nullum crimen sine lege* principle: as acknowledged by Dicey himself, the principle, ever since Enlightenment reformism, had been endorsed by the continental political systems, though Dicey was sceptical of Europe's integral application of the principle.[80]

Secondly, the "rule of law" stood for the individuals' equal subjection to law; as for the above principle, this idea was (theoretically) endorsed also by the entire nineteenth-century legal world, though Dicey believed it was sharply disproved by the presence (in France and in general throughout the continent) of a specific administrative judicial system.[81] Dicey launched a severe attack on the "droit administratif", which needs to be "historicized" by briefly mentioning two aspects: first of all, it should be recalled that Dicey's misunderstanding of the French *droit administratif* "was legendary"[82] and that Dicey himself later softened his criticism throughout the *Introduction*'s various editions; secondly, it ought to be recalled that Dicey was politically and ideologically biased[83] against administrative intervention which, however, was actually developing also in Great Britain, being it prompted (as in Europe) by the need to "govern" society and by the aim of integrating the *classes dangereuses*; under this perspective, Dicey's defence of the "rule of law" as an area free from administrative intrusions was analogous to the continental attempt to strengthen administrative courts to tackle the increasing pressures exerted by the "interventionist state".

Thirdly – and most decisively – Dicey believed that the "rule of law" stood for a peculiar process of founding and attaining freedoms and rights, which was connected with Great Britain's specific kind of constitution and legal system. As illustrated by Bryce, the English constitution was flexible and developed as a result of continuous successive adjustments: its general principles (such as the rights of freedom) "are the result of judicial decisions". Individuals' legal sphere was not abstractly determined once and for all; rather, it has developed "from below", adapting itself to many and various situations, through the intervention of judges, who, being called upon to resolve specific problems, over time have determined its contours.

Hence, Dicey's "rule of law" was an inseparable feature of "judge-made law" and was thus a peculiarly English way of casting and resolving the problem of the relationship between power and law, which was indeed different from the continent (especially the "French model"), this relying on the provisions of a ("rigid") constitution. Dicey conceded that the difference between Great Britain and the continent might appear to be exclusively extrinsic and, as such, irrelevant: if in England or, for example, in Belgium, freedom was guaranteed and arbitrariness was avoided, it did not matter whether this happened as a result of a written constitution imposing such a *status quo* in general terms or as a result of the "law of the land" ensuring such a condition on a case-by-case basis. However, as Dicey sharply underlined, there was a substantial difference as to the decisive problem of guarantees. Dicey argued that solemn constitutional declarations were weak enunciations whose infringement was always feasible, whereas the strength of the English flexible constitution was due to the circumstance that the protection of individuals' legal sphere was not simply theorized but implemented. English legal culture could not conceive of an abstract declaration of rights that neglected their procedural "remedy"; hence, freedoms were developed through the judicial interventions protecting them "in action".[84]

It is at this stage that Dicey was compelled to provide a solution to the most delicate problem: the relationship between power and law, sovereignty and rules and, in his case, between parliamentary sovereignty and the "law of the land", which determined and protected individuals' legal sphere. Just like the continental *Rechtsstaat*, the English rule of law was placed within a specific field of tension marked by the relationship between the sovereign and the law (and the individual's rights). How did Dicey settle the tension without cancelling it?

Dicey's solution lied essentially in the following two considerations. Firstly, parliamentary sovereignty and judge-made law were complementary rather than antagonistic elements within the system's overall logics: parliament could indeed enact law without meeting any opposition, but the law, once enacted, was entirely left to the judge's interpretation, and the judge understood it in the light of his particular sensitivity and of the "general spirit of the common law".[85] Parliament's will was, indeed, formally absolute; yet, when placed within the system's overall functioning, it was also substantially conditioned by judicial interpretation and application.

Secondly, parliament was entitled to change the constitution as it thought proper, it could affect freedoms and suspend the *Habeas Corpus* Act; however, "the suspension of the constitution", being "based on the rule of law", i.e. depending on the "law of the land" which was a judge-made law, "would mean with us nothing less than a revolution".[86]

Even though it would have been a "revolution", it would have nonetheless been a "legal" revolution, since parliament's sovereignty was ultimately absolute and uncontrollable: under such a perspective, the tension within which the "rule of law" theorized by Dicey was placed seemed to dissolve "upwardly", i.e. it was resolved by confirming the role of sovereignty which, in order to exist, could not find insuperable legal hurdles on its way. Under such a perspective, Dicey's "rule of law" and the German formula *Rechtsstaat* seem analogous, not only because they both focused on the tension between power and law, but also because they shared the same dilemma, i.e. the difficult combination between the sovereign's absolute power and a system of restraints functionally linked with the protection of individuals' legal sphere.

However, such an "invariant" coexisted with differences pertaining to the strategies adopted to overcome the usual *impasse*. Whereas Jellinek believed that the dilemma must be solved within the legal realm of the state (relying on the state's self-limitation, the state-person theory, and the legal relationship) and that the safety valve was people, civilization, and history, in other words elements "external" to the legal world (albeit affecting its effective configuration), Dicey believed that parliamentary sovereignty was bound to confront a specific legal structure (which freedom and property primarily depended on), i.e. the "law of the land" or judge-made law, endowed with a genesis and substance of its own: the sovereign could change it, but had nonetheless to confront a legal system which was not (at least directly) referable to his will.

Rather, Gierke's theory could be evoked by Dicey's "rule of law", inasmuch as individual rights, according to the German jurist, were framed within the community and its historical development (even if they can be cancelled ad libitum by the state's ultimate power[87]).

In any event, even if their argumentative strategy differed, both Dicey's "rule of law" and the German formula *Rechtsstaat* shared two basic assumptions: on the one hand, they aimed at protecting individuals' legal sphere; on the other hand, they believed that the system's necessary safety valve must be found in history and society.

Besides the analogies between British and German jurists, Dicey's *Introduction* focused on two specific aspects that were not so clear in continental jurisprudence: firstly, the necessary link between "law" and its "interpretation" and the shortcomings of a theory which concentrated on the creation and not on the effective application of the law; secondly, and consequently, the importance of guarantees and controls and the discovery of the Achilles' heel of continental (and especially French) constitutionalism, which lacked a suitable mechanism for the "enforcement" of constitutional provisions, whereas the United States, despite their distance from the British model's "flexibility", had wisely entrusted judges with the task of safeguarding their constitution.

7 THE RULE OF LAW AND THE CONSTITUTION: KELSEN'S CONTRIBUTION

Being backed on the one hand by the development of the British "rule of law" and on the other by their familiarity with the American constitutional model, in different ways Dicey and Bryce underlined the unresolved problem of continental theories: law's persistent weakness before power's absolutism. While Dicey's attack on the *droit administratif* could be easily rejected (or sent back to the sender, who overlooked an analogous process in his own country), it was more difficult to ignore Dicey's considerations on constitutional law, inasmuch as the problem of legal restraints binding the state–legislator rather than the state–administrator had been left unsolved by continental jurisprudence.

In fact, not even Dicey had completely eradicated the problem, since his idea of sovereignty was analogous to that adopted by continental theories. Yet, Dicey was able to appeal to a constitution which, albeit flexible and modifiable ad libitum by parliament, nonetheless belonged to a legal system which, all in all, offered freedom and property strong (though not insuperable) protection against possible (though historically and politically unlikely) *coups de main* carried out by the sovereign.

Not surprisingly, several continental jurists, both in German-speaking countries and in France, were becoming aware that a mere "administrativistic" application of the "rule of law" theory could not finally solve the problem of the "power–law" link.

In the French legal culture,[88] a rigorous contribution (perhaps the closest to the German tradition of *Rechtsstaat* and unsatisfied with the exclusively "administrativistic" idea of the rule of law) came from the work of an Alsatian jurist, Raymond Carré de Malberg.[89]

Just like Jellinek (or Vittorio Emanuele Orlando), Carré de Malberg believed that the state was a legal being, the personification of a nation: the state presupposed the nation but the nation, far from being provided with an autonomous, albeit embryonic, apparatus, existed only in that it was personified by the state; the state as a legal person was the pivotal figure of public law theory[90] and allowed for the creation (and the very conceivability) of a unitary order.[91]

The state's essence was the sovereign absolute power[92] and such a belief urgently raised the recurrent problem: how could power be compatible with law? How could the sovereign's irresistible force be combined with a system of constraints imposed thereon? The problem was particularly serious given the French parliament's dominant position within the country's constitutional system: as Carré de Malberg bluntly said, "nowadays the French parliament is almighty, just as the English parliament".[93] Parliament was sovereign both in England and France and the problem of the limits of power involved not only administration, but also the activities of legislators.

Carré de Malberg adopted an already proven remedy: he endorsed the self-limitation theory and insisted on the "guaranteeing" importance of the "formal" link between the state and law, i.e. on the fact that the state, being the nation's legal organization, had no choice but to act through law; he consequently believed that the state, as a legal entity, was submitted to its own norms and could, as any other subject, be a holder of obligations as well as rights.

The most insidious objection (advanced also by Duguit)[94] and the theory's main weakness were the merely *octroyée* nature of legal boundaries: given that the state's limitation depended upon the sovereign's self-control (to use Jhering's expression), which could be modified or even cancelled ad libitum, the protection of the individual sphere appeared uncertain, to say the least. Being aware of this weakness, Carré de Malberg deeply investigated the idea of national sovereignty. By originally examining French constitutional history, starting with the Revolution's founding act, Carré de Malberg opposed (what he deemed to be) Rousseau's idea of sovereignty, i.e. "democratic" sovereignty, identified with the totality of individuals constituting the nation,[95] to the sovereignty that was cultivated and realized by the 1789 Revolution; by attributing sovereignty to the nation, the revolution meant to detach it from the monarch and from each single component of the political system so as to attribute it to the state "as such", which personified the nation.

Hence, if "national sovereignty" implied that no sole body, including parliament, could be the holder of sovereignty (this belonging to the state-nation), then parliament's power was scaled down. A "hyperdemocratic" approach, according to which political representation could be conceived of as a mere means of transmission of the electors' wills, was rejected and the old though always troubling threat of a "despotic majority" was kept under control. On such groundings, Carré de Malberg attempted to express the real meaning and develop the full potential of the rule of law.

Although the rule of law had led jurists to urge the development of a *sub lege* administration, Carré de Malberg believed that it was also important to draw a line between *État de droit* and *État légal*. The latter aims at rigidly and generally subduing administration to law, even where no individual rights are involved, and takes the shape of a "special form of government", whereas the distinctive feature of the *État de droit* is its instrumental and functional character: it purports to impose legal constraints on administration in order to strengthen the individual's legal sphere.[96] An *État légal*, therefore, did not perfectly tally with an *État de droit*. On the one hand, *État légal* imposed restraints upon administrative action that were more rigid and generalized than the *État de droit* form of state, which could intervene only to protect individual interests; however, on the other hand, while the *État légal*'s effectiveness was exhausted within the relationship between the administration and the law, the *État de droit* was not so circumscribed: given that its immanent aim and *raison d'être* were the protection of individuals from the abuses of power, the *État de droit*, by following its "natural course", must affect both administration and legislation; its "natural" achievement was the enactment of a "constitution" which could guarantee specific "individual rights to citizens" which no law could impinge on. According to Carré de Malberg, "the rule of law is a system of limitations, not only affecting administrative authorities, but also the Legislative Body". In order to attain a real and complete *État de droit*, the French parliament's "good will" was not enough; rather, citizens' freedoms needed judicial protection against both administrative and legislative actions.[97]

In his *Théorie générale*, Carré de Malberg argued that the *État de droit* ought to control also the *sancta sanctorum* of sovereignty, which tradition identified with legislative power; for such a purpose, not only did he suggest to draw a clear line between the constitution and the law – a distinction which Bryce had already regarded as typical of "rigid" constitutions – but also advocated some form of control guaranteeing the constitution's actual supremacy (and thus avoiding the risk, which Dicey deemed to be very high in "continental" systems, of disregarding high-sounding principles).

Carré de Malberg was not alone in dealing with similar issues and remedies. In the years immediately preceding the First World War (when Carré de Malberg was writing his *Théorie générale*[98]) and in the following decade, Hans Kelsen began to outline his original theory and apply it to the construction and technical instrumentation of the rule of law.[99]

The radical break introduced by Kelsen in the *Rechtsstaat* tradition was grounded on a specific epistemological foundation (which we shall only briefly deal with). Ever since his significant 1911 work (*Hauptprobleme der Staatsrechtslehre*), Kelsen had believed that the distinction between

Sein and *Sollen*,[100] and thus between sciences explicating phenomena on a causal basis and forms of knowledge concerned with the analysis of norms, could guide us in critically reviewing traditional public law theories.[101] The idea of the state as a "real" entity, which was the source of the recurring dilemmas of nineteenth-century jurisprudence, resulted from overlooking of the *Sein/Sollen* distinction.

According to Kelsen, the state was not a "real" entity but a theoretical object created by jurists: to conceive of the state "cannot but mean to conceive of the state as law".[102] The state and the law are thus reciprocally identified: to think of the state as a set of norms – an idea which would be most rigorously formulated in Kelsen's great works of the 1920s (in *Allgemeine Staatslehre* and in *Das Problem der Souveränität und die Theorie des Völkerrechts*) though it had been already substantially outlined in *Hauptprobleme* – allowed Kelsen to get rid of the idea (propounded by Jellinek and tradition in general) of the state's "duplicity" and to dismantle the latter's most consolidated features: the idea of the state as a "really" exceeding and irresistible power, as a subject with a will, with given purposes using all its forces to achieve them.

According to Kelsen, the state is not a real entity, it is a set of norms:[103] to think of the state as "real" perpetuates an archaic and "religious" approach, offering a "substantialistic" and anthropomorphic image of the state which modern epistemology (from Vaihinger to Cassirer,[104] from Mach to Avenarius[105]) has rejected. On the contrary, when the state is deemed to coincide with the legal system and to be its simple "personification", there follows the demise of the aporia that the rule of law has unsuccessfully tried to overcome by combining (through the "self-limitation" theory) the state's "absolute" power with law's binding (and guaranteeing) role. Indeed, the aporia arose from the archaic and mythical image of the state as an exceeding and "really" existing power; it was an aporia capable of outliving the self-limitation *escamotage*, which also Kelsen saw as inefficacious, since it relied on the Leviathan's (ultimate) decision. On the contrary, if the state coincides with the legal system, the key element of the aporia loses ground: the state is not power, it is law, it is a system of norms (and the "personification" of its unity).

Since state and law coincide, it follows that physical and legal subjects, as well as the state's organs, are all subject to obligations imposed thereon by the legal system: "the state's legal obligation is not different from that of other legal subjects"[106] and both the state and any single individual represent "the personification of legal norms", the only difference being that the state personifies the entire legal system, whereas individuals are personifications of partial legal systems.[107]

The famous aporia ceases because its ground – the essential tension between the sovereign, the law and the individual's rights – collapses once the heterogeneity of such elements is dissolved in the unity of the legal system, which is the only legitimate research field of the jurist. The tension between the state's irresistible power and the individual's self-defence ceases to exist: the state coincides with a legal system and individuals are defined with respect to an objective system of norms; the obligation is precisely "the subjectivization of the legal proposition", i.e. the applicability of norms to "a specific individual".[108] Being "internal" components of the legal order, individuals are not holders of "rights" which the legal system has to deal with: human beings are "persons" in that the legal system "establishes their rights and obligations" and lose such a quality once the state decides to "take it from them".[109] To assume the existence of "natural" restraints on the legal system would be tantamount to recalling that natural law theory which, according to Kelsen, is definitely no longer tenable.

By encompassing the traditional *dramatis personae* of the *Rechtsstaat* within the homogeneous dimension of the legal system and by amputating "power" and "subjectivity" as "really" existing elements, Kelsen thus defined his approach to the rule of law. If absolutism is the renounce to a legal theory of the state, the rule of law coincides with the possibility of submitting all the state's activities to the law: the *Rechtsstaat* is "determined in all its activities by the legal system, which is legally intelligible in all its key components".[110]

The rule of law thus stands, first of all, for law's centrality, and for the ensuing opposition to the trend – which was very strong in public law theory of the time – for claiming a wider role for administration than that of mere "executor" of legal norms.[111] Ever since his *Hauptprobleme*, Kelsen had deemed administrative "discretionary power" not to stand for free deviation from norms but rather for a process which, shifting from abstraction to concreteness, determining the content of norms, presupposes them and becomes unintelligible without them.[112] Being an executive activity ("discretional" in that it implements a rule), administration could not be an autonomous source of obligations and rights; on the contrary, it presupposed the legal system, exclusively based on the "legislative process": the system's unity would have been jeopardized if, along with legislation, a "second source of the state's will, autonomous and independent of the first" would have been conceived of.[113]

While in his earlier thinking Kelsen viewed the rule of law as the emblem of both law's centrality and the opposition to the "administrative state" – an opposition combining theoretical suggestions with a strong attack against the *monarchisches Prinzip* in the name of parliament's relevance[114] – he later associated his rule of law theory with his "dynamic" analysis of the normative system,[115] which he elaborated under the influence of Alfred Verdross and Adolf Merkl.[116]

In this perspective, the unity of the legal system did no longer coincide with a set of general norms, but was located within the "dynamic" relationship between "general norms" and "individual norms", being both components of a unitary law-making process.[117] Law-making and law-enforcing are not simply opposed: the judgement depends on the law, "from which it is legally determined"; but the judgement creates law, is an act of law-making, inasmuch as it is referred to those legal acts, e.g. executive acts, which are to be taken *on the basis* of it".[118]

It follows that to conceive of the legal system in a "dynamic" manner, to fully understand its legal characteristics, and thus to understand the rule of law in all its implications, prevents us from focusing on legislation "as such". Legislation is merely a component of the "multi-step" structure outlined by Kelsen; when you look at "the bottom" of the system, you find "individual" norms "applying" legislation, when you look at "the top" of the system, you realize legislation is not the system's apex, rather it is itself the application of a higher norm, i.e. the constitution. And it is precisely the constitution which, albeit briefly mentioned in the *Hauptprobleme*, but not yet dissected in all its potential,[119] became in the 1920s an essential topic of Kelsen's theory.

This dynamic, "stepped" vision of the legal system[120] allowed Kelsen to introduce relevant changes both in constitutional theory (and legislation[121]) and in the foundation of the rule of law. If legislation lost its "absolute" position within the system and became an intermediate step in the law-making and law-applying processes, if it was reinterpreted as the enforcement of a higher norm, then legislative acts were open to control: the "regularity" of any "enforcement" procedure, as well as its "conformity" to the "higher level of the legal system"[122] could then be rightly ascertained. Consequently, according to Kelsen, the implementation of the rule of law lead to the setting up of a judicial body committed to controlling laws" constitutionality. In fact, given the "system's hierarchical structure", "the postulate of statutes' constitutionality was theoretically and technically identical to the postulate of the judgements' and administration's legitimacy" and consequently warranted its assessment by an appropriate institution.[123]

Being a superior norm within a hierarchically structured system, the constitution theoretically and technically allows for constitutional control; the latter, in turn, makes constitutional provisions compulsory.[124] The constitution is the safety valve of the rule of law, whereas statutes represent the application of constitutional provisions.

On these premises, the nineteenth-century traditional rule of law was radically revised and gave way to a new figure – the constitutional *Rechtsstaat* – which, while having some of the former's characteristics, transformed and replaced it.

The dilemma between "power" and "law" (and "rights"), which permeates the lengthy development of the rule of law, was removed (more than solved) by Kelsen using a Gordian technique: demolishing a tradition which had become entangled in the famous aporia by virtue of the "myth" of the "really" active state (we shall not question in this essay whether and how the exorcized "dilemma" troubled Kelsen's reasoning when dealing with the original constitution and the fundamental norm).

Having founded the rule of law on the hierarchical relationship between the constitution and legislation, the link with any prior definition of individual rights (endemic to the former development of the "rule of law") has been severed and the rule of law has acquired a purely formal dimension. It is true that, according to Kelsen, the constitutional *Rechtsstaat* (where the constitution can be modified only by a "qualified majority") is a useful means to protect minorities and to favour the development of democracy,[125] but it is also true that the rule of law fosters democracy by means of its legal and formal structure and not because it is intrinsically connected with pre-existing ("natural") rights finding therein an effective protection against power.

Through the *Stufenbautheorie* and constitutional primacy, the privileged relationship between sovereignty and parliament was interrupted: statute law was no longer the quintessence of sovereignty and both legislative and administrative powers could be controlled by a judicial body. According to Kelsen, the limit to legislative power that traditional doctrine had detected in history, politics, and society, could be legally grounded on the same reasoning justifying the subjection of all the state's organs to control.

Through the constitutional review of legislation, Dicey's objection to continental constitutionalism (redundant in its principles and defenceless in terms of guarantees) loses its sharpness. Guarantees were now provided by control mechanisms that the legal system itself, without appealing to external "safety valves", was able to devise. While Dicey's reasoning endorsed the common nineteenth-century conception of sovereignty and resolved the problem of "guarantees" by resorting to the British judge-made law, Kelsen broke off with traditional German doctrines: he subjected statute law to the constitution and resolved the problem of "guarantees" by introducing control mechanisms within a rigorously unitary legal order.

Under Kelsen's perspective, the preservation of the constitutional *Rechtsstaat* could not depend on formal mechanisms: the protection of the constitution was the task of a judicial body which guaranteed statutes' conformity to the (formal and substantial) restraints established by the constitution itself; the constitution's stability was protected by the requirement of a qualified majority for any modification of it. Beyond the formal sphere, which Kelsen regarded as the only legally relevant ambit, there was the area of social interaction. The future of democracy and of the constitutional *Rechtsstaat* – which purported to be a technically refined and efficient instrument of democracy – depended on the complex interplay of competing interests and motivations and on the rationality and tolerance with which individuals were endowed.

8 THE RULE OF LAW BETWEEN "OBJECTIVE LEGAL INSTITUTES" AND THE "WELFARE STATE"

Kelsen paved the way for a new approach to the rule of law: one that eradicated nineteenth-century dilemmas; demolished the meta-legal vision of power and individuals; focused on the legal system; and established its differentiated, hierarchical normative levels. This enabled the new approach to overcome the dogma of the untouchable majesty of statute law, hallowed the constitution's pivotal role, introduced restraints on legislators' activity and made judicial review feasible.

Kelsen's brilliant contribution was grounded on a sharp distinction between *Sein* and *Sollen* (is and ought) and operated within the boundaries of the system's "formal" dimension: "content-based" constraints binding the system fell outside the scope of the legal discourse, whereas democracy (which Kelsen constantly took into account) was a means for social coexistence which, excluding absolute political beliefs, found its most suitable instrument in the "formal" mechanisms of the rule of law.

Not surprisingly, therefore the widespread anti-formalist (and anti-Kelsen) reaction of the 1920s focused on the problems inherent in a merely "formal" understanding of the rule of law. In fact, it was true that the constitution made the legislator's activities open to control; however, the constitution had no protection other than in the purely numerical and extrinsic "qualified majority" required for its modification. The problem of limits, which the *Stufenbautheorie* had resolved for the legislative power, i.e. at the system's "intermediate" level, affected the system's summit, the level of the constituent power.

The thesis that a merely formal restraint on power's arbitrariness was insufficient permeated the German debate in the Weimar age, and was neatly pointed out by Erich Kaufmann.[126]

After his early neo-Kantian years, Kaufmann decidedly broke away from Rudolf Stammler and Kelsen[127] arguing the deficiencies of a merely "formal" understanding of law: that neo-Kantian "forms and norms" were empty and that there was no path towards their ontological foundation; Kaufmann believed it essential to move away from an "abstract system of forms" towards a "material order of contents" and to relinquish "formal apriorism" which "makes us go astray in the sea of effective reality".[128] His approach was in striking contrast with Kelsen's method and his aim was to understand the real relationships (*Dingbegriffe*) underpinning conceptual relations (*Relationsbegriffe*).[129] According to Kaufmann, it was necessary to go beyond the system's formal and procedural levels to detect its "objective" traits directing both judges' and legislators' choices: constraints on public power ought not to be "merely formal", rather they need to be grounded on a "material order" which can determine the latter's conditions "in a content-based manner".[130]

The concept of "institute"[131] was outlined to overcome a purely normative analysis: the institute was something more than a set of norms; it was enlivened by its own principles, it was the expression of an objective order, of a "logic of things" which judges, ordinary legislators, and the constituent assembly were bound to respect. Under a "formalistic" approach, limits and cross-checks were doomed to give way to the inevitable arbitrariness of a given "will" (if not the ordinary legislator's, at least the constituent super-legislator's). However, if the narrow limits of normativism were overcome, there arose principles, values, and forms of collective life ("institutes") that offered individuals the ultimate and indefeasible "guarantee" against the despotism of power, which formalism was unable to offer.

The "institute" as a "substantial" limit to power's arbitrariness was not the creation of Kaufmann's alone; it was the final outcome of German historicist and organicistic tradition, and also connected (as Kaufmann himself specified) with that idea of *institution* which Maurice Hauriou had innovatively outlined in the late nineteenth century.

According to Hauriou, the legal order must be set against a background of social interaction where the most miscellaneous groups and associations developed. The word "institution" thus stands for any organized social group: a group both demanding and protective towards its members, characterized by a given internal distribution of power and capable of lasting over time. It is within the institution's social and legal microcosm that the rules determining individual members' duties and prerogatives are established.[132]

The institution, rather than the state, is the "original" legal phenomenon: the state presupposes a rich and diverse network of institutions that affects its historical development and is still alive at the height of its splendour.[133] Hauriou's reasoning is "dualistic" and is explicitly in contrast with Léon Duguit's "sociologistic" monism as well as with the "formalistic" monism of Carré de Malberg or Kelsen. The legal order is grounded on the duality between "state" and "nation"; the nation does not exist simply because it is embodied in the state (as propounded by Carré de Malberg), but it is itself a historical reality, visible and operating, "an organized social body",[134] "a set of established situations ..., capable of solidarizing in order to counterpoise the government and constitute a coalition ...",[135] endowed with an autonomous and legal substance of its own.

According to Hauriou, such coordinates defined the rule of law: rather than being grounded on the self-limitation idea, which was internal to the dogma of the state's omnipotence and an expression of a kind of "monism" unable to view anything beyond the state's ambit, the state ought to be founded on an "equilibrium theory", according to which order was the result of interaction between the state and the institutional framework, which the state could not but refer to.[136]

Hauriou did not underestimate the "internal", "endo-state" aspects of the rule of law; as a matter of fact, by relying on the plurality of bodies and powers, nineteenth-century jurisprudence was able to subject administration to law and to provide for the setting up of an administrative judicial system. Within such a perspective, however, it was indeed difficult to impose limits on legislation, even though Hauriou viewed the American model as an interesting example in this respect.[137] The point, however, was that a final and satisfying solution could not be reached without going beyond the state's monad and referring to the dynamics of "social institutions".

According to Hauriou, we must refer to the individuals, interests, groups, social hierarchies, and the gradual setting-up, within social relationships, of "established situations", i.e. institutions that the state's power can govern, coordinate, protect, but not arbitrarily create or cancel.[138] Ergo, freedom does not derive from the state's self-limitation:

Hauriou believed that law and rights were created by society's institutional framework which was both the matrix of the state and the necessary reference point for the latter's action.[139]

The "political constitution" drew its meaning and strength from its relationship with the "social constitution". Individual rights themselves ought to be seen neither as unilateral concessions by the state nor as attributes of an absolute and unrelated subjectivity but rather as protrusions of society: social and normative structures, forms of social relationships, "institutions" precisely. It was the whole set of such statutes, of such "objective legal institutions", that determined individuals' conditions, the *statute* of each French citizen.[140]

The combined interaction between the state's initiative and the spontaneous germination of institutions led to the dynamic equilibrium upon which the success of the rule of law hinged. Consequently, socially consolidated rights might not even be confirmed by a written constitution, as demonstrated (according to Hauriou) by Great Britain's eloquent example; and vice versa: the legal order was not "illiberal" simply because the written constitution lacked a precise enunciation of freedoms, as in the 1875 French constitution. The rule of law was founded not so much on formal apparatuses as on the equilibrium between social institutions and the state's intervention. Hauriou, however, did acknowledge the relevance of a written constitution: in France, the Declaration of Rights was important not for its "individualistic" content, product of its time,[141] but because it greatly reinforced the respect for "objective legal institutions", inasmuch as it was a set of rules superior to ordinary laws and hopefully strengthened by the review of statutes' constitutionality.[142]

If Hauriou and Kaufmann's contexts, outlooks, and concerns were different, though, they shared a two-faceted "antiformalistic" thesis: to demonstrate the flaws of a merely formal definition of the rule of law and to find a way for law to avoid the political arbitrariness that, while kept under control in its "ordinary" legislative manifestation, might show up in the "state of exception" of the constituent's activities. However, useful institutional mechanisms could be – established devices such as administrative courts and more recent ones such as review of statutes' constitutionality – seemed incapable of hindering, by themselves, the sovereign's "despotic drift": there arose again the risk of an "unfounded" legal order, of an order separated from the "logic of things", from a structure embedded in the reality of social relationships, this being the sole bulwark against power's recurrent "excesses".

Not surprisingly, this was a constant concern of jurists debating the constitution of Weimar. We must take into account the 1919 constituent's inconsistent (though innovative and bold) attempt to "constitutionalize" "social rights". This attempt (which was taken over and further by the post–Second World War constitution) had been differently valued by contemporary jurists. Some thought the constitution of Weimar ran aground on a barren compromise between incompatible principles; others thought it displayed a dangerous "interventionist" penchant, threatening traditional freedom and property by means of a long list of "social rights".

Therefore, while anti-formalism and the anti-Kelsen critique of the 1920s searched for restraints on the constituent power, it also, under a somewhat opposed perspective, disapproved of Kelsen's lack of attention towards the creative and dynamic role of power.

Hermann Heller's critique falls within the latter perspective. Heller criticized Kelsen for his attempt to create a theory of the state without a state,[143] leaving sovereignty, power, and decisions at the margins of his discourse. Heller (a supporter of social democracy) wished to keep at a distance from both Marxist orthodox economicism and from Kelsen's formalism, and strove to elaborate a theory accounting for both rules and the authority creating and making them effective, without erroneously making power and obedience legally "invisible".[144] Heller contrasted Carl Schmitt with Kelsen, to claim the existence of a supreme command capable "of definitively and effectively deciding on all matters relating to collective social action within the territory, possibly going also against positive law, and of imposing such decisions on all individuals".[145]

Heller argued that the holder of sovereignty in contemporary constitutional systems was undoubtedly the people, the centre from which radiated Rousseau's "General Will" which supported and legitimized the entire system.[146] Democracy, which was centred on the people's strong and determined will, must be conceptualized by relinquishing both Schmitt's celebration of the people's homogeneity and absolute unity and Kelsen's neutral proceduralism, which brought democracy within the formalism of the constitutional *Rechtsstaat*. Democracy meant sharing a number of fundamental values and principles without, at the same time, excluding different perspectives and strategies; there could be value pluralism and even conflict, as long as they were governed by the acceptance of common rules. Consequently, parliamentarism was neither the institutional projection of ethically "neutral" compromises (as propounded by Kelsen) nor the frail covering (as argued by Schmitt) of conflicts and agreements among "total" parties: its "historical and spiritual foundation" "is not the belief in public debates as such, rather in the existence of a common ground for debates".[147]

Heller argued that the possibility of overcoming the Weimar crisis whilst retaining and furthering its democratic potential depended on the individual's capacity to identify himself with a common set of values; it was within such a context that the rule of law acquired its historical and political impetus.

Heller also claimed that the historical parable of the rule of law was animated by the need to constrain power's arbitrariness and to make the legal consequences of individual actions foreseeable. By appealing to the primacy of law and to the separation of powers, it was possible to introduce check devices – above all, administrative courts – which would secure protection of the individual freedom and property. According to Heller, the most recent attempts to go even further and subject both administration and the legislative power or even the constituent power to a system of restraints were due to the fears of the bourgeoisie, which was aware that the real threat to freedom and property came from the parliamentary assembly, more and more concerned with the interests of the working classes (owing to the introduction of the universal suffrage and the advent of mass parties).

According to Heller, modern society was facing a dramatic dilemma. The first alternative was that the bourgeoisie, frightened by the possibility of a radical and interventionist democracy and unsatisfied with the feeble protection which the formal procedures of the *Rechtsstaat* could offer, threw itself into the arms of an "irrational neo-feudalism",[148] took refuge in the cult of the "strong man" and relinquished democracy and "nomocracy", parliamentarism and the rule of law. The second alternative – the only way, according to Heller, to save the rule of law – required a deep reassessment of the traditional nineteenth-century theory of the *Rechtsstaat* and the acknowledgement that the aim it pursued – the protection of the individual's legal sphere from power's arbitrary intrusions – was a necessary but not sufficient condition for order. To update the rule of law and to suit it to contemporary needs meant to free rights from their original individualistic bias[149] and thus turn the traditional rule of law, focused on the protection of property and freedom, into a social-democratic *Wohlfahrtsstaat*, a social rule of law.[150] It was only by opening up the rule of law to the new realities of "social democracy", by functionally connecting it with rights, that did not coincide with the "classical" rights of liberty and property, that the rule of law could raise from its ashes and become the means for a new legitimacy.

These (mostly German and French) theories of the 1920s virtually conclude the course of the rule of law that began with a "prehistory" in eighteenth-century reformism and was fully realized by mid–late nineteenth-century European theories of public law.

The key points of the "new direction" taken by the rule of law can be summarized as follows.

Firstly, by determining the hierarchical relationship between statute law and the constitution, Kelsen's *Stufenbautheorie* dismantled the dogma of parliament's "absolute" sovereignty (a dogma shared by the main nineteenth-century European legal traditions); moreover, it allowed legal restraints to be imposed on legislative activities and made them open to review, thus reducing the notable differences between the European continental tradition and American constitutionalism. Thanks to Kelsen's pioneering and long overlooked contribution, a radical discontinuity was created in the history of the rule of law, by introducing a new and determining "constitutional moment" and fully realizing the integral "legalization" of the system that had only been imperfectly achieved by nineteenth-century theories.

The theoretical device deployed by Kelsen was the denial of the state's "reality" and its identification with the normative legal system: rather than offering a solution internal to the well-known oxymoron of an absolutely sovereign and legally bound state, he eliminated one of its terms. It was at this stage, however, that there arose the second key point of the debate on the rule of law: Kelsen's uncompromising normativism became the Achilles' heel of the rule of law, inasmuch as this purported to "finally" limit the sovereign's power. The mere formal "hierarchy of norms" thus seemed an ineffective weapon against a form of power which, albeit kept under control in a given area of the system, demonstrated once again its "excessive" nature at a higher level, and could not actually be curbed until attention was shifted from form to content, from norms to social structures, to "institutes", "institutions", and grounding principles.

Thirdly, some aspects of the relationship between rule of law and individual rights changed. According to Heller and Neumann, the state characterized by the rule of law had a privileged relationship with a new class of rights (which began to be called "social"), which gave legal basis to individuals' claim to the state's "positive" intervention. In any case, a salient feature of the rule of law remained unaltered throughout its story, i.e. its functional role, the protection it offered to individuals, often through a precise range of rights. Yet, while the nineteenth-century traditional rule of law was essentially concerned with the protection of freedom and property, under Heller's perspective the *Rechtsstaat*, as *Wohlfahrtsstaat*, was functionally connected with a class of rights which widened and further complicated its original purpose.

Fourthly, in an unusually clear manner (again in Heller's lucid work), there appeared the likelihood – neither remote nor hypothetical, but rather actual and decisive – that the rule of law might be fully exhausted and defenceless against a crisis that allegedly required a radical overstepping of all normative and formalistic hurdles.

9 "RULE OF LAW", "STATE OF JUSTICE", AND "ETHICAL STATE"

The "dictatorship" feared by Heller was soon experienced in Germany, in a much more complex and powerful way than that envisaged by the jurist – whereas Italy precociously provided Heller with an example of an "anti-parliamentary" solution to the crisis of the liberal-democratic state. Undoubtedly, Fascism and National Socialism were not homogeneous and interchangeable phenomena: a historical and comparative analysis of the Italian and German regimes of the 1920s and 1930s would outline a complex picture of both the analogies and differences between them. In any event, an undeniable (albeit unrefined and basic) common trait to such experiences was their hostility towards liberal and democratic traditions. This does not mean, however, that the German and Italian regimes were similar in their summary execution (or ritual sacrifice) of the rule of law.

In Germany, in the years immediately following 1933, the rule of law was at the centre of a harsh debate among jurists;[151] however, it ought to be borne in mind that in all power conflicts that deeply affected the life of the Nazi regime the debate was marked by a tendency to overstate (or make up) ideological differentiations – which were in fact modest or inexistent – in order to use them as weapons again political antagonists.

A number of circumstances led early National Socialism to resort to the idea of the rule of law. On the one hand, examination of the famous formula allowed the protagonists of the debate to come to terms with liberal constitutionalism and to specify their own political beliefs; on the other hand, the same protagonists of the National Socialist "revolution" employed the expression *Rechtsstaat* to reassure groups and intellectuals attached to tradition during the particularly delicate transition towards the new political arrangement.

According to jurists with an old or recent National Socialist penchant, the rule of law was a useful target when attacking "liberalism", upon which it is deemed to be historically dependent: however, not all jurists believed that the downfall of liberalism caused the *Rechtsstaat* to disappear automatically. On the contrary, the possibility of using the notion (and "symbol") of the rule of law in the new German National Socialist world sparked off a multi-voiced debate, dominated by two jurists, Otto Koellreutter and Carl Schmitt, both striving for a pre-eminent position in the new regime.

Although Koellreutter had been a long-time supporter of National Socialism whereas Schmitt had a more complex and troubled past, they both interpreted and valued the "Gesetz zur Behebung der Not von Volk und Reich" of 24 March 1933,[152] which conferred upon the government the power to enact laws and introduce constitutional changes, in the same way. According to both, from this moment, even without a formal abrogation of the constitution of Weimar, the ancient regime was replaced by a new regime grounded on the *Führertum* and the *Volk*.

In 1933, Koellreutter attempted to demonstrate that National Socialism, unlike Fascism (this being founded above all on the state), appealed to the *Volk* (to the people conceived of as a blood and racial unity, a homogeneous reality with a given ideological and territorial identity) and to the *Führer*, who interpreted the *Volk*'s profound needs: hinging upon the link between *Führer* and *Volk*, the National Socialist regime was most pertinently called *Führerstaat*.[153] In the same year, Schmitt began his career as the "Reich's jurist"[154] by publishing *Staat, Bewegung, Volk*,[155] in which his previous liking or longing for the strong, independent, and detached-from-society state (the "total state" in qualitative terms[156]) were replaced by a "triad" view of the state as a mere component of a process grounded on "movement" and on the *Führer* as its interpreter and guarantor. According to both jurists, the new state was a *Führerstaat* which expressed the strength of people whose fundamental trait was the *Artgleichheit*, i.e. qualitative equality or homogeneity stemming from common blood and racial bonds.[157]

Although there seems to be no decisive difference between the two jurists on the new regime's grounding principles, the *casus belli* between them was precisely the rule of law. Koellreutter believed that the transition from what the jurist Gustav Adolf Walz called the *Zwischenverfassung*[158] (the unwarlike, powerless constitution of Weimar) to the new National Socialist order epitomized the transformation of the old liberal rule of law into a new (allegedly "national") *Rechtsstaat*. The new state broke with liberal individualism: while the traditional *Rechtsstaat* was functionally linked with individuals and their rights, the "national" *Rechtsstaat* found its main reference point in the people's life. The circumstance that the

National Socialist order was still a *Rechtsstaat* was proven by the fact that, in the new regime, according to Koellreutter, general laws and the judiciary's independence were still important.[159] Yet, such elements were functionally linked with the people rather than with the individual and could be suspended when necessary, i.e. for the same *salus populi* which legitimized the 1933 act.[160]

Although Schmitt did not deny that general laws and independent judges were still in action in the National Socialist order, he emphasized that all aspects of the new regime had to be interpreted by bearing in mind that equality was no longer merely formal and that laws (including pre-1933 laws that had not yet been abrogated had to be interpreted in the light of National Socialist principles.[161] From this perspective, the notion of the *Rechtsstaat* seemed to Schmitt a misleading characterization of the new regime.

According to Schmitt, the *Rechtsstaat* was a recent expression dating back to the nineteenth century. It arose as the expression of a neatly liberal anthropology, metaphysics, and politics. The "state characterized by the rule of law" was opposed, on the one hand, to the "Christian state", so as to value a purely secular and generally "human" legitimization of the political order, and, on the other hand, to Hegel's state, so as to underline the functional link between the sovereign and the individual. In opposition to such an ideological dimension of the rule of law, a new formulation of the concept, oriented towards its "neutralization and technicalization", took shape, starting with Stahl. Under such a perspective, the state must simply be "subject to law", no matter what aims it pursued, whereas law was a mere form which could be easily suited to any specific content.[162]

According to Schmitt, the colourless, ethically and teleologically indifferent image of the state provided by normativistic formalism was incompatible with the National Socialist belief in a "concrete" order, grounded on the *Blut und Boden* hendiadys.[163] The *Rechtsstaat*, construed according to its proper meaning, seemed to be inseparable from the relativism and agnosticism that had turned the state into a *Gesetzesstaat*, a "legislative state", a state formalistically identified with the barren "creation" and "application" of norms.[164] As a "legislative state", the *Rechtsstaat* was incompatible with the National Socialist state,[165] for which Gustav Adolf Walz had coined the popular formula *völkischer Führerstaat*; Walz himself acknowledged the existence of general laws and of judges enforcing them but insisted on their instrumental value – since the heart of the new order was the people, which was not a heterogeneous and "plural" mass but an *artgleicher deutscher Volk* naturally expressed by the *Führerstaat*.[166]

Given its congenitally "formalistic" nature, the *Rechtsstaat* could not properly be used to denote the new *Führerstaat*. Being historically and conceptually viewed as a "legislative state", the *Rechtsstaat* was in contrast with another kind of state which could have been more suited to the National Socialist regime, i.e. the "state of justice". The liberals' trap ought to be avoided: these would have us believe that the alternative between *Recht* and *Unrecht*, righteousness and wrongfulness, and justice and injustice rotated around the notion of *Rechtsstaat*. On the contrary, the rule of law, assumed to be synonymous with a "legislative state", dismissed "justice" by turning it into a problem of regularity or conformity to law. Suffice it to mention the example of criminal law: although "justice" would call for the punishment of the guilty (*nullum crimen sine poena*), formalism rested upon the empty maxim *nulla poena sine lege*. Therefore, while the "legislative state" was suited to liberals' empty scepticism, the "state of justice" was properly referable to the people's "concrete order".[167]

By relying on such an assumption, Schmitt legitimized the "Night of the Long Knives", when the SA's leaders had been eliminated: the *Führer* acted as a supreme judge before supreme danger. Whereas the rule of law's formalism had ruined the German nation – liberalism had used constitutional guarantees to protect people guilty of high treason – the *Führer*'s concrete justice could save the nation. Undoubtedly, the liberal legal tradition admitted the possibility of suspending guarantees in the name of an "exceptional" need. However, in the new regime, the "state of necessity", far from suspending law, revealed it: Hitler did not act like a Republican dictator "in a legally empty space", confronting an exceptional contingency that, once overcome, would allow the formalism of the rule of law to be restored. On the contrary, his actions were an authentic act of justice: his jurisdiction was rooted in law's primary source, i.e. the people. In cases of extreme need, the *Führer* was the supreme judge and the ultimate means for the realization of law.[168]

The debate on the rule of law would soon be abandoned, since it proved to be useless to a regime which was no longer interested in maintaining a connection, albeit weak, with the past. In any event, the meaning of the National Socialist debate on the rule of law was clear and notable. While the rule of law doctrine had, until then, expressed the possibility of using law (through its refined technical instrumentation) as a means to restrain and control power by making its actions foreseeable and "regular", in the new regime the concept of the *Rechtsstaat*, to be compatible with Nazi ideology, needed to overturn the relationship between power and law. It was power (the *Führer*'s "exceptional" power) that used law to guarantee the *salus populi*. This led to the importance of the "state of necessity". "Necessity" was indeed an old weapon: the Jacobins appealed to it legitimate the suspension of the constitution[169] and it had also permeated liberal legal theories.[170] Yet, under the new regime, it was the "rule" that was internal to the "exception" and not the contrary. Power reigned supreme within this scenario and power's decisions would prevail ("structurally" and not exceptionally) over rules: norms could still have a useful purpose as long as they had a "subordinate" function and merely regulated politically "secondary" relationships. Koellreutter's conservative solution involuntarily ended up by being similar to Fraenkel's idea of the "double state":[171] a state – typical of the National Socialist regime – where the "high" level of unbridled and uncontrollable politics was superimposed (in a useful synergy) on the "low" level of "normal" private and economic relationships.

The interplay between rules and exceptions, law and necessity, was not a prerogative of the German debate on the *Rechtsstaat*; rather, it had already taken place (in both similar and different ways) in Fascist Italy.[172] Schmitt himself emphasizes that, during the German and Italian crisis and the "rejection" of liberalism, attention had been focused on the rule of law; yet, according to Schmitt,[173] the quality of the debate had been higher in Italy, as demonstrated by a book by Sergio Panunzio, published in 1921 and dedicated precisely to the *Stato di diritto*.

Panunzio was the first to clearly express a theory that was to be developed with many variations in the 20-year period of Fascism. He did not wish to overthrow the rule of law, only to limit its relevance and to demonstrate its inadequacy in exhausting, by itself, the entire state phenomenon. According to Panunzio, the system of norms, constraints, and checks was indeed important, but the limits of its application needed to be crystal clear: the rule of law was essentially valid for the "contractual" coexistence of individuals and presumed an ordinary and peaceful everyday life. Yet, history was much more "demanding": exceptional states often arose, such as wars, and in this case the "ordinary logic" of the rule of law was no longer useful. "Each legal criterion is overcome" and the hero takes charge of the situation, the hero whose exceptional personality interprets the nation's "deep" needs "beyond any legal limit and criterion". The state characterized by the rule of law gave way to the "ethical state": "a historical entity and a self-autonomous person, which is the Spirit itself".[174]

The rule of law, the *Stato di diritto*, was not quashed but placed at a lower level in the hierarchy of fundamental legal concepts. It was contrasted with another different and determining kind of state, the "ethical state", the state that was action, dynamism, embodiment of the national community, and, as such, not referable to Kant's idea of a mere coexistence of (private) freedoms.[175] Under such a perspective, the link that the liberal doctrine of the rule of law had established with individuals, deemed to be the beneficiaries of the state's actions and of the system of restraints imposed thereon, changed. The individual (according to Giovanni Gentile, Felice Battaglia, and Arnaldo Volpicelli) was indeed the protagonist of the political process: yet, he was not the selfish individual, the "empirical" individual, or the abstract holder of unchangeable rights and duties, but the subjectivity underlying any different and superficial individuality, the subject who discovers himself as "self-conscience", "overcomes his immediacy", and "discovers his essence".[176] According to Battaglia, the state was the organization of human life as concrete *ethos* and, as such, it cannot be divided (as suggested by Panunzio) into "state characterized by the rule of law" and "ethical state": the state is wholly ethical, inasmuch as it "is founded on the subject becoming a citizen", detecting the state's roots in himself, *in interiore homine*.[177]

Coexistence between the "rule of law" and the "ethical state" was not always easy and painless; indeed, the adoption of an intrinsically "individualistic" formula was harshly criticized by a number of Fascist jurists: suffice it to mention Giuseppe Maggiore who, being receptive to Nazi ideology, criticized the principle of lawfulness in criminal law, regarded the *Duce* as both the embodiment of popular conscience and the source of all laws[178] and fully developed the criticism of individual rights (and of the underlying "individualistic" anthropology) that he had begun before the Fascist era. According to Maggiore, the state was the original act, the realization within history of the Subject's conscience, "the universal subject, the One dialectising itself in the opposition between subject and sovereign".[179] The individual had no autonomous reality and was inconceivable as such, since it was "the whole as universal subjectivity" which conferred upon him his value and meaningfulness.[180] Individuals and their rights did not matter: what counted was the totality and strength of the state, which was "the same immanent energy of the legal process: the act of law *par excellence*".[181]

As we have seen, the period in question was marked by a number of theories sharply rejecting the continuation of the rule of law doctrine within the regime's legal culture. The most widespread approach was different: a clear-cut break with traditional jurisprudence was not claimed and focus was placed on a *topos* of nineteenth-century tradition, i.e. the state's "absolute" sovereignty. In this perspective, the state freely determined itself through law and individual rights stemmed from the state's self-organization. Law was not "a unilateral order imposed on the subject" but an order that the state addressed to itself in its "continuous and unbreakable organizational process and legal development". The state existed in that it organized itself by laying down law: "by virtue of the *legislative act* which the state *really* consists of, the state ... organizes and constitutes itself as a *legal entity*".[182] No pre-state rights and "immortal principles" could be opposed to the state: an "external legal limitation to sovereignty"[183] was not conceivable, the latter being exclusively restrained (and founded in a legally unquestionable manner) by history and by its creative and uninterrupted process.

The link with nineteenth-century doctrines is apparent: the *Rechtsstaat* simply referred to a state which existed and realized itself through law. Such a perspective derived from Stahl's legal philosophy and was often found also in pre-Fascist Italian legal culture.[184] It led to the belief that, while the new regime must reject "all atomistic conceptions of the individual" and of his rights, it must provide a legal definition of the relationship between the individual and the state.[185] Thus, the most widespread trend was to "de-ideologize" the rule of law, freeing it from any liberal-constitutional relic and to identify it (*à la* Stahl) with the "norm-based" or legal nature of the state's activities. The state was empowered to get rid of any single rule but could not live without a legal system, without a normative arrangement rendering its will "regular" and ordered; the state did not encounter any limits to its will and could change the system as its pleased, but it had to deal with history, with "the needs of popular conscience".[186] When the state was obliged to limit freedom to safeguard public interests, this did not depend on an arbitrary decision of the governors, but on "a general, i.e. law's, order".[187]

In other words, the redefinition of the rule of law according to Fascist legal culture relied on three key points. Firstly, the *Stato di diritto* was a state whose will was expressed through law, this not prejudicing the contents of the state's decisions and the scope of its interventions; the functional link between the state and individuals was thus abandoned since it was deemed to be an unacceptable "individualistic" relic of nineteenth-century traditions. Secondly, rather than being concerned with the constitution, the *Stato di diritto* dealt with administration and advocated "justice within administration", which the regime could live with. Thirdly, the rule of law relied upon a clear distinction between "private" relationships and the public domain; such a distinction, though not perfectly coinciding with the National Socialist "double state" – given the different importance attached by Fascism to law and to the "norm-based" state's will – assumed in any event the idea of an "absolute politics" mainly embodied in the state.

10 THE SOCIAL RECHTSSTAAT AND ITS CRITICS: THE POST–SECOND WORLD WAR PERIOD

Even though National Socialism rapidly got rid of the rule of law while Fascism tended to preserve it as an internal and "lower" feature of its absolute and ethical state, both needed to eliminate the rule of law's genetic and conceptual links with nineteenth-century liberal tradition. It is therefore not surprising that it seemed necessary to resort to the principles of lawfulness, legal certainty (and rule of law) even during the last period of Fascism and much more urgently after its collapse, when an urgent need to prepare and "plan" an alternative regime arose.

A book by a young Italian philosopher, Flavio Lopez de Oñate, dedicated to the "legal certainty" was an important premonition of such a need and the indicator of a growing "crisis".[188] Lopez de Oñate's work hinged upon law's relevance. According to Lopez, law allowed for the legal consequences of individual actions to be foreseeable: only if it was consistent and unalterable, not arbitrarily adjusted by external contingencies, could law be seen as the "objective coordination of action"[189] providing individuals with the certainty they need.

The principle of lawfulness used by Lopez de Oñate to criticize a declining though still existing Fascist regime, was akin to that which Piero Calamandrei – who had enthusiastically reviewed Lopez de Oñate's work[190] – appealed to during the period of "power vacuum" which followed the end of Fascism. Calamandrei argued that lawfulness was the most precious legacy of the French Revolution and had been destroyed by both National Socialism and Fascism, the former openly attacking it, the latter "officially and superficially" endorsing it though in fact introducing "a semi-official practice of effective unlawfulness".[191]

Thus, in both Lopez de Oñate and Calamandrei's different though convergent works can be seen a "revival" of the liberal-constitutional tradition that had been fully expressed by the rule of law and by its underpinning principles, i.e. the centrality of law, the independence of the judiciary, and the possibility of foreseeing the legal consequences of individual actions. The circumstance that law was able again to control power was viewed as the most relevant evidence of the end of the recent "totalitarian" nightmare.

Yet, planning an alternative order to a "totalitarian" state soon appeared to be a more complex and demanding task, since "lawfulness" seemed to be hardly separable from the overall arrangement of a new regime: not surprisingly, throughout the historical development of the rule of law, recurrent attempts to technicalize, neutralize, or depoliticize the formula failed and the functional link between the state and the individual's expectations and claims survived.

Therefore, when a new constitutional order entirely incompatible with the defeated "totalitarianism" was sought for, a mere revival of the pre-Fascist tradition and the simple restoration of the "principle of lawfulness" appeared to be reductive proposals. In this context, on the one hand, "lawfulness" required the introduction of new constitutional devices (the hierarchy of norms, the judicial review on constitutionality), which Kelsen had originally theorized in the 1920s; on the other hand, the functional scope of the rule of law, namely the connection between the state and the individual's rights, was once again confirmed, but it took on new meanings, inasmuch as rights were now seen as the pillars of the constitutional order and could no longer coincide with the nineteenth-century "freedom-property" hendiadys.

The rights attributed to the individual were different because the anthropology underpinning post–Second World War constitutions was itself different. In the Italian constitution[192] as well as in the French[193] and the German "Fundamental Law",[194] can be found the imprint of a number of theories (Jacques Maritain's neo-Thomism, Emmanuel Mounier's personalism, Catholic and Protestant neo-natural law doctrines, liberal-socialism) that, in spite of their different philosophical foundations, all firmly believed in the centrality of the "person".[195] The "person" represented the substantial principle which, by being coordinated with the rule of law's "formal" structures, radically differentiated the new constitutional democracy from the "totalitarian state"; it was the "person" which suggested a vision of the subject very different from liberal "individualism" and opposed "solidarity" to "selfishness", and "social" rights to mere "negative" freedom.

Undoubtedly, post-war constitutions had their own specific development and characteristics, according to different contexts. Yet, there were also some common and innovative traits: firstly, the rule of law was inseparable from the judicial review of statutes' constitutionality; secondly, the "original" link between the rule of law and individual rights took on a new meaning, since "new" rights (especially social rights) were added to the "old" rights of "freedom and property".

Such an understanding, which was substantially shared by many European countries, was emphasized in the German *Grundgesetz*, which explicitly focused on a "social" *Rechtsstaat*; and it was by no mere chance that precisely in Germany the debate on the meaning and scope of such an expression was particularly rich and intense.

The connection between the rule of law and a democracy capable of extending the subject's legal sphere beyond the classical boundaries of freedom and property was not new: Heller had already subscribed to such a perspective by adding the adjective "social" to the *Rechtsstaat*. What was innovative was giving the new model a constitutional relevance, and considering it as one of the pillars of the new order. Yet, while it was commonly accepted that the rule of law had now become a constitutional *Rechtsstaat*, it was not taken for granted that the latter was also a social *Rechtsstaat*. While some jurists argued (by appealing to the phrasing and overall logic of the *Grundgesetz*) that the social *Rechtsstaat* was an essential component of the new constitutional democracy,[196] other jurists, such as Ernst Forsthoff, were sceptical towards such an interpretation of the "Fundamental Law".

According to Forsthoff, the underpinning principle of the *Grundgesetz* was the rule of law as such, with its traditional set of principles (the separation of powers, law's centrality, and the judiciary's independence), whereas the "social state" was a politically and socially relevant phenomenon, though not an institution of constitutional rank: administration, not the constitution, allowed for the realization of the "welfare state". According to Forsthoff, "the structure of the Federal Republic's constitution ... is determined ... by the rule of law", whose relationship with the "welfare state" is realized only "through the interplay between the constitution, the legislation and administration".[197] Administration, not the constitution, took care of "the primary needs of life".[198] Forsthoff was influenced by Schmitt, who had "weakened" the constitutional relevance of "social rights" by holding that the constitution of Weimar had chosen the bourgeois *Rechtsstaat* and had deemed only the rights of freedom to be "absolute", whereas "socialistic rights" were conditioned by a number of factual and institutional presuppositions;[199] similarly, Forsthoff believed that the relevance of the adjective "social" ascribed by the *Grundgesetz* to the *Rechtsstaat* should not be "taken seriously" when interpreting the constitution.

In the post–Second World War period, therefore, two different conceptions of the rule of law stood out: while, on the one hand, the new constitutions were appealed to in order to demonstrate the functional link between the rule of law and "social rights", on the other hand a different understanding of such constitutions denied the organic link between "rule of law", "welfare state", and "social rights" and drew a line between the constitutional *Rechtsstaat* and the (administrative and legislative) "welfare state".

A third interpretation was advanced with respect to the relationship between the rule of law and the "welfare state"; rather than simply viewing them "in a disjunctive manner" (ascribing a constitutional relevance to the former and referring the latter to the ambits of administration and legislation), it deemed such forms of state to be directly opposed one to the other. It followed, according to Friedrich von Hayek and Bruno Leoni,[200] that the rule of law was necessarily incompatible with the artificial and despotic intervention of both legislative and administrative powers.

The idea of a crisis of the rule of law caused by legislative inflation now started gaining ground:[201] if the rule of law entailed a system of limits making power's actions foreseeable and subject to control, then it also included, as an essential feature, law's stability and steadiness; however, if law were to become an instrument used to govern society, if it were adapted to individuals' ever-changing needs, then it would cease to represent certainty and would epitomize insecurity. The rule of law would lose its conceptual purity and mingle with the ideals of its "ideal-typical" antagonist, i.e. the "state of justice",[202] precisely the "state of justice" which Schmitt had identified with National Socialism, though it could have been equally identified with the Soviet's model of "socialist lawfulness". Ergo, a review of administrative or legislative action was not enough; rather, the root of the problem ought to be tackled, thus dispelling (despite Dicey's theory) the myth of parliamentary omnipotence and resorting to a rule of law which relied on the technical knowledge of judges and jurists and was sheltered from legislators' unilateral and "arbitrary" decisions.[203]

In the "anti-totalitarian" mood permeating the legal culture of the post–Second World War period, the rule of law's success was proportional to the multiplicity of political models it was associated with: it could appear as the means to combine the enhancement of individual rights with the control of sovereign's arbitrariness, or as the guarantor of freedom and property against an inevitable but dangerous "welfare state", or as a kind of social and legal order radically different from the "artificial" and arbitrary "legislative state".

11 CONCLUDING REMARKS

Many issues concerning the rule of law during the post–Second World War period retain their vitality and relevance today, transformed but still recognizable. The theory of a radical incompatibility between the rule of law and the "welfare state", or (under an opposite perspective) the need to develop and fully accomplish Heller's idea of a social *Rechtsstaat*; the new role of the law, the loss of its Enlightenment "majesty" and its ever-increasing use as a pliable and changeable instrument of government; the judge's role and his relationship with (statute and constitutional) law: all these are issues which have come down to present debates through the filter of 1950s culture, which referred to ideas and suggestions going back even further in time.

In fact, certain themes and topics recurrently feature in the historical development of the rule of law.

(a) In general terms, the rule of law finds its "horizon of meaning" within the power–law link, in the need to constrain and regulate the sovereign's unforeseeable will. More precisely, however, it has expressed the strong and widespread nineteenth-century conviction that law can control power,[204] through the refined legal devices offered by the advances of modern public law science. Given the extraordinary nineteenth-century development of German public law theories, it is not by chance that the concept of the rule of law has been first theorized in that country.

(b) The legalization of power, of which the rule of law purports to be both the means and expression has been carried out by rules and procedures that varied according to national legal cultures and the restraints imposed by different legal systems. Three main areas appear to be particularly distinctive in this respect: the United States, Great Britain, and continental Europe (which, however, had different characteristics depending on whether the revolutionary and post-revolutionary "French model" or the German model were taken into account). Despite the diversity of the political and legal systems involved, the lemma "rule of law" seems in any event to be translatable in various national idioms without losing its semantic field as it shifts from one historical and cultural experience to another.

(c) The strategies used to achieve the rule of law's aim, i.e. to control power through law, have been numerous: there seem to be two distinct conceptions of the "state subject to law", according to whether law imposes merely formal and procedural constraints on the state or whether it compels the state's action to respect specific contents. The difference has had capital importance in the development of the rule of law, for it has affected its meaning and purpose: while, in both cases, power's subjection to law brought benefits to individuals, in the former case the state's action was free to assume any kind of content whatsoever, whereas in the latter a compulsory link between "state" and "rights" was established.

Such a distinction can be useful, in general terms, for guiding and classifying purposes. Two further considerations must nonetheless be borne in mind in employing it. Firstly, the historical development of the rule of law has drawn inspiration more frequently from the "content-based" model rather than from the "formal" model which, in pure and rigorous terms, has been associated with Stahl (for its "original" enunciation) and with Kelsen (for its full elaboration). Secondly, even where the rule of law has been independent of an (explicit or implicit) functional link with individual rights, it could nonetheless have a "content-based" effect: Kelsen's constitutional *Rechtsstaat* was, in itself, a device grounded on the formal hierarchy of norms, but it was also the main instrument for the realization of democracy, as Kelsen himself argued.

(d) Among the many traits ascribed to the rule of law throughout its historical development, there did not seem to emerge a necessary relationship between the rule of law and a specific political and constitutional system: although there was a prevailing historical link between the rule of law and liberal constitutionalism, the twentieth-century development of the *Rechtsstaat* paved the way for different usages of the formula, for it has been referred also to the "Fascist state" or to the "welfare state" of the post–Second World War period.

(e) Although the rule of law is referable to different kinds of state and to different political and constitutional regimes, it nonetheless always expresses a hardly appeaseble tension towards power, which it perceives as the expression of a supreme will and decision. The rule of law appears not so much as an alternative but rather as an antidote to power's voluntarism, i.e. as an instrument which may soften and "tame" the sovereign's will, which nonetheless maintains a pivotal role. Although the rule of law has always expressed, across different countries – such as Dicey's Great Britain, Jellinek's Germany, or Orlando's Italy – a precise "anti-voluntaristic" stance, this has taken different shapes: resort could be made to judge-made law, as in Great Britain; or, as throughout the continent, to advanced institutional engineering (thus first setting up an administrative judicial system and then reviewing statutes' constitutionality).

The rule of law is also an attempt to curb power by correcting its mechanisms "from within". Through it, the nineteenth-century political and legal culture believed two important aims could be attained.

Firstly, the rule of law could help in contrasting Rousseau's and the Jacobin idea of popular sovereignty:[205] that "primacy of the will" which was specified as "tyranny of the majority", primacy of the number, and "democracy without quality". The rule of law strives to combine sovereign power's absolutism with the protection of individuals' legal domain against the will's despotism. Secondly, the rule of law could overcome an ambivalent approach towards administration: in some respects, this appeared as an irreplaceable instrument for social integration and for the settlement of conflicts; in other respects, it was suspected of being too "interventionist" towards freedom and property. Consequently, the rule of law allowed for power to be moderated from within by making its actions controllable and revisable.

(f) It was the idea of the sovereign's absolute will which led to the aporia underpinning the nineteenth-century development of the rule of law, i.e. the irresolvable conflict between the state's absolute sovereignty and the legal constraints which the rule of law identified itself with. While such an aporia remained unsolved throughout nineteenth-century public law theories, the parable of the rule of law was given a new direction by Kelsen's theory, which allowed for the old taboo of the uncontrollable legislative power to be overcome and provided the grounding for the review of statutes' constitutionality. The post–Second World War period brought about a new era for the rule of law's development. On the one hand, fundamental rights were now provided with a safe shield against the legislator's now "controllable" free will; on the other hand, the rights to which the rule of law was now functionally linked went well beyond nineteenth-century traditional freedom and property. This entails a paradox: on the one hand, the rule of law was an antidote to legislators' absolutism but, on the other, it stimulated (being a "social" *Rechtsstaat*, connected with "social rights") state interventionism, thus leading to the "legislative inflation" promptly criticized by the "antivoluntaristic" theorists of the "rule of law" (such as Hayek or Leoni) as jeopardizing legal certainty.

(g) Both the "antivoluntaristic" stance (the need to curb the "decisionism" of power) and the remedy thereof (to resort to judges' control) were recurrent in the nineteenth-century development of the rule of law and in its twentieth-century mutations. Whether it be the American Supreme Court or the common law judge, or the Constitutional Court, or the administrative judge, it is up to the curb power. It is reasonable to assert that such a reiterated belief in the "antivoluntaristic" role of the judge was grounded on an obstinate "Montesquieu-based" image of the judiciary as a "void power", as well as on a typically positivistic theory of interpretation, conceived of as a mere cognitive and deductive operation.

Throughout the history of the rule of law the solution of the enigma of the "subjection of power to law" has been found in the judge's role. It is also not surprising that, in contemporary debate, the problem of the rule of law hinges upon the capital question of legal hermeneutics, i.e. the role of judges and the techniques of interpretation and application of law.[206]

(h) If the recurrent solution in the history of the rule of law has been resorting to the judge in order to control power, there was also a widespread feeling that a "final" solution to the power–law link was hard to find. In the nineteenth century, when the rule of law strove to ensure the judicial review of administration, whereas legislation seemed, by nature, to escape any legal constraint, a "closing valve" to the system was needed. Although the judicial review of administrative action appeared as a notable progress in the long path to subjecting power to law, it did not seem to exhaust the problem of power and its control. Rather, a widespread "philosophy of history" (more exactly a common "sense" of history) fostered, through its faith in "magnificent and progressive futures", the idea of a spontaneous harmony between power, law, and rights, and offered by such means the "closing valve" to the legal system.

Yet, the optimistic historicism of the nineteenth century was doomed to be harshly defeated by the dramatic events of the twentieth century. It was precisely the tremendous impact of totalitarian regimes that urged a rethinking of the limits on sovereignty and pushed "upwards" the process of subjecting power to law, which had began in the previous century, thus stimulating the widespread realization of that constitutional *Rechtsstaat* which made legislators' action open to judicial review and seemed capable of protecting fundamental rights.

However, this did prevent the needs and tensions expressed in the debate of the first 20 years of the twentieth century from reappearing. On the one hand, the characteristic aim of the rule of law (the restraint on the sovereign's uncontrollable will) was pursued by extending the control to the system's higher levels (from administrative control to legislation, and from legislation to the constitution); on the other hand, in a tension with the other trend, merely formal restraints on power were feared to be frail and "unfounded"; the need was felt to interrupt the "process ad infinitum" to which any *Stufenbautheorie* seemed doomed and to find out "ultimate" constraints which could be imposed on power, "absolutely" preserved areas ontologically removed from the despotism of will.

Within the ever-renewed tension between power and law, between formal controls and substantial restraints, between the sovereign's interventionism and order's spontaneity, it might thus be possible to see a "surplus of meaning" from which the rule of law draws its symbolic suggestiveness, and which cannot be encompassed within formal constitutional devices and the boundaries of "pure reason".

"But once more – said the European – what state would you choose?" –The Brahmin answered, "That in which the laws alone are obeyed". "Where is this country?" said the counsellor. The Brahmin: "We must seek it".[207]

NOTES

1. See L. Cohen-Tanugi, *Le droit sans l'État: sur la démocratie en France et en Amérique*, Paris: PUF, 1985.
2. For the many historical similarities between the rule of law and the "citizenship discourse", see P. Costa, *Civitas. Storia della cittadinanza in Europa*, vols. 1–4, Roma-Bari: Laterza, 1999–2001.
3. On the historical and theoretical notion of the rule of law, see A.L. Goodhart, "The Rule of Law and Absolute Sovereignty", *University of Pennsylvania Law Review*, 106 (1958), 7, pp. 943–63; E.-W. Bockenförde, "Entstehungswandel des Rechtsstaatsbegriffs", in *Festschrift für Adolf Arndt zum 65. Geburtstag*, Frankfurt a. M.: Europäische Verlagsanstalt, 1969, pp. 53–76; M. Tohidipur (ed.), *Der bürgerliche Rechtsstaat*, Frankfurt a. M.: Suhrkamp, 1978; B. Barret-Kriegel, *L'état et les esclaves*, Paris: Calmann-Lévy, 1979; J. Raz, *The Rule of Law and its virtue* [1977], in id., *The Authority of Law. Essays on Law and Morality*, Oxford: Clarendon Press, 1979, pp. 210–29; J. Finnis, *Natural law and Natural Rights*, Oxford: Clarendon Press, 1980, pp. 270 ff.; N. MacCormick, "Der Rechtsstaat und die rule of law", *Juristische Zeitung*, 39 (1984), pp. 65–70; F. Neumann, *The Rule of Law. Political Theory and the Legal System in Modern Society* [1935], Leamington: Berg, 1986; A.C. Hutchinson and P. Monahan (eds), *The Rule of Law. Ideal or Ideology*, Toronto/Calgary/Vancouver: Carswell, 1987; L. Ferrajoli, *Diritto e ragione. Teoria del garantismo penale*, Roma-Bari: Laterza, 1989, pp. 889 ff.; M. Stolleis, "Rechtsstaat", in A. Erler and E. Kaufmann (eds), *Handwörterbuch zur deutscher Rechtsgeschichte*, Berlin: Schmidt Verlag, 1990, vol. 4, pp. 367–75; S. Amato, "Lo Stato di diritto: l'immagine e l'allegoria", *Rivista Internazionale di Filosofia del diritto*, 68 (1991), pp. 621–66; M. Fioravanti, "Costituzione e Stato di diritto", *Filosofia politica*, 5 (1991), 2, pp. 325–50; J. Chevallier, *L'État de droit*, Paris: Montchrestien, 1992; B. Montanari (ed.), *Stato di diritto e trasformazione della politica*, Torino: Giappichelli, 1992; M. Troper, "Le concept d'État de droit", *Droits. Revue française de théorie juridique*, 15 (1992), pp. 51–63; I. v. Münch, "Rechtsstaat versus Gerechtigkeit?", *Der Staat*, 33 (1994), 2, pp. 165–84; M. Fioravanti, "Lo Stato di diritto come forma di Stato. Notazioni preliminari sulla tradizione europeo-continentale", in G. Gozzi and R. Gherardi (eds), *Saperi della borghesia e storia dei concetti fra Otto e Novecento*, Bologna: il Mulino, 1995, pp. 161–77; P.P. Craig, "Formal and substantive conceptions

of the rule of law", *Diritto pubblico*, 1 (1995), pp. 35–55; H. Noske (ed.), *Der Rechtsstaat am Ende? Analyse, Standpunkte, Perspektiven*, München/Landsberg: Olzog, 1995; A. Catania, *Lo Stato moderno: sovranità e giuridicità*, Torino: Giappichelli, 1996; H. Hofmann, "Geschichtlichkeit und Universalitätsanspruch des Rechtsstaats", *Archiv für Rechts- und Sozialphilosophie*, Beiheft 65, Stuttgart: Steiner, 1996, pp. 9–31.

4. B. Barret-Kriegel, *L'état et les esclaves*, pp. 27 ff.
5. Plato, *The Statesman*, pp. 494, 505, in *The Dialogues of Plato*, Eng. tr. (with analyses and introductions) by B. Jowett, Oxford: Oxford University Press, 1892.
6. Aristotle, *Politics*, Book IV, pp. 117–18 (Aristotle, *The Politics of Aristotle*, Eng. tr. (with introduction, marginal analysis, essays, notes, and indices) by B. Jowett, Oxford: Clarendon Press, 1885.
7. J.A.N. Caritat de Condorcet, "Réflexions sur ce qui a été fait et sur ce qui reste à faire, lues dans une société d'amis de la paix" [1789], in J.A.N. Caritat de Condorcet, *Oeuvres*, IX, ed. by A. Condorcet O'Connor and M.F. Arago, 1847, anast. reprint, Stuttgart-Bad Cannstatt: Frommann, 1968, p. 447.
8. M. Robespierre, "Rapport du 5 nivôse an II sur les principes du Gouvernement révolutionnaire", in M. Robespierre, *Œuvres complètes*, 10, *Discours. 5. partie*, Paris: Presses Universitaires de France, 1967, It. tr. "Sui princìpi del governo rivoluzionario" (25 December 1793), in M. Robespierre, *La rivoluzione giacobina*, ed. by U. Cerroni, Pordenone: Studio Tesi, 1992, pp. 145–46.
9. J.A.N. Caritat de Condorcet, "Sur le sens du mot révolutionnaire" [1793], in Condorcet, *Oeuvres*, vol. XII, p. 623.
10. N. MacCormick, "Der Rechtsstaat und die rule of law", p. 66.
11. The American rule of law is examined by B. Casalini's essay, *infra.*
12. G. Stourzh, "The Declarations of Rights, Popular Sovereignty and the Supremacy of the Constitution: Divergences between the American and the French Revolutions", in *La Révolution américaine et l'Europe*, Paris: Editions du Centre National de la Recherche Scientifique, 1979, p. 361.
13. I. Kant, "The metaphysics of morals", in I. Kant, *Political Writings*, ed. by H. Reiss, translated by H.B. Nisbet, Cambridge/New York: Cambridge University Press, 1991, pp. 132–3.
14. Ibid., p. 133.
15. Ibid., p. 132.
16. Ibid., p. 135.
17. I. Kant, "On the common saying: This may be true in theory, but it does not apply in practice", in I. Kant, *Political Writings*, p. 79.
18. Ibid., p. 79.
19. I. Kant, "Idea for a universal history with a cosmopolitan purpose", in I. Kant, *Political Writings*, p. 46.
20. Ibid., p. 46.
21. I. Kant, "On the common saying", p. 74.
22. I. Kant, "The metaphysics of morals", p. 143.
23. I. Kant, "On the common saying", p. 79.
24. M. Stolleis, "Rechtsstaat", p. 368; E.-W. Böckenförde ("Entstehungswandel des Rechtsstaatsbegriffs", pp. 53–4) recalls that Carl Theodor Welcker, in 1813, and Johann Christoph Freiherr von Aretin, in 1824, had already used the expression *Rechtsstaat*.

25. B. Constant, *Principes de politique applicables à tous les gouvernements*, ed. by E. Hofman, Genève: Droz, 1980, vol. 1, pp. 22 ff. See also B. Constant, "Principes de politique" (1815), in B. Constant, *Oeuvres*, ed. by A. Roulin, Paris: Gallimard, 1957.
26. See B. Constant, *Commentaire sur l'ouvrage de Filangieri*, Paris: Belles Lettres, 2004.
27. See B. Constant, *De la force du gouvernement actuel de la France et de la necessité de s'y rallier. Des réactions politiques. Des effets de la Terreur*, ed. by Ph. Raynaud, Paris: Flammarion, 1988, It. tr. *Le reazioni politiche*, in B. Constant, *Le reazioni politiche. Gli effetti del terrore*, ed. by F. Calandra, Napoli: E.S.I., 1950, pp. 91, 97.
28. A. Rosmini, *La costituzione secondo la giustizia sociale*, in A. Rosmini, *Progetti di costituzione. Saggi editi ed inediti sullo Stato*, ed. by C. Gray [Edizione nazionale delle opere edite e inedite di A. Rosmini-Serbati, vol. 24], Milano: Bocca, 1952, p. 231.
29. See J. Luther, *Idee e storie di giustizia costituzionale nell'Ottocento*, Torino: Giappichelli, 1990.
30. See M. Ricciardi, "Linee storiche sul concetto di popolo", *Annali dell'istituto italo-germanico in Trento*, 16 (1990), pp. 303–69.
31. The essay by G. Gozzi examines the rule of law in German culture, *infra*; see also I. Maus, "Entwicklung und Funktionswandel der Theorie des bürgerlichen Rechtsstaats", in M. Tohidipur (ed.), *Der bürgerliche Rechtsstaat*, vol. I, pp. 13–81; G. Gozzi, *Democrazia e diritti. Germania: dallo Stato di diritto alla democrazia costituzionale*, Roma-Bari: Laterza, 1999, pp. 35 ff.
32. See M. Stolleis, *Geschichte des öffentlichen Rechts in Deutschland*, II, *Staatsrechtslehre und Verwaltungswissenschaft 1800–1914*, München: Beck, 1992, pp. 152 ff.
33. F.J. Stahl, *Die Philosophie des Rechts*, II, *Rechts- und Staatslehre auf der Grundlage christlicher Weltanschauung*, Erste Abteilung, *Die allgemeinen Lehren und das Privatrecht* [Tübingen, 1878^5], Hildesheim: Olms, 1963, pp. 195–6.
34. Ibid., p. 131.
35. Ibid., pp. 137–8.
36. *Die Polizei-Wissenschaft nach den Grundsätzen des Rechtsstaates.*
37. See M. Fioravanti, *Giuristi e costituzione politica nell'ottocento tedesco*, Milano: Giuffrè, 1979, pp. 95 ff.; M. Stolleis, *Geschichte des öffentlichen Rechts*, p. 258.
38. R. von Mohl, *Die Polizei-Wissenschaft nach den Grundsätzen des Rechtsstaates* [1832], vol. 1, Tübingen: Laupp, 1844^2, p. 10, n. 1.
39. Ibid., pp. 30–2.
40. Ibid., pp. 21–2.
41. M. Stolleis, "Rechtsstaat", p. 372.
42. O. Bähr, *Der Rechtsstaat* [1864], Aalen: Scientia Verlag, 1961, pp. 1–3.
43. Ibid., pp. 32–9.
44. Ibid., pp. 18–21.
45. Ibid., pp. 45–52.
46. Especially by Otto Mayer. On Mayer see M. Fioravanti, "Otto Mayer e la scienza del diritto amministrativo", *Rivista trimestrale di diritto pubblico*, 33 (1983), pp. 600–59.
47. See, for Italy, B. Sordi, *Giustizia e amministrazione nell'Italia liberale. La formazione della nozione di interesse legittimo*, Milano: Giuffrè, 1985; for Germany: W. Rüfner, "Die Entwicklung der Verwaltungsgerichtsbarkeit", in K.G.A. Jeserich, H. Pohl, and G.-C. von Unruh (eds), *Deutsche Verwaltungsgeschichte*, vol. III, *Das deutsche Reich bis zum Ende der Monarchie*, Stuttgart: Deutsche Verlags-Anstalt, 1984, pp. 909 ff.;

for France: F. Burdeau, *Histoire du droit administratif (de la Révolution au début des années 1970)*, Paris: PUF, 1995.
48. See M. Fioravanti, *Giuristi e costituzione*, pp. 243 ff.
49. C.F. von Gerber, *Grundzüge des deutschen Staatsrechts*, Aalen: Scientia Verlag, 1969, It. tr. *Lineamenti di diritto pubblico tedesco*, in C.F. von Gerber, *Diritto pubblico*, ed. by P.L. Lucchini, Milano: Giuffrè, 1971, p. 95.
50. Ibid., pp. 65–8.
51. Ibid., p. 118, n. 18.
52. Ibid., p. 120.
53. See S. Mezzadra, "Il corpo dello Stato. Aspetti giuspubblicistici della *Genossenschaftslehre* di Otto von Gierke", *Filosofia politica*, 7 (1993), 3, pp. 445–76.
54. O. von Gierke, *Labands Staatsrecht und die deutsche Rechtswissenschaft* [1883], Darmstadt: Wissenschaftliche Buchgesellschaft, 1961.
55. Ibid., pp. 37–8.
56. R. von Jhering, *Der Zweck im Recht*, Goldbach: Keip, 1997, It. tr. *Lo scopo nel diritto*, ed. by M.G. Losano, Torino: Einaudi, 1972, pp. 186–7.
57. Ibid., p. 224.
58. Ibid., pp. 226–7.
59. Ibid., pp. 261–2.
60. Ibid., p. 269.
61. Ibid., pp. 270–1.
62. Ibid., pp. 271–4.
63. Ibid., p. 304.
64. See M. Fioravanti, *Giuristi e costituzione*, pp. 391 ff.; M. Stolleis, *Geschichte des öffentlichen Rechts in Deutschland*, II, pp. 375 ff., 450 ff.; G. Valera, "Coercizione e potere: storia, diritti pubblici soggettivi e poteri dello Stato nel pensiero di G. Jellinek", in G. Gozzi and R. Gherardi (eds), *Saperi della borghesia*, pp. 53–118.
65. See G. Jellinek, *System der subjektiven öffentlichen Rechte*, Aalen: Scientia Verlag, 1979.
66. See M. La Torre, "Dei diritti pubblici soggettivi: il paradosso dei diritti di libertà", *Materiali per una storia della cultura giuridica*, 12 (1982), pp. 79–116.
67. G. Jellinek, *Allgemeine Staatslehre*, Berlin: Springer Verlag, 1919, It. tr. *Dottrina generale dello stato*, ed. by M. Petrozziello, Milano: Società Editrice Libraria, 1921, vol. I, pp. 665–7.
68. S. Romano provides an excellent contribution in this respect: "La teoria dei diritti pubblici subbiettivi", in V.E. Orlando (ed.), *Primo trattato completo di diritto amministrativo*, Milano: Società Editrice Libraria, 1900, pp. 160 ff.
69. See *supra*, § 3.
70. J. Lyons, *Introduction to Theoretical Linguistics*, Cambridge: Cambridge University Press, 1969, p. 457.
71. See R.A. Cosgrove, *The Rule of Law: Albert Venn Dicey, Victorian Jurist*, London: Macmillan, 1980; S. Cassese, "Albert Venn Dicey e il diritto amministrativo", *Quaderni fiorentini per la storia del pensiero giuridico moderno*, 19 (1990), pp. 5–82; S. Cassese, "La recezione di Dicey in Italia e in Francia. Contributo allo studio del mito dell'amministrazione senza diritto amministrativo", *Materiali per una storia della cultura giuridica*, 21 (1995), 1, pp. 107–31.
72. The essay by E. Santoro is devoted to Dicey and the rule of law, *infra*.

73. A.V. Dicey, *An Introduction to the Study of the Law of the Constitution*, London: Macmillan, 1959[10], pp. 16 ff.
74. A.V. Dicey, *An Introduction*, pp. 39–43.
75. Ibid., pp. 60–3.
76. Ibid., p. 70.
77. J. Bryce, *Flexible and rigid constitutions* [1901], in J. Bryce, *Constitutions*, New York: Oxford University Press, 1905.
78. A.V. Dicey, *An Introduction*, p. 137.
79. Ibid., p. 407.
80. Ibid., pp. 188 ff.
81. Ibid., pp. 193, 328 ff.
82. P.P. Craig, "Formal and substantive conceptions", p. 40.
83. See in this respect I. Jennings, *The Law and the Constitution*, London: University of London Press, 1959[5], pp. 54 ff.
84. A.V. Dicey, *An Introduction*, pp. 198 ff.
85. Ibid., p. 413.
86. Ibid., p. 202.
87. See *supra*, § 5.
88. The essay by A. Laquièze, *infra*, is devoted to the French model of the rule of law. See also Ph. Raynaud, "Des droits de l'homme a l'état de droit. Les droits de l'homme et leurs garanties chez les théoriciens français classiques du droit public", *Droits. Revue française de théorie juridique*, 2 (1985), *Les droits de l'homme*, pp. 61–73; M.-J. Redor, *De l'état légal à l'état de droit. L'évolution des conceptions de la doctrine publiciste française 1879–1914*, Paris: Economica, 1992.
89. See M. Galizia, "Il 'Positivisme juridique' di Raymond Carré de Malberg", *Quaderni fiorentini*, 2 (1973), pp. 335–509; G. Bacot, *Carré de Malberg et l'origine de la distinction entre souveraineté du peuple et souveraineté nationale*, Paris: Ed. du CNRS, 1985.
90. R. Carré de Malberg, *Théorie générale de l'État, spécialement d'après les données fournies par le Droit constitutionnel français*, Paris: Sirey, 1920, vol. I, pp. 2–7.
91. Ibid., pp. 48–50.
92. Ibid., p. 194.
93. R. Carré de Malberg, *Théorie générale de l'État*, vol. II, p. 140.
94. Duguit criticizes the self-limitation theory by relying on the primacy of both society and the *règle de droit*; see L. Duguit, *Traité de droit constitutionnel*, I, *La règle de droit - Le problème de l'État*, Paris: Ancienne Librairie Fontemoing, 1927[3], pp. 633 ff., 665 ff. See E. Pisier-Kouchner, *Le service public dans la théorie de l'État de Léon Duguit*, Paris: Pichon et Durand-Auzias, 1972, pp. 62 ff.
95. R. Carré de Malberg, *Théorie générale de l'État*, vol. II, pp. 154 ff.
96. R. Carré de Malberg, *Théorie générale de l'État*, vol. I, pp. 488 ff.
97. Ibid., pp. 492–3.
98. See G. Bacot, *Carré de Malberg*, pp. 10–11.
99. G. Bongiovanni's essay, *The rule of law and constitutional justice in Austria. Hans Kelsen's contribution*, *infra*, is devoted to Kelsen.
100. H. Kelsen, *Hauptprobleme der Staatsrechtslehre, entwickelt aus der Lehre vom Rechtssätze*, Aalen: Scientia Verlag, 1984, It. tr. *Problemi fondamentali della dottrina del diritto pubblico*, ed. by A. Carrino, Napoli: E.S.I., 1997, pp. 41 ff. On Kelsen and neo-Kantianism see G. Calabrò, "Kelsen e il neokantismo", in C. Roehrssen (ed.),

Hans Kelsen nella cultura filosofico-giuridica del Novecento, Roma: Istituto dell'Enciclopedia italiana, 1983, pp. 87–92; S.L. Paulson, "Kelsen and the Neo-kantian Problematic", in A. Catania and M. Fimiani (eds), *Neokantismo e sociologia*, Napoli: E.S.I., 1995, pp. 81–98; R. Racinaro, "Cassirer e Kelsen", ibid., pp. 99–110.

101. See M. Fioravanti, "Kelsen, Schmitt e la tradizione giuridica dell'Ottocento", in G. Gozzi and P. Schiera (eds), *Crisi istituzionale e teoria dello Stato in Germania dopo la Prima guerra mondiale*, Bologna: il Mulino, 1987, pp. 51–103; Fioravanti appropriately focuses on the anti-traditional stance of Kelsen's legal theory.
102. H. Kelsen, *Das Problem der Souveränität und die Theorie des Volkerrechts. Beitrag zu einer reinen Rechtslehre*, Tübingen: Mohr, 1920, It. tr. *Il problema della sovranità e la teoria del diritto internazionale. Contributo per una dottrina pura del diritto*, ed. by A. Carrino, Milano: Giuffrè, 1989, p. 20.
103. H. Kelsen, "Staat und Recht. Zum Problem der soziologischen oder juristischen Erkenntnis des Staates", *Soziologische Hefte*, 2 (1922), pp. 18–37, It. tr. "Stato e diritto. Il problema della conoscenza sociologica o giuridica dello Stato", in H. Kelsen, *Sociologia della democrazia*, ed. by A. Carrino, Napoli: E.S.I., 1991, p. 69.
104. See in particular E. Cassirer, *Substanzbegriff und Funktionsbegriff. Untersuchungen über die Grundfragen der Erkenntniskritik* [1910], Hamburg: Meiner, 2000.
105. H. Kelsen, "Das Verhältnis von Staat und Recht im Lichte der Erkenntniskritik", *Zeitschrift für öffentliches Recht*, 2 (1921), pp. 453–510, It. tr. "Il rapporto tra Stato e diritto dal punto di vista epistemologico", in H. Kelsen, *L'anima e il diritto. Figure arcaiche della giustizia e concezione scientifica del mondo*, Roma: Edizioni Lavoro, 1989, pp. 5 ff.
106. H. Kelsen, *Problemi fondamentali*, p. 484.
107. H. Kelsen, *Il problema della sovranità*, pp. 31–2.
108. H. Kelsen, *Problemi fondamentali*, p. 395.
109. H. Kelsen, *Il problema della sovranità*, pp. 67–8.
110. H. Kelsen, "Rechtsstaat und Staatsrecht", *Österreichische Rundschau*, 36 (1913), pp. 88–94, It. tr. "Stato di diritto e diritto pubblico", in A. Kelsen, *Dio e Stato. La giurisprudenza come scienza dello spirito*, ed. by A. Carrino, Napoli: E.S.I., 1988, pp. 214–15.
111. See B. Sordi, *Tra Weimar e Vienna. Amministrazione pubblica e teoria giuridica nel primo dopoguerra*, Milano: Giuffrè, 1987, pp. 88 ff.; B. Sordi, "Un diritto amministrativo per le democrazie degli anni Venti. La 'Verwaltung' nella riflessione della Wiener Rechtstheoretische Schule", in G. Gozzi and P. Schiera (eds), *Crisi istituzionale e teoria dello Stato in Germania dopo la Prima guerra mondiale*, pp. 105–30.
112. H. Kelsen, *Problemi fondamentali*, pp. 560–1. See also H. Kelsen, "Zur Lehre vom Gesetz im formellen und materiellen Sinn, mit besonderer Berücksichtigung der österreichischen Verfassung", *Juristische Blätter*, 42 (1913), pp. 229–32, It. tr. "Sulla dottrina della legge in senso formale e materiale", in H. Kelsen, *Dio e Stato*, p. 233.
113. H. Kelsen, *Problemi fondamentali*, pp. 612–13.
114. See B. Sordi, *Tra Weimar e Vienna*, pp. 157 ff.
115. S.M. Barberis, "Kelsen, Paulson and the Dynamic Legal Order", in L. Gianformaggio (ed.), *Hans Kelsen's Legal Theory. A Diachronic Point of View*, Torino: Giappichelli, 1990, pp. 49–61 and the essays collected in L. Gianformaggio

(ed.), *Sistemi normativi statici e dinamici: analisi di una tipologia kelseniana*, Torino: Giappichelli, 1991.
116. H. Kelsen, *Problemi fondamentali*, foreword to the second edition (1923), pp. 27–8. See A. Abignente, *La dottrina del diritto tra dinamicità e purezza: studio su Adolf Julius Merkl*, Napoli: E.S.I., 1990.
117. H. Kelsen, *Problemi fondamentali*, pp. 25–7.
118. H. Kelsen, "Die Lehre von den drei Gewalten oder Funktionen des Staates", *Archiv für Rechts- und Wirtschaftsphilosophie*, 17 (1924), pp. 374–408, It. tr. "La dottrina dei tre poteri o funzioni dello stato", in H. Kelsen, *Il primato del parlamento*, Milano: Giuffrè, 1982, pp. 88–9.
119. See G. Bongiovanni, *Reine Rechtslehre e dottrina giuridica dello Stato. H. Kelsen e la costituzione austriaca del 1920*, Milano: Giuffrè, 1998, pp. 64 ff.
120. See A. Giovannelli, *Dottrina pura e teoria della Costituzione in Kelsen*, Milano: Giuffrè, 1979; M. Barberis, "Kelsen e la giustizia costituzionale", *Materiali per una storia della cultura giuridica*, 12 (1982), pp. 225–42, M. Troper, "Kelsen e il controllo di costituzionalità", *Diritto e cultura*, 4 (1994), pp. 219–41.
121. Kelsen plays a significant role in the process leading to the 1920 Austrian constitution. See G. Bongiovanni, *Reine Rechtslehre*, pp. 143 ff.
122. H. Kelsen, "La garantie juridictionnelle de la Constitution (La Justice constitutionelle)", Paris: Les Presses Universitaires de France, 1929, pp. 52–143, It. tr. "La garanzia giurisdizionale della costituzione (la giustizia costituzionale)", in H. Kelsen, *La giustizia costituzionale*, ed. by G. Geraci, Milano: Giuffrè, 1981, p. 148.
123. Ibid., pp. 171–2.
124. Ibid., p. 199.
125. Ibid., p. 202.
126. See E. Castrucci, *Tra organicismo e Rechtsidee. Il pensiero giuridico di Erich Kaufmann*, Milano: Giuffrè, 1984.
127. E. Kaufmann, *Critica della filosofia neokantiana del diritto*, ed. by A. Carrino, Napoli: E.S.I., 1992.
128. Ibid., pp. 12–13.
129. E. Kaufmann, "Juristische Relationsbegriffe und Dingbegriffe", in E. Kaufmann, *Gesammelte Schriften*, III, *Rechtsidee und Recht. Rechtsphilosophische und ideengeschichtliche Bemühungen aus fünf Jahnrhunderten*, Göttingen: Schwartz, 1960, p. 267.
130. E. Kaufmann, "Die Gleichheit vor dem Gesetz im Sinne des art. 109 der Reichsverfassung" [1927], in E. Kaufmann, *Gesammelte Schriften*, III, pp. 246–65, It. tr. *L'uguaglianza dinanzi alla legge ai sensi dell'art. 109 della Costituzione del Reich*, in E. Kaufmann, *Critica*, p. 85. See R. Miccù, "La controversia metodologica nella dottrina weimariana dello Stato", in R. Miccù (ed.), *Neokantismo e diritto nella lotta per Weimar*, Napoli: E.S.I., 1992, pp. 155 ff.
131. E. Kaufmann, *L'uguaglianza*, pp. 88–9. See E. Castrucci, *Tra organicismo e Rechtsidee*, pp. 128–9.
132. M. Hauriou, *Principes de droit public*, Paris: Sirey, 1910, pp. 128 ff.
133. Ibid., pp. 228 ff.
134. Ibid., p. 254.
135. Ibid., p. 461.
136. Ibid., pp. 72–3.
137. Ibid., pp. 75–7.

138. Ibid., pp. 78–80.
139. M. Hauriou, *Précis de droit constitutionnel* [1923], Paris: Sirey, 1929^2, pp. 101–3.
140. Ibid., p. 613.
141. M. Hauriou, *Principes de droit public*, p. 558.
142. M. Hauriou, *Précis de droit constitutionnel*, pp. 611 ff.
143. H. Heller, "Die Krisis der Staatslehre" [1926], *Gesammelte Schriften*, II, *Recht, Staat, Macht*, Leiden: Sijthoff, 1971, pp. 3–30, It. tr. "La crisi della dottrina dello Stato", in H. Heller, *La sovranità ed altri scritti sulla dottrina del diritto e dello Stato*, ed. by P. Pasquino, Milano: Giuffrè, 1987, pp. 31 ff. See also H. Heller, *Dottrina dello Stato*, ed. by U. Pomarici, Napoli: E.S.I., 1988, pp. 97 ff.
144. Ibid., pp. 95 ff. See the remarks by P.P. Portinaro, "Staatslehre und sozialistischer Dezisionismus. Randbemerkungen zu Hellers Rechts- und Staatstheorie", in Ch. Müller and I. Staff (eds), *Der soziale Rechtsstaat. Gedächtnisschrift für Hermann Heller 1891–1933*, Baden-Baden: Nomos, 1984, pp. 573–84.
145. H. Heller, *La sovranità*, p. 174.
146. Ibid., pp. 165–7.
147. H. Heller, "Politische Demokratie und soziale Homogenität" [1928], *Gesammelte Schriften*, II, pp. 421–33, It. tr. "Democrazia politica e omogeneità sociale", in H. Heller, *Stato di diritto o dittatura? e altri scritti*, Napoli: Editoriale Scientifica, 1998, pp. 17–18.
148. H. Heller, "Rechtsstaat oder Diktatur?" [1929], in H. Heller, *Gesammelte Schriften*, II, pp. 443–62, It. tr. *Stato di diritto o dittatura?*, in H. Heller, *Stato di diritto*, p. 51.
149. H. Heller, "Grundrechte und Grundpflichten" [1924], in H. Heller, *Gesammelte Schriften*, II, pp. 284 ff.
150. Ibid., p. 291. See W. Schluchter, *Entscheidung für den sozialen Rechtsstaat. Hermann Heller und die staatstheoretische Diskussion in der weimarer Republik*, Baden-Baden: Nomos, 1983^2; I. Staff, "Forme di integrazione sociale nella Costituzione di Weimar", in G. Gozzi and P. Schiera (eds), *Crisi istituzionale e teoria dello Stato*, pp. 11–50. Neumann, too, deals with the "creation of the social rule of law" (F.L. Neumann, "Die soziale Bedeutung der Grundrechte in der Weimarer Verfassung" [1930], in F.L. Neumann, *Wirtschaft, Staat, Demokratie. Gesammelte Aufsätze 1930–1954*, Frankfurt a. M: Suhrkamp, 1978, It. tr. "Il significato sociale dei diritti fondamentali nella costituzione di Weimar", in F.L. Neumann, *Il diritto del lavoro fra democrazia e dittatura*, Bologna: il Mulino, 1983, p. 134).
151. See P. Caldwell, "National Socialism and Constitutional Law: Carl Schmitt, Otto Koellreutter and the Debate over the Nature of the Nazi state 1933–1937", *Cardozo Law Review*, 16 (1994), pp. 399–427; M. Stolleis, *Geschichte des öffentlichen Rechts in Deutschland*, III, *Staats- und Verwaltungsrechtswissenschaft in Republik und Diktatur 1914–1945*, München: Beck, 1999, pp. 316 ff.
152. See C. Schmitt, "Das Gesetz zur Behebung der Not von Volk und Reich", *Deutsche Juristen-Zeitung*, 38 (1933), pp. 455–8.
153. O. Koellreutter, *Grundriss der allgemeinen Staatslehre*, Tübingen: Mohr (Paul Siebeck), 1933, pp. 163–4.
154. See C. Galli, *Genealogia della politica. Carl Schmitt e la crisi del pensiero politico moderno*, Bologna: il Mulino, 1996, pp. 840 ff.
155. C. Schmitt, *Staat, Bewegung, Volk. Die Dreigliederung der politischen Einheit*, Hamburg: Anseatische Verlagsanstalt, 1933.

156. See C. Schmitt, "Weiterentwicklung des totalen Staats in Deutschland" [1931], in C. Schmitt, *Verfassungsrechtliche Aufsätze aus den Jahren 1924–1954. Materialien zu einer Verfassungslehre*, Berlin: Duncker & Humblot, 1985, p. 360; see also G. Preterossi, *Carl Schmitt e la tradizione moderna*, Roma-Bari: Laterza, 1996, pp. 107 ff.
157. C. Schmitt, *Staat, Bewegung, Volk*, p. 42; O. Koellreutter, *Grundriss*, p. 54.
158. G.A. Walz, *Das Ende der Zwischenverfassung*, Stuttgart: Kohlhammer, 1933.
159. O. Koellreutter, *Grundriss*, pp. 108–9, 255–6.
160. See O. Koellreutter, "Der nationale Rechtsstaat", *Deutsche Juristen-Zeitung*, 38 (1933), pp. 517–24.
161. C. Schmitt, "Nationalsozialismus und Rechtsstaat", *Juristische Wochenschrift*, 63 (1934), pp. 716–18.
162. C. Schmitt, "Was bedeutet der Streit um den 'Rechtsstaat'?", in C. Schmitt, *Staat, Grossraum, Nomos. Arbeiten aus den Jahren 1916–1969*, ed. by G. Maschke, Berlin: Duncker & Humblot, 1995, pp. 123–5.
163. Ibid., p. 126.
164. Also Schmitt's disciple, Forsthoff, claims the impossibility of separating the rule of law from its liberal grounding, thus criticizing Koellreutter, "Der deutsche Führerstaat", *Juristische Wochenschrift*, 62 (1934), p. 538. Koellreutter's answer is contained in his "Das Verwaltungsrecht im nationalsozialistischen Staat", *Deutsche Juristen-Zeitung*, 39 (1934), pp. 626–8; see also the remarks by H. Helfritz, "Rechtsstaat und nationalsozialistischer Staat", *Deutsche Juristen-Zeitung*, 39 (1934), pp. 425–33.
165. C. Schmitt, "Nationalsozialismus und Rechtsstaat", pp. 714–15; C. Schmitt, "Der Rechtsstaat", in H. Frank (ed.), *Nationalsozialistisches Handbuch für Recht und Gesetzgebung*, München: NSDAP, 1935, pp. 5–6.
166. G.A. Walz, "Autoritärer Staat, nationaler Rechtsstaat oder völkischer Führerstaat?", *Deutsche Juristen-Zeitung*, 38 (1933), pp. 1338–40.
167. C. Schmitt, "Nationalsozialismus und Rechtsstaat", pp. 713–14.
168. C. Schmitt, "Der Führer schützt das Recht" [1934], in C. Schmitt, *Positionen und Begriffe im Kampf mit Weimar, Genf, Versailles 1923–1939*, Berlin: Duncker & Humblot, 1988, pp. 200–1.
169. See *supra*, § 3.
170. See *supra*, § 5, Jhering's example.
171. See E. Fraenkel, *Der Doppelstaat*, Frankfurt a. M.: Europäische Verlagsanstalt, 1974, It. tr. *Il doppio Stato. Contributo alla teoria della dittatura*, Torino: Einaudi, 1983. Bobbio's observations are to be found in *Introduzione* to the Italian edition, pp. ix–xxix.
172. For greater documentation in this respect, see P. Costa, "Lo 'Stato totalitario': un campo semantico nella giuspubblicistica del fascismo", *Quaderni fiorentini*, (28) 1999, pp. 61–174.
173. C. Schmitt, "Was bedeutet der Streit", p. 121.
174. S. Panunzio, *Lo Stato di diritto*, Città di Castello: Il Solco, 1921, pp. 156–9.
175. See U. Redanò, *Lo Stato etico*, Firenze: Vallecchi, 1927. See also the critique by C. Curcio, *Rivista internazionale di filosofia del diritto*, 7 (1928), pp. 102–4.
176. F. Battaglia, "Dall'individuo allo Stato" [1932], in F. Battaglia, *Scritti di teoria dello Stato*, Milano: Giuffrè, 1939, pp. 48–51.

177. F. Battaglia, "La concezione speculativa dello Stato" [1935], in F. Battaglia, *Scritti*, pp. 164–5. See for similar considerations A. Volpicelli, "Lo Stato e l'etica. Nuove osservazioni polemiche", *Nuovi studi di diritto, economia e politica*, 4 (1931), pp. 163–75; G. Gentile, "Il concetto dello Stato in Hegel", *Nuovi studi di diritto, economia e politica*, 4 (1931), pp. 321–32.
178. G. Maggiore, *Diritto penale totalitario nello Stato totalitario*, Padova: Cedam, 1939, pp. 20 ff.
179. G. Maggiore, *Il diritto e il suo processo ideale*, Palermo: Fiorenza, 1916, pp. 107–10.
180. Ibid., pp. 101–2.
181. Ibid., p. 113.
182. A. Volpicelli, "Vittorio Emanuele Orlando", *Nuovi studi di diritto, economia e politica*, 1 (1927–1928), p. 194.
183. Ibid., p. 202.
184. See e.g. A. Falchi, "I fini dello Stato e la funzione del potere" (1914), in A. Falchi, *Lo Stato collettività. Saggi*, Milano: Giuffrè, 1963, p. 97.
185. C.A. Biggini, *La legislazione costituzionale nel nuovo diritto pubblico italiano*, Ravenna: Arti Grafiche, 1931, pp. 156–7.
186. O. Ranelletti, *Istituzioni di diritto pubblico. Il nuovo diritto pubblico italiano*, Padova: Cedam, 1929, p. 30. See also B. Brugi, "I così detti limiti dei diritti subiettivi e lo Stato", *Lo Stato*, 2 (1931), pp. 699–707.
187. F. Ercole, *Lo Stato fascista corporativo*, Palermo: Ed. del G.U.F., 1930, p. 17. Under such a perspective, the Fascist state may be seen as the highest and most exclusive stage of the parable of the rule of law since Fascism has extended the scope of law to fields, such as labour relationships, which had been left legally "undefended" by liberalism. See F. Battaglia, "Le carte dei diritti", *Archivio di studi corporativi*, 5 (1934), pp. 154 ff. Renato Treves (in an essay published during his exile in Argentina) denounces the verbalistic nature of the Fascist understanding of the rule of law. A response can be found in F. Battaglia, "Ancora sullo Stato di diritto", *Rivista internazionale di filosofia del diritto*, 25 (1948), pp. 164–71. See also R. Treves, "Stato di diritto e Stato totalitario", in *Studi in onore di G.M. De Francesco*, Milano: Giuffrè, 1957, vol. 2, pp. 51–69; C. Treves, "Considerazioni sullo Stato di diritto", in *Studi in onore di E. Crosa*, Milano: Giuffrè, 1960, vol. 1, pp. 1594–5.
188. F. Lopez de Oñate, *La certezza del diritto* [1942], Milano: Giuffrè, 1968, pp. 25 ff. On the "crisis" of intellectuals between Fascism and post-Fascism, see L. Mangoni, "Civiltà della crisi. Gli intellettuali tra fascismo e antifascismo", in *Storia dell'Italia repubblicana*, I, *La costruzione della democrazia: dalla caduta del fascismo agli anni Cinquanta*, Torino: Einaudi, 1994, pp. 615–718.
189. F. Lopez de Oñate, *La certezza del diritto*, p. 48.
190. P. Calamandrei, "La certezza del diritto e le responsabilità della dottrina" [1942], in F. Lopez de Oñate, *La certezza del diritto*, pp. 167–90. See P. Grossi, *Stile fiorentino*, Milano: Giuffrè, 1986, pp. 142 ff.; F. Sbarberi, *L'utopia della libertà eguale. Il liberalismo sociale da Rosselli a Bobbio*, Torino: Bollati Boringhieri, 1999, pp. 115 ff.
191. P. Calamandrei, "Costruire la democrazia (Premesse alla Costituente)" [1945], in P. Calamandrei, *Opere giuridiche*, ed. by M. Cappelletti, Napoli: Morano, 1968, vol. III, pp. 132–3.
192. See U. De Siervo (ed.), *Scelte della costituente e cultura giuridica*, I, *Costituzione italiana e modelli stranieri*, Bologna: il Mulino, 1980; U. De Siervo (ed.), *Scelte della*

costituente e cultura giuridica, II, *Protagonisti e momenti del dibattito costituzionale*, Bologna: il Mulino, 1980; P. Pombeni, *La Costituente. Un problema storico-politico*, Bologna: il Mulino, 1995; M. Fioravanti and S. Guerrieri (eds), *La costituzione italiana*, Roma: Carocci, 1998.

193. S. Guerrieri, *Due costituenti e tre referendum. La nascita della Quarta Repubblica francese*, Milano: Angeli, 1998 (esp. pp. 101 ff.).

194. G. Gozzi, *Democrazia e diritti*, pp. 117 ff. See also F. Lanchester and I. Staff (eds), *Lo Stato di diritto democratico dopo il fascismo ed il nazionalsocialismo (Demokratische Rechtsstaatlichkeit nach Ende von Faschismus und Nationalsozialismus)*, Milano/Baden-Baden: Giuffrè/Nomos Verlag, 1999.

195. See P. Pombeni, "Individuo/persona nella Costituzione italiana. Il contributo del dossettismo", *Parolechiave*, 10–11 (1996), pp. 197–218; F. Pizzolato, *Finalismo dello Stato e sistema dei diritti nella Costituzione italiana*, Milano: Vita e Pensiero, 1999.

196. See W. Abendroth, "Zum Begriff des demokratischen und sozialen Rechtsstaates im Grundgesetz der Bundesrepublik Deutschland" [1954], in E. Forsthoff (ed.), *Rechtsstaatlichkeit und Sozialstaatlichkeit. Aufsätze und Essays*, Darmstadt: Wissenschaftliche Buchgesellschaft, 1968, pp. 114–44; W. Abendroth, "Der demokratische und soziale Rechtsstaat als politischer Auftrag" [1975], in M. Tohidipur (ed.), *Der bürgerliche Rechtsstaat*, vol. I, pp. 265–89. On the continuity between Heller and Abendroth, see G. Gozzi, *Democrazia e diritti*, p. 169.

197. E. Forsthoff, *Rechtsstaat im Wandel. Verfassungsrechtliche Abhandlungen 1950–1964*, Stuttgart: W. Kohlhammer, 1964, It. tr. *Stato di diritto in trasformazione*, ed. by C. Amirante, Milano: Giuffrè, 1973, p. 60. See C. Amirante, *Presentazione*, ibid., pp. v–xxxiv. On the complexity of Forsthoff's work, see B. Sordi, "Il primo e l'ultimo Forsthoff", *Quaderni fiorentini*, 25 (1996), pp. 667–82.

198. E. Forsthoff, *Stato di diritto*, pp. 151–2.

199. C. Schmitt, *Verfassungslehre* [1928], Berlin: Duncker & Humblot, 1970, It. tr. *Dottrina della costituzione*, ed. by A. Caracciolo, Milano: Giuffrè, 1984, p. 227.

200. See B. Leoni, *La libertà e la legge* [1961], Macerata: Liberilibri, 1994 (esp. pp. 67 ff.). See R. Cubeddu, *Introduzione*, ibid., pp. ix–xxxv. See also the review by D. Zolo, *Quaderni fiorentini*, 24 (1995), pp. 394–6. The essay by M.C. Pievatolo, "Leoni's and Hayek's Critique of the Rule of Law in Continental Europe", *infra*, is devoted to Leoni (and to Hayek).

201. Giovanni Sartori (in an illustratively entitled paragraph "From Rule of Law to Rule of Legislators") argues that *ius* ought not to be mistaken with *iussum* and claims the insufficiency of a merely formalistic construction of the rule of law; he also ascribes "legislative inflation" to (what we today would call) a "legislation-centred" conception, deeming this to represent a threat to the rule of law (G. Sartori, *Democratic Theory*, Detroit: Wayne State University Press, 1962, pp. 306–14).

202. G. Fassò, "Stato di diritto e Stato di giustizia", in R. Orecchia (ed.), *Atti del VI Congresso nazionale di filosofia del diritto*, I, *Relazioni generali*, Milano: Giuffrè, 1963, pp. 83–119.

203. Ibid., pp. 115 ff. A separate examination would be needed for Gustav Radbruch's thinking: it is nonetheless worth recalling that he also believes the "secret" of the English rule of law to lie in a class of jurists and judges used to interpreting positive laws in the light of the system's historically rooted values. See G. Radbruch, *Der Geist des englischen Rechts*, Heidelberg: Rausch, 1947, It. tr. *Lo spirito del diritto inglese*, Milano: Giuffrè, 1962, pp. 39 ff.; see also A. Baratta, *Introduzione*, pp. xi ff.; G. Alpa, *L'arte di giudicare*, Roma-Bari: Laterza, 1996, pp. 32–3.

204. See P.P. Portinaro, "Il grande legislatore e il futuro della costituzione", in G. Zagrebelsky, P.P. Portinaro, and J. Luther (eds), *Il futuro della costituzione*, Torino: Einaudi, 1991, pp. 5–6.
205. See M. Fioravanti, "Lo Stato di diritto come forma di Stato", in G. Gozzi and R. Gherardi (eds), *Saperi della borghesia*, pp. 173–4.
206. See in this respect R.M. Dworkin, *A Matter of Principle*, Cambridge (MA): Harvard University Press, 1985, pp. 9 ff.; P.P. Craig, "Formal and substantive conceptions", pp. 54–5. See also G. Zagrebelsky, *Il diritto mite. Legge, diritti, giustizia*, Torino: Einaudi, 1992, pp. 147 ff.; G. Alpa, *L'arte di giudicare*, passim; E. Scoditti, *Il contropotere giudiziario. Saggio di riforma costituzionale*, Napoli: E.S.I., 1999. An excellent critique of the recurrent aporias of the rule of law is to be found in M. Troper, "Le concept d'État de droit", pp. 51 ff.
207. Voltaire, *A Philosophical Dictionary*, in *The Works of Voltaire*, ed. by John Morley, notes by Tobias Smollett, tr. by W.F. Fleming, New York: E.R. Du Mont, 1901, p. 332.

PART II

THE RULE OF LAW IN EUROPE AND THE UNITED STATES

CHAPTER 3

THE RULE OF LAW AND THE "LIBERTIES OF THE ENGLISH": THE INTERPRETATION OF ALBERT VENN DICEY

Emilio Santoro

1 LAW AND THE LIBERTIES OF THE ENGLISH

At the close of the seventeenth century, following the Glorious Revolution and the victory of the Parliamentarians, it was widely believed among the English that the "rule of law" had been established and that individual liberty would therefore be assured. Jurists and political theorists began to maintain that judicial procedures, the public nature of trials, and the rules relating to evidence, together with the role of the jury, ensured solid legal guarantees to those accused of any crime, by protecting the fundamental rights of their countrymen.

The rhetoric accompanying the battle fought in seventeenth-century England against monarchical absolutism did not put direct emphasis on subjective rights and freedom but raised the banner of objective law. Sir Edward Coke's arguments best exemplify this attitude. In his works the cry for liberty is drowned by his exaltation of the "law" as the primary condition for freedom itself: "the law is the surest sanctuary, that a man can take, and the strongest fortress to protect the weakest of all".[1] The objective application of the laws and the action of the courts provide individuals with a protection, Coke's[2] "birth right", that enables everyone to keep safe his goods, lands, wife, heirs, body, life, and honour.

The law invoked by Coke was none other than "common law". Common law was considered to be the source of liberty, the legal apparatus limiting the power of the monarch, and protecting personal freedom. Whig[3] rhetoric owed its legitimacy to the fact that, during the seventeenth century, common law had almost eliminated feudal differences of status, ensuring the near equality of English subjects before the law (with the notable exception of women). The relationship between feudal lords and tenants had, by then, come to be based on abstract rights as defined by the Royal courts, and were beyond a landlord's discretion.[4] Certainly, as Douglas Hay[5] has pointed out, the conquests of the civil war proved to be essential for the protection of the gentry – the newly enriched merchant class, which, during the seventeenth century

P. Costa and D. Zolo (eds.), The Rule of Law: History, Theory and Criticism, 153–199.

had begun to rival landowners for the control of English society – against the greed and tyranny of the monarch. One of the anti-monarchists' main victories was the establishment of a normative framework guaranteeing the protection of basic rights in fundamental areas, such as the transfer of property, inheritance laws, contracts, wills, and writs. The fact that these achievements were grafted on to the well established tradition of common law greatly favoured their stability.

Since its very early stages, common law had been characterized by a system of writs designed to safeguard relations between citizens dealing with each other on a par. A seventeenth-century Englishman might well have had the impression of conducting his life within the framework of horizontal legal relationships among formally equal citizens. The vertical dimension was based on the relationship between the citizen and his sovereign, who could not, by definition, damage or encroach upon the rights of his subjects, which made it impossible for him to be called to judgement or to answer for his actions. In theory, then, citizens' rights were not guaranteed in the case of arbitrary action by the sovereign. But the sovereign's immunity was soon neutralized by the judicial doctrine that, as Blackstone writes,[6] while it was impossible for the king to "misuse his power, without the advice of evil counsellors, and the assistance of wicked ministers, these men may be examined and punished". On the basis of this doctrine a citizen could claim for damages he had suffered from the Crown, i.e. from the state, and though the king in person could not be called into question, the particular minister, or public official, considered responsible for the abuse had to answer for it. The courts did not recognize him as having any particular privileges: ministers and public officials, like any private citizen, had to answer for damages caused. During the eighteenth century, therefore, public authority came to be subsumed in the horizontal dimension of the legal framework: the absolute equality of all before the law was guaranteed. All English subjects, regardless of rank, would be tried by the same judges in the higher courts according to the same principles; as Hay[7] has pointed out, justice could be said to be assured even to the poorest man.

This situation constituted a formidable basis for the legitimization of Whig rhetoric, presenting England as the "kingdom of law and equality". The Whigs, reacting to the monarch's attempt to import legal-political models from the continent in order to legitimize the consolidation of his own power, re-elaborated the relevant tracts of the common law. They upgraded its role from a mere organizational instrument resolving daily legal disputes to the central pivot of the constitution. Whig rhetoric covers this slide: from championing the equality of all Englishmen before the law it passes to the exaltation of the law as the custodian of the nation's liberty. Herein lies the shift that gave birth to the myth of the rule of law and of "the liberty of the English".

In the period that spans from the end of the seventeenth century to the mid nineteenth century, a host of diaries, letters, memoirs, and works by notable jurists reflected this Whig self-glorification. The remarks of occasional travellers bear witness to the admiration that the English legal system aroused among continental visitors. As early as in the eighteenth century, foreigners were struck by the care and attention given by judges to the rights of the accused, a solicitude not equalled in the law courts of any other nation. By the seventeenth century, England was seen as a country, in which torture was practically unknown and where the executive power had already been curtailed by an independent judicial system. England certainly owed this image to the Revolution Settlement and the common law tradition, which imposed limits on the discretionary power of the executive. Above all, however, this perception stemmed from the belief that the common people were quite capable of forcefully reminding the magistrates of the rights of "free-born Englishman", which comprised freedom of association, freedom of the press and, to a lesser extent, religious freedom.

In the 1970s the idea that, following the Glorious Revolution and the Whig victory, 1689 witnesses the emergence of a constitutional system based upon the law and capable of guaranteeing the "rights of Englishmen" became the focus of studies by Edward P. Thompson and his followers, Douglas Hay in particular. The results of their research caused considerable controversy.[8] Thompson and Hay substantially accepted the Whig rhetoric. They maintained that a system of government based on the rule of law actually came into being in England in the eighteenth century and they accepted that this was a fundamental step forward in Western political development. A system of government offering effective protection to the rights of citizens, they argued, had been outlined for the very first time. The lower classes, religious dissidents, and politicians in post-revolutionary England enjoyed a degree of real "constitutional" guarantees and were in a position to appreciate the protection of "the Rule of Law" against the "Rule of Might".

Thompson did emphasize that recognizing the basic historical truth at the heart of Whig propaganda does not amount to the wholesale acceptance of the idea that the revolution heralded the administration of "impartial" justice in English society. Historical research tells us otherwise. Thompson maintained that "the English revolution of the seventeenth century, although defeated in many of its aspirations, created a system of legal boundaries to the power, which, however manipulated, produced a relevant cultural achievement".[9] According to Hay and Thompson, English culture and rhetoric in the eighteenth century were deeply imbued with the concept of "law". Law came to be affirmed as a dominant value, the ideological pivot of a whole society. It undermined religion and laid new foundations for the organization of the society:

> The hegemony of the eighteenth-century gentry and aristocracy was expressed, above all, not in military force, not in the mystification of a priesthood or of the press, not even in economic coercion, but in the rituals of the study of the Justices of the Peace, in the quarter-sessions, in the pomp of Assizes and in the theatre of Tyburn.[10]

Reference to the gallows at Tyburn is significant. Thompson and Hay were keen to point out that the criminal code and its application amounted to a sort of didactic "theatre" allowing Whig ideology to permeate into social life.[11] Hay in particular emphasized that the criminal code, more than any other social institution, made it possible to govern England in the eighteenth century without the need of a police force or of a large army.[12] The guarantees characterizing criminal procedures are certainly surprising when compared with standards in continental Europe at the same time:

> Many prosecutions founded on excellent evidence and conducted at considerable expense failed on minor errors of form in the indictment, the written charge. [...] If a name or date was incorrect, or if the accused was described as a 'farmer' rather than the approved term 'yeoman', the prosecution could fail. The courts held that such defects were conclusive, and gentlemen attending trials as spectators sometimes stood up in court and brought errors to attention of the judge. [...] The punctilious attention to forms, the dispassionate and legalistic exchanges between counsel and the judge, argued that those administering and using the laws submitted to its rules.[13]

The exaltation of the English system, despite its often brutal severity, is more readily understood when it is compared to that of the French. In France the institution of the *lettre de cachet* allowed the police[14] to remove an individual and keep him imprisoned indefinitely, without a specific charge.[15]

Despite the existence of procedural guarantees and trial by jury England should not be seen as the realm of "mild" criminal justice.[16] Here, perhaps more than elsewhere, the need was perceived more keenly to establish criteria and to ensure fixed and moderate[17] punishments proportionally suited to the crime, to create an effective system of prevention that avoided mere displays of arbitrary severity.[18]

The English criminal system in the eighteenth century could certainly not be described as "impartial". The majority of offences were configured in such a way as to almost always end up being committed by the poor. A feeling of equality before the law was nevertheless reinforced by famous cases of gentlemen and nobles on the gallows: their "martyrdom" seemed to demonstrate that law was sovereign in England. It should be added that the poor were also very often the victims, as well as the perpetrators of murder and theft, and that the severity of the law and its zealous application safeguarded their interests, as well as those of the gentlemen who saw to its administration.[19]

The Whig strategy of maintaining order clearly hinged upon the obvious and often harsh concern with the protection of property. This, however, hinged upon the law, and was accompanied by the moral and economic aversion to the creation of a police state.[20] In the course of the eighteenth century the law increasingly provided the reference point, as well as the framework for the new economic and social order. Landed property was regulated by inalienable bonds. Marriage agreements were articulated according to the complexities of common law. Most importantly, the unassailable fortress of the law constituted a formidable obstacle to monarchical absolutism. But, as Hay stresses, the efforts made by the ruling class to appear spontaneously subjected to the rule of law proved to be of the greatest import. This class, in fact, strove to present the law, by virtue of its equity and of the universal character of its norms, organs, and procedures, as the source legitimizing its hold on power. This attitude provoked what Thompson[21] has defined as a process of osmosis between legal ideology and popular culture: the law was perceived as an important conquest in the eyes of the agricultural and mercantile middle classes, and remained an essential point of reference for the yeomen and craftsmen who supported them.

The law was established as a corpus of norms, procedures, and values legitimizing the power of the dominant classes. Thompson[22] points out that, when it takes on the role of a legitimizing ideology, the law inevitably acquires autonomy and an identity, and develops its own logic, "which may, on occasion, inhibit power and afford some protection to the powerless". And so, in his opinion, the legitimizing function bestowed by the Whigs upon the law made it difficult to present the law as a mere instrument serving the interests of one group above another. An openly unjust law would not be able to cover any one party's abuse of power, and would therefore prove useless as a form of legitimization. The law conceived of as a set of norms, procedures, and structures had to be devoid of flagrant manipulation if it were to fulfil a legitimizing function. It had to appear substantially just. Eighteenth-century England was not a society of consensus. The law was employed explicitly to impose the predominance of a certain class, and at the same time – protected this class against the monarchy and represented this class's source of legitimacy. The upshot of this was that the law could not be considered a pliable instrument to be handled by anyone with a share in power. It was from this peculiar context, according to Thompson's analysis, that the figure of the "free-born Englishman" emerged. This individual was assured of the inviolability of his privacy and freedom, and protected by *Habeas Corpus*; he would have been fully convinced of the equality of all men before the law.

During the protracted clash between the monarchy and the parliamentarians, which had successive phases throughout the sixteenth and seventeenth centuries, the law was not an instrument in the hands of either party but rather the prize at stake. By the time the gentry inherited the law as modified by the Glorious Revolution, law had become a bastion against royal absolutism and the abuse of power. In the eighteenth century, the victors considered the law to be the key to the control of power, as well as to safeguarding their goods, property, and wealth. In the course of the revolution Whigs came to believe that only the law could protect their property and lives from the abuse of monarchical power and aristocratic arrogance.[23]

This peculiar historical situation, writes Thompson,[24] engendered the rule of law as "an unqualified good". Thompson admits that in a society divided by class conflict the action of the law does not correspond to justice; but he emphasizes that its positive action should not be belittled, and that the workings of a legal "proceduralization" with recorded acts is a far cry from the mere implementation of brute force.

The instrument chosen by the ruling classes to defend their interests and to legitimize their power had inbuilt mechanisms that prevented them from using it to their exclusive advantage. Whig rhetoric about the law therefore contributed to the creation of the legal ideology connected to the "rights of the free-born Englishman", albeit in a somewhat circular manner. The peculiar nature of law soon lent the rhetoric substance:

> [T]he rulers were, in serious senses, whether willingly or unwillingly, the prisoners of their own rhetoric [...] they played the games of power according to rules which suited them, but they could not break those rules or the whole game would be thrown away.[25]

According to this historiographical current, therefore, the particular development of the Glorious Revolution, which took up the ideological stance of Coke and other jurists, created a situation in which

> Not only were the rulers (indeed, the ruling class as a whole) inhibited by their own rules of law against the exercise of direct unmediated force (arbitrary imprisonment, the employment of troops against the crowd, torture, and those other conveniences of power

with which we are all conversant), but ideological rhetoric, to allow, in certain limited areas, the law itself to be a genuine forum within which certain kinds of class conflict were fought out.[26]

The fact that the law being invoked was identified first and foremost with common law softened the otherwise traumatic impact of the coming of private property in its modern conception, and favoured the establishment of this model. Common law is after all a manifestly historical construction, formed out of layers of judicial precedent and interpretation, and therefore very difficult to change *ex abrupto*. These characteristics dragged "law" into the battlefield where the social conflict was being fought. Together with their legal rhetoric the Whigs used the "law" as the main instrument for imposing a new definition of property: they abolished by decree the habitual but ill-defined rights to the use of land, thus encouraging and reinforcing the practice of enclosure. The struggle between the classes became manifest in the conflict between the written law passed by Parliament and customary law. At the basis, it was a clash between two distinct conceptions and practices of property and its relative rights. The conflict unfolded before the Common Law Courts, and was therefore highly proceduralized. Copyholders – whose right to land had been endorsed by legal decisions – fought effectively in the courts, when they were able to pay a lawyer. In certain cases where they were able to cite common law, they even came out victorious. This situation changed, in part, the nature of the conflict; the emphasis shifted from the question of the property itself to a question of legal procedure. Every time landowners tried to obstruct the judicial path adopted by copyholders, they triggered violent popular reactions. The battle to defend the interests of those expelled from the countryside was transformed into "a fight for their rights", i.e. a campaign for defending their rights in front of a court.[27]

In the wake of Thompson's interpretation, other British historians praised the virtues of the rule of law as a strategy for integrating the social classes. The idea that Whig rhetoric about the rule of law had helped Britain avoid a crisis after the French Revolution gained much favour. It allowed many anti-Jacobins, first of all Edmund Burke, to argue plausibly for the Glorious Revolution against the ideological strain developed by the French Revolution. This, according to Harvie,[28] provides the key to understanding social conflict in the first half of the nineteenth century. Faced with social disorders from 1790 to 1832, the English ruling classes might have chosen to abandon the egalitarian ideology of the *rule of law* and its universal connotations, to abolish the complex system of legal constrains afforded by the Constitution and to transform their power into a violent machinery of repression. Indeed, they took some steps in this direction, as the campaign against Paine, the Combination Acts (1799–1800), the Peterloo Massacre (1819), and the Six Acts (1820) seem to suggest. In the end, however, the ruling classes preferred to take the path of legality instead of shattering their own image and repudiating one and a half centuries of constitutional legitimacy. In contrast to what had happened in other European countries, the government maintained order by applying the law, and did not resort to arbitrary measures. Even at the peak of Chartist[29] agitation, while the lower classes experienced repression, they also enjoyed constitutional protection and legal guarantees. Electoral reform and the extension of the suffrage in 1832 served to revitalize the image of the law and reinforced the idea of a state ruling impartially according to the law. Great Britain was thus able to weather 1848 without any of the dramatic repercussions experienced on the continent. According to Harvie, the Reform Act of 1832 restored the credibility of the law as an impartial instrument to limit social and political conflict.[30] In this interpretation the Reform Act performed the same function that Thompson recognized in the judicial system, which grew out of the Glorious Revolution.

Similarly, McKibbin[31] argues that the preservation and rigorous application of the rule of law saved the legitimacy of the prevailing system in the face of social conflict at the end of the eighteenth and in the early nineteenth century. The struggle between trade unions and entrepreneurs was carried out in a correct legal context, and this once again lent credibility to *fair play* and "the rule of law", which were shown to be more than empty slogans. Those in power recognized that to "tinker" with the law so as to affect the operation of the labour market and tip the balance against the workers, as well as resorting to coercive measures, would prove ideologically indefensible and politically risky. In view of these risks, statesmen such as Peel, Gladstone, and Disraeli aimed to build up a *liberal consensus* founded on the rule of law and designed to make a class-based society acceptable to the lower orders.[32] Their success was largely determined by the pre-existence of an established order of ideas. They did not have to invent a tradition out of nothing: they restored the constitutional myth that had been developed by the Whigs, reviving the rhetoric of the Puritan Revolution and of its aftermath.

2 DICEY'S CONSTITUTIONAL THEORY: THE RULE OF LAW AND PARLIAMENTARY SOVEREIGNTY

Whig rhetoric and historiography covering the political events of the last 300 years in Britain seem to put forward the *rule of law* as the secret which allowed the "rights of the English" first to emerge and then to be gradually affirmed as the fundamental basis of the social order. Paradoxically, however, no jurist had attempted an exact definition of the *rule of law* until the end of the nineteenth century. Up until then, no one had tried to identify the fulcrum of Great Britain's constitutional apparatus, nor had anybody asked what it was that made this system so unequalled in the whole of Europe when it came to maintaining individual freedom. Albert Venn Dicey tackled these issues in his *Introduction to the Study of the Law of the Constitution* of 1885. In this work he described the workings of the English constitutional system and identified the *rule of law*[33] as its main pivot.

Dicey's treatise is remarkable for its clarity, and represents the first strictly legal approach to English public law, which up to then had been dominated by historical studies. These qualities ensured *The Law of the Constitution* an immediate and enduring success. To this day, it is the cornerstone of English constitutional law studies. No previous work can be said to deal with British law from such a perspective – it is almost as though Dicey invented British jurisprudence studies. This impression is further reinforced by the mandatory discussion of Dicey's theories[34] in almost every work on constitutional history and analysis published in the last 30 years. Today in Great Britain jurists and political scientists discuss and criticize the theories embodied in *The Law of the Constitution*, more than 100 years after its appearance.

Reading Dicey today, we must bear in mind the contemporary context in legal theory. Late nineteenth-century legal theory in England had been dominated by the ideas of John Austin. Austin maintained that in order to exist as such, a state required a sovereign body whose competence was not predefined, whose power could not be limited. This theory gained ground easily as it seemed to re-propose, in more general terms, that fundamental element of Whig constitutional rhetoric (second only to the rule of law), i.e. the principle of parliamentary sovereignty.[35] One of the reasons for the success of *The Law of the Constitution* was that it perfectly blended Austin's theory with the Whig tradition rooted in the achievements of the Glorious Revolution; Dicey maintained that both parliamentary sovereignty and the rule of law[36] were the two fundamental principles of the English constitution. Having linked these two ideas, Dicey maintained that *the rule of law* was not capable of limiting the power of the whole state, but of government exclusively. In arguing this, Dicey was close to the notion of the *Rechtsstaat*, which was emerging at the same time on the continent. The rule of law was presented as the best form of protection against the arbitrary action of executive power:

[A] study of European politics now and again reminds English readers that wherever there is discretion there is room for arbitrariness, and that in a republic no less than under a monarchy discretionary authority on the part of the government must mean insecurity for legal freedom on the part of its subjects.[37]

The unlimited nature of parliamentary sovereignty, which is dealt with in the first part of *The Law of the Constitution*, seems, by contrast, to pose few problems. According to Dicey, the principle of parliamentary sovereignty implies that Parliament has the right to make or abolish any law and no organ or individual in Great Britain has the right to ignore parliamentary legislation. In other words the principle of parliamentary sovereignty implies that every Act, or section of an Act, creates new law, or abrogates or modifies an existing one, and must therefore be observed by the courts. On the basis of this principle no person or organ has the right to abrogate or ignore parliamentary legislation, nor to issue rules, requiring enforcement by the courts, conflicting with Acts of Parliament.[38] Dicey opens the chapter on "The Nature of Parliamentary Sovereignty" in this way:

Parliament can legally legislate on any topic whatsoever which, in the judgement of Parliament, is a fit subject for legislation. There is no power which, under the English constitution, can come into rivalry with the legislative sovereignty of Parliament. Not one of the limitations alleged to be imposed by law on the absolute authority of Parliament has any real existence, or receives any countenance, either from the statute-book or from the practice of the Courts.[39]

His interpretation of the legislative sovereignty of Parliament is therefore close to Austin's: Parliament is sovereign as holder of an absolute power, and its power cannot be limited by any agent. Any measure defining the limits of its power would necessarily create a "non-sovereign" Parliament. Dicey makes it quite clear that such a conception of parliamentary sovereignty rules out the distinction, adopted by jurists on the continent, between constitutional (or fundamental) laws and ordinary laws. This distinction is based in fact on criteria that either have to do with the formal aspect of laws, or are related to their mode of production. While in Great Britain

[T]here is no law which Parliament cannot change, or (to put the same thing somewhat differently), fundamental or so-called constitutional laws are under our constitution changed by the same body and in the same manner as other laws, namely, by Parliament acting in its ordinary legislative character.[40]

The English constitution, therefore, which is by definition founded on the sovereignty of Parliament, does not provide a list of fundamental or unalterable rights. The sovereignty of Parliament, according to Dicey,[41]

is incompatible with the existence of a pact defining the competence of *every* authority. The legislative power of Parliament has no limits, *moreover* no organ exists that can annul legislation on the grounds that it has violated constitutional principles, and even less so on the grounds of having overridden the citizen's fundamental rights.[42] Dicey is nonetheless anxious to emphasize that Parliament holds legal, but not political, sovereignty. The latter belongs to the electorate. There does not however appear to be any "constitutional" guarantee protecting the "rights of Englishmen". Parliament is unhampered by any legal restrictions and is only subject to political ones (both internal and external).[43] As with the *Rechtsstaat* theory prevailing on the continent, the legislator is only subject to political control.

The second and more extensive section of *The Law of the Constitution* is devoted to the other essential principle of the constitution, the rule of law. Dicey first analyses the constitutional *status* of the individual's rights to freedom; he gives ample space to personal liberty as guaranteed by the *habeas corpus writs* and dwells in detail on freedom of assembly and freedom of speech and of debate. This section includes a chapter on martial law and Dicey's celebrated discussion of administrative law.

In the fourth chapter of the book, "The Rule of Law: Its Nature and General Applications", Dicey stresses that the supremacy of the *rule of law* determines three fundamental aspects of the United Kingdom constitutional order:

> [I]n virtue of the 'supremacy of the rule of law' in Great Britain no man is punishable ... except for a distinct breach of law established in the ordinary legal manner before the ordinary Courts of the land.[44]

The absorption into the constitution of the fundamental principles of liberalism is therefore attributed to the absolute supremacy of the rule of law. This primacy ensures that the constitution embodies above all else the principle of strict legality: every action by the government infringing upon the sphere of individual liberty or private property has to be ratified by law. Secondly, the constitution lays down the principle of the uniqueness of the legal subject, regardless of status or rank. The reference to the "ordinary courts" in the passage quoted above draws attention to the singularity of Dicey's formulation of the second principle, which underlines the equality of all before the law, as well as the equal subjection of all to the same jurisdiction:

> [W]e mean ..., when we speak of the 'rule of law' as a characteristic of our country, not only that with us no man is above the law, but (what is a different thing) that here every man, whatever be his rank or condition, is subject to the ordinary law of the realm and amenable to the jurisdiction of the ordinary tribunals.[45]

The principle of the rule of law demands more than the mere equality of all before the law: it imposes the submission of everyone to the same laws administered by the same courts. Dicey here splits the liberal doctrine of the uniqueness of legal status into two principles: he insists both on the traditional one that the law should be the same for all and adds that so should the jurisdiction. This second principle causes the English constitutional system to sharply diverge from the continental ones, which normally only recognize the principle of the competence of the judge as established by law.

Dicey's insistence on the importance of the uniqueness of jurisdiction is central to his conception of the rule of law and is also instrumental in his attack on administrative law. He stresses, in fact, that the possibility of the executive making untoward use of discretionary power can only be ruled out if the principle of the same jurisdiction is combined with the principle of legality. The principle of legality does not alone suffice to guarantee the absolute predominance of ordinary law or to exclude the exercise of arbitrary power, privilege, or the abundant use of discretionary power by the government. The only guarantee is provided by "the equal subjection of all classes to the ordinary law of the land administered by the ordinary law courts". Only this equal subjection can preclude the possibility of any exemption of public officials or others from the jurisdiction of the ordinary tribunals; a selective observation of ordinary law is thus prevented and ordinary law remains applicable to all. France is chosen to exemplify the continental system and many examples are provided of how there officials "are, or have been, in their official capacity, to some extent exempted from the ordinary law of the land, protected from the jurisdiction of the ordinary tribunals, and subject in certain respects only to official law administered by official bodies"[46].

Equality before the law and the illegitimacy of administrative law and administrative tribunals are therefore presented by Dicey as two sides of the same coin, in accordance with the tradition of common law dating back at least to Blackstone:

> In England the idea of legal equality, or of the universal subjection of all classes to one law administered by the ordinary courts, has been pushed to its utmost limit. With us every official, from the Prime Minister down to a constable or a collector of taxes, is under the same responsibility for every act done without legal justification as any other citizen. The Reports abound with cases in which officials have been brought before the courts, and made, in their personal capacity, liable to punishment, or to payment of damages, for acts done in their official character but in excess of their lawful authority.[47]

The principle of the uniqueness of jurisdiction neither exempts the activities of public officials from being regulated by *additional* particular laws, which are not to be applicable to the private citizen, nor does it prevent that special courts should try these officials for the infringement of these special regulations. Nevertheless, Dicey insists on the principle that official status should not guarantee privilege. A public official, whatever his rank, cannot exploit his position to escape the duties of the ordinary citizen.[48] This was not found to be the case in continental Europe, and France in particular, where the system of administrative law was based on the principle that controversies involving the government and its officials were not subject to the judgment of the ordinary courts, and should be dealt with by ad hoc organs.[49] By establishing the illegitimacy of administrative law, the *rule of law* guaranteed that the equality and rights of citizens were safer in England than in France; the statement that "all persons are subject to one and the same law, or that the Courts are supreme throughout the state"[50] could not be said to hold true for France.

We now come to the third aspect of the constitution deriving from the supremacy of the rule of law. Dicey considers this not to be a normative principle but an historical fact; it is presented as a specific outcome of the English tradition of common law and therefore a characteristic of the "English Constitution", which sharply distinguishes it from its European counterparts. He affirms that the constitution of Great Britain

> is pervaded by the rule of law on the ground that the general principles of the constitution (as for example the right to personal liberty, or the right of public meeting) are with us the result of judicial decisions determining the rights of private persons in particular cases brought before the Courts; whereas under many foreign constitutions the security (such as it is) given to the rights of individuals results, or appears to result, from the general principles of the constitution.[51]

Dicey does not treat this third aspect of the rule of law as a principle, unlike the others, and omits to stress its normative valence. He rather describes it as a representative of the core of truth in the by and large "erroneous", though constantly repeated, idea that "the constitution has not been made but has grown". Dicey does not make use of this Whig notion, which at the time was still dogma in English legal theory,[52] to legitimize the whole of the constitutional structure. Moreover he wanted to reveal the absurdity, once and for all, of the notion that in Great Britain "the form of government is a sort of spontaneous growth so closely bound up with the life of a people that we can hardly treat it as a product of human will and energy". As John Stuart Mill argued, this idea is logically untenable: every legal norm is the product of active human will, quite unlike a tree that, once planted, continues to grow of its own accord.[53] The important historical fact that can and should be extrapolated from Whig rhetoric concerning the spontaneous development of the constitution is that it was not created all at once. The theory that "the English constitution has not been made but has grown" has the exclusive merit of indicating, if only in "a vague and imprecise way" the *fact* that the constitution is one created by judges, with all the advantages and disadvantages of judge-made law. In particular it casts light on the essential fact that the "liberties of the English" "far from being the result of legislation, in the ordinary sense of that term, are the fruit of contests carried on in the Courts on behalf of the rights of individuals".[54]

The third aspect of the rule of law is therefore not presented as a principle, but as a "formula" clarifying that the laws, which are normally part of the Constitution in continental Europe, in Great Britain "are not the source but the consequence of the rights of individuals, as defined and enforced by the Courts".[55] This "formula" does not fix the limits of the constitutional legitimacy of norms and institutions: it is, rather, a simple reminder that the English constitution is not the fruit of extraordinary activity bent on its creation but "the result of ordinary law". One might think that Dicey here attributes a prescriptive content to this "formula", insofar that it may indicate what he believes to be the correct way forwards. He does not appear to think, however, that the constitution can continue to develop in a jurisprudential manner.[56] In highlighting this third aspect of the rule of law, Dicey's main concern remains to emphasize the different origins of the English and European constitutions.

His real interest is in stressing that, in England, as opposed to Europe, the courts, with the help of Parliament, are the fundamental agents in the constitutional process, and have incorporated rights traditionally guaranteed by common law into the constitution:

> [T]he principles of private law have with us been by the action of the Courts and Parliament so extended as to determine the position of the Crown and of its servants.[57]

In this process courts and Parliament have not played the same role and should not be considered on the same level. Parliament, acting as a legislative body, has limited itself to ordering and incorporating the jurisprudential output of the courts. When it has performed a creative role in the process of incorporating law into the constitution, it has done so in its role as High Court of the country, not as its legislative organ.[58] The process has been one of re-elaboration of common law, not one of creation of new law.[59]

Dicey claims that if judge-made rights were to be codified, the constitution of Great Britain would be identical to those of Europe. He compares the English constitution to the Belgian one, which was approved at the end of the nineteenth century, to demonstrate his thesis. The Belgian constitution was considered a model in so far as it had been designed as "an admirable summary of the leading maxims of English constitutionalism". The idea common in Europe that Great Britain had no constitution at all, and that there are no constitutionally guaranteed rights, argues Dicey, is therefore absurd. If we compare the continental constitutions with English legal provisions, and above all with those of judicial origin, we realize that the English constitution with its fundamental core of rights guaranteeing liberty exists, though it is not sanctioned by any single document. It contains none of the declaration of rights that are typical of the constitutions of other countries. The protection of personal freedom comes from judicial decisions: constitutional rights are no more than the generalization of these decisions.

Dicey's aim is to show that the "English constitution" ensures rights as effectively as the continental ones, and that the difference in the origin of these rights is merely formal, not having a real bearing on their effective guarantee. In the development of his argument, however, the judicial creation of rights slowly ceases to be mere historical fact. Dicey almost imperceptibly shifts the argument and transforms the "formula", which should only serve to remind us of the origin of English rights, to a position of central importance in his conception of the rule of law. The fact that laws ensuring freedom are the circumstantial result of judicial decisions becomes the fundamental guarantee of their enjoyment. The point here is that these laws, described by Dicey as "constitutional principles", are not the fruit of some official proclamation, but were created in response to particular cases brought before the courts. The real problem, he continues, is not that the absence of a written constitution in Great Britain makes for difficulties in the defence of individual rights but that those same rights are badly protected by written constitutions. The relationship between individual rights and the constitution in countries like Great Britain, where such rights are founded on the deliberations of the courts, is very different from the relationship between individual rights and the constitutions of continental Europe, where fundamental charters are produced by a constituent act. In these countries

> the rights of individuals to personal liberty flow from or are secured by the constitution. In England the right to individual liberty is part of the constitution, because it is secured by the decisions of the Courts, extended or confirmed as they are by the *Habeas Corpus* Acts.[60]

According to Dicey[61] the constitutions of the different European countries were devoted exclusively to "defining" individual rights, and gave scant attention to the need to provide for the protection of those rights. Dicey accentuates the effective execution given by the courts to the constitutional dispositions and further stresses the pertinence, especially in matters of constitutional law, of the Latin saying *ubi jus ibi remedium*. Often, in fact, constitutional rights are no more than empty declarations.[62] But the English have a guarantee in that they

> gradually framed the complicated set of laws and institutions which we call the Constitution, fixed their minds far more intently on providing remedies for the enforcement of particular rights or (what is merely the same thing looked at from the other side) for averting definite wrongs, than upon any declaration of the Rights of Man or of Englishmen.[63]

In other words, the judicial production of measures protecting individual rights has a clear advantage both over the legislative process and over the declaration of rights: the judicial alternative, by its very procedures, creates an inseparable link between the methods used to protect rights and the right to be guaranteed. The English constitutional system therefore has the great advantage that laws relating to rights, such as *Habeas Corpus* Acts, only articulate the guarantees created by the courts. These constitutional laws, according to Dicey, do not proclaim any principle or define any right, but "are for practical purposes worth a hundred constitutional articles guaranteeing individual liberty".[64]

Individual rights provided for by the constitutions of continental Europe are mere "deductions" drawn from constitutional principles. The constitutional provision of rights offers the citizen no protection against the suppression or suspension of those rights; in fact, it favours it. This is evident in those countries where the validity of the declaration of rights is frequently suspended. The fact that they are laid down in a special regulatory text, that they are "something extraneous to and independent of the ordinary course of the law", makes them more easy to set aside without upsetting normal legal procedures. Thus constitutional provision that in theory aims to reinforce the protection of fundamental rights by preventing Parliament from tampering with them, and which requires the whole of the constitution to be explicitly modified in order to do so, ultimately undermines them.[65]

History shows that rights regarding personal freedom are better guaranteed in England, where "the law of the constitution is little else than a generalisation of the rights which the Courts secure to individuals",[66] and where it makes no sense to talk of 'fundamental' rights or of some rights more guaranteed than others.[67] The experience of the nineteenth century demonstrates that, where the only safeguard to personal freedom is provided by constitutional principles, the validity of the constitutional charter often ends up being suspended or abrogated. In Great Britain, on the other hand, rights concerning freedom have always been perceived as part of "ordinary law"; it is inconceivable that they could be disregarded "without a thoroughgoing revolution in the institutions and manners of the nation". The historical basis of the judicial production of constitutional rights, the third aspect of the rule of law, represents an important daily guarantee of a citizen's right to freedom even though it is not a precept. It is this third historical-factual aspect that prompts Dicey to maintain that in Great Britain,

> the constitution being based on the rule of law, the suspension of the constitution, as far as such a thing can be conceived possible, would mean with us nothing less than a revolution.[68]

3 THE RULE OF LAW AND PARLIAMENTARY SOVEREIGNTY IN THE TRADITION OF COMMON LAW

Having clarified what Dicey means by the rule of law and by the sovereignty of Parliament we are now faced with a problem of compatibility between these two principles. This is probably the most controversial issue for British constitutionalists.

Writers who are most sensitive to the protection of fundamental rights have severely criticized the conception of parliamentary sovereignty elaborated by Dicey. He stands accused of not having understood that, as August Friedrich von Hayek writes:

> The whole history of constitutionalism, at least since John Locke, which is the same as the history of liberalism, is that of a struggle against the positivist conception of sovereignty and the allied conception of the omnipotent state.[69]

Dicey failed, they argue, to take into account that, without the imposition of precise limits on legislative power, the rights and liberties that the common law traditionally guarantees in Great Britain could be abolished by Parliament overnight. Here Dicey's theory was not only criticized on an "ideological" level but had its legal validity called into question. In the opinion of these critics of Dicey, parliamentary sovereignty is not one of the principles of the English constitution. Geoffrey De Q. Walker, for example, refers to "Dicey's dubious dogma of parliamentary sovereignty", accusing *The Law of the Constitution* of being "like some huge, ugly Victorian monument that dominates the legal and constitutional landscape and exerts a hypnotic effect on legal perception".[70]

Dicey's critics maintain that *The Law of the Constitution* is marred by a legislation-centred reading of the constitutional system. They accuse him of having reduced the principle of the rule of law to a mere "rule of recognition". They interpret the notion of the rule of law in the light of the "sovereignty of Parliament", then Dicey stands accused of affirming that Parliament is "the source of ultimate political authority, which is free from all legal restraint and from which every legal rule derives its validity".[71] These critics read *The Law of the Constitution* as if it maintained that every act produced by Parliament, in accordance with the norms regulating its activity, should have its validity taken for granted by the courts, without assessing its impact on individual rights and legitimate aspirations. Rather than being the father of British constitutionalism, Dicey is held responsible for having propagated Austin's dogma of parliamentary sovereignty, significantly weakening the safeguards on individual rights.

More charitable critics of *The Law of the Constitution* noted the juxtaposition of the principle of parliamentary sovereignty with that of the rule of law. Such juxtaposition leads to a "pragmatic contradiction"[72] that damages the whole constitutional model. Dicey is therefore accused of proposing a substantially weakened version of English constitutional law, founded on contradictory, uncertain and insecure bases.[73] Supporters of this thesis take it for granted that it is impossible to reconcile the emphasis on the rule of law with the theory of the unlimited sovereignty of Parliament. These writers, too, accuse Dicey of not having been able to resist the influence of Austin's legal positivism,[74] which prevented him from elaborating a coherent vision of the constitution.[75] Allan even goes as far as to postulate the existence of two Diceys: the supporter of parliamentary sovereignty on the one hand, and the constitutionalist struggling to free himself from the chains of the Hobbesian authoritarianism received via Austin,[76] on the other.

Whilst it is true that Dicey's reconstruction of the English constitutional system is a product of its time, his critics too have been strongly influenced by their cultural environment. The crisis surrounding the common law in the second half of the nineteenth century heralded the success of Austin's ideas and of a legislation-centred constitutional theory. This theory was eagerly embraced by the Whig rhetoric on parliamentary sovereignty, and gained favour as a result of the extensions of the electorate between 1866 and 1884, which undoubtedly reinforced parliamentary authority. The dogma of parliamentary sovereignty was at that time so well absorbed by English jurists that any conflicting theory appeared as far removed from reality.[77] It is not therefore surprising that

The Law of the Constitution was immediately received as an Austinian work, and that parliamentary sovereignty, rather than the rule of law, was understood to be its supporting theoretical pillar. Dicey's work was conceived, written, revised, read, and discussed in an environment coloured by Austin's all-pervading influence.[78] It is easy to understand that English jurists of the late nineteenth and of early twentieth century gave the *Law of the Constitution* a legislation-centred interpretation, which carried on as the standard interpretation of the constitutional debate until after the Second World War.[79]

The complexity of the ideal of the rule of law in contrast to the theoretical superficiality and the strongly pragmatic approach adopted by Dicey certainly had a hand in making this interpretation *The Law of the Constitution* the most accepted one. It is difficult to deny, however, that Dicey tried to give content to the rule of law, albeit with an almost complete lack of philosophical sophistication, considering it to be, as he did, the cornerstone of the English constitution. Although he failed to make a clear distinction between constitutional theory and the contingent aspects of British legal institutions,[80] the "durable merit"[81] of his analysis lies in the emphasis he put on the general principles of the Constitution, as has been justly pointed out. By maintaining that the rule of law consists in the application by the courts of the "general principles of the constitution", which are no more than the traditional rights to liberty,[82] Dicey insisted on the necessity of studying the English legal system with regard to the protection of civil liberty, and not only paying attention to the limits placed upon the power of government. The fact that Dicey exaggerated the merits of the British system and the protection that it afforded to fundamental rights in comparison with other western democracies does not mean that he represents it falsely.[83]

Dicey's attack on continental constitutionalism, particularly on the French model, was primarily directed against systems with the power to modify constitutional rights "with the stroke of a pen". The notion of parliamentary sovereignty has to be considered in the light of this debate. For Dicey the English system was superior in that it entrusted a judicial body born out of the tradition of common law, besides and before Parliament, with the safeguarding of rights. Then to put Dicey at odds with the tradition that sees "the liberty of the English" as the pillar of the constitution appears to be a gross misinterpretation of his work.

In *The Law of the Constitution* it is evident that Dicey was proud of the tradition of common law that had protected basic liberties and principles of fairness in England earlier than in other countries. It therefore seems legitimate, both on the historical and theoretical level, to separate his theories from the legislation-centred imposition of Austin and to realign them with the tradition of common law. However strong Austin's influence on Dicey may have been he never maintained that Parliament was the source of every legal measure. Dicey is therefore far removed from the theory of Austin and, earlier, of Hobbes, for whom common law was valid in so far as it was tacitly accepted by the sovereign. My aim is to show here that Dicey, quite to the contrary, maintained that the common law courts were the arbiters of parliamentary authority. *The Law of the Constitution* can be seen as an attempt to outline a common law constitution. In the absence of a real constitutional law, consecrated in a written document venerated as the foundation of legal authority, Dicey charged the *rule of law* with the function of conferring constitutional status to those rights traditionally recognized in English common law. In Dicey's framework, more than in the definition he provides, the rule of law reflects and incorporates ideas and values around which common law has gradually developed. The rule of law is in itself a largely meaningless label, because its contents are determined by common law, which, in the end, defines the characteristics of the constitution.

Dicey sought to show that the rule of law and parliamentary sovereignty were the two principles, which gave rise to the development of English constitutional law. He did not recognize any problem of incompatibility between parliamentary sovereignty and the rule of law; on the contrary, the rule of law was presented not only as being absolutely compatible with the sovereignty of Parliament but also as insolubly linked to it. The supremacy of the law is "intimately" bound to the sovereignty of Parliament and both represent the secure guarantee of individual rights provided by the English constitution. Parliamentary sovereignty and the supremacy of the law are presented as equal notions. This however reduces the rule of law to a mere principle of legality. In other words, if the supremacy of the law is made to coincide with parliamentary sovereignty, the rule of law is reduced, as Dicey's critics maintain, to nothing more than a "rule of recognition" making it difficult to maintain that it ensures the respect of "the freedom of the English".

Dicey explicitly deals with the problem,[84] maintaining that parliamentary sovereignty, as opposed to any other form of sovereign power, favours the supremacy of law, while the predominance of rigorous legality requires the exercise, and therefore increases the authority of parliamentary sovereignty.[85] The two principles are not mutually limiting or conflicting but strengthen one another.

Dicey's line of argument is derived from Austin's assumption that a state, by definition, must have a sovereign body: that is an organ whose power is original, not derived from any norm and therefore without any predefined limits. The argument suggests, at least at first, that the rule of law consists in a mere principle of legality: the behaviour of the executive and administrative authorities in general is legitimate only if they conform to the law. With this in mind, Dicey's theory appears obvious: that the sovereignty of Parliament favours the supremacy of ordinary law. His reasoning seems tautological. If a sovereign body must of necessity exist in a state, only the sovereignty of Parliament can guarantee the rule of law. In fact only Parliament expresses its will through Acts of Parliament. The sovereignty of Parliament and the rule of law guarantee that the executive power can do no more than apply laws passed by Parliament.

Dicey, however, affirms that the relationship between the sovereignty of Parliament and the rule of law, presented as the fundamental characteristic of the English constitution, is not automatic. While it is true that the sovereignty of Parliament, as it has developed in England, promotes the supremacy of the law, this is not found to be the case in all countries that have a parliamentary government.[86] Choosing once again the French model by way of comparison, Dicey maintains that the French National Assembly, whose powers substantially correspond to those of the English Parliament, exercises its sovereignty in a "different spirit". The legacy of the Bourbon monarchy and the Napoleonic Empire encouraged it to interfere in the minutiae of administrative practice and to be diffident in the face of judicial independence and authority. But more importantly it was discouraged from opposing "the system of *droit administratif* which Frenchmen – very likely with truth – regard as an institution suited to their country". This meant that the French National Assembly left ample executive, but also legislative, powers in the hands of the government, powers, which the English Parliament never conceded to the government or its officials.[87]

Although the comparison is to some extent forced, Dicey's analysis grasps an important fact about the English constitutional tradition. The difference between the behaviour of the English Parliament and that of the French National Assembly with regard to public administration originated in the fact that English members of the public administration had never lost their status of "servants of the Crown", even after Parliament's power in government increased. According to Dicey, Parliament's behaviour towards public officials was, in 1915,[88] quite the same as when the "servants of the Crown" had depended on the king, that is, on a power that naturally aroused the suspicion and vigilance of Parliament. The compatibility between the rule of law and the sovereignty of Parliament therefore stemmed from the role of Parliament.

Even when in a sovereign position, Parliament was never able to use the powers of the government to interfere with the regular course of the law – unlike the sovereign monarch, who was not only a legislator but also a governor, and therefore head of the executive power. Even more importantly, Parliament regarded with suspicion the exemption of officials from the ordinary responsibilities of citizens or from the jurisdiction of the ordinary courts, and discouraged it; Parliamentary sovereignty was therefore fatal to the development of 'administrative law'.[89]

Here Dicey provides us with an historical guideline to help us understand the basis of his conception of the rule of law. The relationship between Parliament, government, and the judicial body developed in England from the conflict, in which the courts and Parliament allied against the crown. This conflict saw its most intense period in the seventeenth century and culminated in the victory of the alliance of Parliament and the courts, which, from the eighteenth century onwards, had a free hand in drawing up the constitutional order.[90] Dicey stresses that these events show that Parliament had displayed a tendency to protect the independence of the judiciary, whereas, the monarchy had endeavoured to guarantee public officials in the exercise of their powers.[91] The historical evolution led to a situation in which Parliament was sovereign, but had to exercise its sovereignty in accordance with its ally, the courts. The judicial practice engendered by this peculiar relationship and by its historical roots lends plausibility to the conception of the rule of law proposed in *The Law of the Constitution.*

In order to follow Dicey's reasoning it is useful to take a step backwards and re-examine his comparison between the rule of law and the principle of legality: certainly the most ambiguous and controversial element in Dicey's theory. Dicey often seems to take it for granted that the rule of law does not guarantee any fundamental rights, and is limited to protecting the individual from the arbitrary power of government. Comparing the situation in seventeenth-century England with continental Europe, he recognized that many foreign governments were not particularly oppressive, although there was no country in which citizens were thoroughly protected from the exercise of arbitrary power. In other words, Dicey recognized that England's unusual situation arose not so much from its inherent goodness but from the legality of its system of government.[92] It would therefore seem that the rule of law does not directly define the rights attributable to citizens, but limits itself to guaranteeing the predictability of the actions by the state authorities, the certainty of law. The liberty guaranteed by the rule of law would appear to be a residual liberty: the liberty to do what the law does not prohibit. In a system devoid of a declaration of rights and reliant on rule of law alone, there cannot exist a core of fundamental rights that the law is bound to respect.

The rule of law, therefore, does not refer to a list of fundamental and protected rights but comes to be identified with a mere principle of legality.[93] However if we accept this reduction of the rule of law to a principle of legality, it makes no difference, Dicey maintains,[94] whether individuals are protected from the risk of arbitrary arrest thanks to the personal liberty that a constitution affords them in countries like Belgium, or whether the right to personal freedom and protection from arbitrary arrest is part of the constitution as guaranteed by ordinary law, as is the case in England. It is clear that whilst the constitutional provision of fundamental rights can allow Parliament to abrogate these very rights with the stroke of a pen, the rule of law as a mere principle of legality may protect citizens against arbitrary acts from the executive but cannot offer them absolute guarantees on any of their liberties, for Parliament retains the power to pass extremely restrictive laws whenever it chooses. Such a principle in fact only means that interference with life, liberty, and property has to be authorized by law.

The key to resolving this apparent contradiction in Dicey's theory lies in the emphasis it places on the fact that Parliament only expresses its will through the Acts of Parliament. This, claims Dicey, notably increases the authority of the judiciary. The assumption that by definition – and not by virtue of a constitution limiting parliamentary sovereignty[95] – every law enables the ordinary courts to apply it and to check on its application by any administrative authority is crucial to the idea of the rule of law as elaborated by Dicey. As confirmed by Jennings,[96] the fundamental principle of the English constitution is not the sovereignty of Parliament but the rule according to which the courts apply as law that has been approved according to prescribed legal form.[97] This "rule" allows Dicey to present parliamentary sovereignty and the rule of law, as being not only mutually compatible but actually synergic, and to maintain that the supremacy of the law requires the exercise of parliamentary sovereignty.[98]

But he does not stop here. Dicey also states that it is essential for the enforcement of the rule of law that the courts, as has been traditionally the case in England, only refer to their own texts in interpreting the laws:

> A Bill which has passed into a statute immediately becomes subject to judicial interpretation, and the English bench has always refused, in principle at least, to interpret an Act of Parliament otherwise than by reference to the words of the enactment.[99]

This prescription might seem a ritual genuflection to the principle of the subordination of the courts to the will of the legislator, a reaffirmation of the principle that in France led to the brief introduction of the *référé législatif*.[100] The opposite is the case. By referring judges exclusively to the words of the legal text, Dicey sought to remind them that *they must on no account take into consideration the intention of the legislator*: "An English judge will take no notice ... of the changes which a Bill may have undergone between the moment of its first introduction to Parliament and of its receiving the Royal assent."[101] Dicey believes that this hermeneutic, interpretive rule provides the foundation for maintaining judicial authority and the stability of the law.

The concept of the legislator disappearing, leaving only the legislative text is the vital presupposition in the constitutional system outlined by Dicey: it is the precondition, which allows the courts to exercise their own autonomous normative activity. It in fact creates a framework, in which judicial activity does not follow the work of the legislator, but is independent in its purpose.[102] The courts should not execute the will of the legislator but must amalgamate it with the constitutional tradition incorporated in common law. Behind the interpretive rule preventing judges from considering the law as an expression of the will of Parliament lies the understanding that the judges called to interpret the law are influenced not only by feelings typical of the courts, which, as we have seen, are "jealous" of the executive power, but also by the spirit of the common law. It is this dual attitude of the courts, protected by their fidelity to the letter of the law,[103] which represents the strength of Dicey's conception of the rule of law. This same attitude neutralizes the voluntarism inherent to the principle of the sovereignty of Parliament and ensures the protection of the "freedom of the English".

This doctrine, however strange it may appear to a continental jurist, is not at all eccentric: on the contrary, it is in perfect accord with the tradition of common law. The theory that judges should interpret the law in accordance with "the norms and spirit of the common law" goes back to Sir Edward Coke.[104] Carleton Kemp Allen, in his monumental *Law in the Making*,[105] underlined that Coke's maxim is an "essential guide", ensuring continuity in the development of the law and regulating the impact of new legislative provisions in order to include them in the existing constitutional scheme. As Postema[106] recently reminded us, this tradition and the myth surrounding it have created the conviction that a statute can only be absorbed into English law in so far as it can be integrated into common law. This idea was first aired by Sir Mathew Hale,[107] who, together with Coke, might be considered the founding father of common law. In his *The History of the Common Law,* Hale maintains that the role of the judge is to interpret parliamentary legislation as a corpus of acts declaring common law or, at the most, acts correcting some perceived shortcomings.[108] The theory was widely accepted and appears in Blackstone's celebrated *Commentaries*.[109]

Hale's theory is relevant to our discussion of Dicey's conception of the rule of law because he was the first British jurist who treated, if implicitly, the legislative sovereignty of Parliament and grafted it on to the existing legal tradition. This combined the principle of parliamentary sovereignty with the idea that the common law and the customs of the realm are the important substratum of the law.[110] If the norms of parliamentary production do not find a place in this "substratum" they are deprived of any significant influence in the complex regulatory framework and are therefore incapable of damaging the "rights of Englishmen". Hale's writing clearly anticipates the theory Dicey was to make his own. Hale in fact maintains that Parliament has the power to produce new statues but that these have a limited impact and significance unless incorporated into common law.[111] Without this "incorporation" the legislative act is valid, on the strength of constitutional procedure authorizing its production – defined by Dicey as "sovereignty of Parliament" – but exists exclusively as an isolated act, like a temporary disturbance on the surface of law without leaving an enduring impression.

This way of thinking naturally leads to a theory – similar to twentieth-century legal realism – that legislative acts are not automatically law: judges can, with due caution and deliberation, refuse to accept them as such. As Postema[112] writes, Hale's discussion of this matter is "schematic" but it makes it quite clear which rules, according to the tradition of common law, regulate incorporation of new legislative acts into English law. Statutes are seen as normative acts to be inserted into the framework of the principles of common law, operating on the basis of this same framework. When it appears impossible to follow this interpretive method, because the statute is far removed from the framework defined by common law, the judiciary is bound to give a restrictive interpretation to the language of the legislative norms, in order to preserve the regulatory discipline of common law as far as possible. The judiciary must operate from the assumption that Parliament can restrict or enlarge the scope of these norms of common law but cannot change their substance or add new norms completely outside their frame of reference. They can interpret and apply statutes exclusively on the basis of the traditional legal categories of common law and reconstruct legislative norms that appear far removed from the frame of reference in the light of that "artificial reason and judgement of law" that Coke had raised to the specific dominion of the jurists.

Parliament has the constitutional power even to approve a totally new discipline, not normally allowed in common law, but approval alone does not amount to its recognition as "law": it only becomes "law" when the courts include it in common law, substituting pre-existing regulation. Parliamentary sovereignty in a sense implies not the power to *produce* law but rather to *propose* law, with the understanding that while these proposals might have immediate legal validity, the validity might be short-lived.[113] Parliament therefore exercises legislative sovereignty, but the judiciary remains, to use Lewis Carroll's celebrated quip, the real master of law, establishing the rules on the basis of the principles of common law. The classic theory of common law[114] is founded on the idea that "through interpretation" the judiciary exercises constant "control" over legislation. The dominant principle, emphasized by Allen and forever present in the minds of the judiciary, is that common law has a broader scope and is more fundamental than the statutes passed by Parliament, and therefore "wherever possible – and that means every time that the judges deem it to be opportune – legislative enactment should be construed in harmony with established Common Law principles rather than in antagonism to them".[115]

When inserted into Hale's framework, which was soon accepted as the point of reference for the classical theory of common law, Dicey's constitutional theory strikes us as remarkably cogent and coherent. Hale's theories made it clear that parliamentary sovereignty is not the expression of popular sovereignty in the constitutional order outlined by Dicey. Sovereignty, in the final analysis, is not even the prerogative of Parliament defined as an organ of the state. Sovereign are the Acts of Parliament. The "sovereignty of the law", however, does not mean the sovereignty of any formally valid Act of Parliament: only those Acts accepted as law, with their validity recognized by the judges and grafted on to the body of the common law, can be considered sovereign. The context of the common law, not the will of Parliament or of the electorate, is what determines the content of the law. Dicey, in other words, reduces the idea of the rule of law to the principle of legality because he works within a tradition, dating back to Hale, in which a law is established not simply because it has been passed by Parliament and become an Act, but because it has been scrutinized against the standards, values, and principles pertaining to common law. This is the key to understanding Dicey, and it accounts for his acceptance of two apparently contradictory principles: parliamentary sovereignty and the rule of law, the latter interpreted as the protection of fundamental individual rights.

Elaborating his theory of the rule of law Dicey returns to Hale, but identifies the principles, standards, and values of common law, recognized by Hale as the *substratum* of English law, with those of liberal philosophy. Dicey therefore changes the legitimating basis of common law. Common law has to be accepted as the context in which new laws come into being not only because it expresses the law of the land but also because it guarantees rights recognized as fundamental by the liberal tradition; what's more, it does so better than any other legal arrangement. This is the hidden framework, which lurks behind Dicey's comparisons between the English and the liberal constitutions of continental Europe. By showing that the rights usually provided for in constitutions are recognized in common law and by maintaining the superiority of the protection offered by it, Dicey ascribes the centuries-old English legal tradition to a liberal one. The common lawyers, although perhaps unaware of it, created the most impressive liberal legal edifice ever devised. The success of *The Law of the Constitution* in the field of English constitutional law, as well as its theoretical-legal and theoretical-political interest, stem from this attempt to fuse together the common law and the liberal tradition. This operation, at end of the nineteenth century, led to the revitalization of the myth of common law, and created a firm basis for liberal values both from the point of view of legal positivism and of sociology. Liberal values were finally translated into positive law, which is common law, and were validated by a time-honoured legal tradition (which, paradoxically, predated the same liberal doctrines). This framework allows Dicey to assert that in England a violation of constitutional rights could only take place in the case of a revolution that would radically change the existing legal system.

4 THE COURTS AS THE BASTION OF INDIVIDUAL LIBERTY

Once Dicey's constitutional doctrine has been placed in the framework of the classic theory of common law, the juxtaposition of the rule of law, as guarantee of fundamental rights, with parliamentary sovereignty wanes; parliamentary sovereignty is not in fact *formally* incompatible with the traditional role played by the common law courts in defence of justice and liberty. Dicey finds the necessary balance in the idea that the courts cannot formally annul laws produced by Parliament, as this would deny its sovereignty, although they can interpret them restrictively, reducing them, if necessary, to becoming impracticable, should the defence of those individual rights traditionally guaranteed by common law or the defence of the "freedom of the English" make this necessary.

The historical soundness of the fundamental role attributed to the courts by Dicey is even recognized by Jennings,[116] who otherwise harshly criticizes Dicey's notion of the rule of law. Jennings writes:

> To a constitutional lawyer of 1870, or even 1880, it might have seemed that the British Constitution was essentially based on an individualist rule of law, and that the British state was the *Rechtsstaat* of individualist political and legal theory. The Constitution frowned on 'discretionary' powers, unless they were exercised by judges. When Dicey said that "Englishmen are ruled by the law, and by the law alone" he meant that "Englishman are ruled by the judges, and by the judges alone".[117]

Parliament, unlike government, works through the statutes and these, unlike administrative rules, are applied and therefore examined exclusively by the ordinary courts. The courts can only guarantee the effectiveness of the rule of law when the rules are produced in Parliament; or rather only in this case they are able to ensure the values and rights of the common law constitution. According to Dicey, the examining role played by the courts between the promulgation of a statute and its application, the fact that the statute can only be translated by the courts into individual norms, meant that in Great Britain (and this was still applicable at the turn of the nineteenth century) legislation was subject not only to formal and methodical restrictions but also to effective limitations in content and scope. The protection of individual rights guaranteed by the courts represented something that came close to a tried and true scrutiny of constitutionalism: it was the factor allowing Dicey to maintain that the rule of law, defined as the judicial protection of individual rights, and parliamentary sovereignty are not only compatible but complementary.

That Dicey's conception of the rule of law, when read in line with the tradition of common law as outlined by Hale, depicts a system of guarantee is clearly shown by his discussion of periods of crisis. This discussion also makes clear the reasons for Dicey's deep aversion to administrative justice.

Emblematic here is his exploration of the possibility, which came about on a number of occasions, of Parliament suspending the validity of the *Habeas Corpus* Acts, those laws regulating the emission by the courts of *Habeas Corpus* writs. This provision was an order a court would issue to those suspected of holding an individual in detention. The writ insisted that the detained individual be brought to court in order to examine the legality of his imprisonment. The court demanded the release of anyone whose arrest was deemed illegal, or guaranteed that the detained person be swiftly brought to trial. The writ could be requested by the detainee himself or in his name by anyone considering the detention to be illegal. The right to obtain a writ of *Habeas Corpus* was recognized by common law long before 1679, when the first celebrated *Habeas Corpus* Act was approved. As Dicey writes, the *Habeas Corpus* Acts clearly show that English constitutional law is fundamentally judge-made law. These acts can be considered the practical basis supporting the freedom of the citizens of England:

> [T]he *Habeas Corpus* Acts are essentially procedure Acts, and simply aim at improving the legal mechanism by means of which the acknowledged right to personal freedom may be enforced. They are intended, as is generally the case with legislation which proceeds under the influence of lawyers, simply to meet actual and experienced difficulties.[118]

The right to freedom was already guaranteed by common law, but the procedures did not always operate correctly. The *Habeas Corpus* Acts were passed because magistrates or those responsible for illegal detentions would resort to any tactic to avoid issuing or serving the writ. The first *Habeas Corpus* Act, promulgated by Charles II, guaranteed judicial control to all those detainees accused of committing a crime. A person accused of a minor crime had the right, with appropriate guarantees, to remain free while awaiting trial. In the case of more serious crimes, the suspect only had the right to be brought swiftly to trial. The second *Habeas Corpus* Act, passed under George III, further guaranteed the right of those deprived of their liberty without having been accused to turn to the courts: for example, a child separated from the parents, a wife imprisoned by her husband, or the mentally ill forcefully confined in an asylum.[119]

At times of political upheaval, continues Dicey,[120] the power and duty of the courts to issue a writ of *Habeas Corpus* has often been regarded with suspicion or considered a danger by the executive. At such times Parliament responded by approving the *Habeas Corpus* Suspension Acts. These normally blocked the courts from freeing or putting on trial those accused or suspected of high treason. Dicey stresses the limited effect of these Acts. Even though they limited the guarantees designed to protect individual freedom they had nothing to do with the "the suspension of constitutional guarantees" or with a "state of emergency" proclaimed in the countries of continental Europe under similar circumstances. They never sanctioned a complete suspension of the power to promulgate the writs of *Habeas Corpus*, as their name might suggest. Normally a Suspension Act in no way affects the privileges of any person not imprisoned on a charge of high treason: it does not legalise any arrest, imprisonment, or punishment which was not lawful before the Suspension Act passed: it does not in any way touch the claim to a writ of *habeas corpus* possessed by everyone, man, woman, or child, who is held in confinement otherwise than on a charge of crime.[121]

Furthermore these laws always had an annual validity and the power of arrest outside judicial control had to be granted therefore from year to year. Their effectiveness was also limited: during the period of the Suspension Act, the trial of prisoners accused of treason could be constantly postponed. The trial nevertheless had to take place at a certain point and if the arrest was proved to be illegal, those responsible were brought to law. The suspension of *Habeas Corpus* did not therefore legitimize an otherwise illegal provision, but was limited to deferring matters from the legalizing scrutiny of the courts. If Parliament wanted to ensure the immunity of public officials who had acted on the basis of the Suspension Act it had to shield their actions with an Act of Indemnity (as usually Parliament did). This gave public officials confidence about the consequences of actions they had carried while following orders.[122] This Act legalized earlier violations of the law, and was the greatest expression of parliamentary power.

An Act of Indemnity is clearly a manifestation of arbitrary power and when follows a Suspension Act amounts to granting the executive arbitrary power. Dicey maintains, however, that the Suspension Act, even when followed by an Act of Indemnity, did not deprive citizens of their right to freedom. Even though it is an arbitrary act, the Act of Indemnity is promulgated by a parliamentary assembly; "this fact of itself maintains in no small degree the real no less than the apparent supremacy of the law"[123] and with it the control by the ordinary courts. This control is the real guarantee of individual liberty. There is nothing that can prevent Parliament from suspending control of the courts and from conceding a safe conduct to public officials.[124] If there were such a prohibition, Parliament would cease to be sovereign. Freedom is therefore in the arbitrary control of Parliament. The only genuine guarantee of individual freedom lies in the power of the courts to issue writs of *habeas corpus*, and therefore to control the restriction of liberties, provided by common law. The *Habeas Corpus* Acts only incorporated and regularized this power:

The repeal of the Habeas Corpus Acts [...] would deprive every man in England of one security against wrongful imprisonment, but since it would leave alive the now unquestionable authority of the judges to issue and to compel obedience to a writ of Habeas Corpus at common law, it would not, assuming the bench to do their duty, increase the power of the government to imprison persons suspected of treasonable practices, nor materially diminish the freedom of any class of Englishmen.[125]

Therefore even when the *Habeas Corpus* Acts are suspended by a law, which is the clear expression of the will of Parliament to place arrest for certain crimes outside of the boundaries of the protection granted by judicial control, judges have the *duty* to continue safeguarding the freedom of those citizens accused of treason. This does not imply that the law suspending the *Habeas Corpus* Acts is illegitimate or unconstitutional and therefore invalid. It is legitimate in so far as it expresses the constitutional principle of parliamentary sovereignty, but, as it is unreasonable in the light of common law, the courts have the *duty* to minimize its effects. For this reason, the suspension of the *Habeas Corpus* Acts, an extremely serious measure, does not erode the right to freedom – as does the suspension of the constitution in the countries of continental Europe – but only handicaps a particular instrument designed to safeguard personal freedom. It is therefore the specific relationship between statute law and common law that allows Dicey[126] to insist that, notwithstanding the suspension of the *Habeas Corpus* Act, the English continue to benefit from nearly all the guarantees to their freedom. Like Hale, he maintains that the sovereignty of Parliament does not preclude the courts' role as the real masters of law.

Dicey develops his discussion of the Acts of Indemnity on the same lines. An Act of Indemnity, he writes, is the supreme and extreme expression of parliamentary sovereignty: "Legalising illegality". It is approved, both to improve the situation created by the suspension of the *Habeas Corpus* Acts, in cases of emergency – e.g., during an invasion or widespread civil unrest – when Parliament recognizes that, in order to safeguard the very legality, the rule of law has to be violated. In such cases, which lie by definition outside the normal principles of legality, the members of the executive often find themselves obliged to violate the law and they do so claiming Parliament will later heal the violation by an Act of Indemnity.[127] Dicey underlines that this practice, while apparently merely formulaic, is of enormous importance as it unequivocally establishes the principle that even the most arbitrary powers of the executive must always respect parliamentary law. Parliament, as with the Act of Indemnity of 1801, can confer legality on only some behaviours of public officials[128] and this restrains them from committing particularly oppressive or cruel acts. But this principle, more importantly, as with the case of the Suspension Act, means that executive power must act, "even when armed with the widest authority, under the supervision, so to speak, of the Courts":

Powers, however extraordinary, which are conferred or sanctioned by statute, are never really unlimited, for they are confined by the words of the Act itself, and, *what is more, by the interpretation put upon the statute by the judges.*[129]

The simultaneous reference to respecting the statute to the letter and insisting on its judicial interpretation may appear to be contradictory. This apparent contradiction lies at the heart of Dicey's rhetorical strategy. He uses it to demonstrate that the interpretation by the ordinary courts has, in the first instance, the role of adapting the significance of statutes (attributing immunity) to the framework of the principles of common law. Even when exercising its sovereignty to the maximum, Parliament is obliged to exercise its power, if not in accordance with the ordinary courts, certainly mindful of their examination in the light of the canons of common law.

It is evident that Dicey's theory of the rule of law assigns the role of custodians of constitutional rights to the courts, even when we look at his discussion of the exceptional powers granted to the government in times of crisis. Dicey recognizes that there are times when the government, in order to cope with a particular situation, cannot rigidly adhere to the law as interpreted by the judges without putting the public interest at risk. To facilitate the government, Dicey[130] continues, Parliament by an extraordinary statute must confer it with a power ordinarily denied by common law. This procedure does not however remove government power from the control of the courts. The power is attributed to the executive by a statute and consequently the acts it carries out return to the judgement of the ordinary courts, the competent authority for judging the correct application of every statute:

The English executive needs therefore the right to exercise discretionary powers, but the Courts must prevent, and will prevent at any rate where personal liberty is concerned the exercise by the government of any sort of discretionary power.[131]

Even in the case of a concession of exceptional power to the government, the judicial power is not therefore subordinated to the will of Parliament: it is instead an independent power whose role of interpretation guarantees citizens' rights. If the courts, which are traditionally opposed to granting extraordinary powers to government, do not consider the attribution of such powers consonant with the principles of common law, the government and public officials are held responsible for their actions as if the special law had never existed. Once again the validity of the law and the legitimacy of public officials' behaviour depend, as Hale put it, on whether the courts "endorse" the extraordinary statute or not:

Parliament is supreme legislator, but from the moment Parliament has uttered its will as lawgiver, that will becomes subject to the interpretation put upon it by the judges of the land, and the judges, who are *influenced by the feelings of magistrates no less than by the general spirit of the common law*, are disposed to construe statutory exceptions to common law principles in a mode which would not commend itself either to a body of officials, or to the Houses of Parliament if the Houses of Parliament were called upon to interpret their own enactments.[132]

To conclude his examination of the constitutional framework regulating the exercise of extraordinary power in times of crisis, Dicey[133] claims to have achieved his goal, to have shown that in England parliamentary sovereignty has favoured the rule of law, and that the supremacy of the law demands the exercise of parliamentary sovereignty, which Parliament is forced to exercise in a spirit of legality. Certainly his discussion explains his determined opposition to the institution of administrative tribunals. The risk of these tribunals, constitutionally outside the tradition of common law, adopting a supine attitude to the will of the legislator, is very high. Should that happen, as the structure of the English constitution is centred on parliamentary sovereignty, nothing could then guarantee the citizen's right to freedom.

5 DICEY'S NOTION OF THE RULE OF LAW AND THE THEORY OF *RECHTSSTAAT*

In the light of Dicey's theoretical account it might be useful to attempt a comparative assessment of his notion of the rule of law with the theory of *Rechtsstaat*[134] (and the other analogous Euro-continental theories), which was formulated and reached its maturity at about the time *The Law of the Constitution* was published.

The essential element of the theory of the *Rechtsstaat* is the conviction that a virtuous circle exists between the sovereignty of the state, general law and liberty, a conviction that spread as the principle of popular sovereignty gained ground. This virtuous circle was centred on a number of theories: Locke's idea that the limits imposed by the law on individual liberty are limits sought by the rational ego of the subject whose liberty is to be limited,[135] or Rousseau's idea of the General Will, according to which the collective body never seeks, by definition, to limit the liberty of any of its members. This "democratic" ideology combined with Montesquieu's aristocratic conception of the judge as the "mouth of the law", and of the judicial power as "null".[136] These two ideologies, paradoxically, gained strength and gave life to an ideal type of constitutional organization, which could be defined as a unification of the ideas of Rousseau and Montesquieu. This model hinges on the role of Parliament, the sovereign organ in virtue of its connection with the electoral body, and gives judges the role of applying the law, as faithful executors of the will of the legislative body (and therefore ultimately of the people). Judicial power is essentially an instrument for ensuring that the will of Parliament is carried out.

The Rousseau–Montesquieu model, which gained strength in Revolutionary France, spread throughout Europe during the nineteenth century, where it managed to be dominant for 200 years. Despite this success, the progressive disillusionment with contractual doctrine led to increased uncertainty about the bases of this constitutional theory: the idea that the legislator, by his very nature, was set on guaranteeing individual freedom came to be seriously questioned from the end of the eighteenth century. It became increasingly clear that the order most able to ensure freedom rested on the same sovereign power capable of denying it. As Pietro Costa points out in the present volume, a large part of nineteenth-century liberalism is permeated by an uneasiness deriving from an understanding of the fragility of the protection of fundamental rights offered by the legislation-centred paradigm.

In the middle of the nineteenth century German legal theory with Lorenz von Stein and Otto Bähr tried to rein in the state Leviathan, transforming Montesquieu's theory of the division of power into one specifying the diverse functions of the state (administrative, judicial, legislative). As a result the administrative state became subject to the rules of the legislative state and to the judgements of the state as judge, which the teachings of the Enlightenment has already made independent of executive power and subject exclusively to the law. From the second half of the nineteenth century the *Rechtsstaat* (and the other similar continental experiences) was the state in which the principle of legality was recognized not only in adjudication (*nullum crimen sine lege* and *nulla poena sine lege*), as eighteenth-century Enlightenment had maintained, but also in administrative affairs. Even the German legal school had difficulties about the role of the state as legislator, however, relying for its control only on extra-legal elements, such as public opinion, the civic awareness of the people, and the history of the nation. Even the most sophisticated theories of the state-under-law had to resort to ideas such as Rudolf von Jhering's theory of state self-limitation and the theory of subjective public rights proposed by Georg Jellinek.

The thorny relationship between (legislative) power and law was not tackled satisfactorily until the beginning of the twentieth century, by Hans Kelsen. The Austrian jurist on the one hand identified the state with the legal order, depriving it of any voluntarist overtones. On the other hand, he highlighted the hierarchical theory of the legal order and reduced the relationship between the constitution and statutes to one of normality, comparing it to any relation between two rules of different status, requiring appraisal from a legal point of view. In this framework Parliament was no longer a sovereign body but one called upon to act on the basis of precise constitutional norms, which were to define its competence and the procedures it had to follow. The exact compliance with these regulations, and therefore the formal and substantial correctness of the laws, could be controlled by a judicial court. By establishing the hierarchical relationship between the constitution and the law, Kelsen's *Stufenbautheorie* did away with the nineteenth-century dogma of parliamentary sovereignty and, by subordinating it to legal restrictions, made the legislative power subject to judicial control. This paved the way to bringing the European public law and the North American constitutional traditions closer.

The problem Dicey aimed to resolve with his theory of the rule of law did not differ from the one which had long haunted European theorists, namely how to reconcile the protection of citizens' freedom with the sovereignty of the state, and the legislative body in particular. Both Dicey and continental lawyers tried to muster up the two forces, which had defined the arena of theoretical-legal debate over the last four centuries: voluntarism on the one hand, which had found its maximum expression in the absolutist conception of the modern state and the universal, formal, and rationalist conception of law, and liberal individual rights on the other.

Dicey's solution was very different from continental theories because his idea of the rule of law originated in the legal tradition of common law. His solution undermined notions that continental Europeans considered to be crucial to the rule of law. By adhering to Austin, Dicey rejected the idea that the English constitution was founded, as Montesquieu maintained, on the principle of the division of powers,[137] and that Parliament was subject to constitutional law. Dicey also maintained that the rule of law is based on the principle of legality and therefore, like the German *Rechtsstaat*, is primarily meant to limit the discretionary power of the executive. But he also claimed that the rule of law, as a principle of legality, guaranteed the fundamental rights of Englishmen. Paradoxically, he presented the protection of these rights as a corollary of parliamentary sovereignty.

This paradox is resolved by the different role Dicey affords to the judicial power. It is this element that distinguishes Dicey's theory from those on the continent: he flatly refuses the Rousseau–Montesquieu model. Montesquieu's conception of an independent judicial power is far removed from the tradition of common law assumed as a starting point by Dicey. While the Rousseau–Montesquieu paradigm attributes the courts an independence that is only organic, though deemed essential to the neutral application of the will of the legislator, Dicey grants them an independent prescriptive power. In this perspective, as Dicey writes in *Law and Public Opinion*,

> the explanation of a rule may, especially where the rule is followed as a precedent, so easily glide into the extension or the laying down of the rule, or in effect into the extension or the laying down of the rule, or in effect into legislation, that the line which divides the one from the other can often not be distinctly drawn.[138]

The Rousseau–Montesquieu model undermines the traditional role of the defence of individual rights that the courts play in common law. It considers the role of the courts to be an usurpation of political power,[139] as individual rights by definition limit the power of the majority and of rulers to transform their (possibly despotic) will into law. Dicey's conception of the rule of law is sharply opposed to the "phonographic" conception of judicial power, to the idea that the judge merely echoes the legislators' will. He attributes to the courts not only a formally independent power but also an independent normative power meant to protect citizens' rights.

Dicey's rule of law therefore emerges as a judge-made principle. Parliamentary legislation is seen as part of a democratic process. Its legitimacy depends on the respect for certain fundamental rights, the historic "rights of Englishmen". A judge respects the popular will, as expressed through law, because his "normative ideology"[140] embodies the value of democracy (or more simply the principle of parliamentary sovereignty). But the legitimacy of a statute is only a *prima facie* legitimacy: the democratic nature of Parliament should not automatically persuade judges to apply a law approved by it, whatever its contents. The rule of law requires that a formally valid law violating important civil rights should be interpreted by the courts in keeping with the values of freedom and independence which, according to Dicey, are the traditional values guaranteed by common law.

It could be argued that the traditional British constitution produced an alternative model to the one resulting from the French Revolution, which was based on the idea that the constitution allows for the division of powers and by so doing guarantees fundamental rights.[141] The idea that rights are born of judicial protection[142] and that the constitution is no more than the "entrenchment"[143] of this protection is central to Dicey's notion of the rule of law. This entrenchment is independent, at least in principle, from the division of powers (even if achieved historically through the independence of the courts), and is founded on a deep-rooted legal tradition that makes law almost immune to the excesses of legislative voluntarism.

Once placed in the tradition of common law, Dicey's theory opens an important theoretical space, in which it is now possible to reassess the very general notion of the rule of law. The continental experience of the *Rechtsstaat* appears to be an ambitious attempt to subject power to law. Kelsen undoubtedly represents the culmination of this process as he opened the way to a constitutional engineering capable of placing legislative power under judicial control. By placing emphasis on substantial rather than formal aspects, the development of the *Rechtsstaat* can be interpreted as an attempt to harmoniously combine the sphere of sovereign power with the legal sphere of individual freedom, removed from that power. In the course of the nineteenth century this undertaking seemed impossible. Kelsen's theory provided a formal solution to the problem, as it eliminated the dogma of the sovereignty of the legislative body. In his wake, many of the post-war constitutions have been engaged in ensuring not only the right to freedom, but social rights too. Kelsen's formalism soon turned out an unsatisfactory solution. The progressive expansion of state intervention from the 1970s onwards has brought back the Leviathan's menace to the freedom of the individual. Kelsen, in the Enlightenment tradition, saw judicial review as the most effective method of reining in the power of the state. More precisely, he saw the judiciary as best suited to this task because of its being, in Montesquieu's words, a "null power". The judicial body was merely the "mouth of the constitution". Dicey compels us radically to question this conception of the judge's role and to focus on the problems related to the application of the law, construction techniques, legal training, and culture. Starting with Dicey's teaching it might be possible to work at a legal-realist conception of the "rule of law" that might overcome the formalistic dilemmas and the doubts about its effectiveness that have characterized this notion so far.

NOTES

1. E. Coke, *The Second Part of the Institutes of England Containing the Exposition of Many Ancient and Other Statutes*, 3rd edn., London: Crooke, p. 56.
2. Ibid., p. 56.

3. *Whig* was the name given to the political party that, in the course of the seventeenth century, struggled with the Tories for the transfer of power from king to Parliament.
4. William Blackstone in his celebrated *Commentaries on the Law of England* (Oxford: Clarendon Press, 1765–9, vol. 2, p. 77) hails the abolition of military tenures as "a greater acquisition to the civil property of this kingdom than even Magna Carta itself". In his *An Analysis of the Civil Part of the Law* (sects. xix, xxi) he also points out that, at the time he was writing, the equality of all citizens before the law was almost achieved. He sees no need to make a distinction in the relationship between "lord" and "tenant" and the relationship between "lord" and "villein", namely between the landowner and one holding the land on the basis of some agreement, or between the landowner and a serf. We must therefore assume that even villeins, traditionally subject to the discretionary power of the lords, had gained abstract rights that had weight in law. About a century earlier, Coke (*The Second Part of the Institutes of England*, pp. 4, 45) had claimed that the liberties granted by Magna Carta had by then been virtually extended to villeins, who should consider themselves free with regard to everyone except their lord.
5. D. Hay, "Property, Authority and the Criminal Law", in D. Hay *et al.* (eds), *Albion's Fatal Tree. Crime and Society in Eighteenth-Century England*, London: Penguin Books, 1988, p. 32.
6. W. Blackstone, *Commentaries on the Law of England*, vol. I, p. 237.
7. D. Hay, "Property, Authority and the Criminal Law", p. 32.
8. For criticism of Thompson and Hay see P. Anderson, *Arguments within English Marxism*, London: Verso, 1980, in particular pp. 87–99; B. Fine, *Democracy and the Rule of Law*, London: Pluto Press, 1984, pp. 169–89; A. Merrit, "The Nature of Law: A Criticism of E.P. Thompson's *Whigs and Hunters*", *British Journal of Law and Society*, 7 (1980), 2, pp. 194–214; M.J. Horwitz, "The Rule of Law: An Unqualified Human Good?", *The Yale Law Journal*, 86 (1977), pp. 561–7.
9. N. Gallerano (ed.), "Un'intervista a E.P. Thompson", *Movimento operaio e socialista*, 1 (1978), 1–2, p. 85.
10. E.P. Thompson, *Whigs and Hunters. The Origins of the Black Act*, Harmondsworth: Penguin Books, 1977, p. 262.
11. See E.P. Thompson, "Patrician Society, Plebeian Culture", *Journal of Social History*, 7 (1974); D. Hay, "Property, Authority and the Criminal Law", pp. 40–9.
12. D. Hay, "Property, Authority and the Criminal Law", p. 56.
13. Ibid., pp. 32–3.
14. A clear indication that the police were long considered as extraneous to the English system and typically "French" is the entry "Police", included for the first time in the seventh edition of the *Encyclopaedia Britannica* in 1842 (vol. XVIII, pp. 248–56): six columns, out of eighteen, are devoted to a description of the French system. In the following edition, the space devoted to France was even greater (even if slightly less proportionally): covering 15 of the 50 columns (*Encyclopaedia Britannica*, 8th edn., 1859, vol. XVIII, pp. 183–209). The theory was that France had "the most elaborate police machinery that human ingenuity has yet built up, by dint of long-continued application, and under little check from outside".
15. The French legal system of the period was still based on the absolutist principle, making the sovereign, as the author of the *lettres*, the source of all power.
16. Suffice it to remember that the translation of the second edition of *Dei delitti e delle pene* by Cesare Beccaria, in the second half of the eighteenth century, underlined

the fact that "the number of criminals put to death in England is much greater than in any other part of Europe" (Preface to the second English edition of 1769, quoted in W. Holdsworth, *A History of English Law*, London: Methuen, 1938, vol. XI, p. 576).

17. This finds its clearest expression in the call for reform in the pages dealing with criminal law in Blackstone's *Commentaries*. The critical tone in these pages is not discernible anywhere else in the book. Sir William Holdsworth (*A History of English Law*, vol. XI, p. 578) writes that "it was Beccaria's book which helped Blackstone to crystallize his ideas, and it was Beccaria's influence which helped to give a more critical tone to his treatment of the English criminal law than to his treatment of any other part of English law".
18. Hay emphasizes that many of the legislators' objectives were pursued primarily through an "exhibition of power" by magistrates. Such "exhibitions" included the "impartial" application of punishments but also their suspension or commutation in certain select, but frequent cases: so, on the one hand the law was seen to be "the same for all", and on the other, the "people" were shown that their rulers were merciful.
19. D. Hay, "Property, Authority and the Criminal Law", pp. 36–7.
20. Ibid., pp. 17–65; E.P. Thompson, *Whigs and Hunters*, pp. 245–69.
21. E.P. Thompson, *Whigs and Hunters*, pp. 263–6.
22. Ibid., p. 266.
23. Ibid., p. 264.
24. Ibid., p. 267.
25. Ibid., p. 263.
26. Ibid., p. 265.
27. Ibid., p. 260.
28. C. Harvie, "Revolutions and the Rule of Law", in K. Morgan (ed.), *The Oxford Illustrated History of Britain*, Oxford: Oxford University Press, 1984, esp. pp. 421–60.
29. Chartism was a political movement that developed in England in the nineteenth century. It takes its name from the "People's Charter", including the radicals' demands for universal male suffrage, secret ballots, annual elections, payment for Parliamentary members, eligibility not based on the census, and equal size of boroughs. It began as a largely peaceful movement, gathering signatures in support of the Charter, which was presented three times for Parliamentary approval and rejected thrice.
30. The reform of the representative system was followed by a series of laws in the 1830s and 1850s, aimed at adapting state structures to the new requirements of industrial society, or – as Harvie described it – laws to "incorporate" the ascending "provincial" middle classes.
31. R. McKibbin, "Why was there no Marxism in Great Britain?" *English Historical Review*, 99 (1984), pp. 305–26.
32. H. Perkin, *The Origins of Modern English Society*, London: Routledge & Kegan Paul, 1969, pp. 340–407.
33. The rule of law had already been discussed by William Edward Hearn, former Dean of the Faculty of Law at the University of Melbourne, in *The Government of England. Its Structure and its Development* (London: Longmans, 1866, 2nd edn.). Dicey (*Introduction to the Study of the Law of the Constitution* [1915], Indianapolis: Liberty Fund, 1982, p. cxxxviii) acknowledges no debt to Hearn. On the contrary he

maintains that both Hearn and Walter Bagehot, "deal and mean to deal mainly with political understandings or conventions and not with rules of law".

34. See, for example, P. McAuslan and J.F. McEldowney, *Law, Legitimacy and the Constitution. Essays Marking the Centenary of Dicey's Law of the Constitution*, London: Sweet & Maxwell, 1985; I. Harden and N. Lewis, *The Noble Lie. The British Constitution and the Rule of Law*, London: Hutchinson, 1986. Both begin with a section on "Dicey and the rule of law"; the first chapter of P.P. Craig, *Public Law and Democracy in the United Kingdom and the United States of America*, Oxford: Clarendon Press, 1990, is devoted to an analysis of Dicey's thought.
35. Dicey claims that it will not escape the attention of those who study English constitutional law that "Austin's theory of sovereignty is suggested by the position of the English Parliament"; and he adds: "as to Austin's theory of sovereignty in relation to the British constitution, sovereignty, like many of Austin's conceptions, is a generalisation drawn in the main from English law, just as the ideas of the economists of Austin's generation are (to a great extent) generalisations suggested by the circumstances of English commerce" (A.V. Dicey, *The Law of the Constitution*, pp. 26–7).
36. Dicey points out in his Preface to *The Law of the Constitution* that his book is not simply a manual but, as the title indicates, an introduction to the subject based on "two or three guiding principles which pervade the modern constitution of England" (ibid., p. xxv). The two "leading principles" of the English constitution are: "first, the legislative sovereignty of Parliament; secondly, the universal rule or supremacy throughout the constitution of ordinary law" (ibid., p. cxlviii). Less importance, at least prima facie, is given to the third principle: "the dependence in the last resort of the conventions upon the law of the constitution" (ibid., p. cxlviii).
37. Ibid., p. 110.
38. Ibid., p. 4.
39. Ibid., pp. 24–5.
40. Ibid., p. 37.
41. Ibid., p. 78.
42. "There does not exist in any part of the British Empire any person or body of persons, executive, legislative, or judicial, which can pronounce void any enactment passed by the British Parliament on the ground of such enactment being opposed to the constitution, or on any ground whatever, except, of course, its being replaced by Parliament" (ibid., p. 39).
43. For a discussion of the distinction between legal and political sovereignty and of the internal and external restrictions on legislative power, see ibid., pp. 26–35 and 285–9.
44. Ibid., p. 110.
45. Ibid., p. 114.
46. Ibid., p. 115.
47. Ibid., p. 114.
48. Ibid., p. 115.
49. Ibid., p. 120.
50. Ibid., p. 115.
51. Ibid.
52. For a detailed discussion of this idea, which has long dominated English legal history, see E. Santoro, Common law *e costituzione nell'Inghilterra moderna. Introduzione al pensiero di Albert Venn Dicey*, Torino: Giappichelli, 1999.

53. "Political institutions (however the proposition may be at times ignored) are the work of men, owe their origin and their whole existence to human will. Men did not wake up on a summer morning and find them sprung up. Neither do they resemble trees, which once planted, are 'aye growing' while men 'are sleeping'. In every stage of their existence they are made what they are by human voluntary agency" (J.S. Mill, *Consideration on Representative Government*, London: Longman, 1865, p. 4).
54. A.V. Dicey, *The Law of the Constitution*, p. 116.
55. Ibid., p. 121.
56. Dicey states this idea more explicitly in another of his celebrated works, *Lectures on the Relations between Law and Public Opinion in England during the Nineteenth Century* (London: Macmillan, 1914, p. 489): "it might be inferred that the sphere of judicial legislation must gradually become narrower and narrower, and judicial legislation itself come at last completely to an end. This conclusion contains this amount of truth, that no modern judges can mould the law anything like as freely as did their predecessor some centuries ago. No Lord Chief Justice of to-day could occupy anything like the position of Coke or carry out reforms, such as were achieved or attempted by Lord Mansfield. There are whole departments of law, which no longer afford a field for judicial legislation".
57. A.V. Dicey, *The Law of the Constitution*, p. 121 (italics added).
58. On the dual legislative and judicial role of the English Parliament and on the implications for the Anglo-Saxon constitution, see C.H. McIlwain, *The High Court of Parliament and its Supremacy* [1910], New York: Arno Press, 1979. For a criticism of McIlwain's theses, see J. Goldsworthy, *The Sovereignty of Parliament: History and Philosophy*, Oxford: Clarendon Press, 1999.
59. "Such principles, moreover, as you can discover in the English constitution are, like all maxims established by judicial legislation, mere generalisations drawn either from the decisions or dicta of judges, or from statutes which, being passed to meet special grievances, bear a close resemblance to judicial decisions, and are in effect judgements pronounced by the High Court of Parliament" (A.V. Dicey, *The Law of the Constitution*, p. 116).
60. Ibid., p. 117.
61. Ibid., pp. 117–18.
62. "The question whether the right to personal freedom or the right to freedom of worship is likely to be secure does depend a good deal upon the answer to the inquiry whether the persons who consciously or unconsciously build up the constitution of their country begin with definitions or declarations of rights, or with the contrivance of remedies by which rights may be enforced or secured" (ibid., p. 117).
63. Ibid., p. 118.
64. Ibid.
65. Ibid., p. 117.
66. Ibid., p. 119.
67. "Freedom from arbitrary arrest, the right to express one's own opinion on all matters subject to the liability to pay compensation for libellous or to suffer punishment for seditious or blasphemous statements, and the right to enjoy one's own property, seem to Englishmen all to rest upon the same basis, namely, on the law of the land. To say that the 'constitution guarantees' one class of rights more than the other would be to an Englishman an unnatural or a senseless form of speech" (ibid., p. 119).

68. Ibid., p. 120.
69. A.F. von Hayek, *Law, Legislation and Liberty*, London: Routledge, 1973–9, vol. II, p. 61.
70. G. De Q. Walker, "Dicey's dubious dogma of parliamentary sovereignty: A recent fray with freedom of religion", *The Australian Law Journal*, 59 (1985), pp. 283–4.
71. T.R.S. Allan, *Law, Liberty, and Justice*, Oxford: Clarendon Press, 1993, p. 16.
72. D. Dyzenhaus, *Hard Cases in Wicked Legal Systems: South Africa Law in the Perspective of Legal Philosophy*, Oxford: Clarendon Press, 1991, pp. 236–8.
73. R.W. Blackburn, "Dicey and the teaching of public law", *Public Law* (1985), pp. 692–3.
74. For the influence of Austin's positivism on Dicey see M. Loughlin, *Public Law and Political Theory*, Oxford: Clarendon Press, 1992, pp. 13–23.
75. T.R.S. Allan, *Law, Liberty, and Justice*, p. 16.
76. Ibid., p. 2.
77. Ibid., p. 16.
78. For an analysis of the English legal debate at the end of the nineteenth century and Austin's role, see E. Santoro, Common law *e costituzione nell'Inghilterra moderna*, pp. 56–107.
79. It does seem that most critics were opposed to the interpretation of Dicey's theories as developed in the course of the twentieth century, rather than to the theories themselves. Dyzenhaus (*Hard Cases in Wicked Legal Systems*, pp. 236–8), for example, links Dicey's theories with those of the contemporary jurist Sir William Wade, and his criticism is in the end more directed at Wade than at Dicey. Also Dicey's theories were not blamed per se but for having encouraged the dogmatic use of the notion of the "sovereignty of Parliament" (T.R.S. Allan, *Law, Liberty, and Justice*, p. 16). For an analysis of the legal debate and of Dicey's role, see M. Loughlin, *Public Law and Political Theory*, Oxford: Clarendon Press, 1992.
80. T.R.S. Allan, *Law, Liberty, and Justice*, p. 46.
81. N.S. Marsh, "The Rule of Law as a Supra-National Concept", in A. Guest (ed.), *Oxford Essays in Jurisprudence*, series 1, Oxford: Clarendon Press, 1961, p. 241.
82. See A.V. Dicey, *The Law of the Constitution*, chaps. 5–7 and p. 115.
83. Sir Ivor Jennings (*The Law and the Constitution*, 5th edn., London: London University Press, 1967, p. 39), who spent his life constructing an alternative model of English constitutional law to Dicey's, maintained that to say general constitutional principles were founded on jurisprudential decisions is "the very partial representation of the facts". It should be noted that Jennings intends the expression "general principles of the constitution" in a literal sense, choosing as an example "the sovereignty of Parliament". Dicey, on the other hand, only applies this expression to the right to freedom.
84. See chap. XIII. "Relation between parliamentary sovereignty and the rule of law". This chapter caused a stir among English legal theorists: E. Barendt ("Dicey and civil liberties", *Public Law*, 1985, pp. 600–1), described it as "surely one of the least happy chapters of his book".
85. A.V. Dicey, *The Law of the Constitution*, p. 268.
86. Ibid., p. 271.
87. Ibid. In his attempt to highlight the contrast between the French and English systems Dicey's theory is both forced and anachronistic. He bases the compatibility of Parliamentary sovereignty and the rule of law on the fact that the English Parliament

has never directly used executive powers nor nominated executive officials (ibid., p. 269). But, a few years earlier, Walter Bagehot – in his *The English Constitution* [1872], London: Oxford University Press, 1928 – had stressed that Parliament and Government in England formed a single constitutional body.

88. It would be more correct to say "in 1885", when *The Law of the Constitution* first appeared, as Dicey did not return to this theory in later editions. Bagehot's description of the role of "Government" shows that Dicey's description was anachronistic even in 1885. On the various editions of *The Law of the Constitution*, see E. Santoro, Common law *e costituzione nell'Inghilterra moderna*, pp. 9–15.
89. A.V. Dicey, *The Law of the Constitution*, p. 270.
90. As Jennings explains (*The Law and the Constitution*, pp. 158–60), after the Glorious Revolution the border between parliamentary power and the power of the courts was defined by the *modus vivendi* established between courts and Parliament. The judges did not oppose the power of the Long Parliament, the restoration of Charles II, the accession of William and Mary established by the Bill of Rights, or the claims of the House of Hanover in the Act of Settlement. As emerges from Coke's *Reports*, the courts might have opposed these Acts on the grounds of common law but they did not. The limits of their power and those of Parliament never occasioned political conflict. This meant that it was never necessary to give a formal, unequivocal definition to the relationship between common law and Acts of Parliament.
91. A.V. Dicey, *The Law of the Constitution*, p. 270. According to Dicey, evidence of this interdependence was the fact that everybody considered quite normal that judges were, strictly speaking, not irremovable; they could be removed following a decision approved by both Houses. The magistrates accepted with good grace to be "independent of every power in the state except the Houses of Parliament".
92. Ibid., p. 111.
93. It is significant that the section of *The Law of the Constitution* devoted to the rule of law opens with a long quotation from Alexis de Tocqueville exulting the spirit of English legality as superior to that of the Swiss, even though the Swiss have a written (and moreover "rigid") constitution. Dicey sometimes identifies the spirit of legality with the rule of law. He writes, for example, that the peculiar characteristic of English institutions is "the rule of law or the predominance of the legal spirit" (ibid., p. 115).
94. Ibid., p. 117.
95. Dicey, to be coherent, cannot maintain that Parliament has no power to issue a law excluding the competence of the ordinary courts concerning matters the law is regulating. Such a thesis would go against Austin's theory, and admit at least a partial limitation of Parliamentary sovereignty. The existence of a limit to Parliamentary competence, even in recent times, was at the centre of several controversies in the field of administrative law. See, for example, the famous decision in *Anisminic v. Foreign Compensation Commission* ([1969] 2 AC 147), which supports Dicey's conception of the rule of law.
96. I. Jennings, *The Law and the Constitution*, pp. 152–3.
97. Jennings continues by emphasizing that "the courts have no concern with sovereignty, but only with the established law. 'Legal sovereignty' is merely a name indicating that the legislature has for the time being power to make laws of any kind in the manner required by the law. That is, a rule expressed to be made by the Queen, 'with the advice and consent of the Lords spiritual and temporal, and Commons in

this present Parliament assembled, and by the authority of the same', will be recognised by the Courts, *including a rule which alters this law itself*". According to Jennings (*The Law and the Constitution*, p. 156), implicit in Dicey's notion of "legal sovereignty" is that the power of Parliament is neither original nor absolute, but it "derives from the law by which it is established", otherwise it would be difficult to understand what makes it "legal".

98. A.V. Dicey, *The Law of the Constitution*, p. 271.
99. Ibid., p. 269.
100. According to this system, introduced at the time of the revolution, when the law was unclear or there were lacunae, the court was bound to ask the legislator to set the rule clearly.
101. A.V. Dicey, *The Law of the Constitution*, p. 269.
102. The heart of Dicey's constitutional doctrine was well expressed by Lord Wilberforce before the House of Lords during the discussion of *Black-Clawson v. Paperwerke Waldhof-Aschaffenburg* ([1975] AC 591, 629–30, cited by T.R.S. Allan, *Law, Liberty, and Justice*, p. 79): "This power which has been devolved upon the judges from the earliest time is an essential part of the constitutional process by which subjects are brought under *the rule of law – as distinct from the rule of the King or the rule of Parliament*. [...] The saying that it is the function of the courts to ascertain the will or intention of Parliament is often enough repeated. [...] If too often or unreflectingly stated, it leads to neglect of the important element of judicial construction; an element not confined to a mechanical analysis of today's words, but [...] related to such matters as intelligibility to the citizen, constitutional propriety, considerations of history, comity of nations, reasonable and non-retroactive effect and, no doubt, in some contexts, to social needs"(italics added).
103. Some observations by Stanley Fish ("What Makes an Interpretation Acceptable?" in *Is There a Text in This Class? The Authority of the Interpretative Communities*, Cambridge (MA): Harvard University Press, 1980, pp. 353–4) on the importance of fidelity to the text clarify Dicey's theory. Fish observed that invoking the literal meaning of the text only appears to suggest disregarding any interpretation in favour of the text itself. In reality with this strategy "a set of interpretative principles is replaced by another that happens to claim itself the virtue of not being an interpretation". Dicey appears to be perfectly aware that "returning to the text" *a rigore* is not a possible strategy, because in any case the meaning of the "text" will be based on some interpretation. At the same time he seems convinced that this strategy is not invalidated by the fact that nobody can invoke the literal meaning of the text. Its effectiveness depends on the degree to which jurists believe in the importance of the text standing on its own. Dicey appears sure that insistence on this referral to the literal meaning of the text would amount to a return to the interpretive canons of common law. He is therefore able to separate the legislative text from its source and deliver it to the hands of its interpreters (paradoxical in the context of a return to the letter of the law).
104. Jennings (*The Law and the Constitution*, p. 326) maintains that Coke considered common law as normal law and recognized that Parliament, in virtue of its "transcendent and absolute" power, was able to make exceptions to general law or, as the preface of the ninth volume of the *Reports* states, "to take away one of the pillars of the common law". As this colourful language suggests, Coke considered such power quite exceptional and advised Parliament "to leave all causes to be governed

by the golden and straight wand of the law, and not to the uncertain and crooked cord of discretion" (E. Coke, *The Fourth Part of Institutes of the Law of England Concerning the Jurisdiction of Court*, 4th edn., London, 1669, p. 41, quoted in I. Jennings, *The Law and the Constitution*, p. 327). Coke claimed only common law jurists attain to the cognizance of "artificial reason and judgment of law" during his celebrated controversy with James I; for a discussion of Coke's theories related to this dispute and of his notion of "right", see E. Santoro, Common law *e costituzione nell'Inghilterra moderna*, pp. 23–8.

105. C.K. Allen, *Law in the Making*, Oxford: Clarendon Press, 1964, pp. 456–7. The first edition of this work appeared in 1927 and there were six subsequent editions. The quotations are taken from the seventh, published in 1964.
106. G.J. Postema, *Bentham and the Common Law Tradition*, Oxford: Clarendon, 1986, p. 17.
107. Hale's theories are presented and compared with those of Coke in E. Santoro, Common law *e costituzione nell'Inghilterra moderna*, pp. 29–32, 37–41; see also C.M. Gray, Editor's Introduction, in M. Hale, The History of the Common Law, Chicago/London: The University Press of Chicago, 1971, esp. pp. xxi–xxxvii.
108. M. Hale (*The History of the Common Law*, pp. 101–6) also presents the great legislative reforms of Edward the Confessor as a matter of "settling the law", which had become chaotic following the unification of different peoples into the English nation.
109. W. Blackstone, *Commentaries on the Law of England*, vol. I, pp. 85–7.
110. M. Hale, *The History of the Common Law*, p. 46.
111. Hale also emphasizes that the English constitutional framework is in continual evolution and only the reception of a legislative act within common law keeps it from being abolished when it has become incompatible with the new constitutional framework. It is naturally the exclusive competence of the courts to decide on the unconstitutional nature of any law. According to Hale this was the fate of many laws in the past, now almost completely forgotten.
112. G.J. Postema, *Bentham and the Common Law Tradition*, pp. 24–5.
113. This idea, as Postema (ibid., p. 26) makes clear, leaves no room for Bentham's project to reform English law by issuing legal codes. Every reform approved by Parliament can be a real reform of the English law only if the statutes are sanctioned by the courts; therefore it is excluded a priori the idea of a code.
114. By the "classical theory of common law" I mean the one prior to Austin. By the "modern theory of common law" I refer to the one that gained ground from the mid nineteenth century, under the influence of Austin's teaching. This distinction is developed in the second part of E. Santoro, Common law *e costituzione nell'Inghilterra moderna*.
115. C.K. *Allen, Law in the Making*, p. 456.
116. I. Jennings, *The Law and the Constitution*, p. 310.
117. Among continental jurists G. Radbruch (*Der Geist des englischen Rechts*, Göttingen: Vanderhoeck und Ruprecht, 1946) was perhaps the first to propose that the "secret" of the rule of law consists in a class of jurists and magistrates accustomed to interpreting positive laws in the light of historical values engrained in the system. See also the Foreword of A. Baratta to the Italian translation of Radbruch's essay (Milan: Giuffrè, 1962, p. xi ff.); G. Alpa, *L'arte di giudicare*, Rome-Bari: Laterza, 1996, pp. 32–3.

118. A.V. Dicey, *The Law of the Constitution*, p. 134.
119. Dicey (ibid., p. 133) underlines that the procedures recommended in the second *Habeas Corpus* Act, in effect until 1856, were less respectful to the rights of those accused of a crime, and less effective.
120. Ibid., p. 139.
121. Ibid., p. 140.
122. Ibid., pp. 141–4.
123. Ibid., p. 145.
124. Dicey rarely mentions the police, not even listing them in his index, as he regards them as extraneous to the English legal system. It should however be noted that, when he alludes to public officials in general, he is often referring to the authority and power of the police. This strategy is clearly designed to make administrative law appear more of a threat.
125. A.V. Dicey, *The Law of the Constitution*, p. 140, note 29 (italics added). That this thesis, as paradoxical as it might seem, belongs to the tradition of common law, is testified by Dicey quoting the *Commentaries* by Blackstone (*Commentaries on the Law of England*, vol. III, p. 138).
126. A.V. Dicey, *The Law of the Constitution*, p. 120.
127. Dicey (ibid., p. 273) sees this procedure, laboriously established in the course of the eighteenth century, as combining "the maintenance of the law and authority of Parliament with the free exercise of that kind of discretionary power or prerogative which, under some shape or other, must at critical junctures be wielded by the executive government of every civilised country".
128. "Reckless cruelty to a political prisoner, or, still more certainly, the arbitrary punishment or the execution of a political prisoner, between 1793 and 1801, would, in spite of the Indemnity Act, have left every man concerned in the crime liable to suffer punishment" (ibid., p. 145).
129. Ibid., p. 273 (italics added).
130. Ibid., p. 271.
131. Ibid., p. 272.
132. Ibid., p. 273 (italics added).
133. Ibid.
134. As stated in the Foreword, I use the German expression *Rechtsstaat* to indicate the first and perhaps most important politico-constitutional model among the many (*Stato di diritto, État de droit, Estado de derecho*, etc.) that developed in the second half of the nineteenth century in continental Europe. We lack an English counterpart for these terms, perhaps because, as Neil MacCormick maintains, "British constitutional usage avoids much reference to 'the state' as a concept at all, preferring to treat executive government as an emanation from 'the Crown', while legislation depends on a Parliament which was historically the rival of the Crown, not its partner, and the judiciary seek to distance themselves from both" (N. MacCormick, "Constitutionalism and democracy", in R.P. Bellamy (ed.), *Theories and Concepts of Politics. An Introduction*, Manchester: Manchester University Press, 1993, pp. 128–9).
135. See E. Santoro, *Autonomy, Freedom and Rights. A Critique of Liberal Subjectivity*, Dordrecht: Kluwer, 2003, in particular pp. 123–59.
136. Montesquieu, in book XI, chap. 3, of *Esprit des Lois* maintains that judicial power is "in a certain sense nothing" (*en quelque façon nul*).

137. On this matter Dicey (*The Law of the Constitution*, pp. 74, 86) is peremptory: "the principle, in short, which gives its form to our system of government is (to use a foreign but convenient expression) 'unitarianism', or the habitual exercise of supreme legislative authority by one central power, which in the particular case is the British Parliament. [...] All the power of the English state is concentrated in the Imperial Parliament, and all departments of government are legally subject to Parliamentary despotism".
138. Ibid., p. 491.
139. It is this aspect of the doctrine of the separation of powers that Dicey finds incompatible with the English constitutional system. In *Law and Public Opinion* (pp. 59–60), he writes: "democracy in England has to great extent inherited the traditions of the aristocratic government, of which it is the heir. The relation of the judiciary to the executive, to the Parliament, and to the people, remains now much what it was at the beginning of the century, and no man dreams of maintaining that the government and the administration are not subject to the legal control and interference of the judges."
140. I borrow this expression from Alf Ross. Normative ideology, according to Ross (*On Law and Justice*, London: Steven, 1958, pp. 75–6) "constitutes the foundation of the law system and consists of directives which do not directly concern the manner in which a legal dispute is to be settled but indicate the way in which a judge shall proceed in order to discover the directive or directives decisive for the question at issue".
141. Emblematic of this idea is the celebrated article 16 of the "Declaration of the Rights of Man and of the Citizen" of 26 August 1789: "Any society in which the guarantee of rights is not assured, nor the separation of powers determined, has no constitution."
142. In *Law and Public Opinion* (p. 487) Dicey writes: "where there is no remedy there is no right. To give a remedy is to confer a right".
143. See Nelson Goodman (*Fact, Fiction and Forecast*, Cambridge (MA): Harvard University Press, 1983, p. 94 ff. According to Goodman, a predicate is "entrenched" when its use (its "projections") appears natural. Dicey regards the courts of common law as the natural place to "project" the freedom of the English in settling controversies. They are the real guarantors of rights in Great Britain.

CHAPTER 4

POPULAR SOVEREIGNTY, THE RULE OF LAW, AND THE "RULE OF JUDGES" IN THE UNITED STATES

Brunella Casalini

1 INTRODUCTION

Between 1764 and 1776, a conception of the constitution came to prevail in the United States, which represented a real turning point with respect to pre-modern constitutional thought. The constitution would no longer be understood as an assemblage of laws, customs, and traditions, but would instead be considered as a fundamental plan of government, based on a corpus of systematic written norms. The constitution thus assumed a normative character and was no longer merely descriptive. The very word *constitution* came to be used for the first time in those years with its present-day meaning, and the power of the constitution was clearly placed over and above the power of the ordinary legislator.[1] The awareness of the difference between ordinary laws and constitutional laws stood out as one of the most significant changes in the elaboration of the concept of constitution. Further inventions of US constitutional history included the creation of constituent assemblies, the popular ratification of constitutions, the legal acknowledgement of fundamental rights, the introduction of procedures for amending the constitution, and the institution of judicial review of legislation. On the basis of these innovations, essential to the history of modern constitutionalism, was the attempt to clarify the implications of the idea that the constitution was an act of self-determination by the sovereign people. It is this idea, which is the basis of the tension between politics and law in modern constitutionalism,[2] that gives law its central position in how the political identity of the United States was constructed and the cult of law took root, becoming a veritable civil religion. The idea of "rule of law" consequently underwent a significant twist: in order to be able to speak of "rule of law" and not of "rule of men", it was not enough that the fundamental rights of the citizen be removed from the arbitrary will of the legislator, but it now became necessary for the law to be seen as a derivation of popular sovereignty. In the republican conception[3] of the period of the founding of the United States, legal certainty was considered

P. Costa and D. Zolo (eds.), The Rule of Law: History, Theory and Criticism, 201–236.

as a necessary value, but no longer sufficient. Going beyond Montesquieu's idea of liberty as the absence of fear guaranteed by certain, fixed laws in defence of civil rights, the rule of law in the United States came to be considered as the guarantee of a liberty understood first of all as republican self-determination. And liberty presupposed, at least originally, a close connection between political rights and civil rights.

The twentieth-century re-evaluation of the concept of "rule of law" mostly removed the republican implications from the notion of the rule of law, basing it rather on reference to a law of spontaneous production, administered by the Courts of Justice. This implies, for example in Hayek and Oakeshott, a depreciation of parliamentary legislation as a source of law and at the same time a reduction of the constitution to its role as guarantor, exercising restrictions on political power. Law thus appears completely autonomous from politics, capable of self-reproduction and self-legitimization. The United States is considered a paradigmatic example of this modern-day tendency, which seems to imply risk of a shift from the supremacy of constitutions to the supremacy of constitutional courts. This tendency is stronger in the United States than elsewhere due to a peculiarity of the US constitutional tradition: the existence of diffuse control over the constitutionality of the laws, namely the possibility for courts, and ultimately for the Supreme Court, to assume the function of interpreter of the constitution. The Supreme Court became empowered to review, declare unconstitutional, and thus invalidate both the decisions of Congress and those of the legislative powers of the states, on the basis of motivations which extended to the substance of the legislative acts under examination.

The introduction of the "judicial review of legislation", which is –generally considered to go back to the ruling of *Marbury v. Madison* (1803) by Judge John Marshall,[4] resulted in the assigning of considerable powers to the Supreme Court. It is enough to consider, on the one hand, the interpretative margin left by the vagueness of certain constitutional clauses (e.g. formulations such as "due process" and "equal protection of the laws") and, on the other hand, the impossibility of recourse to ordinary legislative procedures to modify the decisions of the Supreme Court, for the extent of its powers to become quite clear.[5] If the unique character of the institution of constitutional review in the United States is the basis of the pre-eminent position held by the Supreme Court, it is necessary nevertheless to recognize that the current situation is above all connected with a change in the Court's perception of its own role.

The prevalent interpretation of the constitution as a model of "constitution-as-guarantor" recognizes, from the very beginning of US history, a pre-eminent role controlling the constitutionality of civil rights laws. In the light of this interpretation, from the time of its introduction (1791) the Bill of Rights, through its defence by the judiciary, has guaranteed US citizens the exercise and enjoyment of fundamental rights.[6] This reading of US constitutional history, however, is at best partial. It is enough to recall that not only Afro-Americans and Native Americans, but also women, Mexican guest workers, and immigrants of Asian origin – i.e. all those who did not have access to citizenship – were excluded until almost the mid twentieth century from the principle of equality before the law, one of the cornerstones of the rule of law.[7] But, it is perhaps even more important to remember that until the introduction of the XIV amendment (1868) the US constitutional system allowed no room for an interpretation of the Bill of Rights that was binding not only for the federal government but also for the states, to which the US federal system delegates most matters of day-to-day importance to citizens (such as from schooling to welfare services and to the family).[8]

The activism of ordinary courts and of the Supreme Court in the defence of individual rights and above all of the rights of minorities is part of the US history of the twentieth century, a history closely connected to the role that the United States took on at the international level in the battle against the spread of totalitarianism in Europe.[9] The real turning point in this direction is represented by a famous footnote in *United States v. Carolene Products Co.*, decided in 1938. It suggested – as Ely puts it – that "the Court should also concern itself with what majorities do to minorities, particularly mentioning laws 'directed at' religious, national and racial minorities and those infected by prejudice against them".[10] If there is no doubt about the advantages US citizens have derived from this change in the perception the Supreme Court has of its own role (it is enough to think of the judgment in *Brown v. Board of Education of Topeka* in 1954, which marked the end of the system of racial segregation), it is equally true that the constitutional debate over the role of the judiciary and the relationship between the "judicial review of legislation" and democracy had never been so intense as in the post–World War II period.

The following pages provide a historical outline of the twists and turns in the US tradition of the rule of law over more than 200 years of constitutional life. My historical reconstruction underlines the connection between the rule of law and "rule of the people" which has existed from the beginning of US constitutionalism. This connection seems to have been to some extent neutralized, even if never denied, both by the difficulty of recourse to the power of constitutional revision, given the muddled nature of Article V, and by the power of being sole and ultimate interpreter of the constitution that the Supreme Court assumed with the ruling *Marbury v. Madison*. The connection which US legal culture continued to maintain with the tradition of common law – despite the Revolution and the recognition of the positive character of the written constitution – contributed to facilitating this process of neutralization of popular sovereignty. On the other hand, the more recent crisis of the tradition of common law is not extraneous to the difficulties which the Supreme Court encounters in the attempt to legitimize its own role.

This historical reconstruction will be followed by an analysis of the main positions which have emerged within the contemporary theoretical debate, whose key issues are the neutral character of judicial interpretation and how the supremacy of the judiciary affects the political system. Attempts to re-establish the neutrality of judicial interpretation aim at preserving the idea that the real existence of the rule of law is tied to the impartial administration of law by the courts. The reflection on the effects of the supremacy of the judiciary is instead connected to the aim of re-legitimizing the political process and rereading the significance of the rule of law in the light of the complexity of the constitutional structure.

2 THE "RULE OF LAW" AND THE "RULE OF THE PEOPLE" IN THE REPUBLICAN THOUGHT OF THE "FOUNDING FATHERS"

The attempt, already undertaken by Edmund Burke in the eighteenth century, to place US constitutionalism in a tradition of historical continuity with respect to the British Constitution has overshadowed the innovations implicit in the writing of the constitution introduced by the American Revolution. The same can be said to have occurred in the retracing of the constitution back to the tradition of the colonial charters. The notes written by Benjamin Franklin in the margins of *Thoughts on the Origin and Nature of Governments* (1769) by Allan Ramsey, however, allow a new reading of the continuity between colonial charters and the constitutions of the revolutionary period. Criticizing Ramsey's assertion that considering the colonial charters as *Pacta conventa* was an absurdity, Franklin stressed that Ramsey's mistake was in overlooking the fact that the colonial charters of Pennsylvania and the Carolinas had actually had John Locke and Algernon Sidney among their inspirers.[11] The link which Franklin established between Locke and Sidney and, on the other hand, between the colonial charters and the idea of contract, sheds light on one of the central areas which connect, in the 1760s and 1770s, the most important figures of the American Revolution to the radical English culture of the seventeenth century. The use of Locke and Sidney to explain the significance of the "true" English Constitution was recurrent in the revolutionary pamphlets. In most cases, knowledge of the radical English thinkers of the seventeenth century by the Americans was due above all to the reception of Locke's and Sidney's ideas present in the writings of the Real Whigs – of authors like John Trenchard, James Gordon, and James Burgh, destined to have a popularity and influence in the United States unknown in England.[12]

In the theoretical elaborations of the Real Whigs, the cult of the "ancient constitution" – as guided by insights already present in the reflections of Locke and Sidney[13] – had been the object of a rereading which is crucial to understand the constitutional reflections of the period of the Revolution in the United States. The value of the English Constitution was traced back, in fact, not to its antiquity, to its immemorial foundations, but to the fact that rational examination revealed in it the presence of the fundamental principles of the law of nature. John Adams, Thomas Jefferson, and many other eighteenth-century North American thinkers could consider themselves as the heirs of the various Lockes and Sidneys in the attempt to reveal the "true" meaning of the English Constitution. Their battle took place on a legal-constitutional terrain, but in the name of a vision of the English Constitution which implied a drastic break with the past, since it asserted unequivocally the principle of popular sovereignty.

The US constitutional debate of the eighteenth and early nineteenth centuries was made even more complex by its revolving around two different conceptions of republicanism, which in turn were connected to two different visions of popular sovereignty. With reference to the conceptual categories elaborated by Philip Pettit, we could speak of a "populist republicanism" (based on a line of thought which, starting from Aristotle extends to Hannah Arendt) and of a "classical republicanism" (associated with the line which goes from Cicero to Machiavelli).[14] The first republican type is, for Pettit, "inherently populist" for it considers people's political participation as a fundamental good. In the perspective of populist republicanism, Pettit maintains, the people should rely on their representatives and public officials only when it is strictly necessary.[15] Populist republicanism is founded on a positive conception of "the people", often using the notion uncritically as representative of a homogeneous public. Populism, on the other hand, alongside the defence of the interests and the common sense of the ordinary citizen, cultivates an attitude of suspicion towards every form of hierarchy and "expertocracy" (i.e. "rule by experts").[16]

On the other hand, "classical republicanism" underlines the element of trust between the people and their elected representatives. In particular, as Pettit writes, this second republican tradition "sees the people as trusting the state to ensure a dispensation of non-arbitrary rule".[17] Unlike the Aristotelian tradition, classical republicanism does not present an edifying image of the ordinary citizen. Individuals are seen as corruptible beings, the bearers of different and conflicting interests. The political process results in filtering opinions through the selection of representatives, while citizens' participation in political affairs is above all their means of preventing the degeneration of the government into a form of tyranny, which is harmful to individual freedom.

The thought of Jefferson and the anti-Federalists can be traced back to the populist conception of republicanism, whereas the constitutional thought of John Adams and the Federalists can be placed within the classical republican vision.

In the radical populist interpretation of Jefferson and Thomas Paine, since the constitution was the expression of the sovereign people, nothing could prevent the people from undertaking periodic constitutional revisions. Central to Jeffersonian constitutionalism was the idea that a republican government must rely on the people's sovereignty as a check on the exercise of power, through instruments such as a written constitution and the brief duration of mandates (and therefore frequent recourse to elections). This vision held implicit, on the one hand, the autonomy of civil society with respect to government, and, on the other, suspicion with regard to every concentration of political power. Considering "self-love" as the main passion of the human being, populist constitutionalism sought not to balance but to reduce political power, through representation and the separation of powers at different levels and in different branches. Jefferson saw the function of the Bill of Rights and the Supreme Court in this context: the former was supposed to place a check on the possibilities of interference by the federal power in the autonomy of the individual states, and the second was supposed to function within the limits of a strict application of the text of the law. If the judiciary could not be reduced to a mere machine, to a technical organ held to a strict application of the text of the law, the judges' power would in fact, according to Jefferson, be able to distort the democratic logic, becoming an inappropriate power within a republican government.[18]

The perspective of John Adams and the Federalists was different. In his *Defence of the Constitutions of Government of the United States of America* (1787–1788), Adams distinguished the republicanism of the French, towards which went the sympathies of Jefferson, from that of the Americans. The French, English, and Americans used the same word "republic", but, Adams maintained, they were not thinking of the same thing. For the French and the English, "republic" was synonymous with democracy or representative democracy: governments that "collect all authority into one centre, and that centre is the nation",[19] or rather a sole assembly, chosen in periods determined by the people and invested with complete sovereignty. For the Americans, instead, the defeat of royal absolutism could not give way to the absolutism of democratic majorities. Adams looked with horror at the omnipotence of a democratic regime governed by irrational passions, which would lead to the rise of new demagogic aristocracies. The republic was, the rule of the people, but the "people" had no existence if not in virtue of their conformity to the fundamental laws and to the principles of justice: the "people", and not a mere "multitude", existed when will and reason converged. Only in this sense could "rule of the people" coincide with the rule of law and contrast with the "rule of men". In order to keep the will of the rulers faithful to the principles of the rule of law, Adams proposed a system of checks and balances that was conceived of as a real instrument of control over passions, and which would channel them in a direction that was not socially harmful. Adams did not deny the value of popular sovereignty but, as the Federalists would also do,[20] he tended to overlook the question of the constituent power, to neutralize its revolutionary results on the political–institutional level.

James Madison would continue in the spirit of Adam's approach and insist on the virtues of checks and balances and of a representative system that, through large electoral districts and the multiplication of political groups, would permit the selection of a qualified political elite, able to resist demagogic temptations and escape the pressures of particularistic and local interests.[21] The filter of the representative system and the constitution of a political body of "optimates" were necessary, according to Madison, in order to maintain the neutral character of political decisions, subtracting them from the passions that resided in the popular mind and which otherwise could induce the people-multitude *to harm themselves*.[22] Madison was opposed to attributing a special role of defence of individual rights either to the Bill of Rights or to the Supreme Court. It was the system of checks and balances, the separation of powers, the creation of large electoral districts, the dialectics between the federal state and the federated states, that he relied upon to neutralize passions and interests, to restrain and channel them in order to bring as much reason as possible to the deliberative process of the majority. Only a law which could be supported with general, neutral arguments could, in his opinion, guarantee the existence of a government perceived as a "rule of law" and not "of men". For Madison, the Supreme Court did not have a privileged role as interpreter of the constitution and its powers had to be limited to the control over manifestly unconstitutional legislative acts.[23] Only the subsequent introduction by Judge Marshall of the "judicial review of legislation", which cancelled the distinction between unjust acts and unconstitutional acts, determined the hierarchical superiority of civil rights over political rights, creating a barrier against the power of democratic self-determination.

3 THE JUDICIAL REVIEW OF LEGISLATION

The distinction between legislative power and constituent power, present in the thought of the "Founding Fathers", could be understood not as "an elitist attempt at limiting popular will in the name of an ideal notion of law", but instead as an instrument to preserve "the 'reserve of power' implicit in people's sovereignty, in the sovereignty of a people whose will could not be represented *in toto* because it is constituted by the sum of single individuals endowed with inalienable rights".[24] The overlapping between rule of law and rule of the people could be interpreted, i.e. as a connection between self-government and the primacy of law. This possibility, however, was to remain purely theoretical at the federal level, due to the freezing of popular sovereignty brought about de facto, on the one hand, by the muddled procedure of constitutional revision foreseen by Article V of the constitution, and, on the other, by the interpretation of rule of law contained in the famous judgment in *Marbury v. Madison* by Judge Marshall, which introduced the judicial review of legislation.[25] From this perspective, it is important to recall the political context in which Judge Marshall produced that judgment.[26] It was, in fact, right in the middle of a heated political struggle, initiated in 1800 by the election of Jefferson to the presidency, between the Republican Party and the Federalist Party over the significance of the American Revolution. Marshall's verdict indirectly represented the response of the Federalists, still entrenched in their positions of power within the courts of justice, to the Jeffersonian interpretation of democracy, to that idea of "permanent revolution" which seemed to refer to the continuity between elections and revolution, on which Jefferson had constructed the significance of his own victory, presenting it as a "second revolution".

The risk that the Jeffersonian position might undermine the constitutional structure at its foundations, as the Federalists believed, emerges from some of the central statements in Jefferson's first inaugural address, where he enumerated the essential principles of the US government, avoiding any reference to the rule of law, underlining that the safeguarding of the people's right to elections was "a mild and safe corrective of abuses which are lopped by the sword of revolution where peaceable remedies are unprovided". He declared his support for "absolute acquiescence in the decisions of the majority, the vital principle of republics, from which is no appeal but to force".[27]

Against the majoritarian conception of democracy, put forward by Jefferson, in the sentence *Marbury v. Madison* Marshall proposed the removal of constitutional law from the political sphere. In that sentence, it was recognized that the people had "an original right to establish for their future government, such principles, as, in their opinion, shall most conduce to their own happiness". The "exercise of this original right", however, as was specified immediately afterwards, ought not to "be frequently repeated". Once they had been established, those principles had to be considered fundamental, "permanent". The constitutional principles, approved by the people, had affirmed the limited character of the legislative power in such a way that an act of the legislature contrary to the constitution had to be considered null and void. If, in the case of conflict between ordinary laws, the courts were obliged to decide what the law was, the same criteria had to apply in the case of conflict between ordinary laws and constitutional laws.[28] In this way the sentence *Marbury v. Madison* made the judicial power – understood as the virtual representative of the constituent people – responsible for the achievement and defence of the fundamental principles of the constitutional order. At the same time, that sentence took away the role of interpreter of the constitution from the legislative power, giving rise to a permanent legal restraint on the power of the majority, analogous to that exercised on individuals by ordinary laws.[29]

During the nineteenth century, the Supreme Court tried repeatedly to respond to its critics and to attacks against it, trying to reproduce within US jurisprudence the aseptic, detached image of the judge of common law.[30] The appeal to the tradition of common law performed a dual function: it checked the radical pressures which could derive from Locke's theory of the contract[31] and legitimized a vision of law which – contrasting with the public vision originally connected to the writing of the constitution itself – was now presented as a privileged sphere of that "artificial" reason which only the judge possessed, in virtue of his specific professional training and expertise. The entire sphere of economic–contractual relations was excluded from the sphere of political decision-making and submitted to the competence of judiciary action. The consequences of this went well beyond economic–contractual relations. It is enough to recall that in the ruling *Dred Scott v. Sandford* in 1857 the Supreme Court established – on the basis of the clause of due process provided for by the Fifth Amendment[32] – that the ownership of slaves was entitled to the same protection as any other type of property ownership.[33]

4 THE LIBERAL CONCEPTION OF THE RULE OF LAW DURING THE NINETEENTH CENTURY

For the entire nineteenth century and beyond, until the New Deal, two constitutional models contended for predominance.[34] The first – prevalent until the years immediately following the Civil War – was founded on the conviction that fundamental rights could be better protected by the clear-cut separation between state powers and the powers of the federal government. The Bill of Rights was therefore used for this entire period (in the way, moreover, the anti-Federalists and Jefferson himself had conceived of it at the time they had proposed it) as an instrument against the extension of federal power and never against the states, never to verify if rights were actually enjoyed by citizens under the republican constitutions of the individual states.[35] The second model became prevalent in the period stretching roughly from the last decade of the nineteenth century to the turning point of the New Deal, following the introduction of the Fourteenth Amendment, with which, for the first time, the supremacy of federal citizenship over state citizenship was affirmed.[36] This model was the result of the particular interpretation that the Supreme Court gave to the clause of due process. Having to establish, in the light of the new amendment, which rights were so fundamental as to require protection at the federal level, the Supreme Court, according to a conception of the state as "night watchman" and neutral arbitrator in socio-economic conflicts, constitutionalized the theory of freedom of contract. In the attempt to return questions which were increasingly assuming a socio-political character[37] to the sphere of private law, the Supreme Court in those years opposed the introduction of the regulation of working hours or labour conditions for vulnerable workers, such as children.[38] The defence of the theory of freedom of contract undertaken by the Supreme Court immediately appeared paradoxical, for it was sharply at odds with the intensifying social conflict deriving from the transformation of the US economy by the creation of great concentrations of industrial and financial enterprises.

The ideological nature of judgments, openly taking sides in favour of laissez-faire, such as in the famous *Lochner v. New York* in 1905,[39] undermined the image of judicial power as neutral and impartial. The doctrine of common law, which had inspired the jurisprudence of the Supreme Court for the entire preceding century, had to face the criticism of the realist, pragmatist movement, which swept away the certainties of the doctrine of natural law.[40] The idea of common law as the objective, impartial expression of a spontaneous state of things, the reflection of a reality to be saved from the distorting interventions of the legislator, was superseded by a law that was no longer perceived as something given once and for all, but instead as something that could be constructed and interpreted, suitable for regulating and directing reality in a normative sense. The idea of a "living constitution", supported by a historicist, evolutionary approach to law, was substituted for the metaphor of the constitution as a "machine", inspired by a mechanistic-Newtonian vision.[41]

5 THE EXPLOSION OF THE TENSION BETWEEN POLITICS AND LAW

The crisis of the nineteenth-century legal paradigm, founded on the tradition of common law, had important effects on US constitutional law in the first decades of the twentieth century. The first result was a new tension between constitutionalism and democracy, between the powers of the Supreme Court and the autonomy of the states, in the same way as between the powers of the Court and those of the federal government. This tension was to become more acute as the central state not only re-enforced its prerogatives and exercised its power of policy-making over national politics in the social and economic spheres, but also took on a more credible democratic appearance with the end of slavery and the introduction of women's suffrage. The ever-clearer perception of the problematic character of the "counter-majoritarian" power exercised by the Supreme Court created pressure in the first decades of the twentieth century for the adoption of the principle of self-restraint – i.e. a greater deference of the judiciary towards the legislative power.

After 1938, however, the Supreme Court managed to carve out a new space of action for itself, transforming itself from defender of property rights to guarantor of other civil rights and defender of minorities. The decisions of the Court introduced at least two new constitutional trends. The first was orientated towards the defence of certain "preferential rights", considered so because they are inherent to the human personality, such as the freedom of expression and the right to privacy. The second was inspired, however, by the idea of equal protection and aimed at securing equal access to fundamental social services for all, through a scrupulous scrutiny of the criteria of eligibility, with the aim of avoiding discriminatory measures.[42] Both of these models led not only to Supreme Court judgments that were strongly intrusive with regard to majority of political decisions, but also to the Court's assumption of a role as an actual co-legislator. Through the partial incorporation of the Bill of Rights into the Fourteenth Amendment and an extensive interpretation of constitutional formulas, the Supreme Court, in fact, produced, in the post–World War II period (and in particular during the Warren period, 1953–1969) a series of new rights, not explicitly foreseen by the constitution (e.g. the right to privacy or the right to abortion).

All this greatly shook the principles of the liberal "state under the law". The nineteenth-century conception of the constitution as rule of law rested on the authority of a law which was apparently neutral and apolitical. The constitutional practice of the twentieth century went above and beyond both the dividing lines between public law and private law, and between law and politics. The recognition of an irremovable element of interpretative judicial discretion and the activism of the Supreme Court have required a rethinking of the role of judicial interpretation of the constitution, as well as of the actual significance, virtues, and limits of the rule of law.

6 ATTEMPTS TO REFORMULATE THE NOTION OF CONSTITUTION AS RULE OF LAW

Some of the positions expressed in the contemporary constitutional debate in the United States are a development and a re-elaboration of legal realism. They are, a consequence of the new consciousness of the indeterminate character of law and its inapplicability in mechanistic terms. Among the heirs of the realist critique of legal formalism, the movement of *Critical Legal Studies*[43] has assumed an important position. For this movement, the liberal conception of the rule of law and the formalist vision of law on which it rests are the expression of the desire to arrive at a justification of law that places it outside disputes over the basic foundations of society.[44] According to *Critical Legal Studies*, i.e. the defence of legal formalism goes back, implicitly, to the idea that the form of law is able to reflect an objective and intelligible moral order, removed from the precarious, conflictual dimension of politics.[45] For *Critical Legal Studies*, this image of law is fictitious: incoherence and indeterminateness are the actual characteristics of laws, and derive from the very way in which laws are produced. They are not emanated, observes Roberto Mangabeira Unger, by an immanent moral rationality, but instead are the result of conflicts, clashes, and compromises among social groups endowed with differing positions of power, bearers of contrasting interests and opinions, and the traces of which remain in the ambiguities of the legislative text. From the thesis of the indeterminacy of legal rules, *Critical Legal Studies* derives that of the political nature of law and judicial activity. Any attempt to determine the best possible interpretation of the constitution, in such a way as to determine the goals that the system legitimizes and permits to be achieved legally, hides an ideological operation, according to *Critical Legal Studies*. In the interpretation of law, the judge always exercises a discretional power, selecting from among the many points of view left open by the law the one which is closest to his own subjective preferences. The need of liberal legalism to determine a single correct rule for the application of law and the impossibility of obtaining this result mark, for *Critical Legal Studies*, the failure of the rule of law.

If *Critical Legal Studies* undertake a direct attack on the idea of rule of law, openly stressing the ideological character of judicial deliberation, various contemporary approaches to the study of US constitutional law attempt a re-evaluation of the idea of "rule of law" through the formulation of theories of interpretation aimed at providing judicial decisions with objective foundations. The outcome of this operation is conditioned by the choice of what in the constitution is to be considered fundamental: its character as a written text, its original intention, the inspiring principles of the constitutional tradition, or the popular will as expressed in constituent periods. From these elements, the judge should be able to deduce general rules under which to subsume the particular case. In each of these cases, even though on the basis of diverse conceptions of the rule of law, there is the attempt to lead the judge beyond politics, or better, beyond a judicial function which performs de facto a legislative role. Here I will examine, in particular, the proposals of Antonin Scalia, Ronald Dworkin, and Bruce Ackerman.

7 ANTONIN SCALIA AND THE RULE OF LAW AS RULE OF RULES

The formalistic conception of the rule of law recognizes the existence of general rules, the coherent, stable application of law, the non-retroactivity of law, and the separation between the organ responsible for the production of legislation and administration, as an intrinsic value of the legal system. The existence of a legal system endowed with such characteristics is said to make the actions and behaviour of rulers predictable and therefore to increase the freedom of the citizen, freeing him from the fear and insecurity that come from living under an arbitrary government. According to the formalistic conception of the "rule of law", the capacity of the legal system to stabilize social expectations favours individual autonomy and human dignity, since it allows individuals to plan their lives. The role of the rule of law in this perspective is purely negative: to minimize the dangers deriving from the arbitrary exercise of political power. In applying the law, the judge must act according to criteria of impartiality and neutrality, without engaging in judgements tied to some substantive conception of justice. When the judge goes beyond the strict application of the norm, he transforms the "rule of law" into the "rule of men", allocating to himself an arbitrary power.

The constitution can be considered an extension and an improvement of the idea of "rule of law", or rather of the principle that the government must act with respect to pre-established legal restraints. The constitution thus becomes, within a formalistic conception of the rule of law, a set of rules aimed at limiting power. The value which is privileged by this reading of constitutionalism is normative stability, considered an essential condition for the citizen's autonomy.[46]

According to Antonin Scalia, today one of the major exponents of a conception of rule of law as the rule of rules, or rather of a formalistic vision of the "state under the law",[47] the tendency of the common law judge to make reference not to the text but to the intention of the legislator, or to some other criterion external to the text of the law, is bound to open the doors to judicial arbitrariness, and to supplant and betray the will expressed by democratic majorities. In Scalia's "originalist" interpretation,[48] a "rule of law" and not "of men" should respect the objective meaning of the text of the law and not go looking for the subjective intention in it presumably expressed by the legislator: "It is the law that governs, not the intent of the lawgiver."[49] The recourse of the judge to the subjective intention of the legislator, extracted perhaps from the acts of the legislative commissions or from parliamentary discussions, is according to Scalia, one of the ways US judges most frequently assume the illegitimate role of co-legislators.

Passing from the interpretation of ordinary laws to that of constitutional norms, the distinguishing element among the various constitutional theories is, for Scalia, the difference between the search for the *original* meaning and the search for the *current* meaning. A "textualist" judge sticks to the original meaning of the text. He can, if he finds it opportune, consult the opinions expressed during the convention of the "Founding Fathers", but only if that enables him to determine the meaning which the text of the constitutional norm had at the moment of its drafting. In his opinion there is no relevance, and there must not be any relevance, in either the original intention of the constituents, or in the meaning which a contemporary reader could give to the text. The search for the "current" meaning is typical of those judges who intend to transform the constitution into a "living constitution", into a constitution which is flexible and adaptable to change. Behind the apparent virtues of flexibility, the notion of "living constitution" conceals, according to Scalia, the danger of arbitrariness by the judiciary and of the indeterminacy of the law. What the constitution meant yesterday it might no longer mean tomorrow. It will not be up to the democratic legislator to decide if it will be so or not, but to a body of judges not democratically elected. This reading of the constitution, which for Scalia is the result of the influence of the system of common law in the sphere of constitutional interpretation,[50] takes for granted that the constitution cannot and must not resist the pressures of social change. Scalia maintains that it loses sight of the ultimate goal of the constitution as a rule of law: to prevent future generations from being able to alter the restraints established by the preceding generations.[51] The argument of flexibility is, from the perspective of textualism, a disguised legitimization of the tendency of US judges to follow the open and arbitrary character of the tradition of common law in constitutional interpretation. It conceals the risk that the constitution ends up meaning simply what judges from time to time believe it should mean.

The negative effects of the legal culture underlying this approach are indicated by Scalia with reference to the education and professional training of judges, the criteria for their selection, and, more generally, in relation to the possible impact of that legal culture on the political system. In US law schools the study of constitutional law is centred not so much on the text of the constitution, as on the cases and decisions of the courts of justice.[52] In the procedures for the selection and confirmation of federal judges, moreover, what is given importance is above all the ideas which the judges profess, or claim to profess "regarding a whole series of proposals for constitutional evolution".[53] A judicial power which is thus exposed on the political level is bound, according to Scalia, to become a slave to the changing tastes of public opinion. Its capacity to perform the function of guaranteeing the rights of minorities would be seriously threatened and the democratic resources of the US Republic would risk being dissipated.[54]

Scalia's critique of the tradition of common law attacks in particular – as Mary Ann Glendon has observed[55] – the degenerative tendencies which it has manifested in the judicial decisions of the last few decades, such as diminishing attention to the rigorous application of the principle of *stare decisis*. The appeal to textualism, however, despite its motivation by appreciable intents and arguments, does not appear to be an adequate answer to the difficulties a judge must face when applying ordinary law, let alone the dictates of the constitution. Scalia's opposition between a rigorous application of the norm and an arbitrary judicial decision seems too extreme.[56] The search for the original meaning of the text, however, leaves open the problem of the gap between its interpretation and its application: once the original meaning of a norm has been determined, there remains the question of what it entails with relation to the specific case. The originalist perspective, moreover, raises difficult theoretical questions about the justification of a historical interpretation of the constitution. It is legitimate to ask oneself, indeed, for what reason the current generations should feel bound by the meaning which the "Founding Fathers" gave to the text of the constitution more than 200 years ago. For what reason, for example, should the Eighth Amendment, which prohibits the infliction of "cruel and unusual punishment", be interpreted not on the basis of what US citizens today consider "cruel", but instead on the basis of the moral perception of the epoch in which that amendment was first written[57]? The binding nature of a constitution does not seem to derive, as the originalist perspective would have it, from the authority of the convictions professed by the "Founding Fathers". If anything, it is tied to the ability of different generations to identify themselves with the text of the constitution, through subsequent reappropriations of its meaning.[58]

8 DWORKIN: THE JUDGE AS INTERPRETER OF CONSTITUTIONAL PRINCIPLES

Dworkin, too, tries to recover a *hard nucleus* of the constitution in order to construct a "government of law" and not "of men". The way chosen to reaffirm the idea of a "rock-solid, unchanging constitution",[59] however, definitively abandons legal formalism: it is not the text of the constitution but rather the principles of constitutional morality that are the objective anchor of Dworkin's substantive conception of the rule of law.

Dworkin's philosophy of law would be difficult to understand – as Duncan Kennedy suggests – without taking the twofold necessity from which it arises into account: on the one hand, to provide a theoretical justification for the contribution made by the Supreme Court to certain important liberal reforms achieved in the second half of the twentieth century; and, on the other hand, to show how this contribution did not undermine the idea of "rule of law". The legitimization of judicial power within the liberal conception of the rule of law is tied, indeed, to the possibility for the judge to act correctly not in purely moral terms, but also in legal terms.[60] The idea of the Court as a "forum of principles" is the solution which Dworkin arrives at through a reformulation of the idea of "rule of law" which seeks to explain within the constitutional system why the judiciary may not obey the legislative power when rights are in question.

In the formalistic conception of the rule of law, the judge has to deduce from the normative texts the rules within which to subsume particular cases. The conception of the constitution as a set of rules admits of normative lacunae. In "hard cases", when faced with a lacuna, the judge seems to have no alternative than to resort to his subjective preferences or evaluations. This element of discretion is precisely why positivist legal scholars suggest an attitude of prudential deference from judges towards policies decided by the legislator. Dworkin distances himself from this notion of the rule of law: the constitution is not a set of rules but rather a set of fundamental principles. The "constitution of principles", as opposed to "the rule-book" conception of the constitution, proposes a substantive notion of the rule of law: it offers substantial criteria of justice for criticizing a society whose laws do not guarantee the rights entailed by a coherent interpretation of the constitution. This substantive conception of the rule of law provides judges with a power of verification and control which seems meant to allow a much wider interference in the activity of the legislative power. Two major risks could emerge: first, an absolute arbitrariness on the part of the judge and, secondly, an upsetting of the democratic logic. Dworkin seeks to demonstrate how his theory avoids both dangers.

If democracy is equivalent to "government of the people", Dworkin maintains that it is, however, possible to distinguish "two kinds of collective action". The first can be considered as deriving from some statistical function of the behaviour of individuals as, for example, when "the foreign exchange market drove down the price of the dollar". In this case, it is not possible to verify a coherent aim of the group of individuals which affects the state of the monetary market. The second form of collective action, instead, has a community character: it derives from a concerted action in which the individual actions converge and merge. "We, the People", the people from which the constitution emanates, is not a "statistical" entity and neither can its will be made to coincide, Dworkin maintains, with the will of the majority. In Dworkin's interpretation of republican liberalism, "We, the People" is a political community "of principle", which takes form as a moral person in the expression of the constitution.[61]

Dworkin in fact understands the constitution as the expression of the moral identity of a "community of principle", a community, i.e. whose members choose to be regulated by common principles, and "not just by rules hammered out in political compromise". For them, Dworkin adds, politics is "a theatre of debate about which principles the community should adopt as a system, which view it should take of justice, fairness and due process".[62] Hypothesizing that the community can act as an entity that is distinct from the persons who compose it, Dworkin's personification of the community is the premise which allows him to claim that the community, acting as an individual, would choose, as a principle of personal ethics, coherence in time. Secondly, Dworkin maintains that the constitution can be seen as a text, or a narration, written by a single author. These two statements justify the view that the attitude of the judge towards the system is similar to that of the interpreter towards a work of literature.

The legal practice is an interpretative practice, and as such – Dworkin admits – it is profoundly political. Dworkin, however, in order to preserve the legitimacy of judicial review, seeks to demonstrate that the nature of the judicial process cannot be reduced to a matter of personal political preferences. Dworkin's appeal to hermeneutic theory is not intended, in fact, to amplify the space for interpretations ad infinitum, but is meant, on the contrary, to demonstrate that it is always possible for the judge to arrive at a "right answer" or rather at a correct, and therefore objective, interpretation in the light of the overall meaning of the constitutional document.[63]

The interpretative practice, Dworkin maintains, does not leave an absolute, arbitrary power in the hands of the judge. The judge must indeed keep to precise interpretative rules. He is bound by the principle of "integrity", or rather by the need to provide interpretations that are coherent with a system of principles which is defensible in the light of the entire structure of the constitution and of preceding constitutional interpretations. Judges, writes Dworkin, must "regard themselves as partners with other officials, past and future, who together elaborate a coherent constitutional morality, and they must care to see that what they contribute fits with the rest".[64] Judges cannot propose an interpretation of the constitution that suits their personal convictions, no matter how attractive it might be. To decide if a theory offers the best justification of the existing law, some limits are established by the "dimension of fit", others by the "dimension of value", which involves moral (or political) argument. According to Dworkin, in the interpretation of clauses such as that of the equal protection of the law it is impossible to offer an interpretation that is independent of some political theory on what should be understood by equality. In this case also, however, the judge cannot resolve these problems of morality by making reference to his own personal political choices or to more general questions of policy. What distinguishes him from the legislator is precisely that the judge must interpret the documents faithfully, whereas the legislator can and, for Dworkin, in general does act in a way that will achieve a particular political result rather than with regard to consistency with constitutional principles.

Compared with formalistic visions of the rule of law, Dworkin's theory has the merit of not removing the connection which exists between politics and law at the level of constitutional interpretation. His justification of the Supreme Court's power of judicial review proposes, however, a new form of dualism: *judicial politics* should move within a space that is not contaminated by *parliamentary politics*, which, according to Dworkin, is normally precluded both from the possibility of deciding in view of the common interest, and from the ability to interpret the principles of constitutional morality correctly.

It is perhaps worth remembering, in contrast with Dworkin's substantive conception of the rule of law, that over the span of US constitutional history the Supreme Court has scarcely adhered to the principle of integrity – i.e. to an interpretation which is coherent with the entire constitutional structure and with preceding constitutional interpretations. Dworkin himself, choosing for his ideal judge the name of Hercules, appears to be conscious of the distance existing between reality and his theory. What is truly problematic is the relationship of opposition which Dworkin delineates between constitutionalism of rights and democracy. Rights act as a power which is permanently in opposition to democracy, not only in its form as parliamentary democracy, but also in that of constituent democracy, so that Dworkin himself goes so far as to assert the uselessness of resorting to the process of constitutional revision for the definition of new rights.[65] For Dworkin the path of constitutional amendments can be disregarded, given that new rights ("unenumerated rights", not provided for, i.e. by the constitution or Bill of Rights) can be more easily recognized and defended on the ground of a better judicial interpretation of the clauses of due process and equal protection. According to Dworkin, in the interpretation of these clauses the very sense of the distinction between enumerated rights and unenumerated rights is missing. Here, we are dealing with general principles of political morality, the application of which cannot depend on the meaning of words but instead must depend on the meaning that a majority of judges decides to attribute to the constitutional ideals of freedom and equal citizenship.

For Dworkin, the law should act as a "means of social integration".[66] However, it is difficult for it to fulfil this task if – as Habermas points out – only the professional ability of judges, whose thought remains closed like a monologue within the courts, is relied upon for the rational reconstruction of the law.[67] A judiciary power which claims, in virtue of its presumed independence from the pressures of public opinion, autonomously to defend individual rights against their possible violation by the political power, risks creating social restraints which citizens will deem arbitrary. The sense of duty that should accompany the birth of every new right cannot find roots outside of processes of recognition activated by democratic decision procedures.[68] In Dworkin's liberal constitutionalism, it is the Court that has the duty of moral deliberation: it is the place where, through the application of the principle of integrity, the moral values expressed by the constitutional tradition are reconstructed in a coherent vision by the judge. In this way an opposition is outlined between the deliberative role of the Court and the prudential role – the mere registration of existing preferences – of the democratic process. On the basis of this opposition, Gutmann and Thompson see a sort of "deductive institutionalism",[69] which rests on the differing nature of the incentives offered to the legislator and to the judge. The argument is simple: since they must aim at electoral consensus, legislators will tend to make choices in the light of the preferences of their own electors; the judge, on the other hand, in order to have his own professionalism recognized, will be more careful to argue his decisions in terms of principle. It is, as Gutmann and Thompson have pointed out, a weak argument. It could be observed, in fact, that legislators are often pushed to making decisions of principle precisely because they are aiming at widespread consensus, while the judge, because of the need to focus his attention on a particular case, runs the risk of pronouncing judgments which do not take their social impact into account. From a normative perspective, the implications of the opposition between legislative power and judicial power point to the prospect of a situation in which parliamentary politics is reduced to a mere system of aggregation of preferences.[70]

9 ACKERMAN: RULE OF LAW AND CONSTITUENT POWER

The vision of the constitution as the "rule of rules" proposed by the "originalist" interpretation of Judge Scalia left open a fundamental question: why should the subsequent generation feel bound by the will expressed by the "constituent fathers"? Dworkin answers this problem in terms of moral theory: the constitution is the nucleus of commitments of principle around which there develops the identity of a political community acting as a moral person. Dworkin's solution is attractive for its capacity to conciliate stability and flexibility, but is founded on the opposition between democracy and constitutionalism: the fundamental nucleus of principles embodied in the constitution is removed from public political discussion and guarded by an elite of judge–philosophers. Ackerman outlines a solution to the problem of the temporal gap left open by originalism, asserting that the constitution sets up a rule of law that binds the ordinary legislator, but cannot bind the source of its own legitimization – i.e. the constituent power. Every generation, as Jefferson maintained, must be able to rewrite the fundamental principles of the rule of law if it does not intend to accept those of the preceding generations. Between one generational change and another, the Court acts as guarantor of the will expressed by the constituent people. The obligation which the people have towards the constitution does not derive, therefore, either from the fact that the constitution is "there", or from the fact that it is "just": it derives from the commitment of the people of the United States to self-government.[71]

Against the customary interpretation of the US Constitution as a typical example of "constitution-as-guarantor", Ackerman proposes a reading of US constitutional history stressing the areas in which the most has been made of the role of popular sovereignty. According to Ackerman,[72] the constitution has left the power of self-determination with the people, outlining a sort of dualist democracy. It is a democracy in which politics runs along two tracks: a higher law-making track, typical of constitutional politics, and a lower law-making track, typical of ordinary politics. In normal times, decisions are left to the government and to elected representatives, while the citizen is not asked for more than a limited commitment: to go to vote and pay taxes. In exceptional moments, however, the constitution allows the people to act as a constituent power. Ackerman's dualist democracy distinguishes, in this way, between two different levels of political rationality: the choices of ordinary politics are entrusted to the compromises and to the logic of the clash of interests in pluralist democracy, while the determining choices for defining the political identity of the nation require the capacity of political leaders to reactivate participation and mobilize consensus.

The utilization of the rationality expressed by popular sovereignty in the moments of constitutional politics and the doubt about the capacity of the legislative process to express the common interest have important consequences for the role which Ackerman assigns to the Supreme Court. During periods of normal political administration, when interest groups prevail, the Supreme Court is called upon to take on the role of "guardian" of the values of the constitution, to act as the interpreter of the public reason expressed by the constituent people.

With his two-track theory, Ackerman denies the existence within US constitutional history of a tension between the power of parliament and the power of judges to invalidate, through the judicial review of legislation, decisions taken by the people's representatives. Alexander Bickel has defined this tension as a "counter-majoritarian difficulty".[73] According to Ackerman, the error of monist theories of democracy (including that of John Ely[74]), from which the idea of a "counter-majoritarian difficulty" derives, is in conceiving of the legislative power as representative of the popular will and democracy as a synonym for the sovereignty of parliament. Unlike in the British tradition, in the US democratic system Ackerman maintains that the "will of the People" and "parliamentary sovereignty" do not coincide. The voice of the popular will makes itself heard only in the moments of constitutional politics. For this reason, according to Ackerman, control over the constitutionality of the laws, far from being inconsistent with the majority principle, performs a democratic function of great importance: it has the responsibility for defending the constitutional results of the particular moments in which the people, normally eclipsed, are present on the public scene.

The dualist theory of democracy is proposed as capable of respecting the democratic sensitivity of the monists and of offering at the same time an alternative to the theories of rights. Contrary to democratic monists, rights foundationalists fear the abuses of the legislative against individual rights and defend the possibility of removing rights from the vicissitudes of political controversies, relying on the courts for their defence. The dualist theory of democracy shares the lack of trust towards transitory majorities, but does not conceive of rights as demands which, for their intrinsic nature, precede and limit the power of the popular will, expressed in "the higher law-making track." According to Ackerman, the constituent people preserve the possibility of reforming or rewriting the fundamental rights contained in the Bill of Rights. If one day, Ackerman supposes, the wave of religious fanaticism which has swept the Arab world should arrive in the West and set off a polemical reaction in the United States, leading to the revision of the First Amendment[75] and to the introduction of a new amendment in which Christianity is elevated to State religion, a judge of the Supreme Court would have the duty to consider such an amendment as an integral part of the constitution. In Ackerman's opinion, the plausibility of this interpretation is supported by the silence of the constitutional text: while the German Constitution explicitly excludes the constitutional revision of fundamental rights, that of the United States is silent in this regard and that is because, unlike in Germany, in the United States the author maintains that "it is the People who are the source of rights".[76] "In this sense, the dualist's constitution is democratic first, rights protecting second".[77]

Being aware of the difficulty of basing this thesis on a textual interpretation of the constitution, Ackerman conceives of the recourse to the constituent power of the people as an "implicit resource" of the constitutional system. Neither Reconstruction, the period in which, at the end of the Civil War, the Thirteenth, Fourteenth, and Fifteenth Amendments were introduced, nor the New Deal appealed to a regular application of the procedures of constitutional revision provided for by Article V of the constitution.[78] In particular, with the Presidency of Franklin Delano Roosevelt, the United States undertook a modern procedure of constitutional revision, consisting in the promulgation of "amendment analogues." Through the strength which he derived from popular consensus and from the support of the Democratic majority in Congress, in order to enact the reforms of the New Deal Roosevelt persuaded the Supreme Court to alter the rulings which had characterized the "*Lochner* Era". To that end, the President made use of the practice of "transformative appointments". In substance the constitutional "revolution" promoted by Roosevelt did not produce written constitutional amendments but instead was accomplished through a new interpretative practice by the Court, facilitated by the nominations of new judges who were more favourable to Roosevelt's policies.

It is above all this impossibility of writing down the transformations introduced by the modern procedure of constitutional revision which assigns to the Supreme Court a role that risks going beyond the techno-bureaucratic tasks Ackerman would attribute to it. It is up to the Court to interpret the will of the constituent people expressed through the channels of constitutional politics. It is the Court which must ascertain that there has come about one of those exceptional moments in which the people or its leaders have thrown the switch which permits a shift from the track of normal politics to that of constitutional politics. It is again the Court that must determine the specific content expressed by the constituent politics and must bring about, finally, a synthesis which makes this content coherent with the preceding constitutional tradition. In theory, only the constituent people can decide which rights are fundamental for defining its own political identity. But as a matter of fact, without a revision of Article V, which allows the will of the national citizenry (and not the will of the states) to amend the constitution, the Court can always transform itself into something different from the simple custodian of the principles of the rule of law established by the constituent people. If, moreover, as Waldron observes:

> [O]nce the people begin disagreeing among themselves about how to interpret their own past acts of higher law making, it is unclear why any particular interpretation of that heritage should be able to trump any other simply because it is endorsed by five judges out of nine.[79]

In other words, it is not clear why the answer of the Supreme Court should prevail over the alternative interpretations offered by the democratically elected representatives of the people.

10 THE IRREDUCIBILITY OF THE CONSTITUTION TO JUDICIAL RULE OF LAW

Against attempts to refound the judicial rule of law through a theory of interpretation which ensures its neutral character, there are efforts by some authors in the direction of a democratic constitutionalism, or rather a constitutionalism which does not take Constitution and political democracy to be in opposition. The rule of law in adjudication is, according to this perspective, one of the values which a constitutional system seeks to promote, but it is not the only one. If, for Ackerman, the constitution is democratic in that it is the emanation of the constituent people, other authors have sought a connection between democracy and constitutionalism, underlining not so much the popular origin of the constitution as its being aimed at creating a democratic government. In these theories, there is an emphasis on the need for a constitutional democracy to allow room for dialectics among powers and democratic decisions. From this perspective, the only legitimate function of the judicial review of legislation is that of supporting the democratic process. It is possible to read in this sense the views of Sunstein, which call for a re-evaluation of the republican perspective present in the *Federalist*. Sunstein proposes an interpretation of Madison in which attention is no longer put only on the struggle among factions guided by the search for selfish self-interest: individuals are not moved only by economic motives, but also by a purely political passion which consists in the will to affirm one's own opinions.[80] Madison's political philosophy adapts in this way liberal elements and republican elements, referring back to a republicanism which is close to the Machiavellian tradition. It is a perspective which Sunstein distinguishes both from civic humanism and from democratic pluralism.[81]

In Sunstein's opinion, Madison had insisted on the possibility of a "virtuous politics" without, however, yielding to overly optimistic assumptions about human nature.[82] In this liberal-republican conception, participation was no longer the supreme good, and neither was freedom principally definable as self-government. According to the "Founding Fathers", Sunstein writes:

> We might understand the Constitution as a complex set of precommitment strategies, through which the citizenry creates institutional arrangements to protect against political self-interest, factionalism, failures in representation, myopia, and other predictable problems in democratic governance.[83]

The constitution performed a function of guarantor against every form of arbitrary government principally because it required the government to "provide reasons that can be intelligible to different people operating from different premises".[84] The constitution, therefore, guaranteed a rule of law in that it ensured a legislation which could be perceived as neutral and therefore able to obtain a general consensus.

The ordinary political process, by virtue of its capacity to produce principled decisions, recovers a central position in this vision, which entails a reconsideration of the role of the Supreme Court within the constitutional plan. In the theories of "rights foundationalists", but also to a certain extent in approaches such as those of Amar and Ackerman, in which the judiciary acts as a temporary substitute for the will of the constituent people during periods of normal politics, the Supreme Court exercises great power as a check on legislative organs. Sunstein's approach reduces the discretionary power of the Court, bringing it back within the plan for the balance of different powers designed by the "Founding Fathers". From the option for a deliberative conception of democracy comes the limitation of the activism of the Supreme Court to two main types of cases: when the rights at stake are crucial in the functioning of the democratic process and when there is the danger that certain minority groups do or will not receive equal treatment within the political process.[85]

The deliberative function taken on by the Supreme Court in the twentieth century through the exercise of the power of judicial review is looked upon with suspicion by Sunstein for two reasons. The first is that constitutional judgments operate by removing the controversial issues to which they respond from the political arena. This operation, as stressed by Holmes,[86] can reinforce a political system, to the extent that it manages to neutralize the struggle among inflexible factions: one can think, for example, of the peace-making effect of having placed religious questions outside the terrain of political struggle. On the other hand, however, the problem arises of the democratic nature of institutions that divert issues which are perceived as potential sources of social division outside of the public arena.[87] Sunstein maintains that "under such a system, democratic processes would operate only when the stakes were low, and the largest issues would be resolved behind the scenes or by particular groups".[88] The second reason is connected to the idea that "in all well-functioning constitutional democracies, the real forum of high principle is politics, not the judiciary – and the most fundamental principles are developed democratically, not in courtrooms".[89] According to Sunstein, the pluralism of contemporary societies seems to obtain better guarantees from a constitutional system in which the controversial issues are not delegated to a restricted group of judges operating on the basis of highly abstract theories, such as to block rather than stimulate the intervention of the democratic deliberative process.

It is worth citing the example of abortion. When in 1973 the Supreme Court decided with *Roe v. Wade* to make abortion a constitutional right, it removed a hot issue from the sphere of political deliberation, but the effects of this decision have been, in the opinion of many, just as controversial on the political level. There are reasons to believe that that ruling has sharpened, instead of neutralizing, the conflict between pro-choice and pro-life forces. In a case like this, in Sunstein's opinion, the Supreme Court should have acted so as to favour a reopening of the dialogue in the political sphere instead of closing the discussion.

What Sunstein writes about *Roe v. Wade* sheds light on his attempt to restore a complex, articulated image of constitutionalism, which values its structural component. A "minimalist" Court, which acts on the basis of "incompletely theorized agreements" – i.e. seeking a ground where for each specific case it is possible to reach a general agreement, without arguing in depth the fundamental principles which may motivate the choice – would respect the pluralism of contemporary societies and be in line with the need to keep a dialectical relationship among the various powers in both their horizontal and vertical separation. In this latter hypothesis, the states' autonomy would be guaranteed within a federal system intended to allow a wide range of political solutions and experiments.[90]

The strictly liberal conception of constitutionalism, stressing its character as guarantor, tends to reduce it to a set of rights that can at any moment be defended and claimed in the halls of justice.[91] In this way it depreciates the active role of citizens and the filtering function of the political process. Furthermore, it ends up by eating away at the root sources of social solidarity and consensus which are necessary for correct, effective functioning of the democratic system. Instead, in Sunstein's republican interpretation, constitutionalism goes well beyond legal certainty and the judicial protection of rights.[92] But this does not mean that the fundamental nature of rights is abandoned: they are instead interpreted either as preconditions or as the result of a correct political process. Sunstein's liberal-republican constitutionalism, although safeguarding the value of the rule of law, nevertheless does not consider it the only or the principal virtue of a political system; it aims, rather, at a dialogue among the constitutional powers which is useful in making the political process more effective and in minimizing its pathologies.

11 CONCLUSIONS

Dworkin, Ackerman, and Sunstein have an important merit: in different ways, they have tried to reckon with the republican interpretation of the rule of law which animated the constitutionalism of the "Founding Fathers", or rather with the idea that the constitution, to the extent that it refers back to a law which the citizen is able to identify with, has much more to do with building the identity of the political community than with legal certainty. Yet, the intersection between civil rights and political rights, which derived from the idea of the constitution as an emanation of popular sovereignty, disappears beyond the horizon of the republican liberalism of Dworkin, where – as we have seen – it is not only the ordinary political process that is depreciated but even the recourse to the procedures of constitutional revision. Ackerman's theory of dualist democracy is more attentive to the risks which arise from the task, attributed to the courts, of periodically reconstructing constitutional identity, even if it is through an expansion of the protection of rights. Ackerman restores full dignity to the principle of popular sovereignty, but he seems to conceive of it as being capable of producing rationality and consensus only when it is expressed in the form of constituent power. It is likely that, especially in a constitutional system over 200 years old, a more frequent resort to constitutional revision could avoid the need for introducing significant innovations outside the procedures provided for by the system. Ackerman's republican-populist perspective ends up, however, by depreciating "normal politics", whether as a moment of creating and reproducing institutional consensus, or as an instrument for guaranteeing rights and resolving social conflicts.

"Normal politics", due to its deep roots in public life, allows legislators to make an evaluation of the impact of their own decisions on the day-to-day life of citizens, something which is not possible during the moments of "constitutional politics", when public issues are addressed in a highly abstract manner. This same capacity for evaluating the impact of their decisions is, to a large extent, also denied the courts of justice, for various reasons: the concentration of judicial activity on individual cases; the technical training of judges; their restricted social origins besides their character, which is not representative of the different components of society. The courts' difficulty in foreseeing and managing the systemic effects of their decisions, as well as collecting information on relevant social issues, should encourage an in-depth consideration of the making the defence of rights the exclusive responsibility of the courts of justice.

The effects of the courts' intervention in issues of affirmative action and abortion on the political system of the United States can be considered exemplary of the contradictory consequences of judicial politics. The constitutionalization of abortion has radicalized the conflict between pro-abortion and anti-abortion advocates, and has created at the same time a paradoxical situation:[93] a change in the jurisprudence of the Court – possible also through the simple practice of "transformative appointments", i.e. the appointment of new judges – could overturn the current situation and take away women's right to abortion. At that point, the way of ordinary legislation would be precluded and the only recourse open to legislators would be the complicated procedure of constitutional revision. No less contradictory are the effects of the Court's actions on the question of minority rights. The actions of the Court in this case appear to have served to conceal the limits of the welfare measures adopted to date in the United States and, above all, to avert attention from the social, economic, and cultural aspects of the ethnic and racial issues.[94]

The judiciary can be an important support for the political process, but the courts should not substitute themselves for collective discussion within the public arena. In political debate it is not only agreement on collective ends that is achieved, but also the choice of the means to pursue the agreed-upon objectives, a choice no less relevant and no less charged with tension. The role of guarantor of individuals' and minorities' rights which the Supreme Court took on during the second half of the twentieth century has contributed to directing political groups towards the judicial solution of political conflicts. The reasons which have pushed and continue to push in this direction are easily discernable, considering the fact that action via the judiciary reduces the number of actors involved in the decision-making process and is in general quicker in the solution of controversial issues than is the legislative procedure.[95] Issues of a political nature, prone to public discussion, tend to be put forward in terms of demands to be made exclusively through the judiciary, with a considerably distorting effect: citizens are encouraged to think that the recognition of rights can be achieved independently of any type of political action or decision.

NOTES

1. On this subject there are different interpretations: Gordon Wood (*The Creation of the American Republic*, Norton (NY): North Carolina Press, 1972), for example, maintains that the first constitutions were written by the ordinary legislator, putting off until 1780 – i.e. until the drafting of the Constitution of Massachusetts – the moment in which awareness of the difference between an ordinary legislative process and a constituent process emerged in a clear and explicit manner. I agree, here, with the conclusions reached in the most recent work by Kruman, who corrects Wood's thesis: cf. M.W. Kruman, *Between Authority and Liberty. State Constitution Making in Revolutionary America*, Chapel Hill/London: The University of North Carolina Press, 1997. On changes in the conception of the Constitution in the United States, see also G. Stourzh, "Constitution: Changing Meanings of the Term from Early Seventeenth to Late Eighteenth Century", in T. Ball and J.G.A. Pocock (eds), *Conceptual Change and the Constitution*, Lawrence (KS): University Press of Kansas, 1988, pp. 35–54.
2. On the tension between politics and law in modern constitutionalism, cf. P.P. Portinaro, "Il grande legislatore e il futuro della Costituzione", in G. Zagrebelsky,

P.P. Portinaro, and J. Luther (eds), *Il futuro della Costituzione*, Torino: Einaudi, 1991, pp. 5–6.

3. On the US republican tradition there are a great number of works. Among the most important works, see B. Bailyn, *The Ideological Origins of the American Revolution*, Cambridge: Cambridge University Press, 1967; G. Wood, *The Creation of the American Republic, 1776–1787*; J.G.A. Pocock, *The Machiavellian Moment: Florentine Political Thought and the Atlantic Republican Tradition*, Princeton (NJ): Princeton University Press, 1975. For a re-evaluation of the modern, innovative character of US republicanism and its roots in John Locke, in contrast with the readings of Pocock, Bailyn, and Wood, see I. Kramnick, *Republicanism and Bourgeois Radicalism. Political Ideology in Late Eighteenth-Century England and America*, Ithaca/London: Cornell University Press, 1990; T.L. Pangle, *The Spirit of Modern Republicanism. The Moral Vision of the American Founders and the Philosophy of Locke*, Chicago/London: The University of Chicago Press, 1990; J. Appleby, *Liberalism and Republicanism in the Historical Imagination*, Cambridge (MA): Harvard University Press, 1993; P. Rahe, *Republics Ancient and Modern. Classical Republicanism and the American Revolution*, Chapel Hill/London: The University of North Carolina Press, 1992; M.P. Zuckert, *Natural Rights and the New Republicanism*, Princeton (NJ): Princeton University Press, 1994; J. Huyler, *Locke in America. The Moral Philosophy of the Founding Era*, Lawrence (KS): University Press of Kansas, 1995; J.P. Young, *Reconsidering American Liberalism. The Troubled Odyssey of the Liberal Idea*, Boulder (CO): Westview Press, 1996.
4. John Marshall was the Chief Justice of the Supreme Court from 1801 to 1835. His jurisprudence was fundamental for the consolidation of the interpretative criteria of the Constitution. The introduction of the judicial review of legislation is attributed to the judgment which he expressed in the case of *Marbury v. Madison*. The case which led to that decision was determined by the refusal of Jefferson and by his Secretary of State, James Madison, to confirm the nominations to the office of Justice of the Peace, among them that of John Marbury, made by President John Adams at the expiration of his term (for this reason also called "midnight nominations").
5. Against the decisions of the Court there is only the difficult and seldom used recourse to constitutional amendments. It should be remembered, moreover, that art. V of the Constitution makes the states and not the federal powers the protagonists in the procedures for constitutional revision. In order to be valid, amendments must be ratified by three-quarters of the states, something which, considering the differing demographic densities of the individual states can produce effects that are paradoxical from a democratic perspective.
6. With the exception of the *Dred Scott* case (1857), with which the Court sanctioned the legitimacy of the exclusion of Afro-Americans from the enjoyment of the rights of citizenship, the Court rarely used the Bill of Rights to nullify acts of the federal legislature until the end of the nineteenth century. Only after the Second World War – and not differently from what took place in the other Western democracies – did the Court mature a particular sensitivity towards questions of personal freedoms and civil rights. For stimulating reading on the use of the language of rights in US history, which underlines the impact of the reaction to totalitarianism on the twentieth-century conception of rights, see R.A. Primus, *The American Language of Rights*, Cambridge: Cambridge University Press, 1999.

7. For a reading on US citizenship which is attentive to its internal contradictions, see R.M. Smith, *Civic Ideals. Conflicting Visions of Citizenship in US History*, New Haven (CT)/London: Yale University Press, 1997.
8. Through the clause in the XIV amendment which prohibits any state from enacting "any law which shall abridge the privileges or immunities of citizens of the United States", the rulings of the Supreme Court in the twentieth century undertook a partial incorporation of the first ten amendments, thus asserting the validity of the contents of the Bill of Rights with regard not only to the federal government, but also to the governments of the individual states; cf. R. Primus, *The Language of Rights*, passim.
9. Cf. R.M. Cover, "The Origins of Judicial Activism in the Protection of Minorities", *Yale Law Journal*, 91 (1982), pp. 1287–316.
10. J. Ely, *Democracy and Distrust: A Theory of Judicial Review*, Cambridge (MA): Harvard University Press, 1980, p. 76.
11. Cf. C.A. Houston, *Algernon Sidney and the Republican Heritage in England and America*, Princeton (NJ): Princeton University Press, 1991, p. 233. For the influence of Sidney on the drafting of the Constitution of Pennsylvania, cf., ibid., pp. 232–3.
12. On the influence of the "real", "independent", or "true whigs" on US constitutional history during the revolutionary period, see C. Robbins, *The Eighteenth Century Commonwealthman*, Cambridge (MA): Cambridge University Press, 1959; T. Colbourn, *The Lamp of Experience: Whig History and the Intellectual Origins of the American Revolution*, Indianapolis (IN): Liberty Fund, 1998; B. Bailyn, *The Ideological Origins of the American Revolution*; R.E. Toohey, *Liberty and Empire, British Radical Solutions to the American Problem, 1774–1776*, Lexington (KY): The University Press of Kentucky, 1978; D.N. Mayer, *The Constitutional Thought of Thomas Jefferson*, Charlottesville (VA)/London: The University Press of Virginia, 1997, chap. II; C.B. Thompson, *John Adams and the Spirit of Liberty*, Lawrence (KS): University Press of Kansas, 1998, chap. IV.
13. On the possibility of retracing this turning point in English constitutional thought to Locke and Sidney, cf. J.G.A. Pocock, *The Ancient Constitution and the Feudal Law. English Historical Thought in the Seventeenth Century*, New York: W.W. Norton, 1967, pp. 236–9. On the break made by Locke with respect to the paradigm of common law, cf. D. Resnick, "Locke and the Rejection of the Ancient Constitution", *Political Theory*, 12 (1984), 1, pp. 97–114; J.R. Stoner, Jr., *Common Law and Liberal Theory. Coke, Hobbes, and the Origins of American Constitutionalism*, Lawrence (KS): University Press of Kansas, 1992, pp. 137–51.
14. With regard to the different families within the republican tradition, see M. Geuna, "La tradizione repubblicana e i suoi interpreti: famiglie teoriche e discontinuità concettuali", *Filosofia politica*, 12 (1998), 1, pp. 101–32.
15. P. Pettit, *Republicanism. A Theory of Freedom and Government*, Oxford: Clarendon Press, 1997, p. 8.
16. Cf. J.M. Balkin, "Populism and Progressivism as Constitutional Categories", *The Yale Law Journal*, 104 (1995), in particular pp. 1945–6.
17. P. Pettit, *Republicanism. A Theory of Freedom and Government*, p. 8.
18. D.N. Mayer, *The Constitutional Thought of Thomas Jefferson*, p. 257; but see in general chap. IX: *A Solecism in a Republican Government. The Judiciary and Judicial Review*.

19. J. Adams, "Defence of the Constitutions of Government of the United States of America", in J. Adams, *Works*, vol. 4, Boston (MA): Little, Brown, 1851, p. 504.
20. The influence of the reflections of J. Adams on Federalist thought is asserted by C.B. Thompson, *John Adams and the Spirit of Liberty*, passim.
21. For an interpretation from a republican perspective of the thought of the Federalists, see D.F. Epstein, *The Political Theory of the Federalist*, Chicago/London: The University of Chicago Press, 1984; G.W. Carey, *The Federalist Design For a Constitutional Republic*, Urbana/Chicago: University of Illinois Press, 1994.
22. Cf. A. Hamilton, J. Madison, and J. Jay, *The Federalist Papers*, ed. C. Rossiter, New York: New American Library, 1961, p. 384.
23. Cf. S. Snowiss, *Judicial Review and the Law of the Constitution*, New Haven (CT)/London: Yale University Press, 1990, chaps. II and III.
24. T. Bonazzi, "Il Demos Basileus e la nascita degli Stati Uniti", *Filosofia politica*, 5 (1991), p. 102.
25. Appleby writes: "Despite the celebration of popular sovereignty in America, the sovereign people were restrained once the constitution was ratified"; cf. J. Appleby, *Liberalism and Republicanism in the Historical Imagination*, p. 219.
26. The historical context in which the Marshall judgment is situated, or rather the background constituted by the battle between Federalists and Republicans over the Constitution, is seldom remembered. For an in-depth analysis, see P. Kahn, *The Reign of Law. Marbury v. Madison and the Construction of America*, New Haven (CT)/London: Yale University Press, 1997.
27. T. Jefferson, *Public and Private Papers*, introduction by T. Wicker, New York: Vintage Books, The Library of America, 1990, pp. 168–9. For the significance of Jefferson's inaugural speech and the challenge which this presented for the Federalist interpretation of the Revolution, see also P. Kahn, *The Reign of Law*, passim.
28. *Appendix: William Marbury v. James Madison, Secretary of State of the United States*, in P. Kahn, *The Reign of Law*, pp. 254–6.
29. S. Snowiss, *Judicial Review and the Law of the Constitution*, p. 119.
30. S.C. Stimson, *The American Revolution in the Law: Anglo-American Jurisprudence Before John Marshall*, Princeton (NJ): Princeton University Press, 1990, p. 144.
31. On this thesis there is agreement in the works of Stimson (*The American Revolution in the Law: Anglo-American Jurisprudence Before John Marshall*) and Stoner (*Common Law and Liberal Theory*). On the same topic, see also C.L. Tomlins, *Law, Labor and Ideology in the Early American Republic*, Cambridge (MA): Cambridge University Press, 1993, in particular pp. 93–4, 104–5.
32. The Fifth Amendment establishes, among the various guarantees for the protection of the freedom and security of the individual, that no person may be "deprived of life, liberty, or property, without due process of law".
33. Cf. J. Nedelsky, *Private Property and the Limits of American Constitutionalism: The Madisonian Framework and its Legacy*, Chicago: The University of Chicago Press, 1985, p. 225; R.M. Smith, *Liberalism and American Constitutional Law*, Cambridge (MA): Harvard University Press, 1985, p. 73.
34. Cf. L. Tribe, *American Constitutional Law*, Mineola (NY): The Foundation Press, 1978.
35. The Federal structure has acted as a powerful restraint on the protection of fundamental rights, and in part it continues to do so, given the competitive and not cooperative character of US Federalism. Being in direct rivalry among themselves in

questions of investment and production, within a system which permits special interests to negotiate in order to obtain from state legislative and judicial organs the most favourable conditions for them, it is difficult for the states to manage to maintain high standards of regulation of working conditions; cf. H.N. Screiber, "Constitutional Structure and the Protection of Rights", in A.E. Dick Howard (ed.), *The United States Constitution. Roots, Rights and Responsibilities*, Washington, DC/London: Smithsonian Institution Press, 1992, p. 195. On the same topic, see also H.A. Linde, *Citizenship and State Constitutions*, pp. 381–96.

36. In sect. I, the Fourteenth Amendment affirms: "All persons born or naturalized in the United States, and subject to the jurisdiction thereof, are citizens of the United States and of the State wherein they reside. No State shall make or enforce any law which shall abridge the privileges or immunities of citizens of the United States; nor shall any State deprive any person of life, liberty, or property, without due process of law, nor deny to any person within its jurisdiction the equal protection of the laws."
37. Cf. M.J. Horwitz, *The Transformation of American Law, 1870–1960: The Crisis of Legal Orthodoxy*, Oxford: Oxford University Press, 1992, pp. 10–11.
38. For the opposition of the Court to the regulation of child labour, cf. S.M. Griffin, *American Constitutionalism*, Princeton (NJ): Princeton University Press, 1996, pp. 88–9. The sentences of the Court during the "Progressive Era" against the legislation on child labour are often taken as an example of the ability of the Supreme Court to block for decades reforms which were widely supported by public opinion, see J. Agresto, *The Supreme Court and Constitutional Democracy*, Ithaca (NY): Cornell University Press, 1984, pp. 28–9.
39. With this ruling, the Court declared unconstitutional the legislation introduced by the State of New York for the regulation of the working hours in bakeries. The sentence is considered emblematic of the conservative role played by the Court at the beginning of the twentieth century (the "*Lochner* Era", from the name of that sentence), blocking the introduction of legislation more favourable to the working class; cf. S.M. Griffin, *American Constitutionalism*, pp. 100–1.
40. Cf. M.J. Horwitz, *The Transformation of American Law, 1870–1960: The Crisis of Legal Orthodoxy*, passim.
41. Cf. M. Kammen, *A Machine that Would Go of Itself: The Constitution in American Culture*, New York: Alfred A. Knopf, 1986.
42. I refer here to the analysis by L. Tribe, *American Constitutional Law*; see, in particular chaps. 11 and 16.
43. On the movement of the C.L.S., see A. Carrino, *Ideologia e coscienza. Critical Legal Studies*, Naples: ESI, 1992.
44. R.M. Unger, "The Critical Legal Studies Movement", *Harvard Law Review*, 3 (1983), p. 563.
45. Ibid.
46. For this reading of US constitutionalism, cf. R.S. Kay, "American Constitutionalism", in L. Alexander (ed.), *Constitutionalism. Philosophical Foundations*, pp. 16–63.
47. Cf. A. Scalia, "The Rule of Law as a Law of Rules. Oliver Wendell Holmes Bicentennial Lecture", *Harvard Law School*, 56 (1989), 4, pp. 1175–88.
48. What counts in the originalists' interpretation is history. For the originalists, then, as John Arthur explains, "the question to be asked in interpreting vague constitutional language is how those who originally wrote the words understood them";

J. Arthur, *Words that Bind: Judicial Review and the Grounds of Modern Constitutional Theory*, Boulder (CO): Westview Press, 1995, p. 23. On the originalist perspective, see R. Bork, *The Tempting of America. The Political Seduction of the Law*, New York: The Free Press, 1990; R. Berger, *Government by Judiciary: The Transformation of the Fourteenth Amendment*, Indianapolis (IN): Liberty Fund, 1997.

49. A. Scalia, "Common-Law Courts in a Civil-Law System: The Role of United States Federal Courts in Interpreting the Constitution and Laws", in A. Scalia, *A Matter of Interpretation. Federal Courts and the Law*, ed. by A. Gutmann, with comments by G. Wood, L.H. Tribe, M.A. Glendon, and R. Dworkin, Princeton (NJ): Princeton University Press, 1997, p. 21.
50. Ibid., p. 38.
51. Ibid., p. 40.
52. Ibid., pp. 3–9.
53. Ibid., p. 47.
54. Ibid., pp. 46–7.
55. M.A. Glendon, "Comment", in A. Scalia, *A Matter of Interpretation. Federal Courts and the Law*, pp. 95–114.
56. An attempt to reformulate textualist originalism, attentive to the distinction between the interpretive question and the normative question, or rather to the problem of the directive which must be drawn from the constitutional text with relation to the specific case, is found in M. Perry, *The Constitution in the Courts. Law or Politics?* Oxford: Oxford University Press, 1994.
57. Cf. C.R. Sunstein, *One Case at a Time. Judicial Minimalism on the Supreme Court*, Cambridge (MA): Harvard University Press, 1999, pp. 237–41.
58. On this point, cf. G. Palombella, *Costituzione e sovranità. Il senso della democrazia costituzionale*, Bari: Dedalo, 1997, pp. 25–9.
59. The idea of the Constitution as a "rock-solid, unchanging constitution" is formulated by Scalia; cf. A. Scalia, "Common-Law Courts in a Civil-Law System: The Role of United States Federal Courts in Interpreting the Constitution and Laws", p. 47. For the non-adherence of Dworkin to the idea of a "living constitution" cf. R. Dworkin, "Comment", in A. Scalia, *A Matter of Interpretation. Federal Courts and the Law*, pp. 122–3.
60. Cf. D. Kennedy, *A Critique of Adjudication (fin de siècle)*, Cambridge (MA): Harvard University Press, 1998; see, in general, pp. 119–30.
61. R. Dworkin, *Freedom's Law. The Moral Reading of the American Constitution*, Cambridge (MA): The Belknap Press of Harvard University Press, 1996, pp. 19–20.
62. R. Dworkin, *Law's Empire*, Cambridge (MA): The Belknap Press of Harvard University Press, 1986, p. 199.
63. Cf. R. Dworkin, "On Interpretation and Objectivity", in R. Dworkin, *A Matter of Principle*, Cambridge (MA): Harvard University Press, 1985, chap. 7.
64. R. Dworkin, *Freedom's Law*, p. 10.
65. Cf. G. Palombella, "Giudici, diritti e democrazia", *Democrazia e diritto*, 1 (1997), p. 248.
66. Cf. J. Habermas, *Faktizität und Geltung. Beiträge zur Diskurstheorie des Rechts und des demokratischen Rechtsstaats*, Frankfurt a. M.: Suhrkamp Verlag, 1992, Eng. tr. *Between Facts and Norms. Contribution to a Discourse Theory of Law and Democracy*, Cambridge (MA): The MIT Press, 1996, p. 222.
67. Ibid., pp. 222–3.
68. Ibid.

69. A. Gutmann and D. Thompson, *Democracy and Disagreement*, Cambridge (MA): The Belknap Press of Harvard University Press, 1996, p. 45.
70. Ibid., pp. 45–6.
71. F.I. Michelman, "Constitutional Authorship", in L. Alexander (ed.), *Constitutionalism. Philosophical Foundations*, p. 77.
72. B. Ackerman, *We The People. Foundations*, Cambridge (MA): The Belknap Press of Harvard University Press, 1991; B. Ackerman, *We The People. Transformations*, Cambridge (MA): The Belknap Press of Harvard University Press, 1998.
73. Cf. A. Bickel, *The Least Dangerous Branch: The Supreme Court at the Bar of Politics*, Indianapolis: Bobbs-Merrill, 1962.
74. J. Ely, *Democracy and Distrust*.
75. The First Amendment, as is well known, confirms the respect of freedom of religion as well as freedom of expression.
76. B. Ackerman, *We The People. Foundations*, p. 15.
77. Ibid., p. 13.
78. Ackerman offers a detailed analysis of the period of Reconstruction and of the New Deal; see B. Ackerman, *We The People. Transformations*, passim.
79. J. Waldron, "Review of B. Ackerman, *We The People: Volume I, Foundations*", *Journal of Philosophy*, 90 (1993), 2, p. 153.
80. Cf. D.F. Epstein, *The Political Theory of the Federalist*, chap. III.
81. C.R. Sunstein, "Interest Groups in American Public Law", *Stanford Law Review*, 38 (1985), p. 42.
82. Cf. C.R. Sunstein, *The Partial Constitution*, Cambridge (MA): Harvard University Press, 1993, p. 21.
83. Ibid.
84. Ibid., p. 24.
85. Ibid., pp. 143–4. Here Sunstein reconsiders and re-elaborates the theory of Ely, tying it to a different conception of democracy (no longer the model of pluralist democracy but instead that of deliberative democracy).
86. S. Holmes, "Precommitments and the Paradox of Democracy", in J. Elster and R. Slagstad (eds), *Constitutionalism and Democracy*, Cambridge (MA): Cambridge University Press, 1997, pp. 195–240.
87. Cf. C.R. Sunstein, "Constitutions and Democracies", in J. Elster and R. Slagstad (eds), *Constitutionalism and Democracy*, p. 340.
88. Ibid.
89. C.R. Sunstein, *Legal Reasoning and Political Conflict*, Oxford: Oxford University Press, 1996, p. 7.
90. Cf., for example, C.R. Sunstein, *One Case at a Time. Judicial Minimalism on the Supreme Court*, p. 114.
91. For a highlighting (in tune with the positions of Sunstein) of the limits of the liberal conception of constitutionalism as an outline of the rights that act as a power in opposition to, and in permanent conflict with, the democratic idea, see G. Palombella, "Giudici, diritti, democrazia", passim.
92. For a similar interpretation of constitutionalism, see R. Bellamy, "The Political Form of the Constitution: Separation of Powers, Rights and Representative Democracy", *Political Studies*, 44 (1996), pp. 436–56.
93. On the effect of radicalization of the conflict produced by the constitutionalization of the right to abortion, cf. P. Raynaud, "Tyrannie de la majorité, tyrannie des

minorités", *Le débats*, 69 (1992), p. 56. The article also takes into consideration the contradictory effects of the judicial policy of affirmative action.

94. Cf. G.A. Spann, *Race Against the Court. The Supreme Court and Minorities in Contemporary America*, New York: New York University Press, 1993.
95. Cf. C.P. Manfredi, *Judicial Power and the Charter: Canada and the Paradox of Liberal Constitutionalism*, Norman (OK)/London: University of Oklahoma Press, 1993, in particular chap. VI, which pays considerable attention not only to the distorting effects of judicial action on political discourse, but also to the difficulties of the judiciary in controlling the systemic effects of its own decisions.

CHAPTER 5

RECHTSSTAAT AND INDIVIDUAL RIGHTS IN GERMAN CONSTITUTIONAL HISTORY

Gustavo Gozzi

1 *RECHTSSTAAT* AND RULE OF LAW: AN ENDLESS CONTROVERSY

Lorenz von Stein, one of the most important theorists of the *Rechtsstaat* in the German-speaking area, wrote in 1869 that the *Rechtsstaat* was a peculiarly German creation.[1] Von Stein saw the origins of the notion in the work of Robert von Mohl, who had reconstructed the history of the concept of *Rechtsstaat* from Hugo Grotius onwards.[2]

What exactly did Stein mean? Did he mean that only the concept of *Rechtsstaat* was peculiarly German, while there remained, notwithstanding the various formulations, a single, identical state-form? Or did he mean that the concept referred to a specific constitutional history that made it impossible to compare the typical German state-form with other forms of state? In my view, the second interpretation corresponds to Stein's intended meaning.[3] As my first task, then, I will attempt to support this point.

The question has also been addressed by Neil MacCormick, who, however, reaches conclusions quite different from those that will be defended here. MacCormick claims, in fact, that a comparison of the German and English cases shows that *Rechtsstaat* and rule of law, despite their different constitutional histories, rest upon the same underlying *principles*.[4] MacCormick singles out the following in particular: (1) the principle of legality, which is the same in the different contexts; (2) the principle of the general validity of legal precepts;[5] (3) the principle of the public nature of laws; and (4) the principle of non-retroactivity. These principles, aside from specific constitutional histories, make up the same Western constitutional tradition.

However, when MacCormick discusses the significance of these principles, he identifies them with the *political values* underlying the legal system. These values, he claims, vary according to the different constitutional histories. Thus for England the values are rooted in the tradition of common law, which was elaborated by the courts and, which laid the

P. Costa and D. Zolo (eds.), The Rule of Law: History, Theory and Criticism, 237–259.

foundations of the rule of law. In Germany, on the other hand, the doctrine of the *Rechtsstaat* precludes the possibility of the primacy of law over the state.[6] Indeed, it is precisely in the relationship between law and state – which in the German case is settled with the primacy of the state – that the most significant feature of the doctrine of the German *Rechtsstaat* emerges. Conversely, the English doctrine of the "government of law" is most clearly distinguished by grounding the rule of law on the superiority of law as proclaimed by the courts of justice.

A position similar to MacCormick's is defended by Hasso Hofmann. Hofmann, although he acknowledges that the term *Rechtsstaat* is specifically German and does not correspond to the English phrase "rule of law", claims that the two terms are part of an overall development of liberal thinking and political systems in Europe and North America.[7] Important milestones in this overall development are the works of Locke and Montesquieu.

The central principle that makes it possible to proclaim the universality of the *Rechtsstaat* is, according to Hofmann, the separation of powers, which is derived from the assumption of a *regimen mixtum*, in other words, from the underlying principle of balance.[8] On the basis of these observations, Hofmann regards the emergence of the *Rechtsstaat* as the achievement in history of an idea that may well lay claim to universal validity. The issue of the *Rechtsstaat*, then, belongs to the internal history of the constitutional development of the West. Consequently, if any attempt is made to assert the relativism of the concept, reference should be made not to the various national constitutional histories of the Western world, but rather, in Hofmann's view, to other cultures. In particular, Hofmann stresses the different conceptions of human rights in the Western traditions and in other cultures: suffice it to mention the emergence in the West of an individual morality as opposed to the centrality of an objective ethics (*objektive Sittlichkeit*) in other cultures (e.g. in Asian or in African cultures).

Hofmann's last point can hardly be denied but what does appear to be problematic in his account is his attribution of both concepts to the same *liberal thought*. If we are to fully grasp the difference between the two forms of state, what requires investigation, rather – aside from the issue of principles – is the system of political and constitutional relations that held among the forces in play.

Thus Franz Neumann writes: "The essence of the *Rechtsstaat* consists in the separation of the political structure from the legal system, which alone must guarantee, independently of the political structure, liberty and security. This separation is also what distinguishes the German concept of *Rechtsstaat* and the English doctrine, in which the sovereignty of the parliament and the rule of law are interconnected".[9]

Neumann goes on to argue that the English bourgeoisie had succeeded in transforming its will into law through the Parliament, while the German bourgeoisie had found the laws already in place and strove to refocus and interpret them in order to achieve as much liberty as possible with respect to a more or less absolute state. On this basis, he concludes: "The German doctrine could be called liberal-constitutional, and the English one democratic-constitutional."[10]

Neumann recognizes, then, the difference between the two conceptions, but his conclusion is rather problematic as he ends up by reducing the German doctrine of the *Rechtsstaat* solely to its liberal version, thus omitting the conservative perspective and neglecting the complex constitutional solution that emerged after the foundation of the *Reich* in 1871. Finally, before embarking on an investigation of the German model, we need to examine one particular aspect of the English model, if we are to achieve a thorough understanding of the differences between the two constitutional perspectives.

Albert Venn Dicey, in his fundamental work *Introduction to the Study of the Law of the Constitution* (1885), set out three basic characteristics of the rule of law: (1) the supremacy of ordinary law; (2) equal status before the law; and (3) the derivation of constitutional rights from the individual rights proclaimed by courts of justice and parliament.[11]

It is certainly the third feature that links the meaning of "rule of law" to the specific constitutional history of England. Dicey held, in fact, that the English Constitution was pervaded by the rule of law "on the ground that the general principles of the Constitution (e.g. the right to personal liberty or the right of public assembly) are with us the result of judicial decisions determining the rights of private persons in particular cases brought before the courts".[12] He went on to claim: "Our Constitution, in short, is a judge-made Constitution and it bears on its face all the features, good and bad, of judge-made law".[13]

Dicey elaborated these considerations by comparing English constitutionalism with the situation on the European continent. While in most European countries the foundation of rights was a Declaration of Rights, in England rights were based on the law of the land: they were generalizations of judicial decisions confirmed by the laws of parliament, such as the *Habeas Corpus* Acts.

Thus while on the continent – Dicey considered in particular the French and the Belgian constitutions – it was possible to modify the constitution following a special procedure, in England rights belonged to the constitution, in the sense that they were grounded in the ordinary law of the land, and could "hardly be destroyed without a thorough revolution in the institutions and manners of the nation".[14] In short, Dicey highlighted the peculiarity of the English case, which he finds in the specific constitutional guarantees of rights. This distinction was also valid for the German doctrine of the *Rechtsstaat*, which in its final version, as we shall see, allowed no primacy of law over the state. The German case was also characterized by a particular evolution of the form of the *Rechtsstaat*: from the liberal perspective of the first half of the nineteenth century to the consolidation of a substantially conservative conception following the foundation of the *Reich* in 1871.

2 THE IDEA OF *RECHTSSTAAT* IN EARLY GERMAN CONSTITUTIONALISM

An analysis of the transformations in the German doctrine of rights during the nineteenth century may help to reveal the specificity of the *Rechtsstaat* and its profound difference from the English case. If in England, rights – as Dicey claimed – were the result of judicial decisions that had contributed to forming the "law of the land", in the German states, the interpretation of rights varied from country to country and underwent a complex evolutionary process characterized, on the one hand, by the passage from natural law doctrine to positive law doctrine and, on the other, by the replacement of the liberal perspective with an essentially conservative view in the second half of the century, which was in turn marked by the primacy of the state over law. An investigation into these transformations will make it possible to highlight the constitutive elements of the German doctrine of the *Rechtsstaat*.

In general, it can be said that until 1871 there was, in the German territories, a predominance of liberal ideas.[15] Let us begin, then, by attempting to define this *liberal* interpretation of the *Rechtsstaat*, paying particular attention to the doctrines of fundamental rights.

The southern German constitutions (Bavaria, 1818; Baden, 1818; Württemberg, 1819; Hessen-Darmstadt, 1820) reflected a process of *positivization* of fundamental rights. In these charters, in fact, there was no reference either to *Urrechte* (original rights) or to *Menschenrechte* (human rights); but only to *bürgerliche und politische Rechte*[16] (civil and political rights) or to *staatsbürgerliche Rechte*[17] (citizens' rights). The constitutional documents gave expression to a positivized conception of fundamental rights; theory, on the other hand, was still split between natural law doctrine and positive law doctrine, and this tension was relieved only in the second half of the century.

The beginnings of the theory of the *Rechtsstaat* were also marked by the opposition between conservative and liberal perspectives. The former conception was expressed in the work of Friedrich Julius Stahl, who grounded his doctrine of the *Rechtsstaat* on the monarchic principle.[18] He is the source of the following well-known definition of the *Rechtsstaat*: the *Rechtsstaat* "must determine with precision and with certainty the boundaries and the limits of its activity, as well as the free sphere of its citizens, according to the modalities of law".[19]

This was a *legal* formulation of the *Rechtsstaat*, which became widespread during the nineteenth century and was taken up also by authors of liberal orientation.[20] Providing a *political* definition of the limits of state action was, however, the responsibility of the monarch, who was considered the interpreter of that Christian vision of the world that, in Stahl's view, was the foundation of the legal system. In this conception rights were merely concessions by the sovereign, and only as such did they constitute limits to the power of the government.[21]

The liberal doctrine of the *Rechtsstaat*, on the other hand, was divided between natural law and positive law doctrines. On the liberal front the different grounding of rights – natural law or positive law – expressed the tension between *doctrine*, which strove for the recognition of the inalienable rights of man, on the one hand, and on the other the consideration of the *constitutional reality* dominated by the monarchic principle and resistant to the principles of the constitution-based state.

The natural law perspective was quite heavily influenced by the legal doctrine of Kant,[22] especially in the work of Carl von Rotteck. Rotteck's conception, built upon a natural law foundation, joined individual original rights with the reality of the state in the doctrine of the *Rechtsstaat*. He recognized, in fact, the rights, which each individual bears in the state "not as a citizen, but as a legal entity" and, which could be conceived of even "without the state".[23] These were rights over which a majority decision had no legal power.

Among these rights Rotteck included in particular the right of personality or freedom and noted that an individual, on entering a state, became a free member of a free association in which he could confirm and safeguard his rights.[24] In short, following Kant, for Rotteck inalienable rights belonged to man as such, but could be realized only within the union of the state.

Rotteck, like Carl Welcker,[25] developed the natural law perspective up to the elaboration of an abstract rational *Rechtsstaat*, which he was forced to adapt, however, to the existing reality of the constitutional monarchy.[26]

Unlike Rotteck, Mohl developed his conception of the *Rechtsstaat* from a perspective of positive law.[27] In his analysis of the 1819 Constitution of Württemberg, he treated the reality of the state as a condition, which imposed itself on human behaviour. Moreover, in his study of public law in Württemberg he never spoke of original rights but only of citizens' rights (*Rechte der Staatsbürger*).[28]

Mohl's analysis focuses on the written constitution and on the rights it confers on the citizen. Only the *Rechtsstaat* – as distinct from the state of patrimony, despotism, and theocracy – had citizens. These citizens were granted a legal property (*rechtliche Eigenschaft*),[29] by virtue of which they enjoyed precise rights laid out in the Constitution (of Württemberg, in Chap. III): equality before the law, protection of personal freedom, freedom of thought, freedom of conscience, protection of property before the state, freedom of movement, and freedom of enterprise.[30] The absence of reference to other rights, such as the right of assembly, did not, however, exclude them. In a later work, in fact, Mohl elaborated the general principles of the *Rechtsstaat* and extended the rights conferred on citizens, including in particular the active and passive right to participation in the political process, religious freedom, and the freedom to create associations.[31]

The identification of the general principles of the *Rechtsstaat* derived, in Mohl's work, from the precise delineation of the aims of this form of state: in the first place, the preservation of the legal system throughout the state; in the second place, support for the rational purposes of individuals, in cases in which their means are inadequate,[32] but also intervention on behalf of each member of the state in the "freest possible exercise and use of his forces".[33] The identification of the aims of the state led Mohl to overcome the natural law approach and to interpret a specific positive legal system – that of Württemberg – according to his constitutional ideal.[34]

The problems we pointed out in the analysis of political theory appeared also in the German doctrine of public law in the first half of the nineteenth century. The doctrine of public law also revealed different foundations of rights. The natural law perspective underlay the work of Johann Christoph Freiherr von Aretin,[35] whereas other authors, such as Friedrich Schmittener, while attributing a natural law character to rights, maintained that these rights, as such, expressed a merely ethical force; in order to become rights they had to be recognized by the state legal system through legislation and under the protection of the judiciary.[36]

The guarantee of rights was the essential criterion of the *Rechtsstaat*. Heinrich Zoepfl wrote that by *Rechtsstaat* was meant "the idea of a state in which individual liberty is fully guaranteed".[37] Aretin declared that the *Rechtsstaat* was a constitutional state "in which one governs according to the general rational will and one aims solely for the common good. By common good we mean the broadest freedom and security of all the members of the civil society".[38]

According to Aretin, it was the constitutional monarchy that best realized this form of the state, since it solved the great problem of how to reconcile "the power necessary to govern with the broadest possible freedom of the citizens".[39] But who determined the possible space for freedom? The answer to this question made it possible to outline the architecture of the state-form, progressively defining the idea of the *Rechtsstaat*.

Zoepfl held that subjects could claim their *Volksrechte* (people's rights) from the sovereign. The legislative power made it possible to guarantee the people's rights by posing them as natural limits (*natürliche Grenze*) to state power.[40] The people, in fact, had a right to autonomous legal production, in which it expressed its ethical conscience (*sittliches Bewusstsein*) by participating in legislation through the process of popular representation. Thus the German doctrine of the *Rechtsstaat* gradually laid the foundations of rights in *legislation* through representation. In this connection Dieter Grimm writes: "Popular representation was the means by which early constitutionalism established the relationship between fundamental rights and the legislature".[41]

Finally, the doctrine of public law posed the problem – crucial for the *Rechtsstaat* – of the relationship between statute law and constitution. Zoepfl declared that the constitution expressed "the concept of legal principles that are valid in a state from the point of view of the form of sovereignty (*Beherrschungsform*) and government, that is from the point of view of the organization of the state's power and the rights of the people and their reciprocal relationships".[42] Aretin asserted that the constitution was "the law of all laws" (*das Gesetz aller Gesetze*),[43] whose precepts bound both the legislature and the representative assembly. In particular, Aretin pointed out that certain constitutions, such as that of Württemberg, declared null and void all laws that were in contrast with the constitution.[44]

The constitution as foundation of the *Rechtsstaat* was recognized also in the work of one of the most important exponents of German liberalism, Carl von Rotteck. "The essence of the constitution", he wrote, "consists in the national representation (*National-Repräsentation*), which must express the interests and the rights of the people against the government". Only this representation was adequate to the task of "realizing the idea of the true general will and turning a state of force (*Gewalt-Staat*) into a *Rechtsstaat*".[45]

Yet the superiority of the constitution over statute law – which was one of the essential principles of the *liberal doctrine* of the *Rechtsstaat* and which could have become the basis for the compatibility between *Rechtsstaat* and democracy – did not take hold[46] in the reality of German constitutional history, and even the *constitutional* foundation of fundamental rights was abandoned for a merely *legislative* foundation of rights in the realization of the *Rechtsstaat*, which consolidated itself in the second half of the nineteenth century.

The positions of liberalism were given political voice in the constitutional debates of Paulskirche[47] and went into crisis with its failure. The *Rechtsstaat* was conceived of as a state of fundamental rights that considered liberty as the highest value.[48] All the debates of Paulskirche echoed this line; the national assembly wanted to make fundamental rights the basis of German unity. Thus the delegate Georg Beseler, a liberal exponent of the centre-right wing, who, together with Friedrich Christoph Dahlmann, head of the Constitutional Commission, declared that the fundamental rights had to be guaranteed constitutionally and that, on this basis, it was possible to leave the police state behind and give birth to the *Rechtsstaat*.[49]

In June 1848 the Constitutional Commission drafted an outline of a Declaration of the Fundamental Rights of the German People, which asserted the principle of equality before the law and rejected class privileges, thereby eliminating any residue of feudalism.[50] On 27 December of the same year, the Declaration of the Fundamental Rights was proclaimed. In commenting on the introductory law, Theodor Mommsen stated that the Declaration, "the *Magna Carta* of the German nation, guarantee of liberty for all future generations, truly contains what it promises: the *fundamental rights* of the German people".[51]

However, the Declaration of Rights was rejected by Prussia, which already had its own constitution, ratified in December 1848, while Bavaria and Hannover refused to publish it. Finally, the Fundamental Rights were declared devoid of validity by the Federal Declaration of 23 August 1851.[52] It was the end of the constitutional experience of Paulskirche.

3 THE CRISIS OF THE LIBERAL DOCTRINE OF THE *RECHTSSTAAT*

The Paulskirche failure prevented the establishment of a liberal conception of the *Rechtsstaat*, proclaiming the superiority of the constitution among the sources of law and the pre-state character of rights (although the doctrine did not lack, as we have seen, positive law readings in the interpretation of rights). These principles were asserted in the doctrine but they were not applied in German constitutional history in the nineteenth century. The end of Paulskirche marked the beginning of the crisis of the liberal perspective and the liberals ended up accepting a compromise with the monarchic principle that guaranteed the rights of individuals in civil society.

This position found expression in the work of Johann Kaspar Bluntschli, who held that the natural liberty of man was a legal freedom (*rechtliche Freiheit*), that is limited by law, and that consequently the political problem consisted in finding "the right connection between freedom and the legal system".[53] Legal freedom meant two things: *Volksfreiheit* (people's freedom), which was realized in the state, and individual freedom, which was grounded "in the individual life of the soul" (*in dem Individualleben der Seele*) that is in a reality that the state was neither called on nor able to dominate.[54]

The relationship between the public law and the two meanings of freedom determined the different state forms. Bluntschli accepted the primacy of the constitutional monarchy, which did not permit the "freedom of the people" to become the "power of the people" (as in democracy), and did not allow individual freedom to stray into anarchy. In constitutional monarchy, by contrast, the "freedom of the people", namely political freedom, was an institution of the state, while individual liberty belonged to private law and guaranteed the legal sphere of the individual. In this way the terms of the compromise were clearly set out: on the one hand, constitutional monarchy was accepted; on the other, the state was obliged to "respect and guarantee individual freedom in the same way as all private law".[55]

Joseph Held, too, distinguished between civil rights and political rights. The former – among which the right to property and personal freedom – were not attributed to the individuals by the state but belonged to each person as such.[56] Political rights, on the other hand, derived from the state and could be granted only by the state; in this sense they were not strictly speaking rights but rather *duties*[57] that subjects had toward the state. This understanding was also to be given to employment in public office, participation in political elections, etc.

The liberal position, then, tended to guarantee, ultimately, from a standpoint of positive law, the security of individuals' rights and the autonomy of civil society, but it had to accept the compromise with the constitutional monarchy. After 1848, the most systematic formulation of the compromise with constitutional monarchy, which was accepted by liberal doctrine, appeared in Otto von Bähr's work on the *Rechtsstaat*.

The first and fundamental step towards the creation of a *Rechtsstaat*, according to Bähr, was the issue of a fundamental law (*Grundgesetz*) or a constitution. The aim of a constitution, he wrote, was "the definition of the rights and obligations with which the state, represented by its organs, presents itself before individuals and the formulation of the rules which govern the acts of the legal system within the organism of the state".[58] Bähr continues to give formal expression to the superiority of constitutionally posited principles, which determined the activity of the organs of the state and the whole of relations between the state and the citizen, but at the centre of his construct, as will soon be clear, lay the form of legislative power.

Bähr used the foundation of the constitution to outline the structure of the *Rechtsstaat*: in the first place, legislation. Laws established fixed rules in changing social relations. "Legislation must take on the most sacred good of the nation, the law".[59] And just as law came to maturity in the conscience of the nation, so could legislation not be the product of a single individual, but rather had to be the result of an agreement between people and sovereign.

However, Bähr warned, law and legislation could find their true meaning and genuine force (*Macht*) only where "they find a judicial authority designed for their realization".[60] Accordingly, Bähr elaborated his doctrine of the *Rechtsstaat* on the principle of *representation* and on the need for a *separation of powers*. But his systematic construction went further. He pointed out, in fact, that, in addition to legislation and judicial authority, there was also the executive power, which expressed "the life of the organism of the state". The judicial power and the executive power were both subject to law, but in different ways. The judge represented the legal system and his decisions were *objective law*, while the executive power intervened not from the standpoint of the objective legal system but rather on the basis of the *subjective interests* that it represented on any given occasion.

It followed that adjudication and administration had to be separate functions and that the safeguarding of the legal system performed by the judiciary was to be given priority. It was therefore necessary that the administration be subjected to judicial power; this, wrote Bähr, "is an essential condition of the *Rechtsstaat*".[61] Bähr's logical treatment of the question led him to identify the principles of *administrative justice*.[62] This was undoubtedly one of the most important developments in the liberal doctrine of the *Rechtsstaat* to ensue from the principle of legality and from the need to subordinate the administration to a judicial authority of public law in order to safeguard citizens' rights before the administrative authority of the state.[63]

For Lorenz von Stein, Bähr had the merit of recognizing the centrality of popular representation in the legislative process and of having supported the independence of the judiciary from the sovereign. In a more recent examination of Bähr's work, on the other hand, Michael Stolleis argues that by restricting the concept of *Rechtsstaat* to the safeguarding of rights in administrative disputes Bähr *formalizes* the doctrine[64] and makes it *non-political*. This, according to Stolleis, is what characterizes the specific German variant of the rule of law.[65] Given the considerations we have made thus far – with particular reference to the crisis of the liberal doctrine of the *Rechtsstaat* – we are certainly induced to embrace Stolleis's interpretation.

The foundation of the Second Empire in 1871 gave birth to new constitutional relations and the acknowledged superiority of the monarchic principle became the foundation of a conception that completely perverted the doctrine of the *Rechtsstaat*.

4 THE *RECHTSSTAAT* AND SUBJECTIVE PUBLIC RIGHTS

Beginning with Carl Friedrich von Gerber, passing through Paul Laband up to Georg Jellinek, the conception of *Rechtsstaat* underwent a profound transformation that marked the definitive defeat of the liberal standpoint. The work of Gerber anticipated the orientation that was consolidated with the foundation of the Second Empire. In his well-known essay from 1852, Gerber recognized that the state did not absorb the entire social life of men, since much of this life remained outside the orbit of the state. There were, therefore, "people's rights", which constituted limits for state power, but these were not rights proper, i.e. subjective rights: these rights, he wrote, "remain merely negations, restricting state power in the limits of its faculties; they are to be considered only as limits of the monarch's rights from the standpoint of the subjects".[66]

In a later work this perspective was made systematic. Gerber stated explicitly, in connection with the rights of the individual, that they were in no way to be considered "rights in a subjective sense, rather they are *legal propositions*, that is *precepts of objective law*".[67] The issues at stake were freedom of conscience, freedom to profess a scientific conviction, freedom of the press, freedom of education and occupational choice, freedom to go before one's natural judge, freedom of assembly and association, freedom to expatriate, and individual freedom of the person.

The individual liberties of the liberal tradition, which, from Locke to Kant, had been recognized as belonging to men by virtue of their common humanity, were now conceived of as a mere reflex of objective precepts, that is as an expression of general laws. In this way, the balance between the legal system and personal freedom that had been a mainstay of liberal doctrine was overturned. Only the sovereignty of the state held sway, and the *Rechtsstaat* was transformed into *Staatsrecht* (the law of the state). In this connection Gerber stated quite clearly: "the force of the will of the state, the power of the state, is the law of the state. Public law is therefore the doctrine of the power of the state".[68]

After the foundation of the Empire, Laband picked up on Gerber's doctrine, but formulating as *given* the premises that Gerber had merely anticipated.[69] In his words: "rights to freedom or fundamental rights are precepts for the power of the state, which the state gives itself. These rights constitute limits for the competence of officials and guarantee the individual his natural freedom of behaviour in certain spheres, but they do not constitute subjective rights of citizens. They are not rights, for they have no object".[70]

It was Jellinek's task to formulate the doctrine of the *Rechtsstaat* in the era of Wilhelm II. Although he substantially shared the positive law approach of his predecessors, he distinguished himself from the doctrine of rights of Gerber and Laband. Jellinek introduced the distinction between (1) *status passivus*, (2) *status negativus*, (3) *status positivus*, and (4) *status activus*, which constituted at the end of the nineteenth century, the most systematic formulation of the doctrine of *Rechtsstaat* and individual rights.

The *status passivus* (or *status subjectionis*) referred to the situation of the individual who has only duties – such as the obligation to perform military service – and no rights. The *status negativus* (or *status libertatis*) was the condition of a man who possessed the right to freedom. But these rights were not conceived of from a perspective of natural law; rather, the standpoint was that of historicism. "Although some would like to make them appear as though they were the product of a general theory of man and state", he wrote, "nonetheless, in their specific legislative form, they [fundamental rights] can only be explained *historically*".[71]

This meant, at the same time, that constitutions acknowledged no rights as pre-existing to the state and that constitutional precepts were merely prescriptions addressed to the legislator. It is true that Jellinek admitted that certain statutory precepts, such as those that recognize freedom of religion, could have immediate validity, but in general constitutional prescriptions required, in order to be valid, the actual action of the legislator. In this sense, Jellinek concluded, the fact that the laws enacted in conformity with constitutional precepts turned to the advantage of individual interests was an effect of objective law, not the satisfaction of any subjective legal claim.[72]

From Jellinek's positive law perspective it was the law that provided foundation for the rights to freedom. Indeed, he wrote that "every freedom is nothing but the exemption from illegal constraints".[73] Nonetheless, Jellinek distinguished his position from that of Gerber who, it will be recalled, had resolved the rights to liberty into objective law. This position was tenable, according to Jellinek, only in a period prior to the institution of administrative courts; the creation of these agencies, however, had made it possible to recognize and safeguard "the interest of the individual that was hidden in the formulas of the fundamental rights".[74]

The *status positivus* (or *status civitatis*) referred to the state conferring on the individual subjective public rights, that is to say a precise legal capacity: the capacity to "activate precepts in the legal system" (*Normen der Rechtsordnung in Bewegung zu setzen*) so as to spur the intervention of an authority to annul an illegal administrative act".[75]

Finally, the *status activus* (or *status activae civitatis*) consisted in ascribing political rights to the citizen.

This systematic account of the *Rechtsstaat* in the era of Wilhelm II in the second half of the nineteenth century rested on several precise principles:

1. The state possessed its own legal personality. Personality meant, for Jellinek, the capacity to possess rights. The state had its own will in which it expressed the will of a community. The conception of the state as a "legal personality" was common to both Jellinek and Laband.[76] This position implied the superiority of the state over the legal system. Jellinek stated, in fact: "It turns out that the state is a purposeful entity constituted by human individuals ... which ... possesses its own will ...; it also turns out that the legal system, on the basis of the above-mentioned de facto condition, which exists independently, is able to regulate the formation of the will of the state. In this way, the state, *by creating its own legal system*, establishes itself as a subject of law".[77]

2. The state attributed to the individual a legal personality and, at the same time, the capacity to demand legal protection from the state. Jellinek pointed out that the person who granted the legal protection and the one who was obliged to provide it were the same, i.e. the state. It followed that the state could fulfil its obligation only by "limiting its activity with respect to its subjects".[78]
3. The rights conceded by the state were individual rights – subjective public rights – which represented "an expansion of natural freedom" and could be in no sense conceived of, as in Gerber's doctrine, as a mere "reflected right" of objective law.

These points allow us to assert that the Jellinek's conception expressed in the most systematic way the German doctrine of the *Rechtsstaat* in the second half of the nineteenth century, a doctrine centred on the sovereignty of the state, on the legislative – and not constitutional – foundation of rights, and on the criteria of administrative justice. Certain principles of the liberal tradition – the pre-state status of rights, the primacy of the constitution – had been completely lost.[79]

5 *RECHTSSTAAT* AND DEMOCRACY: COMPATIBILITY OR IRREMEDIABLE OPPOSITION?

The foregoing considerations have shown the controversial character of the German doctrine of the *Rechtsstaat*. Attention has been directed to the liberal standpoint, the conservative interpretation (Stahl), and the solution found through the compromise between liberalism and conservatism. It was this last approach, which finally held sway, largely due to the systematic work of Jellinek.

The great variety of doctrinal positions helps explain the current difficulty in presenting an adequate interpretation, especially about the relationship between *Rechtsstaat* and democracy. Can the two doctrines be compatible, and, if so, what conception of the *Rechtsstaat* can democracy coexist with? The plurality of answers serves to show how difficult the problem is, which derives both from the present-day evolution of democracy and from the lack of clarity on the various nineteenth-century interpretations of the *Rechtsstaat*.

Werner Kägi accepts the possible coexistence of the two doctrines in the state-form of constitutional democracy,[80] in that the underlying principles of both are oriented toward the same end. For this to be possible, for Kägi, democracy must not be conceived of in Rousseau's terms as "totalitarian democracy"; rather, the majority principle must operate within the limits of law. The people must not place itself above the constitution and the law, but must recognize rights that exist prior to and above the state; it is on this basis that a democratic *Rechtsstaat* may be built.[81]

However, this position expresses only a *doctrinal* point of view. In particular, it takes into account only the liberal interpretation, which builds the *Rechtsstaat* on the foundations of pre-state rights, and considers democracy only in the version supplied by Rousseau. What is needed is an examination of the actual constitutional reality in the German area.

In nineteenth-century German constitutional history, liberalism reached a compromise with the constitutional monarchy, on the basis of which the House of Representatives and the Upper House, on the one hand, and the monarchy, on the other, both contributed to the exercise of the legislative function. Legislative precepts excluded the possibility of a separation between politics and law in the sphere of legislation.[82] In this constitutional context, dominated by positive law, the legality of the administration and the "statutory reservation" were the principles of the *Rechtsstaat* specifically designed to protect individuals from possible arbitrary action by the administration.[83]

After the First World War the unlimited power of parliaments aroused the fear that majorities might violate the constitution. During the Weimar Republic, the *Staatsgerichtshof* (the Constitutional Court of the Reich) had been called on, on the basis of article 19 of the Constitution, to examine issues of constitutionality that might arise within a *Land* or between *Länder*, or between the *Reich* and the *Länder*. What is more, there were other courts that were involved in examining questions of constitutionality, such as the *Reichsgericht* (the Supreme Court of Appeal).

It was only after the Second World War that Germany instituted a centralized *richterliches Prüfungsrecht* (judicial examination) of constitutionality, which was entrusted exclusively to the *Bundesverfassungsgericht* (Federal Constitutional Court). It is this turning point – which marks the primacy of the Constitution over the legislator – that establishes the insuperable contrast between the *constitutional democracy* of today and the German *Rechtsstaat*, and makes democracy compatible with certain liberal interpretations of the *Rechtsstaat*.[84]

The democracy established in post-war Germany elevated the Federal Constitutional Court to "guardian of the Constitution" and made of it a constitutional organ in the process of formation of political will. The establishment of a system of constitutional justice eliminated all possible tension between legality and legitimacy, and secured their full coincidence.[85]

It is worth pointing out that the conception of the constitution has also undergone a transformation in German constitutional democracy with respect to the *Rechtsstaat*: the Constitution no longer represents merely a limitation of state power with respect to the freedom of the citizen; rather it constitutes also "the legal positivization of the fundamental values of the life of the community".[86] We are dealing with values or principles of justice, which postulate a "validity for all spheres of law";[87] their realization, i.e. the creation of the social premises that can make each individual's freedom effective, is the necessary condition of individual freedom.[88] It is above all this overcoming of *formalism* that makes the *Rechtsstaat* incompatible with the reality of contemporary constitutional democracy.

The constitutionalization of fundamental rights and the primacy of the constitution over statute law, then, make the gap between the *Rechtsstaat* and constitutional democracy unbridgeable, or rather they impose a redefinition of the contents of the doctrine of the *Rechtsstaat*. Thus Grimm introduces the concept of a *material* as opposed to a *formal Rechtsstaat*. Only the former, in his view, can coexist with democracy. It consists in assuming a *double legality*: that of the constituent democratic decision, which lays down the principles of the constitutional system and that of the legislative power. The first decision is based on a broader consensus than can be attained by the legislator with majority decisions. Contrasts between the two levels of decision can be resolved only by the Constitutional Court.

The error of those who, on the other hand, claim a new formalization of the *Rechtsstaat*[89] – and, in Grimm's opinion, a consequent return to a positive law approach – consists in asserting the unlimited freedom of the legislator. Rather, Grimm maintains, two-tiered legality (*zweistufige Legalität*) "is none other than a synonym for constitution".[90]

In the post-war period, Konrad Hesse, before Grimm, had also distinguished between formal and material elements of the *Rechtsstaat*. He had observed that the *Rechtsstaat* provides for the primacy of law, but he added that in the German Fundamental Law of 1949 the primacy of the law was identified with the primacy of the Constitution and that "this separates substantially the principle of the present *Rechtsstaat* from previous conceptions".[91] The constitutional limitation of state powers corresponds to the conception of the *formal Rechtsstaat*, but the Constitution binds the state agencies not only formally but also *materially*, by establishing ties of precise legal *contents*.

In short: the *Rechtsstaat*, on the one hand, shapes the reality of the state through the constitution and legislation and, on the other, obliges all powers of the state to pursue the contents of law.[92] In particular, Hesse notes, the contents are those of the equality and dignity of the person. This joining of formal and material elements is the foundation of the "social *Rechtsstaat*".[93]

Finally, Hesse admitted that the *material Rechtsstaat* is compatible with democracy, since the principles of the former were in his view also the principles of the democratic system. The *Rechtsstaat* and democracy are underpinned by two different forms of legality, the former on the *institutional* level and the latter on the *political* level. Democracy, in fact, must realize through a participatory political process the principles that the *Rechtsstaat* sets out as constitutional precepts. It appears clear, then, that a reutilization of the concept of *Rechtsstaat* in the age of democracy can only take place on the basis of a profound transformation of the concept. The notion should be understood as constitutional (not legislative) and material (not formal) *Rechtsstaat*: a transformation, which makes it utterly different from the nineteenth-century *Rechtsstaat*.

NOTES

1. L. von Stein, *Die Verwaltungslehre* [1869], vol. 1, *Die vollziehende Gewalt*, Zweite ungearbeitete Auflage, Aalen: Scientia Verlag, 1962, p. 296.
2. R. von Mohl, *Die Geschichte und Literatur der Staatswissenschaften*, Erster Band, Erlangen: Verlag von F. Enke, 1855, pp. 229 ff. Actually, before Mohl, K. Th. Welcker had used the term *Rechtsstaat* in *Die letzten Gründe von Recht, Staat und Strafe* [1813], Aalen: Scientia Verlag, 1964, p. 25. Cf. E.W. Böckenförde, "Entstehung und Wandel des Rechtsstaatsbegriffs", in id., *Staat, Gesellschaft, Freiheit*, Frankfurt a. M.: Suhrkamp, 1976, p. 66.
3. The same view is held by E.W. Böckenförde, op. cit., p. 85.
4. N. MacCormick, "Der Rechtsstaat und die rule of law", *Juristen Zeitung*, 39 (1984), p. 67.
5. MacCormick notes that, in the German tradition, this principle is recognizable in the work of Kant, *Metaphysiche Anfangsgründe der Rechtslehre* [1797], in particular §42, and, in the English tradition, in the work of Locke, *The Second Treatise of Government*, §136; cf. N. MacCormick, op. cit., p. 68.
6. This position had been upheld by Gustav Radbruch, who saw in the primacy of law over the state a return to natural law; in G. Radbruch, *Rechtsphilosophie* [1914], 5th edn., Stuttgart, 1956, §26, p. 284.
7. H. Hofmann, "Geschichtlichkeit und Universalitätsanspruch des Rechtsstaats", *Archiv für Rechts- und Sozialphilosophie*, Beiheft 65, Stuttgart: Franz Steiner Verlag, 1996, p. 9. On the European form of the *Rechtsstaat*, see M. Fioravanti, "Lo Stato di diritto come forma di Stato. Notazioni preliminari sulla tradizione europeo-continentale", in R. Gherardi and G. Gozzi (eds), *Saperi della borghesia e storia dei concetti fra Otto e Novecento*, Bologna: Il Mulino, 1995.
8. H. Hofmann, op. cit., p. 27.

9. F. Neumann, *Die Herrschaft des Gesetzes*, Frankfurt a. M.: Suhrkamp, 1980, p. 204.
10. Ibid., p. 210.
11. A.V. Dicey, *Introduction to the Study of the Law of the Constitution* [1885], 10th edn., New York: St. Martin's Press, 1967, pp. 202–3.
12. Ibid., p. 195. Jennings criticized certain aspects of Dicey's reconstruction. In particular, he observed that, in connection with Dicey's assertion that the constitution consisted essentially in the recognition of the rights of individuals, it was necessary to highlight also the extension of the intervention of public authorities in the sphere of private actions. Jennings added that – with regard to Dicey's analysis of the relationships between legislative power and judicial power – if parliament did not accept the interpretation given by the judges, it could always modify the contents. Cf. I. Jennings, *The Law and the Constitution* [1933], London: University of London Press, 1959, pp. 55–8. Jennings pointed out that the English Constitution contained the political ideas of its builders and, from this perspective, expressed the principles of the victory of the parliament over the Stuarts. The sovereignty of the parliament derived from a political movement that had been recognized as law of the land. This was the meaning to attribute – on his view – to Dicey's assertion that law determined the Constitution. In this sense – according to Jennings – Dicey was merely enunciating the individualistic theories of nineteenth-century Whigs; ibid., p. 314. On Jennings's critique of Dicey cf. J. Harvey and L. Bather, "Über den englischen Rechtsstaat. Die 'rule of law'", in M. Tohidipur (ed.), *Der bürgerliche Rechtstaat*, Frankfurt a. M.: Suhrkamp, 1978, vol. 2, p. 359 ff.
13. A.V. Dicey, op. cit., p. 196.
14. Ibid., p. 201.
15. Cf. W. Wilhelm, *Metodologia giuridica nel secolo XIX* [1958], Milano: Giuffrè, 1974, p. 158.
16. Cf. The Bavarian Constitution of 26 May 1818, title IV, §9, in W. von Rimscha, *Die Grundrechte im süddeutschen Konstitutionalismus*, Köln-Berlin-Bonn-München: Carl Heymanns Verlag, 1973, p. 218.
17. Cf. The Constitution of Baden of 22 August 1818, II, §7, in W. von Rimscha, op. cit., p. 220, and the Constitution of Württemberg of 25 September 1819, chap. III, §21 in E.R. Huber (ed.), *Dokumente zur deutschen Verfassungsgeschichte*, Stuttgart/Berlin/Köln/Mainz: W. Kohlhammer, 1978, vol. 1, p, 190.
18. Cf. F.J. Stahl, *Das monarchische Prinzip*, Heidelberg: Verlag der akademischen Buchhandlung, 1845. Stahl held that "the monarchic principle is the foundation of German public law and of the German science of the state (*Staatsweisheit*)", ibid., p. 34. From a historico-constitutional point of view, the monarchic principle had been formulated in the *Wiener Schußakte* of 1820 where, in article 57, one reads: "since the *deutsche Bund* consists, with the exception of the free cities, of sovereign princes, in conformity with this fundamental concept the entire power of the state (*Staats-Gewalt*) must be assigned to the head of state (*Oberhaupt des Staats*), and the sovereign may be bound to collaborate with the ranks (*Stände*), on the basis of a territorial-rank constitution, only in the exercise of certain rights", in E.R. Huber, op. cit., p. 99. In this way the monarchic principle was formulated as "the fundamental principle of the new German constitutional public law", as Treitschke put it, cited in E. Kaufmann, *Studien zur Staatslehre des monarchischen Prinzips*, Leipzig: Brandstetter, 1906, p. 37. In this connection cf. W. von Rimscha, op. cit., p. 93.

19. F.J. Stahl, *Die Philosophie des Rechts* [1833–1837], vol. 2, *Rechts- und Staatslehre auf der Grundlage christlicher Weltanschauung*, Tübingen: Mohr, 1878, p. 137.
20. The legal definition of the *Rechtsstaat* as it was formulated by Stahl appeared, for example, in the work of a liberal writer like O. von Bähr.
21. Cf. W. von Rimscha, op. cit., p. 95.
22. The importance of Kant for the doctrine of the *Rechtsstaat* is decisive. Kant rejected any eudemonic conception of the state – which went back to Aristotelian tradition – and identified the purpose of the state not so much in the happiness of its citizens as in the harmony between the liberty of each individual and a universal law. Cf. I. Kant, *Über den Gemeinspruch: Das mag in der Theorie richtig sein, taugt aber nicht für die Praxis* [1793], Frankfurt a. M.: Vittorio Klostermann, 1992, in particular p. 39 ff. Although Kant did not use the term *Rechtsstaat*, but rather *rechtlicher Zustand* (legal state), after the publication of *Metaphysische Anfangsgründe der Rechtslehre* (1797) Kant and his followers were described as "die kritische oder die Schule der Rechts-Staats-Lehre" (the critical school or the school of the doctrine of the *Rechtsstaat*), in J.W. Placidus, *Literatur der Staatslehre – Ein Versuch*, Straβburg, 1798. In this connection cf. M. Stolleis, "Rechtsstaat", in A. Erler and E. Kaufmann (eds), *Handwörterbuch zur deutschen Rechtsgeschichte*, vol. 4, Berlin: Erich Schmidt Verlag, 1990, p. 367.
23. C. von Rotteck, *Lehrbuch des Vernunftsrechts und der Staatswissenschaften* [1830], vol. 2, Stuttgart: Halberger'sche Verlagshandlung, 1848, p. 135. The same positions were upheld by P. Pfizer in the entry "Urrechte oder unveräu·erliche Rechte" (original or inalienable rights), in C. von Rotteck and C. Welcker (eds), *Das Staats-Lexikon* [1834–1843], vol.12, Altona: Verlag von Johann Friedrich Hammerich, 1848, p. 689. Pfizer wrote: "The proponents of natural law define as inalienable rights those innate rights of man that cannot be lost, neither through contract nor by renunciation".
24. C. von Rotteck, *Lehrbuch*, p. 136.
25. C. Welcker, *Grundgesetz, Grundvertrag, Verfassung*, in C. von Rotteck and C. Welcker (eds), *Das Staats-Lexikon* [1834–1843], vol. 6, Altona: Verlag von Friedrich Hammerich, 1847, p. 162.
26. Cf. W. von Rimscha, op. cit., p. 103.
27. Elsewhere I have stressed the natural law perspective of R. von Mohl, exemplified by his including in the doctrine of the *Rechtsstaat* also the work of Hugo Grotius. In this connection, cf. G. Gozzi, *Democrazia e diritti. Germania: dallo Stato di diritto alla democrazia costituzionale*, Roma-Bari: Laterza, 1999, p. 36.
28. R. von Mohl, *Das Staatsrecht des Königreichs Württemberg*, Erster Band, Tübingen: Laupp, 1840, p. 312 ff.
29. Ibid., p. 316.
30. Ibid., p. 314.
31. R. von Mohl, *Enzyklopädie der Staatswissenschaften*, Tübingen: Laupp, 1859, pp. 329–31.
32. Ibid., p. 325.
33. R. von Mohl, *Die Polizeiwissenschaft nach den Grundsätzen des Rechtsstaates* [1832–1833], vol. 1, Tübingen: Laupp, 1844, p. 8. Mohl conceived of the *Rechtsstaat* also as a *Polizei-Staat*. The *Rechtsstaat* should not strive, in his view, only to protect rights. This is how Mohl defined the notion of *Polizei*: "The concept refers to all the different agencies and institutions designed to remove, by means of the power of the

state, the external obstacles which hinder the development of the forces of man and which the individual is not able to overcome"; ibid., p. 11. For Mohl, the *Rechtsstaat* should not limit itself to guaranteeing rights, but it should also strive for the realization of well-being; cf. M. Stolleis, "Rechtsstaat", p. 370.

34. W. von Rimscha, op. cit., p. 92.
35. J.C. Freiherr von Aretin, *Staatsrechts der konstitutionellen Monarchie*, vol. 1, Altenburg: Literatur-Comptoir, 1824, p. 153 ff.
36. Cf. F. Schmittener, *Grundlinien des allgemeinen oder idealen Staatsrechts*, Giessen: Georg Friedrich Heyer's Verlag, 1845, p. 558. In this connection and, more in general, for an analysis of the doctrines of rights of early German constitutionalism, cf. D. Grimm, "Die Entwicklung der Grundrechtstheorie in der deutschen Staatsrechtslehre des 19. Jahrhunderts", in id., *Recht und Staat der bürgerlichen Gesellschaft*, Frankfurt a. M.: Suhrkamp, 1987, p. 314. I owe largely to Grimm's essay the following considerations in this paragraph.
37. H. Zoepfl, *Grundsätze des allgemeinen und des constitutionnell-monarchischen Staatsechts* [1841], Heidelberg: Akademische Verlagshandlung von C.F. Winter, 1846, p. 56. Zoepfl's position, which was first close to the liberals and later to the conservatives, are analysed by M. Stolleis, *Geschichte des öffentlichen Rechts in Deutschland*, vol. 2, München: Verlag C.H. Beck, 1992, p. 91 ff.
38. J.C. Freiherr von Aretin, op. cit., p. 163.
39. Ibid., p. 164.
40. H. Zoepfl, op. cit., p. 227. Also Zachariä conceived of rights as limits to governmental power. In particular, Zachariä recognized a natural liberty, which, however, could not be unlimited (*unbeschränkt*). It was the law that established the limits; cf. H.A. Zachariä, *Deutsches Staats- und Bundesrecht*, Erste Abtheilung, Göttingen: Vandenhoeck und Ruprecht, 1841, p. 227 ff., in particular p. 237. On the contradictions in Zachariä's position, split between adhesion to the principles of Kantian philosophy and the conservative perspective, cf. M. Stolleis, *Geschichte*, p. 170.
41. D. Grimm, op. cit., p. 319.
42. H. Zoepfl, op. cit., p. 244.
43. J.C. Freiherr von Aretin, op. cit., p. 229.
44. §91 of the Constitution of Württemberg proclaims: "All laws and provisions which are in contrast with the present constitution are null and void. The other are subject to constitutional revision (*verfassungsmägießen Revision*)", in E.R. Huber, *Dokumente*, p. 198. In this connection, R. von Mohl noted that the citizen was bound to obey laws only if they were passed in conformity with the Constitution and if they had a constitutional content, and he recalled that the Constitution of Württemberg, §21, established that the citizen was bound to obedience only in conformity with the Constitution (*verfassungsmägießen Gehorsam*); cf. R. von Mohl, *Das Staatsrecht*, pp. 324, 326: cf. also D. Grimm, op. cit., p. 316.
45. C. von Rotteck, *Constitution*, in C. von Rotteck and C. Welcker (eds), *Das Staatslexikon* [1834–1843], vol. 3, Altona: Verlag von Johann Friedrich Hammerich, 1846, p. 527.
46. In this connection cf. R. Wahl, "Der Vorrang der Verfassung", *Der Staat*, 1981, p. 491 ff. Of the same opinion U. Scheuner, "Die rechtliche Tragweite der Grundrechte in der deutschen Verfassungsentwicklung des 19. Jahrhunderts", in E. Forsthoff, W. Weber and F. Wieacker (eds), *Festschrift für Ernst Rudolf Huber*, Göttingen: Verlag Otto Schawartz, 1973, p. 155.

47. Following the German general elections, which were held in the States of the Confederation with a predominantly majority system, a meeting was held on 18 May 1848 that marked the beginning of the activities of the first national assembly of the German people. The aim was to draft a new constitution of Germany, and work began with the fundamental rights. In December 1848 the fundamental rights came into force for all of Germany. The constitutional problem was intertwined with that of the state-form and, more precisely, with the relationship between Austria and Prussia. The issue was whether Austria should enter the new state and renounce its unity or whether, on the contrary, it should maintain its unity, reducing its ties with Germany to relationships of international law. On 27 March 1849 a constitution was approved that excluded Austria, and Friedrich Wilhelm IV was offered the crown of the Empire. But his refusal to accept the imperial power that was offered by a democratically elected assembly marked the definitive crisis of the national assembly of Frankfurt. On the events of the Paulskirche cf. H. Lutz, *Zwischen Habsburg und Preußen. Deutschland 1815–1866*, Berlin: Siedler, 1985. See also J.-D. Kühne, *Die Reichsverfassung der Paulskirche*, Frankfurt a. M.: Metzner, 1985.
48. Cf. G. Haverkate, "Deutsche Staatsrechtslehre und Verfassungspolitik", in O. Brunner, W. Conze and R. Kosellek (eds), *Geschichtliche Grundbegriffe*, Band 6, Stuttgart: Klett-Cotta, 1990, p. 75. On the issue of the Paulskirche cf. A.G. Manca, *La sfida delle riforme. Costituzione e politica nel liberalismo prussiano (1850–1866)*, Bologna: il Mulino, 1995, especially the first chapter.
49. Cf. the statement by G. Beseler, in F. Wigard (ed.), *Verhandlungen der deutschen constituirenden Nationalversammlung zu Frankfurt/M.*, vol. 1, Frankfurt a. M., 1848, p. 701.
50. Cf. Artikel II of the *Entwurf. Die Grundrechte des deutschen Volkes*, in J.G. Droysen (ed.), *Die Verhandlungen des Verfassungs-Ausschusses der deutschen Nationalversammlung*, Leipzig: Weidmann'sche Buchhandlung, 1849, p. 374.
51. See Mommsen's comment on the Introductory Law of the declaration of 28 December 1848 in Th. Mommsen, *I diritti fondamentali del popolo tedesco*, ed. by G. Valera, Bologna: il Mulino, 1994, p. 118.
52. The deliberation states: "The so-called fundamental rights of the German people ... cannot be considered legally valid", in E.R. Huber (ed.), *Dokumente zur deutschen Verfassungsgeschichte*, vol. 2, Stuttgart-Berlin-Köln-Mainz: W. Kohlhammer, 1986, p. 2.
53. J.C. Bluntschli, *Allgemeines Staatsrecht*, München: Verlag der literarisch-artistischen Anstal, 1852, pp. 667–8.
54. Ibid., p. 669. In this connection cf. D. Grimm, op. cit., p. 324.
55. J.C. Bluntschli, *Allgemeines Staatsrecht*, p. 670.
56. J. Held, *System der Verfassungsrecht der monarchischen Staaten Deutschlands mit besonderen Rücksicht auf den Constitutionalismus*, part 1, Würzburg: Verlag der Stahel'schen Buch- und Kunsthandlung, 1856, p. 253. On Held, see D. Grimm, op. cit., pp. 324–5.
57. J. Held, op. cit., p. 256.
58. O. von Bähr, *Der Rechtsstaat*, Kassel and Göttingen: Georg H. Wigand, 1864, p. 49.
59. Ibid., p. 12.
60. Ibid., p. 12.
61. Ibid., p. 54.

62. In this connection, O. von Bähr recognizes the importance of the principles enunciated by R. von Gneist in *Das heutige engl. Verfassungs- und Verwaltungsrecht*, Berlin: Springer, 1857.
63. In the copious literature on the question, see in particular L. von Stein, "Rechtsstaat und Verwaltungsrechtspflege", *Zeitung für das privat- und öffentliche Recht der Gegenwart*, 6 (1879). Stein recognizes the originality of Otto von Bähr's work compared with the "academic" treatments of the doctrine of the *Rechtsstaat*, just as, for example, that of Mohl. Stein, who introduced the distinction between constitution and administration, asserted that the mere constitution was not sufficient to guarantee a people liberty. What was needed, above all, was a jurisdiction that safeguarded the rights and the liberty of individuals against the administration as well; ibid., p. 316.
64. The formalization of the *Rechtsstaat* in the second half of the nineteenth century continued also with the creation of administrative law as an autonomous discipline, due above all to Otto Mayer; cf. M. Stolleis, "Rechtsstaat", p. 372.
65. Ibid., p. 371.
66. C.F.W. von Gerber, "Sui diritti pubblici" [1852], in id., *Diritto pubblico*, Milano: Giuffrè, 1971, p. 67.
67. C.F.W. von Gerber, *Grundzüge des deutschen Staatsrechts* [1865], Leipzig: Tauchnitz, 1880, reprint Hildesheim/Zürich/New York: Olms-Weidmann, 1998, p. 34 (the second italics are mine).
68. Ibid., p. 3.
69. D. Grimm, op. cit., p. 334.
70. P. Laband, *Das Staatsrechts des deutschen Reiches* [1876–1882], vol. 1, Tübingen: Laupp, 1876, reprint of 5th edn., Tübingen, 1911, Aalen: Scientia Verlag, 1964, p. 151.
71. G. Jellinek, *System der subjectiven öffentlichen Rechts* [1892], Tübingen: Mohr, 1905, p. 95.
72. Ibid., p. 97.
73. Ibid., p. 103.
74. Ibid., p. 102. For these reasons Jellinek, criticizes the theses of Laband, who, as we have seen, denied the existence of subjective rights, cf. Jellinek, op. cit., p. 102, n. 2.
75. Ibid., p. 106.
76. P. Laband, *Das Staatsrechts des deutschen Reiches* [1876–1882], vol. 1, Tübingen: Laupp, 1876, reprint of 5th edn., Tübingen 1911, Aalen: Scientia Verlag, 1964, p. 94. Laband observed that the conception of the state as juridical personality of public law implied that the subject of the power of the state was the state itself. He went on to say that Jellinek also shared his position (ibid., p. 95). Finally, Laband claimed that the sovereign was the only representative of the state. It was on this representation of the state that sovereignty was founded, thus only the *Kaiser*, on Laband's view, could act on behalf of the *Reich* (ibid., p. 229). Substantially similar assertions are to be found also in Jellinek. Indeed, he claimed that the state "is the only association that rules by virtue of a force which is intrinsic to it, original, legally derived from no other force", in G. Jellinek, *Allgemeine Staatslehre*, Berlin: Verlag von O. Häring, 1900, p. 158. Jellinek added that "any power of state domination can come only from the state itself" (ibid., p. 370). Finally, with respect to the sovereignty of the state, the monarch was the supreme organ of the state. He was holder of a right of the sovereign "conferred by the state", G. Jellinek, *System*, p. 150.
77. G. Jellinek, *System*, p. 32 (italics mine).
78. Ibid., p. 67.

79. Böckenförde asserts, in contrast, that the doctrine of the *Rechtsstaat* in the second half of the nineteenth century continued to be the liberal doctrine. It was a purely *formal* concept of the *Rechtsstaat*, which survived until the end of the Weimar Republic; cf. E.W. Böckenförde, "Entstehung und Wandel des Rechtsstaatsbegriffs", p. 76. A different view is expressed by Haverkate, who stresses the conservative character of the concept of the *Rechtsstaat* in the second half of the century; cf. G. Haverkate, "Deutsche Staatsrechtslehre", p. 74.
80. W. Kägi, "Rechtsstaat und Demokratie", in *Demokratie und Rechtsstaat. Festgabe zum 60. Geburtstag von Zaccaria Giacometti*, Zürich: Polygraphischer Verlag A.G., 1953, p. 107. Also Bäumlin posits the reciprocity of democracy and *Rechtsstaat* on the basis of a common horizon of values. Thus, according to this interpretation, the responsibility of those governing towards those governed in the democratic state-form corresponds to the centrality of the dignity of the person in the *Rechtsstaat*; cf. R. Bäumlin, *Die rechtstaatliche Demokratie*, Zürich: Polygraphischer Verlag, 1954, p. 91.
81. Ibid., pp. 129, 136.
82. G. Leibholz, "Demokratie und Rechtsstaat", in *Schriftenreihe der Landeszentrale für Heimatdienst in Niedersachsen*, Heft 5, Bad Gandersheim, 1957, p. 28.
83. Ibid., p. 28. Thoma also identified in the principle of legality the foundation of the *Rechtsstaat*; cf. R. Thoma, "Rechtsstaatsidee und Verwaltungswisseschaft", *Jahrbuch des öffentlichen Rechts der Gegenwart*, 4 (1910), p. 196 ff.
84. On this interpretation cf. G. Bongiovanni and G. Gozzi, "Democrazia", in A. Barbera and G. Zanetti (eds), *Le basi filosofiche del costituzionalismo*, Roma-Bari: Laterza, 1997, p. 215 ff.
85. G. Leibholz, op. cit., p. 11.
86. G. Böckenförde, op. cit., p. 81.
87. Entscheidung des Bundesverfassungsgerichts (BVerfGE) 7, 198 (205).
88. G. Böckenförde, op. cit., p. 79.
89. The conception of a formal *Rechtsstaat* has been supported by public law experts and political scientists of left-wing orientation (Abendroth, Maus, Preu·, etc.); cf. D. Grimm, "Reformalisierung des Rechtsstaaats als Demokratiepostulat?" *JuS* (1980), 10, p. 706.
90. Ibid., p. 708. The polemical reply to the conception of the *Rechtsstaat* in a material sense formulated by Grimm highlights how this perspective tends to establish the primacy of the constitutional judge over the legislator and how, on the basis of an "evaluative" examination of the modes of behaviour of individuals, the judge ends up by "juridifying" the political potential of conflict; cf. F. Hase, K.-H. Ladeur and H. Ridder, "Nochmals: Reformalisierung des Rechtsstaats als Demokratiepostulat?" *JuS* (1981), 11, p. 796. On the contrary, the formalization of the *Rechtsstaat* establishes, according to these authors, the centrality of the process of legislation and, as a consequence, the enhancement of the "conditions of formation of an opinion and of a will which is social-decentralized, political and non-state, scientific, cultural", ibid., p. 795.
91. K. Hesse, "Der Rechtsstaat im Verfassungssystem des Grundgesetzes", in M. Tohidipur (ed.), op. cit., vol. 1, p. 293.
92. Ibid., p. 299.
93. Hesse's reconstruction is based on the German Fundamental Law (*Grundgesetz für die Bundesrepublik Deutschland*), where, in art. 28, par. I, one reads: "The constitutional system of the *Länder* must draw on the principles of the republican, democratic and social *Rechtsstaat* in conformity with the present Fundamental Law". Hesse identifies the *Grundgesetz* as the constitutional foundation of the "social *Rechtsstaat*".

CHAPTER 6

ÉTAT DE DROIT AND NATIONAL SOVEREIGNTY IN FRANCE

Alain Laquièze

In contemporary French public law doctrine, the notion of *État de droit* has two broad meanings:

1. The state acts exclusively in a legal manner, i.e. it operates by means of law. Since it is sovereign, the state founds and delimits the national legal system, namely all of the rules it dictates to itself and those that derive from them. As the source of law, the state is competent to define its own competences.
2. The state is subjected to law: the objective pursued is that of framing and limiting the state by means of law. Political power is framed by law, by means of the following guarantees: separation of powers, which implies in particular the independence of the judiciary from political agencies; proclamation of rights and liberties; and judicial review of legislation and administrative acts.[1]

These two meanings, which complement more than contradict each other, are traditionally attributed to the *État de droit*, a concept elaborated by jurists and designed for use by them. The French term is nothing but a literal translation of the word *Rechtsstaat*, which received its first theoretical treatment in the works of the German jurists Robert von Mohl[2] and Friedrich Julius Stahl,[3] before the *Rechtsstaat* became a commonplace of legal doctrine beyond the Rhine in the second half of the nineteenth century (Carl Friedrich von Gerber, Rudolf von Jhering, Paul Laband, Georg Jellinek), which in turn was to have decisive influence on the public law scholars in the Third Republic.[4]

The idea of a state limited by law was not unknown before the nineteenth century. Its seeds were already sown in the *ancien régime*. But while in the modern period jurists made use of the theory of the rule of law to place limits on the power of the state and, in particular, to limit the omnipotence of parliament that derives from the theory of national sovereignty, jurists prior to 1789 were primarily concerned to lay legal foundations for the omnipotence of the monarch, the rights of the king, in the face of the resistance the King encountered in the ordinary exercise of his power.

P. Costa and D. Zolo (eds.), The Rule of Law: History, Theory and Criticism, 261–291.

From the sixteenth century, royal authority was considered absolute. But the term "absolute" was understood not as a synonym of dictatorial or tyrannical but rather in the sense of independent, of "free person", free from any restriction. If the monarchy was independent from any human restriction, the absolute government of the monarch, however, was not considered as an arbitrary government. The monarchic writer Louis de Bonald, following Bossuet, wrote at the beginning of the nineteenth century:

> [A]bsolute power is a power which is independent from the men over whom it is exercised; arbitrary power is a power that is independent from the laws by virtue of which it is exercised.[5]

No doubt, absolute monarchy was grounded in a rigorous and complete notion of sovereignty, whose principles were the foundation of the state. It is hardly necessary here to recall the works of French jurists who, from Bodin to Jacob Nicolas Moreau, presented monarchic sovereignty as the monopoly of coercive power, exclusively in the hands of the sovereign, and which, as a consequence, ruled out the separation of powers or a compromise among them. Cardin Le Bret, counsellor to Richelieu, expressed this idea in a formula which is actually an axiom: "The King is the sole sovereign in his Kingdom, and sovereignty is as indivisible as the point in geometry."[6]

Nonetheless, this doctrinal will to condemn any form of counterbalance of power, any resistance to the overwhelming power of the king, does not mean that the monarch's power was unlimited. The French monarchy was, to use Bodin's words, a "royal or legitimate monarchy", namely a monarchy in which "subjects obey the laws of the Monarch and the Monarch the laws of nature, and the subjects have natural freedom and the ownership of property". These natural rights, however, owing to their abstract character, did not seem to be easy to defend in the event that they were violated by the king, unless an appeal was made to some hypothetical right to resist.

In a society dominated by an intense corporate life, individual rights had necessarily to be subordinated to reason of state. Individual freedom, understood as the right to go where one likes or to act as one pleases, was not at all guaranteed. The king could restrict or suppress this freedom with a simple *lettre de cachet*. Freedom of conscience, freedom of speech, and personal property were also scantily guaranteed in legal terms for subjects whose "body and property" belonged to the King.[7]

Although individual rights were not protected from the power of the sovereign – one could, therefore, only trust in the moderation of a monarch whose action aimed at the common good – it is true that the French monarchy was provided with a legal status, if not indeed a constitution, in spite of the term not having the meaning contemporary jurists give it. The "monarchic constitution" was not a written document, with a systematic exposition of rules about the government of the state, but rather a mosaic of customary provisions, the most important being the fundamental laws of the kingdom about the devolution of royal power and the inalienability of royal property. Thus there coexisted a law of succession (the principle of heredity and of the first born, the principle of masculinity, the principle of Catholic faith), a law of the inalienability of the crown, and a law of the inalienability of the property of the crown, and the monarch had to respect all these laws.

Moreover, the power of the sovereign encountered legal limits in customary law, which was very important as regards private law, and likewise in the particular statutes of the provinces. Monarchic power also had to come to terms with certain decision-making agencies, such as the States General, which, however, had not been convened since 1614, and the provincial States, which continued to assemble regularly in Brittany, Languedoc, Artois, Flanders, and Béarn. The king also had to deal with the activism of the sovereign courts and in particular with the parliament of Paris, which, at the time of the Fronde and later in the reign of Louis XV, demanded the right to be involved in the elaboration of laws.[8] Despite these limits, the king remained the sole holder of sovereignty, and it was to him that the final decision fell.

The Revolution was not to alter the terms of the problem substantially. Certainly, there was a break with the past, in that the holder of sovereignty was no longer the monarch but the nation. But the change in sovereign did not alter the nature of sovereignty, which remained unlimited. Furthermore, on the one hand the discovery, during the Reign of Terror, that the people too could be oppressive and, on the other, chronic diffidence towards direct democracy led many authors to distinguish between nation and people and to exalt the representative model. The construction of the theory of national sovereignty, already underway in Sieyès but completed by the *doctrinaires* (Royer-Collard, Guizot),[9] attributed power of a quasi-royal nature to the representative organs which have the function to make the law, i.d. the supreme expression of the general will.

The incontestable character of statute law, which remained dominant in French legal literature throughout the nineteenth and into a good part of the twentieth century, was already present in the 1789 Declaration of the Rights of Man and of the Citizen, precisely at the time when the revolutionaries were intent on building a hierarchical legal system in which the Declaration was to have a higher value than the constitution, which, in turn, was to stand above statute law. The Rousseau-like mysticism of the law can be found in many articles of the Declaration that systematically refer to the legislative act to specify conditions for the exercise of the proclaimed rights and their delimitation.[10] It is found again in the enunciation of individual rights heading the charters of 1814 and 1830, a circumstance which led the jurist Hello to write in 1848: "The law keeps the promise of the Charter, that is, it serves to guarantee our rights".[11]

The Second Empire, like the Third Republic, resorted to statute law when affirming fundamental freedom, such as freedom of assembly, freedom to organize in trade unions, and freedom of association. The supreme nature of legislation, passed by a parliament acting in the name of the nation, was further accentuated by the absence of any real counterbalancing power. The judiciary occupied a subordinate position. The negative memory left by the judicial *parlements* of the *ancien régime* did not encourage the executive power to concede broad powers to judges. The judges, who were regularly purged with each change in the government, enjoyed neither the independence nor the powers necessary to limit the action of the state. It is not surprising, then, that the American model of judicial review of legislation received little attention, despite the efforts of Laboulaye.[12]

As a consequence, the judicial protection of individual rights from the abuse of legislators, an essential characteristic of the rule of law as we understand it today, was not at all assured. It is not that the public law theorists of the nineteenth century naively believed that legislation, like the king, could not operate badly. A liberal such as Benjamin Constant knew well that a law could be oppressive. Distancing himself both from Rousseau's conception of unlimited sovereignty and from Bentham's utilitarianism, which denied the existence of unalterable and indefeasible natural rights, Constant held that a retroactive law or one prescribing actions contrary to moral rectitude should not be applied. But this refusal to apply an oppressive law was given voice, in fact, through the exercise of the individual right to "resist oppression", a right which is purely illusory in practical terms, unless one contemplates revolution.[13] As for the rest, Constant, in his defence of the limited sovereignty of the state, relied on the control that citizens exercise over their representatives.[14]

The issue of the oppressive law, though raised by certain illustrious representatives of liberal thinking – in addition to Constant, we should mention in particular Edouard Laboulaye – did not become central to the debate until the end of the nineteenth century. If state power was considered dangerous, this indicated above all a problem with the executive. It is understandable, then, that some authors defended "mixed government" and the parliamentary regime, a state in which a responsible executive is placed under the strict control of deputies.

The public law scholars of the Third Republic underlined the weakness of the French state, dominated as it was by the theory of national sovereignty and legislation as expression of the general will. This theory undermined the safeguard of individual freedom. The Alsatian jurist Raymond Carré de Malberg, in his *Contribution á la théorie générale de l'État*, published in 1920, gave a precise characterization of what he called the "legal state" as opposed to a genuine *État de droit*. Together with him, other eminent jurists, working in the first three decades of the century, elaborated the concept of *État de droit*, which was intended to be not merely "a weapon against the system of the legal state"[15] but also fertile terrain for a considered reflection on the legal nature of the state and its relationships with law.

In the following sections we will examine the decisive contribution of the – essentially public law – doctrine of the Third Republic to the construction of the concept of *État de droit*, but we will not fail to investigate the more recent doctrinal debates on the *État de droit*. Even 100 years after its invention in France, the concept of the *État de droit* continues to stimulate controversies and, at times, polemics. While some hold that it is being fully achieved, others believe that it is quietly dissolving. Perhaps it is nothing but a horizon, a goal which is by definition impossible to reach.

1 THE DOCTRINE OF THE THIRD REPUBLIC: THE CONSTRUCTION OF THE CONCEPT OF *ÉTAT DE DROIT*

The elaboration of the concept of *État de droit* by jurists of the Third Republic certainly responded to an immediate desire to combat the system of the legal state, which was characterized by fidelity to the sovereignty of legislation. However, this elaboration also led to a reflection on the relationship between state and law.

1.1 The État de droit versus the État légal

In his *Contribution à la théorie générale de l'État*, Carré de Malberg identified two principal differences between the *État de droit* and the *État légal* which were both still present in the France of the Third Republic. The first difference lay in the fact that, while the *État de droit* operated solely in the interest of the citizens and to safeguard their rights, the system of the *État légal* was linked to a political conception according to which the administrative authority was, in all cases and in all matters, to be subordinated to the legislative organ, in the sense that it could only act in execution of, or on concession of, a law. According to this conception of the fundamental organization of powers, the administration was always obliged to seek the legitimacy and the primary source of its activity in a legislative text.

The second difference lay in the fact that the *État de droit* had a broader range than that of the *État légal*. The latter tended merely to guarantee the supremacy of the will of the legislative body and had no implication beyond the subordination of the administration to the law. The *État de droit*, on the other hand, being a safeguard of citizens' rights, was not limited to subjecting administrative authorities to administrative regulations and to laws, but aimed also to subject legislation to constitutional rules.[16]

The doctrinal critique of the *État légal* was above all a critique of the unlimited power of the parliament in the Third Republic. The theory of national sovereignty was intended to limit the power of the government and to prevent those in power from believing they were the sole holders of authority. But the development of the parliamentary system, which tended to weaken the executive, and the extension of the right to vote in the course of the nineteenth century had generated confusion between the holders and the exercisers of sovereignty; in other words, there had emerged an identification between the nation and its representatives. As a consequence, national sovereignty had become sovereignty of the assemblies. And the assemblies, bolstered by their popular legitimacy, could pass whatever laws they wanted.[17]

It is understandable, then, that a considerable part of French doctrine, with the significant exception of Carré de Malberg, resisted the German theory of the self-limitation of the state, developed especially by Jellinek, according to which the power of the state was not limited by an external authority but by the state itself, i.e. by the law which only the state could make. Since the parliament was the main source of laws at the time, obliging the state to respect the law which it itself had created did not entail any limitation on parliamentary omnipotence. Léon Duguit summarized the prevailing view when he wrote that "a limit that can be created, modified or suppressed at the discretion of those to whom it is applied is no limit at all".[18]

The theory of the *État de droit* as it was developed from the early twentieth century presented a number of elements which assigned a primary role to legal mechanisms and pushed into the background political guarantees like the imperative mandate and the referendum, both tainted with a plebiscitary character. Most importantly, a hierarchic structure of norms was asserted that did not merely establish the subordination of administrative acts to statute law but also subjected legislation to the constitution or even to a declaration of rights with supraconstitutional value.

Since the constitutional laws of 1875 were not preceded by a declaration of rights, the question of the legal status of the 1789 Declaration inevitably caused a doctrinal division. The debate on this issue involved two sides. There were those, such as Adhémar Esmein and Carré Malberg, who denied any legal status to the 1789 Declaration. For these legal positivists, the Declaration was nothing but a set of abstract maxims waiting to be specified by future constitutional and legislative texts and devoid, themselves, of any legal sanction. Separate from a constitutional text, it could be nothing but a declaration of principles, a pronouncement of philosophical truths that could not be considered as legal prescriptions with the efficacy of the rules of positive law. Esmein distinguished "declarations" (which recognized in general individual rights as "above and before positive laws") from the safeguarding of rights by means of genuine positive and obligatory laws. More precisely, Esmein contrasted declarations to provisions laid down in a constitutional text, which effectively assure this or that individual right to citizens. Examining the various French constitutions beginning in 1791, the author of *Eléments de droit constitutionnel* showed without difficulty that most of these documents, from the constitution of 1791 to that of 1870, made explicit provision for the guarantee of rights. The same could be said of the American Constitution and, in Europe, of practically all written constitutions.[19]

Authors like Duguit and Maurice Hauriou, on the other hand, defended the legal status of the 1789 Declaration and its supremacy with respect both to legislation and to the constitution. From this clearly natural law perspective, the Declaration merely recognized pre-existing individual rights and, by proclaiming them, granted them a supraconstitutional status. Duguit wrote:

> The system of the declaration of rights tends to define the limits imposed on the action of the state and, to that end, formulates certain higher principles which both the constitutional legislator and the ordinary legislator must respect. These higher principles are by no means created by the declaration; the declaration solemnly ascertains them and proclaims them. [...] In the system of 1789, there are three categories of law arranged in hierarchical order: the declaration of rights, the constitutional laws and the ordinary

laws. The constitutional legislator is subordinated to the declarations and the ordinary legislator to the constitutional legislator. *A fortiori*, the ordinary legislator is bound by the declaration of rights.[20]

Duguit added, challenging Esmein's view, that the Declaration of Rights preserved, in the Third Republic as well as in 1789, the status of positive law, which bound even the constituent power. This claim, however, appears to be more the manifestation of a conviction than the result of rigorous demonstration.[21]

In the first edition of his *Précis de droit constitutionnel*, Hauriou wrote:

Declarations do not have a merely moral value, as is often claimed; they have a legal status. Certainly, they are not sufficient to consecrate in practical terms the freedoms they proclaim, since they only contain the principles and do not assure the organization in detail, without which any sort of application is impossible, but the declaration of principle that they contain has a value, since it legally establishes the principle of the freedom proclaimed and contains a commitment of the state not to suppress this principle and to promulgate organic laws, necessary for the practical regulation of that freedom. Declarations of rights do not only have legal status; they also have constitutional status. Certainly, the declarations are not incorporated in the text of the constitution, they are the preamble, but this means that they contain constitutional principles that rank higher in order than the written constitution.[22]

Although the supreme status of the 1789 Declaration was asserted more emphatically in the first edition of the *Précis de droit constitutionnel* than in the second, in the latter the author stressed that the Declaration continued to preserve its character as a rule of positive law. The Declaration became, in fact, "the constitutional text of the social constitution".[23]

Asserting the legal status of the 1789 Declaration had two advantages. First, it undermined the theory of the self-limitation of the state, since it was admitted that certain natural rights external to the state were legally binding on the state itself. Second, claiming that the legislator had to respect not only the constitutional text, which contained only rules concerning institutional relationships, but also certain individual rights cleared the path for a more penetrating control over legislation.

But what was the conceptual framework, in a state marked by a pronounced centrality of legislation, for the effectiveness of this hierarchy of norms and for an efficacious guarantee of the individual rights placed at the top of the hierarchy? The issue was raised, then, of the means of reviewing legislation, a decisive instrument in the building of an *État de droit*. Since examination carried out by a political organ was unanimously rejected, due to the negative experiences with the Senate in the First and Second Empires,[24] attention was naturally turned towards some sort of judicial verification. The idea of a special constitutional court, charged with reviewing legislation, was rejected by most jurists.

For Duguit, an institution of this kind, entrusted with extensive prerogatives in questions of referring and annulment, would become a political organ capable of acquiring too much power within the state.[25] Similarly, for Hauriou, a constitutional court, given its exclusive purpose, would overshadow the legislator.[26] This was a classic critique of the judicial review of legislation, which had already appeared, for example, in Tocqueville.[27] In short, a constitutional review moving in this direction did not seem feasible. In these conditions it is not surprising, then, that many of the parliamentary bills in favour of a special constitutional court which were presented between 1903 and 1907, especially on the initiative of the deputy Charles Benoist, and then submitted again in the 1920s had no success.[28]

Charles Eisenmann proposed the institution of a special constitutional court in his essay *La justice constitutionnelle et la haute Cour constitutionnelle d'Autriche*, published in 1928. If the Austrian system seemed preferable to him, it was because it did not allow the question of constitutionality to be raised in simply any court case and because it provided a single, definitive solution. It was a single solution in that it assured the unity and, by consequence, the visibility of judicial decisions. It was definitive in that it allowed the annulment of irregular laws, i.e. their definitive elimination from the legal system. Eisenmann added:

> Let no one claim that the legislator is precluded from creating law. No, he is still free to create whatever he likes, but everything that he validly creates will be regular law. What is more, in this way the certainty of law is guaranteed by means of the uniformity and homogeneity of legislative law.[29]

Nonetheless, Eisenmann's work, which drew on Kelsen and which was at the same time a critique of the natural law positions of Hauriou, Duguit, and Gény, was to have only very limited influence on the French doctrine of his day. It was not until the Fifth Republic, and the institution of a genuine centralized review of legislation, that the thought of the great Austrian jurist became widespread.

Most authors in the Third Republic held that if there had to be a review of legislation, this should be carried out by the ordinary judge, who applied the technique of the objection of unconstitutionality. This conclusion was reached by way of arguments of legal logic. In 1912, Joseph-Barthélemy and Paul Duez, in an opinion on a Rumanian law of 1911, wrote:

> The power and the duty of courts not to apply unconstitutional laws in a given trial does not need to be consecrated in a specific text; indeed, one would need a formal text to take the power to review legislation in general away from judges.

These authors saw this as a "logical, natural consequence of the judicial function".[30] Similarly, Duez drew all the consequences from the assertion of the existence of a hierarchy among state norms. For Duez,

> Legislation and Constitution have the same legal nature: both found or organize, in a general, abstract, impersonal manner, rules of law. There is only a hierarchical differentiation between the two: constitutional rules, placed on a higher legislative step, bind ordinary legislation, just as the latter determines the limits to which administrative regulations are subjected, the latter being a lower status legislative act. From a legal perspective, the review of legislation against the constitution seems to be similar to the review of regulations against legislation.[31]

Reviewing a statute against the constitution was, as a legal operation, no different from reviewing a regulation against legislation. Hauriou also accepted this position when he explained that "the declaration of the unconstitutionality of a statute is not qualitatively different from the declaration of the illegality of administrative regulations".[32]

Legal logic seemed to suggest, then, that the ordinary judge should be able to carry out a review of legislation, even in the absence of a precise text that empowered him in this sense. There were many who shared this view. Considering that the revolutionary texts prohibiting the interference of the courts in the exercise of legislative power were no longer valid,[33] they admitted that the judge should have at least the competence to verify the existence of a law; he had the power to make sure that the law was enacted in a legal and constitutional manner.[34] This was an examination of the external regularity of the law, which did not concern the merit of the law; it was not a material examination of the law. One can hardly avoid pointing out, however, an ambiguity in the thinking of French public law theorists of the Third Republic. Although they were aware that the emergence of a true *État de droit* required the material review of legislation by a judge, they had difficulty justifying such a review on the basis of positive law.

There were two main obstacles to the organization of a genuine judicial review. First, the principle of the separation of powers, since 1789, prohibited the judge from interfering with the legislative function. French public law continued to be dominated by the fear that a political judge might usurp power. Hauriou attempted to dispel this worry by arguing that the French system was based on the duality of judicial systems – a consequence of the principle of the separation between administrative and judicial authorities – and limited the role of the judge to specific controversies. The judge's function was limited to litigation, he argued, and could not extend to the judicial creation of general rules and, consequently, to a possible government by judges. Moreover, since both the ordinary judge and the administrative judge had to take a stand on the constitutionality of laws, they should agree upon the grounds of their respective decisions; this would necessarily lead to the search for a compromise. Thus Hauriou concluded:

> In these conditions, judges would play no political role whatsoever, as, on the one hand, they would create no rule of law and, on the other, they would carry out no preventive action. Political power can be defined as that which creates law preventively.[35]

In support of his position, Hauriou found in the decisions of the Tribunal of Conflicts, Council of State, and Court of Cassation evidence that French courts had carried out an examination of the merit of the constitutionality of laws or, at least, an interpretation of constitutional texts.[36]

The second factor that blocked evolution towards a material review of legislation was the absence of adequate norms of reference. There was, in fact, no constitutional text during the Third Republic that set precise limitations to legislation. Neither the constitutional laws of 1875, which are remarkably concise, nor the 1789 Declaration of the Rights of Man and of the Citizen, whose legal status, as we have seen, was contested by many authors (which raises doubts as to the customary nature it was supposed to have acquired through the creation of an *opinio juris*) laid the foundations, without prior revision of the constitution, for the material review of legislation.

In this connection, an investigation into the decisions of the Council of State of the time is revealing. If the Higher Administrative Court recognized, in 1913, with the Roubeau decision, the legal status of the 1789 Declaration by means of the system of the general principles of law, it did so only with the aim of annulling an administrative regulation that contradicted the principle of equality. This did not mean, however, that the Declaration had constitutional status. Indeed, this is exactly the point made by an insightful commentator on the decisions of the Council of State who observed that, in this case, the status of the Declaration was not constitutional but legislative.[37]

In any case, Carré de Malberg was the most far-sighted of all since he held that only a constitutional amendment modifying Article 8 of the act of 25 February 1875, which established the procedure for the revision of the constitution,[38] would allow the introduction of a genuine review of legislation. Carré de Malberg rightly saw that instituting this sort of judicial review, as far as it would lead to a revolution in French public law, was not conceivable without a textual basis.[39]

The impact of doctrinal constructions on the political life of the time was to remain quite limited, at least as regards the full acceptance of a hierarchy of norms and its corollary, the review of legislation. However, the doctrine was followed to some extent in the direction of a more thorough examination of administrative action by the administrative judge. This doctrinal exhortation in favour of a close judicial review of administration constituted another element in the elaboration of the concept of *État de droit*.

Some authors supported the *recours pour excès de pouvoir*, the annulment of administrative acts which could be demanded by private parties. In order to subject the state to law in an effective manner, it was necessary to distinguish, within the sphere of the state, between the authority that created law and the authority charged with sanctioning violations of the law. For this reason the *recours pour excès de pouvoir* could not be considered the same as a *recours gracieux*, since this would be appealing to the goodwill of the administration, with no requirement that the administration obey the law. The *recours pour excès de pouvoir* was, consequently, a suit of litigation before a judicial authority. This position perfectly fitted the idea that the administration should be obliged to respect the law.[40]

In addition to arguing that the *recours pour excès de pouvoir* was contentious in nature, public law doctrine supported the extension of the acceptability of this type of suit, in particular to include taxpayers and associations. It was clear, then, that the doctrine approved judicial decisions that tended in this direction.[41] Similarly, public law doctrine was favourable to the extension of the types of acts subjected to the *recours pour excès de pouvoir*. It may in fact seem perplexing, in the name of the constitutional state, that the public power could not be subjected to law in all its manifestations and that there should be administrative acts which were not susceptible to legal examination. Thus some authors were led to contest in particular the category of "government acts". This was the case of Léon Michoud and Henri Berthélemy, who denied the existence of a homogeneous category of acts exempt from the *recours pour excès de pouvoir*. If certain acts were not susceptible to suit, they argued, this occurred on a specific occasion for a particular reason. For example, vicissitudes of war were events of *force majeure* which allowed neither damage claims nor grounds for annulment. Above all, these authors criticized the notion of government acts imposing an artificial distinction between governmental and administrative functions.[42]

Finally, it was in the name of the *État de droit* that jurists contested the old theory of the exemption of public power from liability for damages to private parties. This theory, whose justification lay in the idea of sovereignty, was no longer admissible once sovereignty was considered as limited and once, in particular, the *recours pour excès de pouvoir* against acts of the state was recognized as legitimate. For this reason, the authors took a stand in favour of the theory of risk in administrative matters,[43] for the accumulation of liability, which allowed a person damaged by a state official to bring a claim against the administration,[44] and of the liability of the state as legislator (although Duguit was alone in supporting this last point). The other authors rejected the liability of the state as legislator as politically and financially inopportune. They feared, indeed, that such a responsibility might end up blocking legislation, increasing the expenditures of the state, and giving the judge excessive political importance, since it would be up to the judge to establish the amount of damages in the event of ascertained responsibility of the state as legislator.[45]

1.2 The État de droit: a general theory of law and state

Like the German theory of the *Rechtsstaat*, the French theory of the *État de droit* raised the problem of the nature of the state. In the wake of Michoud, who in *La théorie de la personne morale*[46] appealed to the German legal literature to defend the thesis of the moral personality of the state, French public law doctrine progressively adopted this conception, with the important exceptions of Duguit and Jèze, who considered the notion an empty abstraction. For Carré de Malberg the thesis of the legal personality of the state advanced by Michoud was "the very condition of the modern system of the *État de droit*".

However, the French and the German conceptions of the state as a legal person were not identical. In the German literature, the notion of the personality of the state entailed that the organization of a people in a state gave rise to a legal entity that was wholly distinct not only from the individuals *uti singuli* who made up the nation but also from the national body of citizens. Certainly, the nation was one of the elements that participated in the formation of the state. But once constituted, the state was not the personification of the nation; rather it personified only itself. Not being the subject of the rights of the nation, it was only the subject of its own rights. For certain eminent German authors like Jellinek and Laband, only the state was a legal person, while the German people was not a subject of law.

This theory separating the state and the nation could not be adopted in France, because of the very principle of national sovereignty as it was conceived by the French Revolution. By attributing sovereignty, that is state power, to the nation, the Revolution made the two notions intrinsically connected. As Carré de Malberg stressed:

By proclaiming that sovereignty, that is the power characteristic of the state, resides essentially in the nation, the Revolution in effect implicitly consecrated, at the basis of French law, the fundamental idea that the powers and rights of the state are ultimately but the rights and powers of the nation itself. The state, then, is not a legal subject that stands apart from and opposed to the nation: once it has been admitted that the powers characteristic of the state belong to the nation, it must also be admitted that there is identity between the nation and the state, in the sense that the state cannot but be the personification of the nation.[47]

In these conditions, the nation had no distinct legal existence. The members themselves of the nation could not be considered in their relationships with the person-state as entirely extraneous third parties.[48] Since the terms "state" and "nation" merely refer to two different faces of the same person, the state was, in Esmein's words, "the legal personification of a nation".[49]

The thesis of the moral personality of the state was contested in particular by Duguit in his two major works on *L'État*, published in 1901–1903.[50] His critique reappeared in *Traité de droit constitutionnel.* Starting with the observation of society, Duguit, a disciple of the sociologist Durkheim, recognized on the one hand the existence of social solidarity, which gave rise to rules of objective law that each individual was held to obey. On the other, there was individual will, which could be realized only in conformity with the rules of objective law. For Duguit, the quality of legal person could only be attributed to human beings, since only they truly exist and have a will. Consequently, to speak of the personality of the state meant to drift into abstraction and fantasy. Since the state had no real existence, there were only those who govern and those who are governed, and the former were distinguished from the latter only because they were the stronger of the two. Power was only de facto power; it came from the fact that the governors were stronger, and it was legitimate only when it acted in conformity with positive law. To cite a formula used by Duguit: "The state is simply the individual or the individuals invested de facto with power, the governors."[51]

Michoud vigorously rejected Duguit's position. He stressed that legal science was made up of abstractions and is premised upon theories that classify real facts and induce from them general rules. He noted subtly that Duguit also used imaginary creations when he employed the expressions "those who govern" and "those who are governed", which, in reality, were not as distinct as he made them out to be. Moreover, to claim that the will of the governors prevailed over that of the governed solely because the former were stronger led to a risk of escalation: some could be tempted to impose their will by force, if they felt it was more in conformity with the rules of the law. Michoud considered the theory anarchic and incompatible with the needs of society.[52] It would end up turning the state into a phenomenon of pure force and not a necessarily limited subject of law.

If the conception of the state as a person came to prevail in the doctrine, it should not be thought that it appeared in only one form. Michoud, rejecting the contribution of the *Willenstheorie*, held that the state was a subject of law not because it possessed a will – a collective will would be impossible to demonstrate in any case – but because it was the holder of rights corresponding to the national collective interest, which was not identical with the particular interests of the individual members of the nation. The emergence of a moral person presupposed, then, simply that within a group there existed, on the one hand, a collective interest, distinct from the individual interests of its members, and on the other, an organization capable of expressing a will that could represent and defend this interest. Here, the will of the moral person was not the natural will of the collective whole but the product of the legal organization of the community, since it was by means of this organization that the community provided itself with representatives or with organs designed to express its will.[53]

Carré de Malberg certainly came close to agreeing with Michoud when he stated, against the proponents of collective will, that a will was not a natural property of a collective whole. Realistically, any will expressed in the name of a moral person was purely individual. It was only after the union of individuals was organized legally – on the basis of a deed – that the moral person was provided with a will. There was, however, an essential difference between Carré de Malberg and Michoud. For Michoud, the unifying organization that gave life to will was simply a secondary element in the expression of moral personality. The fundamental element remained the existence of a collective interest distinct from individual interests. In this hypothesis, the moral personality was a social reality before being a legal reality, and this social reality was founded on the collective interest. For Carré de Malberg, in line with his legal positivist perspective, the moral personality was, by contrast, an exclusively legal reality, founded on purely formal elements: the unifying organization was the only founding element of the moral personality.[54]

The issue of the *État de droit*, then, led French doctrine to raise questions about the relationship between the state and the law. Authors like Esmein and Carré de Malberg believed that there could be no law without the state. Persuaded by the German theory of self-limitation, Carré de Malberg held that the state was the sole creator of law as it alone possessed a power of material coercion which guaranteed the execution of the legal rule and repressed the failure to apply it. There could be, then, no power capable of legally limiting the state, least of all natural law, as it was entirely devoid of any means of coercion. The state, therefore, was the source of law which limited its own power. Carré de Malberg made a point of adding that it was through its legal nature that the power of the state was subjected to law and thus limited.[55]

This theory of self-limitation met significant reservations in French doctrine, as it was not considered to guarantee an effective limitation of state power. The *État de droit*, then, required solid foundations, and law had to be considered a reality distinct from the state. The appeal to the principles of natural law, already proclaimed in the 1789 Declaration, was a solution. This was the path chosen by Michoud, who maintained that the powers of the sovereign state were limited by a higher rule of justice which did not come from the group but rather preceded it. In his words:

> We admit that even above the limit that emerges from the social conscience of the group there is another limit of an entirely ideal nature which is that of natural law, and that this limit not only imposes itself on the organs of the group but would impose itself on the group itself, if the latter could decide in some way other than through its organs.[56]

The question of natural law, discredited at the beginning of the twentieth century by the growing success of sociology, was bound to be replaced by the idea of objective law in French doctrine. The existence of stable and unchanging norms, grounded in an unalterable "nature", was deemed incompatible with social dynamics. Thus attention was directed to social conscience in search of a true foundation for legal obligation. Duguit's analysis was certainly an expression of this point of view. Discarding all the "metaphysical" notions of public law (sovereignty, moral personality, subjective law), Duguit believed that the foundations and limits of the powers of the governors lay in objective law, which originated in social reality. Thus law was a social fact which took shape spontaneously in the conscience of men under the influence of two sentiments: sociability, which exhorted men to punish acts that were harmful to social solidarity; and justice, which strove to preserve equality for all. In this hypothesis, the state or, to use Duguit's terminology, those governing no longer played a determining role in the production of legal norms.[57]

This conception of objective law, whose source lay in social reality, reappeared in the works of the international law scholar George Scelle, the sociologist Gurvitch, and the public law scholar George Burdeau. But despite its popularity, this theory of the "social hetero-limitation" of the state met numerous objections. Not only was the theory criticized for providing an inadequate explanation of how the rules of law take shape within society, but doubts were also raised as to the solutions the theory proposed to limit the powers of the governing over the governed. Once it was admitted that the recognition of the validity of the acts of the governors depended not on a determined legal system but on a sentiment that emerged within society, only two alternatives were left: either a legitimate right to resist against oppression, with the obvious risk of anarchy; or, to avoid running this risk, a presumption that the acts of the governors are compliant with objective law, with resistance against oppression becoming a purely theoretical option.[58]

In the end, these reflections on the *État de droit* hinged upon the theme of the legitimization of state power, since the dominant relationship of the governing over the governed was transformed into a legal relationship. The extent to which state power and the obligation of the governed to obey were accepted depended on success in framing them legally. The problem in particular was the legitimization of public law and administrative law, since the study of the *État de droit* led to an awareness of the particular nature of state power and, therefore, of the need to provide a specific legal framework in derogation of common law. This legitimization had to also take the role of jurists into account, since jurists had become major actors in this modern *État de droit*, which resulted from the progress of civilization as opposed to the barbarity of the police state. More than the lawyer or the law professor, it was the judge who turned out to be the main figure in this government of jurists.[59]

This last lesson of the elaboration of the constitutional state in the Third Republic was slow to take hold. The image of a competent and impartial judge, capable of taking a stand against political power, did not become real in French society until the last decade of the twentieth century, which is a clear sign of how current the terms of the debate are.

2 THE CONTEMPORARY DISCUSSION ON THE ÉTAT DE DROIT

It would be mistaken to believe that we are now witnessing the end of the history of the concept of the *État de droit*. As the notion is an essential element of liberal Western societies, it could hardly escape the rekindled interest of doctrine in the wake of the collapse of communism. What is more, in French law a transformation has taken place which, especially with the expansion in the decisions of the Constitutional Council, has deeply eroded the belief in the myth of legislation, understood as the sole expression of general will. While some contemporary authors evoke the achievement of the *État de droit*, others, pointing to the multiplication of legal systems and norms, are more inclined to speak of its dissolution. Given these two points of view, it is the role of legal doctrine to search for solutions to improve the *État de droit* in France.

2.1 Accomplishment or dissolution of the État de droit?

The institution of the review of legislation was certainly one of the most important elements in the advancement of the *État de droit* in France under the Fifth Republic. It is significant that the introduction of a review of legislation in the Constitution of 4 October 1958 was followed, a few years later, by the recognition of the legal status of the preamble of the same constitution, which in turn refers to the 1789 Declaration and to the preamble of the Constitution of 1946.[60]

This can scarcely be pure coincidence. It must be seen, rather, as proof that an effective legal examination of legislation requires the assumption of individual rights as principles of constitutional rank, as was pointed out by the public law theorists of the Third Republic and some members of the constituent assembly of 1958, in particular Pierre-Henri Teitgen. Nonetheless, it is clear that the myth of legislation as expression of the general will was slow to die, since, after 1971, doubts were still raised as to the constitutional status of all the rights proclaimed in the 1789 Declaration. The Constitutional Council, in the decision of 16 January 1982, confirmed that the Declaration enjoyed full constitutional status and subjected the legislator, as well as "*all the organs of the state*",[61] to the Constitution or, rather, the complex of constitutional norms of which the constitutional text was *stricto sensu* but one component.

One contemporary constitutional scholar, Louis Favoreu, has seen in this the full and complete achievement of the *État de droit* in France, in that the legislator is held to respect higher rules by a judge who could subject him or her to sanction. While in the *État legal* the respect for the hierarchy of norms was founded on the principle of legality, in the *État de droit* this respect rests on a "principle of constitutionality", which has replaced legality. Legislation is no longer "the source of the sources"; rather, it is "no longer anything but one source among many others" (Alessandro Pizzorusso). The constitution has become the central text that distributes the normative competences, under the surveillance of the constitutional judge, a situation which prevents legislators from freely extending or restricting their own competences as they did before. This is, then, quite distant from the theory of national sovereignty, understood as a theory of parliamentary sovereignty.

Constitutionality has substituted legality as the vehicle of the essential values of society. It is constitutionality, and no longer legality, that is considered as guarantor of the essential content of fundamental rights. With the recognition of the constitutional status of both the 1789 Declaration and the Preamble of 1946, there is a reduction in the range of application of Article 34 of the French Constitution, which provides, in particular, that the law should establish the rules about "the fundamental guarantees granted to citizens for the exercise of public liberties". There is also a reduction in the importance of, and interest in, the general principles of law, principles which span laws and stand above decrees, forged by the administrative judge to allow a closer control over administrative acts.[62] In this perspective, legality becomes a simple component of constitutionality.

It was, moreover, again Favoreu, who saw to the reprint in 1986 of Eisenmann's work *Justice constitutionnelle et la Haute Cour constitutionnelle d'Autriche*, which made it possible to assess the modernity of Eisenmann's position and which contributed to the further diffusion of Kelsen's views among French constitutional scholars. It is worth noting that the manual *Droit constitutionnel*, edited by Favoreu, contains a book entitled *L'État de droit*, which is heavily influenced by Kelsen: the state is now merely a legal system or a "normative system which is globally effective and provided with sanction". As a result, the state becomes confused with law, which makes the *État de droit* entirely pleonastic, at least in its material dimension. All that is left is a formal conception of the *État de droit* that rests on the hierarchy of the norms.[63]

One could maintain, moreover, that the *État de droit* has been completely and definitively achieved in France since the ordinary judge and the administrative judge have agreed to examine legislation with respect to treaties, even subsequent ones.[64] By now, and given the subordinate character of legislation, the questions to raise seem to be only questions of jurisdiction, relating to the functions of the constitutional council, the ordinary judge, or the administrative judge. Could an administrative judge, for example, one day decide to accept an action founded on the unconstitutionality of a law?[65] All this seems increasingly plausible since, in parallel with this evolution, the administrative judge has further strengthened his control over the administration, for example with the near disappearance of the category of the so-called measures of internal order.[66]

Nonetheless, some scholars[67] are far from being convinced by these steps forward made by the *État de droit* and point their finger at its dysfunctions, which, in their view, will lead towards its gradual dissolution.

Thus the inflation of legal norms, which is not typical of France but must be measured with the yardstick of the European model of the welfare state, has been harmful to their comprehensibility and has hindered citizens' access to the law. In its public report of 1991, the Council of State pointed out that between 110 and 120 laws were passed every year compared with the 80 per year at the beginning of the Fifth Republic, and that there were some 80,000–90,000 applicative decrees in force. Similarly, it has been calculated that, in the last 30 years, the average length of normative texts has increased by 35%.[68]

Indeed, there has been a multiplication of diverse and increasingly technical texts which, trying to be more faithful to changing reality, are renewed ever more quickly. The increase in the number of rules, then, is accompanied by an increase in their instability. This paves the way for a legal system which, as has been noted, is no longer characterized by being "systematic, general and stable, the traditional features of the system which testified to its 'rationality'".[69]

But some also complain that the legal rules, and above all the laws, are poorly written, that their contents are often too programmatic and imprecise, which is detrimental to the prescriptive character of the rules of law. This soft, flexible law damages both the credibility of texts and their effectiveness. The legislator, whose work is often called into question, indirectly assigns a far from negligible role in rewriting the law to that authorized interpreter who is the judge.

Not only is there a profusion of texts, but the sources of law are also multiplying: law no longer originates exclusively internally; increasingly there are European Union and international sources, and such law of external origin is at times applied on national territory without any ratification measures. And what should be said about the plethora of fundamental principles, consecrated and guaranteed by French constitutional texts, the European Convention on Human Rights, and the Charter of Fundamental Rights of the European Union, which multiply the number of courts liable to intervene in this sphere (Constitutional Council, European Court of Human Rights, Court of Justice of the European Communities, etc.)?

There can be little doubt that an increasingly fragmentary and complex legal system is apt to lose its efficacy. The *État de droit* itself is unavoidably affected by this evolution. How can private parties benefit from its advantages if they do not know their rights with precision or if access to these rights becomes ever more difficult? It should be pointed out that recent legal debate has been quite concerned with the notions of security of law and legitimate trust, which are presented as effective means to protect citizens against excessively abrupt changes in the laws in force and provide them with more readable and transparent normative texts.[70] This debate will surely be further fuelled by the steps made in the decisions of the Constitutional Council, which has seen the accessibility and intelligibility of laws as a goal of constitutional rank.[71]

Is it necessary, as Jacques Chevallier suggests, to accept in any event an *État de droit* that is intrinsically bound to be imperfect and incomplete, and which carries the seeds of self-destruction, since the enactment of too much law kills the law?[72] In short, law, in this view, suffocates what it was designed to protect. One could go even further and say, as Michel Troper does, that either the *État de droit* is a tautology or it is a contradiction in terms. In a word, it is impossible.[73] For Troper, it is illusory to hold that the state can be limited by the law. Either the law is a product of state will, and in that case there will be no limitation of the state, unless this is what the state wants (and here we return to the classic critique of the thesis of self-limitation); or the state is limited by a law that is external to it, i.e. by natural law. But in this case the theory of the *État de droit* is incompatible with sovereignty and democracy. If one admits, indeed, that democracy is a system in which the people are sovereign, and that sovereignty is an unlimited power, a people which is subjected to higher rules ceases to be sovereign.

Furthermore, since the rules of natural law cannot be known directly, in order to identify and interpret them uniformly men would be needed who are specially authorized to this end; this, in turn, entails choices based on value judgements. Since the content of natural law cannot be the object of certain knowledge, it would be necessary for specific persons – and here one must think of judges – to make decisions which actually cannot but express their preferences. In other words, "the *État de droit* thus conceived is not ... a state subjected to law but a state subjected to the judge".[74]

2.2 *Is it possible to improve the État de droit?*

If one follows the arguments of Troper, any attempt to improve the *État de droit* is a vain enterprise, since the *État de droit* is in any case purely a linguistic illusion. Even if one rejects the ultimate consequences of this reasoning, one can hardly deny the pertinence of placing the judge at the centre of this state supported and limited by law.

Never in the past had French society, little attracted as it was by the realm of legalism and litigation, placed such importance on the judge. The rapid rise of judicial power, even in the most controversial political affairs, has led some to say that it has become a "third power",[75] situated between the people and its representatives. Of course, there might be reason for concern over this omnipresence of legal operations, which reflects a certain social pathology and a crisis of the political sphere. Some authors, who have seen the judge as an executioner, with no legitimacy, have in any case expressed their concern.[76]

The question of the legitimization of judges is fundamental, given that they have new powers that have led them to censure political acts, and even question the actions of certain political representatives. As regards the Constitutional Council, some of whose decisions, particularly in the 1980s, have been criticized for usurping the legislative power, the doctrinal literature has worked out a number of solid arguments to justify the Council's role as the reviewer of legislation. The review of legislation is first of all entirely democratic to the extent to which it allows the parliamentary minority to express itself and to contest a decision of the parliamentary majority before the constitutional judge. Moreover, and the claim has been substantiated by the decisions of the Constitutional Council, the review of legislation can serve to defend the competences of the legislature against the trespassing of the government. What is more, a constitutional court contributes to the balance between democratic institutions establishing, for each organ of the state, the extension and the limits of its constitutional jurisdiction. The Constitutional Council expressed this idea clearly when, in the decision of 23 August 1985, it declared that "legislation expresses the general will only if it respects the Constitution". One could even claim that the constitutional judge contributes to the functioning of a better democracy by participating in the creation of legislative norms. By virtue of its ability to interpret and even to censure the law partially or wholly, the Constitutional Council could be considered a genuine co-legislator.[77]

Finally, it has been pointed out that the members of the Constitutional Council are appointed by political authorities and that their legitimacy depends on the acceptance of the agencies subjected to their control, as well as by the consensus of public opinion.[78] Actually, however, the issue of democratic legitimization is less pertinent to the constitutional judge than to the ordinary judge, and in particular to the civil judge, who stands in the front line of political affairs. Some authors argue that the source of legitimacy is to be sought in the dimension of impartiality, essential to the function of judging: an impartiality that must be guaranteed by true independence in career advancement and must find expression in the distance between the judge and the parties in the case. Moreover, legitimacy – so goes the argument – derives from the judge's ability to represent common values and to bring out the fundamental principles of liberal democracy, especially watching over respect for the law and the guarantee of individual rights.[79]

Another option for reinforcing the legitimacy of judges is to have them elected by citizens. But aside from the fact that the election of the judiciary is diametrically opposed to the French tradition, it is far from certain that a reform of this kind would underpin legitimization. Moreover, wouldn't an electoral procedure, which forces candidates to engage in an electoral campaign and to commit themselves to programmes, risk damaging the primary vocation of the judge, which is impartiality?

There appear to be three paths towards improving the legitimacy of the judiciary. The first involves the reinforcement, if necessary, of the independence of the judge. A recent plan for constitutional reform moved in this direction, proposing a radical break between government and investigating judges. It proposed, more precisely, that public prosecutors should be appointed by the executive, with the approval of the Higher Council of Justice,[80] thus conferring on this institution the true power of appointment. The project was also designed to prevent the Minister of Justice from giving any sort of instructions to the attorney's office within the context of an investigation. However, this reform was sunk at the beginning of 2000. The government's eternal fear of judges and the desire to preserve a centralized judicial policy certainly played an important role in a debate which was not free from ulterior political motives.

Another path involves the search for the responsibility of the judge as a consequence of the extension of his competence. The difficulty allegedly lies in finding a viable solution. Certainly, one could object that this responsibility already exists and is provided by the statute of the judiciary, which lays down a system of civil, criminal, and professional responsibilities. But wouldn't it be necessary, with a further gesture of courage, to institute a genuine constitutional responsibility for judges? This is the position argued by Denis Salas:

> Judicial power cannot be recognized in its entirety, de facto, unless there is an equivalent sanction at a symbolic level. How can one call for an external check on politicians if, at the same time, it is tolerated that judges are judged only by their own peers? Does political responsibility exist only for politicians? A Higher Council of Justice with a more open composition would not be sufficient. We would need to conceive of either a new procedure consecrated in the Constitution or a Higher Council composed exclusively of non-judges. When the time comes, the judge would be required to justify his most serious errors before a predominantly political audience. The democracies with a strong judiciary have long recognized this sort of responsibility: this is the case of impeachment in the common law countries and *Richteranklage* in Germany.[81]

We are dealing with a major enterprise requiring a revolution in mentality. It is hardly likely that such an endeavour will be successful in the near future. But on this point the examples drawn from comparative law, particularly in the countries near France, may be of considerable aid.

One might well ask, however, whether the most effective way to consolidate the authority of the judiciary, and consequently of the *État de droit*, might not simply be to provide supplementary means in terms of personnel and space. The inadequate number of judges, who are no more numerous than at the beginning of the century while the number of cases has exploded, at times forces some courts to apply the rule of collegial collaboration with elasticity. Thus a decision signed by three judges may actually have been studied by only one. The obvious lack of judges leads in any case to serious delays in procedure. Recent studies have shown that the main criticism levelled against the judicial system by those awaiting a decision was in regard to the time required to deal with the cases and to appoint the judges. It is evident that the function of judging today seems more like clever *bricolage* than rational organization. If the judges do not have adequate means to perform their jobs, it is clear that responsibility lies with the political power that controls the purse strings.

An improvement in the *État de droit* also requires a renewed consideration of individual rights and of the best ways to guarantee them. It would be useful to put order in the multitude of rights called fundamental, recognized by the European Court of Human Rights, Constitutional Council, Council of State, and Court of Cassation.

The limitless extension of fundamental rights raises an insurmountable obstacle: in general, not everything can be fundamental; otherwise nothing is fundamental any longer. Moreover, not all fundamental rights can be equal, since there may be incompatibilities, and one may have to give way to another. In other words, the more the character of "fundamentality" is spread out over different rights, the greater is the risk of collision between the fundamental character of rights and the need to relativize them. Etienne Picard has proposed instituting a "scale of fundamentality".[82] At the top of this scale Picard places the principle of the pre-eminence of law, which establishes the pre-eminence of the fundamental rights. At its side stands the principle of human dignity against all forms of degradation, which was recognized as a constitutional principle by the Constitutional Council in July 1994. Picard writes:

> These then are the two combined principles which found the fundamental rights in that they must be, in principle, pre-eminent and can, all things considered, prevail on the practical terrain: the pre-eminence of the person founds the pre-eminence of his rights; the pre-eminence of the law is simply the pre-eminence of rights.[83]

The merit of this "scale of fundamentality" lies in its attempt to found a substantial hierarchy of fundamental rights which is free from a purely formal vision of the hierarchic structure of the legal system. And although the substantial hierarchy of fundamentality cuts across this formal hierarchy, since certain principles can be consecrated by norms of a different status, it is evident that the formal hierarchy has been to a considerable extent conditioned by the substantial hierarchy: thus the Constitution consecrates the "more" fundamental principles, statutes concern the "less" fundamental principles, regulations deal with principles of even lesser importance, and so forth.

In sum, a reflection on the identity and value of fundamental rights is of the utmost importance as it confers content and spirit on a purely formal hierarchy of norms that otherwise seems at times useless. It is precisely because the *État de droit* is not merely a legal system, a system of norms, that reflection on fundamental rights is necessary; the more so if it is true that their constitutional consecration in the various European countries, France among them, has been a source of freedom for individuals, if not indeed of social peace.

Could fundamental rights bind not only the legislator but also the constituent power? At stake here is the issue of supraconstitutionality. Stéphane Rials, in an essay which appeared in 1986 in *Archives de Philosophie du Droit*, rekindled a debate which had died out back in the 1930s.[84] Arguing from a natural law perspective, the author seeks to provide an inventory of supraconstitutional principles that could be applied in judicial review of constitutional laws. He singles out a principle of respect for the life and dignity of the person, a principle of the organization of power entailing its regular circulation as well as procedures to temper it, and, finally, a principle of "subsidiarity" according to which organizations are subsidiary with respect to the person.

The project, however, has attracted no followers.[85] French doctrine has decidedly rejected supraconstitutionality, above all in the name of its adherence to positive law. In France, the judicial review of constitutional legislation is impossible, as the judge receives power from the Constitution and not from the law itself, as is the case in the countries of the common law tradition. In the decision of 2 September 1992 the Constitutional Council recalled that the constituent power is sovereign and has therefore the faculty to abrogate, modify, or complete provisions of constitutional rank, subject only to certain limits of scope – the republican form of government – and time. Supraconstitutionality has also been perceived as a danger for democracy, since the sovereign people would yield to a government of judges.[86] On the issue of supraconstitutionality France surely lags behind countries such as Germany and Italy.

One could ask, in conclusion, whether the conception of *État de droit*, understood as incompatible with democracy and national sovereignty, is not outdated, since there is a growing supranationality of rights, also recognized by French judges, who do not hesitate to draw inspiration from international and European courts to forge new fundamental rights. The current debates on the principle of precaution and the principle of legal certainty constitute a significant illustration of this phenomenon. The *État de droit* which is emerging is a state that foregrounds the judges, or, more precisely, the dialogue, or even the dispute between national and European courts. It gives prominence to fundamental rights which tend to become independent of the Constitution and of sovereignty, as though these were two sides of the same coin. In this situation, the conception of a French *État de droit* tends gradually to disappear. Indeed, it would be quite difficult today to oppose the *État de droit* to the *Rechtsstaat* as the jurists of the Third Republic did in a period admittedly marked by patriotic exaltation.

NOTES

1. See G. Burdeau, F. Hamon, and M. Troper, *Droit constitutionnel*, Paris: Librairie Générale de Droit et de Jurisprudence, 1995, pp. 88–9; P. Pactet, *Institutions politiques. Droit constitutionnel*, Paris: Armand Colin, 1998, pp. 43–4 and 125–8.
2. R. von Mohl, *Die Polizeiwissenschaft nach den Grundsätzen des Rechtsstaats*, 3 vols., Tübingen: Laupp, 1832–4.
3. F.J. Stahl, *Die Philosophie des Rechts* , Hildesheim: Olm, 1856, p. 1963.
4. On this influence, which is far from a slavish imitation, see J. Chevallier, *L'État de droit*, Paris: Montchrestien, 1999, esp. pp. 11 ff.; P.-M. Gaudemet, "Paul Laband et la doctrine française de droit public", *Revue du droit public* (1989), 4, pp. 957 ff.
5. Cited in P. Sueur, *Histoire du droit public français XV–XVIII siècle*, Paris: Presses Universitaires de France, 1989, vol. 1, p. 123.
6. C. Le Bret, *De la souveraineté du Roy*, Paris: J. Quesnel, 1632.
7. See the penetrating treatment in F. Olivier-Martin, *Histoire du droit français des origines á la Révolution*, Paris: Domat Montchrestien, 1948, pp. 340–2.
8. On the Fronde of the deputies during the reign of Louis XV see in particular M. Antoine, *Louis XV*, Paris: Fayard, 1989.
9. See G. Bacot, *Carré de Malberg et l'origine de la distinction entre souveraineté du peuple et souveraineté nationale*, Paris: Ed. CNRS, 1985; see also S. Rials, "Constitutionnalisme, souveraineté et représentation", in id., *La continuité constitutionnelle en France de 1789 à 1989*, Paris: Economica et Presses Universitaires d'Aix-Marseille, 1990, pp. 49–69.

10. See J. Chevallier, op. cit., pp. 24–5.
11. C.-G. Hello, *Du régime constitutionnel dans ses rapports avec l'état actuel de la science sociale et politique*, Paris: A. Durand, 1848, vol. 2, p. 42.
12. See E. Laboulaye, *Histoire des États-Unis*, Paris: Charpentier, 1867, 3 vols (esp. vol. 3); see also A. Dauteribes, *Les idées politiques d'Edouard Laboulaye 1811–1883*, unpublished manuscript, Montpellier I, 1989, 2 vols. Laboulaye's position may be compared to that of Tocqueville, who, in the first *Démocratie en Amérique* (1835), discusses the American review of legislation but does not consider the practice to be exportable to France.
13. See B. Constant, *Ecrits politiques*, Paris: Gallimard, 1997, esp. pp. 510 ff.
14. Ibid., esp. pp. 616 ff.
15. J. Chevallier, op.cit., p. 31.
16. See R. Carré de Malberg, *Contribution*, vol. 1, pp. 490–2.
17. On the critique of the *État légal*, see M.-J. Redor, *De l'État légal á l'État de droit. L'évolution des conceptions de la doctrine publiciste française 1879–1914*, Paris: Economica et Presses Universitaires d'Aix-Marseille, 1992, part 1: *La doctrine face à l'État légal*, pp. 33 ff.
18. On the theory of the self-limitation of the state, see R. Carré de Malberg, *Contribution*, vol. 1, pp. 231 ff.; L. Duguit, *Traité de droit constitutionnel*, Paris: E. De Boccard, 1927, vol. 1, pp. 104–5; M.-J. Redor, *op. cit.*, pp. 80–4.
19. See A. Esmein, *Eléments de droit constitutionnel français et comparé*, Paris: Sirey, 1921, vol. 1, pp. 553 ff; R. Carré de Malberg, *Contribution*, vol. 1, pp. 579 ff.
20. L. Duguit, *Traité*, vol. 3, pp. 603–4.
21. See C. de La Mardière, "Retour sur valeur juridique de la Déclaration de 1789", *Revue française de droit constitutionnel* (1999), 38, esp. p. 235.
22. M. Hauriou, *Précis de droit constitutionnel*, Paris: Sirey, 1923, p. 245.
23. M. Hauriou, *Précis de droit constitutionnel*, Paris: Sirey, 2nd edn., 1929, p. 625.
24. On the Senate in the First and Second Empires see J. Barthélemy and P. Duez, *Traité de droit constitutionnel*, Paris: Economica, 1985, pp. 203–6; A. Ashworth, "Le contrôle de la constitutionnalité des lois par le Sénat du Seconde Empire", *Revue du droit public* (1994), pp. 45 ff.
25. L. Duguit, *Traité de droit constitutionnel*, vol. 3, pp. 715–16.
26. M. Hauriou, *Précis de droit constitutionnel*, 1929, p. 271.
27. In the first *Démocratie en Amérique* Tocqueville had already written: "If the judge had been able to attack the laws in a general and theoretical way, if he had been able to take the initiative and censure the legislator, he would have clamorously entered the political scene; he would have become the champion or the opponent of a political party and have aroused all the passions that divide a country to take part in the struggle" (*Démocratie en Amérique*, Paris: Flammarion, 1981, vol. 1, p. 171.).
28. See M. Verpeaux, "Le contrôle de la loi par la voie de l'exception dans les propositions parlementaires sous la III République", *Revue française de droit constitutionnel* (1990), 4, pp. 688 ff; J.-P. Machelon, "Parlementarisme absolu, État de droit relatif. A propos du contrôle de constitutionnalité des lois en France sous la III République (positions et controverses)", *Revue administrative* (1995), pp. 628 ff.
29. C. Eisenmann, *La justice constitutionnelle et la haute Cour constitutionnelle d'Autriche*, Paris: Economica, 1986, p. 292.
30. *Revue du droit public*, 1912, pp. 142–3, cited in G. Drago, *Contentieux constitutionnel français*, Paris: Presses Universitaires de France, 1998, p. 137.

31. P. Duez, "Le contrôle juridictionnel des lois en France. Comment il convient de poser la question", in *Mélanges Maurice Hauriou*, Paris: Sirey, 1929, esp. p. 225.
32. M. Hauriou, *Précis de droit constitutionnel*, 1929, p. 269.
33. At issue in particular are the act of 16 and 24 August 1790, title II, art. 10, of the Constitution of 3 September 1791, title III, chap. V, art. 3 and art. 127 §1 of the Penal Code.
34. We cite in particular Gaston Jèze, Henri Berthélemy, Paul Duez, Maurice Hauriou, Joseph-Berthélemy (for bibliographic information see Guillaume Drago, op. cit., pp. 141–2). See also J. Laferrière, *Manuel de droit constitutionnel*, Paris: Domat Montchrestien, 1943, pp. 315–16, who still argues this position.
35. M. Hauriou, *Précis de droit constitutionnel*, 1929, p. 281.
36. Ibid., pp. 282–7. See also the note by Hauriou on the Tichit decision of 1912 (cited in M.-J. Redor, op. cit., p. 219), in which, in order to relativize the effects of the review of legislation, Hauriou observes that the judge merely uses his faculty to interpret the law: "The judge who makes a pronouncement about the conflict that emerges, in a certain matter, between a fundamental law and an ordinary law does not interfere with the exercise of legislative power, does not make a regulatory decision, neither stops nor suspends the execution of a law: the law remains executive; the judge regulates a conflict between two laws and in reality it is one law that suspends the application of the other in a specific case".
37. See the comment by Gaston Jèze on the Roubeau sentence of the State Council of 13 May 1913, pp. 685–8. See also Christophe de la Mardière, op. cit., pp. 250 ff.
38. Article 8, paragraph 1, of the constitutional law of 25 February 1875 provided that: "The Chambers shall have the right, with separate deliberations taken in each of the same with an absolute majority of votes, spontaneously or on request of the president of the Republic, to declare that there is reason to revise the constitutional laws."
39. R. Carré de Malberg, "La constitutionalité des lois et la Constitution de 1875", *Revue politique et parlementaire*, 132 (1927), pp. 339 ff.
40. On this issue, see M.-J. Redor, op. cit., pp. 186 ff.
41. On the question of the extension of the *recours pour excès de pouvoir*, cf. F. Burdeau, *Histoire du droit administratif*, Paris: Presses Universitaires de France, 1995, pp. 256 ff.
42. L. Michoud, "Des actes de gouvernement", in *Annales de l'enseignement supérieur de Grenoble*, Paris: Larose et Forcel, 1889, p. 82, cited in M.-J. Redor, op. cit., p. 213.
43. This theory of risk, supported in particular by Hauriou and Fernand Larnaude, was firmly established in the sentence of the Council of State, Cames, issued 21 June 1895, *Receuil Sirey* (1897), 3, p. 33, conclusion by Romieu, comment by Hauriou).
44. Gaston Jèze supported the system of accumulation of responsibility in numerous articles in the *Revue du droit public* from 1910 onwards. The Council of State consecrated the system with the Lemonnier decision, dated 26 July 1918, *Recueil Sirey* (1918–1919), 3, p. 41, conclusion by Blum, comment by Harriou; *Revue du Droit Public* (1919), 41, conclusion by Blum, comment by Jèze. See also F. Burdeau, op. cit., pp. 319 ff.
45. See M.-J. Redor, op. cit., pp. 251 ff.
46. L. Michoud, *La théorie de la personne morale*, 2nd edn., Paris: Librairie Générale de Droit et de Jurisprudence, 1906–1909, p. 1924.

47. R. Carré de Malberg, *Contribution à la théorie générale de l'État*, vol. 2, pp. 1 ff.
48. See L. Michoud, *La théorie de la personnalité morale. Son application au droit français*, Paris: Librairie Générale de Droit et de Jurisprudence, 1924, vol. 1, pp. 36 ff, vol. 2, pp. 1 ff.
49. For A. Esmein, *Eléments de droit constitutionnel français et comparé*, vol. 1, p. 1: "The state is the legal personification of a nation: it is the subject and the support of public authority." Similar assertions appear in Michoud, op. cit., vol. 1, pp. 313 ff.: "The nation has no distinct legal existence; the state is merely the nation itself (the collectivity), organized legally; it is impossible to imagine how it could be conceived as a subject of law distinct from the state."
50. L. Duguit, *L'État, le droit objectif et la loi positive*, Paris: Fontemoing, 1901; L. Duguit, *L'État, les gouvernements et les agents*, Paris: Fontemoing, 1903.
51. L. Duguit, *L'État, le droit objectif et la loi positive*, p. 259.
52. L. Michoud, *La théorie de la personnalité morale*, vol. 1, pp. 45–53. Cf. R. Carré de Malberg, *Contribution*, vol. 1, pp. 20 ff. The Michoud–Duguit controversy continued for some time. See in particular L. Michoud, "La personnalité et les droit subjectifs de l'État dans la doctrine française contemporaine", in *Festschrift Otto Gierke*, Weimar: Hermann Böhlaus Nachfolger, 1911, pp. 493 ff.; L. Duguit, *Les transformations générales du droit privé depuis le Code Napoléon*, Paris: Alcan, 1920. See also L. Duguit, *Traité de droit constitutionnel*, Paris: E. De Boccard, 1927, vol. 3, pp. 616 ff.
53. Cf. A. Paynot-Rouvillois, "Personnalité morale et volonté", *Droits* (1999), 28, pp. 17 ff. and 25.
54. Ibid., pp. 26–7. See how Carré de Malberg treated the question in *Contribution*, vol. 1, pp. 31 ff.
55. Ibid., vol. 1, p. 229: "Sovereignty is not pure brute force: it is the product of a balance of forces, a balance which has become sufficiently stable to generate a lasting organization of the collective whole. The state supposes essentially this organization; it supposes, that is, an organized force. What this means is a force that is regulated by legal principles, which is called upon to function in certain ways and by means of certain organs, and which is, consequently, limited by law. Since the state cannot be realized without this legal order, it follows that it can only be conceived as subordinate, as regards its continuity and functioning, to the maintenance of a rule of law. Whatever power can emerge and subsist only through the institution and the application of a legal rule is necessarily a power limited by law".
56. L. Michoud, op. cit., vol. 2, pp. 57–8.
57. Cf. Chevallier, *L'État de droit*, pp. 35–8.
58. For a critique of Duguit's theory, see in particular R. Carré de Malberg, *Contribution*, vol. 1, pp. 236–7.
59. On the defence of judges and jurists, see M.-J. Redor, op. cit., pp. 260 ff.
60. See the comment on the decision in L. Favoreu and L. Philip, *Les grandes décisions du Conseil constitutionnel*, Paris: Dalloz, 1999, pp. 252 ff.
61. See the decision of 16 January 1982.
62. See L. Favoreu, "Légalité et constitutionnalité", *Les Cahiers du Conseil constitutionnel* (1997), 3, pp. 73 ff. See also L. Favoreu (ed.), *Droit constitutionnel*, Paris: Dalloz, 1998, pp. 343–6.
63. Cf. L. Favoreu, *Droit constitutionnel*, pp. 107–8.

64. See, for example, the decisions of the Court of Cassation, Joint session, of 24 May 1975, Société des Cafés Jacques Vabre, and of the Council of State, Session of 20 October 1989, Nicolo.
65. Although the exceptional examination of constitutionality, which had been the object of a draft of constitutional amendment in 1990, appears to be a significant element in reinforcing the *État de droit*, as a guarantee of individual rights provided for in the preamble of the Constitution.
66. At issue is the jurisprudence of the Council of State taken in Assembly, Hardouin and Marie, 17 February 1995: the acceptability of an appeal by a detainee or by a soldier against a detention measure.
67. See J. Carbonnier, *Flexible droit*, Paris: Librairie Générale de Droit et de Jurisprudence, 1971; J. Carbonnier, *Droit et passion du droit sous la V République*, Paris: Flammarion, 1996; J. Chevallier, "Vers un droit post-moderne? Les transformations de la régulation juridique", *Revue du Droit Public* (1998), 3, pp. 659 ff.
68. See the report of the Council of State, 1991, general considerations: "De la sécurité juridique", *Études et Documents du Conseil d'État*, (1992), 43; see also B. Mathieu, *La loi*, Paris: Dalloz, 1996; Colloque de l'Institut de France sous la présidence de Jean Foyer, *Les abus du juridisme*, Paris: Palais de l'Institut, 1997.
69. See J. Chevallier, *L'État de droit*, p. 102.
70. On the principle of legal certainty, see the articles by B. Pacteau, "La sécurité juridique, un principe qui nous manque?", *Actualité Juridique. Droit Administratif* (1995), special issue on *Le droit administratif*, pp. 151–5; M. Fromont, "Le principe de sécurité juridique", *Actualité Juridique. Droit Administratif* (1996), special issue *Droit administratif et droit communautaire*, pp. 178–84.
71. Decision n° 99–421 DC of 16 November 1999, *Journal Officiel*, 22 December 1999, p. 19041.
72. See J. Chevallier, *L'État de droit*, p. 150.
73. See M. Troper, "Le concept d'État de droit", *Droits* (1992), 15, pp. 51–63.
74. Ibid., p. 57.
75. The expression is used by D. Salas, *Le tiers pouvoir. Vers une autre justice*, Paris: Hachette Littératures, 1998, pp. 169 ff.
76. See A. Garapon, *Le gardien des Promesses. Justice et démocratie*, Paris: Odile Jacob, 1996; A. Minc, *Au nom de la loi*, Paris: Gallimard, 1998.
77. See M. Troper, "Justice constitutionnelle et démocratie", in *Pour une théorie juridique de l'État*, Paris: Presses Universitaires de France, 1994, pp. 329 ff.; G. Drago, *Contentieux constitutionnel français*, pp. 106 ff., D. Rousseau, *Droit du contentieux constitutionnel*, Paris: Montchretien, 1995, pp. 412 ff.
78. See L. Favoreu, "De la démocratie à l'État de droit", *Le Débat* (1991), 64, pp. 158 ff.
79. See D. Salas, op. cit., pp. 183 ff.
80. Article 65 of the Constitution of 1958 provides for the institution of a Higher Council of Justice charged with giving its opinion on the appointment of judges. Following the enactment of the constitutional law of 27 July 1993, the Higher Council of Justice is composed of two sections, one competent for the judges and the other for the public prosecutors.
81. D. Salas, op. cit., pp. 218–19.
82. See E. Picard, "L'émergence des droits fondamentaux en France", *Actualité Juridique. Droit Administratif* (1998), special issue on *Les Droit fondamentaux*, pp. 6 ff. and 32.

83. Ibid., p. 32.
84. S. Rials, "Supraconstitutionnalité et systémacité du droit", *Archives de Philosophie de Droit* (1986), 31, pp. 57–76.
85. Stéphane Rials himself, perhaps impressed by the work of Troper, has revised his position. The substance of natural law no longer seems knowable to him, and any search in this direction becomes an act of will, by definition arbitrary, on the part of the interpreter and not an act of acquiring knowledge. See S. Rials, "Entre artificialisme et idolâtrie. Sur l'hésitation du constitutionnalisme", *Le Débat* (1991), 64, pp. 163–81. See also the analysis by X. Dijon, *Droit naturel*, Paris: Presses Universitaires de France, 1998, vol. 1: *Les questions du droit*, esp. pp. 73–81.
86. Cf. G. Vedel, "Souveraineté et supraconstitutionnalité", *Pouvoirs* (1993), pp. 79–97.

CHAPTER 7

RECHTSSTAAT AND CONSTITUTIONAL JUSTICE IN AUSTRIA: HANS KELSEN'S CONTRIBUTION

Giorgio Bongiovanni

1 INTRODUCTION

I shall deal in this essay with the historical and theoretical process that led to the introduction of constitutional justice in the Austrian Constitution in 1920. Austrian literature about constitutional history is unanimous in ascribing the articles on *Verfassungsgerichtshof* to Hans Kelsen[1] and in deeming him to be, even from a theoretical point of view, the "creator of constitutional justice" (*Vater der Verfassungsgerichtsbarkeit*).[2] Kelsen himself has often confirmed such a circumstance and, when referring to the Austrian constituent process, he has described the setting up of the Court as "his own very personal creation" and the Court itself as "his cherished work".[3]

The introduction of judicial review may be seen as one of the most important outcomes of Kelsen's analysis, which he began with the *Hauptprobleme* of 1911,[4] and its underlying deep re-assessment of German public law theory and concepts. A pivotal feature of such critical thinking is Kelsen's profound re-elaboration of the idea of the "rule of law ". He criticizes the German conception of the *Rechtsstaat* and its theoretical and "political" assumptions and proposes what he claims is a legal configuration of state and constitutional democracy.

From the first perspective, Kelsen stresses that the "German" conception of the *Rechtsstaat* is grounded on the dogma of the state's legal personality and on the ensuing pre-eminence of state over law. Kelsen examines both the implications of the public/private relationship and the "traditional" theoretical differentiation between two areas of legal relationships in relation to the personality and pre-eminence of the state. The primacy of the state over law is mirrored in a number of theoretical assumptions connoting the *Rechtsstaat*: firstly, the conceptualization of law as an imperative, an order from an original sovereign authority; secondly, a theory of rights and freedoms grounded on the difference between natural freedom and legal freedom[5] and the related determination of "public subjective rights" resulting from the state's "self-obligation"

P. Costa and D. Zolo (eds.), The Rule of Law: History, Theory and Criticism, 293–319.

(*Selbstverpflichtung*); thirdly, a view of the separation of powers, stemming from the need to safeguard the monarchical principle and administrative autonomy, that seriously hinders the principle of legality through the "privileges" of public administration; lastly, an overall reduction of the legal meaning of the *Rechtsstaat* to judicial "remedies" against public administration.[6] In this respect, Kelsen's critique seems to be connected with the Austrian constitutional situation and, above all, with the specific Austrian theorization and the critique by several authors of German accounts.[7]

From the second perspective, Kelsen develops a different historical and legal-constitutional conception of the *Rechtsstaat*. Its grounds are, on the one hand, the sovereignty of the legal system and the necessary legal foundation of all powers; on the other hand, the denial of the public/private distinction and the ensuing equality of all legal subjects. In historical terms, Kelsen's account starts with denying state sovereignty in connection with the "compromise" aspect of the legal system and, therefore, the pluralism of public law dynamics. The result of this first stage of Kelsen's argument is the definition of the "formal" dimension as the key feature of the *Rechtsstaat*. By adopting a dynamic conception of the legal system, Kelsen further develops this feature in connection with the historical accomplishment of democratic systems: in this context, the *Rechtsstaat* acquires a "substantial" meaning connected with the primacy of the constitution and rights. Hence, two stages may be discerned in Kelsen's theorization of the *Rechtsstaat*: the first is mostly related to the "formal" dimension of this concept, whereas in the second he develops its "substantial" aspects, in connection with the accomplishment of democracy. Kelsen's overall argument ultimately leads to the idea of constitutional justice, viewed as a "condition of existence" for democracy. The essential idea of democracy changes with Kelsen's emphasis on its "constitutional" features.[8]

2 *RECHTSSTAAT* AND *STAATSRECHT*

Soon after the publication of the *Hauptprobleme*, in a number of works,[9] Kelsen focuses on the relationship between German public law and the meaning of *Rechtsstaat*. Such works, which systematize several points of Kelsen's 1911 publication, focus on the meaning of *Rechtsstaat* within German public law and question its "political" and theoretical assumptions. Kelsen first examines the "trends of the most recent theories on law", especially administrative theories, which proclaimed, the "impossibility of a legal understanding of the state" with respect to its "primary activity", i.e. monarchical administration, this being conceived of as "the state's free performance of activities to achieve its aims".[10] According to Kelsen, since the rule of law is seen as simply a collection of "postulates of law's politics" (*rechtspolitische Postulate*) which "may be more or less realized", it is limited to the "remedies" available against potential administrative abuses.[11] The above doctrines' attempt to remove "precisely such relationships of the state, precisely such part of political power" from the legal system, i.e. to legitimize administrative "freedom", is not only an expression of specific "political thoughts" but is also rooted in the idea that "the state is above all other subjects"[12] and thus has a "surplus-value" (*Mehrwert*) in its relationship with its "subjects".[13] Hence, the German doctrines' meaning of *Rechtsstaat* hinges upon the state's role and centrality, the state being a sovereign "subject" with which legal relationships are to be set up. The idea of the state having a leading role in the dynamics of public law, confirmed at the end of the nineteenth century by administrative theory, is coupled by German thinkers with a conceptualization of the state as the original and thus sovereign authority, as well as the sole representative of public and general interests. Such an understanding of the state is the key point (using Kelsen's words) of the "traditional" doctrine, this being focused on an original subject around which public law relationships rotate.[14] Such arguments have an extremely important consequence: in German public law, the relationship between law and the state is overturned and the latter's pre-eminence over the former is affirmed. The relationship between "the state's power and law" (*Staatsgewalt und Recht*) is settled by conceiving of the state as the creator of law; therefore, legal limitations of state powers are mere "political postulates" that the state may or may not impose upon itself. As pointed out above, from such a perspective the rule of law is primarily concerned with the legal remedies available against the abusive sovereign acts by the state.

Kelsen argues that this approach, putting the state before law, is grounded on two premises: the idea that the state is a subject different from other entities and stands above them all and the belief that the state represents the general interest. The former idea is mirrored in the conception of the state's sovereignty; the latter in the identification of "state" and "society", which in turn entails the idea of the state's will. According to the first premise, the state implies a "power relationship" between the commander and the commanded. The state is endowed with "sovereign power", it is the "first cause: it is a will which causes other acts of will; it is a subject commanding other subjects, it is "above" them, i.e. "superior" to them; being so, it is neither commanded nor caused by any other will".[15] The state is "public strength" (*öffentliche Gewalt*) or "intensive power" (*intensive Macht*) and thus its "existence is independent of law": according to Georg Jellinek's "two-sided theory" (*zwei-seiten Theorie*), the state "as a social fact is power".[16] The state is original power: according to Jellinek, "a state arises when a given entity (*Gemeinwesen*) is able, through its original power (*ursprüngliche Macht*) and original coercive means (*ursprüngliche Zwangmitteln*), to exert power (*Herrschaft*) over its members and territory".[17] As pointed out by Kelsen, such a vision entails "a right to dominate ... quite evidently belonging to the state".[18]

The second premise hinges upon what Kelsen calls the *Substrat* of the "state-person idea", i.e. the existence of "a unitary will of the state".[19] Kelsen treats this premise in connection with Jellinek's view that the state's unitary will is a "teleological unity" (*teleologische Einheit*) of the different wills expressed by the state's many organs. Such a unitary will results from the pursuit by agencies of the state of its "constant aims" (*konstante Zwecke*),[20] i.e. society's collective interests. According to Kelsen, this is tantamount to claiming the existence of a "common conscience" (*Gesamtbewusstsein*) mirroring the unification of society's social aims, these being merely interpreted by agencies of the state's. The state represents society's "common and general interests", i.e. a fact of social life, which is to be implemented by the state's agencies.[21] In other words, the state expresses society's purportedly homogeneous common conscience, which is specified by the state's actions. The belief in the state's unitary will has a further implication: as specified by Jellinek, the "common interest" (*Gemeininteresse*) stems from the community (*Volksgemeinschaft*), which is deemed to be "identical to the state".[22] Ergo, the state and society are not separate entities: the existence of a homogeneous society allows it not to be differentiated from the state, this being the society's direct expression.[23] The general interest is thus identified with the state's interest.

The above theory entails a number of corollaries discussed by Kelsen. Firstly, if the state is the original subject representing the general interest, then law is an order or imperative from that interest. In Jellinek's account of law's essential and distinctive traits, legal provisions are the result of an "acknowledged external authority", whose "compulsoriness" (*Verbindlichkeit*) is guaranteed by "external powers" (*äußere Mächte*).[24] Legal provisions are "an imperative requiring subjects' conforming behaviour", both because such an imperative "comes from the state" and because it is grounded "on the latter's factual power and on its physical and psychological strength".[25] The circumstance that a legal provision is an order (*Befehl*) brings about what Jellinek defines the "most complex problem of the entire doctrine of the state",[26] i.e. how the state, even in its legislative function, may be bound by law. As is known, reference is made to an analogy with "ethical autonomy": the state is not bound by "other acts of will" (*andere Willensakte*), i.e. by other provisions, but rather by "reason's self-legislation" (*Selbstgesetzgebung der Vernunft*), i.e. "the state's self-obligation to abide by its laws" (*Selbstbindung des Staates an seine Gesetze*).[27] The state's subjection to law, which is a fundamental requirement of the *Rechtsstaat*, is conceived of as an ethical principle or *politische Postulat* rooted in the notion of "ethical autonomy"; and it is mirrored, in legal terms, in the state's being self-limited by laws it itself enacts. It follows that law's primacy over the state is theoretically very limited: if the state is identified with society, and is the sole source of law, then provisions placed on a higher level than legislation cannot exist, and there is a difficulty in defining legislative limits with respect to individual rights. Moreover, the establishment of legal relationships is grounded on the distinction between public and private domains, these domains having different relationships among different entities. In other words, public law relationships are conceived of as relationships between unequal entities (the state and its subjects), whereas private law relationships are between equal subjects.

According to Kelsen, such a distinction originates from the introduction of Roman law into Germany and from the ensuing characteristics of German public law.[28] Reference is made to the theoretical account given in Paul Laband's *Rektoratrede*. According to Kelsen, Laband's analysis exhibits both a double conception of the relationship between state and law, and a view of the specificity of the public/private distinction.

Kelsen notes that Roman law is regarded as both a new law for the organization of the state, which establishes the state's legal structure and relationships, and as an element – through the principle *princeps legibus solutus est* – of the "power of domination" (*Herrschaftsgewalt*) which is above the legal system and "free from law".[29] Moreover, Kelsen argues that such a double conception involves a distinction between *jus publicum* and *jus privatum*: the distinction was not known before the reception of Roman law, and is reflected in the "profound difference" between the "law of the state" and the "law of its subjects", these being ambits with substantially different legal relationships. The double conceptualization of the relationship between state and law further entails a sharp distinction between judicial (*Justiz*) and administrative (*Verwaltung*) domains. In the legal thinking of late nineteenth century and, in general, in German administrative law, administration is viewed as a form of power whose complete "legal understanding" and subjection to law are not feasible. Because administrative activities are "free activities" aimed at attaining the state's "aims", they are independent of legal provisions, i.e. they precede law. The administrative relationship is thus an unequal relationship: the "legal surplus-value" of the state's power finds its expression in the administrative relationship, since administration is the state's core and guarantee of unity.[30]

Kelsen examines three lines of thinking for the above understanding of administration: firstly, Otto Mayer's suggestion to set up "special" legal institutions, such as "public law transactions", to express the specificity of the "public" and of the state's "legal surplus-value";[31] secondly, the use of Laband's distinction[32] between formal and material statutes, with the latter's enactment being conceptualized as a prerogative of the monarch and his bureaucratic apparatus. As has been noted, this is an attempt to allow administration to pass material legislation without the legislative procedure, thus retaining "the power to establish laws and legal obligations in parallel with formal legislative power".[33] This is matched by the idea of administrative discretion, which is conceived of as "the state's free activity within law" which may be exercised by the "monarch and the government" in the public interest.[34] Thirdly, and in direct connection with the "rule of law", Kelsen studies the views of jurists, such as Richard Thoma, who argued for the "administrative freedom" (*Freiheit der Verwaltung*) to deal with the state's increasing administrative and economic functions, i.e. with the liberal state becoming a *Kulturstaat*.[35]

As we have seen, Kelsen traces these positions back to specific political "aims" and "reasons". He claims that administrative autonomy, which implements – in the monarchical-constitutional state – the idea of the state's independence from law, restores the centrality of the *monarchisches Prinzip* and preserves some authoritarian remainders of the police state. As a matter of fact, the circumstance that some aspects of administrative activity are not subject to law corresponds to its dependence on the monarchical executive power and the monarch, and is reflected, in terms of relationships among constitutional bodies, in the monarch's superiority over law and, therefore, in the centrality of the monarchical principle. Kelsen emphasizes the centrality of this principle in German doctrines and the fact that it "reserved significant powers to the king, the executive and administration on the grounds that the monarchy-bureaucracy institutional complex represented the "State", i.e. the fundamental core of political experience".[36] Hence, as Adolf Merkl says, the *deutsche Staatsrechtslehre* is tainted with a "monarchical prejudice".[37]

From this account also emerge the limitations of the German understanding of the *Rechtsstaat*. They affect, first, the principle of legality and, second, the conception of individual freedom and rights. As for the principle of legality, legal theory admits of no higher norm binding legislation to respect individual rights and allows administration an extensive freedom from law's effective primacy. The former view leads to the denial that the constitution is superior to legislation, which makes the boundaries of the legislative power (seen as the joint function of monarch and parliament expressing the state's will) hardly ascertainable. The latter view makes the principle of legality precarious through a number of instruments meant to secure freedom of action for the monarchical administration. As for the conception of individual freedom and rights, which we shall only briefly deal with,[38] this is entirely built upon the public/private distinction.[39] In Jellinek's systematization of public subjective rights, individual rights in the private domain are connected with the idea of natural freedom, i.e. an ambit which the state is "indifferent" to. On the contrary, individual rights in the public domain are thought of as "creations" of the state which, by self-limitation, allows the development of individuals' "legal" rights. Being variable according to the state's will, legal rights have a mere legislative determination. Hence, individual "public" rights are the result of the state's will and express, as Kelsen noted, the "essential difference" (*Wesenverschiedenheit*) between the state and other legal subjects.[40]

The premises and limitations of the German understanding of the rule of law lead to a vision of the *Rechtsstaat* that, as we have seen, amounts to a set of (especially administrative) remedies against the sovereign state's will. We might apply Kelsen's remarks on the reception of Roman law and the traits of German public law to this understanding of *Rechtsstaat*, too: "What kind of public law can it be that does not impose any positive legal norms or legal obligations upon the state?"[41]

3 KELSEN'S CONCEPTION OF *RECHTSSTAAT*

Kelsen develops his conception of *Rechtsstaat* by appealing to the ideas of constitutionalism and by acknowledging the need for a general updating of its functions,[42] thus overcoming the German model's deep ambiguities and limits. Kelsen's "restoration" draws inspiration from previous Austrian doctrines, in particular from Friedrich Tezner's administrative legal theory.[43] Tezner, within the Austrian context, had suggested a new vision based on a rigid understanding of legality and on a "judicial" model of public administration. Kelsen's model of the rule of law is developed both by providing a different historical account of its meaning in the emergence of the modern state, and by detecting its key traits, which Kelsen synthesizes in their *formal* dimension. From the first perspective, the rule of law is seen as a "legal (and state-based) constitution" [*Rechts-(und Staats) Verfassung*)], i.e. as a superior constitutional order that is a precondition for the "equilibrium" of a pluralistic, rather than a homogeneous, society. From the second perspective, the *Rechtsstaat* is identified with the legal system's sovereignty and is thus seen as the "logical premise" (*logische Voraussetzung*) for "the complete legal understanding" of "the state's law" (*Staatsrecht*).

As mentioned above, the influence of Austrian doctrine on Kelsen's conception concerns the principle of legality and the elaboration of a "judicial" model of public administration. The principle was at the heart of the debate on administrative discretion that followed the setting up of an Administrative Tribunal (*Verwaltungsgerichtshof*) in Austria in 1875. The Tribunal's jurisdiction did not extend to "matters over which administration had a discretional power". In construing this provision, two different stances were taken: one by Edmund Bernatzik who, from the premise of administrative freedom, denied the accountability of administrative discretional activities; and the other by Tezner, who instead proposed to limit the above exception and establish the verifiability of all administrative activities.[44] Within the debate, which was especially concerned with discretional activities and their relation to the "public interest", two different conceptualizations of administration were opposed: a traditional one grounded on administrative freedom and another viewing administration as rigidly bound by the primacy of law.[45] Despite such different visions, the Austrian debate was marked by a common trait, namely the equation of administration and adjudication and their equal submission to law. Suffice it to recall Bernatzik's words: "within free administrative discretion, the criterion for the distinction between "adjudication" and "administration" cannot be detected".[46] In any event, the leading figure of the debate was indeed Tezner, who believed that the equation between administration and adjudication called for adequate legal framework for administrative action, thus arguing – as early as at the end of the nineteenth century – the need for administrative procedures.[47] Tezner's reasoning, grounded on a particular view of legality freed from the traditional conceptualization of administration, later became a key reference of Kelsen's account of the rule of law.

As noted above, this account has a historical-constitutional dimension. This dimension surfaces in the *Hauptprobleme* in connection with the development of state and law. Contrary to German doctrine, Kelsen does not believe that the state, rather than law, is an "original authority", the former being the *prius* and the latter the *posterius*, i.e. that the state develops before law. Such an argument "must be firmly rejected" in that "historical research proves that the development of law and state is not separate" and it is implausible to consider "the state as creator of law", i.e. as being historically "an institution preceding law".[48] Kelsen takes his analysis even further by examining the rise of the modern state and by denying that it represents a break with the medieval political and constitutional world. Although Kelsen does not provide a complete historical account, he demonstrates, on the one hand, that the new concept of state stands for "the expression of given political postulates not recognized by the system ..., which contradict the legal system"; on the other hand, that the state expresses an "autocratic system, built upon the interests of the prince and his retinue, which contrasts with a *democratic* legal order", with the aim of achieving, "in contrast with the legal (and state-based) constitution [*Rechts-*(*und Staats-*) *Verfassung*], a wider scope of action for the sovereign's free discretion".[49] Hence, the modern state denies the constitutional limits of power and embodies the political postulate that the state is a subject of power.

Kelsen's denial of the state's sovereignty has two implications. On the one hand, the rule of law is identified with the legal system's sovereignty and the state's subjection to law in its activities. As pointed out by Kelsen, and contrary to German administrative legal doctrines, the meaning of the rule of law may be truly understood by bearing in mind "one single essential point: the subjection of the state, in all its expressions, to the legal system, i.e. the political principle of law's exclusive power".[50] As we will see when dealing with its formal traits, the rule of law is grounded on the "the necessary legal foundation of each power" and on the denial of "autocratic powers", i.e. powers lacking "explicit legal groundings" and "a formal assignment of competences".[51] On the other hand, the *Rechtsstaat* refers to a different understanding of political and constitutional dynamics, which underlines the pluralistic dimension of these dynamics. As has been stressed,[52] the concept of *Rechts- (und Staats-) Verfassung* (with which the notion of *Rechtsstaat* is identified), employed by Kelsen to depict the political and constitutional organization preceding and following the rise of the modern state, views the legal system as "a normative system of conflicts ..., as the organized sum of claims and obligations" and, therefore, as the legal expression of social pluralism. Reducing political and constitutional dynamics to the state's sovereignty means to deny such a pluralistic dimension as well as law's mediating role. Kelsen argues that political dynamics, from the rise of the modern state until the constitutional state, are grounded on the "pluralistic distribution of power" and on "the search for an agreement among different political and social forces through contractual mediation"; within such a context, there is no room for "statuality", i.e. for the "unity, sovereignty and compactness of the state-public powers". Hence, the legal system guarantees equilibrium and pluralism, and cannot be replaced by the will of any sovereign subject. The legal system "is more or less like a compromise",[53] it expresses the "common rules" of political life and of different subjects' "legal status", it is a means for "protecting one's rights and initiating judicial procedures".[54] The legal system's sovereignty thus allows for "the state and other subjects bound by law to be coordinated amongst themselves".[55] The concept of *Rechtsstaat*, seen as *Rechtsverfassung*, epitomizes the role of law and the legal system as mediating structures and the conditions of pluralism.

Kelsen's account is matched by his analysis of the formal nature of *Rechtsstaat*: from this perspective, the *Rechtsstaat* represents the legal system's sovereignty and becomes the condition for building public law. The "formal" meaning embodies the essential traits that the rule of law must have with respect to different kinds of state: it specifies the "essence of the rule of law" (*Wesen des Rechtsstaates*).[56] The formal characteristics of the rule of law may be summed up in the following two points: (a) *Rechtsstaat* implies "the difference between a legal norm and a state act, with the latter being determined by and formally separate from the former";[57] (b) legal norms establish a legal relationship, i.e. correlative duties and obligations, among different subjects bound thereby.[58] The *Wesen* of *Rechtsstaat* thus takes shape, firstly, in the primacy (sovereignty) of the legal system and, secondly, in the fact that there can be no obligation without a corresponding legal norm. It is thus assumed that "the state can only 'want' and 'act'" (*der Staat kann nur "wollen" und "handeln"*) according to what is established by the legal system, and that nobody has a legal obligation that is not related to a legal norm. These two principles mean that, "under the rule of law," the state person "can be thought of as endowed with obligations and rights, which is bound like all other individuals"[59] by law. Rights and duties, i.e. legal relationships among individuals, including the state, are determined by the legal system, i.e. by a system of norms.

The "formal" conception of the rule of law as a logical premise of public law also has a number of significant consequences for the legal character of the state's various actions and for the system's unity. Firstly, an act of the state is valid only if there is a normative authorization

(*Ermächtigung*) by the constitution or by law, and not merely the state's presumed will. Secondly, since norms express "legal relationships" (*Rechtsverhältnisse*) among individuals and these relationships are considered merely in their formal dimension (as granting rights and duties), all pre-legal conditions (power, strength or sovereignty) connoting norms materially and subjectively (quality of individuals involved in the relationship) are excluded from legal consideration and imperativist theories can be rejected. Thirdly, the unity of the legal system depends on all state actions stemming from the system of norms. Fourthly, it is possible to develop a unified conception of legal subjectivity, equating different executive acts of the legal system (deeds, judgements, legal transactions), and to reject the public/private distinction and the public law doctrines connected with it.

This conceptualization highlights the discontinuity between Kelsen's understanding of the rule of law and German doctrines. Unlike the latter's premises, Kelsen's notion of *Rechtsstaat* is characterized by the direct link between the system's sovereignty and the equalization of all legal subjects. By giving up the centrality of the state-person, Kelsen "abandons the whole nineteenth-century tradition of remedies"[60] and upholds a principle of legality that is not limited by the state's role. The idea of the rule of law is specified in connection with the relationship between law and administration: administration has a mere "executive" role and administrative action can no longer be presumed lawful and viewed as intrinsically incompatible with judicial review. Furthermore, denying the idea of the state's will leads to the rejection of Jellinek's account of "public" individual rights. Under the rule of law, the equal relationship among different subjects rules out the possibility of rights being "granted" by the state or derived from the state's "self-limitation". Self-limitation is considered to be a "non-legal" (*unjuristisch*) concept that cannot be the basis of an individual's legal status.[61] Thus, the model of the rule of law advanced by the *Reine Rechtslehre* overcomes nineteenth-century conceptions and, through the idea of the legal system's exclusive sovereignty, paves the way for a conceptualization of the constitution as the legal system's higher source.

4 *RECHTSSTAAT* AND CONSTITUTION

The "formal" conception of the rule of law, developed by Kelsen in the 1910s, was elaborated in the following years through a dynamic conception of the legal system, acquiring a "substantial" dimension as a theory of the meaning of the rule of law within democratic systems. The substantial dimension is developed from a double perspective: in a more technical and legal sense, through the conception of a hierarchical legal structure (*Stufenbau*) and the primacy of the constitution; and through the analysis of the real meaning of constitution. According to Kelsen, the formal/substantial distinction[62] epitomizes the difference between the *general meaning* of the rule of law and its content-based *specifications* in different legal systems; it follows that the hierarchical structure, the primacy of the constitution and the analysis of its meaning represent the content-based dimension of twentieth-century democracies. In other words, the formal argument is pushed further in connection with the changes in public law dynamics. The concept of constitution (*Verfassung*) and the dynamic conception confirm and conclude Kelsen's account of the rule of law and the lawful organization of the state, which had first been outlined in his *Hauptprobleme* and his subsequent writings.

A parallel reading may see Kelsen's argument as a theory of "constitutional democracy", i.e. a theory about how the rule of law is implemented within democracies and how "democracy and constitutionalism" can coexist.[63] Kelsen's account of constitutional democracy is grounded on a new definition: democracy is severed from the idea of popular sovereignty and, in the light of the new the pluralism and freedom that now characterize society; majority decisions are constrained, and pluralism guaranteed, by individuals' rights. As seen above, the "substantial" dimension of the *Rechtsstaat* is double-sided: it implies (a) the idea of the legal system's hierarchical structure; and it regards (b) the concept and function of the constitution.

(a) The "doctrine of the hierarchical organization" of the legal system (Stufenbaulehre) and of the constitution as a higher norm is associated with a new interpretation of the traditional partition of state functions into three powers. Kelsen criticizes the ideological aspects and the political consequences of this partition.[64] These aspects of the theory of the separation of powers, which is the ideology of constitutional monarchies, are spotted in the content-based conceptualization of legislation as the "free" determination of the state's aims and in the vision of the executive power as "placed on the same level" (Gleichgeordnete) as the legislative power. Premised upon "historical and political considerations ... grounded on the essence of 'sovereignty' and 'state'".

This theory leads Kelsen to deny the possibility of a "legal control of legislative activities"[65] and to view administration as an activity only partially bound by law.

On the contrary, the hierarchical conception of the legal system – and, related to it, the primacy of the constitution – allows for the rigid separation of powers to be overcome, for it conceives of all state actions as executing the constitution and, by providing "a solid unifying platform subjecting powers to law, ensures the respect of mutual boundaries and the mutual coordination of powers".[66] The constitution becomes the "foundation of the unity" of the state[67] and is the means for the complete subjection of power to law. Moreover, legislation can thereby be considered an entirely legal function, and thus subjected to the judicial review of its compliance with the constitution, in both formal and substantial terms. The coincidence between the legal system's sovereignty and the primacy of the constitution requires constitutional justice to guarantee the lawfulness of all state functions and the coherence of the legal system.[68] The hierarchical conceptualization of the legal system and the idea of constitution make it possible to extend "judicial procedures to areas traditionally not keen on or resistant to legal involvement, i.e. to controversies where law is no longer the criterion but the object of judgement".[69] According to Merkl, the legal system's hierarchical structure highlights the fact that "the legislator has a superior, i.e. the constitution".[70] Lastly, the arguments of the Hauptprobleme show that the hierarchical structure makes administrative action fully subject to law, for it is conceived of, just like all other state actions, as a completely legal and executive function of the legal system. Within this paradigm, administration is entirely equated with adjudication, in line with the "judicial" model of public administration, which had already taken hold in the Austrian school.

Hence, the Stufenbaulehre and the superiority of the constitution over all other legal sources correspond both to the complete subjection of power to law and to a specific arrangement of powers. As we will see below, from the point of view of the arrangement of powers, the hierarchical system describes in legal terms both the democratic system's structure and parliament's centrality: as has been pointed out, such a "hierarchical construction of the state's functions" (Stufenbau der Staatsfunktionen)[71] has an immediate constitutional impact. Therefore, such a construction represents Kelsen's final development of the model of the rule of law which was first propounded in the Hauptprobleme: in line with the rule of law and with the legal system's sovereignty, all state actions are thought to be legally determined functions, i.e. performed on the basis of specific legal authorizations.

(b) The second aspect of the "substantial" dimension of the rule of law is the analysis of the concept of constitution. This analysis is intertwined with that of the constitution's function: Kelsen sees the primacy of the constitution as a requirement of democratic pluralism; moreover, he develops a "constitutional" conception of democracy, i.e. of the limits of popular sovereignty.

The concept of constitution is examined from two perspectives: one dealing with the organization and relationship among the state's several powers; the other with the content-based relationship between the state and individuals. To this end, Kelsen defines the concept of constitution by specifically referring to the limitations it imposes on the legislative process: within this ambit, he examines the distinction between form and content and argues for the content-based dimension of the constitution. Indeed, the constraints imposed by the constitution on the legislative process are not limited to the procedural rules required for lawmaking; they also concern the rules "governing, not the creation, but rather the content of laws". A line therefore must be drawn between a narrow conception of the constitution, i.e. "the necessary foundation of legal rules governing the reciprocal behaviour of the state's members", and "the notion of the constitution in its broadest meaning", whose "original if not exclusive aim" is to draw "principles, directives and limits affecting the content of future laws". The concept of constitution is thus not limited to "norms concerning legislative bodies and procedures"; rather, it refers to the content dimension of "individual fundamental rights or freedoms".[72] It follows that the constitution "is not only a procedural rule but also a substantial rule". In other words, the concept of constitution is twofold: it encompasses both the organization of the state's powers and fundamental rights.

Kelsen examines the above conceptualization of the constitution in connection with the new forms of pluralism and freedom brought about by the advent of democracy. As regards pluralism, Kelsen focuses on social pluralism and its political impact by concentrating (in *Vom Wesen und Wert der Demokratie*) on people and popular sovereignty.[73] Together with his criticism of nineteenth-century doctrines and his understanding of the legal system as guaranteeing "equilibrium" among conflicting forces, Kelsen argues that a people cannot be sociologically or politically conceived of as representing either the unity or the substratum of the state's will; rather, a people is a "multiplicity of distinct groups" divided by "national, religious and economic contrasts".[74] This paves the way for Kelsen's most relevant political contention: social pluralism leads to "one of the most important elements of actual democracies, i.e. in the coexistence of political parties", upon which "modern democracies are entirely grounded".[75] In democratic systems, the state's will is but the "result of political parties' wills". This matches changes in public law dynamics: in democratic-pluralistic systems, the relationship between the state and individuals is mediated by "collective groups, such as political parties, which synthesize the equal wills of individuals".[76]

These changes parallel what Kelsen calls a "metamorphosis in the conception of freedom".[77] Such an "alteration in meaning" is due to the fact that, in order to become the "principle" of democracy, freedom is no longer to be seen as "negative" but as "social or political" (positive) freedom. Kelsen thoroughly reassesses the idea of freedom: its classical conceptualization as "negative" freedom, i.e. as a domain for individual autonomy protected against the state's intrusion, gives way to the idea of "positive" freedom, i.e. "individual participation in the state's power".[78] There ensues a new relationship between freedom and equality, in that democracy becomes a system that seeks to "synthesize" these two values.[79] As has been underlined,[80] Kelsen's new conception of freedom ought to be understood in the light of the shift from the liberal state to the democratic-social state. "Positive" freedom overcomes the liberal antithesis between freedom and equality: participation in "creating the legal system" requires, for different subjects, equal opportunity of choice. Hence, political freedom requires individual free choice, which is attainable only if it is not hindered by economic or social restraints.

It follows that "'negative' freedom is a good not intrinsically but only if it is a part or aspect of the broader concept of 'positive freedom'".[81] This entails the following two considerations: on the one hand, positive freedom implies individuals' autonomous choices within the political world; on the other, autonomous choice is feasible only if minimum "substantial" equality is guaranteed.[82] This, in turn, establishes an unbreakable link between democracy and social rights[83] and substantially connotes the former. If "the system is founded on positive freedom" then "the principle of 'freedom from deprivation'"[84] and the "co-existence" of social rights within the democratic political world become the system's essential traits. Kelsen develops this argument by critically evaluating the "atomistic-individualistic conception": democratic freedom does not presuppose the isolated individual, of the liberal tradition, but an individual who finds his essential dimension in "collective associations".[85] Therefore, positive freedom synthetically epitomizes a vision of subjects as social "individuals".

The link between the constitution, pluralism and freedom leads Kelsen to see the constitution as a requirement of democracy. The fact of pluralism requires the supremacy of the constitution as a higher "procedural rule"[86] governing the dynamics of democracy. By formally setting out the "law-making process", the constitution determines, within the political parties' pluralistic system, the rules of democratic interplay.[87] Hence, constitutional supremacy is strictly connected with pluralism and the need for rules about the correct formation of political will, which cannot be left in the hands of variable political majorities. From this point of view a rigid constitution is the "guarantee" of political will being formed correctly.

Moreover, the constitution – conceived of not as a "procedural" rule about "by whom" and "how" decisions may be taken but rather as a "substantial rule" – is intertwined with the "guarantee" of pluralism and with the classical problem of "the arbitrariness of the majority".[88] In this respect, the inclusion of fundamental rights in the constitution protects minorities. For the protection of minorities is "the essential function of the so-called fundamental rights and freedoms, or human or citizens' rights, which are guaranteed by all modern constitutions of parliamentary democracies".[89] Within the pluralistic-democratic system characterized by positive freedom, fundamental rights are no longer just "a means for the protection of individuals against the state"; rather, they are also "a means for the protection of minorities".[90] Pluralism requires the majority's will to be subject to a "content-based" limitation guaranteeing both freedoms and rights[91] and the pluralism of political wills. Unlike in monarchic-constitutional states, rights no longer protect individuals' spheres of freedom from the state;[92] rather, they guarantee minorities and limit the majority's power.

In other words, the primacy of the constitution has a double value: on the one hand, it "guarantees" the procedural rules leading to the formation of political wills; on the other, it protects minorities and guarantees pluralism in democratic systems. Since individuals' "positive" freedom requires the constitutional regulation of the expression and content of political wills, the superiority of the constitution becomes the correlated element of democracy. This account of the relationship between constitution and democracy has two further implications for the concept of constitution and the changes in the concept of democracy. Kelsen's constitutional model views the constitution as the "supreme guaranteeing legal norm" rather than as a "first principle of unity or political order",[93] for it values the given of social pluralism and rejects any kind of substantial unity. The constitution does not result from the decision of a specific subject; rather, it is an "authorless constitution"[94] that "ascertains the relative equilibrium reached so far by groups striving for power".[95]

This conception of the constitution affects the relationship between the constituent and the constituted, i.e. the role of the constituent power. The idea of the constitution as authorless and as a "guarantee" separates the constituent and the constituted: the validity (grounding) of the constitution does not stem from the constituent power but it is founded on a norm with respect to which "the constituent power is only a mere fact".[96] The constituent power is thus only "a boundary-like and analytical concept solely used to denote a theoretical requirement of the constitution"[97]: within a "guaranteeing" constitution, there is no room for the "Jacobin" (and generally democratic-radical) idea that the constituent power is enabled to review the constitution; rather, the constituent process "gives rise to common rules" setting the "forms and limits" of power. Accordingly the constituent process does not imply the sovereignty of any given subject but rather of a "legal" rule establishing a legal "equilibrium" among different subjects.[98]

As to the notion of democracy, Kelsen's view on the organization of governmental powers confirms the theory's "guaranteeing" role: the constitution appears as "balanced" in that it is functionally conceived to ensure the equilibrium of powers and not, as is the case of the "monist" constitutions, to single out a sovereign "organ" within the state's powers.[99] Therefore, parliament is central but not sovereign,[100] since the system is aimed at equilibrium among powers. It follows that the very notion of democracy changes: democracy is no longer represented by Rousseau's popular sovereignty expressed through the majority principle; rather, it is conceived as a "majority-minority" principle consistent with a limitation of majority power.[101] Democracy thus acquires a "constitutional" dimension: it is not identified with popular sovereignty and the principle of majority, but is achieved through the limits to such a power and the "compromise" between majority and minority. If the majority principle is connected with the idea of freedom rather than sovereignty, it "logically" rests on the protection and defence of minorities. The democratic system is built upon alternations of political stances and thus on pluralism. Therefore, the principle of majority turns out to be a majority-minority principle: it does not coincide with the numerical power of votes but with the possibility for a minority to become a majority. Starting with the role of fundamental rights, such a conception implies continuous dialectics among different stances and, ultimately, the guarantee of minorities;

this calls for a system which, as we shall see, involves counter-powers against the majority's power.

5 THE ROLE OF CONSTITUTIONAL JUSTICE

This account of the rule of law and the role of the constitution underpins Kelsen's idea of constitutional justice. For Kelsen the review of legislation is a legal requirement of the supremacy of the legal system and the primacy of the constitution. He argues that "a constitution not guaranteeing the annulment of unconstitutional acts is not, technically speaking, completely binding".[102] "The jurisdictional guarantee, i.e. constitutional justice", is therefore a technical means "to ensure the regular performance of the state's functions". Being grounded on the legal system's hierarchical structure and on the idea of legislation as the "application of law", constitutional justice consists in an assessment of the "regularity" of statutes, i.e. of the "correspondence between a lower and a higher grade of the legal system". It is one of the main "guarantees of the constitution ..., i.e. a basic guarantee of the constitutionality of statutes" and of annulling "unconstitutional statutes".[103]

In democratic-pluralistic systems, constitutional justice is the main legal instrument that makes the constitution effective and enables it to guarantee democracy. Kelsen thus underlines the political implications of constitutional justice: pluralism and equilibrium among powers. For constitutional justice has a direct political function as a limitation of legislative power: it is "the institution of control" which effectively guarantees minorities.[104] Constitutional justice is the "condition of existence" of the democratic republic: for democracy requires that legal control be tightened against the "domination" of majority. According to Kelsen, constitutional justice "by ensuring the constitutionality of law-making and in particular the material constitutionality of the laws, ... is an effective protection of minorities against the majority's abuses". The judicial protection of the constitution is the "adequate instrument" to safeguard minorities and to implement a democratic system whose essence is not "the majority's omnipotence" but "constant compromise amongst the groups that majority and minority represent in parliament". It makes opposition possible against "the majority's dictatorship, which is not less dangerous for social peace than the minority's".[105]

Together with its guaranteeing role, Kelsen stresses that constitutional justice, being independent "as much of parliament as of government", meets the demand for the mutual control of powers and, therefore, the requirement of a balanced constitution. Its judicial organization, as a

Constitutional Court being a counter-power against the legislative and the executive, is connected with the meaning of the "separation of powers" in the "democratic republic": constitutional justice allows for the "distribution of powers among different agencies, not so much to isolate them from each other but to allow their mutual control". In other words, constitutional justice and the Constitutional Court do not contradict "the principle of the separation of powers at all"; rather, they are its "accomplishment", for not only do they prevent a "concentration of excessive power in the hands of a single agency – which would be detrimental to democracy" – but they "guarantee the regular operation of all agencies".[106]

The link between the review of legislation and the constitution's guaranteeing and balancing role is but one aspect of Kelsen's argument. For he also deals with the Constitutional Court's room for invalidating legislation. This raises the issues of the limits and characteristics of judicial review and its relationship with legislative power, in turn raising the problem of the scope and character of the Court's interpretation of the constitution. It is the problem of determining the tasks and limits of constitutional justice: whether the Court should have a mere "controlling" function or a broader and directly political role. The latter aspect is more directly relevant for Kelsen's model of the Constitutional Court: whether it configures a more "political" or a more "judicial" Court (though the distinction is merely orientating). This calls for an analysis of different issues including, at least, the nature of the Court's review, the subjects entitled to request it, the Court's members and the legal consequences of its judgements. While Kelsen's model has been mostly deemed to be "non-political", for he circumscribes the Court's jurisdiction *vis à vis* legislative power, it should be noticed that, both in his contribution to the Austrian Constitution and in his subsequent works, Kelsen endorses a plurality of perspectives. This is true about the distinction between abstract and specific review and, more directly, about the characters of the Court's interpretation of the constitution.

The distinction between abstract and specific review mirrors the alternative – which generally characterizes judicial action – "between the objective protection of the legal system ... and the protection and guarantee of individual entitlements"; in the case of judicial review, the objective interest is the "protection of the constitution". The difference between the two models is that in the former case, "the doubt as to law's constitutionality appears abstract and theoretical, and no specific material interests are involved", whereas in the latter case the "interests of actual legal subjects are involved".[107] It follows that, in the first case, the review concerns the law's "abstract" flaws, whereas in the second case "the detriment to the individual's right is directly taken into account" and judgement is grounded on the law's "specific flaws" leading to such a detriment. There is no doubt that Kelsen's model, based on the review by a central Court, is an "abstract" check: the monopoly of an agency devoted to reviewing legislation means that "the constitution is almost automatically expunged from the range of instruments normally available to judges in the performance of their duties"; therefore, constitutional justice tends to perform an objective review disconnected from the specific protection of rights.

While this appears to be important and perhaps prevalent in Kelsen's thinking, Kelsen conceives of constitutional jurisdiction as providing a direct protection of rights, too. This may be shown in connection with the establishment of the Austrian Court. The development of the *Verfassungsgerichthof* and its conceptualization as a "guarantor of the constitution" rather than a mere instrument for the equilibrium between *Bund* and *Länder* – during the proceedings of the constituent assembly's subcommittee – results from an increase in the number of ways of requesting a review of legislation. Indeed, it is only through Kelsen's proposal of the possibility of the Court activating itself through an *ex officio* procedure (*amstwegiges Verfahren*)[108] that the review of legislation acquires a broader meaning of "objective" protection of the constitution; the Court takes on the role not only of guaranteeing equilibrium among different levels of Federal legislation but also of checking the constitution's overall enforcement.[109]

Similar considerations apply to the Court's interpretative possibilities. Though Kelsen's approach is generally construed in the light of his well-known arguments about the need for the constitution to avoid using "vague formulas" or indeterminate principles such as "ideals of fairness, justice, equality, morality, etc.",[110] it should be added that such considerations do not provide a complete picture of his thinking. While Kelsen deems a non-programmatic constitution to be necessary so as to avoid a "shift of power" from the legislator to the constitutional judge, he also insists on the connection between this position and the protection of rights. In other words, Kelsen's critical considerations almost exclusively concern "programmatic" norms rather than "provisions about the content of laws, to be found in the declarations of individual rights".[111]

Moreover, while Kelsen believes that the constitution establishes limits within which legislators may act, he also underlines the possibility of the Court choosing among different interpretative options and thus among different values. Although Kelsen views the Court's role as a check for "conformity of the lower rule to the rule immediately above it", another equally important aspect of his thought is a more political evaluation of the Court's activity.[112] This approach is particularly present in some passages of Kelsen's answer to Carl Schmitt, where a conception of the Constitutional Court as an agency deciding on "actual" conflicts of interest is explicitly accompanied by a choice for specific options. Kelsen argues that when a rule leaves "ample room for discretion", the Court's activity "is not directly, or not only, concerned with the issue of constitutionality; but also deals with the opportunity of the disputed rule"; in such a case, interpretation should refer to "the best way of individual or general law-making within the constitution's overall framework".[113] Hence, the Court's judgement represents the "development of the constitution in a given direction", because each individual judgement by the Court concerns an "existing conflict of interests" and is affected by the "sociological reality which the controversy arises from: in other words, the fact that, just like in all other legal acts, in a Court's decision – and especially of a Court which is the guardian of the constitution – there is a clash of conflicting interests, and each judgement has an impact on conflicting interests, i.e. it favours one of them or mediates between them".

The above considerations, besides being decisive for configuring the role of the Constitutional Court[114] as judicial, epitomize a "political" and expansive understanding of constitutional justice. It follows that Kelsen's thinking can hardly be framed within a specific single view or defined by one univocal character. Indeed, Kelsen's stance includes different specifications as to the nature and functions of the Court and mirrors a number of different political and institutional needs. This approach shows Kelsen's awareness of some critical issues of constitutional justice: on the one hand, important aspects of its configuration seem unlikely to be specified without considering the constitution's characteristics; on the other hand, this connection depends also on political relations and on the overall constitutional arrangement of the form of government, i.e. on whether the constitution is "monistic" or "pluralistic". From this perspective, Kelsen's theory ought to be seen as providing an "open" definition of constitutional justice, to be specified on the basis of actual constitutional relations: in other words, the Court's configuration varies according to the political and constitutional setting it is placed in.

NOTES

1. See R. Walter, *Die Entstehung des Bundes-Verfassungsgesetzes 1920 in der Konstituirenden Nationalversammlung*, Wien: Manz, 1984; F. Ermacora, "Österreichs Bundesverfassung und Hans Kelsen", in A. Merkl, *et al.* (eds), *Festschrift für Hans*

Kelsen zum 90. Geburtstag, Wien: Deuticke, 1971; G. Stourzh, "Hans Kelsen, die österreichische Bundesverfassung und die rechtsstaatliche Demokratie", in R. Walter (ed.), *Die Reine Rechtslehre in wissenschaftlicher Diskussion*, Wien: Manz, 1982; G. Schmitz, *Die Vorentwürfe Hans Kelsens für die österreichische Bundesverfassung*, Wien: Manz, 1981.

2. For this opinion, see A. Merkl, "Hans Kelsen als Verfassungspolitiker", *Juristiche Blätter*, 60 (1931), p. 385; W. Antoniolli, "Hans Kelsen und die österreichische Verfassungsgerichtsbarkeit", in *Hans Kelsen zum Gedenken*, Wien: Europaverlag, 1974; however, H. Haller questions such a circumstance in *Die Prüfung von Gesetzen*, Wien/New York: Springer, 1979.
3. H. Kelsen, "Wiedergabe einer Sendung des österreichischen Rundfunks, 8 Mai 1973", in *Hans Kelsen zum Gedenken*, pp. 47 ff.; Kelsen speaks about "*sein persönlichstes Werk*" and about "*sein geliebstiges Kind*".
4. H. Kelsen, *Hauptprobleme der Staatsrechtslehre* (1911), Aalen: Scientia, 1960.
5. A. Merkl, "Idee und Gestalt der politischen Freheit", in *Demokratie und Rechtsstaat. Festgabe zum 60. Geburtstag von Zaccaria Giacometti*, Zürich: Polygraphischer Verlag A.G., 1953; A. Baldassarre, "Libertà", in *Enciclopedia giuridica*, Roma: Istituto della Enciclopedia italiana, 1991.
6. Cf. B. Sordi, *Tra Weimar e Vienna*, Milano: Giuffrè, 1987, pp. 108–9: Sordi underlines that this view is generally connected with antiparliamentary debates.
7. The leading figure is Friedrich Tezner. For the criticism of Gneist, see also J. Redlich, *Englische Lokalverwaltung*, Leipzig: Duncker & Humblot, 1901.
8. Kelsen is certainly the first author to develop a systematic critique of German public law doctrines and of the conceptualization of the *Rechtsstaat*: such a critique paves the way for twentieth-century debates on the relationship between law and democracy. In this respect, Kelsen significantly refers to the work of Adolf Merkl, who ought to be seen as co-author of the Kelsen's critique.
9. See H. Kelsen, "Rechtsstaat und Staatsrecht", *Österreichische Rundschau*, 36 (1913), It. tr. "Stato di diritto e diritto pubblico", in H. Kelsen, *Dio e Stato*, Napoli: ESI, 1988; H. Kelsen, "Zur Lehre vom Gesetz im formellen und materiellen Sinn, mit besondere Berücksichtung der österreichischen Verfassung", *Juristische Blätter*, 42 (1913), It. tr. "Sulla dottrina della legge in senso formale e materiale", in H. Kelsen, *Dio e Stato*; H. Kelsen, "Zur Lehre vom öffentlichen Rechtsgeschäfte", *Archiv des öffentlichen Rechts*, 31 (1913).
10. H. Kelsen, *Hauptprobleme der Staatsrechtslehre*, p. 493.
11. See H. Kelsen, "Zur Lehre vom öffentlichen Rechtsgeschäfte", p. 75, on "administrative courts, personal liability of the state's bodies for damages arising out of unlawful behaviour, the state's liability for its bodies' unlawful acts" (*Verwaltungsgerichte, persönliche Haftung der Organe für rechtswidrigen Schaden, Haftung des Staates für Unrecht seiner Organe*).
12. H. Kelsen, "Rechtsstaat und Staatsrecht", It. tr. p. 218.
13. H. Kelsen, "Zur Lehre vom öffentlichen Rechtsgeschäfte", p. 192.
14. See M. Fioravanti, "Kelsen, Schmitt e la tradizione giuridica dell'Ottocento", in G. Gozzi and P. Schiera (eds), *Crisi istituzionale e teoria dello Stato in Germania dopo la Prima guerra mondiale*, Bologna: il Mulino, 1987.
15. H. Kelsen, *Das Problem der Souveränität und die Theorie des Völkerrechts. Beitrag zu einer Reinen Rechtslehre*, Tübingen: Mohr, 1920, It. tr. *Il problema della sovranità e la teoria del diritto internazionale. Contributo per una dottrina pura del diritto*, Milano:

Giuffrè, 1989, p. 12.
16. H. Kelsen, *Der soziologische und der juristische Staatsbegriffe* (1922), Tübingen: Mohr, 1927, pp. 114–15.
17. G. Jellinek, *Allgemeine Staatslehre*, Berlin: Häring, 1905, p. 476.
18. H. Kelsen, *Das Problem der Souveränität und die Theorie des Völkerrechts. Beitrag zu einer Reinen Rechtslehre*, It. tr. p. 98.
19. H. Kelsen, *Über Grenzen zwischen juristischer und soziologischer Methode*, Tübingen: Mohr, 1911, It. tr. *Tra metodo giuridico e sociologico*, Napoli: Guida, 1974, p. 52.
20. G. Jellinek, *System der subjektiven öffentlichen Rechte*, Tübingen: Mohr, 1905, p. 26.
21. H. Kelsen, *Hauptprobleme der Staatsrechtslehre*, pp. 172 ff. Jellinek views the people as one of the State's organs; the State's unitary will is thus the people's unitary will.
22. G. Jellinek, *System der subjektiven öffentlichen Rechte*, p. 234. See also M. Fioravanti, *Giuristi e Costituzione politica nell'Ottocento tedesco*, Milano: Giuffrè, 1980, pp. 404 ff.
23. According to H. Kelsen (*Hauptprobleme der Staatsrechtslehre*, p. 173), such a conception, which reduces social dynamics to the State's, was first propounded by Gerber. See A. Baldassarre, "Diritti pubblici soggettivi", in *Enciclopedia giuridica*, Roma: Istituto della Enciclopedia italiana, 1989.
24. G. Jellinek, *Allgemeine Staatslehre*, pp. 325–6.
25. H. Kelsen, *Hauptprobleme der Staatsrechtslehre*, pp. 223.
26. G. Jellinek, *Allgemeine Staatslehre*, p. 462.
27. Ibid., 466. According to H. Kelsen (*Hauptprobleme der Staatsrechtslehre*, p. 405), self-obligation is underpinned by the problem of lawmaking.
28. See H. Kelsen, "Zur Lehre vom öffentlichen Rechtsgeschäfte"; H. Kelsen, "Rechtsstaat und Staatsrecht", passim.
29. H. Kelsen, "Zur Lehre vom öffentlichen Rechtsgeschäfte", p. 65.
30. B. Sordi, *Tra Weimar e Vienna*, p. 47.
31. H. Kelsen, "Zur Lehre vom öffentlichen Rechtsgeschäfte", p. 192.
32. P. Laband, *Das Budgetrecht nach den Bestimmungen der Preußischen Verfassungs-Urkunde*, Berlin: Guttentag, 1871. With respect to such a distinction, see H. Kelsen, "Zur Lehre vom Gesetz im formellen und materiellen Sinn, mit besondere Berücksichtung der österreichischen Verfassung", passim.
33. B. Sordi, *Tra Weimar e Vienna*, p. 172.
34. On such aspects, see H. Kelsen, *Hauptprobleme der Staatsrechtslehre*, pp. 500–1.
35. R. Thoma, "Rechtsstaatsidee und Verwaltungsrechtswissenschaft", *Jahrbuch des öffentlichen Rechts der Gegenwart*, 4 (1910).
36. M. Fioravanti, *Costituzione*, Bologna: il Mulino, 1999, p. 152.
37. A. Merkl, "Die monarchische Befangenheit der deutschen Staatsrechtslehre", *Schweizerische Juristenzeitung*, 16 (1919–20).
38. For a detailed analysis of these matters, see Gustavo Gozzi's essay in this volume.
39. For an analysis of this aspect, see H. Kelsen, *Hauptprobleme der Staatsrechtslehre*, pp. 629 ff.
40. According to H. Kelsen (*Hauptprobleme der Staatsrechtslehre*, p. 646), speaking of "public" rights implies a difference between the State and other legal subjects.
41. H. Kelsen, "Zur Lehre vom öffentlichen Rechtsgeschäfte", p. 62.
42. H. Kelsen, "Zur Lehre vom Gesetz im formellen und materiellen Sinn, mit besondere Berücksichtung der österreichischen Verfassung", It. tr. p. 231.

43. In the first foreword to Hauptprobleme, Kelsen acknowledges and thanks Tezner, "though", he writes, "words are not enough to thank him". Tezner is also a critic of Jellinek, who advances considerations further developed by Kelsen on the *zwei-seiten Theorie*. See F. Tezner, "Die wissenschaftliche Bedeutung der allgemeinen Staatslehre und Jellineks Recht des modernen Staates", *Annalen des Deutschen Reichs für Gesetzgebung, Verwaltung und Volkswirtschaft*, (1902). Lastly, in terms of constitutional analysis, Tezner was quite likely the first scholar to mention the *Hauptprobleme* in *Die Volksvertretung*, Wien: Manz, 1912.
44. E. Bernatzik, *Rechtssprechung und materielle Rechtskraft* (1896), Aalen: Scientia, 1964; F. Tezner, *Zur Lehre vom dem freien Ermessen der Verwaltungsbehörden als Grund der Unzuständigkeit der Verwaltungsgerichte*, Wien: Manz, 1888.
45. On the *Frage des öffentliches Interesse*, cf. B. Sordi, *Tra Weimar e Vienna*, pp. 195–7; A. Piras, "Discrezionalità amministrativa", in *Enciclopedia del diritto*, Vol. XIII, Milano: Giuffrè, 1964.
46. E. Bernatzik, *Rechtssprechung und materielle Rechtskraft*, p. 47.
47. F. Tezner, *Handbuch des österreichischen Administrativverfahrens*, Wien: Manz, 1896.
48. H. Kelsen, *Hauptprobleme der Staatsrechtslehre*, pp. 406–7.
49. H. Kelsen, "Das Verhältnis von Staat und Recht im Lichte der Erkenntniskritik", *Zeitschrift für öffentliches Recht*, 2 (1921), It. tr. "Il rapporto tra Stato e diritto dal punto di vista epistemologico", in H. Kelsen, *L'anima e il diritto*, Roma: Edizioni Lavoro, 1989, pp. 46–7.
50. H. Kelsen, "Zur Lehre vom öffentlichen Rechtsgeschäfte", p. 75.
51. M. Fioravanti, *Costituzione*, p. 151.
52. M. Fioravanti, "Stato", in M. Fioravanti, *Stato e Costituzione*, Torino: Giappichelli, 1993, p. 65.
53. H. Kelsen, "Gott und Staat", *Logos. Internationale Zeitschrift für Philosophie der Kultur*, 11 (1922–1923), It. tr. "Dio e Stato", in H. Kelsen, *Dio e Stato*, p. 157.
54. M. Fioravanti, "Stato", p. 70.
55. H. Kelsen, "Zur Lehre vom öffentlichen Rechtsgeschäfte", p. 73.
56. H. Kelsen, *Hauptprobleme der Staatsrechtslehre*, p. 438.
57. H. Kelsen, "Zur Lehre vom öffentlichen Rechtsgeschäfte", p. 206.
58. Ibid., p. 88.
59. H. Kelsen, "Rechtsstaat und Staatsrecht", It. tr. p. 218.
60. B. Sordi, *Tra Weimar e Vienna*, p. 110.
61. H. Kelsen, *Hauptprobleme der Staatsrechtslehre*, pp. 400 ff.
62. H. Kelsen, *Allgemeine Staatslehre*, Berlin: Springer, 1925, p. 91.
63. M. Fioravanti, *Costituzione*, p. 151.
64. H. Kelsen, "Die Lehre von der drei Gewalten oder Funktionen des Staates", *Archiv für Rechts- und Wirtschaftsphilosophie*, 17 (1923–1924), It. tr. "La dottrina dei tre poteri o funzioni dello Stato", in H. Kelsen, *Il primato del parlamento*, Milano: Giuffrè, 1982, p. 82. Kelsen maintains that this doctrine has the "political intent to obtain and preserve a particularly privileged position for whoever historically holds given powers or performs given functions or holds given rights". On the separation of powers, see W. Kägi, "Von der klassischen Dreiteilung zur umfassenden Gewaltenteilung (Erstarrte Formeln – bleibende Idee – Neu Formen)", in *Verfassungsrecht und Verfassungswirklichkeit. Festschrift für Hans Huber zum 60. Geburtstag*, Bern: Stämpfli & Cie, 1961, pp. 151–73, and also the extensive study by G. Silvestri, *La separazione dei poteri*, Milano: Giuffrè, 1984.

65. Cf. H. Kelsen, "La garantie juridictionnelle de la Constitution (La justice constitutionnelle)", *Revue du droit public et de la science politique*, 35 (1928), It. tr. "La garanzia giurisdizionale della Costituzione (La giustizia costituzionale)", in H. Kelsen, *La giustizia costituzionale*, Milano: Giuffrè, 1981, pp. 151–2. Kelsen notes that in constitutional monarchies "the problem of the constitutionality of laws" does not lead to "practical concerns", since it is believed – a belief shared also in democratic-constitutional regimes – that the "sovereign", through his sanctions, "should verify the constitutionality of law-making", in that the sovereign's ratification is the expression of the state's unitary will.
66. B. Sordi, "Un diritto amministrativo per le democrazie degli anni Venti", in G. Gozzi and P. Schiera (eds), *Crisi istituzionale e teoria dello Stato in Germania dopo la prima guerra mondiale*, p. 123.
67. H. Kelsen, "Die Lehre von der drei Gewalten oder Funktionen des Staates", It. tr. p. 109.
68. H. Kelsen, "La garantie juridictionnelle de la Constitution (La justice constitutionnelle)", It. tr. p. 202.
69. B. Sordi, *Tra Weimar e Vienna*, p. 187.
70. A. Merkl, "Die Unveränderlichkeit von Gesetzen – ein normologischen Prinzip", *Juristische Blätter*, 46 (1917), It. tr. "L'immodificabilità delle leggi, principio normologico", in A. Merkl, *Il duplice volto del diritto*, Milano: Giuffrè, 1987, p. 134.
71. T. Öhlinger, *Der Stufenbau der Rechtsordnung*, Wien: Manz, 1975, p. 30.
72. H. Kelsen, "La garantie juridictionnelle de la Constitution (La justice constitutionnelle)", It. tr. pp. 153–4.
73. H. Kelsen, *Vom Wesen und Wert der Demokratie*, II, Mohr, Tübingen 1929, It. tr. "Essenza e valore della democrazia", in H. Kelsen, *La democrazia*, Bologna: il Mulino, 1981, pp. 50 ff.
74. Ibid., p. 51.
75. Ibid., p. 52.
76. Ibid., p. 56.
77. Ibid., pp. 39 ff.
78. Ibid., p. 46.
79. Ibid., p. 40.
80. A. Baldassarre, "Diritti sociali", in *Enciclopedia giuridica*, Roma: Istituto della Enciclopedia italiana, 1989.
81. Ibid., p. 6.
82. For a similar view, see N. Bobbio, *Il futuro della democrazia*, Torino: Einaudi, 1984, Eng. tr., *The Future of Democracy*, Minneapolis (MN): University of Minnesota Press, 1987. On the close relationship between Kelsen's theory and Bobbio's analysis, see D. Zolo, *Il principato democratico*, Milano: Feltrinelli, 1992, pp. 121 ff (Eng. tr. *Democracy and Complexity*, Cambridge: Polity Press, 1992).
83. In this respect, and with respect to social rights stemming from positive freedom and universal suffrage, see M. Luciani, "Sui diritti sociali", *Democrazia e diritto*, 4 (1994); 1 (1995).
84. A. Baldassarre, "Diritti sociali", p. 7.
85. H. Kelsen, *Vom Wesen und Wert der Demokratie*, II, It. tr. p. 57.
86. H. Kelsen, "La garantie juridictionnelle de la Constitution (La justice constitutionnelle)", It. tr. p. 154.

87. H. Kelsen, *Allgemeine Staatslehre*, p. 321, where Kelsen underlines that, in the process leading to the establishment of the democratic system, the constitution becomes the general rule ordering the formation of the State's will.
88. H. Kelsen, *Vom Wesen und Wert der Demokratie*, II, It. tr. p. 83.
89. Ibid., p. 94.
90. Ibid., p. 95.
91. As we have seen, Kelsen's idea of positive freedom also envisages a detailed list of social rights. In this respect, it ought to be recalled that the fifth project for the Constitution of the Austrian Republic, drafted by Kelsen in 1919, contains a wide catalogue of social rights. On these issues, see G. Schmitz, *Die Vorentwürfe Hans Kelsens für die österreichische Bundesverfassung*, passim; G. Bongiovanni, *Reine Rechtslehre e dottrina giuridica dello Stato*, Milano: Giuffrè, 1998, pp. 167 ff.
92. Such a protection is limited by the legislative connotation of rights. On rights within the liberal *Rechtsstaat*, see M. Fioravanti, *Appunti di storia delle costituzioni moderne*, Torino: Giappichelli, 1991.
93. M. Fioravanti, "Costituzione e Stato di diritto", in M. Fioravanti, *Stato e Costituzione*, p. 187.
94. Ibid., p. 152.
95. H. Kelsen, "Der Drang zur Verfassungsreform", *Neue Freie Presse*, October 6 (1929), It. tr. "Le spinte alla riforma costituzionale", in H. Kelsen, *La giustizia costituzionale*, p. 49.
96. M. Dogliani, "Potere costituente e revisione costituzionale", in G. Zagrebelsky *et al.* (eds), *Il futuro della Costituzione*, Torino: Einaudi, 1996, p. 257.
97. Ibid.
98. On constituent power see M. Fioravanti, "Potere costituente e diritto pubblico", in M. Fioravanti, *Stato e Costituzione*.
99. On the distinction between a monist constitution and a balanced one, see M. Fioravanti, "Le dottrine dello Stato e della Costituzione", in R. Romanelli (ed.), *Storia dello Stato italiano*, Milano: Donzelli, 1995.
100. M. Fioravanti, *Costituzione*, p. 154.
101. H. Kelsen, *Vom Wesen und Wert der Demokratie*, II, It. tr. pp. 94 ff.
102. H. Kelsen, "La garantie juridictionnelle de la Constitution (La justice constitutionnelle)", It. tr. p. 199.
103. Ibid.; Kelsen's theory represents a decisively new approach with respect to nineteenth-century public law jurisdictions. It marks the passage from *Staatsgerichtsbarkeit* to *Verfassungsgerichtsbarkeit*, i.e. to an effective ascertainment of constitutionality. Jellinek's suggestion as to an enlargement of the functions of the Austrian *Reichsgericht* is to be associated with the former view (*Staatsgerichtsbarkeit*); see G. Jellinek, *Ein Verfassungsgerichtshof für Österreich*, Wien: Hölder, 1885.
104. H. Kelsen, "La garantie juridictionnelle de la Constitution (La justice constitutionnelle)", It. tr. p. 201.
105. Ibid., pp. 202–3.
106. Ibid., pp. 173–4.
107. M. Luciani, *Le decisioni processuali e la logica del giudizio costituzionale incidentale*, Padova: Cedam, 1984, pp. 238–9.
108. See B. Caravita, Corte "*giudice a quo*" *e introduzione del giudizio sulle leggi. La Corte costituzionale austriaca*, Padova: Cedam, 1985, passim. Caravita focuses on

the decisive role of the principle of *amstwegige Verfahren* in the interpretation of the Austrian model of constitutional review. The author's analysis is fundamental both for the genesis of the Austrian model and for a more general interpretation of Kelsen's theory.

109. On the meaning of the *ex officio* procedure, with respect also to the protection of individual rights and *Verfassungsbeschwerde* (individual appeal), see H. Kelsen, G. Fröhlich and A. Merkl, *Die Verfassungsgesetze der Republik Österreich*, V, Wien-Leipzig: Deuticke, 1923, with reference to arts 139, 140, 144 of the Austrian constitution; A. Merkl, "Die gerichtliche Prüfung von Gesetzen und Verordnungen", *Zentralblatt für juristische Praxis*, 39 (1921).
110. H. Kelsen, "La garantie juridictionnelle de la Constitution (La justice constitutionnelle)", It. tr. pp. 189–90.
111. Ibid., p. 190.
112. B. Caravita, *Corte "giudice a quo" e introduzione del giudizio sulle leggi. La Corte costituzionale austriaca*, pp. 160 ff.; D. Grimm, "Sul rapporto tra dottrina dell'interpretazione, giustizia costituzionale e principio democratico", in C. Roehrssen (ed.), *Hans Kelsen nella cultura filosofico-giuridica del Novecento*, Roma: Istituto della Enciclopedia italiana, 1983; C. Mezzanotte, *Corte costituzionale e legittimazione politica*, Roma: Tipografia Veneziana, 1984.
113. H. Kelsen, "Wer soll der Hüter der Verfassung sein?", *Die Justiz*, 11–12 (1930–1931), It. tr. "Chi dev'essere il custode della Costituzione?", in H. Kelsen, *La giustizia costituzionale*, p. 259.
114. Ibid., p. 260: "in this respect, it is particularly important that the State's will, which is manifested in the Constitutional Court's judgement, be formed through a process giving voice to existing conflicting interests"; "so that the contentious procedure is at least useful in casting light on the effective situation of the different interests". Of course, Kelsen provides other reasons legitimating the judicial procedure: the guarantee of the Court's independence and the fact that its activity is concerned, above all, with the application of law and only partially with lawmaking.

PART III

THE CONTEMPORARY DEBATE

CHAPTER 8

THE PAST AND THE FUTURE OF THE RULE OF LAW

Luigi Ferrajoli

1 RULE OF LAW, LEGAL STATE, AND CONSTITUTIONAL STATE

The phrase "rule of law" is commonly given two different meanings that should be kept rigorously distinct. In the broadest, or weak or formal sense, it means any legal system in which public powers are conferred by law and wielded in the forms and by means of the procedures the law prescribes. In this sense, which corresponds to the German *Rechtsstaat*, all modern legal systems in which public powers have a legal source and form are "legal states" in a merely formal meaning of the "rule of law".[1] In the second, strong and substantive sense, "rule of law", instead, stands only for those systems in which public powers are also subject to (and hence limited or constrained by) law not only in their form, but also in the content of their decisions. In this meaning, prevalent in continental Europe, the phrase "rule of law" denotes legal and political systems in which all powers, including legislative power, are constrained by substantive principles normally provided for by the constitution, such as the separation of powers and fundamental rights.

I shall argue that these two distinct meanings correspond to two distinct normative models relating to two different histories. Both of them developed in Europe and each was the outcome of a paradigm shift in the conditions of existence and validity of legal norms. These two models are: (1) the ancient positivist model of the legal state that emerged together with the modern state and the principle of legality as a criterion for recognizing the existence of law; and (2) the new positivist model of the constitutional state which resulted, in the wake of the Second World War, from the spread throughout Europe of constitutional charters stating criteria for the recognition of the validity of law, and of the review of ordinary legislation by a Constitutional Court.

The significance of the former shift is obvious. It was generated by the state monopoly over legal production and hence by the purely positivist justification of law. No less radical was, however, the latter shift which,

P. Costa and D. Zolo (eds.), The Rule of Law: History, Theory and Criticism, 323–352.

as we shall see, affected the same structural aspects as the former. I shall illustrate three modifications produced by each of the two paradigm shifts from which the two different models derive: (a) in the nature of the law (b) in the nature of legal science, and (c) in the nature of judicial decision. Consequently, I shall identify three paradigms – pre-modern law, the legal state, and the constitutional state – and analyse the changes that took place in these three aspects of each of them during the shift from one paradigm to the other. By contrast, I shall not go into the specific tradition of English rule of law; although the rule of law in the strong, substantive meaning was first exhibited in England, the English tradition has always been linked to the tradition of common law and thus cannot be identified either with the legal state or the constitutional one.[2] In conclusion, I shall deal with the present crisis of these two models of the rule of law, a crisis now faced with a new paradigm shift of still uncertain form and outline.

2 LEGAL STATE AND LEGAL POSITIVISM

The distinctive feature of pre-modern law was its form, not so much legislative as judge-made and doctrinal, being the product of judicial tradition and knowledge that had accumulated through the centuries. In the Middle Ages common law had no unitary and formalized system of positive legal sources. There were certainly statutory sources: acts, ordinances, decrees, statutes, and the like, but these derived from diverse, concurrent institutions – Empire, Church, princes, free cities, or corporations – none of which had the monopoly of legal production. The conflicts among them – the struggles between Church and Empire or between Empire and free cities – were conflicts for sovereignty, namely the monopoly or at least supremacy in legal production. But, they were never resolved univocally until the birth of the modern state and the supremacy of this institution and its legal system over all the others. In the absence of unitary sources and in the presence of a plurality of concurrent legal systems, the unity of law was assured by doctrine and judicial decisions, by way of an evolution and updating of the old Roman law tradition within which the various statutory sources were arranged and coordinated as materials of the same kind as legal precedents and the opinions of learned doctors. Clearly, such a paradigm – inherited from Roman law but in this way similar to extra-European consuetudinary law – had enormous institutional and epistemological implications.

The first of these implications concerned the theory of validity, namely the identification of what we can call the norm of recognition of existing law. Within a doctrinal and judge-made legal system a norm exists and is valid not because of its formal source, but for its intrinsic rationality or substantive justice. *Veritas, non auctoritas facit legem* is the formula that can express the validity of pre-modern law and is opposite to that championed by Hobbes in his renowned polemic *A Dialogue between a Philosopher and a Student of the Common Law of England.*[3] By then the student of law was right. Whenever an exhaustive and exclusive legal system is bereft of positive sources, a legal norm is not valid by the authority but the authoritativeness of who establishes it; hence, its value is identified with its "truth", in the broad sense, obviously, of rationality or conformity with precedent and tradition, in other words, with the common sense of justice.

The second implication regards the nature of legal science and its relationship with law. Within a system of doctrinal and judge-made law, legal science becomes immediately normative and identifies with the law itself. There is no "positive" law which is the "object" of legal science and of which legal science is the interpretation or descriptive and explicative analysis. There is only law handed down by tradition and constantly reworked by scholars. From this there follows a third implication that judicial decision does not consist in the application of a body of law "given" or presupposed as something that exists on its own, in harmony with the modern principle of the judge's subjection to the law, but in the doctrinal and judicial production of that body of law. This brings with it all the consequences of a flawed legality, especially in criminal matters: the lack of certainty, the enormous discretion of judges, inequality, and the lack of guarantees against arbitrariness.

This shows how extraordinary was the revolution which took place with the establishment of the principle of legality through state monopoly of legal production. It was a paradigm shift involving the form much more than the content of legal experience. If the Napoleonic Code or the Italian Civil Code is compared with Gaio's *Institutiones*, the substantive differences would seem relatively few. What changes is the kind of legitimization: no longer the authoritativeness of the scholars but the authority of the source of production; no longer truth but legality; not the substance (or intrinsic justice) but the form of the normative acts. *Auctoritas, non veritas facit legem*: this is the conventionalist principle of legal positivism as expressed by Hobbes in the *Dialogue* mentioned earlier; the opposite of the ethical-cognitivist principle of natural law.

Legal naturalism and legal positivism, natural law and positive law can well be seen as the two cultures and legal expressions underlying these two opposing paradigms. The millenarian predominance of natural law as a "strand of thought according to which for a law to be a law it must conform to justice"[4] cannot be understood without taking the outlines illustrated here of pre-modern legal experience into account. In the latter, when there were no positive sources, natural law was resorted to as a system of norms that were intrinsically "true" or "just" as "common law"; in other words, as the legitimating ground of legal doctrine and judicial practice.[5] This is why the pre-modern theory of law could be but natural law; whereas the legal positivism of Hobbes's formula corresponded then, in a seeming paradox, to an axiological or philosophical-political claim of thought, i.e. of rationality and justice – the demand for re-establishing law upon the principle of legality as both a meta-norm for recognizing existing law and a first and irreplaceable boundary to arbitrariness, legitimizing power through its subordination to law and protecting equality, liberty, and certainty.

The modern rule of law was established in the form of the legal state when this claim was realized historically with the establishment of the principle of legality as the sole source of valid, and indeed existing, law. By virtue of this principle and the codifications implementing it all legal norms exist and are valid, in that they are "posited" by authorities invested with normative competence. Their language is no longer spontaneous and, so to speak, itself "natural", as in pre-modern law shaped by natural law, but an artificial language whose rules of use are themselves established by the laws, both regarding the forms of the normative linguistic acts – statutes, judicial decisions, administrative provisions, and contracts – and the meanings they express and produce. This turned the paradigm of law, legal science, and judicial decision upside down.

In the first place, with the principle of legality the very notion of "validity" of the norms changes and is dissociated from those of "justice" and "truth". Therefore, the criterion for identifying existing law changes, too: a norm exists and is valid not because it is intrinsically just, let alone "true", but because it has been enacted by a body authorized by law. This shift, expressed in what we usually call the "separation of law and morals", came about through a long process of secularization of law promoted in the early modern era by the doctrines of Hobbes, Pufendorf, and Thomasius, and reached maturity with the French and Italian legal Enlightenment and the openly legal positivist doctrines of Jeremy Bentham and John Austin. This separation is the ground of the formal conception of validity as logically independent from justice – the distinctive feature of legal positivism. It also grounds the unity of the legal system. From whatever starting point, even the most marginal, whether it be a legal deed (e.g. the purchase of a newspaper) or a legal situation (e.g. a parking prohibition), there is a law behind it, either because it immediately regulates the former and constitutes the latter or because it regulates the normative acts which in turn regulate or constitute that deed or situation.

In the second place, the nature of legal science changes: it ceases to be an immediately normative discipline and tends to become cognitive, i.e. explicative of an object – positive law – separate and autonomous from it. Over and above the similarities of content, our manuals of private law are as different from the civil treatises of the pre-modern era as they are from the works of Roman jurists because they are no longer immediately normative systems of theses and concepts but interpretations, comments, or explications of the civil code, and only on this basis can they be argued and upheld.

Finally, the nature of judicial decision changes – it becomes subjected to the law and is legitimized exclusively by such subjection and thus by the principle of legality. This confers a somewhat cognitive characteristic to judgment, too, which is called upon to ascertain, on the basis of the rules of use that the law itself lays down, the facts foreseen and stated by the law, e.g. offences. It is precisely the conventional character of law expressed by the Hobbesian formula which transforms judgment into cognition or ascertainment of what the law prescribes in accordance with the symmetrical and opposing principle of *veritas non auctoritas facit iudicium*. It also grounds the whole combination of guarantees – from legal certainty to equality before the law and freedom against arbitrariness, from the independence and impartiality of judges to the burden of proof being on the prosecutor, and to the rights of the defendant.

3 CONSTITUTIONAL STATE AND RIGID CONSTITUTIONALISM

While this first shift of legal paradigm was expressed in the establishment of the principle of legality, because of the legislator's omnipotence, the second shift occurred over the last half century with the subordination, guaranteed by a specific judicial check of legitimacy, of legislation itself to a superior law, namely the constitution, which is of a higher order than ordinary legislation.

There follow three changes in the model of the legal state, parallel to the latter's changing of pre-modern case law: (a) in the nature of law, whose positive character extends from legislation to the norms regulating its content and thus causes a dissociation between validity and being in force, as well as a new relationship between the form and substance of decisions; (b) in the interpretation and application of the law, where this dissociation involves a change in the judge's role as well as in the forms and conditions of his subjection to the law; and (c) in a legal science that is no longer simply descriptive, but plays a critical and propositional role regarding its very subject matter.

The first change concerns the theory of validity. In the constitutional state, statutes are not only subject to formal norms about their production, but also to substantive ones about their meaning. Thus, statutes whose meaning clashes with constitutional norms are inadmissible. The existence or being in force of norms that in the older legal positivist paradigm had been dissociated from justice now is dissociated from validity too, for a norm may well be formally valid and thus in force but substantively invalid because its meaning clashes with substantive constitutional norms, such as the principle of equality or fundamental rights. More precisely, while the rule for recognizing a norm as in force remains the old principle of legality concerning the form of law-making exclusively, which we can thus call the principle of formal legality or mere legality, the rule for recognizing validity is much more complex for it contains what we can call the principle of substantive legality or strict legality. This principle also compels the substance that is the contents or meaning of the norms produced, to be coherent with the principles and rights laid down in the constitution.

The second alteration, consequent to the first, concerns the role of case law. The incorporation of principles and fundamental rights into the constitution and thus the possibility of norms becoming invalid by being in contrast with them, changes the relationship between judge and statute law. No longer is it an a-critical unconditional subjection to whatever it is the content or substance of statute law but a subjection, first and foremost, to the constitution and thus to the law only insofar as its is constitutionally valid. Therefore, interpretation and application of the law is also and always a ruling on the law itself that the judge, whenever he is unable to implement it constitutionally, has the obligation to censure as invalid by denouncing its unconstitutionality.

The third alteration, regards the epistemological paradigm of legal science. As much as it changes the conditions of validity, this alteration requires that legal science be no longer merely explicative and value-free but also critical and project-oriented. Under the old paradigm of the legal state, the critique and design of the law was only possible from the outside – at the level of ethics or politics, or simply opportunity or rationality – there being no room for substantive internal flaws in positive law: neither inconsistencies among norms (for it was the later law that remained in force), nor incompleteness (for the lack of constitutional constraints made legislative non-compliance impossible), were possible. On the other hand, within a complex normative system such as that of the constitutional state, which not only regulates the forms of production, but also the meaning of norms, incoherence and incompleteness, antinomies, and lacunae are flaws that stem from the different normative levels of its formal structure. It is obvious that these flaws, which are not only possible, but also to a certain extent inevitable, act retrospectively on legal science, giving it the political and scientific role of ascertaining what the flaws are from the inside and suggesting the necessary corrections. More precisely: legal science has to ascertain the antinomies caused by norms that violate the rights of liberty as well as the lacunae caused by the lack of norms supporting social rights, and call for the annulment of the former because they are invalid and the enactment of the latter because they are due.

Constitutionalism taken seriously, as the drafting of law using law itself, confers to legal science and case law a pragmatic function and dimension unknown to the legal reasoning of the old dogmatic and formalistic legal positivism: ascertaining antinomies and lacunae, promoting their overcoming by means of existing guarantees, and drafting the guarantees that are needed but absent. This confers legal culture a civil and political responsibility to its object, giving it the task of pursuing the overall coherence and completeness – i.e. the effectiveness of constitutional principles – by judicial or legislative means, though without any prospect of this being wholly achieved.

It is clear that the subjection of legislation to the constitution introduces an element of permanent uncertainty concerning the validity of the former, depending on the judicial assessment of its coherence with the latter. At the same time, however, and contrarily to popular belief, this restricts the uncertainty of its meaning by reducing the power of interpretative discretion of both courts and legal science. Indeed, under the same conditions, and depending on whether or not there are principles laid down by a rigid constitution, the same legal text involves a narrower (in the former) and wider (in the latter) range of legitimate interpretations. Take, for example, a norm like the one in the Italian criminal code which punishes the imprecisely defined offence of *vilipendio* (defamation, often of an institution): "Whomsoever commits defamation ... etc." Without a constitution, the meaning of a norm like this is totally indeterminate since "defamation" could mean any manifestation of thought that asserts as "vile" the institutions the norm protects. With the constitution, and in particular the constitutional principle of free speech, even granting that a norm against "defamation" could still be valid, it cannot be construed so as to apply to all expressions of thought, even if these are offensive to these institutions, instead of simple insults.

Finally, there is a fourth change – perhaps the most important but which I shall merely hint at here – produced by the paradigm of rigid constitutionalism.[6] While in the theory of law this paradigm involves revising the concept of validity because of the dissociation between the formal force and the substantive validity of decisions, in political theory it involves a correlative revision of the purely procedural concept of democracy. The transformation of principles and fundamental rights into a constitution, constraining legislation, and conditioning the legitimacy of the political system to their protection and implementation has grafted a substantive dimension on to democracy in addition to the traditional political, formal, or merely procedural one. I mean to say that the substantive dimension of validity in the constitutional state translates into a substantive dimension of democracy itself, of which it is both a limit and a complement: a limit because the fundamental principles and rights are prohibitions and obligations imposed on the power of the majority which would otherwise be absolute, and a complement because these very prohibitions and obligations are as many guarantees that go to protect the vital interests of all against the abuse of such powers, which, as the last century has shown, could otherwise overturn democracy itself, along with rights.

I wish to add that while rigid constitutionalism brings about an internal change to the ancient positivist model, it is also a supplement to the rule of law as well as to legal positivism itself: it is the rule of law and legal positivism in their most extreme and developed state, as it were. Indeed, as we have seen, the change it brings about has given legality a twofold artificial and positive character; no longer only of the "is" of law, in the sense of its state of "existence", but also of its "ought", namely its conditions of "validity", they, too, being made positive constitutional law on the law in the shape of legal limits and constraints to law-making. This has been the most important achievement of contemporary law: regulation not only of the forms of legal production, but also of the contents of the norms produced, and therefore a broadening and completion of the very principle of the rule of law through the subordination of the formerly absolute legislative power to law.

4 INSTITUTIONAL AND CULTURAL SHIFTS

At this point, we can identify these two paradigm shifts that we have described with a structural change in the principle of legality and, consequently, in the rules of formation of legal language. The distinctive trait of legal positivism that distinguishes modern from pre-modern law is, as we have seen, precisely the positive character that comes from what has been called the principle of formal legality or mere legality, by means of which a norm exists and is valid exclusively for the legal form of its production. The distinctive trait of legal constitutionalism with respect to merely legislative legal systems is, in turn, no less structural a feature; the subordination of legislation itself to law through what I have called the principle of substantive legality or strict legality, by means of which a norm is only valid and in force insofar as its contents do not clash with the fundamental principles and rights laid down by the constitution.

I expressed the first of these two structural differences – between pre-modern law and the positive law of the legal state (or rule of law in the weak sense) – by saying that, whereas the legal language of uncodified legal systems is a "natural" language, that of positive law is an "artificial" one; all its rules of use are stipulated and agreed on positively. It is the criminal laws, for example, that tell us what is "theft" and what is "murder"; they are substantive norms about the production of judicial decisions and condition their validity, together with the "truth" of their assumptions. Similarly, it is the norms of the civil code that tell us what a contract – a mortgage or a sale – is, and thus, all together, form the substantive norms for the production of civil judgements that ascertain the validity of contracts. This collection of norms about production is the basis of formalism and legal positivism, expressed by the principle of mere legality: law can in no sense be derived from morality or nature or other normative systems but is wholly an artificial object "posited" or "produced" by human beings and thus depending on their responsibility, on how they consider, draft, produce, interpret, and apply it.

The second structural difference (between the positive law of the legal state and the positive law of the constitutional state, or the rule of law in the strong sense) can also be expressed in relation to legal language. It is that now not only does legal language codify and discipline through norms of higher order the procedural norms on the production of linguistic normative acts, but also the substantive norms on the meaning or content they are able to express; not only the syntactic rules on the formation of the symbols – laws, rulings, and other binding legal acts – but also the semantic rules that constrain the meaning, precluding that which cannot be validly decided and obliging that which must be decided. In short, not only the rules on "how" law is pronounced, but also on "what" it can and cannot say. The substantive conditions of validity of laws, that the pre-modern paradigm found in the principles of natural law and the earlier positivist paradigm had replaced with the purely formal principle that valid law is enacted law, come into the legal system again as positive principles of justice enshrined in norms of a higher order than legislation. Indeed, if the rule of law is based on the principle of strict legality, the laws are themselves regulated by norms on their production. Therefore, not only do they condition by their language the validity of the decisions expressed in legal language but, as expressions in legal language, in turn have their own validity conditioned by norms of a higher order that regulate their meaning as well as their form. It is in these substantive norms on meaning that the foundations of the constitutional state lie, whether they impose limits, as in the rights of freedom, or obligations, as in social rights. It is in them that the legal paradigm of constitutional democracy shows up through the democratic convention: besides the rules of the democratic game, the game itself, besides the method and form of democracy, the democratic project itself.

However, these two shifts were not only produced by political revolution and legal and institutional innovation – the rise of the modern state and then the introduction of rigid constitutions and specialized agencies of constitutional justice – but also by cultural developments, i.e. theoretical revolutions that changed the conception of law in the imagination of jurists and in common sense. This is what took place in the first major modern legal revolution, the rise of legal positivism as both a model and a conception of law in opposition to the old, pre-modern case law. Although anticipated by contract theories of law as a "device" or "contrivance"[7] in political philosophy and by the legal positivist theories of Bentham and Austin, its success in legal culture was difficult and anything but taken for granted. Suffice it to consider the stiff opposition to codification raised by the most important legal school of the nineteenth century – the Pandectist School, who were schooled on the idea of the *System of Modern Roman Law* according to the meaningful title of the work by its leader Friedrich Savigny – who strongly argued for the law to be separate from legislation and the immediately constructive and normative role of legal science.

The same holds true about constitutionalism. Its institutional and even theoretical premises were largely present well before today's European constitutions provided for and guaranteed their own rigidity by special procedures for constitutional amendment and the review of legislation. There was the example of the Constitution of the United States which, from the outset – as far back as the renowned 1803 ruling of *Marbury v. Madison* on an unconstitutional law – was a rigid constitution guaranteed by the judicial control of the Supreme Court. It obtained this guarantee, however, not so much from its conception as a law of a higher order than legislation as from being the outcome of a federal treatise that neither Congress nor individual states could deviate from. Furthermore, most European countries had constitutions that were formally rigid since their amendment required aggravated procedures With the exception of the 1920 Austrian constitution, none of these, however,[8] provided for any special judicial review of the constitutionality of laws. One can even postulate "the natural rigidity of constitutions" as has happened recently,[9] even when they, like the Italian Albertine Statute, are devoid of norms on how to amend them. This idea seems perfectly obvious to us today since a flexible constitution, namely one that can be validly amended by ordinary procedures, is in fact not a constitution but an ordinary law, whatever name it goes by, and even if it is written in stone. It is, however, a fact that this theory was upheld in 1995, and not in 1925 (when Mussolini rode roughshod over the Statute with his liberticidal laws without any jurist raising his voice in warning against a *coup d'état*), nor in the 1950s (when the Italian court of cassation held that constitutional principles and rights were only programmatic). Even at a theoretical level, all the premises of democratic constitutionalism were in the doctrine of the greatest theoretician of legal positivism, Hans Kelsen, who not only theorized the step structure of the legal system, but also elaborated the guarantee of the judicial review of legislation, in his plan for the Austrian constitution of 1920.[10] It is, however, again a fact that Kelsen himself was the most fervid believer in not only the "pure" and value-free nature of legal theory, but also the archaic legal positivist theory – which, as we have seen, is untenable in systems with a rigid constitution – of the equivalence of the validity and the existence of norms, which prevents substantively unconstitutional norms from being declared invalid.[11]

In sum, in the legal culture of the nineteenth and early twentieth centuries, legislation, whatever its content, was considered the supreme unlimited and illimitable source of law. Constitutions, whatever we may think today of their "natural" rigidity, were not perceived as rigid constraints on the legislator but solemn political documents or, at most, ordinary laws. Just consider the devaluation and incomprehension by Jeremy Bentham, one of the greatest exponents of legal liberalism, on the Declaration of 1789. In a pamphlet titled *Anarchical Fallacies*,[12] Bentham asked himself whatever could such a document be that begins with the proclamation "all men are born free and equal" and then goes on to list a whole series of principles of justice and natural rights, if not a minor philosophical treatise set forth in articles and the upshot of a "confusion" of words that "can scarcely be said to have a meaning."[13]

For he claimed that "there are no such things as natural rights", "rights anterior to the establishment of government" that "existed before laws, and will exist in spite of all that laws can do".[14] Bentham did not realize that, through that Declaration, positive law was changing its nature before his eyes. The Declaration itself was positive law and those principles of justice it proclaimed, once stipulated, were no longer principles of natural but of positive law, which obliged the political system to respect and protect them.

Even so, after their legal nature was recognized, constitutions were long held to be simple laws subject to amendment and thus, as was the case in Italy, violation by the legislator. Indeed, it was not until 50 years ago that the idea of a statute about statutes and a law about law began to enter the common sense of jurists. It was beyond the bounds of imagination that a statute could constrain statutes, since the latter were the only, hence omnipotent, source of the law – the more so since they had been democratically legitimized as the expression of the parliamentary majority and thus popular sovereignty. This meant that the legislator in turn, as well as the policy of which legislation was both the product and the tool, was considered omnipotent. A merely formal and procedural conception of democracy ensued, which was identified solely with the power of the people, namely, the representative procedures and mechanisms meant to achieve majority will.

It was only after Second World War and the defeat of Nazi-fascism that, with the introduction of judicial guarantees of the repeal of unconstitutional laws by ad hoc courts and not their simple non-application in individual cases as in the United States,[15] the meaning and normative scope of the rigidity of constitutions as norms of a higher order than ordinary legislation was recognized and sanctioned. It was no coincidence that this guarantee was first introduced in Italy and Germany, followed by Spain and Portugal, where, after the Fascist dictatorships and the massive popularity they enjoyed, the role of the constitution as a limit and constraint on the power of the majority was being rediscovered in accordance with the notions embodied two centuries earlier in Article 16 of the Declaration of 1789: there is no constitution in which "the guarantee of fundamental rights is not assured or the separation of powers provided for"; the two principles and values that Fascism denied and which are, in turn, the denial of Fascism.

This is the reason why we can talk about having "discovered" the constitution only over recent decades; in Italy, for example, in the sixties, after the constitutional court awoke the constitution from the hibernation the Court of Cassation had placed it in. Constitutionalism was not part of the scientific terrain of jurists in the nineteenth century, nor in the early half of the twentieth century, and has only recently penetrated legal culture and been grafted on to the old legal positivist paradigm. Indeed it is on this terrain that we have the clearest confirmation of the pragmatic dimension of legal science: norms and principles are nothing more than meanings and do not exist merely by virtue of their legal enunciation but also, and more so, as meanings shared by legal culture and common sense. I would add that our legal culture is still largely old positivistic and non-constitutional, and the paradigm of the constitutional state is still very much to be developed both in theory and institutionally.

There is an interaction between institutional and cultural shifts. Legal and political philosophies are always a reflection, a constitutive and, so to speak, a performative factor of the actual legal experiences of their times natural law, despite all its variations, was the dominant legal philosophy of the pre-modern era for as long as there was no formalized system of sources based on the state monopoly of legal production; legal positivism took over after codification and the birth of the modern state; constitutionalism is, or at least is becoming, dominant today, after the introduction of judicial guarantees of constitutional rigidity. Each of these stages corresponded to a change in the legitimization of law and its criteria of validity; from the immediately substantive basis of pre-modern case law, when the validity of a legal case depended on the (subjective) assessment of the (objective) justice of its contents, through the purely formalistic basis of the legal state, in which the validity of a norm only depended on the legal form of its production, up to the both formal *and* substantive formula of the constitutional state, in which the validity of laws depends not only on their sources and forms conforming to the norms for their production, but also on their content complying with the principles laid down by constitutions, which are of a higher order.

Three cultures, models of law and notions of validity, therefore, each corresponding to a different political system: the *ancien régime*, the legal state, and the constitutional state. But also three different epistemological paradigms of judicial decision and legal science, and three different increasingly complex models of political legitimization. With the first institutional revolution, the existence and validity of law were dissociated from its justice since the a priori assumption that it was immediately just, based on the wisdom of its doctrinal and judicial development, had ceased. For the first article of the social contract founding the positive legal order was that a law formally pre-establish, against judicial arbitrariness, what is forbidden and punishable, so that the judge was constrained in applying by the need to accept the premises the law itself laid down. But the second article, produced by the second institutional revolution, was that the same law be constrained to substantive principles of justice, that it must allow, or must forbid, something that is permitted or forbidden by fundamental constitutional rights. With this second revolution, the existence of law, too, is dissociated from its validity, for the a priori assumption that a norm is valid merely by virtue of how it is said and not also of what it says no longer holds. The substantive and nomostatic dimension of law that had been expunged by early positivism began to penetrate the legal system again, in the broader legal positivism of the constitutional state: under the guise not of an arbitrary sense of right but of limits and constraints placed on the legislator as positive constitutional norms.

5 THE CURRENT CRISIS OF BOTH MODELS OF THE RULE OF LAW

Both models of the rule of law illustrated here are today in crisis. I shall identify two aspects and two sets of factors of this crisis, one affecting the legal state and the other the constitutional state: in other words, the rule of law in both the weak and strong sense, or the law itself in its positive form both legal and constitutional. In both cases, the crisis manifests itself in as many forms of regression towards a pre-modern type of case law.

Firstly, the crisis affects the principle of mere legality which, as we have said, is the norm of recognition of the legal state. It derives, in turn, from two factors: legislative inflation and dysfunctional legal language, both expressions of the crisis of the regulative and conditioning capability of the law and therefore of the "artificial reason" that Thomas Hobbes set against the *iuris prudentia* or wisdom of the "subordinate judges" of his time.[16] In Italy, for example, there are now many tens of thousands of state and regional laws in force, and thousands of laws and decrees passed every year. The result of this exponential growth – the outcome of a politics that has degraded legislation to administration and has by now no vision of the difference between the two functions as to sources and content – is the twilight of codifications and a growing uncertainty in and ungovernability of the entire legal system. Criminal law, especially, has grown at such a pace that its very effectiveness and guarantee mechanisms, its capability for regulating and preventing offences, and repressive abuses have been upset. The Rocco Code, dating from 1930, is still in force in Italy; to this the Republic, in half a century, has added an infinity of special, emergency, and occasional laws, produced by a political and unplanned use of criminal laws good only for exorcizing problems: from anti-drug legislation to the countless laws prompted by the unending state of emergency, firstly terrorism then mafia, up to the latest "security acts" passed only for their symbolic value. On the other hand, in the general ineffectiveness of non-criminal control, no important law has been left without its own criminal clause, to the point that the constitutional court saw fit to issue a declaration of criminal law bankruptcy in the form of Ruling N 364 of 1988, by which it dismissed the classic principle of the inexcusability of *ignorantia legis* in criminal matters as unrealistic.

The other factor of crisis in the principle of legality has been the disorganized language of the laws expressed in increasing vagueness, obscurity, and long-windedness. Here, again, Italian criminal law is emblematic. The Rocco Code had undermined the principle of determinacy through ambiguous, imprecise, and value-based expressions, in particular when referring to crimes against the person of the state, with meanings that could be extended ad infinitum in judgment. Semantic indeterminacy, however, reached heights of real inconsistency in the special legislation of the republican era that brought about a further dissolution of criminal language with single articles of law many pages long, intricate normative labyrinths, uncoordinated contradictory references, obscure formulas interpretable in more than one way, normally resulting from compromise or, worse still, the decision to rely on judicial application for normative choice.

The result of this disaster is a maximal criminal law – maximal extension, maximal inefficiency, and maximal arbitrariness – of which all the political functions that are classically associated with the principle of legality are withering away: predetermination of offences by the legislator and hence legal certainty and the judge's subjection to law; protection of citizens against judicial and police arbitrariness and their equality before the law; mandatory prosecution, the centrality of trial, and its role as a means for verifying or confuting acts committed instead of preventive penalization; and, lastly, the efficiency of the judicial machinery, choked up with an infinite number of fruitless, costly paper cases whose outcome only serves to blur the distinction of lawful v. unlawful in common sense and to take time and resources away from more important inquiries that are increasingly bound to end in that form of surreptitious amnesty that is the expiry of limitation period. In short, it is the conditioning role of the principle of mere legality that in today's "age of decodification"[17] is undermining the primacy of legislation, hence of politics and representative democracy, to the advantage of administration, the judiciary and negotiation, i.e. sources of neo-absolutist power which are no longer subordinated to the law. The rationality of the law, which Hobbes countered with the "*juris prudentia*, or wisdom of subordinate judges" typical of the old common law, has been done away with by the legislation of even more subordinate legislators; the growth of discretion in legal practice had precisely the effect of reproducing a law of prevalently judicial, administrative, or private making, along the lines of the old model of pre-modern law.

The second and no less important aspect of the crisis concerns the principle of strict legality – the regulated and conditioned character of legislation itself – with which I have here identified the norm of recognition of the constitutional state. Again, in Italy, in recent years the constitution has been subjected to concentrated attack and repeated transgression – from the damage wrought to Article 138 on its revision by the various attempts at institutional reform, up to the violation of Article 11 with the participation in the Kosovo war – which have impaired its authoritativeness and constraining strength. Furthermore, this is not a slight dip in the effectiveness of the 1948 constitution but a crisis of the very idea of constitution as a system of limits and constraints and, more generally, of the value of rules as such; these are increasingly resented and disparaged by political and economic powers as inappropriate shackles on popular sovereignty and the free market.

There is also another, even more evident, crisis factor, which concerns the constitutional state. This is the end of the national state as the exclusive monopoly of legal production: the source of law has shifted beyond national borders and this has brought about a crisis in the unity and coherence of the system of legal sources and the guarantor role of state constitutions. The old pyramid structure of the sources – headed by the constitution, followed immediately by ordinary laws and then regulations and other administrative and contractual sources – has been replaced with a conglomeration of legal sources from various different systems, from the European Union to the United Nations, but nonetheless directly or indirectly in force.

Emblematic – by being advanced in the substance of the rule of law although not so in form, either weak or strong – is the process of European integration. In one sense, the European Union is still an amorphous legal and political system, whose traits contradict both principles of democratic constitutionalism: adequate political representativeness of the organs of the Union endowed with greater normative powers and the rigid subordination of their decisions to a check of validity which is clearly anchored to the protection of fundamental rights. In another sense, the process of European integration has shifted the decision-making places traditionally reserved to national sovereignty outwith state boundaries; not only on economic and monetary issues, but also in commercial relationships, immigration, consumer protection, environmental protection, and social policies. It is estimated that almost 80% of legislative production is now directly or indirectly of community origin.[18]

I shall speak later of the perspectives that this process opens which, in the long term, are certainly progressive, thanks also to the European Charter of Basic Rights approved in Nice in December 2000. In the meantime, until a constitutional re-establishment of the Union comes about, this incomplete integration is putting the traditional hierarchies of sources of law under strain and is weakening national constitutions, owing to the EU's lack of political responsibility and constitutional review. On its basis, norms produced outwith the state – treaties, regulations, directives, and rulings – come into force in state legal systems, prevailing over national parliamentary laws and even claiming prevalence over their constitutions. This deforms the constitutional structure of national democracies, in terms both of the political representativeness of the new legal sources, as well as their constitutional constraints: in short, the whole paradigm of the constitutional state.

The democratic deficit of the Union is seen first and foremost in the community legal system. The new sources refer back to agencies that are not directly representative, such as the Council and the Commission, which make decisions through mechanisms that are not transparent and which are deeply affected by lobbies that are all the more powerful the richer and better organized. However, the absence of representativeness and political responsibility has a retroactive effect on the national legal systems that the new sources become part of: through the greater distance between the public and the normative agencies of the Union; through the low level of influence national parliaments can exert on the choices their governments make in participating in complex decision processes that often culminate in decisions made by majority vote and not unanimous agreement; through disinformation and lack of interest in European issues among both political classes and public opinion.

The constitutional review of community sources is as much weakened.[19] Not only do these sources come into force in national systems directly – the regulations as directly applicable norms and the directives as the frame for them but also with immediate effectiveness[20] – but, according to the decisions of the Court of Justice, they are of a higher order than all the norms of national[21] law, including constitutional ones.

The Italian constitutional court ruled against this at the beginning but later substantially accepted it, with the provision that community norms be subordinated to the supreme principles of the Italian republican constitution.[22] It thus comes about that non-legislative norms are not subordinated to legislation but of a higher order than legislation and even able, at least according to the Court of Justice, to deviate from the constitution. This generates more normative inflation and, most importantly, the opening of new areas of neo-absolutist power in contrast with every principle of the rule of law. There is, therefore, a danger that the blurring of roles between national and European legal sources will produce a twofold form of dissolution of legal modernity: the formation of an uncertain community case law by concurrent conflicting courts and regression into the pluralism and overlapping of legal systems and sources that was characteristic of pre-modern law. Expressions such as "principle of legality" and "statutory reservation" are becoming progressively meaningless.

Finally, there is the crisis of the embryonic international constitution formed by the UN Charter and the many conventions on human rights. The principle of peace, which is the fundamental norm and the rationale of the United Nations, has been destroyed by the two wars western powers unleashed during the last decade – the Second Gulf War and the Kosovo War – and by overriding the United Nations in favour of North Atlantic Treaty Organisation (NATO) as the guarantor of a world "order" increasingly marked by the growth of inequality, concentration of wealth, and the expansion of poverty, hunger, and exploitation in the rest of the world.[23]

After all, the whole process of worldwide economic integration that goes under the name of "globalization" can be easily read as a vacuum of public law produced by the absence of limitations, rules, and checks over the strength of major state, military, and private economic powers. Without institutions capable of dealing with these new relationships, the law of globalization is increasingly shaped after the private, contractual forms of law instead of the general, abstract public ones,[24] which shows how much economics dominates politics, and how much the market dominates the public sphere. Thus, the neo-absolutist regression in external sovereignty of the major powers (only) is accompanied by a parallel neo-absolutist regression of the major transnational economic powers; this is the return of a regressive neo-absolutism that shows up in the vacuum of rules that is openly accepted by present-day globalized anarchic capitalism as its fundamental rule – a sort of new *Grundnorm* for economic and industrial relations.

6 THE FUTURE OF THE LEGAL STATE: PROSPECTS FOR REFORM

The decline of national states, the loss of the normative role of law, the multiplication and confusion of legal sources, the thwarting of the principles of formal and substantive legality, and the demise of politics and its capability for forward planning are undermining both paradigms of the rule of law: legal state and constitutional state. It is impossible to foresee what the outcome of this crisis will be, whether destructive, leading to the law of the jungle and survival of the fittest, or whether this will prove to be a transitory crisis that will lead to the emergence of a third, broader model of the rule of law. The only thing we know is that, whatever the outcome is, it will depend on the role that legal and political reason will be able to play. Evolution towards a strengthening rather than a dissolution of the rule of law pivots on re-establishing legality – ordinary and constitutional, and state and supra-state – in order that it be able to meet the challenges it faces on the two fronts described above.

The first challenge, that the crisis of the principle of mere legality is undermining the legal state, calls upon the critical, propositional, and constructive role of legal reason to re-establish ordinary legality. I shall identify two possible lines for reform, one pertaining to the liberal area of the rule of law and the other to its social dimension.

The former concerns criminal law, a terrain on which, and not by chance, the liberal rule of law was born. An effective way of stemming the flood of legislation that has put such a strain on the guaranteeing role of criminal law would be to strengthen the principle of mere legality, by replacing the simple statutory reservation – the principle that a criminal law may only be created through a parliamentary statute – with a code reservation, the idea being to enact a constitutional principle that no norm can be introduced for offences, punishments, and trials unless through an aggravated procedure, in the form of amendments or supplements to the text of the criminal, or criminal procedure, code.[25] This would not simply be a reform of the code but a recodification of the whole body of criminal law. It would be based on a meta-legal guarantee against abuse by special legislation, which could put an end to the present chaos and protect the codes – which Enlightenment culture saw as a relatively simple and clear system of norms for protecting citizens' rights against the arbitrariness of "subordinate judges" – from the arbitrariness of today's "subordinate" legislators. The criminal and criminal procedure codes would become the exhaustive and exclusive normative texts of the whole criminal matter; and, each time, legislators would have to take on the responsibility for their being coherent and systematic. This would enhance legislators' regulatory power over both citizens and judges. The ensuing drastic depenalization – starting with the paper-laden, bureaucratic criminal law made up of a conglomeration of misdemeanours and petty offences often punished with fines – would be compensated by the overall increased certainty, effectiveness, and guarantees.

Restoring and strengthening the principle of mere criminal legality and hence the regulatory and conditioning capacity of the law refers back to the reform and reinforcement of the principle of strict legality; a principle by means of which, as we have seen, the law itself must be regulated and conditioned by meta-legal guarantees: not only by the classical substantive principles of determinacy, materiality and offensiveness as semantic rules for the formation of legal language but also, in this case, a formal principle of legislative production for constraining it to unity, coherence and to the greatest possible simplicity and intelligibility. It is, moreover, only by re-establishing legality through these principles – determinacy in content and code reservation in the form of production – that the proper relationship between legislation and judicial decision can be restored on the basis of a rigid *actio finium regundorum*. In an apparent paradox, legislation and hence also politics can assure the separation of powers and the judge's subjection to the law, and thus meet the constitutional requirement of the absolute statutory reservation, if and only if legislation itself is in turn subordinated to the law, namely, guarantees (first and foremost, determinacy) that can limit and constrain the decision. This is tantamount to saying that the law can be effectively conditioning if and only if it is itself conditioned legally. This is the old Enlightenment formula detracts nothing from its value. That all this held true two centuries ago, when codification made the shift possible from the judicial arbitrariness characteristic of the old case law to the rule of law, makes it no less valid today when legislative inflation has practically pushed the criminal system back into the uncertainty of pre-modern law.

Re-establishing the legality of the welfare state is more difficult and complex. The welfare state did not develop, in Italy and elsewhere, through the subjection to law characteristic of the rule of law, so much as through the steady expansion of governmental institutions, the growth of their political discretion and the unsystematic accumulation of special laws, specific measures, administrative practices and acts of patronage that have been grafted on to the old structure of the liberal state, deforming it. The upshot was a heavy complex bureaucratic intermediation of welfare provisions that is responsible for their inefficiency and, as shown by not only Italian experience, illegal degeneration. There is no denying that the public provision of social services involves the development of costly bureaucratic apparatuses but these can be appropriately pruned and simplified by building a social rule of law which, no differently from the liberal rule of law, is based on the maximum subordination of its provisions to law not only in their form, but also in their content. This could be made possible by making provisions as universal as social rights, rather than dependent on discretionary and selective bureaucratic intervention.

In this prospect, the most fruitful indication put forward by the most interesting studies on the reform of the social state, in my view, is a general principle that combines well with a strengthening of mere legality and its conditioning role through the contents, which are in turn conditioned, imposed on legislation itself. According to this principle, a social right can be guaranteed all the more completely, simply, and effectively in legal terms, at the least cost, and given maximum protection from political and administrative discretion and the arbitrariness and corruption they feed, the less bureaucratic mediation that is needed for its satisfaction; this reduction is achieved by the social right being recognized to apply equally to all through laws as general and abstract as possible. The paradigmatic example in this sense is the statutory satisfaction, in universal generalized terms, of the social rights to subsistence and welfare by a minimum guaranteed wage to all those of majority age upwards.[26] But a similar framework is also found in generalzsed, free, and mandatory forms of social welfare, such as health care and education for all, which now are variously paid for by the public sphere in accordance with the paradigm of equal rights to health and education. In these cases automatic provisions, together with subjection to law, guarantee to the highest degree the certainty of law and rights, the equality of citizens and their immunity from arbitrariness. Naturally, these social guarantees have a high cost; the cost of actually satisfying the corresponding rights is compensated for, besides the minimum living standards and substantive equality it secures, by fewer resources wasted on enormous parasitic bureaucracies that today manage social welfare, sometimes corruptly, on the basis of discrimination and power.

Unfortunately, little hope can be held out for these prospects of reform. Today, changing the welfare state according to the universalistic model of the statutory guarantee of social rights runs against the prospective privatization of the public sphere and the free-market options that prevail in political culture and the ruling classes. Similarly improbable would be a re-establishment of criminal legality based on the guarantee of the code reservation. While criminal legislation is sliding back towards pre-modern law, criminal doctrine looks on in silence as havoc is wreaked with its subject matter and takes comfort in the "realist" fallacy that criminal law cannot be any different from what it is. Improbable, however, does not necessarily mean impossible. We should not mix up inactivity and realism unless we wish to hide the responsibility of both politics and legal culture, reducing to "unrealistic" or "utopian" what we will not or cannot do. We should admit, instead, that the cause behind the crisis is the unwillingness of politics and the propositional inactivity of culture, one following the other as each other's alibi, putting at risk not only the future of the rule of law, but also of democracy itself.

7 THE FUTURE OF THE CONSTITUTIONAL STATE: CONSTITUTIONALISM WITH NO STATE

The second challenge faced by the rule of law regards its constitutional dimension. It is the crisis of the principle of strict legality produced by states losing their sovereignty, with the dislocation of legal sources outside borders and the ensuing weakening of the guarantees provided by national constitutions. It calls for a rethinking of constitutionalism and legal guarantees, i.e. of the places, forms, and degree of rigidity with which constitutions can condition legislation by constraining it to guarantee the fundamental rights and the principles of equality and justice they lay down. We have seen how these places are no longer only state but supra-state and are today occupied at European and world level by agencies that actually make decisions with no political responsibility and under uncertain constitutional constraints. This weakens both dimensions of constitutional democracy: the formal dimension of political democracy, because non-representative agencies are being endowed with growing powers of decision-making, and the substantive dimension of the constitutional state, because those agencies are not subordinated to law and there are no secure checks on the constitutionality of their decisions.

Faced with these processes, first and foremost that of European unification, a nostalgic attitude of sterile opposition leads nowhere. What is certain is that markets will not withdraw behind national boundaries and phenomena of supra-state, international integration and interdependence will increase, not decline. The only possible answer to this challenge, therefore, is to promote legal and institutional integration in addition to the economic and political integration that, whether we like it or not, is not only happening, but is also irreversible. Faced with the crises of the national state and constitutionalism, we are forced to the realization that the only alternative to the decline of the rule of law and new forms of market and political absolutism is a stateless constitution that can deal with the new localizations of power and decisions. While it is true that today's state constitutions are no longer capable of fulfilling their role of guarantor, it is useless to fight a tardy rearguard action in defence of the state and the autonomy of its now outdated legal system. Attention should rather be focused on developing European constitutionalism on the one hand and, on the other, an international model of constitutionalism that can restrain the absolutism of the new powers.

International constitutionalism is the more difficult and improbable long-term prospect. The demise of opposing political blocs, which could have been an excellent prelude for a new world order based on the primacy of the United Nations and the guarantee of human rights enshrined in many international charters, heralded instead the decline of the United Nations, the conversion of NATO to the armed wing of rich western countries against the increasingly impoverished countries of the rest of the world and the reinstatement of war as a means for resolving international conflict and defending our democratic fortresses against the pressure of the growing "huddled masses" kept outside their borders. The only step forward towards an international rule of law was the Treaty of Rome of 17 July 1998 setting up an international criminal court empowered to deal with crimes against humanity. The fact remains that the only alternatives to a future world of war, violence, and exponential growth of poverty and crime, in which our very democracies would be put at risk and deprived of their legitimacy, are a legal project of world constitutionalism, which is already outlined in the UN Charter, and the resolution by major powers to take it seriously.

The prospects of extending the constitutional paradigm to the European Union are somewhat more realistic. Despite many limitations and difficulties, there is an ongoing constituent process in the Union which has sped up considerably over the last 10 years. The latest and most significant step was the approval in Nice on 7 December 2000 of a European Charter of basic rights; besides traditional liberties and civil rights, this provides a long list of social rights a well as last-generation rights on privacy, the protection of the human body, and the preservation of the environment. This document has been merely proclaimed and not yet formally incorporated in the treaties. However, its political value and de facto compulsory nature, consequent to its unanimous approval by the European Council, Commission and Parliament, are unquestioned. Moreover, in legal terms, too, it is probable that its norms already be incorporated into Article 6 of the Treaty of Union which for "general principles of Community law" refers to basic rights "resulting", besides from the European Convention on Human Rights of 1950, "from common constitutional traditions of Member States": these are precisely those very "common constitutional traditions" that the Convention, which was set up by the European Council of Cologne on 3–4 June 1999, had to identify within the charter it would develop. It can therefore be argued that not only is this charter a first, highly important step towards the development of a true European constitution, but it is now also law in force, legally binding on the Union and its member states, as well as for the Luxemburg Court of Justice, more and more clearly bound to become a European constitutional court.

Of course, the new Charter of Rights will be insufficient to redraft European law along the lines of a constitutional state. For that, a rational re-establishment of the entire power organization of the Union will be necessary, based on the one hand on the classic principle of the division of power and, on the other, on a more exact distribution of competence along federal lines between European and state agencies. To build a European rule of law, therefore, it is necessary to proceed in the opposite direction from a national rule of law: constitutionalism not as a complement of the legal state but, instead, as its premise. Only when the constitutional integration of Europe has taken place – only when its jurisdiction is extended well beyond the basic economic issues and is made to include a legislative function of the European parliament – will it become possible to promote increasingly advanced forms of legislative integration.

Today, legal integration proceeds with community sources being superimposed on state ones, thus aggravating the tangle of norms and the crisis of the principle of legality in its formal no less than in its substantive dimension. The main factor in this integration is the role played by the Court of Justice which, helped by the involvement of state courts brought about by the direct introduction of community norms into state systems,[27] is forming a prospectively judge-made European law. It is clear, however, that there is no substantive reason why integration should not take place legislatively: why, in particular should the Union have as many basically similar codes or systems of civil and criminal law as member states, without arriving at a European civil[28] and criminal[29] codification, at least within the scope of its jurisdiction. This would enhance not only the protection of rights and the process of political unification, but also free exchange itself, the security of commerce, and the protection of community interests and goods, which is part of the treaty's aims and falls under the Union's jurisdiction. The main obstacle standing in the way of unification of codes, or at least of the formation of federal codes and judicial systems with a clearly distinct scope from that of state codes, is, obviously, criminal law. In systems like Italy's it is reserved to legislation by representative agencies, but this requirement could be met at community level if the European parliament were empowered with legislative functions. In short, it would be possible for a European rule of legislative law to develop as an alternative to the present trend towards a community-wide case law confusedly mixed up with national legal systems. The European Charter can certainly contribute to reaching this goal since the rights it guarantees outline a public space that goes well beyond the limited scope of the treaties.

This would obviously be a third paradigmatic shift. After case law, the legal state and the constitutional state, a fourth model: the rule of law raised to supranational level, with nothing of the old form of the state but retaining the form and substance of its articulated constitutional structure in the principles illustrated above of mere and strict legality. Of course, it would make no sense to talk of the forms that the system and hierarchy of the sources of a hypothetical supranational, specifically European rule of law would take on. Within the perspective of a constitution and a public sphere that are no longer national but supranational, we can only imagine that a constitutional space of an order higher than any other source could serve as the basis for re-establishing strict legality, similarly to the model of the constitutional state that is the limit and necessary dimension of, and intrinsic constraint to, all legitimate power. For it is precisely this space that hosts the public sphere, identifiable with the interests of all – either because they are general or because they correspond to fundamental and hence universal rights – whose guarantee the legitimacy of all public powers depends on. Re-establishing mere legality on the model of the legal state, through a reorganization of the underlying system of sources and corresponding powers on the basis of a clear redefinition and division of their competences and relationships of hierarchy and subsidiarity, depends on the articulation of the public sphere at its various levels and dimensions.

On the prospect of this third, broader model of the rule of law outlined by supranational charters of rights, however, political studies have raised theoretical doubts concerning and identified obstacles to both its viability and desirability. The necessary premise for a European or even global legal and constitutional state would be one single people, civil society, or public sphere, that does not exist;[30] therefore, a supranational legal integration, even though only limited to protecting basic rights, would amount to an imposition (which at best would remain on paper) of a single normative model, undermining pluralism of cultures, traditions, and legal experiences.

Apart from the idea of a basic political and cultural homogeneity underlying our national states, which in my opinion is false, this objection implies a conception of constitution as an organic expression of a *demos*, or at least of pre-political links and a shared sense of belonging among its recipients. I think that this communitarian belief should be overturned. A constitution is not for representing the common will of a people but for guaranteeing the rights of all, even when this runs counter to popular will. Its function is not to express the existence of a *demos* or its presumed cultural homogeneity, collective identity, or social cohesion but, quite the opposite, to guarantee by those rights the peaceful coexistence of different and potentially conflicting individuals and interests. Its basis of legitimacy, as opposed to that of ordinary laws and governmental decisions, does not come from majority consensus but from an even more important and fundamental value: the equality of everyone in basic liberties and social rights, i.e. in vital rights conferred to all, as limits and constraints precisely against the laws and governmental acts of contingent majorities.

Shared sense of belonging and constitution, political unification, and legal enforcement of equality are, furthermore, closely bound together as the experience of our own democracies has shown. It is true that the effectiveness of any constitution requires a minimum of cultural and pre-political homogeneity that, as regards the European Convention on Human Rights, is perceptible precisely, and perhaps especially, in the common constitutional traditions of the member states of the Union. But the opposite is also even truer: it is in an understanding of equality of rights as a guarantee of protecting differences of personal identity and curtailing material inequalities that a perception of others as one's equal can take root, and with it the shared sense of belonging and the collective identity of a political community. It can even be said that the equal protection of rights is not only necessary, but also sufficient for forming the only "collective identity" worth pursuing, namely one based on mutual respect instead of the mutual exclusion and intolerance generated by ethnic, national, religious, or linguistic identities. The main ingredient of political unification is legal rather than economic or monetary unification.

In short, if by "public sphere" we mean that which is in the interests of all as opposed to the private sphere that concerns individuals' interests,[31] it must be acknowledged that it mainly requires the protection of equality and those rights of all that are fundamental rights. The public sphere and civil society are thus not the premise but the effect of the constitution. It is with the constitution, i.e. the social contract, whereby it is agreed upon to protect the basic rights of everyone, that society emerges from the state of nature and a public sphere emerges as the locus of politics and a sphere of equality, distinct from the private sphere that is, by contrast, the place of economics and the sphere of inequality and difference. This is why we can say that a European public sphere will not exist for as long as Europe remains a mere common market – an area of free exchange – but will come into being precisely when equality in those rights for all that are basic rights is established and protected. Even less so will a worldwide public sphere exist as long as human rights laid down in the many conventions and declarations stay on paper, unprotected, and the law of the jungle continue to prevail in international political and economic relations.

The reasons that keep us from being optimistic about the prospects of extending constitutionalism to the international level are not, therefore, theoretical. They are all exclusively political. There is nothing to stop us believing that the idea of an international rule of law is in theory attainable. Its attainability only depends on politics, and precisely on the will of the economically and militarily strongest countries. This is what the real problem boils down to: the crisis of the project of peace and equal rights that politics itself had laid down at the end of the Second World War. The paradox lies in the crisis of political planning taking place in an age of transition in which it is certain that, in the course of just a few decades, the integration processes presently developing will lead in any case to a new world order. Politics and law hold the key to the quality of this new order: whether the West shuts itself up as in a besieged fortress, inequality, and poverty grow and new fundamentalism, wars, and violence develop, or the will prevails within the international community to give renewed momentum to that rational project of a constitutional order that the peace and the very security of our democracies depend on.

NOTES

1. See H. Kelsen, *Pure Theory of Law*, Berkeley (CA): University of California Press, 1967.
2. "Constitutional state" and "rule of law in the strong sense" are not synonyms. The rule of law in the strong sense implies that the law is in fact – even though not by right – subjected to normative principles such as fundamental liberties and the separation of powers. This can take place, as the example of England shows, because these principles have taken social and cultural root notwithstanding the absence of

a written constitution. The bi-univocal tie, today accepted virtually everywhere, between rule of law in the strong sense and constitutionalism stems from the fact that written and rigid constitutions have made these principles "positive" in nature. In doing so they have given legal guarantee to the subordination of public powers to these principle, not only in terms of spontaneous alignment by judges and legislators, but also in their formulation in positive constitutional norms and the control by a constitutional court on their possible violation. Despite the absence of a constitution, in England the experience of the rule of law realized a model of rule of law in the strong sense, to the extent of having been the inspiration for the whole evolution of the rule of law in continental Europe and the United States. However, that model has remained outside the continental development of the *Rechtsstaat* (state-under-law) and of the paradigmatic shifts that marked it.

3. The formula *auctoritas, non veritas facit legem* appears in the 1670 Latin translation of the *Leviathan* [1651]: T. Hobbes, *Leviathan, sive de Materia, Forma et Potestate Civitatis Ecclesiasticae et Civilis*, in *Opera Philosophica quae Latine Scripsit Omnia*, ed. by W. Molesworth (1839–1845), reprint Aalen: Scientia Verlag, 1965, vol. 3, chap. 26, p. 202. But Hobbes states very much the same maxim in *A Dialogue between a Philospher and a Student of the Common Law of England* [1681], in *The English Works*, ed. by W. Molesworth (1839–1845), reprint by Aalen: Scientia Verlag, 1965, vol. 6, p. 5: "It is not wisdom, but authority that makes a law".
4. This definition of natural law doctrine has been suggested by N. Bobbio, *Teoria della norma giuridica*, Torino: Giappichelli, 1958, §12, pp. 49–54.
5. "Natural law", wrote Bobbio, "was conceived of as "common law" (Aristotle called it *koinòs nomos*), and positive law as a special, or particular law in a certain civitas; therefore, on the principle that particular law prevails over general law (*lex specialis derogat generali*), positive law prevailed over natural law every time the two came into conflict"; cf. N. Bobbio, *Il positivismo giuridico* [1961], Torino: Giappichelli, 1996, pp. 13–14.
6. Cf. my *Diritto e ragione. Teoria del garantismo penale* [1989], Roma-Bari: Laterza, 2000, pp. 898–900, 904–7, 926.
7. One recalls the first page of the *Leviathan* in which the state is called "an Artificial Man" and the laws "an artificial *Reason* and *Will*" (T. Hobbes, *Leviathan* [1651], Harmondsworth: Penguin, 1985, Introduction, p. 81). "Commonwealths, or civil societies and governments", writes Locke, are "the contrivance and institution of man" (*A Second Letter Concerning Toleration* [1690], in *The Works of John Locke in Nine Volumes*, London: Rivington, 1824, vol. V.
8. As is known, the introduction of the constitutional court into the Austrian Constitution of 1.10.1920 (arts. 137–48) was the work of Hans Kelsen, who was asked by the government to develop the whole project. He himself was a member of the court for many years and a permanent referee. See in particular H. Kelsen, "La garantie juridictionnelle de la Constitution (La justice constitutionnelle)", *Revue du droit public et de la science politique*, 35 (1928).
9. See A. Pace, *La causa della rigidità costituzionale*, Padova: Cedam, 1996.
10. On Kelsen's theoretical and institutional contribution to the affirmation of the constitutional paradigm see G. Bongiovanni, Reine Rechtslehre *e dottrina giuridica dello Stato. Hans Kelsen e la costituzione austriaca del 1920*, Milano: Giuffrè, 1998.
11. H. Kelsen, *General Theory of Law and State* [1945], New York: Russell & Russell, 1961.

12. J. Bentham, *Anarchical Fallacies*, in *The Works of Jeremy Bentham*, J. Bowring (ed.), Edinburgh: William Tait, 1838–43, vol. 2.
13. Ibid.
14. Ibid.
15. On the difference between a centralized control of the constitutionality of laws through the power of the constitutional court to cancel unconstitutional laws in general (which was a feature of the Austrian constitutional model), and the American model, which empowers all judges to refuse the application of unconstitutional norms only in single, specific cases, while they stay valid and can be applied elsewhere, cf. H. Kelsen, "Judicial review of legislation: a comparative study of the Austrian and the American constitution", *Journal of Politics*, 4 (1942), 1.
16. T. Hobbes, *Leviathan*, cit., XXVI, p. 317: "it is not that *Juris prudentia*, or wisedome of subordinate Judges; but the Reason of this our Artificiall Man the Commonwealth, and his Command, that maketh Law". See also the ending of n. 3.
17. See N. Irti, *L'età della decodificazione*, Milano: Giuffrè, 1979.
18. Cf. M. Cartabia and J.H.H. Weiler, *L'Italia in Europa. Profili istituzionali e costituzionali*, Bologna: il Mulino, 2000, p. 50.
19. On the check of legitimacy by the European Court of Justice and the Italian constitutional court cf. M. Cartabia and J.H.H. Weiler, op. cit., pp. 73–98. 163–90.
20. The system of Community sources is traced by art. 249 of the Treaty.
21. This principle was established by the Court of Justice in its decision of 15.7.1964, case 6/64 *Costa/Enel*.
22. The Italian Constitutional Court has progressively aligned itself with the decisions of the European Court of Justice through a series of admissions of increasing weightiness regarding the prevalence of Community norms on Italian ordinary law, by virtue of the "limitations of sovereignty" that Italy consented to in accordance with art. 11 of the Constitution.
23. On the legitimization of war as a tool for protecting human rights see D. Zolo, *Invoking Humanity: War, Law and Global Order*, London/New York: Continuum International, 2002. See also my "Guerra 'etica' e diritto", *Ragion pratica*, 13 (1999), pp. 117–28.
24. See M.R. Ferrarese, *Le istituzioni della globalizzazione. Diritto e diritti nella società transnazionale*, Bologna: il Mulino, 2000.
25. I upheld the principle of "code reservation" in penal issues in "La pena in una società democratica", *Questione giustizia*, (1996), 3–4, pp. 537–8. According to this principle, any parliamentary decision concerning penal issues should assume the form of a Penal Code or an organic reform of it.
26. As is known, this proposal has been widely debated in sociological and political literature; cf.: J. Meade, "Full Employment, New Technologies and the Distribution of Income", *Journal of Social Policy*, 13 (1984), pp. 142–3; R. Dahrendorf, *Per un nuovo liberalismo*, Roma-Bari: Laterza, 1990, pp. 135–47, 156; M. Paci, *Pubblico e privato nei moderni sistemi di Welfare*, Napoli: Liguori, 1990, pp. 100–5.
27. Cf. M. Cartabia and J.H.H. Weiler, op. cit., pp. 60–76.
28. This is the direction legal research is moving in today, prompted by two resolutions by the European Parliament, of May 1989 and May 1994. They suggested, as an essential component to the common market, the harmonization of certain areas of private law in member states with the prospect of a common European code of private law. A commission of legal experts, convened to draft a project of European

Civil Code, coordinated by Christian von Bar, presented a new version of the *Principles of European Contract Law* at the end of 1999, published in Italy with an introduction by G. Alpa, "I principi del diritto contrattuale europeo", *Rivista critica del diritto privato*, 18 (2000), 3.

29. On the initiative of the European Commission a group of legal experts, headed by Mireille Delmas-Marty, developed a project of a *corpus juris* for the penal protection of financial interests within the European Union. See G. Grasso, *Verso uno spazio giudiziario europeo*, Milano: Giuffrè 1998; L. Picotti (ed.), *Possibilità e limiti di un diritto penale dell'Unione europea*, Milano: Giuffrè 1999.
30. In this sense, cf. D. Grimm, "Una costituzione per l'Europa?", in G. Zagrebelsky, P.P. Portinaro, J. Luther (eds), *Il futuro della costituzione*, Torino: Einaudi, 1996, pp. 339–67; D. Zolo, *Cosmopolis: Prospects for World Government*, Cambridge: Polity Press, 1997, pp. 129–34.
31. Ulpiano: *Publicum jus est quod ad statum rei Romanae spectat, privatum quod ad singulorum utilitatem* (D 1.1.1.2.).

CHAPTER 9

BEYOND THE RULE OF LAW: JUDGES' TYRANNY OR LAWYERS' ANARCHY?

Pier Paolo Portinaro

1. Like many categories of the modern political lexicon, the expression *Rechtsstaat* or "rule of law" seems to be doomed to implode because of historically stratified empirical referents and because of the complexity of contemporary legal systems. Anyone who has read the most recent legal literature on the matter will have seen over a hundred normative assumptions which, all together with no identifiable system or common canon, and selected with great variation from author to author, are taken as building blocks or obligatory premises for conceiving the *Rechtsstaat* (or the "rule of law").[1] Legal scholars, too, disagree on what constitutes the "dogmatic principle on which the *Rechtsstaat* (or the 'rule of law') stands", such as which other sub-principles are to be subsumed into it and what relationship it may have with other aspects of a constitutional legal system, e.g. fundamental rights and the principle of democracy. Indeed, it is no coincidence that this state of confusion and uncertainty had led some to suggest getting rid of the concept as an outdated and unusable ideological anachronism.[2]

In its narrowest and strictest sense, the concept of the *Rechtsstaat* is a product of the development of German state doctrine (which culminated in that peculiar weakening and legal dematerialization of its subject, which is the doctrine of the sovereignty of law).[3] In its broadest sense, however, as historians of political thought never fail to remind us, it relates back to the venerable philosophical tradition of the "government of laws" in the double meaning of government *per leges* and government *sub lege*,[4] and thus ends up getting confused with constitutionalism. On the common (to European legal systems) obeisance to the "principle of nomocracy", which states that laws and not men must reign supreme, the idea of the *Rechtsstaat* (or the "rule of law") crops up wherever progress is made towards setting a legal limit, either natural or accepted through usage, to the wielding of political power; it gains acceptance by acknowledging pluralism in legal systems and norms, drawing life from the polarity between positive law and rules of conduct that deal with *ethos* or *mos*.[5] Besides, many historians, when attempting to reconstruct the

P. Costa and D. Zolo (eds.), The Rule of Law: History, Theory and Criticism, 353–369.

concept and practice of the rule of law, which is the Western world's laboratory for legally disciplining power, see an older constitutionalism behind its modern version.[6] Despite drawing vitality from this tradition, however, the concept of "rule of law" is a pure product of modern thought. Indeed, it is quite correct to argue that "the idea of 'rule of law' comes into being whenever the idea of 'government of laws' interacts with the concept of sovereignty of the modern nation state".[7]

However, this qualification, which denotes a further stage in the development of Western institutions, is also insufficient for grasping the peculiarity of the *Rechtsstaat* (or the "rule of law"). A state in which no alternative power can limit the sovereignty of legislative power, besides recourse to natural law or to some principle of transcendent law, cannot yet be called a *Rechtsstaat* acting according to the rule of law. This is arrived at by establishing a *potestas irritans actus contrarios* and attributing it to the judiciary. This *potestas*, however, can only come into effect when the independence of the judiciary is recognized (in the history of Great Britain, for instance, with the Act of Settlement of 1701), and especially when the power of the representatives of the people to politically control the government is established. It is only with the birth of modern representative institutions, which were spawned by the great political revolutions, that conditions were created for a substantive legalization of politics. And, no less, the *Rechtsstaat* plays a moderating role of political containment and neutralization *vis-à-vis* the revolutionary energies that brought about modern parliamentary democracies; it is the product of a transformation that leads "from the primacy of the legislator as a political agent personifying the general will to the primacy of law as a legal source, as a formal, neutral expression of the authority of the state".[8]

In the strict sense, therefore, the concept of *Rechtsstaat* only serves to identify a specific period of the history of the nineteenth century post-revolutionary state and to represent the specific legal expression of the liberal middle class, freed from the restrictions and hierarchies of the old regime but also weakened with respect to the revolutionary ideology of popular sovereignty. The idea of *Rechtsstaat* achieves that synthesis of statism and liberalism that was to emerge as the ideological key to an age of extraordinarily flourishing legal science.[9] It was especially the German theory of civil society and state that laid the foundations for what was to become the doctrine of the rule of law in the proper sense for generations of continental European jurists.[10] The special focus on the idea of sovereignty and legal personality of the state made it possible to overcome the *gubernaculum/jurisdictio* dualism that still weighed on early conceptions of modern constitutionalism, including that of Montesquieu. However, the old-style polarization typical of the constitutionalist tradition lived on in the opposition described by the theorists of the *Rechtsstaat*: *richterliche Rechtsfindung* and *politische Rechtssetzung*.[11]

If we also turn our attention to the twentieth-century concept of constitutional democracy, we find three ideas underpinning the theory of the *Rechtsstaat* (or the "rule of law") incorporated within it: (1) the law gives shape to and in so doing limits state powers – the *pouvoirs constitués*; (2) legal sovereignty is exercised according to the model of the government by law, hence the principle of "statutory reservation" becomes the central tenet of the classical doctrine of the *Rechtsstaat* (or the "rule of law");[12] (3) judicial protection functions through the constitutional acknowledgement of the right to bring any abuse by private or public powers before a court. On this basis it is easy to understand how the two traditions, the German *Rechtsstaat* and the Anglo-American rule of law, have become closer, blending within the modern-day theory of constitutional democracy. The marriage of the continental European legal tradition with the Anglo-American common law–based one, in which the role of the *jurisdictio* has always been significant, seems to be functional to the recent expansion of judicial power, more of which will be discussed later. It is also true, however, that so many opinions have been formed around these fundamental assumptions that the idea of the rule of law almost seems to have imploded, as we have stated previously. Despite this, no other principle has emerged capable of representing and synthesizing the plurality of norms dealing with the leading ideas of modern-day constitutionalism within a coherent and unified construct.[13]

2. The polysemy of traditions, which go to make up the concept of "rule of law" has often been countered by the trend towards simplification, in particular in the legal debate of the early twentieth century. On the one hand, its origins were perceived as being within the medieval legal universe because that was the earliest form of what would be called the judicial state (as in the "state as guarantor of the law", according to Fritz Kern's however ambiguous definition, repeated by many authors) while, on the other, it was recognized as the specific legal foundation of the bourgeois society of today. Furthermore, if we examine classical theories, we are obliged to acknowledge that there have been many changes in the doctrine of the "rule of law" since the outset, which sometimes emphasized the legislative (Robert von Mohl), the administrative (Rudolf von Gneist), and the legal component (Otto Bähr),[14] thus paving the way not only for diversified assessments but also distortions

in argumentation. The doctrine of the liberal rule of law had successfully put an end to the "pernicious oscillation between the absolute power of a sovereign and the basic absolute rights of the individual introduced by natural law",[15] but had not been immune to other, albeit somewhat less dangerous oscillations.

As Carl Schmitt, for example, wrote in the early 1930s: "The judicial state has the semblance of a *Rechtsstaat* [or rule of law] insofar as judges pronounce the law directly and sustain it, even against the legislator who produces the norms, and against his laws".[16] On this basis, naturally, it was easy to criticize the rule of law as fundamentally conservative and substantially extraneous to the functions of government. On the other hand, however, its capacity for innovation in the interest of the middle class and economic modernizing interests was also underlined, almost to emphasize its constitutive ambiguity,. With the concept of sovereignty, the centrality of legislation entered the politics of great monarchies, and the modern state took on the characteristics of a legislative state. "What had been perceived in the states of continental Europe from the nineteenth century onwards as *Rechtsstaat* [or 'rule of law'] was in fact merely a legislative state, more precisely a parliamentary legislative state".[17] Here too, however, the emphasis on the legislative component ended up being polemically meant to confine the era of the rule of law within a period still dominated by a natural law belief in the universality and rationality of the law.

Simplifications of this kind, naturally, supported a critique of the rule of law as being substantially apolitical or anti-political in nature and hence weak and yielding to revolutionary political forces. The rule of law, thus, came into conflict with the *Machtstaat*, the state of officialdom (*Beamtenstaat*), and the ethical state of which it is merely an idealistic transformation.[18] Monarchies based on military and civilian bureaucracies on the one hand and plebiscitary democracies on the other were the traditional regimes that such historical simplifications and polemical arguments were made to serve. However, such arguments miss the underlying meaning of a concept that modern theory has introduced to explain a diverse legal-political system in which, as Niklas Luhmann has highlighted, the law is safeguarded from excessive political interference in terms of both constraints and limits of governmental decisions and the political neutrality of the judiciary. Constraints on political decisions and neutrality of judges entail each other in the framework of the rule of law. "Political neutrality of the judiciary only makes sense insofar as it is impossible, in technical-decisional terms, for the whole law to keep adapting to the swings in political consensus. And this in turn is partly impossible since a judiciary independent from politics guards the need to keep a highly complex law coherent, and rejects the grand simplifications of politics".[19]

Except for these qualifications, it must be said that definitions like "legislative state" or "judicial state" have not lost all their heuristic potential, if for no other reason than for being counter-ideal types for highlighting the specificity of present-day institutional changes. Still today, the nineteenth century political subject tends to be defined using the phrase "legal state" as opposed to the "constitutional state", which appeared in the twentieth-century, especially after the tragedies caused by totalitarianism: the basic difference was that the former relied on legislative policies only for the guarantee of basic rights, while the latter depended on a constitution, and one garrisoned by an agency reviewing legislation.[20] Many interpreters thus see again the prevailing present-day tendency in western political systems, and the peculiarity of some of them in particular (e.g. Germany), as an evolution from a parliamentary legislative state into a democratic judicial state.[21] It was on this very change that twentieth-century debate on the future of the rule of law was centred.

Being a legislative state, or an administrative state subject to the principle of "statutory reservation", the classic *Rechtsstaat* kept its state substance solidly by being a sovereign subject. The sovereignty of contemporary *Rechtsstaat* (or rule of law), by contrast, seems increasingly constrained and doubtful.[22] In such a changed situation, therefore, the classical diagnoses, which have become more and more popular in recent years point towards a "judicialization" of politics that would inevitably bring about an undue politicization of the magistracy and judicial agencies.[23]A crucial factor of this development would be a judicial body (a constitutional court as outlined by Hans Kelsen just after the First World War[24]) playing the role of "guarantor of the constitution" and entrusted not only with the review of legislation but also with promoting the actualization of the constitution and the achievement of basic rights. Critics of this constitutional innovation have repeatedly seen this very desire or need to curtail the scope of legislation and devolve it to the judiciary as the clearest manifestation of the crisis of the classical *Rechtsstaat* (or rule of law).[25] On the other hand, advocates of the review of legislation have focused on the ideological characteristics of the classical doctrine of the division of powers, pointing out how the body enabled to nullify unconstitutional laws, was indeed set up as a tribunal but, by virtue of its function, was to be considered an "organ of legislative power".[26]

On the other hand, at international level too, growing and exaggerated hopes have increasingly been pinned on the judiciary for it to be a tool in the struggle against state-committed crimes (war crimes and crimes against humanity) in the wake of a proceduralist trend of which, again, Kelsen was the most authoritative theorist, and which triggered a major theoretical/political diatribe.[27] What is called into question here seems not so much judicial bodies expropriating politics as their subservience to ideals of power and hegemonic interests with strong political connotations. In this arena, too, however, there have been an erosion of the powers of the executive (in particular on two traditional norms of international law, namely the immunity of states from judicial review and the "immunity of the organs") and a growing discretionary power and unprecedented activism of the judiciary, as well as a broader scope for criminal prosecution.[28]

3. The twentieth century, as many tendencies of its early years had suggested, drew to a close with a shifting of the balance of power towards the judiciary, a greater presence of justice in society as a whole and a widespread, growing preoccupation about a degeneration which, in the eyes of many, was producing a sea change in the "rule of law".[29] As at the beginning of the century, and especially just after the First World War, there had developed a debate on the "judicial state" and "government by judiciary",[30] so now one speaks increasingly of "judicial democracy" and "judicial guardianship", or even, in extreme terms with populist nonchalance, of judicial "despotism" and "totalitarianism", and "tyranny" or "dictatorship of the judges".[31] Today, in particular, there is a significant semantic shift. Whether it is invoked in the name of governability and the majority principle, or exorcized as the spectre of authoritarianism, plebiscitary democracy no longer has its counterpoint in representative democracy, but in judicial democracy. In particular, government by judges is again being talked about in terms of a greater politicization of the judiciary which, in the eyes of many critics, is working as a Jacobin weapon for rooting the corrupt out from the social body, or even as a conservationist force for the constitutional settings of the welfare state. On the opposite side, but again within the context of what is now a transversal anti-political party diatribe,[32] and in response to populist calls for politics to make its voice heard again by appealing directly to the people, the issue again emerges of constitutional guarantees and neutral bodies for safeguarding rights and the constitution.

It is a fact that the range of decisions that the political systems of complex societies have delegated to law courts or quasi-judicial institutions has grown in recent years: given that these societies can no longer be rationally governed in a bureaucratic and hierarchical way, nor can they be entirely entrusted to spontaneous, self-regulating mechanisms, judicial bodies find themselves playing a crucial role in a social landscape full of contrasting (and simultaneous) tendencies towards legalization and deregulation, regulation and de-institutionalization. The judge is increasingly becoming an institutional *factotum* with tasks not confined to ruling on controversies but also to settling issues that other public bodies and social institutions do not consider important enough or are unable to tackle satisfactorily. On the other hand, recourse to a judge does offer comparative advantages to citizens using the institutions over addressing over powers: the judicial power is less invasive, more open, more widespread, and less discretionary than political power proper.[33]

Various individual factors may be seen at the basis of this expansion of judicial power; the usual pre-requisites for it include the dynamics of a democratic legal system, an invigorated independence of the magistracy, a widespread culture of rights, a "revolution of growing expectations"; the equally influential pathological factors include corruption of the political classes, government inefficiency, weakness of the parliamentary opposition, which all force the magistracy to a supplementary role.[34] This can explain why intervention by the magistracy has begun to take on the semblance of legislative stopgaps and has often been interpreted as a frontal attack by the judges on the legislator and one which is not limited to ruling on single cases. At the same time, western political systems – and none so markedly as Italy – have witnessed a heightening of the role of other forces, which are (or seem) "neutral", such as the presidency of the republic or of the parliamentary houses, which inevitably leads to their becoming overexposed.[35]

Alessandro Pizzorno, a sociologist aware of the institutional dimension and the way politics works, has recently summed this up referring to a plurality of tendencies: (1) "the increased participation of judges in drafting laws"; (2) "the increased tendency of legislative and administrative bodies to delegate delicate issues to the judiciary"; (3) "broader public access to justice for resolving controversies which were traditionally dealt with by social and administrative authorities"; (4) "establishment, largely by European parliamentary democracies, ... of a review of legislation carried out by an ad hoc judicial body"; (5) the emergence and spread of a practice definable as "check for political rectitude" or "check for virtue" by the judiciary.[36] To these we must add the proliferation of "conflicts of responsibility" within a social scenario, which has been aptly defined as "organised irresponsibility".[37] Indeed, the expansion of judicial power in contemporary societies also stems from a shift in the economics of human suffering, in the sense that the latter increasingly seems to be a result of civilization, and especially of industrialization and the impact of major technologies. Overall, there is an increase in collective damages caused by an indeterminate number of actions by an indeterminate number of actors, against which ever more strong is the demand to identify the culprits and ever more problematical the attribution of individual and collective responsibility.[38] Furthermore, the scientific uncertainty in judicial rulings about responsibility in complex social processes does nothing but increase disputes, which call for a judicial settlement.[39]

In some cases, including paradigmatically Italy, the phenomenon of the rise in the power of the judiciary is largely a matter of its overexposure rather than an increase in its strength. This, on the one hand, stems from the never-ending "crime emergency" and on the other from the collapse of a political class discredited by a corruption that had become part and parcel of the system.[40] We should not be speaking here of the risk for the rule of law to be toppled by a judicial attack but rather of the attempt to reinstate normality in a situation, which has been characterized historically by what, albeit with various interpretations, has been called the "double state".[41]

4. It would be easy and somewhat misleading to concentrate on the anomalies of the Italian situation to illustrate the changes which, over recent decades, have affected how law and politics have interacted in constitutional democracies. Rather, it would be more appropriate to consider the development of the German constitutional democracy, about which doctrine has pointed to two complementary tendencies. On the one hand there is the "politicization of constitutional adjudication" by virtue of recognizing to the court "competences which are not only for reviewing legislation but also for actively promoting the 'actualization of the constitution' in the sense of 'an objective legal system of values'".[42] The passage from the idea of the constitution as guarantee to one of the constitution as indication or "directive" (Böckenförde spoke of *dirigierende Verfassung*) is at the basis of this evolution. One the other hand, however, there is an evident "judicialization of politics",[43] since legislative proposals and political decisions are affected by considerations of what positions the court could reach and what its reactions would be. Where conflict on norms exists, the court's word is final and thus it holds the ultimate sovereign power, while politics ends up merely as an excrescence of constitutional law, coinciding with "the increasingly extensive interpretation of the constitution".[44]

We can take the position of Ernst-Wolfgang Böckenförde as paradigmatic here. Böckenförde, a constitutional scholar of the Schmittian school and a judge at the court of Karlsruhe from 1983 to 1996, claimed that the passage from the classic legislative state to one watched over by constitutional case law jeopardizes the separation of judicial and legislative power, and thus both the liberal core and the democratic substance of the rule of law. There emerges a tendency towards a "judicial state of constitutional judges", which broadens the discretion of the judiciary and places the institutional equilibrium of the rule of law at risk in terms of citizens' autonomy. He points out that the court has become a "strong political (non-party) body, an Areopagus of the constitution; what sovereignty it holds by virtue of its competence for a final binding decision is increased".[45] This development comes into conflict with the democratic moment: the ever delicate balance between democracy and rule of law, which had been broken in the first half of the last century in favour of plebiscitary democracy, seems now to be skewed in favour of what could be best described as a "rule of rights". Constitutional justice is charged with being more preoccupied with guaranteeing human rights and the principle of the welfare state than with the principle of democracy. However, basic rights themselves are now being construed by constitutional case law in terms of "norms of principle", which inevitably come into conflict with the classical synthesis of democracy and rule of law. "Whoever wishes to hold firm on the determining function of a popularly elected parliament for making law – instead of rebuilding the constitutionalist framework to favour a state based on the *jurisdictio* of the constitutional court – has also to hold firm that fundamental rights (enforceable by courts) are 'merely' individual rights of freedom *vis-à-vis* state power and not also objective (and binding) norms of principle in all areas of law".[46]

Underlying Habermas's idea of the constitutional court as "custodian of deliberative democracy"[47] and Rawls's as "paradigm of public reason"[48] there is a similar mistrust of possible paternalistic involutions in constitutional justice, the belief that legal discourse can develop interpretative strategies that favour argument within the decision-making process but "cannot *replace* political discourse, which serves to lay the basis for norms and programmes and always requires the inclusion of all interested parties".[49] It is a fact that the existence of constitutional courts has had a deep impact on the conception of law in western democracies[50] and has favoured a sort of widespread review, even in countries with a centralized system of reviewing legislation, and encouraged judges to wield their interpretative powers (what is called "adjusting interpretation" of the provisions of law).[51] But, notes Rawls, the constitution "is not what the court says it is; it is what those who act constitutionally in the other branches of government allow the court to say about it".[52]

Against these risks, authors like Ottfried Höffe, call for judicial self-restraint and an ethos of judicial self-control.[53] In so doing, however, he obviously underestimates what Luhmann had pointed out many years before (although he, too, erred on the side of unilateralism), namely that "law has become too complex and the organisation of the professions too differentiated for there to be any practical significance in unity of training and professional orientation".[54] Whichever way the question is viewed, it is the moralization of the constitution through a certain conception of fundamental rights and of the role of institutions in actualizing them that enables the judge, as custodian of the constitution, to play a strategic role in contemporary power frameworks. The judge becomes custodian of a constitution in which the *potestas coercitiva* of law fades and gives way to its *potestas directiva*: and this is the major shift in the development today of the rule of law.[55]

The republican communitarian basis on which constitutional discourse is increasingly set in contemporary democracies is an indication of this moralizing tendency of which the wielders of judicial power seem to be the last custodians as the other legal professions become ever more technical. For example, the undeniable resurgence of the issue of the common good in contemporary political theory is fostered by the idea that constitutions deal extensively with issues of human values and commitments towards solidarity, responsibility, and mutual respect (from which judges draw extensively in motivating their rulings). Thus, it is the task of politics to reconcile interests of the custodians of the judicial state to give a higher definition of common good.[56] It is equally undeniable that for many the new frontier of the rule of law seems to be the legal ascertainment of truth in so-called truth commissions. "In the constitutional state", wrote, for example, Peter Häberle, "the principle of the *rule of law* in all its forms builds what is perhaps the sturdiest bridge towards the unending process of seeking the truth".[57] One does wonder, however, if this moral casting of public discourse implies a real risk of judicial hegemony for contemporary democracies or whether the most serious threats to the survival of the rule of law are to be sought elsewhere.

5. Does progress, then, proceed in the light of these developments and with the emergence of new agencies of international justice towards a planetary judicial state or at least, in Kelsen's terms, toward a supranational centralization of the judicial function? Little (indeed nothing for the former) leads us to such a conclusion. At most, what appears is a dissociation between these dynamics of expansion of judicial power and the localization of real powers in the material constitution of societies

and the international community. The globalization process seems to proceed more towards the supremacy of lawyers' partisan and mercenary "expertocracies" that take strategic advantage of the opportunities and resources of a litigation society than towards a government or an international "regime" of judges. Western state institutions have proven and still prove difficult to export. This has led to the establishment of the *Machtstaat* (military and repressive apparatuses, coercive organization, and disciplining techniques) and not of the rule of law; the military state is not hard to export but it is difficult to transplant a judicial democracy that does not degenerate into serving the aims of a politicized justice. More than the figure of the (constitutional) judge with scales for balancing different values and ethical/legal principles, it is the "merchant of law" who now dominates the field, expanding his/her power quantitatively and qualitatively.[58]

Alongside jurists specialized in adjudication, in the practice of worldwide civil society, we now find specialists in political lobbying working at major federal or national centres of executive power and litigators specialized in business cases. These are indeed the categories of lawyers who are acquiring an increasingly high profile in the arena of globalization.[59] Against the *ethos* of impartiality serving truth-seeking and the general interest, the legal Machiavellianism of these legal strategists takes them step by step far from the cultural foundations of the western Christian constitutional state (setting them at irreversible loggerheads with the jurist custodians of the constitutions). But above all, they place their skills at the service of transnational corporations of power against which the de-legitimized national state institutions seem ever less able to erect barriers of guarantee to defend the fundamental rights of individuals who have unfortunately found themselves caught up in the wheels of globalization.

The problem for the rule of law at the dawning of the 21st century is not, therefore, the risk of abuse of power by public bodies, but the threats from major concentrations of private power (starting from data protection and the discipline of information flows).[60] Privatisation processes have radically redrawn the map of economic constitutions, first and foremost in the countries in which a rapid dismantling of collectivist economics has occurred.[61] Furthermore, however, they are posing a serious threat to the social and cultural foundations of those constitutional democracies which, in the course of the twentieth century, conserved and creatively innovated the heritage of the classic rule of law that gave legal shape to western liberal civilisation. The real guardians of the new order are now monetary agencies and financial institutions above and beyond democratic control and imbued with a somewhat selective perception of the principles of the rule of law.[62]

It is undeniable that those who care about the rule of law are in the first instance sensitive to the private dimension. Such, for example, is the conception of Friedrich August von Hayek that belongs to the common law tradition and has become paradigmatic for the neo-liberalism (or libertarianism) of globalization according to which the function of the judge is limited to issues of spontaneous order so that the judge is but an aid to the natural process of selection of norms in a market society.[63] What the legal philosophy of Hayek (and his many and repetitive epigones) seems to ignore is the concentration of powers in a market society that is very far from the harmonious idealizations of the moral philosophers of the good Scottish school. It is not *super partes* tribunals or magistrates whose professional duty is to seek out truth and impartiality that today settle legal controversies, but large organized law firms capable of mobilizing appropriate political support, and real multinationals of commercial law.

The "spontaneous" evolution of open societies seems oriented towards a "dual system of justice", in which a "tailored" justice for the wielders of economic power is set alongside a "mass justice for 'ordinary' consumers".[64] It is precisely this new dualism that threatens the survival (and credibility) of the rule of law in the political systems of the age of globalization. Momentous rulings that can cause hardship to large multinational corporations are more the exception than the rule. There is therefore a danger of passing from a democracy supervised by constitutional judges[65] to a civil society of legal corporations that is in fact a litigation society, in which the interests of the most powerful, and the most reckless strategies always come out on top. Such a society would be bereft of the counterweight which, to safeguard the coherence of a highly complex legal system, erects protective barriers against "the grand simplifications of politics", and it would also lack counterweights against the new, transnationally organized forms of large-scale crime.

In the light of these developments, the critique of judicial expertocracy runs the risk of being aimed against the wrong target. If anything, it is obvious why judges are facing the offensive firepower of converging forces: they are seen as the custodians not only of a commutative justice that aims to abate the inequalities of globalization[66] and a distributive justice that aims to ease the straining of a society characterized by competition and conflicts of private interests, but also of a retributive justice and, as such, they are malevolently seen as an oligarchy of avengers. In particular, they appear on the one hand as the guarantors of the liberal-social-democratic compromise that underlies the contemporary rule of law – as well as civil, political, and social rights – while on the other the champions of a check for legality (and public morality) that clashes with the tendency, held by many to be physiological, towards the corruption inherent in the dynamics of globalized markets, working under extremely heterogeneous cultural, social, and political conditions. And yet the worldwide civil society that is emerging with great difficulty and conflict, has need for, not so much of the national civil societies Hegel looked to in his classical synthesis, but of an administration of justice and a class of competent, determined, and impartial jurists.

NOTES

1. K. Sobota, *Das Prinzip Rechtsstaat. Verfassungs- und verwaltungsrechtliche Aspekte*, Tübingen: Mohr Siebeck, 1997, p. 527. In this work, the author performs a useful exercise in analysing and classifying legal rulings (from the principle of proportionality to the principle of publicity and so on for a total of no fewer than 142 items), which have been set (in some way) in relation to the concept of rule of law. Cf. E. Schmidt-Assmann, "Der Rechtsstaat", in J. Isensee and P. Kirchhof (eds), *Handbuch des Staatsrechts*, Heidelberg: Müller, 1995, vol. I, pp. 987–1043.
2. See Ph. Kunig, *Das Rechtsstaatsprinzip*, Tübingen: Mohr Siebeck, 1986. In the literature of the second half of the twentieth century interest in the rule of law has been replaced by the doctrine of human rights, see again K. Sobota, op. cit., pp. 8–9. This is well documented in Italian literature: the latest example is the debate on fundamental rights initiated by Luigi Ferrajoli in the journal *Teoria politica* (1998–2000). On fundamental rights, see also P. Häberle, *Le libertà fondamentali nello Stato costituzionale*, Roma: Nis, 1993 (part tr. of *Die Wesensgehaltgarantie des Art. 19 Abs. 2 Grundgesetz*, Heidelberg: Müller, 1983).
3. Cf. E.-W. Böckenförde, "Entstehung und Wandel des Rechtsstaatsbegriffs", in id. *Staat, Gesellschaft, Freiheit. Studien zur Staatstheorie und zum Verfassungsrecht*, Frankfurt a. M: Suhrkamp, 1976, pp. 65–92; M. Tohidipur (ed.), *Der bürgerliche Rechtsstaat*, Frankfurt a.M,: Suhrkamp, 1976; M. Stolleis, *Geschichte des öffentlichen Rechts in Deutschland*, vol. II, *Staatsrechtslehre und Verwaltungswissenschaft 1800–1914*, München: Beck, 1992. For French literature see M.J. Redor, *De l'Etat legal à l'Etat de droit. L'evolution des conceptions de la doctrine publiciste française 1879–1914*, Paris: Economica, 1991.
4. Cf. N. Bobbio, "Governo delle leggi e governo degli uomini", in *Il futuro della democrazia*, Torino: Einaudi, 1991, pp. 175 ff.; L. Ferrajoli, *Diritto e ragione. Teoria del garantismo penale*, Roma-Bari: Laterza, 1989, pp. 895 ff. For two classic analyses see F. Neumann, *Die Herrschaft des Gesetzes*, Frankfurt a. M.: Suhrkamp, 1980; M. Villey, *La formation de la pensée juridique moderne*, Paris: Montchrestien 1975.
5. Cf. P. Prodi, *Una storia della giustizia. Dal pluralismo dei fori al moderno dualismo tra coscienza e diritto*, Bologna: il Mulino, 2000, p. 12.
6. See C.H. McIlwain, *Constitutionalism: Ancient and Modern*, Ithaca (NY): Cornell University Press, 1947; N. Matteucci, *Lo Stato moderno. Lessico e percorsi*, Bologna:

il Mulino, 1993. For a recent synthesis M. Fioravanti, *Costituzione*, Bologna: il Mulino, 1999; see also id. "Costituzione e Stato di diritto", in *La scienza del diritto pubblico. Dottrine dello Stato e della costituzione tra Otto e Novecento*, Milano: Giuffrè, 2001, p. 577.

7. E. Santoro, Common law *e costituzione nell'Inghilterra moderna. Introduzione al pensiero di Albert Venn Dicey*, Torino: Giappichelli, 1999, p. 2, and the contribution by the same author in this book.
8. Cf. M. Fioravanti, "Lo Stato di diritto come forma di Stato. Notazioni preliminari sulla tradizione europeo-occidentale", in id., *La scienza del diritto pubblico*, p. 863.
9. Ibid., p. 867.
10. Cf. H. Hofmann, "Geschichtlichkeit und Universalitätsanspruch des Rechtsstaats", *Der Staat*, 34 (1995), pp. 132. On the polarity of natural/positive law in the theory of the rule of law see D. Klippel (ed.), *Naturrecht im 19. Jahrhundert. Kontinuität-Inhalt-Funktion-Wirkung*, Goldbach: Keip, 1997.
11. H. Hofmann, *Das Recht des Rechts, das Recht der Herrschaft und die Einheit der Verfassung*, Berlin: Duncker & Humblot, 1998, p. 40.
12. I here refer to the literature discussed in my "Legalità (principio di)", in *Enciclopedia delle scienze sociali*, Roma: Istituto dell'Enciclopedia Italiana, 1996, vol. V, pp. 216–25 and to R. Guastini, "Legalità (principio di)", e "Legge (riserva di)", in *Digesto delle discipline pubblicistiche*, vol. IX, Torino: Utet, 1994, pp. 84–97 and 163–73.
13. K. Sobota, op. cit., p. 527.
14. See: K. Sobota, op. cit. (particularly the whole second part of the volume); R. Ogorek, *Richterkönig oder Subsumtionsautomat? Zur Justiztheorie im 19. Jahrhundert*, Frankfurt a.M.: Klostermann, 1986.
15. Cf. M. Fioravanti, "Costituzione e Stato di diritto", p. 590.
16. Cf. C. Schmitt, *Legalität und Legitimität*, München-Leipzig: Duncker & Humblot, 1932, It. tr. "Legalità e legittimità", in *Le categorie del 'politico'*, Bologna: il Mulino, 1972, pp. 213, 215 ff.
17. Ibid., pp. 211–12. Along these lines E. Forsthoff, *Rechtsstaat im Wandel*, München: Beck, 1976; E.-W. Böckenförde, "Entstehung und Wandel des Rechtsstaatsbegriffs", passim.
18. For a critical reconstruction see L. Ferrajoli, *La sovranità nel mondo moderno. Nascita e crisi dello Stato nazionale*, Milano: Anabasi, 1995.
19. Cf. N. Luhmann, *Politische Planung*, Opladen: Westdeutscher Verlag, 1971, p. 49.
20. See L. Ferrajoli, "Garanzia", *Parolechiave*, 19 (1999), p. 20.
21. Cf. E.-W. Böckenförde, *Staat, Verfassung, Demokratie. Studien zur Verfassungstheorie und zum Verfassungsrecht*, Frankfurt a.M: Suhrkamp, 1991, p. 190.
22. Cf. N. Matteucci, *Lo Stato moderno*, p. 79: "the post-modern state can be described and synthesized as the decline of sovereignty or, more appropriately, sovereign power".
23. The most radical diagnostics and criticism of the expansion of the political power of the judiciary was produced by Carl Schmitt; see C. Schmitt, *Der Hüter der Verfassung* [1929], Berlin: Dunker & Humblot, 1969; id., *Verfassungslehre*, München/Leipzig: Duncker & Humblot, 1928.
24. See G. Bongiovanni, *Reine Rechtslehre e dottrina giuridica dello Stato. Hans Kelsen e la costituzione austriaca del 1920*, Milano: Giuffrè, 1998.

25. See L. Lombardi, *Saggio sul diritto giurisprudenziale*, Milano: Giuffrè, 1967; M. Cappelletti, *Giudici legislatori?*, Milano: Giuffrè, 1984; id., *Les pouvoirs des juges*, Paris-Aix: Economica, 1990; R. Wassermann, *Die richterliche Gewalt. Macht und Verantwortung des Richters in der modernen Gesellschaft*, Heidelberg: Schneider, 1985; G. Orrù, "Giudici sovrani?" in M. Basciu (ed.), *Crisi e metamorfosi della sovranità*, Milano: Giuffrè, 1996.
26. This, as is known, is the thesis of H. Kelsen, propounded in the course of his controversy with Carl Schmitt and the traditional *Staatslehre*.
27. Cf. D. Zolo, "Il globalismo giudiziario di Hans Kelsen", in id., *I signori della pace. Una critica del globalismo giuridico*, Roma: Carocci, 1988, pp. 21–48; id., *Invoking Humanity. War, Law and Global Order*, London/New York: Continuum International, 2002, pp. 99 ff. For an overall account see M.L. Volcansek (ed.), *Law Above Nations. Supranational Courts and the Legalization of Politics*, Graimesville: University Press of Florida, 1997.
28. For significant precedents cf. A. Cassese, *Violenza e diritto nell'era nucleare*, Roma-Bari: Laterza, 1986, pp. 151 ff. On the issues of international criminal justice see G. Vassalli, *La giustizia internazionale penale. Studi*, Milano: Giuffrè, 1995; F. Lattanzi and E. Sciso (eds), *Dai Tribunali penali internazionali "ad hoc" ad una Corte permanente*, Napoli: Editoriale Scientifica, 1995; S. Clark and M. Sann (eds), *The Prosecutions of International Crimes*, New Brunswick: Transaction Publishers, 1996; O. Höffe, *Gibt es ein interkulturelle Strafrecht? Ein philosophischer Versuch*, Frankfurt a.M: Suhrkamp, 1999.
29. See C.N. Tate and E.T. Vallinder (eds), *The Global Expansion of Judicial Power*, New York: New York University Press, 1995; see also "The judicialisation of politics: a world-wide phenomenon", *International Political Science Review*, 15 (1994), 2; A. O'Neill, *The Government of Judges: The Impact of the European Court of Justice on the Constitutional Order of the United Kingdom*, Firenze: European University Institute Press, 1993; J. Weiler, "The quiet revolution: the European Court of Justice and its interlocutors", *Comparative Political Studies*, 26 (1994), pp. 510–53.
30. Cf. L.B. Boudin, "Government by judiciary", *Political Science Quarterly*, 26 (1911), pp. 238–70 and the literature on oligarchy and bureaucracy of the judiciary including books such as G.E. Roe, *Our Judicial Oligarchy* (1912); E. Fuchs, *Schreibjustiz und Richterkönigtum* (1907); E. Lambert, *Le gouvernement des juges et la lutte contre la législation sociale aux Etats-Unis* (1921). For a history of the "social litigation system" see E.A. Purcell, jr., *Litigation and Inequality. Federal Diversity Jurisdiction in Industrial America, 1870–1958*, New York/Oxford: Oxford University Press, 1992.
31. For bibliographical information see: E. Bruti Liberati, "Potere e giustizia", in E. Bruti Liberati, A. Ceretti and A. Giasanti (eds), *Governo dei giudici. La magistratura tra diritto e politica*, Milano: Feltrinelli, 1996, pp. 190 ff.; see also L.M. Friedman, *Total Justice*, New York: Russel Sage, 1994; A. Garapon, *Le gardien des promesses. Justice et démocratie*, Paris: Jacob, 1996.
32. See K. von Beyme, *Die politische Klasse im Parteienstaat*, Frankfurt a.M.: Suhrkamp, 1993.
33. Cf. C. Guarnieri and P. Pederzoli, *La democrazia giudiziaria*, Bologna: il Mulino, 1997, p. 9, with reference to R.C. Cramton, "Judicial lawmaking and administration in the Leviathan state", *Public Administration Review*, 36 (1976), pp. 551–5. On the discretionary power of the judiciary see A. Barak, *Judicial Discretion*, New Haven: Yale University Press, 1989.

34. Cf. C.N. Tate, "Why the expansion of judicial power", in C.N. Tate and E.T. Vallinder (eds), *The Global Expansion of Judicial Power*, pp. 28 ff. On Italy cf. S. Righettini, "La politicizzazione di un potere neutrale. Magistratura e crisi italiana", *Rivista italiana di scienza politica*, 25 (1995), pp. 227–65; S. Rodotà, "Magistratura e politica in Italia", in E. Bruti Liberati, A. Ceretti and A. Giasanti (eds), *Governo dei giudici*, pp. 17–30; G. Gargani and C. Panella, *In nome dei pubblici ministeri. Dalla Costituente a Tangentopoli: storia di leggi sbagliate*, Milano: Mondadori, 1998. For the German debate see Ch. Koller, *Die Staatsanwaltschaft. Organ der Judikative oder Exekutivbehörde? Die Stellung der Anklagebehörde und die Gewaltenteilung des Grundgesetzes*, Frankfurt a.M.: Lang, 1997.
35. On the role played by independent administrative authorities see A. Predieri, *L'erompere delle autorità amministrative indipendenti*, Firenze: Passigli, 1997; F. Bassi and F. Merusi (eds), *Mercati e amministrazioni indipendenti*, Milano: Giuffrè, 1993.
36. A. Pizzorno, *Il potere dei giudici. Stato democratico e controllo della virtù*, Roma-Bari: Laterza, 1999, pp. 12–13. On the phenomenon of the growth and strengthening of judicial power see K. Holland (ed.), *Judicial Activism in Comparative Perspective*, London: MacMillan, 1991; the cited monograph *The Judicialisation of Politics: A World-wide Phenomenon*; C.N. Tate and T. Vallinder (eds.), *The Global Expansion of Judicial Power*; A. Ceretti and A. Giasanti (eds), *Governo dei giudici. La magistratura tra diritto e politica*.
37. See U. Beck, *Gegengifte. Die organisierte Unverantwortlichkeit*, Frankfurt a.M.: Suhrkamp, 1988.
38. See V.W. Lübbe, *Verantwortung in komplexen kulturellen Prozessen*, Freiburg: Alber, 1998.
39. Cf. F. Stella, *Giustizia e modernità. La protezione dell'innocente e la tutela delle vittime*, Milano: Giuffrè, 2001, pp. 309 ff.
40. See D. Della Porta, *Lo scambio occulto. Casi di corruzione politica in Italia*, Bologna: il Mulino, 1992.
41. See: C.G. Rossetti, *L'attacco allo Stato di diritto. Le associazioni segrete e la Costituzione*, Napoli: Liguori, 1994; T. Klitsche De La Grange, *Il doppio Stato*, Soveria Mannelli: Rubbettino, 2001.
42. Cf. G.E. Rusconi, "Quale 'democrazia costituzionale'? La Corte federale nella politica tedesca e il problema della costituzione europea", *Rivista italiana di scienza politica*, 27 (1997), p. 279.
43. Cf. J. Isensee, "Die Verfassung als Vaterland. Zur Staatsverdrängung der Deutschen", in A. Mohler (ed.), *Wirklichkeit als Tabu*, München: Oldenbourg, 1989, pp. 11–36; E.-W. Böckenförde, "Grundrechte als Grundsatznormen. Zur gegenwärtigen Lage der Grundrechtsdogmatik", in id., *Staat, Verfassung, Demokratie*.
44. See J. Ipsen, *Richterrecht und Verfassung*, Berlin: Duncker & Humblot, 1975; D. Simon, *Die Unabhängigkeit des Richters*, Darmstadt: Wissenschaftliche Buchgesellschaft, 1975; F. Müller, *Richterrecht*, Berlin: Duncker & Humblot, 1986; M. Reinhardt, *Konsistente Jurisdiktion. Grundlegung einer verfassungsrechtlichen Theorie der rechtsgestaltenden Rechtssprechung*, Tübingen: Mohr Siebeck, 1997; G. Orrù, *Richterrecht. Il problema della libertà e autorità giudiziale nella dottrina tedesca contemporanea*, Milano: Giuffrè, 1984.
45. E.-W. Böckenförde, "Grundrechte als Grundsatznormen", p. 191. On the relationship between democracy and rule of law cf. ibid., pp. 365 ff.
46. Ibid., p. 194. Cf. E.-W. Böckenförde, "Verfassungsgerichtsbarkeit. Strukturfragen, Organisation, Legitimation", in *Staat, Nation, Europa. Studien zur Staatslehre, Verfassungstheorie und Rechtsphilosophie*, Frankfurt a.M.: Suhrkamp, 1999, pp. 157 ff.

47. J. Habermas, *Faktizität und Geltung. Beiträge zur Diskurstheorie des Rechts und des demokratischen Rechtsstaat*, Frankfurt a.M.: Suhrkamp, 1992, p. 288.
48. See J. Rawls, *Political Liberalism*, New York: Columbia University Press, 1993, pp. 127 ff.
49. J. Habermas, *Faktizität und Geltung*, p. 279. On the relationship between democracy and rule of law see id., *Die Einbeziehung des Anderen*, Frankfurt a.M.: Suhrkamp, 1996.
50. For an overall account see G. Zagrebelsky, *Il diritto mite. Legge diritti giustizia*, Torino: Einaudi, 1992.
51. Cf. R. Romboli, "Giudicare la legge? La legge 'giusta' nello stato costituzionale", in E. Ripepe (ed.), *Interrogativi sul diritto 'giusto'*, Pisa: SEU, 2000, p. 106. See also E.-W. Böckenförde, "Grundrechte als Grundsatznormen", p. 186.
52. J. Rawls, *Political Liberalism*, p. 130.
53. Cf. O. Höffe, "Wie viel Politik ist dem Verfassungsgericht erlaubt?", *Der Staat*, 38 (1999), pp. 182 ff; E-W. Böckenförde, "Grundrechte als Grundsatznormen", pp. 191 ff.
54. Cf. N. Luhmann, *Politische Planung*, p. 52.
55. See: G.F. Schuppert and C. Bunke (eds), *Bundesverfassungsgericht und gesellschaftlicher Grundkonsens*, Baden-Baden: Nomos, 2000; H. Vorländer, "Die Suprematie der Verfassung. Über das Spannungsverhältnis von Demokratie und Konstitutionalismus", in W. Leidhold (ed.), *Politik und Politeia. Formen und Probleme politischer Ordnung*, Würzburg: Königshausen & Neumann, 2000, pp. 373 ff.
56. Cf. G. Frankenberg, *Die Verfassung der Republik. Autorität und Solidarität in der Zivilgesellschaft*, Frankfurt a.M.: Suhrkamp, 1997, p. 21; P. Häberle, "Die Gemeinwohlproblematik in rechtswissenschaftlicher Sicht", in id., *Europäische Rechtskultur. Versuch einer Annäherung in zwölf Schritten*, Frankfurt a.M.: Suhrkamp 1997, pp. 323–54.
57. P. Häberle, *Diritto e verità*, Torino: Einaudi, 2000, p. 99.
58. See Y. Dezalay, *Marchands de droit: la restructuration de l'ordre juridique international par les multinationales du droit*, Paris: Fayard, 1992; G. Teubner, "Nach der Privatisierung? Diskurskonflikte im Privatrecht", *Zeitschrift für Rechtssoziologie*, 19 (1998), pp. 8–36.
59. See Y. Dezalay, op. cit., passim.
60. See S. Rodotà, *Tecnologie e diritti*, Bologna: il Mulino, 1995; id., *Tecnopolitica. La democrazia e le nuove tecnologie della comunicazione*, Roma-Bari: Laterza, 1997.
61. See the fundamental J.A. Kämmerer, *Privatisierung. Typologie - Determinanten - Rechtspraxis - Folgen*, Tübingen: Mohr Siebeck, 2001.
62. See S. Strange, *Mad Money: When Markets Outgrow Governments*, Ann Arbor: University of Michigan Press, 1998.
63. See F.A. von Hayek, *Law, Legislation and Liberty*, London: Routledge, pp. 1973–9. Francesco Viola underlines that according to Hayek the function of the judge is not to recognize rights but to protect expectations; cf. F. Viola, *Autorità e ordine del diritto*, Torino: Giappichelli, 1987, p. 173.
64. See Y. Delazay, op. cit., passim.
65. "Supervised" in the sense the concept is used by H. Willke in his *Supervision des Staates*, Frankfurt a.M.: Suhrkamp, 1997. By the same author see *Atopia. Studien zur atopischen Gesellschaft*, Frankfurt a.M.: Suhrkamp, 2001.
66. See L. Gallino, *Globalizzazione e disuguaglianze*, Roma-Bari: Laterza, 2000.

CHAPTER 10

THE RULE OF LAW AND GENDER DIFFERENCE

Anna Loretoni

1 PREMISE

The philosophical and legal project of modernity has been described by many authors in terms of a gradual establishment of individualism. The experience of the modern individual, set free from the traditional social bonds that would place her within a preset order, is that of an isolated ego. According to Norbert Elias's insightful account, in previous stages individuals perceived themselves as members of communities, classes, and family groups with a predominance of "we-identities", whereas with modernity individual identity (the "I-identity") has come to play a decisive role. Thus, the experience of modern identity is totally new: it is no longer circumscribed by the clear-cut and rigid boundaries of a fully controllable environment, but is rather the reflective outcome of an open-ended individual project.[1] Yet, it now appears that the group identity processes[2] that seemed to connote only the pre-modern stages of social development are instead a constant of Western democracies – a paradoxical product of modernity, according to some authors – which is far from being a contingent relic. Hence, today's critical reflection on the rule of law has to deal with this issue.

The emergence of differences claiming recognition in the public space – both legal and political – calls for the allocation of goods and resources to individuals with a specific collective identity. This is a crisis factor, or anyhow an unprecedented challenge, for the role and function of law in contemporary societies. Above all, the increasing presence of groups on the political scene has put under significant strain the traditional characteristics of the rule of law in its liberal, nineteenth-century version. This strain has even led some authors to speak of a crisis, if not the very end, of the classical formulation of the rule of law.[3]

The traditional features of law were shaped against a social background very different from the present one: it was a highly individualistic social arrangement where collective identities were rather unusual. The many examples of so-called sector legislation, lobbied for

P. Costa and D. Zolo (eds.), The Rule of Law: History, Theory and Criticism, 371–386.

by groups capable of organizing their interests, were interpreted as overcoming the "principle of generality and abstractness"[4] of law. What is more, contemporary legislators face an increasingly differentiated reality, not only in terms of interests but of values, and this too is due to the presence of groups with very different interests and cultures. It follows that legislators are led to assume pluralism itself as the starting point of their action, i.e. as a datum to be taken into account. This becomes even more important when the law concerns matters directly affecting the realm of private life or personal freedom. The heterogeneity of lifestyles – another typical trait of contemporary societies – makes it difficult, for example, to assume one generalized and standardized model of interpersonal relationships, unlike what might happen in less diverse social contexts.[5] This is the significance of claims in the field of social rights, for example, by groups pressing for the official recognition of a full range of personal choices and not only – as it has long been the case – of the heterosexual family model.[6] The old conceptualization of the welfare state, which viewed the family as the pillar of society, should be revised in the light of a different view of affective relationships allowing, at the very least, for the idea of plural family models.[7]

A deeper reflection on the issue of "collective rights" requires considering how radically the claim for recognition of collective identities challenges, in the legal field, one of the central assumptions of the classical notion of the "rule of law", i.e. the individual as the sole reference – starting and end point – of law-making. Moreover, this is one element that calls into question both the liberal and the democratic understanding of the rule of law, since the latter has, in fact, retained the original individualism. Accepting to challenge of responding to the issue of group identity leads us to welcome a conception of law that is not confined to the protection of individual freedom, well-being, and security – regardless of differences, e.g. the conditions of the so-called minority cultures – but demands more from the state, i.e. the legal protection of collective identities.[8]

2 THE FEMINISM OF DIFFERENCE

Various theories have tried to legitimize the transformations introduced by the reality of different groups and their claims for public recognition, and feminism is undoubtedly one of the most relevant.[9] What liberal theorists view as a corruption of the rule of law paradigm – in its liberal, democratic, and social versions – is taken by feminists to be something which results from the very limitations of the universalistic conception of law and is even desirable, in certain respects. If there is a common trait of feminist thought, from its philosophical to its psychological and political-legal versions, this is the critique of the idea of universality and neutrality, typical of liberal thinking and deeply embedded in its theoretical paradigms. Through a process of deconstruction and unveiling, feminism has been able to identify within law, especially within the neutral and impartial conception of legality typical of liberal thinking, a form that confers an appearance of neutrality to theoretical categories that in fact entail an implicit adherence to a given political and ideological model.

As is well known, this critical approach to law was not part of women's earlier reflection and politics. So-called emancipationist feminism viewed the legal discourse, in particular the attainment of political and social rights, as conducive to a more egalitarian condition of women within society and their full citizenship. In that context, the theoretical issue was mere formal inequality and the aim was extending to women the range of rights once reserved exclusively to men. In political discourse, too, women's condition was thematized not in terms of its specific difference – as has been the case since the 1980s – but in terms of exclusion from a world that was not challenged or questioned but only criticized for its partiality. The demand was for inclusion and no radical changes were envisaged. Nevertheless, ever since "difference" has become a value, as modern feminism's distanced itself from so-called emancipationist feminism, women's thought has sought to unveil – behind paradigms, categories, and values – the apparent neutrality of the legal discourse, showing how at its core reigned a specific normative vision of the agent. Anything but sexless, neutral, colourless, and destitute of a specific membership to a social class, the modern individual of the Western societies is heavily conditioned by all these factors: it has taken up the characteristics established by the dominant groups.[10]

Starting with the premise of a different gender identity, feminist thinking has criticized the notion of equality as assimilation and homologation. In particular, given that law defines what is legitimate and what is not, it applies a binary logic with very strong effects in terms of exclusion and discrimination. What the feminist movement demands from the traditional logic of law is an increased sensitivity to the specific character of subjective identities, the abandonment of *false* universalism and the adoption of an approach able to see individuals in the context of their specific social relations. Martha Minow's "social-relations approach",[11] for example, is in line with this trend. By acknowledging the dilemmas resulting from the plethora of differences characterizing each social context, Minow proposes a legal model that no longer functions in terms of opposing alternatives rooted in generalizing categories. She transposes to the normative level the peculiarities of the various situations and contexts and centres her proposal on the specific social location of each individual. Hence, feminism definitively breaks away the classical paradigm of liberal law and questions the very model of individual rights, seeing them as a reflection of the specific liberal vision of the individual.

Whilst recognizing the effectiveness of strategies seeking to affirm specific female rights, it is sometimes argued that such attempts have inadequate or even perverse effects. Instead, the ideas of "care" or "responsibility towards"[12] are advanced, by arguing that they are better suited to represent individuals' relational nature and the characteristics of specific situations in which they find themselves. According to Wolgast, since individuals are atoms indistinguishable one from the other, their rights must be equally so: in other words, the concept of individual rights is a natural consequence of atomism.[13] Therefore, emphasis is placed on the discourse of rights increasingly becoming a conceptual grid used to interpret reality as a whole: a grid not lacking in value or utility but with limits that should be recognized. Claiming a specific right puts its holder in a position entitling him or her to demand something from another being. However, the problems with "equal" law stem from the assumption that relationships among individuals take place between autonomous subjects who are, above all, in a position of absolute parity. According to this model, each individual is responsible for himself or /herself, even when he or she is in a blatantly inferior position. A telling example of such logic is the case of patients' rights, where the doctor's responsibilities towards the patient are seen as unrelated to the latter's necessary condition of dependency from the former. The patient is thought of as if he or she were a healthy person and the specifics of his or her conditions are not reflected on the normative level. By referring to the common humanity connecting individuals, liberal theories of justice equally fail to consider individuals in their distinctive particularities.[14] It seems that what is relevant is not what differentiates a given individual and makes her a unique being but rather what she shares with all other individuals and what makes her similar to them.

The individualistic structure of the modern theory of rights derives from the very nature of modern constitutions, which are grounded, as recalled by Habermas, on the rationalistic jurisprudence that sees citizens as deciding between them to set up a community ruled by positive law.[15] Similarly, it is the individual person that is the holder of individual rights, independently of her social relations and her belonging to diverse groups. While at the legal level only individual rights can be brought before a court, in the political arena it is always collective players that interact and debates on choices affecting the community or some of its parts, not individuals as such. It is precisely this reality, increasingly apparent in modern democracies, that has caused deep questioning of the idea of the rule of law and especially of the liberal conception of rights as exclusively individual. As is well known, in his debate with Charles Taylor on the need to acknowledge collective forms of identity, Jürgen Habermas claimed that the rule of law cannot require that the state actively promote given conceptions of a "good life" – as advocated by communitarians – not even on the basis of the alleged falseness of liberal neutrality. Nonetheless, he believes that the protection of individuals often entails the protection of the social contexts where individual identities may be guaranteed. In such cases, the formalism of the rule of law is not upheld *sic et simpliciter* and its action for the defence of individuals is made more complex by the awareness of the existing links between the individual and collective domain. In the case of the "welfare state", for instance, the traditional conception of the rule of law as merely the protection of the individual from the always-likely spillover effect of power is superseded. As Habermas argues, by focusing on the intimate link between the rule of law and democracy, it becomes obvious that the "system of rights" cannot ignore either social inequalities or cultural differences. For individual holders of rights are endowed with identities that ought to be conceived of intersubjectively. "Individuals (and thus also legal subjects) acquire an identity only through phenomena of social interaction."[16]

The above perspective underlines the importance of different life contexts in which individuals effectively realize their recognized rights and thus it is not necessary to employ – as proposed by Taylor – a counter-model to correct the traditional individualistic understanding of the system of rights. In other words, formalistic liberalism, whereby individual identities are conceived of as monads, despite its short-sightedness, has self-corrective features that save it from having to abandon the individualistic paradigm of the rule of law in the name of acknowledging collective identities – which, in the end, could produce even more serious damage to individual freedoms.

3 PUBLIC AND PRIVATE: A SUPERFICIAL DIVIDE

Ambiguity has been said to be constitutive of law: legal obligations both constrain and set free.[17] The relationship between feminist thinking and law seems to confirm this ambiguity, apparent not only in the historical succession from "emancipationist feminism" to the "feminism of difference". Indeed, the ambivalence of the legal discourse can be often observed among scholars endorsing the "feminism of difference" approach, and gives rise to two strands of thought: some authors, in spite of their cautious approach to law, are willing to exploit its potential, whereas others believe that law is absolutely incapable of providing adequate answers to women's issues. Scholars of the first group have produced valuable new contributions to the legal discourse and among them we should recall at least the contributions of Adrien Howe and Catharine MacKinnon.

Starting with a non-atomistic conception of individuals that questions the traditional separation between the public and private domains, Howe elaborates the interesting formula of "social injury".[18] This stands for a violation having a collective effect, regarding women as a group. Therefore, a new way of interpreting the single offensive act is introduced into the classical liberal language of law, the offensive deed being not only the act of an individual person against another but rather something referring to a specific social and political context that goes beyond the act itself. Although only individual rights are brought before legal courts, by questioning the boundaries between the public and private domain, the concept of social injury allows an individual violation to be traced back to the wider context of women's social status, thus shedding light on what earlier had been confined to the domestic realm and construed only as an individual experience. In this respect, the private domain is put in a different relation with the collective and public dimension of women's experiences. This reflection fully highlights the fact that the power of law and its effective impact on the expectations of social actors are assessed on a symbolic level, too. As recalled by Tamar Pitch, if norms are symbols, actors seeking to change norms have not only practical but also symbolic purposes. It is precisely this dimension that becomes decisive in the venture for social transformation and full recognition of women's subjectivity that the "feminism of difference" is struggling for.[19]

The reflections of the American legal scholar Catharine McKinnon are similarly insightful. Although she expresses a moderate trust in law as an adequate instrument to improve women's status, she also questions its premises and principles. As is well known, besides striving for the acknowledgement of pornography as an offence against women, McKinnon has mainly dealt with the difficult issue of sexual harassment. With respect to the latter, her position may be ascribed to the feminist line of thinking that does not deny the utility of law. A law against sexual harassment gives victims the possibility of publically voicing the injustice they have suffered, and provides them with a legal ground on which they may obtain compensation. The innovation is indeed significant: a kind of behaviour once deemed to be *normal* is now construed as an *offence*. The link between the legal and the social is clear in this case: the legal prohibition of sexual harassment has made it not only legally but also socially unacceptable. Before the intervention of law, the facts constituting the offence had no social existence and had no cognitive form or coherence: such an injury against women was simply something that normally happened. Once law recognized sexual harassment as a practice of sexual discrimination, it removed it from the "elementary language" used by women to express sexual abuse, and gave it a shape, a background in a number of experiences accumulating and connecting with each other.[20]

The common traits of the feminist critique of the rule of law and the critique by critical legal studies are often underlined. Both theories question the concept of neutrality, not only of the law-making but of the judicial functions. Not even the judge is a neutral being: in construing the law, the judge makes a discretionary choice of a given point of view (among the many left open by written law) which best fits her individual preferences. Moreover, the performance of a judge is far from the normativist scheme of the objective and mechanical application of law. Therefore, if the judge cannot be seen as the guarantor of the rule of law, one might wonder what role does or should she perform. The answer provided by feminists such as Martha Minow is similar to that suggested by Duncan Kennedy, whereby the detection of the political aims lying behind the mystifying façade of law is the premise from which judges may be corrected and required to do "the right thing", that is, to have legal programmes which are better than the legislation's current ones and even better than the ones endorsed by current judges.[21] Hence, like critical legal studies, some feminists turn the judge into an actor of social change: a good judge is well aware of the discretionary power at his disposal and acts pragmatically so as to favour reform. A commitment to programmes of "affirmative action" for women, to a fairer social redistribution and a greater decentralization of political and economic power with a view to a wider democratic participation, these are all aims that fall within the radical agenda of critical legal studies and feminism close to them.

4 THE FAMILY: A NON-DIVIDABLE SETTING

When questioning the current legal regulation of the relationship between the sexes, feminist thinking redefines the private ambit by criticizing the distinction between public and private domains. In analysing the family, feminist thinking has particularly focused on the notion of a "patriarchal system" that places women within the domestic ambit of childbearing and care, the reign of biological necessity governed by *physis*. Instead, the public sphere, the *polis*, where male subjectivity is constructed, represents the kingdom of rationality and political and economic relationships, which goes beyond the natural givens of the domestic sphere of affections. These two separate spheres are complementary with respect to a system that hierarchically orders the genders' respective functions and identities.

As regards such a structuring/separation, law historically chose either not to intervene, leaving outside its scope the family domain, considering it an autonomous sphere, or to strengthen and legitimate the patriarchal model. In both cases, patriarchy has been maintained as a sort of "state of nature" within the wider context of the "civil status".[22] The 1970s feminist slogan "the personal is political" must be interpreted in light of this: the aim was to bring to the foreground a number of family relationships that had traditionally been excluded from public observation and thus kept unaltered because confined to an impermeable private domain. While the political arena has been subject to radical changes for centuries, the power structure between genders within the family has remained essentially intact. The possibility of uncovering this world previously hidden from the political scene and legal discourse, has shed light on the collective nature of women's experiences within the family and has led to the sharing – this being literally meant as "placing in common" – of this condition. Thus, by making the private public, free and responsible choice, which seemed a prerogative of the public sphere, has become possible in the family sphere, too. I believe that MacKinnon's criticism of the idea of privacy must be interpreted in this light: if privacy is employed as an instrument for isolating women, then it will be perfectly suited for perpetuating male dominance over women – and not only over their bodies – and will risk supporting the non-intervention of law within the family sphere. The private ambit, which isolates and separates us, is thus a political ambit, a common ground for inequality and marginalization.[23]

The idea that what is presented as natural and beyond history and culture is, in truth, a socially constructed element, including gender identity and relations, is thus gradually embraced by feminist thinking. This is conspicuous in Susan Moller Okin's account: according to this perspective, gender construction mainly occurs socially and is explicable in terms of roles, especially women's function of primary parent.[24] The 1980s emphasis on a specific female capacity to be responsive to specific contexts and to the dimension of care, by virtue precisely of women's generative qualities, is thus radically rejected. According to the above authors, this position has involuntarily strengthened the stereotypical idea of women and has further contributed to the separation of the masculine and feminine spheres. An example in this respect is provided by the encyclical *Mulieris dignitatem* of Pope John Paul II, where women's identity is conceived of in the light of their specific ability to take care of others and to perform a "naturally" maternal function.

At least up and until the first half of the twentieth century, the idea of a separate sphere, belonging by nature to the female gender, was quite widespread across Western political and legal thought. In the case of the United States, which is quite likely the most thoroughly scrutinized area in this context, the decision in the case *Bradwell v. Illinois* (1872) stands out. Invoking the Fourteenth Amendment, passed a few years earlier (1868), Myra Bradwell asked to be admitted to the Bar of Illinois, seeking access to the legal profession that had been previously denied to women. The US Supreme Court upheld the decision of the Supreme Court of Illinois, which had denied Myra Bradwell, as a woman, the right to join the Bar. The Supreme Court's reasoning is interesting precisely because, rather than narrowly construing the constitutional guarantees embedded in the Fourteenth Amendment, it resorted to special reasons justifying different treatment of women, on the basis of their belonging to a different and separate sphere, i.e. the family. By appealing to allegedly notable differences between men's and women's fields of action: the opinion of Judge Bradley perfectly mirrored the ideology of the separate sphere. Women belong to the domestic ambit and their role is to take care of the family: given that this is imposed by "nature", by "the law of God" or by "divine will", the law cannot be expected to intervene in this respect. In the name of a family model grounded on the patriarchal principle of inequality, this judgement established the dependent status of women, together with their exclusion from civil and political life.[25]

The separation of spheres has therefore allowed the family not to be seen as an integral part of the social world. Thus, the incoherence between an egalitarian outer world and a blatantly unequal family could not trouble most theorists who did not take the private ambit to be a specific concern of their thinking.[26] According to the patriarchal system, women and minors find their social place within the home, seen as their natural and biological environment, whereas men are set within the domain of political and economic relationships. The latter is the realm of freedom, a freedom construed as emancipation from necessity, as a higher setting reserved for the development of the species. Underlying the exaltation of women's maternal role there was the wish to privatize the family, to make it separate from the market that, starting from the Industrial Revolution, was establishing itself as an area where private interests, typical of individualistic ethics, were to prevail. In the meantime, the family has been gradually perceived as an area of self-sacrifice, of cooperation, able to turn individuals' selfishness into an ethics of altruism.[27] For this reason, as it has already been pointed out, this separation does, in fact, unite two complementary worlds. According to this approach, law is the perfect partner for a culture that views women only as mothers and wives, subject to their husbands' power and substantially destitute of legal protection.

5 THE CRITIQUE OF THE WELFARE STATE

According to some feminist thinkers, among the many contradictions of the liberal political and legal paradigm the conception of justice as the equal distribution of goods, including rights, as if these were goods to be equally distributed among individuals, stands out. To reduce rights to goods or to conceive of them as property is not only wrong but even detrimental. Rather than being objects, rights are relationships and institutionally defined rules: they establish what a person can do vis-à-vis another one and do not refer to what the person materially possesses. Therefore, injustice is not the mere withdrawal of goods; rather – and much more problematically – it implies a restriction of freedom and, above all, an injury to dignity.[28]

The above radical critique ought to be connected with a feminist theory of law freed from both the formalistic view of the liberal rule of law and the legal paradigm of the welfare state. To conceive of the legal paradigm uniquely as a distributive paradigm for material goods is misleading, though this is precisely what most authors are taking for granted. Two contradictions of the paradigm are emphasized: firstly, the paradigm overlooks the institutional context of the distribution and takes it for granted; secondly, when the paradigm is extended to non-material goods, these end up being misrepresented. It should be specified that an "institutional context" is construed as one including, for example, the family, which is one of the main social units affected by distributive issues; this area is indeed taken at face value, without questioning the roles that have crystallized within it over time. According to Iris Young, to refer to what are in fact processes, bonds, and relationships between individuals as social goods misrepresents social justice, as a matter of static schemes rather than social processes generating actual situations. This is, once again, due to the influence of the classical paradigm of liberal individualism, whereby individuals receive goods or own property rather than entering into relation with each other, or against one another.

Arguing from the notion of "oppression", which is largely used by contemporary liberation movements, such as feminism itself or black or lesbian movements, the political discourse cannot be reduced to the language of liberal individualism that dominates legal theory and politics. Think, for example, of the oppressive conditions in which women live: the mere awareness of the potential of becoming the victim of violence just for being a woman is not only troubling but significantly restricts women's freedom.

Is it reasonable to conceive of such experiences as cases of social injustice, or should we believe that this does not significantly affect individual rights, opportunities and self-esteem? If we pay attention not only to individual acts of violence, but also to the social context in which they take place and are somehow legitimated, we cannot but answer in the affirmative to the above question. As a matter of fact, injustice stems from systemic violence in that it targets women as members of a specific group.[29] The oppressive nature of violence does not lie in the direct victimization of the individual, but in the awareness shared by all group members of being exposed to this risk precisely by virtue of their collective identity.

Hence, one wonders, what kind of solution is the distributive paradigm able to provide? It may confidently be asserted that the distributive conception of justice is the least apt to grasp the problem of discrimination against women because, among other reasons, it begs the question of the political, legal, and cultural institutions that somehow encourage, tolerate, or in any event allow violence against specific groups. By generally taking the context of injustice for granted, distributive mechanisms do not bring any relevant correction to the causes of injustice and objectively perpetuate the oppressive conditions of disadvantaged groups or individuals who are only partially integrated within society because of, *inter alia*, their systematically devalued identity.

6 CONCLUSIONS

The traditional problem of the relationship between social and legal change is further complicated by many feminist reflections on law.[30] This problem essentially becomes more radical and one wonders whether law *qua talis* can accommodate women's discourse, and the demands and the aspirations of a new identity, such as the one reflectively elaborated by the "feminism of difference". *Pace* communitarians, this strengthens the belief that female identity, quite likely more momentously than other modern forms of identity experience, is above all an oppositional identity. The flight from liberal abstract universalism cannot induce us to accept the idea of a subject rigidly confined within the traditional boundaries of the community she belongs to, and whose identity is founded by ascription. This model is undermined by all forms of modern identity, even more by the female one, which has developed precisely through radical criticism and dissent.[31]

By relying on law's traditional machinery, then, can we represent women's freedom or are we doomed to thwart their expectations? The question of the very role of law has been particularly examined by Carol Smart but underlies the entire literature on women's issues.[32] For example, Italian feminists show an ambivalent attitude towards law whenever they debate about a significant law affecting women's conditions or their public and/or private image. Think, for example, of the law against sexual abuse, or the bills on sexual harassment (which have not been passed yet), or laws concerning reproduction. In such instances, the real question at stake has often been whether the legal discourse can be effective, rather than useless or even detrimental, as a means for establishing female identity. In this respect, some more radical Italian feminists, who are especially critical of institutions in general – including political representation – have focused on the notion of "legal void", i.e. an area where law is indifferent or absent. Together with the critical acknowledgement of the risk entailed in the legal regulation of the private sphere, the notion of "legal void" stands for the achievement or preservation of an area of freedom.[33]

Here, just as in other contexts, a position of radical distance from the legal discourse is crucial. As an expression of patriarchal power over women, law is said to be a useless or harmful instrument. It ends up by imprisoning women and their specific situations within rigid categories and generalized standards that, in the end, turn out to be formalistic and detached from reality and thus of no use. Moreover, there is scepticism about criminal law as a remedy for certain injuries, since in many instances – e.g. sexual abuse – the damage cannot be socially redressed through punishment alone. In such cases, institutions should be able to offer a much more articulated solution. Apart from punishing the offender, attention should be paid to the support needed by the victim of the abuse. The reason behind the many "shelters" aimed at protecting women against violence and maltreatment, planned and run by women's associations with the aid of local institutions, is also the acknowledgement of the *limitations* of law or, more specifically, of an exclusively criminal law approach.[34] The scope of criminal law ought to be drastically reassessed and many offences pertaining to interpersonal relations – sexual abuse, sexual harassment, insult, etc. – should be dealt with by civil law. On the basis of interpersonal conflicts which are often only contingent, law should be asked to provide for "extrajudicial" solutions and thus to be less invasive in certain spheres of life. That the burden of deciding if legal proceedings are to happen in domestic violence cases often rests with the victim epitomizes a specific conception of the individual, grounded on responsibility and free choice rather than on protection. Regarding such offences, the state has no higher interest in punishing than that of the victim, and justifying punishment on the grounds of a threat to the community cannot be considered adequate, failing the victim's concurring will.[35]

Even if the legal discourse's intrinsic tendency to standardization and formalism should not be overlooked, law's capacity to modify actual gender relations and thus cause significant power shifts over time should not be underestimated. Think, for example, of the recognition of women's self-determination in the reproductive field, which was made explicit – albeit not without limitations – by the abortion law, and of the kind of gender relationship that such a law proposed and strengthened. Not to speak of this law's considerable symbolic power. On the basis of a dynamic and agonistic view of law, we may see norms as arising out of groups' expectations (in our case women's) and able to bring about change and innovation.[36]

Nonetheless, we must not forget that, when dealing with matters pertaining to the reproductive sphere, we enter an area of strong differences, especially in terms of ultimate values. This has led some authors to favour the cultural model of judge-made law over the model that makes statute law the core of the legal system, since the former seems to better fit the value-pluralism that seems bound to become a key characteristic of democratic societies.[37] This model takes judge-made law to be more pliable, more open, more accommodating of contexts and specific situations, more capable of considering different points of view and of taking people for what they really are in their relationships of mutual dependency.

Yet, although this preference might be shared in some respects, it risks granting judges an excessive freedom to make totally discretionary decisions. Advocates of the judge-made law model usually respond to such objections by referring to the principles of democratic constitutions and thus to the idea of a constitutional rule of law. Such principles are thought to be the general coordinates within which judges perform their role and social function. Nevertheless, judges still retain a somewhat creative role. Here, it is not a matter of mechanically applying the relevant rule to the specific case by following a logical deductive process going from the general rule to the individual case. This approach, originating in legal positivism, would allow only for a "correct" application of law, complying with the legislators' true intention. Instead we should accept a sort of legal uncertainty, which ought not to be understood as a degeneration resulting from judges' excessive powers. It is law itself, in a social and political context much more diverse than that of the liberal rule of law that cannot but embody this new uncertainty, precisely by becoming mild and following the way of reasonableness.[38] The pressures put on law by "hard cases" (the many issues such as life, death, and bioethics), about which values and meanings sharply differ, make the principle of law's omnipotence both obsolete and undesirable. Transferring some power from legislative assemblies to judicial practice, as an area of greater prudence would be the proposal suggested by the analysis so far. The contemporary debate on the rule of law appears to make the issues of legal hermeneutics and the judicial function crucial. A higher profile for the judicial function is certainly desirable, provided that there is a public sphere where the performance of judges can remain subject to critical discussion.

NOTES

1. See N. Elias, *Die Gesellschaft der Individuen*, Frankfurt a. M.: Suhrkamp, 1996.
2. For the idea of collective identity, see P.L. Berger and Th. Luckmann, *The Social Construction of Reality*, London: Doubleday, 1966; B. Henry, "Fra identità politica e individualità", in F. Cerutti (ed.), *Identità e politica*, Roma-Bari: Laterza, 1996, pp. 167–83.
3. See D. Grimm, *Die Zukunft der Verfassung*, Frankfurt a. M.: Suhrkamp, 1991; E.-W. Böckenförde, "Entstehung und Wandel des Rechtsstaatsbegriffs", in E.-W. Böckenförde, *Staat, Gesellschaft, Freiheit. Studien zur Staatstheorie und zum Verfassungsrecht*, Frankfurt a. M.: Suhrkamp, 1976.
4. See G. Zagrebelsky, *Il diritto mite*, Torino: Einaudi, 1993.

5. See A. Giddens, *The Transformation of Intimacy*, Cambridge: Polity Press, 1992.
6. By "lifestyle" I do not mean, in this context, to refer to something superimposable on identity, in that not every lifestyle has a clearly defined identity-based sense of belonging; in this respect see D.H. Haraway, *A Cyborg Manifesto: Science, Technology and Socialist-Feminism in the Late Twentieth Century*, New York: Routledge, 1991.
7. There has been a wide debate in Italy on art. 29 of the Constitution: "The Republic acknowledges the rights of the family as a natural society grounded on marriage", which *a contrario* places in a subordinate condition all other possibilities of living together, e.g. cohabitation, homosexual couples, and singles.
8. See J. Habermas and Ch. Taylor, *Multiculturalismo. Lotte per il riconoscimento*, Milano: Feltrinelli, 1998; A. Honneth, *Kampf um Anerkennung*, Frankfurt a. M.: Suhrkamp, 1992.
9. See in particular the analysis by I.M. Young, *Justice and the Politics of Difference*, Princeton (NJ): Princeton University Press, 1990.
10. See A. Facchi, "Il pensiero femminista sul diritto: un percorso da Carol Gilligan a Tove Stang Dahl", in G. Zanetti (ed.), *Filosofi del diritto contemporanei*, Milano: Raffaello Cortina Editore, 1999.
11. M. Minow, *Making All the Difference: Inclusion, Exclusion and American Law*, Ithaca (NY)/London: Cornell University Press, 1990.
12. For the notion of "care" in its wider English meaning, see C. Gilligan, *In a Different Voice*, Cambridge (MA): Harvard University Press, 1982; for the notion of "responsibility towards" see E.H. Wolgast, *The Grammar of Justice*, Ithaca (NY): Cornell University Press, 1987.
13. See E.H. Wolgast, op. cit., passim.
14. See S. Benhabib, "The Generalized and the Concrete Other: The Kohlberg-Gilligan Controversy and Feminist Theory", in S. Benhabib and D. Cornell (eds), *Feminism as Critique*, Minneapolis (MN): University of Minnesota Press, 1987.
15. See J. Habermas and Ch. Taylor, op. cit., passim.
16. Ibid., p. 70.
17. The phrase is in J. Habermas, *Faktizität und Geltung*, Frankfurt a. M.: Suhrkamp, 1992.
18. See A. Howe, *The Problem of Privatized Injuries: Feminist Strategies for Litigation*, London: Routledge, 1991.
19. See T. Pitch, *Un diritto per due. La costruzione giuridica di genere, sesso e sessualità*, Milano: Il Saggiatore, 1998.
20. C. McKinnon, "Feminism, Marxism, Method and the State: Toward Feminist Jurisprudence", *Signs*, 8 (1993).
21. D. Kennedy, *A Critique of Adjudication*, Cambridge (MA): Harvard University Press, 1998.
22. C. Shalev, *Birth Power. The Case for Surrogacy*, New Haven (CT)/London: Yale University Press, 1989.
23. See C. McKinnon, *Feminism, Marxism, Method and the State: Toward Feminist Jurisprudence*, p. 213.
24. See S. Moller Okin, *Justice, Gender and the Family*, New York: Basic Books, 1989; N. Chodorow, *The Reproduction of Mothering*, Berkeley/Los Angeles (CA): University of California Press, 1978.
25. The issue is largely developed by S. Moller Okin, op. cit.

26. See C. Saraceno, "Le donne nella famiglia: una complessa costruzione giuridica. 1750–1942", in M. Barbagli and M. Kertzer (eds), *Storia della famiglia italiana*, Bologna: il Mulino, 1992.
27. See F. Olsen, "A Finger to the Devil: Abortion, Privacy and Equality", *Dissent*, 38 (1991), 3, pp. 377–82.
28. The most radical criticism of the distributive paradigm is by I.M. Young, *Justice and the Politics of Difference*, passim.
29. According to data provided by Anti-Rape Associations, more than a third of American women are subject to sexual assault or to attempted sexual assault at least once in their life; see again I.M. Young, *Justice and the Politics of Difference*.
30. A distinct sensitivity in this respect marks the work by T. Pitch, *Un diritto per due*, passim.
31. In this respect, I take the liberty of referring to my "Identità e riconoscimento", in F. Cerutti (ed.), *Identità e politica*, pp. 97–112.
32. See C. Smart, *Feminism and the Power of Law*, London: Routledge, 1989.
33. See L. Cigarini, "Sopra la legge", *Via Dogana*, 5 (1992).
34. In this respect, see the contribution by the Female Jurists Group, Virginia Woolf B, "Per un diritto leggero. Esperienze di giustizia e criterio di equità", *Democrazia e diritto*, (1996), 1.
35. What plays a decisive role is the contrast between freedom and autonomy on the one hand, protection and control on the other. For an analysis of the paternalistic approach of Western criminal law towards the female gender, see M. Graziosi, "Infirmitas sexus. La donna nell'immaginario penalistico", *Democrazia e diritto*, (1993), 2.
36. Although it refers to a perspective which is different from the one concerning genders, the reasoning by L. Ferrajoli, *La sovranità nel mondo moderno*, Milano: Anabasi, 1995, draws inspiration from such an overall conception of law.
37. See S. Rodotà, *Tecnologie e diritti*, Bologna: il Mulino, 1995.
38. See G. Zagrebelsky, *Il diritto mite*, pp. 200–13; G. Alpa, *L'arte di giudicare*, Roma-Bari: Laterza, 1996.

CHAPTER 11

MACHIAVELLI, THE REPUBLICAN TRADITION, AND THE RULE OF LAW

Luca Baccelli

Since the people wish to live according to the laws, and the powerful to control the laws, it is not possible for them to agree.

(Niccolò Machiavelli, *Florentine Histories*)

The influence of laws, where they have any real effect in the preservation of liberty, is not any magic power descending from shelves that are loaded with books, but is, in reality, the influence of men resolved to be free; of men, who, having adjusted in writing the terms on which they are to live with the state, and with their fellow-subjects, are determined, by their vigilance and spirit, to make these terms be observed.

(Adam Ferguson, *An Essay on the History of Civil Society*)

The social and institutional history of the twentieth century has forced a redefinition of the concept of the rule of law as developed from the legal theory of the preceding century. The Second World War marked a particular turning point. The defeat of Nazi Germany and its allies initiated the spread of political democracy which, through decolonization, went on until around the end of the century. Its main effects were the democratization of Portugal, Greece, Spain, and Latin America; the end of the socialist regimes in Eastern Europe; the collapse of the Soviet Union; the end of Apartheid; and the fall of many authoritarian regimes in the Third World. These are radically different circumstances from the nineteenth-century liberal political systems, founded on a limited electoral base, in which the notions of rule of law and of *Rechtsstaat* were developed. The picture becomes even more varied if one considers the success of contemporary constitutionalism. Kelsen's solution to the problem of the connection between law and power – the introduction of rigid constitutions and of judicial review of legislation – placed the relationship between the rule of law and "popular sovereignty" in a new perspective and expressed in new terms the problem of the status and role of judicial power. Furthermore, post-war European constitutions included in their basic principles a wide range of social rights, and, more generally, "social citizenship" entailed the enjoyment of a series of benefits and services guaranteed and provided by the state.

P. Costa and D. Zolo (eds.), The Rule of Law: History, Theory and Criticism, 387–420.

The discussion around "the rule of law" therefore, beginning with the post–Second World War period, cannot but involve the meaning and the functions of the "democratic state", the "constitutional state", and the "welfare state". In relation to the idea of the rule of law as a legal and political structure in which power is exercised "on the basis of", "by means of", and "in the framework of", the law, the power of the state was redefined with regard to its holders, its legitimacy, those at its receiving end, and the means by which it is exercised. All this, however, ended up by bringing the very functions and meaning of "law" into question. In today's complex "risk societies", the legal system takes on characteristics which significantly differentiate it from that normative instrument analysed and theorized by jurists in the 1800s, an instrument formally rational and reliable as to procedure.

At the beginning of the new millennium, it is impossible to disregard the international and multicultural perspective. The rule of law is a creation of the social experience, political practice, and legal doctrine of a small number of Western countries. Today, however, the rule of law is also proposed as a guiding principle in international relations. Moreover, in the era of economic globalization and cultural Westernization, the problem arises of the "exportability" of the legal-political model of the rule of law beyond the cultures and societies which produced it. On the other hand, migrations stretch the limits of the legal systems inspired by the principle of the rule of law with unprecedented problems, as well as presenting the challenge of multiculturalism.

As a response to this scenario, there has emerged a widespread political-theoretical strategy which joins a "minimalist" approach with a sort of "return to the principles". There are many who maintain that the democratization of political processes, the expansion of public services, the constitutionalization of social rights, and the principles of material justice and substantial equality all end up by attributing to the state functions and powers no longer based on law and no longer enforceable within the realm of law. The transformations which the legal system has undergone, on the other hand, would threaten the very cornerstone of the rule of law: the certainty of law. It would be possible to respond to the crisis of the rule of law, therefore, only by drastically reducing public involvement and lessening the demand for economic benefits and social services. Many see this adjustment as an inevitable consequence of the process of globalization and of the subsequent redefinition of the boundaries between politics and economics. On the other hand, a "lightening" of the rule of law would seem likely to favour its diffusion, too. If the cumbersome democratic, constitutional, and welfare state poses serious theoretical and practical problems within the sphere of the very political and legal culture which produced it, one could maintain that *a fortiori* it would cause those problems elsewhere. In this sense those societies furthest away from the cultural, legal, and political experience of the West would converge more readily on the acceptance of a "minimal rule of law".

The aim of this chapter is to pose questions about the meaning that an analysis of the conceptual "prehistory"[1] of the rule of law could assume in dealing with these problems. At first glance a clear distinction, if not a divide, between the "rule of law", the "democratic state", and the "welfare state", would seem appropriate. Since its inception, the ideal of the "rule of law" – in contrast to the "rule of men" – has seemed indeed to imply an anti-democratic prejudice and to be linked to an anti-egalitarian political anthropology. In particular, the early-modern republican tradition of political thought – one of the breeding grounds for the rule of law – has seemed to express, by means of the principle of mixed government, a radical critique of democracy. Attributing to elites a political role radically differentiated from that of "the people", excluding economic and social issues from the sphere of politics, and sharing an organic notion of the body politic that considers discord and conflict *tout court* as pathologies can be seen as elements of that critique.

I would like to question this image, in the light of the idea that, even though many writers seen as belonging to the republican tradition share opinions of this sort, significantly different positions also emerge. In particular, the figure of Niccolò Machiavelli himself – the eponymous author of this tradition – stands out with specificity and originality irreducible to common theoretical assumptions and shared linguistic conventions. In the works of Machiavelli, the notion of the rule of law is central; but it assumes quite different meanings with respect to many republican authors to whom he is compared (Section 1). I do not maintain that such a notion can constitute the basis for a theory of the rule of law capable of facing the problems of modern social and legal systems. I argue, rather, that a critical distance should be assumed with respect to modern attempts to construct "neo-republican" political philosophies that re-propose concepts and principles of the early-modern tradition. Nevertheless, historical inquiry, the investigation into the genealogy of terminologies and key concepts, can help us to cast the contemporary debate in a different light. This historiographical depth facilitates the development of unusual and original ways to tackle and conceptualize theoretical problems.

I hypothesize, therefore, that a consideration of the republican tradition, and in particular of Machiavellian theory, can make a significant contribution to the contemporary discussion concerning the rule of law. I will try to illustrate this thesis with regard to themes such as the conception of individual rights (Section 2.1), the welfare state (Section 2.2), the role of the judiciary (Section 2.3), the relationship between the rule of law and democracy (Section 2.4), and the very concept and function of law (Section 2.5). My further hypothesis is that the discussion of these issues can contribute to the development of an idea of the rule of law that is differentiated from the traditional social-democratic and welfare paradigm. However, this should not imply a return to the classical liberal and elitist concepts. Finally, I shall maintain that this idea is more valid in an intercultural context than "minimalist" neo-liberal hypotheses (Section 2.6).

1 THE RULE OF LAW: FROM THE "MACHIAVELLIAN MOMENT" TO MACHIAVELLI

The classical ideal of the "government of law", at the root of the notion of *rule of law*, seems to imply an anti-democratic prejudice from its very inception in Greco-Roman political-legal thought. In Aristotle's *Politics*, the concept is introduced in the context of a critique of radical and "demagogic" forms of democracy, in which it is the poor multitude that governs, rather than the laws.[2] Cicero puts the law above and beyond popular deliberation, ascribing it in the manner of "natural law" to a normative "natural" plane, and therefore unattainable: the laws of which *omnes servi sumus ut liberi esse possimus* express the supreme reason inherent in nature, eternal, preceding the formation of the state.[3] The ideal of the rule of law pervades medieval political thought and reappears in "republican" writers at the beginning of modern times. In these writers, critique of democracy is connected to the institutional choice of mixed government, understood as a constitutional structure in which the different components of the citizenry – the monarchy, the "best" and the "many" – are allocated the political role for which they are suited.[4] The "republican" critique of democracy continues up to the works of Kant, the philosophical *auctoritas* of the first theorists of the *Rechtsstaat*.[5]

More importantly, within this tradition the critique of democracy expresses an anthropology of inequality. The Aristotelian idea that men are by nature unequal and precisely for this reason are social beings, "political" beings, is the theoretical matrix of the thesis that within the citizenry only the "chosen few", the "best", the *optimates* are capable of political deliberation; by contrast, the "many" reveal themselves to be suited only to the choice among alternatives already drawn up.

This distinction refers to a sort of political division of labour, again found in the Platonic-Aristotelian line: the diverse components of the citizenry ought to play the role for which they are suited, take their proper place in the complex order of things, and seek their "natural" end. Mixed government in this sense, through such a division of labour, permits an ordered harmony in the *body* politic (it can be maintained that this conception still permeates the structural paradigm of the state[6]). This idea runs through the political thought of Florentine "civic humanism" and, in particular, the works of the political thinkers closest to the elite of *optimates*, beginning with those of Francesco Guicciardini; it re-emerges, formulated with great clarity, in James Harrington's *Oceana*. According to Harrington, in every republic there is a "natural aristocracy", excellent in quality and virtue, naturally inclined to political deliberation and endowed with free time for the affairs of government. On the other hand, the people are by nature fit for choosing between the alternatives proposed and examined by the aristocracy.[7] To "the few" – the aristocracy, the nobility, the elite – is attributed the power to propose and discuss, while "the many" – the people – can only elect the governing body and choose among the options that are presented to them, after a preliminary discussion and selection by "the few".

Critique of democracy, elitist anthropology, and theory of mixed government are joined in these writers with a notion of order that expresses a clear aversion to – we could say "obsession" with – every form of political conflict. In Aristotle's *Politics* the idea emerges that the prevalence of the middle class guarantees that factions do not upset the *polis*,[8] and this critique of "tumultuous" republics recurs in early-modern political thought. The tendency towards "sedition" and the recurrence of "tumults" are for Harrington *sic et simpliciter* a pathology of the social body; but the causes of the conflict may be removed if an adequate "balance of property ownership" is introduced: it is in this way possible to create a "perfect" and "immortal" commonwealth.[9] In Kant the establishment of the "republican" form of government will come to mean not only the exclusion of the principle of resistance, but also the illegitimacy of every form of public opposition to the sovereign power.[10]

This view of the rule of law as a critique of the democratic principle should fit, unforced, within the picture of early-modern republicanism outlined by John Pocock in *The Machiavellian Moment*. As we know, Pocock's work reconstructs an alternative political paradigm to the contract theory of "natural law": a republican idea with a characteristic conceptual vocabulary, in which key words recur such as *vivere civile* [civic life], civic virtue, corruption, fortune, and occasion. According to

Pocock, the common matrix of republicanism – from Florentine civic humanism to writers such as Guicciardini, Machiavelli, and Giannotti, up to Harrington, eighteenth-century British political thought, and the theorists of the American Revolution – is Aristotelian practical philosophy. Republicans share the concept of man as *zoon politikòn* and consequently the idea that political participation expresses his "true nature"; and they propose at the institutional level the theory of mixed government, in turn rooted in the political anthropology sketched above. In this framework, republican "virtue" tends to express an ideal of moderation and a clear distinction, if not opposition, between the spheres of politics and economics. This would hold true in different phases of republican political thought: from Machiavelli to the Commonwealth men of the 1700s, hostile to commercial and financial capital, to the republican tradition in the United States.[11]

The historians of political thought who have outlined the characteristics of the republican model, beginning with Pocock, have shown a great deal of caution in applying the results of their historiographic research to contemporary theoretical debate. Pocock's interpretation of early-modern republicanism as political theory inspired by Aristotle, however, has been widely utilized by contemporary communitarians as a political translation of their theses on social cohesion, the ethics of virtue and of the common good, the formation of individual identity, and the obligation of belonging to the community.[12] Recently a normative "neo-republican" political theory has been proposed, as a model inspired by classic republicanism, for politics and institutions.[13] How could such a theory contribute to the debate about the rule of law? In the light of what we have said up to this point, this theory would seem to support an opposition between the principles of the rule of law and those of popular sovereignty, as well as between the rule of law and democracy, viewing the latter as a particularly insidious form of the "rule of men". In addition to this anti-democratic vision, the republican tradition would seem to re-propose the classic opposition between the sphere of politics and the sphere of economics; that is, it would seem to suggest the traditional exclusion of economic themes from the "public" sphere of political praxis, and therefore to accept the incompatibility of public intervention in the economy, and the welfare state, with the ideal of the "rule of law". Finally, if republicanism may be considered a communitarian theory, a possible neo-republican conception of the rule of law would seem to imply a vision – organic and particularistic – of the body politic as a "concrete, substantially integrated community", which would express a well-defined common *ethos*.[14] This vision would appear to be hardly capable of being "universalized" outside the historical and cultural context in which it was developed.

The most recent historiography has, however, made Pocock's interpretation, inspired by a linear vision of the "Machiavellian moment", problematic. In the body of works labelled as republican, different lineages have been identified, distinct ideological families have been defined, and deep lines of division have been brought to light. Among the authors who utilize republican political language, for example, there are several concepts of liberty, alternative visions of politics, optimistic and pessimistic anthropologies, and different ideas of the order/conflict relationship.

First of all, not all early modern republicans can be considered neo-Aristotelian. Quentin Skinner has identified in some Italian writers of the thirteenth century the traces of a well-defined political ideology inspired by Roman republican thought. This ideology emerged *before* the Latin translation of *Politics* and *Nichomachean Ethics* made Aristotelian practical philosophy available to European intellectuals. While in the tradition of Aristotle and Aquinas man is *zoon politikòn* and develops his moral potential through political activity, Skinner holds that, for the neo-Romans, politics is an *instrument* for achieving disparate purposes. This yields two different conceptions of liberty: Aristotelian "positive" liberty[15] is challenged by a conception of liberty that expresses non-dependence and the absence of domination. This second view of liberty, Skinner again points out, was developed by a series of "neo-Roman" writers of the sixteenth, seventeenth, and eighteenth centuries and for a long time constituted an alternative to the "negative" view of liberty developed by Hobbes and taken up again by modern liberalism.[16] This reinterpretation of republicanism is based above all on the reading of the texts of Machiavelli.[17] But it can be maintained that Machiavelli had characteristics that make him stand out from other republican writers and make his complete assimilation into the "Machiavellian moment" problematic.[18]

These differences within the republican paradigm and the peculiarities of the works of Machiavelli should be kept in mind, particularly when dealing with the theme of government by law. In this perspective, Machiavelli's theory of political conflict takes on special meaning. As is well known, Chapter IV of Book I of his *Discourses* introduces a radical new idea to the history of European political thought: it is the revolutionary thesis that, under certain conditions, political conflict can produce positive effects. In the case of the Roman Republic, the conflict between the two main parties (*umori*) of the citizenry – that of the patricians and that of the plebeians – produced "laws and institutions conducive to public liberty". The radical nature of this theoretical innovation can be measured by the reactions that it provoked: not only self-proclaimed adversaries of Machiavelli, but even writers belonging to different tendencies of republican thought, such as Guicciardini, and thinkers, such as Rousseau, who were in large part inspired by Machiavelli, kept their distance from him on this point. Particularly significant is the position of Harrington: the same writer who had exalted Machiavelli as the restorer of "ancient prudence" expressed by "government *de jure*", i.e. in the "empire of laws and not of men",[19] criticizes him explicitly and directly on this point.

From the perspective of the republican theory of "mixed government", the rule of law and political conflict seem to be in opposition, or at least strong tension, with each other. It is therefore understandable that interpretations that emphasize the importance of the rule of law in the works of Machiavelli – going so far as to consider it the truly significant element of his republicanism – have attempted to understate the significance of his positive evaluation of conflict, in the light of the thesis that, even for Machiavelli, the rule of law means moderation.[20]

One could point out, in response, how Machiavelli emphasizes the competitive element of politics, an element with an irreducible implication of violence that would undermine every institutional defence.[21] But, looked at closely, this would mean reproducing for the umpteenth time the oscillation that has characterized the history of the critical literature on Machiavelli,[22] as well as oversimplifying his position. It seems to me much more important to recognize the real centrality of the theme of the rule of law and to pose the problem of its compatibility with the Machiavellian theory of conflict.

The idea that the citizenry is irrevocably split into different components representing different parties (*umori*) turns out to be central and recurrent in the works of Machiavelli, starting with *The Prince*,[23] and this cannot be ignored. Different parties have different interests and ends, which bring them inevitably into conflict: Machiavelli indeed abandons the Platonic-Aristotelian-Thomist anthropological model underlying the organicist idea of the body politic. In the traditional model, humans are by nature *unequal* and precisely for this reason tend to associate with each other. They are drawn together into natural relationships of dominance/subordination (man/woman, father/children, master/slave), from which the political socialization that forms the state develops.[24] They are the "limbs" of a body politic, each one with his or her specific function and "natural place" in the overall order.

Machiavelli's anthropology, on the other hand, recognizes an uncontrollable tendency towards conflict, rooted in the imbalance between the inexhaustibility of human wants and the scarcity of resources with which to satisfy them.[25] The parties of the citizenry are not limbs of a body, joined by an organic link; they are social components in real or potential conflict.[26] This conflict can assume different forms – virtuous or degenerative – but it is in any case a fact of politics, including the politics of republics.

Machiavelli insists that the diverse components of the citizenry have different interests and are characterized by different "ends". Nevertheless this does not mean that they are endowed with different capacities for political deliberation. "Commoners" and "gentlemen" are equally fit for political activity, and among the institutions of the Roman Republic that receive the most praise are those that attributed the power to propose and discuss laws to the plebeians.[27] We are far from the typical pro-optimate republicanism, very far, for example, from Guicciardini's vision of the rule of law, according to which "only the able and deserving should govern".[28]

Attributing equal political capability to all citizens strains the traditional theory of "mixed government", even to the point of changing its meaning. The theory was meant to limit the risks of government by the people but Machiavelli reverses the idea, arguing that the greatest danger for the political community is represented by the uncontrollable tendency of "gentlemen" to impose their dominance. In his *Discourses*, he establishes a connection between the republic and "equality", maintains that "gentlemen" are dangerous for the republic,[29] and declares the political superiority of the people over the prince and the institutional superiority of the republic over the principate. Machiavelli's analysis of the dynamics of conflict is intended to emphasize the political capacity of the people, more than to identify a point of equilibrium between the two parties. And if at times Machiavelli seems to condemn "ambition" on the part of the people as if it were on a par with the nobles' thirst for power, he also points out that, without the "appetites" of the plebeians, Rome would have lost its liberty much more quickly.[30] It is difficult to overestimate the importance of this clarification. Machiavelli reaffirms the virtuous effect of conflict, the idea that laws in defence of liberty are born from the juxtaposition of passions that need to be balanced one against the other. This means that the very ambition of the plebeians, which Machiavelli at times seems to abhor, has virtuous effects. "Mixed government", thus, does not express an organic ideal, or the Aristotelian principle of *mesotes*, of the "just means"; it expresses, rather, the idea of checks and balances, the articulation of powers in such a way that "one keeps watch over the other".[31]

All of this is strictly connected to the theme of the rule of law: Machiavelli abandons the traditional Aristotelian-Thomist celebration of monarchy to affirm that people under the rule of law are more virtuous than is a prince in the same position and to deny that the "licentious" forms of democracy constitute – again, according to the traditional vision – the worst form of tyranny.[32] What most stands out, with respect to the recurrent link between the rule of law, mixed government, and critique of democracy, is that in Machiavelli the people have a role as political protagonist, and that this role is undertaken through political conflict. It is in fact by political conflict that the popular element initiates institutional innovation. The "laws that are made in favour of liberty" are born precisely from the "discord" between the two chief parties of the republic.[33]

Therefore, the conflict which expresses the fundamental parties of the citizenry and is channelled into "laws and orders" is physiological, even healthy. Under other conditions, however, conflict becomes pathological and dangerous. In this case reciprocal fear is activated and the ruinous formation of "sects" takes place.[34] In the critical literature on Machiavelli, the distinction between these two forms of conflict has often been interpreted in the light of the ideal of moderation (which in turn was expressed in the principle of the rule of law) – the virtuous forms of conflict are held to be those which are less radical and violent, those which can be resolved by peaceful means, through "discussing" rather than "fighting"; and it would be the "ambition", therefore, of the plebeians that sets in motion the spiral which leads to violent conflict. But Machiavelli states that the way to tyranny opens up not when conflict becomes radicalized but rather when the people choose to entrust the protection of their interests and, even more, the revenge against their enemies, to a powerful person.[35] Machiavelli, in short, rather than juxtaposing "radical" forms of conflict with "moderate" ones, distinguishes between conflict that arises from the juxtaposition of well-defined social groups, expressing the fundamentally different interests within citizenry, and conflict stemming from the search for personal power, which is connected to the formation of clienteles, factions, and armed groups. The first is virtuous and produces liberty; the second is pathological and leads to tyranny. In the genesis of potentially destructive forms of conflict, "inequality" is indicated as a strongly negative factor; indeed it is at the origins of the formation of factions and cliques. This idea is linked directly to the theme of the "rule of law". In particular, in his *Florentine*

Histories, generally presented as the expression of a "moderate" turn in Machiavelli's works,[36] it is stated quite clearly that lords and nobles are, by their very nature, in opposition to the rule of law: the enmity between the people and the "powerful" is insurmountable "because, since the people wish to live according to the laws, and the powerful to control the laws, it is not possible for them to agree".[37] The people therefore seem spontaneously and "naturally" predisposed to respect the rule of law, and the "powerful" to impose the "rule of men". The overturning of the traditional theory is evident.

A reinterpretation of Machiavelli's republicanism in this sense could open the way to a different interpretation of his contribution to the genealogy of the idea of the "rule of law". The "rule of law" in Machiavelli does not mean moderation; nor does "mixed government" mean attributing a subordinate role to the people. Rather, the "rule of law" provides the institutional framework for conflict to take place in virtuous forms. Within this framework, conflict has a feedback effect on the institutional framework, and is expressed in the "laws and orders" that favour liberty and the power of the republic. For that very reason, conflict under the "rule of law" is not a degenerative factor but rather acts to counteract the entropic tendency of the republic towards "corruption".

This Machiavellian conflict-based theory also embodied in some early-modern republican writers that "constitution-enforcing conception of rights" of which Skinner and James Tully spoke. In this conception, individual rights have the function of forcing the public powers "to act within a known and recognized constitutional structure of lawfulness", and therefore "to subject their governors to a rule of law".[38] It is important to note, however, that rights perform this function insomuch as they express the activism of citizens in defence of their liberty. According to Adam Ferguson, for example, moderation and a conciliatory disposition can be transformed into political indifference, and complacency in the enjoyment of one's rights can jeopardize liberty. Liberty and rights are never guaranteed once and for all. Vigilance is necessary not only to win them but also to make them effective, as is the capacity for active mobilization, the "vigilant jealousy of the rights": constant readiness to "oppose usurpations"[39] and to defend one's security is necessary. Liberty is thus defended more by difference and conflict than by the search for the common good.[40] And among the chief advantages of the republican form of government is the very fact that it keeps open the possibility for conflict and mobilization.[41] It is evident that such an "active" and competitive conception of rights can be connected to the republican idea of liberty as resistance to domination. Indeed, this conception is an alternative both to the natural law view of rights as the natural endowment of individuals, existing before the formation of the state, and to the positive law conception of rights as "reflected effects" of state power or the result of the state's self-imposed limitation, present in the nineteenth-century theory of the *Rechtsstaat*.

I have highlighted these aspects of the conceptual "prehistory" of the rule of law in the early-modern republican tradition to suggest a possible interpretative approach, an alternative to Pocock's "Machiavellian moment" (actually above all a "Harringtonian moment"), which leads from Machiavelli's democratic theory of conflict to Ferguson's conception of rights as the expression of active mobilization and conflict. In Section 2, I wish to show how we can consider some themes of the contemporary debate on the rule of law in the light of this approach.

2 THE RULE OF LAW AND THE "STRUGGLE FOR RIGHTS"

The development of the "republican" paradigm resulted from the attempt to reconstruct the evolution of political vocabularies against the background of the "forms of life" and the linguistic contexts in which they were used,[42] and this work of historiographic reinterpretation has recently been used in an attempt to construct a neo-republican normative political philosophy. The deep differences that run through republicanism with regard to institutional solutions, philosophical references, and political anthropology itself should clearly indicate the difficulties that theoretical operations of this kind run up against.[43] More specifically, it does not seem possible to delineate a compact republican theory of the rule of law. I believe, however, that the historiographic awareness of how Machiavelli and some of his heirs connected the principle of the rule of law to political conflict and individual rights allows us to gain a useful and different interpretative perspective on some of the central issues of contemporary debate. In the following pages, I wish to show how this vision of the rule of law offers interesting starting points for tackling themes such as the status and foundation of individual rights; the relationship among rule of law, the welfare state, and democracy; the role and powers of the judiciary; and the conception of law itself. The problem of "exporting" the rule of law could be seen in a new light, too.

2.1 The rule of law and rights

It is debatable whether a necessary connection between individual rights and the rule of law exists. Since the goal of the rule of law, however, is the legal protection of individuals, it appears natural that for this purpose it should use the deontological figure of individual rights and the legal tools that this makes it possible to adopt. But the "prehistory" and the conceptual history of the rule of law show how from time to time very different conceptions of individual rights have been adopted: from customary rights of common law, through "natural" rights of the natural law and Enlightenment tradition, to "reflected effects" of the state's will (or "self-limitation") in the theorists of the *Rechtsstaat* in the second half of the 1800s and the different conceptions present in contemporary legal philosophy.

Today it is generally accepted that the constitutional (and democratic) state incorporates a range of individual rights in its basic principles. The idea of an inextricable connection between the rule of law and human rights is vigorously expressed in the most recent attempt to develop a systematic theory of *Rechtsstaat*, that of Jürgen Habermas.[44] For Habermas, human rights, the rule of law, and popular sovereignty are "co-original" sources, representing different facets of the same historical process of establishment and evolution of modern law. Furthermore, basic rights are the necessary functional condition for the constitution of a "law code", which requires the guaranteeing of private and public autonomy. For Habermas there is no law, one could say, without rights. In the third place, basic rights express the utilization, through a "logical genesis of rights", of the general normative principle of discourse theory – the "D Principle"[45] – in the political-legal realm.[46] Habermas points out, however, that individual rights need the state's power to become effective and, on the other hand, the state's power needs the law both for performing its functions and for ensuring its legitimacy. It is through law that the organized power of the state arises and can achieve collective goals. But it is only through the state that the law can exercise "its function of stabilizing behavioural expectations".[47] The idea of this mutual exchange is expressed by the notion of the "rule of law".[48]

The connection between the foundation of individual rights and the rule of law appears, therefore, very tight in Habermas (perhaps too much so). His theory of the "rule of law" seems, in fact, to be inextricably connected to the "discourse-justification" of basic rights grounded in discourse theory. Habermas does not speak about natural human rights; basic rights no longer express the Cartesian "monological" rationality: they are, rather, the preconditions and the results of the application of dialogic procedural rationality to the political-legal sphere. Nevertheless they make up normative data which logically and axiologically precede the institution of the state and express a form of rationality (in this case, communicative). In this sense, it can be seen that Habermas's "discourse justification" represents a "post-metaphysical" reformulation of the rationalist approach to individual rights typical of modern natural law theory. But as we have seen, it is possible to find in early-modern political-legal experience another conception of rights, alternative to legal rationalism and relating to the "sentiment" of affirming one's own dignity and resisting arbitrary domination. I advance the hypothesis that this alternative conception offers a significant contribution to the contemporary debate on basic rights.

Contrary to the idea, widespread in traditional legal positivism, that the language of rights is totally translatable into that of duties, it has been argued that there is an irreducible semantic surplus of rights over duties.[49] In order to characterize and interpret such excess, Joel Feinberg has made reference to the "activity of claiming". The idea is that the specific meaning of rights derives from the act of claiming them, in the sense that having rights enables us "to stand up like men, to look others in the eye, and to feel in some fundamental way equal to anyone else".[50] According to Feinberg, an element of "claiming", connected to the concept of human dignity, is therefore characteristic of rights. But at the same time, it must be pointed out that the very origin of rights and their development have to do with claiming and conflict. In Frank Michelman's constitutional theory, itself inspired by early-modern republicanism, rights – conceived of as "a relationship and a social practice"[51] – emerge from, and are based on, the process of development and transformation of legal principles: that process which Michelman calls "political jurisgenesis". Basic rights, therefore, are on the one hand a precondition of citizenship – understood as active membership in the political and legal community – and on the other hand its product.[52] These considerations can be associated with the thesis, expressed by Norberto Bobbio and taken up by Luigi Ferrajoli, on the origin of rights from social conflict and political demands.[53]

Habermas's theory has the merit of considering the "rule of law" essentially as a "rule of rights". The potential of this approach, however, appears limited by its origins in legal rationalism. Basic rights remain a product of reason, even if it is communicative reason, and take us back to the abstract realm of a priori, back to what Habermas considers the quasi-transcendental premise of communication. The idea of the "rule of rights" could instead be utilized in the light of the activist and conflict-based notion of individual rights that I have mentioned: rights could be seen as the result of demands, struggles, mobilizations against situations of oppression and suffering, and as the expression of the human feeling of self-affirmation and dignity, more than as the expression of principles of rationality. In this way it seems possible to utilize fully an element which Bobbio himself presented as one of the most significant aspects of the modern success of the language of rights: a sort of Gestalt change, the assumption of an *ex parte populi* perspective in place of the traditional *ex parte principis* perspective expressed in the language of duties.[54]

On the other hand, if we also take the "constitution-enforcing" conception of rights from the republican tradition, another important element comes into play. From the perspective of modern rational law theory, rights – expression of "human nature" – constitute a "property" of the individual. Consequently the individual can also renounce them, alienate them, or transfer them to the state. There emerges here a paradox that is implicit in the natural law notion of natural rights,[55] evident, for example, in the contract theories of Hobbes and Rousseau. On the other hand, in the republican view, the active exercising of rights is meant to compel the state to act within the constitutional structure. There is therefore a dialectic exchange between the activism of individuals and groups and the transformations of the constitutional framework. The rule of law is the necessary condition for the activity of claiming, and it is the activity of claiming that makes the rule of law effective. On the other hand, the fact that claiming occurs "under the rule of law", within a perimeter determined legally even if still evolving, is one of the conditions for social conflict not to degenerate or become entropic and destructive. In this sense the rule of law could be understood not only as the "rule of rights" but also, more specifically, as the institutional framework and normative precondition for the "struggle for rights".

2.2 *The rule of law and the welfare state*

One of the most recurrent themes of the twentieth-century debate concerns the compatibility of the rule of law with the welfare state. During the 1900s, two models faced each other: one that can be defined as a liberal "minimalist" model and the other, a social-democratic/welfare state model. Neo-liberal criticism places the entire sphere of social rights (and perhaps even that of the political rights typical of representative democracies) beyond the threshold of admissibility compatible with the rule of law. The traditional model of the welfare state has also been criticized both for its failures and in reference to the need to extend the catalogue of rights in the direction of "third"- and "fourth"-generation rights (cultural, ecological, biological).

Recently there has been an attempt to reply to the neo-liberal criticism without endorsing the traditional welfare model. One proposed theoretical strategy is that of placing the different generations of rights in one evolving line. In this perspective, the emergence of democracy and the welfare state does not mean the introduction of new principles, such as those of social justice or collective responsibility, potentially in conflict with the traditional liberal principle of autonomy. In particular, Habermas has tried to extend his "logical genesis of rights" beyond the traditional social rights, to include the rights of the "third" and "fourth" generations.[56] For Habermas political and social rights do not limit autonomy, but instead guarantee the "enforcement of equal individual liberties for all".[57]

The conception of social rights as the linear evolution of civil and political rights has been criticized from various perspectives. Both critics "on the left" as well as theorists of the "law and economics" approach have maintained that there is a notable difference between civil and political rights on the one hand, and social rights on the other: the latter require direct state action to provide services and benefits and their cost makes them more "conditional opportunities"[58] than rights proper, enforceable through legal action. Against this it has been objected, effectively in my opinion, that every type of right has a cost.[59] But it is difficult to deny that neo-liberal criticism contains at least a grain of truth, not only because the extension of welfare services makes the state a powerful and pervasive reality, which limits the space of "negative" liberties; and not only because welfare policies – especially in Italy – have demonstrated only a limited capacity to achieve the objectives of redistribution and substantial equality. Even the most effective welfare state models have stereotyped social needs and have imposed certain social models (family-centred, gender-biased, ethnocentric). On the other hand, over the past few years there has been not only more consensus on the language of rights but also a sort of inflation of rights and above all of right-holders (from non-human animals, or even vegetables and minerals, up to the pre-embryo). There has been talk of "mistaken rights", maintaining that other legal concepts and deontological figures (from responsibility to care) are more suitable than individual rights for regulating certain spheres;[60] and perverse effects have been seen (the proliferation of right-holders can end up limiting more traditionally understood individual rights).

One possible solution to these problems – indirectly inspired by the republican tradition – ascribes priority to political rights as "reflexive" rights: while civil and social rights can be granted paternalistically, political rights contain the capacity for independent claims and are the prerequisite for obtaining other rights. Axel Honneth used the concept of "struggle for recognition" to maintain that the definition of needs and groups to be protected cannot come down "from above" but must come from interested parties.[61] Issues of this type, together with analogous elaborations of feminist inspiration, have been taken up by Habermas himself. It is questionable, however, whether Habermas's "logical genesis" is the best theoretical framework for these positions; they seem more congruent with a conflict-based conception of rights. If rights are conceived of as the expression and legal formalization of claiming, not only do political rights (not limited to the active and passive electorate) become more valuable but so do – in a different form – civil and social rights. To acknowledge that rights are never completely guaranteed, that they require constant mobilization to become effective, and that they are not based on an absolute foundation or universalistic perspective is also to admit that there cannot be a clear dividing line between first-generation rights and social rights. The effectiveness of every category of rights requires an investment not only in economic terms but also of communicative resources, and the mobilization of the interested parties. And social rights are themselves a precondition for the activity of claiming to be undertaken effectively.

An explicit reference to the conflict-based tradition of republicanism, therefore, allows us to better define the critique of paternalistic notions of rights and the rule of law; it also allows us to see the classic rights of liberty in a different light. It is possible to reinterpret the sense in which these protect private autonomy by understanding it as a reserve of identity and a moral resource, a key element for "entering" the public space and advancing one's own claims. Here, too, we can make a connection with Michelman's "republican" theory: not only racial discrimination but also discrimination according to gender or sexual orientation inhibits the possibility of entering the arena of civil society and claiming one's rights. In commenting on the famous case of *Bowers v. Hardwick*, Michelman points out that the laws against "sodomy" not only violate an intangible, intimate space of every individual but also inhibit the presence of homosexuals in the public space. A typically "liberal" right such as that of privacy is thus connected to the principle of active citizenship, in a process of "cross-fertilization".[62] On the other hand, in this perspective political and social rights are in turn the condition for establishing the rights of liberty. If rights are not the "natural" faculties of individuals to be exercised "against" the state, but are rather an instrument for successful claiming within a constitutional framework, then state action to make them effective is not something adjunctive or secondary. The catalogue of rights would in any case be open to successive claims, so as to broaden the range of rights. But this would not necessarily open the way to an excessive inflation of rights: an activist, conflict-based conception of rights implies valuing what differentiates the language of rights from other normative codes (and therefore also implies the recognition that in certain situations other normative codes are more adequate) and excludes an unlimited multiplication of right-holders. Furthermore, if it is claimants who identify the reasons for their hardships and suffering, who articulate their needs and expectations, defining and redefining themselves in the process, then the stereotyping effects and arbitrary classifications typical of paternalistic welfare state models are avoided.

2.3 The rule of law and democracy

In an important essay, Michelman deals with the problem of the relationship between the rule of law and democracy from a "republican" perspective. He points out that the idea of self-government and of the rule of law are both indisputable principles of constitutionalism; therefore, they must coexist in some way, however problematic their relationship might be.[63] Michelman's proposed solution hints at a sort of convergence between the process of self-constitution of the people, of the self-governing "self", and of the process of lawmaking: the way in which the people – endowed with sovereignty – constitutes itself as such is in some manner governed by law. It is a question of that "jurisgenerative"[64] process that has already been mentioned.

These insights could be further developed. The problem of the relationship between the rule of law and democracy cannot but involve the question of the very meaning of democracy in contemporary societies. As is well known, the classic theory of democracy as "government by the people", the expression of popular will and sovereignty, has been challenged by the elitist critique of the founders of political science. Over the twentieth century this challenge was answered, on the one hand, by the theorists of "democratic elitism", from Weber to Schumpeter, Dahl, and Sartori, and on the other hand by radically "participatory" theories.[65] The latter are evermore difficult to propose in complex societies but the assumptions of procedural theories of democracy have also been challenged on grounds of their "broken promises", "evolutionary risks", and unexpected effects.[66] We are witness to the progressive reduction in the claims of democratic theory, and especially to its moving away from the ethical-political values underlying the classic notion of "government by the people".

However, theoretical alternatives may be possible. In the contemporary debate there are many different versions of "deliberative democracy" that criticize the economic approach of twentieth-century political science and the consequent reduction of politics to a mere clash of interests. The democratic process is seen as a public space where principles and values are compared and moral issues are discussed. The contributions of Habermas, who proposes a "proceduralization" of the principle of popular sovereignty, are linked to such conceptions[67]: democracy is identified with openness and "permeability" of institutions to the communicative processes of civil society. With reference to the republican tradition, and in particular to the idea of liberty as non-domination, Philipp Pettit develops an idea of democracy as "contestability".[68] Again, however, Habermas takes us back to the heaven of normative abstractions: the "democratic principle" that establishes popular sovereignty and human rights is but the translation of the general "principle D" into the political-legal sphere.

In developing his idea of the constitutional state Habermas put forward an interesting "siege model", emphasizing social activism and the communicative processes of citizenship; but in his major work he gives central place to the question of the "permeability" of institutions and the conformity of legislative bodies to the deliberative model.[69] Analogously, Pettit raises the issue of how institutions can allow contestations, and responds by referring precisely to the "deliberative" notion of democracy, to the perspective of agreement, to the ideal of a "republic of reason", to the principle of *audi alteram partem*, up to the point of attributing value and legitimacy only to what he defines as "debating contestations". The idea of contestability seems to dwindle into a sort of self-discipline on the part of contestants, while the receptiveness of institutions, which shows paternalistic traits, comes to the foreground. For both authors, the engine of the process seems to be housed more in openness of institutions than in citizen activism.[70]

Some of Habermas's and Pettit's ideas could perhaps be developed from the perspective of a conflict-based view of the rule of law into an alternative to the "classic" theory of democracy that does not progressively move away from its promises and normative premises. In other words, the alternative to democratic elitism or polyarchy would not be a re-proposal of popular participation at all levels of decision-making but a model that keeps institutions open to input coming from the agencies of society. In this light, the rule of law becomes the guarantee of "permeability" and openness in institutions. The degree of democracy is not identified with the number of decisions formally submitted to majority rule in elective assemblies but involves a plurality of factors including an active public sphere, as well as effective legal protection of free expression within this sphere.

In the light of recent developments of democratic theory, the problem of the relationship between constitutionalism, the rule of law, and democracy in one way is played down while in another way it needs to be radicalized. On the one hand, the contrast is not between pure and absolute principles: if we recognize that popular sovereignty as demanded by classical theory cannot be achieved it is easier to accept the idea that there are legal principles which substantiate the rule of law and limit the principle of majority rule. On the other hand, historical perspective shows how without the rule of law and the guarantee of basic rights democracy turns into an authoritarian illusion.[71] If rights are conceived of as principles that are never completely guaranteed and which therefore require active mobilization, it becomes clear that, without democratic forms of activism, without an instance of effective resistance to domination, the very rule of law itself may deteriorate.

2.4 *The power of judges*

Closely related to the question of the relationship between the rule of law and democracy is the debate on the role of the judiciary and, in particular, of constitutional adjudication, in legal systems with forms of judicial review of legislation, especially the constitutional courts of Germany, and the United States "Judicial paternalism" has been suspected both in the documents of the *Bundesverfassungsgericht* and in the positions of the American constitutional theorists;[72] the proposed antidote to this is a strictly deontological notion of basic rights, *à la* Dworkin.[73]

In the American political-legal debate of the past few decades, the idea that Supreme Court Justices should be "strict constructionists" is generally associated with a conservative position.[74] Bruce Ackerman, on the other hand, sees the Court as a privileged interlocutor for "We the People": in the "revolutionary" phases of higher law-making the people resumes its constituent power, while relying on the Court's work in times of ordinary law-making. Michelman's theory appears more interesting: the "jurisgenerative" process does not develop only in exceptional cases,[75] and the agent in that process is not necessarily the people acting as a whole. Particularly instructive in this regard is the history of decisions against racial discrimination. At the beginning, African-Americans formed a marginal social group in the process of redefining its self-identity. As this process led to the emergence of a stronger African-American sense of identity – albeit that there were and are sharp disagreements among African-Americans themselves over what this means – African-Americans not only began to challenge "such partial citizenship as the Constitution granted and allowed them" but also claimed and utilized that "partial citizenship". The judiciary, in this process, "drew on interpretive possibilities that the challenger's own activity was helping to create".[76]

Michelman considers the problem of constitutional innovation and judicial review of legislation so as to avoid both the attribution of omnipotence to the ordinary legislator and the re-proposal of a static, conservative vision of the role of constitutional courts, which can be seen both in the repealing of laws introducing social protections – typical of the *Lochner* era of the Supreme Court – and in the theory, re-proposed in *Bowers v. Hardwick*, that legislative assemblies have the right to make laws in matters of collective morality.[77] This viewpoint considers as a pre-political and pre-legal given what in reality is a product of specific policies, social activities, and legal decisions. This ends up favouring practices of marginalization. On the other hand, what Cass Sunstein defines as a "liberal republican conception" of constitutional adjudication supports the claims of socially disadvantaged and marginalized groups.[78] In the dialectics between the communicative processes of society and law-making, the judiciary plays an active role. Both positions avoid, however, falling back into a "paternalistic" conception of the role of constitutional judges. It is evident that they can be innovatory only insomuch as they are the counterpart of individuals, processes, and movements present in society.[79] In this way it is possible to oppose the tendency, widespread in contemporary politics and theoretical debate, to delegate the solution of vital problems the political system cannot deal with to a judicial "expertocracy" and "government by judges".

A conflict-based conception of the rule of law would be at odds with the conservative approach that limits the function of the judiciary to the protection of existing social and political arrangements. On the other hand, in complex modern societies an increase in the scope of judge-made law is probably inevitable. It is evident, however, that it makes a difference whether judges – and in particular, the justices of the constitutional courts – play the conservative role of strict constructionists, or attribute to themselves an authoritative role as direct representatives of "We the People" or as prophets of the collective ethos, or, finally, if they propose themselves as partners of the individuals and groups engaged in the "struggle for rights". If the constitutional system is conceived of as an evolving entity – related to the claims of citizens, to the transformations of the ethos of cultural-moral pluralism, to value conflicts, and to the processes of defining and redefining principles and individuals – constitutional adjudication can be meaningfully connected with the "jurisgenerative" process. The judiciary – by virtue of the interpretation and reinterpretation of constitutional principles – can press for or anticipate the legislative action of parliamentary majorities but cannot replace individual and collective agents. In this sense, constitutional courts can play a "progressive" and reforming role; but this idea is also compatible with the courts' defending – in a somewhat "conservative" way – the constitutional rights of minority groups. So conceived, the judiciary represents an anti-majority but not anti-democratic principle. It constitutes one of the agencies – along with the legislative assemblies, the executive, the local governments – that participate in the interplay between claims "from below" and normative development through the instruments of the legal system.

2.5 *Which law?*

As we have seen, the problem of the crisis of the rule of law concerns the very conception of law. Albert Venn Dicey pointed out an opposition between administrative law and the rule of law, and Friedrich von Hayek considered the contemporary prevalence of "legislation" over law irreconcilable with the rule of law. Bruno Leoni has gone so far as to consider only judge-made law of "spontaneous" formation compatible with the rule of law: the maximizing of liberty is identified with the minimizing of the scope of legislation and of the decisions of the majority expressed by "representatives" of the people.

The emergence and development of the welfare state would seem to support positions of this type. The legal system is significantly transformed by the introduction of specific measures of redistribution. The adoption of laws that are in practice administrative measures and, more generally, the tendency towards legislative inflation, move away more and more from the model of the "law" as a general and abstract norm to which the ideal of legal certainty referred. According to Dieter Grimm, for example, the introduction of substantive values into the Constitution and the social aims of the state express a political model quite different from that of the *Rechtsstaat* of the 1800s, which did not include any criteria of substantive justice. For Grimm, all of this brings about a crisis of the rule of law. The lack of imperative means and enforceable norms calls into question the force of law as the legal limitation of power, and erodes the classic distinction between "state" and "civil society".[80]

Faced with this scenario, one strand of contemporary political theory resorts to "anarchical-capitalistic" hypotheses of the overcoming of the state in the global market. Even if this position is considered regressive and utopian, the problems created by the transformation of the legal medium remain. These transformations are inevitable: classic nineteenth-century law does not have the "requisite variety" for the legal regulation of modern complex and diverse "risk societies", affected by the processes of globalization. This is true *a fortiori* for "spontaneous" judge-made law, irremediably conservative, adequate only for traditional societies that are very slow to evolve. In the face of economic and financial globalization, this kind of law seems passively to support existing social processes rather than enabling their control and regulation.

These problems could be reconsidered in the light of the conflict-based model. There is no doubt that, in contemporary societies, a redefinition of the respective roles of statute law and judge-made law is both inevitable and an opportunity we can take advantage of. Well known are the theories favourable to "light" legislation, to laws that define the framework for administrative decision and adjudication, to "mild" law and "flexible" law.[81] From this perspective, law appears above all as the framework for social actors to express themselves, to pursue their own aims, and to affirm their own values, making their coexistence possible in so far as they are anchored to some basic principles within an irreducibly pluralistic framework. We must ask, however, who the actors are and what social processes are pertinent. A conflict-oriented approach to the rule of law evidently distances itself from "statism" and "centralism", from the idea that the increase in public guarantees coincides with the expansion of state control over citizens' lives. In a legislative framework defined in the light of constitutional norms and social demands, public measures are the expression of social practices and claims from below. From this perspective, there is no room for Leoni's academic opposition between the "spontaneous" production of law by civil society and legislation, seen as authoritarian per se. We must ask what (relative) spontaneity is in question.

Leoni contrasts the notion of "legal certainty" in the sense of "precision", which originated in Greek democracy and was later to influence modern continental legal experience, with the idea of "certainty" developed from Roman law and then taken up by common law. In the first case, the "rule of law" refers to the existence of "certain" written laws. Such laws, however, can change overnight through the majority decision. In the second case, the law is not seen as legislators' arbitrary work but as resulting from spontaneous elaboration by social actors. This is a matter of "ascertaining" rather than making the law; and it is precisely this function that was performed, respectively, by Roman jurists and English judges. In this context, the "certainty of law" meant the absence of sudden and unexpected changes. Roman citizens and English subjects enjoyed therefore, Leoni maintains, a liberty analogous to that of entrepreneurs in a free market governed by stable rules.[82]

In support of his theory, Leoni cites the testimony of Cato the Censor, who contrasted Greek political systems, created by special legislators, with the Roman Republic, which took form over centuries, benefiting from the experience of many generations.[83] Machiavelli also points out that the Roman legal system was not the work of a single lawmaker but came about via spontaneous reactions to contingent events.[84] The form of spontaneity Machiavelli refers to, however, comes from the juxtaposition of two "humours"; the "great" who seek exclusive power and the "people" who defend liberty. It is this opposition that produces the "laws and institutions conducive to public liberty": not by market relationships but by political and social conflict.

2.6 The rule of law and intercultural dialogue

In the era of globalization a further problem arises: which model of the rule of law is best suited to intercultural dialogue and which arguments for it could be accepted most readily by cultures furthest from the Western political and legal tradition?

It could be maintained that "lightness" favours exportability: a "minimal rule of law", reduced to the essentials of formal equality and the protection of civil rights, could be presented as the most promising candidate for intercultural dialogue; a rule of law reduced to its essence could be more readily the focus of a form of "overlapping consensus". One might ask, however, if the traditional rights of liberty, rooted in western individualism, are not precisely the most difficult part to "translate". A look at documents such as the *African Charter on Human and People's Rights* or the *Universal Islamic Declaration* could be useful in this sense: the distance from the individualism of Western liberal tradition is evident and, instead, social rights and so-called "collective rights" are emphasized.[85] Moreover, it is difficult to imagine that for poorer societies a model of the rule of law without social services would be particularly attractive. It seems more likely that the appeal of Western socio-political systems and legal models has to do – in addition to its guarantees of individual liberty – with the historically achieved forms of protecting weaker individuals.

Some contemporary authors try to resolve the problem at the level of theoretical foundations. The language of rights and the institutional model of the rule of law are said to express the principles – universal and self-evident – of moral law,[86] or to be recognized unanimously in a hypothetical global "original position",[87] or to prove to be at the same time the necessary premises of the functional code of law, the expression of the evolutionary acquisitions of legal modernity, and the result of a rational agreement under ideal discourse conditions.[88] It can be maintained, however, that all these attempts at universal foundation actually refer to a well-defined historical, social, and cultural context.[89] Justly criticized also is the very idea of founding the rule of law in a unilaterally deontological perspective, which is expressed in a conception of rights as unchangeable and inviolable, as in Dworkin's idea of "rights as trumps": it is plausibly claimed that this conception of rights makes their political and social acceptability problematic, especially in the Eastern cultures and poor countries.[90]

On the other hand, some authors who rigorously take on the problem of intercultural dialogue seem to follow just as impenetrable a path when they look for common normative idioms or higher horizons of justice – in terms of "homomorphic equivalents" or "transcendental exchange" – in which to "translate" the Western language of individual rights and of the rule of law, as well as other normative idioms.[91]

In this respect, too, a conflict-based approach to the rule of law could be a useful point of view. First, the republican inheritance does not necessarily refer to an exclusive – not to say "ethno-nationalistic" – conception of collective identity. The "self" of self-government is established in the process of claiming and of giving an institutional application to the results of the claiming, therefore by means of the "struggle for rights". It is not, all in all, the expression of a closed collective ethos but rather the result of legal and political practices that can be changed and elaborated. On the other hand, the claim that the rule of law is founded on universally valid principles does not support but rather hinders an encounter of this type. Presenting the institutions of the rule of law as the expression of a higher rationality is unlikely to be the best way to make it acceptable to non-Western legal cultures. Probably to be preferred is the attitude, "frankly ethnocentric",[92] which expresses a value judgement in favour of the rule of law but also recognizes the relativity of the arguments for it.

In many situations, individuals and groups tend, in a more or less spontaneous way, to be submissive, to find reassurance in dependence. On the contrary, the language of rights privileges the action of rising up and reacting, of proclaiming one's dignity: a sentiment as common as it is specifically "human". The utilization of this sentiment could make the language of rights attractive. There is no doubt that "activism" has Western roots but it is plausible to maintain that it is precisely the claiming element of the language of rights that is also appreciated in non-Western cultures. If the rule of law is conceived of as the institutional structure that creates and stabilizes conditions for developing, activating, and implementing specific judicial techniques necessary for individuals and groups to get involved in the "struggle for rights", it could become attractive even outside the cultural experience that produced it.

In a conflict-based perspective, it is possible to consider two further questions concerning the impact of migration on national legal systems and the problem of protecting individuals from the power of non-state agencies. In a framework of constitutional guarantees of basic rights, the answer of the rule of law to the problems posed by immigration to Western countries should consist, first of all, in supporting and legally protecting the activity of making claims, the "struggle for rights" of immigrant groups and individuals. On the other hand, in the era of globalization the power of non-state agencies is undoubtedly increasing at a national and supra-national level: from multinational corporations to technocratic institutions, to the media and telecommunication networks and major transnational law firms that seem to escape legal regulation and instead produce law "on their own".[93] The classic model of the rule of law – designed to protect individuals against state power – seems inadequate. In the face of this also, valuing conflict, and thus giving legal protection to flexible forms of resistance to new powers and to the production of counter-powers, appears to be a plausible solution to the problem of finding a suitable conception of the rule of the law for the immediate future.

NOTES

1. See Pietro Costa's contribution in this volume.
2. Cf. Aristotle, *Politics*, 1292a–1293a, 1295a–1296b; it is worth pointing out that in Aristotle there also comes into play the question of the relationship between productive activities and practical action (*poiesis* and *praxis*), social segmentation, the availability of "free" time from work for politics: the worst forms of democracy, those which are furthest from the ideal of the rule of law, are those in which the institute of *mistophoria* permits even the workers to participate in the assemblies; the best forms of democracy are those of the *polis* of peasants, who have little time for politics and allow themselves to be governed by the middle class. Cf. also Plato, *The Statesman*, 300c–303b.
3. M. Tullius Cicero, *Pro Cluentio*, 53, p. 146; M. Tullius Cicero, *De Re Publica*, III, 22, p. 33; M. Tullius Cicero, *De Legibus*, I, 16, pp. 43–4.
4. For the development of the interpretative model of early-modern republicanism, see J.G.A. Pocock, *The Machiavellian Moment. Florentine Political Thought and the Atlantic Republican Tradition*, Princeton (NJ): Princeton University Press, 1975.
5. Cf. I. Kant, *Die Metaphisik der Sitten* [1797], in I. Kant, *Gesammelte Schriften*, Berlin-Leipzig: Reimer, 1907, vol. 4, pp. 319, 321–2.
6. Cf. N. Bobbio, "Organicismo e individualismo: un'antitesi", in A.M. Petroni and R. Viale (eds), *Individuale e collettivo. Decisione e razionalità*, Milano: Cortina, 1992.
7. Here classic Aristotelian themes re-emerge, such as that of the incompatibility between productive functions and politics, between *poiesis* and *praxis*. Political deliberation is the monopoly of the nobles in so far as they have free time and are rich and

therefore interested in the destiny of the republic, while the people are incapable of undertaking political initiatives on their own. For Harrington, attributing to the people the faculty of debating means "making themselves as much an anarchy as those of Athens" (J. Harrington, *The Commonwealth of Oceana*, in id., *The Commonwealth of Oceana and a System of Politics*, Cambridge: Cambridge University Press, 1992, p. 147). The republics with a "natural" aristocracy such as Sparta, Rome, and Venice are contrasted with, and preferred to, those with a "plebeian" tendency such as Athens, Switzerland, and Holland.

8. Cf. Aristotle, *Politics*, 1295a–1296b.
9. Cf. J. Harrington, *The Commonwealth of Oceana*, p. 71. This approach is evident right from the first pages of the *Preliminaries*. Harrington re-proposes Aristotle's *apologia* of democracy of peasants (cf. *Politics* 1318b–1319b). These are democracies characterized by scarce participation in the assemblies, and for this reason they are less exposed to "shakings and turbulency" (J. Harrington, *The Commonwealth of Oceana*, p. 5).
10. As is well known, Kant formulates a "practical principle of reason" according to which "the presently existing legislative authority ought to be obeyed, whatever its origin". Even in the face of serious despotic acts on the part of the sovereign power, which call in question the very constitutional power itself, popular uprising is not legitimate: "subjects may indeed oppose this injustice through complaint (*gravamina*), but not by resistance". Kant also excludes every right to "sedition", "rebellion", "tyrannicide" because "the sovereign has only rights against his subjects and no duties" (I. Kant, *Die Metaphisik der Sitten*, p. 319); according to Kant neither is permitted an "active resistance" through public demonstrations that go beyond mere parliamentary opposition: "no active resistance (by means of the people coming together arbitrarily; to coerce the government to take a certain course of action, and so itself performing an act of executive power) is permitted, but only *negative* resistance, that is, a *refusal* of the people (in parliament) to accede to every demand the government puts forth under the pretext of the good of the state" (ibid., p. 322).
11. Cf. J. Pocock, *The Machiavellian Moment*, pp. 208–11, 423–61, 477–86, 521–2, 527 ff.
12. Cf. A. MacIntyre, *Is Patriotism a Virtue?*, Lindley Lecture, Kansas City: The University of Kansas, 1984; M. Sandel, "Introduction", in M. Sandel (ed.), *Liberalism and its Critics*, Oxford: Basil Blackwell, 1984; M. Sandel, "The Procedural Republic and the Unencumbered Self", *Political Theory*, 12 (1984), 1; M. Sandel, *Democracy's Discontent. America in Search of a Public Philosophy*, Cambridge (MA): Harvard University Press, 1996; C. Taylor, "What's Wrong with Negative Liberty", in id., *Philosophy and the Human Sciences*, Cambridge: Cambridge University Press, 1985, pp. 211–29; C. Taylor, "Cross-purposes: The Liberal-Communitarian Debate", in N. Rosenblum (ed.), *Liberalism and the Moral Life*, Cambridge (MA): Harvard University Press, 1989.
13. Cf. P. Pettit, *Republicanism. A Theory of Freedom and Government*, Oxford: Clarendon Press, 1997.
14. Cf. J. Habermas, *Faktizität und Geltung. Beiträge zur Diskurstheorie des Rechts und des demokratischen Rechtsstaats*, Frankfurt a. M.: Suhrkamp, 1992, Eng. tr. *Between Facts and Norms. Contribution to a Discourse Theory of Law and Democracy*, Cambridge: Polity Press, 1996, p. 280; both Philip Pettit and Maurizio Viroli criticize the assimilation of communitarianism and republicanism. Viroli considers attributing an Aristotelian ascendancy to republicanism as "a grave historical error" (M. Viroli, *For Love of the Country: An Essay on Patriotism and Nationalism*, Oxford: Clarendon

Press, 1995; and M. Viroli, *Repubblicanesimo*, Roma-Bari: Laterza, 1999, Eng. tr. *Republicanism*, New York: Hill & Wang, 2002). Pettit (*Republicanism*, p. 8) distinguishes the republican tradition from "the sort of tradition – ultimately, the populist tradition – that hails the democratic participation of the people as one of the highest forms of good and that often waxes lyrical, in a communitarian vein, about the desirability of the close, homogeneous society", even though he does not fail to affirm that the republican ideal of liberty as non-domination would satisfy both liberals and communitarians.

15. The reference is to I. Berlin, *Four Essays on Liberty*, Oxford: Oxford University Press, 1969.
16. Cf. Q. Skinner, "Ambrogio Lorenzetti. The Artist as a Political Philosopher", *Proceedings of the British Academy* (1986), 72, pp. 1–56; Q. Skinner, "Machiavelli's *Discorsi* and Pre-Humanist Origins of Republican Ideas", in G. Bock, Q. Skinner, and M. Viroli (eds), *Machiavelli and Republicanism*, Cambridge: Cambridge University Press, 1993, pp. 121–41; Q. Skinner, "The Paradoxes of Political Liberty", in S. McMurrin (ed.), *The Tanner Lectures on Human Values*, Cambridge: Cambridge University Press, 1986, vol. VII, pp. 225 50; Q. Skinner, "The Italian City Republics", in J. Dunn (ed.), *Democracy: The Unfinished Journey 508 BC to AD 1993*, Oxford: Oxford University Press, 1992; Q. Skinner, *Liberty before Liberalism*, Cambridge: Cambridge University Press, 1998.
17. Cf. N. Machiavelli, *Discorsi sopra la prima Deca di Tito Livio*, I.16, in N. Machiavelli, *Tutte le opere*, Firenze: Sansoni, 1992, Eng. tr. *Discourses on The First Decade of Titus Livius*, in N. Machiavelli, *The Chief Works and Others*, Durham-London: Duke University Press, 1989, pp. 235–8.
18. Louis Althusser's theme of Machiavelli's "loneliness" (cf. L. Althusser, "Machiavel et nous", in id., *Ecrits philosophiques*, Paris: Stock/IMEC, 1995, vol. II) was taken up by M. Geuna, "La tradizione repubblicana e i suoi interpreti: famiglie teoriche e discontinuità concettuali", *Filosofia politica* (1998), 12, 1, pp. 130–2; cf. V.B. Sullivan, "Machiavelli's Momentary 'Machiavellian Moment'. A Reconsideration of Pocock's Treatment of the *Discourses*", *Political Theory* (1992), 20.
19. Cf. J. Harrington, *The Commonwealth of Oceana*, pp. 8–9.
20. "Machiavelli's republicanism is a commitment to a well-ordered popular government. By a well-ordered, or moderated, republic he means, in accordance with Cicero's concept of orderliness or moderation, a republic in which each component of the city has its proper place" (M. Viroli, *Machiavelli*, Oxford: Oxford University Press, 1998, p. 125). Viroli insists on the idea that Machiavelli stigmatizes not only the "arrogance" of the nobles but also the ambition of the people. The reference is to the social struggles following Roman agrarian laws and to the whole history of Florentine conflicts, with the "exaggerated demands" of the people. For Viroli, the social conflict that becomes an armed struggle is the chief danger for a republic; on the other hand, the virtuous forms of conflict end in laws that promote the common good. Conflicts, for Viroli, support public liberty "only in so far as they do not violate the main prerequisite of civil life – that is, the rule of law and the common good" (ibid., p. 127).
21. In order to criticize the interpretation that Viroli gives Machiavellian republicanism as inspired by the ideal of rule of law, it would be easy to cite chapter XVIII of *The Prince*, where Machiavelli refers to "two ways of fighting: one according to the laws, the other with force. The first is suited to man, the second to animals ... because the

first is often not sufficient, a prince must resort to the second" (N. Machiavelli, *De Principatibus*, in id., *Tutte le opere*, Eng. tr. in *The Chief Works and Others*, p. 64). Or one can cite chapter XII: "and because there cannot be good laws where armies are not good and where there are good armies, there must be good laws, I shall omit talking of laws and shall speak of armies" (ibid., p. 48). Moreover, it is debatable whether the 'wise' gentleman of the *Istorie fiorentine* (III.5) actually represents Machiavelli's viewpoint. In the same vein it could be legitimately maintained that it is the nihilistic egalitarianism of the *ciompo* [wool carder] which gives voice to Machiavelli's theory. (N. Machiavelli, *Istorie fiorentine*, III.13, in Id., *Tutte le opere*, Eng. tr. *The Florentine Histories*, in *The Chief Works and Others*).

22. Cf. G. Procacci, *Machiavelli nella cultura europea*, Roma-Bari: Laterza, 1995.
23. "In every city these two opposing parties [*umori*] exists ... the people desire not to be bossed and oppressed by the rich [*grandi*]; the rich desire to boss and oppress the people. As a result of these two opposed desires, one of three effects appears in the city: princely rule or liberty or license" (N. Machiavelli, *De principatibus*, Eng. tr., vol. IX, p. 39).
24. Cf. Aristotle, *Politics*, 1252a–1253a.
25. Cf. N. Machiavelli, *Discorsi*, Preface, Eng. tr., vol. II, p. 323.
26. From this point of view one ought not to interpret in an excessively literal manner the medical metaphor implicit in the use of the term "humor", as occurs in A.J. Parel, *The Machiavellian Cosmos*, New Haven (CT)/London: Yale University Press, 1992.
27. Machiavelli sees very favourably the possibility, long guaranteed to Roman citizens, of proposing new laws at the discussion of the *comitia* and of acting on them "either for or against". "A Tribune, and any other citizen whatever, had the right to propose a law to the people; on this every citizen was permitted to speak, either for or against, before it was decided. This custom was good when the citizens were good, because it has always been desirable that each one who thinks of something of benefit of the public should have the right to propose it. And it is good that each one should be permitted to state his opinion on it, in order that the people, having heard each, may choose the better. But when the citizen became wicked, such a basic custom became very bad, because only the powerful proposed laws, not for the common liberty but for their own power, and for fear of such men no one dared to speak against those laws. Thus the people were either deceived or forced into decreeing their own ruin" (N. Machiavelli, *Discorsi*, Eng. tr., vol. I, chap. 18, p. 242).
28. "The fruit of liberties and the end for which they were instituted is not government by everyone – for only the able and deserving should govern – but the observance of just laws and order, both of which are more secure in a republic than under the rule of one or few" (F. Guicciardini, "Ricordi", C 109, in id., *Opere*, Torino: UTET, 1970, Eng. tr. *Maxims and Reflections of a Renaissance Statesman*, New York: Harper & Row, 1965, p. 69).
29. Cf. N. Machiavelli, *Discorsi*, Eng. tr., vol. I, chap. 55, pp. 306–10.
30. "And though we showed above how the enmities at Rome between the Senate and the multitude kept Rome free by producing laws in support of liberty, and therefore the result of this Agrarian law seems out of harmony with my belief, I say that I do not for that reason abandon my opinion. To a great extent the ambition of the rich, if by various means and in various ways a city does not crush it, is what quickly brings her to ruin. So if the quarrels over the Agrarian Law took three hundred

years to make Rome a slave, she would perhaps have been brought much sooner to slavery if the people, with this law and with its other cravings, had not continually checked the ambition of the nobles. This also shows how much more men esteem property than they do positions of honour" (N. Machiavelli, *Discorsi*, Eng. tr., vol. I, chap. 37, p. 274).

31. Ibid., Eng. tr., vol. I, chap. 2, p. 199.
32. "If, then, we are discussing a prince obliged to keep the laws and a people chained by the laws, we shall see more worth in the people than in the prince. If we are to discuss either people or prince when unrestrained, fewer defects will be seen in the people than in the prince, and they will be smaller and easier to remedy" (N. Machiavelli, *Discorsi*, Eng. tr., vol. I, chap. 58, p. 317). Machiavelli's "popular" option also emerges quite clearly in what appears as his more "moderate" writing: the *Discursus florentinarum rerum* for Pope Leo X. In this text Machiavelli outlines for Florence a possible constitutional model of transition that provides for the revitalization of the republican institutions under a kind of short-term protectorate of the Medici. Here Machiavelli is undoubtedly inspired by the ideal of "mixed government" but inclined in favour of the people. In particular, he proposes the reopening of the "hall" of the Great Council, the key institution and symbolic seat of the Florentine republic of the people. In other words, he proposes the maximum of possible democracy under the given conditions (cf. N. Machiavelli, *Discursus florentinarum rerum post mortem iunioris Laurentii Medices*, in id., *Tutte le opere*, Eng. tr. *A Discourse on Remodeling the Government of Florence*, in id., *The Chief Works*, pp. 110–12).
33. "I say that those who condemn the dissensions between the nobility and the people seem to me to be finding fault with what as a first cause kept Rome free, and to be considering the quarrels and the noise that resulted from those dissensions rather than the good effects they brought about; they are not considering that in every republic there are two opposed factions, that of the people and that of the rich, and that all the laws made in favour of liberty result from their discord. We easily see that this was true in Rome, because from the Tarquins to the Gracchi, more than three hundred years, the dissensions in Rome rarely caused exile and very rarely bloodshed" (N. Machiavelli, *Discorsi*, Eng. tr., vol. I, chap. 4, pp. 202–3).
34. Cf. ibid., vol. I, chap. 7: "[I]njury would have been done by individuals to individuals. Such injury produces fear; fear seeks for defence; for defence partisans are obtained; from partisans rise parties in states; from parties their ruin." In vol. I, chap. 8: "From whence it came that on every side hate sprang up; hate went on to divisions; from divisions to parties; from parties to ruin" (Eng. tr., p. 216).
35. Ibid., Eng. tr., vol. I., chap. 40, pp. 279–84.
36. In more than one place in the *Istorie fiorentine*, the "license" of the people is condemned on a par with the "ambition" of the rich and powerful (the *grandi*), and the division into sects appears to be the basic reason for the degeneration of civic life. For an opposing viewpoint cf. F. Del Lucchese, "Disputare e combattere. Modi del conflitto nel pensiero di Machiavelli", *Filosofia politica* (2001), 1.
37. N. Machiavelli, *Istorie fiorentine*, II.12, Eng. tr., pp. 1093–4.
38. J. Tully ("Placing the 'Two Treatises'", in N. Phillipson and Q. Skinner (eds), *Political Discourse in Early Modern Britain*, Cambridge: Cambridge University Press, 1993, p. 261) points out how even Locke expresses such a concept of rights. Cf. Q. Skinner, "The State", in T. Ball, J. Farrand, and S. Hanson (eds), *Political Innovation and Conceptual Change*, Cambridge: Cambridge University Press, 1989, pp. 114–16.

39. A. Ferguson, *An Essay on the History of Civil Society* (1767), Cambridge: Cambridge University Press, 1996, p. 245.
40. "To bestow on communities some degree of political freedom, it is perhaps sufficient, that their members, either singly, or as they are involved with their several orders, should insist on their rights .... Amidst the contention of party, the interests of the public, even the maxims of justice and candour, are sometimes forgotten; and yet those fatal consequences that such measure of corruption seems to portend, do not unavoidably follow. The public interest is often secure, not because individuals are disposed to regard it as the end of their conduct, but because each, in his place, is determined to preserve his own. Liberty is maintained by the continued differences and opposition of numbers, not by their concurring zeal in behalf of equitable government" (A. Ferguson, *An Essay on the History of Civil Society*, pp. 124–5).
41. Cf. ibid., p. 211; "the influence of laws, where they have any real effect in the preservation of liberty, is not any magic power descending from shelves that are loaded with books, but is, in reality, the influence of men resolved to be free; of men, who, having adjusted in writing the terms on which they are to live with the state, and with their fellow-subjects, are determined, by their vigilance and spirit, to make these terms be observed" (ibid., p. 249).
42. Cf. the methodological essays of the principal exponents of the so-called 'Cambridge School': J.G.A. Pocock, *Politics, Language, and Time*, New York: Athenaeum, 1972; J. Dunn, "The Identity of the History of Ideas" (1968), in P. Laslett, W.G. Runciman and Q. Skinner (eds), *Philosophy, Politics and Society. Fourth Series*, Oxford: Blackwell 1972; J. Tully (ed.), *Meaning in Context. Quentin Skinner and His Critics*, Cambridge: Polity Press, 1988.
43. For a less systematic but at the same time very interesting use of the republican tradition in political theory, cf. R. Bellamy, *Liberalism and Pluralism. Towards a Politics of Compromise*, London: Routledge, 1999; R. Bellamy, *Rethinking Liberalism*, London/New York: Pinter, 2000.
44. Cf. J. Habermas, *Faktizität und Geltung*, passim; J. Habermas, *Die Einbeziehung des Anderen*, Frankfurt a. M.: Suhrkamp, 1996, Eng. tr. *The Inclusion of the Other: Studies in Political Theory*, Cambridge (MA): MIT Press, 1998; J. Habermas, "Stato di diritto e democrazia: nesso paradossale di principi contraddittori?", *Teoria politica* (2000), 16, 3.
45. Principle D is formulated in these terms: "Just those action norms are valid to which all possibly affected persons could agree as participants in rational discourses" (J. Habermas, *Faktizität und Geltung*, Eng. tr., p. 107).
46. Ibid., pp. 135–6.
47. Ibid., p. 143.
48. "The self-referential act that legally institutionalizes civic autonomy is still incomplete in essential respects; it cannot stabilize itself. ... The co-original constitution and conceptual interpenetration of law and political power call for a more extensive legitimization, one requiring legal channels for the sanctioning, organizing, and executive powers of the state itself. This is the idea of government by law [*Rechtsstaat*]" (J. Habermas, *Faktizität und Geltung*, Eng. tr., pp. 132–3).
49. See: A. Ross, *On Law and Justice*, London: Steven & Sons, 1958, pp. 168–9; H.L.A. Hart, "Are there any Natural Rights?", now in J. Waldron (ed.), *Theories of Rights*, Oxford: Oxford University Press, 1984, pp. 80–3; N. MacCormick, "Rights in Legislation", in P.M.S. Hacker and J. Raz (eds), *Law, Morality and Society. Essays in*

Honour of H.L.A. Hart, Oxford: Clarendon Press, 1977; M. La Torre, *Disavventure del diritto soggettivo*, Milano: Giuffrè, 1996, p. 338.

50. J. Feinberg, "The Nature and Value of Rights", in id., *Rights, Justice, and the Bonds of Liberty. Essays in Social Philosophy*, Princeton (NJ): Princeton University Press, 1980, p. 159.
51. F. Michelman, "Justification (and Justifiability) of Law in a Contradictory World", in J.R. Pennock and J.W. Chapman (eds), *Nomos XXVIII. Justification*, New York/London: New York University Press, 1986, p. 91.
52. Cf. F. Michelman, "Law's Republic", *The Yale Law Journal* (1988), 97, 8, p. 1505. Participating in the political process of "jurisgenesis" there are institutionalized deliberative assemblies, the judiciary (*in primis* the constitutional court) and all the arenas of public debate open to citizens which brings about a "potentially transformative dialogue" (ibid., p. 1531).
53. Cf. N. Bobbio, *L'età dei diritti*, Torino: Einaudi, 1992, Eng tr., *The Age of Rights*, Cambridge: Polity Press, 1996; L. Ferrajoli, *Diritti fondamentali*, Roma-Bari: Laterza, 2001.
54. Cf. N. Bobbio, *L'età dei diritti*, Eng. tr., pp. 53–61.
55. Cf. R. Tuck, *Natural Rights Theories*, Cambridge: Cambridge University Press, 1979.
56. Cf. J. Habermas, *Faktizität und Geltung*, Eng. tr., pp. 122–23.
57. Ibid., p. 401.
58. Cf. J.M. Barbalet, *Citizenship*, Milton Keynes: Open University Press, 1988; D. Zolo, "La strategia della cittadinanza", in D. Zolo (ed.), *La cittadinanza. Appartenenza, identità, diritti*, Roma-Bari: Laterza, 1994. The School of Law and Economics is critical of the excessive proliferation of rights; cf. R.A. Posner, *Economic Analysis of Law*, New York: Little, Brown, 1986.
59. Cf. F. Vertova, "Cittadinanza liberale, identità collettive, diritti sociali", in D. Zolo (ed.), *La cittadinanza*; S. Holmes and C.S. Sunstein, *The Cost of Rights. Why Liberty Depends on Taxes*, New York/London: Norton, 1999.
60. Cf. E. Wolgast, *The Grammar of Justice*, Ithaca (NY): Cornell University Press, 1987.
61. "The concrete relations of recognition mirrored in the mutual attribution of rights always emerge from a 'struggle for recognition'; this struggle is motivated by the suffering incurred by, and the indignation against, concrete cases of disrespect. As Axel Honneth has shown, experiences of insults to human dignity are what must be articulated in order to attest to those aspects under which equals must be treated equally and unequals treated unequally in the given context. This contest over the interpretations of needs cannot be delegated to judges and officials, not even to politicians" (J. Habermas, *Faktizität und Geltung*, Eng. tr., p. 426).
62. Cf. *Bowers vs. Hardwick*, 478 U.S. 186 [1986]. Michelman bases the protection of sexual freedom on the consideration that prohibiting homosexuality means inhibiting "not just a certain sort of inclination that 'anyone' might feel, but a more personally constitutive and distinctive way, or ways, of being". In this way the development of "an aspect of identity demanding respect" is hindered (F. Michelman, "Law's Republic", p. 1533) denying, therefore, citizenship to certain individuals. From this viewpoint privacy becomes a political right. Such "cross-fertilization of the constitutional-legal notion of autonomy – simple personal liberty – by the first-amendment inspired value of freedom of association nicely represents the republican penchant for rights that bridge the personal and the political". From this viewpoint

privacy is seen "not only as an end (however controversial) of liberation by law but also as such liberation's constant and regenerative – jurisgenerative – beginning. The argument forges the link between privacy and citizenship" (ibid., p. 1535).

63. Ibid., pp. 1499–500.
64. Ibid., pp. 1502, 1513.
65. Cf. D. Held, *Models of Democracy*, Cambridge: Polity Press, 1987.
66. Cf. N. Bobbio, *Il futuro della democrazia*, Torino: Einaudi, 1984, Eng. tr. *The Future of Democracy*, Minneapolis (MN): University of Minnesota Press, 1987; D. Zolo, *Democracy and Complexity*, Cambridge: Polity Press, 1992; P.P. Portinaro, *La rondine, il topo e il castoro*, Venezia: Marsilio, 1993.
67. Cf. J. Habermas, "Volkssouveränität als Verfahren" (1988), now in id., *Faktizität und Geltung*, Eng. tr. "Popular Sovereignty as Procedure", in *Between Facts and Norms*, pp. 463–90.
68. Cf. P. Pettit, *Republicanism*, esp. pp. 183–205.
69. Cf. J. Habermas, *Faktizität und Geltung*, passim.
70. Cf. P. Pettit, *Republicanism*, pp. 187–90.
71. Cf. L. Ferrajoli, *Diritti fondamentali*, passim.
72. Cf. J. Habermas, *Faktizität und Geltung*, Eng. tr., pp. 307–8.
73. Ibid., p. 309. "The making of norms is primarily a justice issue, subject to principles which establish what is equally good for all" (J. Habermas, *Faktizität und Geltung*, Eng. tr., p. 282).
74. In the history of the Supreme Court, "interventionist" phases in which the Court tends to exercise a leading role are distinguished from phases in which the Court tends to follow, or not to challenge, the executive and legislative branches. In the so-called "Lochner Era" (from the well-known sentence in which the legal regulation of the working hours of bakers was declared unconstitutional), the Supreme Court contrasted the attempts to introduce forms of protection for workers and regulatory actions in the economy with a rigid re-proposal of the principles for freedom of business and commerce. This phase of "conservative activism" was overcome, following the clash with the Roosevelt administration, at the beginning of the 1930s. After such an epoch of "liberal restraint" it was thanks to Chief Justice Warren that the Court returned to a leading role through a series of verdicts against racial segregation and in favour of civil rights. Against this "liberal activism", Richard Nixon declared during the presidential election campaign of 1968 that the justices of the Court had to play a role of "strict constructionists". The systematic nomination of conservative judges on the part of President Reagan and President George Bush, Sr. is recent history. Court sentences such as *Bowers* express in the "Lead Opinion" the idea of illegitimacy of an active intervention by judges in the interpretation and evolution of constitutional principles.
75. F. Michelman, "Law's Republic", p. 1521.
76. Ibid., p. 1530.
77. Cf. *Bowers v. Hardwick*. According to the Lead Opinion, there is no right to sodomy on the part of homosexuals. Sodomy has been prohibited by "millennia of moral teaching", by Common Law and by the criminal law of a great many of the states and, in any case, the majority of the population, through democratic procedures, has the right to impose its viewpoint of moral decency. Moreover, the Lead Opinion continues, the Supreme Court cannot take upon itself the illegitimate role of legislative innovation. On the theme cf. R. Dworkin, "Liberal Community", *California Law Review* (1989), 77.

78. C. Sunstein, "Beyond the Republican Revival", *Yale Law Review* (1988), 97, p. 1539.
79. From this point of view, the position of Michelman and Sunstein differs from Bruce Ackerman's theory of law-making on "two tracks". See B. Ackerman, "The Storr Lectures: Discovering the Constitution", *The Yale Law Journal* (1984), 93; B. Ackerman, *We the People. 1. Foundations*, Cambridge (MA): Harvard University Press 1991. On these questions cf. Brunella Casalini's contribution in the present volume.
80. Cf. D. Grimm, "Der Wandel der Staatsaufgaben und die Krise des Rechtsstaats", in D. Grimm, *Die Zukunft der Verfassung*, Frankfurt a. M.: Suhrkamp, 1991.
81. Cf. G. Zagrebelsky, *Il diritto mite*, Torino: Einaudi, 1992.
82. Cf. B. Leoni, *Freedom and the Law* (1961), Indianapolis: Liberty Fund, 1991, pp. 83–7.
83. "Our State, instead, is the fruit not of the personal creation of one man alone, but of a great many: it was not founded in the course of the life of an individual, but in the course of a line of centuries and of generations. For this reason, he said that there has never been in the world a man so intelligent as to foresee everything and even if they succeeded in consolidating all their brains into the head of only one man, it would be impossible for that person to take charge of everything at the same time without having the experience that comes from the practice of a long period of history" (M. Tullius Cicero, *De Re Publica*, vol. II, chap.1, p. 2).
84. "But let us come to Rome. In her case, in spite of her not having a Lycurgus to organize her at the beginning in such a way that she could continue free for a long time, nonetheless so many unexpected events happened, on account of the disunion between the plebeians and the Senate, that what an organizer had not done was done by Chance" (N. Machiavelli, *Discorsi*, Eng. tr., vol. I, chap. 2, p. 200).
85. See F. Belvisi, "Universal Legal Concepts? A Critic of 'General' Legal Theory", *Ratio Juris* (1996), 9, p. 1; F. Belvisi, "La crisi dell'universalismo giuridico come conseguenza del rapporto tra diritto e cultura", in V. Ferrari, M.L. Ghezzi, and N. Grindelli Vigogna (eds), *Diritto, cultura e libertà*, Milano: Giuffrè, 1998.
86. See J. Finnis, *Natural Law and Natural Rights*, Oxford: Clarendon, 1980; J. Finnis, *Moral Absolutes: Tradition, Revision and Truth*, Washington (DC): The Catholic University of America Press, 1992.
87. Cf. J. Rawls, "The Law of Peoples", in S. Shute and S. Hurley (eds), *On Human Rights. Oxford Amnesty Lectures 1993*, New York: Basic Books, 1993.
88. Cf. J. Habermas, *Faktizität und Geltung*, passim.
89. Cf. L. Baccelli, *Il particolarismo dei diritti. Poteri degli individui e paradossi dell'individualismo*, Roma: Carocci, 1999, chap. 3.
90. Cf. A. Sen, "Legal Rights and Moral Rights: Old Questions and New Problems", *Ratio Juris* (1996), 9, 2.
91. Cf. R. Panikkar, "La notion des droits de l'homme est-elle un concept occidental?", *Diogéne* (1980), 120; O. Höffe, "Déterminer le droits de l'homme à travers une discussion interculturelle", *Revue de métaphisique et de morale* (1997), 4.
92. Cf. R. Rorty, "Human Rights, Rationality, and Sentimentality", in S. Shute and S. Hurley (eds), *On Human Rights*; R. Rorty, "Giustizia come lealtà più ampia", *Filosofia e questioni pubbliche* (1996), 2, p. 1.
93. Cf. M.R. Ferrarese, *Le istituzioni della globalizzazione*, Bologna: il Mulino, 2000.

CHAPTER 12

LEONI'S AND HAYEK'S CRITIQUE OF THE RULE OF LAW IN CONTINENTAL EUROPE

Maria Chiara Pievatolo

History is a great resource for anyone who deems formalistic conceptions of the rule of law insufficient. Relying on a given tradition and understanding its development seems to protect law from static and abstract theories that try to shape its content and forms as a system. Whoever thinks he has history on his side will see both natural law and legal formalism as unilateral conceptions. The former suggests values and references, which may be theoretically outdated and practically ineffective, whereas the formal structures underlying the latter theory[1] run the risk of being nothing more than powerless containers of formally uncontrollable political decisions.[2] A theorist who ignores history – or, rather, deliberately runs the risk of being overcome by history – is doomed to be a theorist without history. Yet, whether this is true or not depends on how this history is told.

There is an extensive literature on the version of neo-liberal thinking grounded on methodological individualism, whose most prominent authors are the Austrian Friedrich A. von Hayek and the Italian Bruno Leoni. As regards the rule of law, this version may be interesting for it seems to provide an understanding of law that is so deeply rooted in history that it can do without a critically aware axiologic background, a formal account, and even a relationship with formally determined institutions. When applied to law, the fundamental idea of methodological individualism is that the rule of law consists of principles that nobody has chosen consciously but which are the unintentional evolutionary outcome of individual actions. Law is formed just like paths in a wood: each walker tries to pass through leafy branches and repeated passage creates paths which others may rely on and which "work" much "better" to achieve everyone's goals than purpose-designed routes. Law and history are not in conflict since legal norms make up a "spontaneous order" of naturalistic regularities selected by evolution.

This interpretation of law – says Hayek – is inferential or reconstructive in character: we do not really know how a particular path has been formed but we can infer how this generally happens since we know how

P. Costa and D. Zolo (eds.), The Rule of Law: History, Theory and Criticism, 421–439.

our fellow human beings behave when looking for a path, and, in the light of this, we are able ideally to build a genealogical model. Yet, if this account is inferential, then what Hayek sees as a spontaneous order – from the point of view of the walker looking for a path – may appear to others as irregularity and disorder. Just think of the mushroom-seeker, for whom beaten paths are barren, or of those concerned with preserving the soil from erosion. We can tell many stories and infer many different models of order, depending on our viewpoint, which will lead us to deem this or that principle to be decisive. Whoever thinks he has "the" history on his side has, in fact, only the genealogy he reconstructs by taking a viewpoint or a particular interest of his to be decisive.

The metaphor of the "spontaneous" emergence of pathways suggests an opposition between two ideas of law: either a deliberate project grounded on political institutions or a spontaneous order in which political institutions are merely instrumental and may become superfluous or even damaging. Such a bipartition rejects the continental *Rechtsstaat*, the constitutional democratic state, and totalitarian (especially socialist) systems in favour of a single "genuine" form of the rule of law, namely, the English version, founded on tradition and case law. As regards law-making, there is a proper rule of law only when decisions about what is law are essentially or exclusively made by judges and legal scholars within the context of an organic tradition, rather than by legislative bodies.[3] Only the rule of law guarantees the "government of law": all the rest is "government of men", whether they are, quite indifferently, democratic majorities, governors or officials of a state ruled by administrative law, or totalitarian dictators. On the one hand, there are men with their arbitrary decisions; on the other, there are law and tradition, whose determinations go well beyond what individuals know and want. The relationship between history and law, as political form and choice, is not a problem for the law is actually "the" history.

Assuming the rule of law to be, as Pietro Costa writes in the introduction to this volume, a set of mechanisms used to mediate, modulate, and check the relationship between power and individuals, we may wonder whether the above assimilation between law and history – or, rather, *a* history told at a given time, in a certain place, and in a certain manner[4] – really provides a model of conceptually determined legal mediation. For the theory of the rule of law as a spontaneous order arises and arose within theoretical and political contexts of conflicting philosophies of history, facing important and controversial revolutionary experiences, such as the French and Russian ones. Within such contexts, the confrontation between traditionalist philosophies of history, on the one hand, and progressive and prophetic stances, on the other, might seem a current issue. However, now that the time of confrontations is over, it must be questioned whether the theory of rule of law as spontaneous order can offer a definite model capable of outliving its controversies.

1 THE GOVERNMENT OF LAW AS A GOVERNMENT OF MEN

Hayek's juxtaposition between a spontaneous (legal) order and an artificial human order mirrors the classic opposition between a government of law and a government of men, which is to be found in Plato's *Statesman*.[5] Among other things, Plato's opposition also deals with law's relationship with history. The anonymous protagonist of *Statesman* recounts the following myth: in order to demonstrate his support of Atreus, who is arguing with his brother Thyestes over an inheritance, Zeus changes the course of the stars and sun, making the latter rise in the east rather than in the west, as it had until then. Such a reversal of the universal order brought about a change to the past world's overall order, when the master of gods was Chronos rather than Zeus.[6]

During the rule of Chronos, politicians were shepherds and governed without laws, and indeed were divine figures. The humanity they guided had a life cycle similar to that of a vegetable: it arose from the earth, blossomed, de-structured itself, and ultimately disappeared. As Plato suggested, however, politicians can no longer be seen as divine shepherds. They are like their subjects, in terms of their education and upbringing.

A just constitution – as argued by Plato – is characterized by magistrates who are experts in their art, so that the government is in the hands of intelligent individuals. A law cannot comprise what is best and fair for all individuals or decide what is best and fair for each single individual. In the light of the differences among men and among their actions, given that nothing human is unchangeable, the legal art cannot enunciate a simple rule that is valid at all times and in all cases. Law can be compared to an authoritarian and ignorant man who demands unswerving and unquestioning obedience to his orders, even when new situations arise. A law for many people must be generic and loose with respect to individual situations. However, if law proves to be inadequate in response to social change, society's intelligent leaders are justified in breaking it, though public opinion may require them first to persuade citizens that changes are warranted. The relationship between the government of law and that of men is akin to that between the medicine manual and the doctor: the former's instructions are generic but if we cannot consult a doctor we must refer to them even though we are aware that they are inadequate.

Does Plato prefer the government of law or the government of men? At first sight, the myth seems to suggest that law is a mere makeshift solution conceived to remedy governors' unreliability: we would gladly do without law if politicians were wise and capable of dealing with the particularities of men and their situations without resorting to rough general rules. Yet, the political and divine shepherds' government was very different from ours: the cycle of human life and human flourishing – as American neo-Aristotelians say – followed the simple model that we have compared to the natural botanical cycle of growth, bloom, and decay and for this, without controversies or the need for deliberation over problems.

Things are now different: humanity develops, culturally and historically, through open relations, even in its reproduction. Hence, a model grounded on a naturalistic understanding of human development and flourishing is of no use. Neither is a god's wisdom useful, since the world develops on its own. While the universe in the past was ordered and could be reduced to rules, now it is complex and chaotic. A god no longer governs, men do. This brings about the problem as to the government of law: human reality is cultural and historical; hence, a naturalistic perspective is counterproductive, since men cannot be treated as plants and cannot be endowed with a god's wisdom. Hence, the government of law is preferable, precisely *because men govern.* Laws are of no use to govern harmony, since this already has its regularities; they are useful to regulate chaos. Laws would be meaningless if there were only divine creatures, plants and animals similar to plants, rather than men, histories, and cultures.

As revealed in Plato's myth, there are at least three main features of the historical condition:

1. There is no longer an immutable order that is established once and for all; therefore, there is no longer a botany of humanity grounded on unquestionable and fixed flourishing models: human realization itself, once it enters the historical ambit, becomes problematic.
2. Correspondingly, there is no divine wisdom in the historical world: the paternalistic pastoral government of the age of Chronos was not oppressive, because men were vegetable-type creatures, without a history, to be grown according to a botany, which had been for ever established.
3. The government of law is suitable to history; the former, faced with the unstable world it is supposed to rule, is human and not divine, textual and thus semantically closed, authoritarian and rough with respect to a changeable, rather than fixed, reality.

Even though the historical condition – the lack of order and of the corresponding wisdom grounded on 'botanic' formulas valid for ever – requires law as a closed system ordering chaos, it also reveals its inadequacy, since the environment of law goes beyond what law itself claims to fix and formalize. A theory of the rule of law, which is fully aware of historical conditions, should question the manners and instruments, which might allow it to come to terms with its own limits: the limits which make law necessary though not exhaustive.

Not only does the myth told in *Statesman* provide a not-particularly-edifying account of the historical condition, but it also represents, in an apparently edifying way, the non-historical and vegetative condition of the age of Chronos. Even the latter is a history, which someone is interested in recounting. It is a kind of history where changes can be mirrored by a foreseeable formula established by a governor in whom power and knowledge are concentrated. To reduce history to a naturalistic formula is itself a way to deal with and exorcize it that, according to the foreign narrator of the myth, is an alternative to the way that justifies the government of law.[7] The government of law is a historical and human order; the government of men may be conceived only as a non-historical and divine model. When opting for the government of law, we ought to be aware that it is historically and humanly conditioned and circumscribed, and that its internal forms and reasons are insufficient; when choosing the government of men, we need to view the universe as non-historical and accept that governors are endowed with divine wisdom.

In *Statesman*, such options are the two elements of a dilemma, in that to choose one option means to exclude the other. However, it might be argued that it is sufficient to find the formula of law's historical development in order to unite what Plato thought was incompatible, thus obtaining a government of law, or rather a rule of law, endowed with superhuman wisdom. In order to be successful, such a theory would have to provide a formula of the rule of law capable both of accounting for history's development and, above all, of being rigorously determined in its contents. For an appeal to history with an episodic and vague content would be tantamount to surreptitiously appealing to the government of men.

Against such a background, the justification of the rule of law grounded on the historical and philosophical formula of the spontaneous order is worth examining. Its analysis will help us in understanding whether it can offer a definite contribution to the discussion on the rule of law, or whether it may be endowed with a given content only by secretly (maybe consciously) relying on the government of men or, more precisely, of far-from-divine notables and judges.[8]

2 RULE OF LAW AND LEGAL HISTORICISM

According to the Italian philosopher of law Guido Fassò, the rule of law may be defined in two ways, depending on whether the perspective of *lawfulness* or *legitimacy* is taken into account.[9] Under the technical and formal perspective of lawfulness, the rule of law characterizes a state limited by law, which checks and circumscribes the state's sovereignty. Under the legitimacy perspective, the rule of law characterizes a state grounded on substantive justice, which ought to be thought of as superior to the technical and formal requirements of mere lawfulness.

Natural law doctrines, as seen by Fassò, deal with the rule of law both as a feature of a lawful state and of a just state. Yet, given their rationalist and non-historicist outlook, natural law doctrines remain abstract, non-historical, and arbitrary – although they do express the need to combine lawfulness with legitimacy. Both, lawfulness without legitimacy and legitimacy without lawfulness, lead to arbitrariness, i.e. to denying the restraint on sovereignty and the quest for certainty, which the rule of law is grounded on. If a law is defined only on a formalistic level, it is open to any content formally compatible therewith; on the contrary, mere substantive legitimacy replaces the government of law with of the government of men, or rather of one man or some men who are supposedly able to infer or know justice. On the other hand, if we purported – like natural law doctrines – to bind law according to content-based and rationalistic criteria, we would make it rigid and historically arbitrary.

In the light of the above, we might conclude that the rule of law, no matter what is meant by it, conceals arbitrary power – since the very limitation of sovereignty, which the rule of law arises from, ends up by ultimately being an arbitrary limitation. Fassò, nonetheless, believes that history might provide the requirements of limitation, certainty and guarantee of individual rights – which are abstractly expressed by natural law doctrines – with a non-arbitrary content. However, in order to do so, the conception of law needs to be enlarged, i.e. law ought not to be identified with rules, will, arbitrariness; rather, it ought to include the specific and particular aspects of case law and custom.

In this respect, Fassò refers to Bruno Leoni, who believes that the rule of law inspired by natural law doctrines and the French Revolution, by reducing all law to acts of parliament excludes citizens' participation in the law-making process and jeopardizes legal certainty because of legislative pollution. Law can be certain only if it is a spontaneous social creation, administered by notables or *honoratiores* not bound by written laws.[10] Rather than the rule of legislative or formal law, there ought to be a rule of social spontaneous or free law. Such a system can assume and mirror society's widespread values, since it is "spontaneous" both in the selection of judges and jurists – which is based on the parties' approval –and in the declaration of law, founded not on legislators' express will, but rather on precedents and customs. Law is not wanted by any given individual but is found within society's historical structure. For if law were wanted by a given individual it would be arbitrary. Being instead found within an order, it guarantees individuals against the state's power; as it is the case in the British tradition of common law – if we overlook, as Leoni himself significantly does, the political role of parliament in creating this tradition.[11]

We might wonder whether it is correct to view this neo-liberal legal historicism as an attempt to come to terms with history by integrating or surrogating the government of law with the government of men. Here men are not Plato's divine shepherds but judges, officials, and notables. There is no guarantee that such figures are less authoritarian than the law they are supposed to complement historically: being themselves men within a historical setting, it is subjectively and objectively impossible for them to deviate from the botany of humanity, which is typical of a kind of knowledge transcending history. If this kind of legal historicism reduced the government of law to the government of men, a historicist rule of law would be, quite simply, a paternalistic and not very justified regime of notables.

Yet, the theory of the spontaneous order claims it can explain how good laws (i.e. able to cope with historical mutations) "grow" and how men can complement their development. The historicist rule of law would risk making citizens' rights empty rhetoric only if it were proven that the theory is programmatically vague. Indeed, a theory whose aim – to detect the law of the historical development of human societies – is out of proportion with respect to its chosen theoretical means[12] may be a form of authoritarian paternalism.

3 THE RULE OF LAW AS A SPONTANEOUS ORDER: THE ISSUE OF INDIVIDUAL FREEDOM

Theorists of the spontaneous order are usually deemed to be interested in the "uncompromising protection of individual freedom".[13] In *The Constitution of Liberty*, Hayek clearly depicts his ideal state of liberty, namely a state where coercion is reduced to a minimum, so that all individuals may act in line with their own projects rather than being subject to other individuals' will. This concept of freedom is negative, for it denotes the lack of hindrances, and exclusively concerns – as specified by Hayek – the relationship among men. Coercion is when an individual's environment and circumstances are so controlled by others that he cannot pursue a coherent project of his own – at best, he can choose the lesser damage – but must serve other people's aims. Coercion is wrong since it destroys an individual's capacity for thinking and evaluating and makes him an instrument of others' purposes. An action is free when it is based on data that cannot be arbitrarily moulded by others; in order to guarantee free individual action, a private domain, which nobody can interfere with, must be secured.[14]

If taken seriously, Hayek's conception of freedom is hardly attainable within a historical context. Freedom is viewed as a free area whose data are not under others' control or influence but are completely open to individuals' choices. Yet, such a free area does not exist within society: even life is the result of other people's choices. Similarly, Hayek's theory whereby employees are free in so far as they can choose a given employer among many competing employers, if unemployment does not go beyond a certain level,[15] is not consistent with his negative idea of freedom. The environment of the worker's choices is determined by others: it matters very little whether the latter are effectively or only nominally competing among them in trying to attract him. What really matters is that the situation in which the worker has to make his choice is decided by others and not by himself.

It follows that Hayek's idea of freedom is not negative because it defines an individual domain of non-interference; rather, it is negative because it defines something that does not exist within society. On the other hand, the manipulation of individuals is something that Hayek's liberalism can hardly do without. A free society grounded on a legal system requires people to be responsible for their actions: i.e. that they are legally imputable in that they are permeable to law's normal coercive instruments.[16] In other words, their manipulation is essential under the rule of law: liberal beings are not stoical wise beings, capable of abstracting their passions and organizing their own area of non-interference within the stronghold of their reason; rather, they *must* be so weak that the scope of the celebrated concept of negative freedom is practically null.

Nonetheless, there is an aspect of Hayek's negative freedom that might endow his idea with a non-ironical meaning. Hayek is keen on specifying that his conception of freedom is applicable only to relationships among men. Therefore, for negative freedom to exist, it suffices to prove that the conditions in which an individual makes his choices are not the immediate product of someone else's deliberation, but the output of an impersonal and, in this respect, naturalistic process. Therefore, the more an individual's range of choices is defined by forces and processes deemed as impersonal and over-personal, the more the individual is "free", i.e. no human being voluntarily interferes with this range. Quite paradoxically, we are free as long as the world we live in does not depend on our choices – i.e. as long as we view our culture and society as a natural output, beyond individual control.[17] Furthermore, since individuals make choices and decisions, the less such choices and decisions affect the context of our choice directly and intentionally, the freer we are.

Such an idea must hold true also for negative freedom whose boundaries and guarantees, if they are not to be oppressive and arbitrary, must be seen as the output of an impersonal process and not as the immediate result of someone's thoughts and choices. According to Hayek, the most reliable theory on freedom is the British one, formulated by the eighteenth-century Scottish school (David Hume, Adam Smith, and Adam Ferguson) and by some English contemporary thinkers (Josiah Tucker, Edmund Burke, William Paley) in that it purports to understand the common law tradition and spirit: the law and freedom it guarantees are a conscious production but the output of selection and evolution processes hardly controlled by individual reason: society is conceptualized as a living organism, which normally grows and develops "on its own".[18] Quite coherently, Leoni argues that the only acceptable definition of freedom is the lexical one, whereby "freedom is a word employed in ordinary language to indicate particular kinds of psychological experiences".[19] Such a definition, which essentially appeals to a widespread and shared *idem sentire*, is justified precisely because such an *idem sentire* results from an evolution and a tradition legitimating it, and not from someone's theoretical and practical choice.

The *theoretical* delimitation and justification of freedom on the grounds of tradition suggests that, for Hayek and Leoni, there is no autonomous domain of practical reason within which, interest in, and reflection on, freedom are to be found. As Hayek argues in *The Constitution of Liberty*, the justification of individual freedom is mainly grounded on the acknowledgement of our ignorance of a large number of factors on which the achievement of our aims and well-being depends. If we were omniscient, if we were able to know what might affect the attainment of our future, as well as current wishes, freedom would have no collective usefulness since experimentation would not be required. On the other hand, Hayek adds, where knowledge is limited, freedom is necessary to leave room for unpredictability: the development of civilization depends on maximizing the likelihood of incidents, which leads to working out, through evolutionary selection, better rules overall.[20]

When Hayek speaks about omniscience, he does not mean individual omniscience but a supposed collective omniscience: not surprisingly, he uses the first person plural and justifies individual freedom as a means to experiment and select rules needed for "civilization" itself. The meaning of freedom is exclusively associated with a common knowledge deficit that makes individual experimentations and inventions highly recommended for the development of a collective entity, i.e. "civilization". A hypothetical "civilization" with an already perfect, complete, and finished body of notions would have no reasons for allowing individual freedom.

Hayek's reasoning seems to suggest that his understanding of freedom has neither practical value nor a genuinely individual meaning. If practical reason were independent of theoretical reason, if the value and meaning of what we do were at least partially independent of what "civilization" collectively knows, omniscience would not eliminate freedom as a condition for the possibility of choices, moral laws, and the associated technical decisions. These should be a problem even in a "civilization" *theoretically* able to know all the elements of its environment. If individual autonomy were something we were to come to terms with beyond its evolutionary meaning, someone's omniscience should not impinge upon the value of someone else's free experiments and choices.

The holistic and functionalistic ease with which the passage of *The Constitution of Liberty*[21] stating this position ignores the practical meaning of freedom leads us to assume that, strictly speaking, Hayek's interest in freedom is morally and politically null. If we were to take Hayek's considerations seriously, we should conclude that individuals knowing the development laws of the spontaneous order do not value liberty as such but only as a means, as long as they are aware of their ignorance.

4 THE RULE OF LAW AS A SPONTANEOUS ORDER: LAW'S NATURAL CHARACTER

Law, being a system of regularities distinct from legislation, i.e. from the explicit and voluntary production of norms by a somehow legitimated authority, is a spontaneous order. It is spontaneous in that the regularities it is made of are not the result of a deliberate project – individuals "following" such regularities need not even be aware of them – but are formed and selected through an evolutionary process: a given behaviour becomes a regularity when the group adopting it outlives and prevails over other groups. The world of law, language, market, and of many other cultural institutions is to be thought of as the result of human action rather than human planning. No human mind is able to plan a spontaneous order, since no human mind is capable of calculating the infinite complexity of interactions and correlations that may take place between one single element of the system and all other elements.[22] It follows that the approach of the common law judge, who draws the law for each individual case from a number of principles already existing within tradition and does not claim to create it, is the most respectful of the social order.

Hayek draws a line between two kinds of social order: *taxis* is an "artificial" order resulting from an organization planned for a specific purpose; *kosmos* is an order made of spontaneously created regularities, which is typical of self-organizing and self-governing systems. "An order not deliberately made by man *does exist*" – yet, such a circumstance, says Hayek, is not widely acknowledged because it has "*to be traced by our intellect*".[23] The reconstruction process of an order – be it an order of rules or woodland paths – is an inferential process. So why cannot it be argued that the *kosmos* is a mere *taxis* of ours, i.e. a construction *of ours* whereby we, as theorists, seek to ascribe a given meaning to reality's multiplicity?

Such a reasoning, albeit not extraneous to Hayek's work, would be deleterious in this context, since legislation and law, *taxis* and *kosmos* or, more generally, scientific theories open to discussion and natural truths that individuals must abide by (because too complex for our limited minds) would become virtually undistinguishable. The vegetable order of law would lose its epistemological legitimization. Therefore, in this case, the rhetoric of ignorance is relinquished in order to firmly claim that the system is not a cognitive construction of ours; rather, it has an objective existence of its own. The system's viewpoint is treated as an absolute viewpoint.[24] There is no way out of the system.

That even an order grounded on deliberately created rules can be spontaneous is proven by the fact that its particular manifestations will always depend on factors that were not known or could not have been possibly known to whoever planned such rules.[25]

Hence, according to Hayek, human culture and society are spontaneous orders; our minds are too limited to understand their complexity and foresee their development; also, the establishment of artificial rules, by interacting with a complex world, falls within a spontaneous order. Ergo, in the perspective of the spontaneous order, what is the difference between a common law judgment, a statute enacted by a democratically legitimated parliament, and a tyrant's edict?

If we take the effects of the above acts into account, we can see that neither judges nor lawmakers nor tyrants have a privileged viewpoint with respect to the complexity of the potential consequences of their actions. Within a spontaneous order, nobody can exhaustively justify his choices at the time he makes them. Justification is something on which evolution, with hindsight, has the last word; it follows that he who makes legal choices has no precise criterion that might legitimate them and must thus grope his way as if in the dark. The only legitimating criterion is retrospective. According to Hayek's outlook, judges will say that in making decisions they are not acting creatively but merely discovering what already existed, whereas democratic legislators and tyrants will variously appeal to one or more wills or procedures. This does not rule out that evolution (through its inscrutable processes) may end up by "vindicating" the output of a conscious will rather than of an act of interpretation or recognition.

None of the suggested legitimating criteria is able, in itself, to circumscribe the content of legal choices: legitimacy concerns the future effects and the link of a given choice with that of an antecedent, which may be either cognitive or voluntary. This means that the same legal act may be seen as the output of liberal wisdom, if the author appeals to the spontaneous order, or of an intolerable tyranny, if the author acknowledges that it is the result of will or imposition.[26] Hence, in order not to breach others' negative freedom we only need to convince them that our choices fall within a naturalistic order.

5 THE RULE OF LAW AS A SPONTANEOUS ORDER: THE INDETERMINACY OF NORMS

The spontaneous order acts in an inscrutable manner, and may be (only generally) recognized and explained with hindsight: it follows that there can be no criterion defining normative behaviours or acts producing or falling within a spontaneous order. This, however, exclusively regards the law-making process. Hence, we need to examine whether Hayek's system allows for determined criteria to identify the typical norms of a spontaneous order[27] according to their contents; this must be done by bearing in mind that, given Hayek's mistrust in a planning reason, the genesis of rules remains in any event crucial. Hence, we should ask whether there is a close relationship between the characters of the typical rules of a spontaneous order, their spontaneous genesis and their justification based on that genesis.

As explained by Hayek, the typical rules of a spontaneous order arise as simple natural regularities, i.e. rules, which individuals unconsciously and practically abide by. They become norms, i.e. linguistically articulated prescriptive rules, only when intellect develops and the need is felt to correct deviating behaviour and settle disputes about them. These rules induce individuals to behave in such a way as to make society feasible; with the proviso that society's feasibility is not logical but naturalistic-evolutionary, and may take place only *ex post*, i.e. through the survival of societies following the norms in question.[28]

The rules of a spontaneous order are independent of any purpose and are universal, i.e. applicable to an undetermined number of possible cases; they enable individuals to pursue their aims both because they ensure a (partly) foreseeable environment and also because they guarantee a reserved domain for everyone. These rules provide no criterion to delineate individuals' reserved domain, since the latter is *produced* by them and is not their premise; even though, generally speaking, actions concerning the sole individual should not be punished. Such a reserved domain ought not to be treated as the domain of morality: the only difference between legal and moral norms is the presence or absence of enforcing procedures recognized by an established authority: a naturalistic understanding of law, as a set of regularities, does not certainly allow us to distinguish between legal and moral regularities. Therefore, says Hayek, if there is a set of norms whose habitual respect leads to an actual order of actions, and some norms are given legal value by authorities, whereas others are merely respected in practice or implied by other validated norms (in that the latter attain their purpose only if the former are observed), the judge may, at his own discretion, deem implied norms to be legally valid, even if no judicial or legislative authority has passed them yet.[29]

A spontaneous order exists independently of individual choices and knowledge and, as such, cannot be explicitly organized in a systematic and exhaustive body of norms: at most, its underpinning principles can be determined, similarly to what common law judges do. Hayek believes that judges decide by examining the logic of each individual situation that is based on the needs of the existing order of actions. This logic is, in turn, the unintentional result and the rationale of all norms judges are expected to view as settled. The common law tradition makes law foreseeable, since judges are bound by widespread beliefs about what is fair, independently of their being legally acknowledged or not. Judges' trained insight – says Hayek quoting Roscoe Pound – constantly directs them towards fair outcomes: the idea that judicial decisions are the result of logical inferences is ascribable to "constructivist" rationalism that treats all rules as being deliberately created. Law is thus made up of all the rules whose binding nature would be recognized if they were explicitly expressed in words.[30]

Hayek's appeal to judges' insight, the idea that the law cannot and should not be viewed as a systematic set of norms intelligible to the human mind, and the uncertain demarcation between law and morality, suggest that such a conception of the rule of law may work, i.e. be given substantive content, only through the surreptitious *and thus critically uncontrollable* involvement of the government of men. Nonetheless, there are at least two elements, which might provide the rule of law with a precise identity: firstly, its rules have no precise purpose; secondly, they are universal.

The first characteristic would make sense if purpose were intrinsic to all rules and could be detected just as rules are first detected, says Hayek, as regularities. Yet, at least since Kant's Copernican revolution, this has been far from obvious: the aim of a rule – or rather the many aims a rule might be used for – is not a sort of intrinsic quality of the rule but stems from the relationship between a deliberating agent and the rule itself. Any given rule might be examined with a merely theoretical interest, for a descriptive or explicative purpose, or may be connected with different practical aims: for instance, the rule fixing the lethal dose of a drug may be connected both with the aim of poisoning and that of medical treatment. A more *à propos* example is provided by Hayek, who claims that the principles of a spontaneous order must be respected if the survival of the group as an entity endowed with a certain order is desirable:[31] if a given aim may be connected also with the normative system of a spontaneous order, it follows that no rule – either descriptive, technical, moral, or legal – entails in itself a connection or a lack of connection with given purposes as part of its irrevocable character.

As regards the universality of rules,[32] this could be a criterion independent of the arbitrary decisions of judges or legislators interested in promoting and preserving the spontaneous order if it were something more than a mere ethnographic-sociological concept. When speaking of the criterion of universality of a given norm Hayek does not certainly mean that it can be formally universalized, only that it is coherent or consistent with the rest of the system of accepted values. This does not depend on a given reasoning but on inevitably arbitrary sociological generalizations[33] – especially because the perception itself of a line of conduct as a problem proves that the sociological generalities which choices should be grounded on do not (or no longer) work.[34]

If the above account is correct, the concepts of evolution, spontaneous order and rule of law lack a definite content unless they are filled by men's choices. What is more, men's choices run the risk of being arbitrary since the emphasis on men's ignorance and thus on the impersonal and inscrutable nature of order and of its development entail, as a sort of side effect, the absolute vagueness of the criteria for legal decision and interpretation.

Although Hayek and Leoni employ arguments that may be largely referred to the same historical and theoretical environment, they institutionally[35] disagree on both the need for legislators' intervention to correct case law and on the possible replacement of the state with an anarchical-capitalistic hypermarket. Leoni, who is essentially more keen on the latter approach, believes that the rule of legislative law turns law itself from a boundary and limitation of power into an instrument of power, subject to majorities' particularistic and episodic interests.[36] Law's guaranteeing role may be restored, thus freeing it from political haggles and legislative inflation, only if it is taken away from the state and back to the social spontaneity of judicial rulings and of the selection of legal scholars and notables, in line with the model of Roman law and, more generally, of the market. Yet, why should we believe that the power of legal scholars and executive officials is less arbitrary than that of political legislators?

Leoni defines law as the normality of social behaviours, i.e. as the set of claims, which might be predictably satisfied.[37] Yet, while law is a social phenomenon, many decisions affecting individuals' lives and choices are not taken exclusively by parliaments or, in general, by the state. Therefore, to remove law from the state may eliminate only problems arising from the state, not the general problem of power and how to check it; hence, unless it is naturalistically assumed that society is harmonious and that individuals' interests are homogeneous, the less such a problem is public and formal, the more dramatic it is.

According to Hayek's metaphor, the world of law is a dense wood through which walkers going towards their individual destinations create paths that are equally useful for all. Theorists of the spontaneous order, albeit disagreeing on the need for intervention by a forester and of what kind, agree that the creation of paths is a spontaneous process in all individuals' interests: the power that we need to check, justify, and possibly eliminate is exclusively the forester's power. However, these theorists ignore the problem that, when walkers who have treated the wood as a pass-through area realize that their paths have created an order that is good and useful for "all", they themselves exercise a power that needs to be legitimated at least as much as the forester's. Those who view the wood differently, for example, as a means for preventing soil erosion, or as a botanic oasis, or even as a living creature deserving respect, might regard the beaten paths as the product of arbitrary and questionable decisions. To believe the contrary is to assume dogmatically that all individuals visit the wood only to walk through it.

6 THE RULE OF LAW AND DEMOCRACY

A speculatively conscious form of legal historicism might offer food for thought on the rule of law, since it might urge legal philosophy to analyse the relationship between law as a formal structure and its political, social, and cultural environment, and political philosophy to examine the interplay between formal and informal powers hiding within the state and society.[38] Which elements of law should be treated as unalterable, and why? And how and where can we guarantee that they are not altered?

The theories of the spontaneous do not help answering these questions. Their understanding of negative freedom – freedom as lack of environmental interference by other individuals' deliberate actions – leads them to identify the domain of freedom with the domain in which only naturalistic regularities are in force, i.e. regularities *thought of* as unalterable and not open to control. Under Hayek and Leoni's perspective, when power has an impersonal naturalistic justification, it is not coercive. Once actually existing socialism has lost its appeal, constitutional democracy, precisely because it explicitly legitimates itself as a construction and a pact,[39] is *the* enemy of freedom,[40] against which there stands the spontaneous order exemplified by the market and by a law formulated accordingly. The spontaneous order, which may be thought of as impersonal and non-deliberate, is the absolute guarantee of individual freedom; in order to attain it, it suffices to eliminate the explicitly deliberative manifestations of political power.

Such an idea stems directly from the theoretical need to give social content to negative freedom, this being descriptively[41] meant as the absence of manipulation of the conditions for individuals' choices. These axioms of negative freedom bear a paradoxical political consequence: if the *only* enemy of individual freedom is the deliberative aspect of law, which is typical of democracies, then the democratic project of the rule of (legislative) law, whereby citizens should only be bound by laws they have consented to, has been so completely realized that no other power within society can manipulate it through a coercive relationship. In other words, according to this account the democratic rule of (legislative) law has eliminated all informal powers, and in society there are no more patriarchal families, mafias, masonries, oligopolistic multinationals, and media concentrations, which are able to manipulate individuals' choices for their own purposes. Only this blindness, which results from a naturalistic understanding of the social world, may lead us to think that, once the legislative production of law is eliminated or reduced to a minimum, absolute individual freedom is favoured – rather than freedom only from state interference but not from other less visible and less controlled authorities. The more the government of law is conceived of as uncontrollable and spontaneous, the more the government of men is justified, in courts and elsewhere.

NOTES

1. Legal positivism is often underpinned by a moral and political choice to limit morality and, therefore, in a certain way, also to limit law; in this respect, it is worth mentioning U. Scarpelli, *Cos'è il positivismo giuridico*, Milano: Comunità, 1965, pp. 127–34.
2. On this issue, see Hayek's criticism of legal positivism in general and of Kelsen's philosophy of law in particular, in *Law, Legislation and Liberty*, London: Routledge & Kegan Paul, 1976, vol. II, pp. 44–8.
3. B. Leoni, *Freedom and the Law*, Indianapolis: Liberty Fund, 1991, p. 22.
4. We might view the neo-liberal theory on spontaneous order as an extreme twentieth-century version of the great legitimating ideologies discussed by J.-F. Lyotard, in *La condition postmoderne*, Paris: Editions de Minuit, 1979.
5. As maintained by M. Dogliani (*Introduzione al diritto costituzionale*, Bologna: il Mulino, 1994, pp. 33–72), modern constitutionalism arises with the crisis of the principle of tradition, which renders an artificial organization of the political world both necessary and feasible.
6. Plato, *Statesman*, 268d ff.; for a historical and philosophical *excursus* on technocracy, see P.P. Portinaro, "Tecnocrazia", *Filosofia politica*, 3 (1995).
7. Plato, *Statesman*, 269c ff.; the cosmos may rotate in one way or in the opposite way, though not in both ways.
8. P.P. Portinaro (op. cit.) and D. Zolo, in his essay "A proposito di *Legge, legislazione e libertà* di Friedrich A. von Hayek", *Diritto privato*, 1 (1996), 2, note that Hayek, through his constitutional engineering suggestions – in the third volume of *Law, Legislation and Liberty* – ends up by endorsing the government of Guardians, which he previously declares that he thoroughly despises. Also Bruno Leoni (*Freedom and the Law*, p. 22), an Italian follower of the Austrian school with an anarchical-capitalistic penchant, enthusiastically endorses a law made by gentlemen, on the basis of the Roman law model.
9. G. Fassò, *Società, legge e ragione*, Milano: Comunità, 1974, pp. 13–52.
10. Ibid., p. 41.
11. It is worth underlining that it is possible to neglect the English parliament's role precisely because its power is deemed not to be the output of an agreed and wanted constitution, but rather an element of a given and immemorial tradition. See in this respect M. Fioravanti, *Costituzione*, Bologna: il Mulino, 1999, pp. 142–3.
12. R. Bellamy (*Liberalism and Modern Society*, Oxford: Polity Press, 1992, pp. 222–3) notes that Hayek, on the one hand, anti-rationalistically exalts spontaneous and non-planned evolution and, on the other, tries to assume a particular form of "spontaneous" evolution as a rigid evolutionary model.

13. R. Cubeddu, *Introduzione* to B. Leoni, *La libertà e la legge*, Macerata: Liberilibri, 1994, p. xii (It. tr. of B. Leoni, *Freedom and the Law*).
14. F.A. Hayek, *The Constitution of Liberty*, London: Routledge & Kegan Paul, 1960, pp. 11–21.
15. Ibid., pp. 118–30.
16. Ibid., pp. 71–84.
17. When Hayek claims that in a society of free men, where individuals can use their competences to achieve their aims, social justice is meaningless because the distribution of material benefits is not determined by human will, he applies exactly such a strategy (*Law, Legislation and Liberty*, vol. II, p. 96).
18. F.A. Hayek, *The Constitution of Liberty*, pp. 39–54.
19. B. Leoni, *Freedom and the Law*, p. 47.
20. F.A. Hayek, *The Constitution of Liberty*, pp. 29–30. It is worth quoting its original text: "the case for individual freedom rests chiefly on the recognition of the inevitable ignorance of all of us concerning a great many of the factors on which the achievement of our ends and welfare depends. If there were omniscient men, if we could know not only all that affects the attainment of our present wishes but also our future wants and desires, there would be little case for liberty. And, in turn, liberty of the individual would, of course, make complete foresight impossible. [...] Humiliating to human pride as it may be, we must recognize that the advance and even the preservation of civilization are dependent upon a maximum of opportunity for accidents to happen [...] All institutions of freedom are an adaptation to this fundamental fact of ignorance."
21. L. Infantino, editor of F.A. Hayek, *Conoscenza, competizione e società* (Soveria Mannelli: Rubbettino, 1998), includes this passage (see n. 21) in his anthology on Hayek, believing it to be important and illustrative.
22. F.A. Hayek, *Law, Legislation and Liberty*, vol. I, pp. 11–12.
23. Ibid., vol I, p. 38 (italics mine).
24. It is nearly superfluous to underline the assonance of such a claim with the theoretical and much more sophisticated work by N. Luhmann (*Soziale Systeme*, Frankfurt a. M.: Suhrkamp, 1988, p. 30).
25. F.A. Hayek, *Law, Legislation and Liberty*, vol I, p. 46.
26. Such reasoning conceals law's voluntary and political implications, and might prove to be useful to hide extra-legal power. It is by no chance that Hayek and Leoni's are severely critics of democrats, reformers, and revolutionaries who are ingenious enough to acknowledge the reality of those implications. As a result of their naturalistic outlook on society, Hayek and, even more, Leoni view formal political powers as the only cause of oppression. Freedom stands for no governmental coercion, thus leaving social relationships of power unaltered (cf. M. Stoppino, "L'individualismo integrale di Bruno Leoni", in B. Leoni, *Scritti di scienza politica e teoria del diritto*, Milano: Giuffrè, 1980, pp. xlvi ff).
27. F.A. Hayek, in *Law, Legislation and Liberty*, vol. I, pp. 1–7, explicitly states that spontaneous orders internally contain a typical law of their own.
28. Ibid., vol. I, pp. 70 ff.
29. Ibid., vol. II, pp. 56–7.
30. Ibid., vol. I, pp. 115–22.
31. Ibid., vol. I, pp. 80–1.

32. Hayek, however, adds a further element: all merely behavioural norms are negative, in that they always impose bans and quasi-obligations, which are not the result of voluntary activities, with the exception of family law (ibid., vol. II, p. 36) and a few other cases. Whereas norms establishing how to purchase or transfer property, make contracts or wills etc. only define the conditions under which the law grants the protection of the behavioural norms, rendering them open to sanctions and ensuring that relevant situations are legally recognized (ibid., pp. 34–5). Yet, this is irrelevant for our purposes, both because it is an empirical generalization and because many private law norms, especially when connected with family and marriage, directly impose (sometimes burdensome) obligations, even where there would be room for individual choice. See for instance the feminist critique – applicable to common law systems – in L.J. Weitzmann, *The Marriage Contract*, New York: The Free Press, 1981.
33. F.A. Hayek, *Law, Legislation and Liberty*, vol. II, p. 27.
34. See J. Waldron, "Particular values and critical morality", *California Law Review*, 77 (1989), 3, pp. 562–89.
35. On these issues, see above all Hayek's criticism of Leoni (*Law, Legislation and Liberty*, vol. I, p. 88n) as to the need for legislation (and thus for the State) to support the judicial function. On this matter Hayek follows C. Menger, *Untersuchungen über die Methode des Sozialwissenschaften und der politischen Ökonomie insbesondere*, It. tr. *Sul metodo delle scienze sociali*, Macerata: Liberilibri, 1996, p. 266); for a historical account see R. Cubeddu, "Sul concetto di Stato nella Scuola austriaca", *Diritto e cultura*, 1 (1998), pp. 3–35.
36. See in particular Hayek's foreword to B. Leoni *Freedom and the Law*.
37. B. Leoni, *Il diritto come pretesa individuale*, now in B. Leoni, *Le pretese ed i poteri: le radici individuali del potere e della politica*, ed. by M. Stoppino, Milano: Società aperta, 1997 pp. 119–33.
38. See G. Palombella, *Costituzione e sovranità. Il senso della democrazia costituzionale*, Bari: Dedalo, 1997.
39. M. Fioravanti, *Appunti di storia delle costituzioni moderne*, vol. I. *Le libertà: presupposti culturali e modelli storici*, Torino: Giappichelli, 1991, pp. 138–9.
40. See, e.g. B. Leoni, *Freedom and the Law*, p. 130: "the more we reduce the large room occupied by collective decisions in politics and law, with all the paraphernalia of elections, legislation and so on, the more we establish a situation similar to what prevails within the language ambit, within the ambit of the common law, of the free market, fashion, customs, etc. where *all* individual choices suit each other and no single choice is less important than others."
41. According to theories of spontaneous order, freedom can be hardly seen as something different from a descriptive and theoretical element, since the only admissible yardstick is the descriptive and theoretical one of evolutionary success. G. Marini, reviewing the Italian version of B. Leoni, *Freedom and the Law* in *Il pensiero politico*, 29 (1996), pp. 332–3, notes that "ethical matters cannot be assimilated to the genetic processes illustrated for law and even less for language (in line with a hidden trend in these pages), without introducing serious philosophical problems certainly affecting the most sensitive ethical domains, such as criminal law, politics, economy".

PART IV

THE RULE OF LAW AND COLONIALISM

CHAPTER 13

THE RULE OF LAW AND THE LEGAL TREATMENT OF NATIVE AMERICANS

Bartolomé Clavero

The state is a cultural construct, not a natural product, and it is a European invention. The concept was created by a part of humanity which was convinced that it represented humanity in its entirety, and was intent on imposing itself upon the rest of humanity through the political institution of the state, among other means. Beginning in the eighteenth century, its different legal expressions went forth from Europe as ways of imposing a European presence and culture. Consequently "the rule of law", "the constitutional state", "the rule of rights", "the rule of the different rights of freedom", or similar formulas aiming at the subordination of political institutions to the legal system, can have very different meanings in Europe than for the rest of humanity.

And so it is that the state, even "the state of rights" or the "state of freedoms", presents a problem that is difficult to understand or even to formulate if our perspective remains European. From this perspective, the most interesting experiment is the American continent, with its states (from Canada to Argentina) founded by a population of European origin faced with native populations that, initially, were a majority but who were destined to become foreigners in their own lands. This chapter aims to show how this came about using an approach based on the supremacy of law and including freedom as its premise.

1 CONSTITUTIONAL EXCLUSION: THE USA AND CANADA

The United States inaugurated the constitutional history of the continent with an intransigent policy towards the indigenous populations which preserved their own culture: in short, exclusion. As to specifically legal effects, there was no conception of any communication with a population which was alien to European culture. Communication, however, was unavoidable, because of the presence of such populations and also because of the expansionism of the new states, which certainly did not facilitate matters. This is well known, if only from the cinema. One

P. Costa and D. Zolo (eds.), The Rule of Law: History, Theory and Criticism, 443–466.

should not look, however, for a historiographic reconstruction of a legal-constitutional type. It would prove to be a disappointing enterprise.[1]

In this case the antecedent was the colonial experience. The English monarchy had not dominated in a direct way over any native people and the United States did not have legal precedents of this type within its borders. Before the Independence, in 1763, a solemn proclamation had recognized the "territory" as an indigenous, legal, and political system, not on the basis of a right of the population but rather as the expression of the colonial aspect of the monarchy, of its "sovereignty, protection, and dominion"; the territory was an object subject to the *sovereignty* and *protection* of the Crown. The entire territory inhabited by the Indians of North America was "reserved" for them, as a gracious concession on the part of Great Britain, which claimed powers in the name of this same *protection*. The declaration of 1763, considering the Indians incapable on principle of alienating their lands, permitted them to do so only to the benefit of this monarchy and of this *sovereignty*, which in this way extended and applied itself beyond its own colonies, beyond the Atlantic strip which had been occupied until then, thus marking out a boundary.[2]

The opposition of the colonies themselves to such a boundary was one of the major factors that sparked the struggle for independence but, by that time, a legal situation had been created that the new United States would inherit, including the same claim to sovereignty. The definitive Federal Constitution, that of 1787, would make manifest this intention, attributing to Congress the competence "to regulate commerce with foreign nations, among the several states, and with the Indian tribes" (Article 1, Section 8, part 3); this was interpreted extensively, along the lines of a subrogation in the sovereignty, with regard to that sort of "third kind", the Indian tribes, which were neither foreign nations nor an integral part of the state. The indigenous peoples were initially not considered a part of the United States but they were in any case subject to Federal sovereignty. The constitutional rulings of the Federal Supreme Court would formulate this position within just a few decades, maintaining that these peoples constituted "domestic dependent nations"; that is, they were *nations*, but *domestic* and *dependent*, "in a state of pupillage", placed under a *guardianship* that was in a certain sense "family-like", in so much as they were permanently considered to be *minors* with regard to the United States.[3]

The *Indian tribes* were here understood as *nations* and therefore capable of self-government, except for their incapacity, in so much as they were *wards*, to negotiate and stipulate agreements with any other than their *guardian*, the Federation of the United States. From this perspective, relations could be established and developed between "nations" and "Nation", between the Indian *nations* and the United States *Nation*. The *guardianship* was intended in such a way that the former could only undertake relations in a stable manner with the latter, among all the nations on earth. The indigenous peoples possessed territories, had governments and their own systems. They maintained *international* relations with the United States, which were compulsory relations in principle and of a precise significance. They were held above all to peace, in such a way as to legitimize the war which the United States waged on those indigenous peoples who did not abide by what had been established. The normative procedure for the realization of such relations would thus be *international*, that of *treaties* in the strict sense of the term. Shortly before the Constitution of 1787, offers of incorporation into the Federation[4] were made to the Indian peoples.

Before the Federal Constitution another step of constitutional significance was made, the invention of the "Territory", as an alternative to the "State", with the precise aim of avoiding a formal autonomous constitution. It was a transitional system, until colonization developed or the Indian population was reduced. It was a context in which the terms of treaties did not count and neither did the principle of territorial recognition contained in the colonial proclamation of 1763. The United States arrogated to itself the right to plan and manage the areas of western expansion that were not part of the states of the interior. From this perspective, the making of treaties could be undertaken in terms, rather unbalanced, of the concession of reservations, government authorizations and ways of applying guardianship. With the Constitution of 1787 this order of ideas was already present.[5]

The situation did not change for decades. The practice of treaties remained until 1871, giving rise to less formal agreements, more directly subject to the decisions of the Federal powers. The possibility of founding at least one indigenous state remained alive, especially in the Oklahoma Indian Territory, but it was reduced in the following years but was definitively abandoned in 1907, when the territory constitutionally became another state, without the indigenous people having any part in it. The relationship between "guardian" and "ward" thus contained the whole of the relationship between indigenous people and the United States. In the period around the turn of the century, there ensued a further erosion of the indigenous peoples' position, caused by the practice of treaties and reinforced by keeping their own territories and governments. If these continued to exist, it was under the colonial condition of *reservation* and *guardianship*.[6]

Relations were established in *international* terms, which implied a principle of not inherently degrading legal recognition, even though relations were still based on colonial-type assumptions. Through these relations, established by means of treaties, the Indian side could maintain its own idea of law, starting from the attribution of a different meaning to words. The common term *nation* could be perfectly well be taken as a sign of legal equality. And other terms as well might not have a pejorative or derogatory accent. The *reservation* could be understood as the land which the indigenous people conserved for themselves while making available or ceding another part of its own territory. From this perspective, *guardianship* might also be seen as assistance which was negotiated and accepted in exchange for peace and lands, legitimizing in this way a defensive war. And not only word-meanings were in play but also signs of another type. Gestures of friendship and exchanges of respects could have a wider meaning not perfectly coinciding with the meaning of a text written in a foreign language, even if it was a *lingua franca* such as English. The sharing of tobacco smoke could be legally more meaningful than a legal text. All of this in any case was law.[7]

It was a law which did not have prevalence over that of the United States, nor was it on equal terms with it. The *reservations* remained dependent and under the guardianship of the United States, without having contributed to or provided consensus for its constitutionalism and without integrating with it. During the period around the turn of the century, between the end of the period of the treaties and the birth of the state of Oklahoma, the indigenous peoples of the *reservations* continued to be *nations* in so much as they were excluded from *the* Nation. Their members were not citizens of this *Nation*. Continuing to be in force was the requirement of conversion not only to a public order but also to the private order of property and the family. That was the requirement for access to citizenship, or better, for its imposition. This period was characterized by an aggressively integrationist political strategy, based on the privatization of lands and destruction of the communities, a strategy that was not definitively carried to completion and which resurfaced periodically during the twentieth century. And recourse was not lacking to churches in the exercise of a guardianship geared to an acculturation that was meant to be not only civilizing but also soul-saving.[8]

The inhabitants of the indigenous reservations received US citizenship in 1924, not at their own request but through the decision of the United States itself, which created, as a consequence, resistance. The more general *international*, or better interstate context was beginning to change. Until then a sovereign conception of the state and a territorial conception of sovereignty were generally accepted. In 1919, however, the League of Nations was established and it began to concern itself with the destinies of peoples not constituted into states, or *minorities* as it defined them. In 1923 some indigenous Americans attempted to attract the League's attention. In this context the United States proceeded towards a goal which was, as will be seen later, a point of departure for other American states: incorporating the indigenous population into citizenship, without taking into account their self-determination or respecting their rights. Only later, in search of improved legitimacy, and without changing the fundamental basis of the system, were specific rights of the native populations examined, rights which the US state has always controlled the right to define, to allocate, to subject to conditions, and to shape.[9]

When the culturally indigenous peoples finally received citizenship and certain rights, they constituted a minority within the United States. And their territories, which these peoples governed internally, were reservations, not states. They were *internal dependent nations*, nations subject to Federal powers but not part of the Federal system constituted by another nation, the Nation with the capital "N". The first approaches of some treaties were lost with the "short-circuit" of their international premises. And the Constitution remained silent, except for the enigmatic reference to the "third kind", the "Indian tribes", which as we know had no states of their own and were not foreign states. No United States Federal amendment has made reference to the question. Judicial rulings could proceed calmly to constitutionalize a substantially colonial position.[10]

The constitutional case of neighbouring Canada was more open. Originally it consisted of colonies which did not join the process of independence and therefore did not react against the English proclamation of 1763. The point of departure was quite distinct. The current constitutional norm of 1982 expressly contains those rights or freedoms recognized by the proclamation of 1763[11] in favour of "the aboriginal peoples of Canada", *les peuples autochtones du Canada*, recognition which extends to treaties and other agreements.

Keeping this proclamation in force, together with its constitutional value, can be significant from a comparative perspective. Remember that the proclamation did not limit itself to the recognition of territory and rights. This second aspect proved more problematic. The declaration started from an explicit affirmation of *sovereignty* which placed colonial law above indigenous law, the latter recognized in as much as it was determined by the former, while the contrary could not be conceived of, despite the fact that it was the law of a native population residing in its own territory. All of this, moreover, implied the projection of a guardianship that devalued the position and reduced the rights of the indigenous population, since the "dark side" of the proclamation of 1763 continued to weigh, with its constitutional recognition, on the Canadian system.[12]

Given this situation, what about the rule of law with regard to two Anglo-American zones such as the United States and Canada? How can there be an effective law for them which is as common to the Indio-American side as to the Euro-American, and recognized by both peoples? Apart from the constitutional pretensions and illusions of the counterpart of European origin, what possibilities were there for setting up a system able to offer a real guarantee? It is evident that Anglo-American constitutionalism was and is rooted in a European colonialism that is, as such, incapable of establishing a rule of law which is able to involve all of the interested population. But it is better not to draw hasty conclusions: it is in fact necessary to widen our panorama to the rest of the American continent and, given its colonial matrix, also establish our observation point outside of it.

2 CONSTITUTIONAL INCLUSION: LATIN AMERICA

It has already been noted that the Latin American point of departure is different or even apparently, opposite: it is a question of inclusion. The states that became independent of the Spanish monarchy did so in the name of their entire population, and not only those of European origin. These states originated in a colonial system that had already established a direct dominion over the native population, setting up, expressly and effectively, a mechanism of *guardianship*. Now some Constitutions were written with the premise of a single *Nation*, on the basis of an implicit or even explicit *nationality* and also a citizenship shared with the indigenous population. Incorporation, however, did not take place. Instead there was exclusion, produced by specific legal mechanisms and other means that do not concern us here.

It is not easy to avoid becoming lost among the diversity of cases, found in this part of the American continent (from Mexico to Argentina) that today calls itself Latin. We need to build up a general picture. The point of departure of the plan of inclusion was expressed rather clearly in one of the first Constitutions of this area, that of Venezuela in 1811. It was developed on the supposition of a common citizenship and produced the effect of the explicit cancellation of the status of *guardianship* over the indigenous people, of the "privileges of the minor" which "in seeking to protect them, instead jeopardized their development, as shown by experience".

In defence of this innovation, a long article preceded it devoted to that "part of the citizenry until now called *indios*". There emerges an attempt at a cancellation of still greater significance: a programme of conversion, first religious and then cultural, of the *indios*. The need is underlined to "make them understand the close connection with all the other citizens" and the need to share rights "based on the simple fact of being people equal to all the others of their species". The programme of an indigenous "deculturation" through constitutional acculturation was applied by the Constitution itself, in view of the "distribution of the property of the lands which had been conceded". It was thus understood that there was no territorial dominion which did not come from private property.

The first Latin American constitutions were for the most part of this sort, but many others did not result in such drastic cancellation. The Constitution of Ecuador of 1830 was the clearest. It considered the indigenous an "innocent, abject and miserable class" and declared "the venerable priests as their natural guardians and fathers", maintaining in this way the system of *guardianship*. The Declaration of Rights of Guatemala, of 1839, went no less far in this direction. It specifically proclaimed that "protected in particular are those who due to sex, age or incapacity cannot know and defend their own rights", so that not only women, but also other adults were considered as minors. There remained expressly understood "indigenous people in general", incapable of knowing their own rights and therefore presumably also of understanding an institution that was as alien to their culture as was private property.

The position of qualitative *minority* of the indigenous populations (which however constituted the quantitative *majority*) and the corresponding guardianship, both state and ecclesiastical, were not manifested in such an open way constitutionally, but they represented the current politics. Venezuela itself, having started off with the absolute affirmation of equal citizenship, passed in 1864 to the constitutional formula of state *guardianship* through the system of *territories*, then arriving at the way of the Church in 1909: "the Government may negotiate the arrival of missionaries who will settle in the areas of the Republic where there are indigenous to civilize". The current Venezuelan Constitution of 1963 goes further, offering a further coverage: "the law will establish the exceptional system required for the protection of the indigenous and their progressive incorporation into the life of the Nation" (Article 77).

Both in Mexico and in Argentina, and in other cases or phases of the federal development of Latin American states, the system of the *territorios*, which invention of the United States, served to claim and impose dominion over the independent indigenous population. The influence of federalism was not alien to this design. And the *international* law of the time favoured it, not conceiving of the possibility of recognizing as *Nations* in conditions of equality peoples endowed with territory and rights and predating the arrival of the Europeans. This external factor, which had important internal consequences will be considered subsequently. From the latter perspective, within the different constitutions which speak of the state and boundaries without taking into consideration nations, there exists quite a range of positions between the extremes of total subjugation and full independence.

There were a great variety of practices, from agreements to war, passing through every sort of mediation and settlement, and with the common denominators of evolving and developing at the margins of programmes and constitutional mandates; and by the creating and maintaining an arbitrary, uncontested power on the part of the state and weak, uncertain rights on the part of the indigenous people, whose autonomy was based on customs and practices but not assured by any power of its own or by recognition. From one system to another, from the explicit willingness of some states to the hypocrisy of others, it doesn't seem that a general law was established. What was the possibility for a rule of law actually to extend itself to the entire Nation?

The premises of these results were evident in the initial proclamations of general citizenship. Indigenous incorporation had to mean the abandonment of indigenous culture. Without this, there was no recognition of rights; with this requisite came a definitive loss of autonomy. Expressed in other terms, the state of *guardianship*, a guardianship which was quite significant because it aimed not only at religious conversion but also at a legal transculturation, was always understood as a necessary phase of transition towards this type of community and citizenship. There is not then so much difference between the first and the last extreme of Venezuelan constitutional evolution. There is certainly not much difference in the basic principles of citizenship and guardianship. What distinguishes one approach from another, the Anglo-American model from the Latin American one, is a question of accent, not of paradigm. Both move between inclusion and exclusion, the former colonial and the latter constitutional.

Both prefer to avoid an explicit constitutional commitment; it will be seen, however, that this commitment is not entirely lacking and it is always significant. Canada resorts to amendments, while the United States resists this approach. The constitutional texts of Uruguay, Chile, and Costa Rica remain silent, even in their most recent versions of 1997.

During the nineteenth century, constitutional manifestations were always sporadic. They always focused on religion, the "conversion to Catholicism", as that of Argentina stated in 1853, or the "conversion to Christianity and to civilization", as that of Paraguay specified in 1870: a programme for indigenous peoples which involved the loss of their own culture and other no less concrete hardships, such as the confiscation of lands or, in case of resistance, extermination.

With the new century the picture seemed to change. In Ecuador, in Peru, and again later, in Brazil, Bolivia, Ecuador, and Guatemala, legal formulations which were a bit more respectful of the indigenous presence began to appear; since these were autonomously organized, they did not incorporate the constitutional presumptions, even if there was no compromise on what regarded the powers of the state and on the consequent uncertainty of any right which did not derive from it. Ecuador began, with demanding declarations in 1906 and 1929: "the Public Powers must protect the Indian ethnicity with regard to the improvement of its social life". Peru followed in 1920: "the State shall protect the indigenous ethnicity", "the Nation recognizes the legal existence of the indigenous communities" and "the law shall emanate the corresponding rights". The State *protects*, the Nation *recognizes* and the Law determines *rights*. The Peruvian Constitution of 1933 dedicated an entire article to the *indigenous communities*, recognizing their "legal existence and legal personality" as well as "the integrity of property" and autonomy in the administration of revenues and properties in conformity with the law: "the state shall emanate the civil, penal, economic and administrative legislation which the indigenous have need of". In 1934 Brazil offered a constitutional recognition of the possession of lands by the *indios*.

In 1938 Bolivia, like Peru, added an adjective – *legal*, which denotes subordination to the state – to a noun – *comunidad*, which stands for a whole having its own order – and introduced a reference to legislation that is to the determining role of political decision. In addition there was the obligation to institute "indigenous school nuclei, including the economic, social and pedagogical aspects" that served as a chapter in the "education of the *campesino*". All of this was included in the section on the "peasant condition", without any recognition of an autonomous culture and within a perspective which tended simply to cancel it. Nor did the position of the constitution of Ecuador in 1945 appear any different when it declared that "in the schools of the areas with a predominance of the Indian population, in addition to Castilian, Quechua or the corresponding native language shall be used". The subsequent constitution of 1946 changed the language so as to lower the level of compromise to the point of reducing it to a mere registration: educational instruction "shall devote particular attention to the indigenous ethnicity", without any other specification.

In the same year, 1945, Guatemala affirmed in its constitution the existence of "indigenous groups", declaring of "national utility and interest" policies aiming at their economic, social, and cultural improvement and entrusting the safeguarding of their "necessities, conditions, practices, usages and customs" to the state. In 1965 the state committed itself "to the socio-economic betterment of the indigenous groups with the aim of their integration in the national culture". Until 1945 the perspective was still that of a cancellation of the indigenous culture, even though guarantees on common property and appreciation for popular art were added. In 1967 the Constitution of Paraguay declared that "the national languages of the republic are Spanish and Guaranì", adding that "Spanish will be used officially", while skipping over the other.

After 1972 the Constitution of Panama offered a further development of these same positions (Articles 84, 104, and 120–123). It recognized "cultural models" and not only the languages of the "indigenous groups", just as it guaranteed "the collective property of the indigenous communities". These were aspects which remained entrusted to the state, since only the general objectives were enunciated. Its policies would have to develop "in accord with the scientific methods of cultural change". The positive recognitions themselves were to be understood as transitory. Prematurely however a constitutional reform of 1928 had conceded the creation of "special statute zones" which offered to the indigenous communities a measure of autonomy under guardianship and guaranteed by the law. Some of these "zones" were able to equip themselves with a statute of their own, citing then current *international* law on *human rights* with the aim of reinforcing themselves constitutionally with regard to the law of the state.[13] But of this suprastate dimension more will be said further on.

There followed a wave of more or less innovative constitutional declarations. In 1978 the Constitution of Ecuador added to the guardianship of linguistic aspects the recognition of "community property" as one of the fundamental sectors of the economy. In 1982 the Constitution of Honduras declared that "the state shall preserve and stimulate the native cultures", attending to "the protection of the rights and interests of the indigenous communities existing in the country" (Articles 172, 173, and 346). In 1983 the Constitution of El Salvador affirmed that "the native languages which are spoken in the national territory are part of the cultural heritage and will be the object of conservation, diffusion and respect" (Article 62). In these cases, at least more dignified formulations were utilized, without speaking explicitly of *guardianship*, without giving constitutional expression to an approach of a "tutelary" sort. *Culture* is spoken of where once one spoke of lack of civilization.

In 1985 the Constitution of Guatemala widened the panorama with the recognition of the "right of persons and communities to their own cultural identity, in accordance with their own values, language and customs", consequently reformulating the rules about property: "the indigenous communities or communities of other types which have historically held land as property and have by tradition administered it in a special manner will maintain that system" (Articles 58, 66–76, and 143). There appears to be a change in perspective in so much as the recognition seems based on the individual's right and is therefore not uncertain or transitory; this innovation however did not become effective, since everything remained dependent on a "specific law" which, regardless of its actual application, it to the discretion of the state to realize this right.

It was a terrain on which other recognitions would appear, with sometimes significant integrations. In 1987 the Constitution of Nicaragua introduced a system of territorial autonomy by means of legislative acts for the area where the indigenous population is predominant (Articles 8, 11, 89–91, 180, and 181). In 1988 the constitution of Brazil entrusted to legislation the identification and determination of land boundaries (Articles 49.16, 215, and 231). In 1991 the Constitution of Colombia, considering "the ethnic and cultural diversity of the Nation", consented autonomy through legislation and organized the participation of an indigenous minority in the legislature (Articles 7, 10, 171, 176, 286–288, 329, and 330). In 1992 Mexico provided for the recognition not only of language and customs, but also of actual cultures: "the Mexican Nation has a multicultural composition which assumes its form originally from its native populations" (Article 4). Reaching the goal requires ordinary legislation. At the same time, however, some guarantees for community property provided for in the Mexican Constitution of 1917 (Article 27.7) were cancelled out.

Also in 1992 Paraguay reinforced its recognition of multiculturalism: "this Constitution recognizes the existence of indigenous peoples, defined as groups with a culture preceding the formation and organization of the Paraguayan state", which is translated into the rights to "ethnic identity" and to "community property". "Paraguay is a multicultural and bilingual State", and this was to be made effective through a law (Articles 62–67, 77, and 140). In 1993 Peru constitutionally recognized "the ethnic and cultural plurality of the nation", but in the Constitution itself the orientation was towards a multilingual approach which was weighted in favour of Castilian and towards a system of "peasant and native communities" which tended, as in the Mexican case, to favour privatization masked by the constitutional recognition itself (Articles 2.19, 17, 48, 88, 89, and 149).

In 1994 the Argentine Constitution went as far as to recognize the presence and the identity of indigenous cultures and lands, entrusting to law the regulation of the question (Article 75.17). In the same year Bolivia declared itself constitutionally "multi-ethnic and multicultural" as well as a "unitary Republic". The Bolivian constitution recognizes "the social, economic and cultural rights of the indigenous peoples who live in the national territory" or of the indigenous communities, understood more specifically as collective subjects with legal personality (Articles 1 and 171). The problem is relegated less to legislation, but it is still the state which reserves for itself as political subject the power to create and administer law, even for matters concerning peoples organized as autonomous communities.

Ecuador went even further. In addition to the recognition in 1996 of multiculturalism, it produced in 1998 a new and truly innovative constitution, thanks to the attention paid to indigenous rights and culture (Articles 1, 3.1, 23.22, 24, 62, 66, 69, 83–91, 97.20, 191, 224, and 241). The recognition of the plurality of cultures and of their respective "equity and equality" was presented as a way to "reinforce national identity in diversity" within a framework of "interculturalism". The idea of a common national substratum also made progress: "the indigenous peoples, who define themselves as nations with ancestral roots, and the black or Afro-Ecuadorian peoples are part of the Ecuadorian state, one and indivisible". "Castilian is the official language"; "the ancestral idioms" are as well "for the indigenous peoples, according to the terms established by law". This was the recurrent emphasis, like a sort of exceptional parenthesis, in the various chapters of the Constitution. Among the rights provided for, there was that of "participating in the cultural life of the community" and that to "identity, in accordance with the law".

While Latin American constitutionalism has developed in Castilian, there is an article in the Ecuadorian Constitution of 1998, under the title of "duties and responsibilities", in an idiom which is different from the second constitutional language of the Americas, that is English, and different also from the other current languages, Portuguese and French, an idiom which is not even European: *Ama quilla, ama llulla, ama shua,* that is "do not be lazy, do not lie, do not steal" in Quechua, the principal lingua franca among the indigenous languages of the Andean region, including above all Peru and Bolivia. There is also an extension of the motto. It may seem an extemporaneous and negligible passage in a constitutional text, but it is a pertinent and relevant sign as an expression of a sense of community.

On the basis of the data up until 1998, it cannot be said that the indigenous presence has been ignored by most of the constitutions. A certain constitutionalism, however, based on the culture of difference and authority, continues to ignore it. Up until this point, though this process is "adventurous" in constitutional terms it has had scant results for indigenous peoples. The self-identification of some peoples as a *nationality* in conditions of equality with others, without excluding those of a European origin, appears indirectly in Ecuador today to be a form of self-denomination bereft of a precise significance in terms of constitutional recognition and of clear institutional impact. In the whole framework of the Ecuadorian constitution, the indigenous presence is taken into account, but it is not in terms of this that the constitutional framework is restructured. The problem already emerges in the chapter on rights, where *rights* do not appear as such, in a strict sense, since their realization is always entrusted to legislation, so that the indigenous condition is subordinated to the ordinary measures of political institutions. These institutions appear more extraneous than indigenous, more bounded than common.

To complete the Latin American panorama, it is also worth mentioning, if only summarily, an international instrument of recognition of the indigenous presence which is assuming constitutional value in some states of this area. The reference is to Pact 169 of 1989 of the International Labour Organization regarding the "Indigenous and Tribal Peoples in Independent Countries", currently ratified by Mexico, Colombia, Bolivia, Costa Rica, Paraguay, Peru, Honduras, Guatemala, and Ecuador. For the sake of brevity, it can be said that this Pact assumes a degree of recognition of native peoples equivalent to that of the most recent constitutional developments previously illustrated. It is a law of these states. In some, as in Costa Rica, it can compensate for the lack of constitutional indications. In others, as in Honduras, it can increase their significance. In any case, it reinforces them. In no case does it change their nature. It continues to be a dispensation conceded by those who resist the recognition of the rights of the peoples already residing in their territory. However there are compromises. There is a sense to the fact that some states, such as Chile, resist both constitutional recognition and the ratification of this Pact, and prefer to resort to the easier procedures of ordinary law.

From a constitutional point of view, within a more legal vision of the state, there exists, if not an actual autonomous right of the indigenous, at least a right to obligatory recognition, which not only legitimizes but also determines a common system of relations. This has little to do with multiculturalism, with a paradigm which can really establish a rule of law, if the nation itself is not open to pluralism, does not begin to recognize existing diversities, the plurality of cultures, and collective subjects endowed with their own systems and powers. The effective rights of native peoples arose and to a large extent continue to be relegated to the margins of constitutions, beyond the reach of the constitutional mandates of the states. Can a non-illusory rule of law mature under these circumstances?

3 THE RULE OF THE LAW OF NATIONS: ALL OF AMERICA

Is it possible to have a rule of law for the American continent which does not imply a situation of *apartheid* (since that is the result) for native peoples, for those who possess territory, community, and entitlements which precede the European presence and the formation of the states? Does an American rule of law exist which is not an illusion of the nations, harmful for the peoples? Perhaps. *Apartheid* itself, as has been demonstrated very clearly in South Africa, can perfectly well be a rule of law, the law of a state which adheres to a system and respects it.

On the American continent there exists in fact a *status iuris gentium*, above all a rule of the law of nations, of international law in all its extensions. We have already had to make reference to the fact that, at the end of the nineteenth century, the American states were able to enjoy the advantages of a general interstate system, which supported and favoured a presumption of sovereignty and the claim of its distribution over the entire area of the Americas, as if there did not exist independent territories of indigenous peoples or actual populations in these territories, as if their presence were literally invisible. This is an important factor in understanding the illusion of the rule of law on the American continent. The position assigned to native peoples was not the invention of the state, of each state on its own. Between exclusion and inclusion, there is a basic coincidence which is at least symptomatic.[14]

Guardianship, and all that this implies in terms of reduction of role and neutralization of rights, was an invention of the *ius gentium*. This *ius* was a law which, since medieval times, had conceived of Europe as the one and only humanity, without taking into account the rest of the world's peoples, and which presented itself as *ius naturale*, as natural law, therefore as an obligatory order. And the guardian, as we know, had at his disposal many discretional powers. He was presumed to know the interests of his ward better than the ward did himself. As once with the Monarchies and the Churches, by then the Churches and the states knew what the native peoples of America needed. Thus no law could be invoked to oppose the discretion of the guardianship. Even when this was not made explicit or established, as in some initial cases or in other recent developments, this basic position was maintained. The states felt that they were invested not only with power but also with science in managing the indigenous population, like a passive humanity incapable of attending even to its own interests.

The degradation of some *gentes* with respect to others and the Europeans was not a constitutional invention. It derived from the preceding centuries and was even aggravated on the eve of certain crucial moments, when that which would be called the rule of law was already taking form. Recourse was made to the most respected authority in the period of the formation of many American states, an authority well known to the world, both Anglo-Saxon and Latin: the *Droit des Gens* by Emmerich de Vattel.[15] Around the middle of the eighteenth century, a rather clear way of defining the rule of law, including the constitutional state, was arrived at. And yet here we find restrictive formulations which lead to the colonial exclusion of the indigenous population, of the human beings present in the American territory before the Europeans.

We must analyze above all the category of *Nation ou État*, of a *state* identified with the *Nation*, the political institution created by men to protect themselves and procure benefits and security by uniting their forces, and endowed to fulfill this aim with the power of sovereignty or self-government, as a true *sovereign state*. The form in which all of this materializes is the constitution, that which forms the *constitution of the state*. These categories are all defined in such general terms that it seems as though all of humanity can make recourse to the national, state, and constitutional formula, to obtain for themselves a good guardianship. However the dependence on a *foreign* state is a warning sign. Regardless of other applications, the theme at hand already emerged in some way in a context which was not exactly that of the plausibility of the nation and of the possibility of the state and of the constitution.

We are speaking of America. We see it cited in a chapter on "the natural obligation to cultivate the earth" or in another devoted to the problem of "whether it is permissible to occupy a part of a country in which there are only nomadic peoples and in small numbers", where prejudice towards the indigenous population signals that the answer to the question will be in the affirmative. This was "a celebrated question, raised to a large extent by the 'discovery' of the New World": already the idea of *discovery* reinforced the prejudicial scenario. It was from this context that the answer arose: "the peoples of Europe, too restricted in their own countries, finding a territory of which the savages have no particular need and make no current and continual use, may legitimately occupy it and establish Colonies". If there were reservations, it was because of Spanish colonialism, not Anglo-Saxon, to the extent to which the former went too far in its direct domination of native peoples. In this case nothing was said of *guardianship*, which already existed for some and would arrive for others, because we are already in the original constitutional position of exclusion, which was the basis of the early United States constitutionalism.

It was Europe, extended into the "New World", which was the subject of this law of nations, of peoples. *Les peuples de l'Europe*, the peoples of Europe, are those which count, and which can count, taking advantage of their rights as nations, of the institution of the state, and of the constitutional system. The rest are *les sauvages*, savages, people who are presumed to be without culture, populations with inferior credentials, bereft of their own law in a strict sense, rooted in their own territory, and faced with the European presence. It is a normative framework based on a specific cultural presumption, with the consequence that aspects which are so important for the existence and protection of all, such as the nation, the state and the constitution, are not accessible to all peoples. Those peoples who remain independent in America and have a non-European culture cannot claim a position of legal and political equality with the population of European provenance and culture; only from the latter can nations, states, and Constitutions arise.

Let us make a jump back in time, undoubtedly opportune, given that there exists a certain continuity.[16] The international, interstate, or interconstitutional scenario which has been delineated continued substantially at least until 1960, until the date of the Declaration on the Granting of Independence to Colonial Countries and Peoples of the General Assembly of the United Nations, despite the Universal Declaration of Human Rights itself, which in 1948 had in fact maintained this colonial discrimination among the peoples, as if it were indifferent with regards to individual liberties (Article 2.2). In 1960 this Declaration asserted that "the subjection of peoples to alien subjugation, domination and exploitation constitutes a denial of fundamental human rights", to then go so far as to recognize that not only established states, but also "all peoples have the right to self-determination" (Articles 1 and 2). It was a step forward that, at the time, was not sufficient but which would end up concerning the native peoples of the American continent.[17]

According to the United Nations, the qualification of *foreign* attributed to decolonization excluded from the very beginning, for the American continent, the hypothesis of any colonial relation existing inside the states of that continent. The very criteria used to identify the new peoples capable of affirming themselves as nations and constituting themselves as states are of a colonial sort: populations external to the borders of the colonizing states and in conformity with the borders which divided up the colonies themselves. The people can be understood as the population which constitutes the state but, in this way, the assimilation between the two parts is taken for granted, ignoring the problem of another entity within the state. The term *Nation*, as in the very name of the United Nations, whose members are actually states, perpetuates this problem.

With the Universal Declaration of Human Rights of 1948, and the decolonization compromise of 1960 that was undertaken in its name, under the impetus of the United Nations itself, the American states were pushed well beyond the point to which they had meant (as has been seen) to arrive. Reference has been made to the 1989 Conference of the International Labour Organization, a specialized organ of the United Nations. Since 1958, the human rights have been developed; meanwhile, controversies have emerged which have produced case law in this regard inside the United Nations itself. Both Declarations and that of case law are relevant.[18]

Two legal instruments regulate the development of human rights, the Covenant on Civil and Political Rights of 1966, and the Declaration on the Rights of Persons Belonging to National or Ethnic, Religious, or Linguistic Minorities of 1992, to which has been added the Declaration on the Rights of Native Peoples, which though only a project, has already been formalized. The Covenant of 1966 is more relevant in this regard than that, parallel and simultaneous, on Economic, Social, and Cultural Rights, despite the adjective "cultural", because it is the former more than the latter which recognizes the right to a particular culture, and not a culture of universal character. Moreover, it adds a protocol which establishes the Human Rights Committee, a judicial body more independent than the common system of checks realized through exchanges and encounters between states and the United Nations.

Both Conventions inserted as a first article the declaration of the rights of all peoples to self-determination. In this way they require (just as the annex on the judicial body) for them to enter into force, contrary to the Declarations, a special and therefore more binding ratification on the part of the states.

The Covenant on Civil and Political Rights, apart from the first article on the collective right to self-determination already cited, consists of a list of individual rights, including the right to one's own culture: "In those States in which ethnic, religious or linguistic minorities exist, persons belonging to such minorities shall not be denied the right, in community with the other members of their group, to enjoy their own culture, to profess and practise their own religion, or to use their own language" (Article 27). As this is not a collective right, it inheres in the individual person and not in the *minority* as such. It is necessary to be a *people* to be able to count on the rights recognized by this covenant, those of the first article. Human Rights Committee, to which the citizens of the states that accept its jurisdiction can apply and adjudicates the problems that arise.

This Committee has already received claims to the right to self-determination, declared in the first article of the Covenant on Civil and Political Rights, by a certain number of peoples not constituted as a state, as occurred with the initiative of the native populations of Canada. Canada immediately ratified these rights. The Human Rights Committee cannot respond to these requests for a procedural reason. The United Nations which constituted it, the Protocol of the Covenant which empowered it, the Covenant itself which structured it and the states which accept it without reserve acknowledge the legitimacy only of individual rights and not collective ones. In other words, the Committee cannot pass judgement on the right of peoples expressed in the first article, but only on individual cases as provided for in the remaining articles.[19]

This is not, however, a denial of the substantial existence of this primary collective right, but only of the possibility of taking advantage of it through this judicial channel. Case law expressly declares that the recognition and the exercise of the right to self-determination is not fulfilled and exhausted with decolonization, the criteria of which it clearly avoids making any recourse to. The Human Rights Committee does not maintain that the requirement is met only in the case of "alien subjugation, domination and exploitation", as asserted, with all its consequences, by the first article of the Declaration of 1960. Now it is understood that the question exists, because of the differences among peoples, even in a context of greater contiguity or in the case of inclusion in the same state. The criteria of decolonization have rightly been overcome. For this judicial agency of the United Nations, the problem remains open.

The Human Rights Committee is also producing case law on Article 27, relative to the right to a particular culture, a right whose entitlement is individual and whose exercise is social. Up until now there have not been sufficient cases to delineate a line of interpretation. Given the tension, characteristic of this article, between the individual right and the collective context, it is not possible in any case to go so far as to take into consideration a collective right, different from that of the state, which gives force to an individual claim, but a direction is nonetheless indicated. The right to culture no longer appears only as a right to one's own language or to other forms of communication and coexistence, but also includes, for example, a right to one's own territory and to the ways of utilizing one's own resources. That also is considered culture and so is protected by Article 27, approaching the realm of collective rights which are not acknowledged, as we have already said, for reasons more of a procedural than a substantial character.[20]

There are other innovations in the United Nations: for example the question itself of the *minority*, of this category which serves to determine the scope of Article 27 of the Covenant on Civil and Political Rights. It is not a new concept for the indication of a human group. It had already been utilized by the preceding agency, the League of Nations. The United Nations has used this term since its origin, indeed it gave the name to one of its most active institutions, the Sub-Commission on Prevention of Discrimination and Protection of Minorities. It is a term which serves to identify the existence of groups endowed with a precise constitution and culture of their own, but without their own state. The criterion therefore is from the beginning qualitative, not quantitative. It can be and indeed is applied without hesitation, by the United Nations, even to populations which are a majority within the corresponding state, which however is a state that identifies with a different culture. That a minority from the legal point of view may be a de facto majority according to the standards of state evaluation happens at times in Latin America, despite all immigration policies.

Though a language of a *tutelary* sort is lacking, a certain continuity exists with the more clearly colonial language of the permanent underaged *minor*. Given that the concept of qualitative *minority* is, moreover, extended to the rest of the population, regardless of whether it is quantitative or not, it is possible to understand the activity of the above-mentioned Sub-Commission for the purpose of protection. There are many cases in which states do not secure any protection and therefore the *minority* is by definition deprived of the possibility of helping itself on its own. But decolonization does not cease to influence our problem. There are *minorities* that, once recognized as *peoples*, disappear when states are formed; and there are others that, without having had recognition, remain more visible precisely because they have been excluded from such transformation. The fact is that over the last few decades the Sub-Commission on Prevention of Discrimination and Protection of Minorities has not only seen its work increase, but it has also had to forcefully pose the problem of its object and aims, with an urgency unthinkable in more openly colonialist times.

The key question is the existence of peoples, not only of minorities, deprived of guarantees from the human rights perspective, a perspective defined not in 1948 but in 1966. The form in which the Conventions are laid down, with a first article on a collective right, the right of peoples to their own self-determination, and an extension of individual rights, delineates the underlying theme. With respect to the declaration of 1960 on decolonization, the point of departure is not reiteration, but integration. Individual human rights are established assuming collective human rights as a premise. The right of each people to their own freedom is a requisite of individual freedom. Reference is made, that is, to individuals whose existence is established, life develops, identity is formed not within an undifferentiated humanity, but within a specific culture, national or adopted. Otherwise the states themselves would be enough. Perhaps even one would be enough.

Other than decolonization, the principal question before the United Nations is that of the native peoples, peoples colonized and integrated without any determination on their own part in constitutional states which continue to be alien to them. It is necessary to remember that, according to statistics issued by the United Nations itself, this condition, which may be called *indigenous*, concerns about 400 million individuals, 40 million of whom are on the American continent. But the problem of rights is not quantitative; it is above all qualitative. A characteristic, though not an exclusive one, of the American continent is that the constitutional order, originally and still so in some states, has ignored the presence not only of that particular part of the population but also of the rest of the population. There exist many peoples without any recognition who are even today deprived of the human right of self-determination, of a right which is the social premise of individual freedom.

The United Nations has dealt with the problem, arriving at the formulation of a project for the Declaration of the Rights of Indigenous Peoples, which is of twofold interest because it does not limit itself to a proposal to recognize them as peoples.[21] The recognition of peoples as collective subjects endowed with self-determination is the first innovation. But there is another no less substantial, which is attention paid to the problem of what happens when people and state do not coincide. A distinction has to be drawn between these two concepts and it is necessary to explore the possibility of how they can be made compatible, without cancelling the right of the people to self-determination. In other words, the process which opens up, making possible the formal emergence of these subjects, the peoples, is a process of proliferation not of *sovereignty* but of *autonomies*, autonomies which however are recognized and guaranteed internationally before the respective states. The people and not the state take responsibility not only for their own rights but also for the level and the form of communication and participation. Internal autonomy itself becomes the expression of self-determination, whether the inclusion of the people in the state is maintained or whether this collective freedom, when it can be expedient, is exercised.

For the moment, this is a project. Within the ambit of an international law of human rights, it is with the Human Rights Committee and in its case law that the greatest importance and topical relevance resides. There are, however, other innovations. Everything that has been proposed and deliberated concerning the rights of native peoples, collectivities that cannot be adequately described by the category of *minority*, has certainly had an influence on a new instrument (not on a mere project) in the development of human rights: the Declaration on the Rights of Persons Belonging to National or Ethnic, Religious or Linguistic Minorities, issued in 1992.

This new instrument is expressly presented as the evolution of the before-mentioned Article 27 of the Covenant on Civil and Political Rights. Its title does not seem to promise much in the way of innovation when it specifies how individual rights and also the rights of "persons who belong to minorities" are to be treated. One undoubted innovation is the qualification of *national* for the word *minority*, whereas *nation* had until then corresponded only to states, as continues to be the case in the name of the United Nations, is placed before those of ethnic groups, religion, and language, which had already appeared in the previously-mentioned article of 1966. And there is a substantial innovation, although not at the beginning. The rights which are declared are actually of individual entitlement and of collective use, with the contradiction which we have already seen to occur when there is not, as in this case, a right attributed to the collectivity itself. The minority continues to be the sphere of the liberties of individuals whose culture cannot count on the protection of their own state. There are those who are lucky to have this protection and those who cannot take advantage of it collectively and must therefore rely to a large degree upon a state of a different culture.

This innovation however applies to an indigenous population that, there not yet being any Declaration which regards it, remains a *minority*, continuing to avail itself of the treatment provided for in the international order. Now, by means of the Declaration on the Rights of Persons Belonging to National or Ethnic, Religious or Linguistic Minorities, there is a commitment that "the measures adopted by the states to guarantee" such rights must not be contrary to the principle of equality (Article 8.3), that is to a canon which is part not only of constitutions but also of the human rights in the Universal Declaration of Human Rights. Within the state, this basic principle is defined with respect to groups. It is clear what that can imply: there is a change in measurement. The equality of individual rights, which is allegedly universal, must be evaluated not by the state, as in constitutional practice, but by the *minority* itself. It is impossible that legally autonomous peoples should not obtain a space within the constitutional states, because that would be an attack against the equality of citizens, according to a common argument used by native peoples in the whole American continent. Equality is measured by the minority, so by the peoples as clearly distinct from the state.

The minority is thus a measure of itself, which modifies the category itself. How can it continue to call itself *minority* if, on the essential question of rights, it is dealing not with something extraneous but with itself? Individual equality is collective, the equality of all the individuals in a cultural space of their own in the same measure, without any discrimination or exclusion. There are no *gentes* who are more cultured with greater rights and others who are in need of acculturation, as the Universal Declaration of Human Rights itself in substance presumed. This has been the presumption of colonialism since the times of *ius gentium* in Medieval Europe.

What kind of rule of law has been the result and what one might be possible? With regards to the past (a past which in any case has continued up until our times), we have an answer. The future is a greater unknown but suggestions coming from the evolution of constitutionalism throughout the whole American continent are not lacking, nor are those coming from the development of the human rights system at the initiative and impetus of the United Nations. If we keep in mind and put together both phenomena, if we stop looking at the constitutional question in the European mirror, and if we understand that a constitutionalism which goes beyond Europe passes today by way of international law, there are answers. Other hypotheses are not necessary.

Between state law and international law, between constitutional rights and human rights, today the necessity arises for some states which have interiorized colonialism constitutionally to reorganize themselves, not merely recognizing a "presence" to which to attribute some rights, but giving rise to a new constitutionalism which, in the area of individual liberties, will not limit itself to privileging the collective entitlement (the states already do that with their own orders), but instead makes the most of the actual existence of peoples who differentiate themselves by their own cultures.

The protection of individual rights depends exclusively on the rule of law within each nation state and ends up harming the individual himself, since, as happens on the American continent, the *people* who form the nation state and identify with its culture are neither the entire population within its borders nor the original population. Expressions of collective autonomy, only *the rights of the peoples* (where not only the first term but also the second is in the plural and not the singular), assumed as the basis and aim of individual rights, can establish *a rule of rights* void of those old colonial claims from which the European rule of law has not been able to free itself.

NOTES

1. S.L. Harring, *Crow Dog's Case: American Indian Sovereignty, Tribal Law, and United States Law in the Nineteenth Century*, Cambridge: Cambridge University Press, 1994, pp. 8–10; J.R. Wunder, *"Retained by the People": A History of American Indians and the Bill of Rights*, New York: Oxford University Press, 1994, pp. 251–62.
2. R.N. Clinton, "The Proclamation of 1763: Colonial prelude to two centuries of Federal-State conflict over the management of Indian affairs", *Boston University Law Review*, 69 (1989), pp. 329–85.
3. P.P. Frickey, "Marshalling past and present: colonialism, constitutionalism, and interpretation in Federal Indian Law", *Harvard Law Review*, 107 (1993), pp. 381–440; J. Norgren, *The Cherokee Cases: The Confrontation of Law and Politics*, New York: McGraw-Hill Case Studies in Constitutional History, 1995; D.E. Wilkins, *American Indian Sovereignty and the U.S. Supreme Court: The Masking of Justice*, Austin (TX): University of Texas Press, 1997, pp. 19–63.
4. F.P. Prucha, *American Indian Treaties: History of a Political Anomaly*, Berkeley (CA): University of California Press, 1994, pp. 59–66.
5. H.R. Berman, "The concept of Aboriginal rights in the early legal history of the United States", *Buffalo Law Review*, 27 (1977–1978), pp. 637–67; M. Savage, "Native

Americans and the Constitution: the original understanding", *American Indian Law Review*, 16 (1991), pp. 57–118.

6. M. Henriksson, *The Indian on Capitol Hill: Indian Legislation and the United States Congress*, 1862–1907, Helsinki: Societas Historica Finlandiae, 1988, pp. 190–220; J. Burton, *Indian Territory and the United States, 1866–1906: Courts, Government and the Movement for Oklahoma Statehood*, Norman (OK): University of Oklahoma Press, 1995.
7. R.A. Williams Jr., *Linking Arms Together: American Indian Treaty Visions of Law and Peace, 1600–1800*, New York: Oxford University Press, 1997.
8. M. Henriksson, *The Indian on Capitol Hill*, pp. 96–116; J.R. Wunder, op. cit., pp. 27–41, 147–77.
9. J.R. Wunder, op. cit., pp. 48–51, 124–46.
10. I.K. Harvey, "Constitutional law: congressional plenary powers over Indian affairs. A doctrine rooted in prejudice", *American Indian Law Review*, 10 (1982), pp. 117–50.
11. Part I, sect. 25; part II, sect. 35: "Any rights or freedoms that have been recognized by the Royal Proclamation of October 7, 1763"; "droits ou libertés reconnues par la Proclamation royale du 7 octobre 1763".
12. P. Macklem, *Indigenous Difference and the Constitution of Canada*, Toronto: University of Toronto Press, 2001.
13. B. Clavero, *Ama Lunku, Abya Yala. Constituyencia indígena y código ladino por América*, Madrid: Centro de Estudios Políticos y Constitucionales, 2000.
14. E. Keene, *Beyond the Anarchical Society: Grotius, Colonialism and Order in World Politics*, Cambridge: Cambridge University Press, 2002.
15. E. Jouannet, *Emer de Vattel et l'émergence doctrinale du Droit Internationale Classique*, Paris: Editions A. Pedone, 1998.
16. S.J. Anaya, *Indigenous Peoples in International Law*, New York: Oxford University Press, 1996.
17. H. Hannum, *Autonomy, Sovereignty, and Self-Determination: The Accommodation of Conflicting Rights*, Philadelphia (PA): University of Pennsylvania Press, 1990.
18. H. Hannum, *Autonomy, Sovereignty, and Self-Determination*, pp. 74–103; S.J. Anaya, *Indigenous Peoples in International Law*, pp. 39–182.
19. D. McGoldrick, *The Human Rights Committee: Its Role in the Development of the International Covenant on Civil and Political Rights. With an Updated Introduction*, Oxford: Clarendon Press, 1994, pp. 14–16, 247–68.
20. D. McGoldrick, *The Human Rights Committee*, pp. lxiii, 158–9, 203–4, 249–50, 256.
21. S.J. Anaya, *Indigenous Peoples in International Law*, pp. 207–16.

CHAPTER 14

THE COLONIAL MODEL OF THE RULE OF LAW IN AFRICA: THE EXAMPLE OF GUINEA

Carlos Petit

Videant Consules, ut ne [!] quid detrimenti Respública capiat.
(Royal Order enacted in San Sebastian on 2 August 1912)

1 SALUS REGUM ET SALUS REI PUBLICAE

"His Majesty the King Don Alfonso XIII (may God protect him), Her Majesty the Queen Doña Victoria Eugenia, and Their Royal Highnesses Prince of the Asturias and the infants Don Jaime and Doña Beatriz, ... are still in good health". Yet, the white inhabitants of Santa Isabel were far more interested in the governor's decree, published in the central pages of the *Boletín Oficial de los Territorios Españoles del Golfo de Guinea* on 1 September 1911, than in the Premiership's "official" announcement concerning the Royal Family, which is the opening article of the magazine.[1] "Since the harvest of cocoa is about to start, and there is a shortage of labour, which might cause the loss of a great part of the harvest and severely affect the interests of both landowners and the Colony in general, if no adequate measures are taken to avoid this"; and considering, in the light of the recent insurrections in Balachá, that "it would not be proper for the *bubis*, the Bantu race inhabiting the main island of the colony, not to make an effort to work on the land, since such an inertia might be interpreted as the fear that what happened in the past might happen again and as a stimulus to the belief that one is set free of all boundaries imposed by our Sovereignty"; and considering, moreover, that "to make natives work civilizes them and makes them abandon their lazy habits, and that in the name of civilization they must be firmly compelled to work", the Most Excellent Mr. D. Angel Barrera y Luyando, navy lieutenant, Governor General of the Spanish Territories in the Guinea Gulf, stressed that other decrees issued in the past on this matter were still in force (30 August 1907 and 9 September 1909) and compelled the black *bubis* of Fernando Póo to draft labour agreements ("agreements to be signed with their masters") for the harvesting of cocoa.

P. Costa and D. Zolo (eds.), The Rule of Law: History, Theory and Criticism, 467–512.

A month later, Their Majesties were "still in good health" but cocoa was left to grow on trees. His Excellency Governor Barrera informed the public of some provisions executing the decree issued on 9 August by the Governor General, about the work of the *bubis* (11 September 1911, *Boletín* of 1 October). It is detailed, providing important new information which demands analysis.

The issue was about labour relationships between masters and farm labourers; however, the total lack of contractual rules turned the Military Authority into the immediate addressee of such provisions. Since it was clear, as from the decree issued in August, that the Colonial Guard was the last resource to ensure their application and effectively realize the mobilization of the *morenos*, the *Instructions* firstly dealt with the Governor's "Delegates" and the "Commanders of Postings" (instructions A and following), who are divided among districts to carry out "standard operations" (instr. F), and compelled to mutually assist each other and "to make daily reports on new opportunities and developments they become aware of" (instr. G). Within a context of conflicts and resistances, the reader of such draconian provisions is compelled to wonder what had happened "among the populations of Balachá in July last year", as reported in the decree of 9 August. Being cautious in foreseeing "the subversive behaviour of the *naturales*", which would be urgently communicated to the Government and would lead to the detention of "whoever appeared to be the main instigator" (instr. I), and firmly wishing to prevent ("with energy") any potential aggression which the Guard's commanders should not "provoke in any way" (instr. J), Governor Barrera's *Instructions* did not deal with the issues of harvesting, contracts, and farms and simply turned into harsh governmental provisions for guaranteeing public order.

The lack of freedom to work ultimately turned the opaque social question which caused the shortage of labour in Guinea into a purely military matter. According to the *Instructions*, the military authorities were entrusted with the task of distributing farm labourers among the many landowners of the territory according to their needs, and of successively checking their performances (instr. C), by controlling the lists of *negros* assigned to each property, their agreements with their masters and the ensuring that some working conditions which today might appear quite burdensome were respected: *bubis* (the inhabitants of the island of Fernando Póo) had to work 5 days a week, 10 hours a day (instr. L), "so that they may be free on Saturdays and Sundays and may work in their *besés*", for a minimum wage of one peseta a day "including lunch" (instr. D). The lists of labour agreements (instr. D) and any breach of norms and negligent behaviour (instr. K), in particular the failure to respect one's duty to work, which called for "the penalty applied to whoever ignores the Governor General's provisions" (instr. Q), had to be communicated by the Commanders of the posting to a protective figure, the *curador colonial*, which we will deal with later on.

The Governor's guards were not the only subjects supposed to abide by his orders. In a more limited but not less firm manner, the *Instructions* compelled also the "*batukos* or chiefs of the *bubis* population" to collaborate, these being instructed as to the need to abide by the August decree and to pay special attention to the advantages of being paid by piecework, with a daily wage estimated in 1 peseta and 50 cents per person. "In this manner, an entire family may go harvesting and earn excellent wages, thus uniting all family members" (instr. B): such a "preference" for being paid by piecework, when carefully examined, illustrates how the official press was moulded to serve the needs of particular interests.[2] In any event, "Commanders of postings will be particularly careful, will take all peaceful measures and will rely on the country's leading figures" – reference is undoubtedly made to missionaries, Catholics, and Protestants, who, "with the aim of assisting the Government in its management, must urge their respective believers to contribute to the harvesting of cocoa" (instr. R) – "in order to persuade *naturales* to submit to the Governor General's orders" (instr. H). Failure to collaborate by the tribes' chiefs will be "exemplarily punished", in such a way as to be determined, in the light of precedents and circumstances, by the Governor "who paternally watches over *naturales*" (instr. N). Such instructions date back to 1 October 1911.

2 DE REGIMINE COLONIAE AB HISPANIS DEDUCTAE

This is what the 200 white inhabitants of Santa Isabel read on 1 October 1911, upon opening the *Boletín Oficial de los Territorios españoles del Golfo de Guinea*, an administrative magazine which had recently been issued (precisely on 1 March 1907) on Governor Luis Ramos-Izquierdo's initiative. The above magazine was not the only one available in the colony: apart from the pioneer *El Eco de Fernando Póo* (24 November 1901 to 10 March 1902), founded by Enrique López Perea, vessel tenant, former deputy governor of Elobey and expert writer on the colony's problems,[3] *La Guinea Española* was also published on the island at the beginning of Angel Barrera y Luyando's government (1911–1924): such a fortnightly magazine – as is the rule for such peculiar Hispanic-African journalism – was founded in 1903 by the *claretianos* (Missionaries Sons of the Virgin Mary's Immaculate Heart), the Catalan Catholic congregation officially entrusted with the evangelization of the black population.[4] Moreover, there also existed *La Voz de Fernando Póo*, a lively graphic magazine produced in Barcelona, which was the main reading of Guinea's landowners. First published (on 15 June 1910) with too expressive a title (*Boletín del Comité de Defensa Agrícola de Fernando Póo*), it soon had to change it: "not being able to attract public attention as a result of the many professional and propagandistic magazines nowadays circulating everywhere, the title has been changed thus allowing for our modest publication to be placed side-by-side with widely popular press and to offer different opportunities to disseminate our work and therefore create a public opinion on Guinea".[5] The above magazines, which circulated in the colony in the period in question, are currently kept – in more or less complete collections – in Spanish newspaper libraries, thus providing a wealth of information from which we can draw the legal texts we are most interested in.[6]

The situation we are dealing with does not date back too much earlier than the beginning of the twentieth century. Being included within the Spanish domain as a result of its assignment by Portugal under the Treaty of Pardo (1778), and almost sold to England in the nineteenth century,[7] the "Spanish Territories in the Gulf of Guinea" (the official title used by metropolitan law) – which had been until then neither very important nor very well known[8] – first began to be attractive after the Spanish loss of the Antilles, the Philippines, and the Carolines or, in other words, after the settlement of Spain's international controversy with France (Treaty of Paris, 27 June 1900) which radically reduced Spain's claims to the African continent.[9] There does not appear to have been, before Primo de Rivera's dictatorship, a notable presence of Spanish people or at least any effective Spanish control on the non-insular part of the small colony.[10]

Until then, the official aim of exploiting Guinea and organizing its government had only resulted in mere experiments of different impact. Among them, the organic decree and statute on property, enacted in 1904 by the Minister of State Faustino Rodríguez Sampedro, stands out. In the light of its long validity (the decree was modified only under the Second Republic), prior governmental norms appear as mere fleeting signs of a period of trials.[11]

As a matter of fact, the Royal Decree of 1904, "a real colonial charter, though not matching the Portuguese Colonial Acts or the English Crown's colonial Constitutions of its autonomous colonies",[12] set up a long-lasting organization and contained the statute through which

Governor Barrera was able to exert his ample powers on the *bubis* of Fernando Póo. Since we wish to deal with this development, we should briefly pay attention to it.[13]

The disastrous 1898 war and the 1900 Treaty are the reasons behind a regulation which appears to reformulate previous provisions: the first event – the national disaster – brought about the extinction, for want of any object, of the Ministry of Overseas Affairs and the ensuing transfer of colonial matters to the portfolio of the Home Office, after an early attempt to delegate such matters to the Premiership; the second event – the unfavourable settlement of a typical expansionist conflict – led to the definition of Spain's borders in Africa; such a settlement, "by definitively leaving the continent's territories under our sovereignty, compelled us to take into account the special conditions of the tribes inhabiting the region and the resources offered thereby".[14]

It is within such a colonial environment, placed (not only metaphorically) at the edge of the Spanish state, that the political limitations of the liberal state characterized by the rule of law are overcome.[15] Failing a parliament, either local or metropolitan, competent in law-making, the law-making Central Administration referred to the proposals suggested by a mere "Advisory Committee", which was only legitimated to examining legal measures by its members' technical competence.[16] Such proposals were generally followed, with the exception of the tricky problem of popular representation: "to set up alongside the general Government of Fernando Póo, a Colonial Council which, representing the interests so far created, guarantees a greater respect and satisfaction thereof" was something that statistical data proved to be unattainable; for popular participation to become effective "there is not a sufficient number of Spanish family heads for whom there should be an election [...] and this calls for a limitation to the trend of setting up local Councils for the management of local matters".

Owing to local circumstances resulting in the lack of self-government (which led to the rise of interests groups and a militant periodical press), the colony's life hinged upon the Governor General, appointed by the King and freely nominated by the Cabinet upon the Ministry of State's proposal (Article 2). Being the sole "representative of the National Government", "entrusted with the colony's government and administration, he may dispose of the area's naval and land forces [...], all Authorities and employees are subject to the Governor, who is responsible for the safety and preservation of order in the territories entrusted to him and, as 'Deputy Real Patron', is endowed with all powers inherent in such a position". Article 4 of the Royal Decree of 1904, which contains the expressions quoted above, carefully lists a large number of functions entrusted to the Governor. Some of them were connected with the hierarchical superiority of his status (to carry out inspections in the territory, to keep relationships with other authorities, to send reports to the Government, to suspend officers for justified reasons, to grant leaves, and to employ temporary personnel), whereas other exorbitant functions (to publish and execute any provision, including international agreements, to suspend capital punishment and propose pardons) were grounded on the Governor's delegated authority, belonging to the State's highest level of jurisdiction. Colonial internal peace and external safety were undoubtedly the supreme values of the colonial system planned in 1904 and, for this reason, the Royal Decree in question authorizes the Governor General – who, in practice, is a professional soldier – to take "all measures he deems necessary" to preserve order by "[...] duly informing the Ministry of State".[17] There was no rule of law in criminal matters (the Governor may "issue decrees to correct mistakes, preserve social peace, control and maintain good government; this within the limits, as far as punishment is concerned, established by the Ministry of State"); rather, the Governor's assessment of local conditions was upheld. It was up to the Governor General, after hearing the merely advisory opinion of the Authorities' Council (Article 12, 1st), the decision to "suspend (through acts) the enactment and execution of provisions communicated by the Ministry of State when, in the Governor's opinion, they might detrimentally affect the Nation's general interests or the particular ones of the territories he is in charge of; which he will promptly give account of to the above Ministry". Governmental powers in the metropolitan territory will never be so wide as in Guinea, not even in the harshest years of Moderatism.[18] We are now in full Restoration times, though it would appear that we are dealing with the old Laws of the Indies.

3 IUS PUBLICUM EUROPAEUM IN ORBE AFRICANO

It is not by chance that these highly praised laws were printed and circulated in Spain at the end of the century.[19] In the generous regulation of governmental powers made by Faustino Rodríguez Sampedro in 1904, there undoubtedly remained some principles (and some solutions) of previous norms enacted in Guinea;[20] above all, the important case of the Antilles had an impact on it. It could be easily said of the Antilles regulation, precisely when Leopoldo O'Donnell began enacting colonial African law (R.D. 13 December 1858), that up until now, the main trait of Spanish colonial administration has been and continues to be that all its authorities carry out judicial and administrative functions together, whether they be Captain Generals or delegated Superintendents, governors or chief mayors. Territorial hearings give advisory votes on the most serious problems and on matters of good government; for this reason, there are some mixed courts [...] The Captain General's authority, who represents the Crown in Overseas provinces, is unlimited in all areas of public administration, justice or war.[21]

This inevitably entails, as far as individual freedom is concerned, "that there is a people for whom normal life almost coincides with the suspension of individual guarantees".[22] Some changes took place in the middle of the century and even a fleeting autonomous regime for the Antilles was set up; yet, this more tolerant side of the Spanish experience in the United States never reached Africa.[23]

What makes Guinea stand out in this period is the detailed description of the prerogatives of colonial authorities. It is not just a mere issue of administrative logorrhoea. The Governor's competences were so specifically regulated and the establishment of his exceptional powers seemed so natural, as if they were Guinea's common law, because the 1904 Royal Decree, i.e. a "Colonial Charter" which marked a new epoch, appears as a real provision of the *government*, i.e. created by the government without the legislative power's concurrence and meant to favour the very wide powers of colonial Spanish authorities. The political participation of the colonized was only possible through the "Council of Authorities", made up of administrative agencies only endowed with advisory powers (arts. 9–12);[24] no municipal life was guaranteed other than through "local Councils", which depended (in the very definition of their functions) on the Governor General's full discretion (Article 14–22); there was no provision for the institutional presence of the colonized[25] apart from what the Governor deemed to be legally relevant. No or little importance was attached to ordinary justice (Article 23): being in the hands of temporary personnel appointed by the Governor and compatible (still in 1904) with the judicial powers of the latter's delegates,[26] it was also affected by a lack of professional judges as a result of poor wages and the harshness of local life.[27]

It follows that the institutional groundings for individual freedom were rather weak. "In the territories of the Guinea Gulf, the rights granted to Spaniards by the Monarchy's Constitution are valid": such a document, dating back to 1876, is a doctrinarian text which, as it is known, systematically subordinates individual rights to statute law, for instance when there is a state of siege, which may be decided by the

Government independently of parliament.[28] It is not surprising that, in a colony "of exploitation", the general reference to the 1876 Charter was completed in 1904 with the explicit proclamation of individuals' free professional initiative, together with a general right of petition which, although not compensating for the lack of freedom, gave voice to the press manifesting landowners' interests: "all Spaniards, whether natural or not, living in the territories of the Guinea Gulf, are entitled to (1) begin their profession and exert it as they think best, in conformity with law and (2) make petitions, individual or collective, to the Authorities. Such a right cannot be exercised by the Armed Forces" (Article 29).

In a few words, the normative framework of constitutional freedom in the small colony of Guinea was more and more distant from metropolitan law and coincided with the 1904 organic Statute and with its future local regulatory developments.[29] The actual situation of such remote portions of national sovereignty affected freedom ab initio and enshrined the intrusion of the Governmental Authority, both directly through the Governor and indirectly, though not less effectively, through the Ministry of State.[30]

Individual freedom, together with the framework of regulations and material conditions allowing for its effective enjoyment, was thus in the hands of governmental power – of Power *tout court*. The normative framework was the *ius publicum europaeum* enacted by the European powers that met in Berlin in 1885 and commonly accepted as the basis for partitioning the African continent. With respect to the situation in Guinea, we can limit our analysis to the *colonial constitution* imposed by Europe on Africa.[31]

Firstly, the constitution unashamedly did without the representative rhetoric which had been traditionally used in metropolitan political laws.[32] After the fleeting Spanish democratic experience (1868–1874), there could emerge a *liberal system of colonial government* "whereby the executive power in the colony does not claim or exert greater functions than those of European representative governments", but a similar *system* – widespread, though not prevailing, in English colonies – was considered dangerous even in its original land. Elsewhere (in Spain and France), an *administrative system* prevails, this being characterized by the lack of participating institutions: "a system where governmental authority is limited only by advisory Councils or bodies or by the intervention of the judiciary, an example of which is represented by the *Real Acuerdo* of the Spanish law of the Indies".[33] Although the colonies' participation in metropolitan assemblies was desirable – and achieved for the Spanish Antilles – it seemed that "the principle of virtual representation ... for external provinces inhabited by semi-civilized races different from the European one and where settlers coming from the motherland represent only a small minority"[34] was to be upheld. Things could not be clearer. Despite the rhetorical assimilation between the Spanish and Guinean systems, the African constitution leaves little room for positive freedom. With a great ostentation of coherence, the Spanish colonial literature between the nineteenth and twentieth centuries simply expressed a mere *administrative*[35] vocation.

The metropolitan "exploitation" of the colony shifted towards mere "administration", though it claimed to be directed at "harmonizing" the countries' respective legal systems; such an assimilation was presented as a characteristic of Latin populations though, in truth, it was deeply marked by contradictions: such a so-called *assimilation*, in fact, would have denied the colonial reality itself.[36] While the principle was generically upheld in Spain, it was always thwarted with respect to the particular law of Guinea: the Peninsula's legislation was not valid in the colony, unless otherwise decided by the Executive Power.[37] The situation was similar with respect to the Spanish purported penchant for racial fusion.[38] What is more, according to the Treaty of Congo (1885), in order to "administer" African lands, Latins and Anglo-Saxons were not even required to effectively occupy the territory.[39] If such a possibility was generically appealing and called for a new geographic outlay, this means that the polyvalent Executive power intervened by planning, under the guise of geography, what it did not wish to realize in politics.[40] Colonial law, hiding behind a geographical and scientific legitimacy, thus avoided legislative assemblies: jurists acknowledged that "even when the ordinary legislative power affirms its competence in these matters, in practice the provisions concerning colonies enacted by the executive are a greater number than those enacted by the legislative power".[41]

Geographical explorations require a commanding unit, rapid operations, and great effectiveness. Therefore, the second element of the colonial constitution in which, as we have seen, freedom had very little room, was the relinquishment of the separation of powers, i.e. of the old revolutionary idea which was supported – more or less convincingly – by European constitutions upholding the rule of law. Jurists were perfectly aware of such a situation: "the manifest inferior civilization of the colonized" was a universal public law principle and "almost necessarily calls for a somewhat despotic power, though a line must be drawn between legitimate and beneficial despotism on the one hand and unfair despotism on the other".[42] Not many differences are to be found among colonies, since many English Crown colonies fit such a description (from Gibraltar to Hong Kong, from Labuan to Gambia, from Sierra Leone to Trinidad-Tobago).[43] When norms must be suited to facts, the African situation required a more practical approach, in that resort was made to the Executive Power: "the Governor has general competences, being himself the representative of both metropolitan and colonial interests; he has legislative competences as well as competences relating to the administration of justice; he has military powers; he is endowed with all rights that the first governmental agent must have for the purpose of preserving colonial order and public safety".[44] Therefore, the colonial Governor's solid standing always included the "right to enact regulating provisions having ... a substantial legislative value".[45]

Given that *laws* (in formal sense) were reduced to *administrative regulations*, the chance for parliament to take decisions affecting the colony was coherently and accordingly limited: even in Congo (where the *Charte coloniale* of 18 October 1908 – a formal law – had turned Leopold's feud into a Belgian national dominion), the intervention of the Brussels Chambers was an extraordinary occurrence.[46] Not to speak of the countries which had only recently been admitted to the "colonial feast", such as inflexible Germany[47] or adventurous Italy.[48] That was the age of representative governments and public opinion; yet, the colonial constitution seemed to exhibit a sort of political "ineffability", which certainly made up its third characteristic:

> it is widely acknowledged by all colonial peoples and by most public law doctrines concerned with colonial administration, that metropolitan parliaments are not competent in colonial law-making [...] in countries such as England, where the widest powers for decentralization have been granted and where self-government is best implemented, parliament is not forbidden to create colonial laws; indeed, it is entitled to do so, though it rarely exerts such a right, not being used to doing so and also being aware of its incompetence in this respect.[49]

In Spain, the *Cortes* dealt with Guinea only on an episodic and indirect basis; under the regime of the 1888 Royal Decree, the debate on a particular section of a financial law regarding overseas territories, lacking a specific reference to African colonies, allowed the representative Rafael María de Labra to express his suggestions for the

> colony's development [...] firstly, the autonomist extension of Councils; secondly, the enlargement of the number of councillors, thus including also members of the black race and in general all human classes; thirdly, the gradual replacement of government-appointed councillors with councillors elected by the people; fourthly and lastly, the full and real proclamation in Fernando Póo, and in all colonies of Guinea, of public freedom, of individual natural rights and of the constitutional immunities granted to Spanish citizens.[50]

Let us examine such suggestions. The reference to colonies within parliament inevitably brings about issues of power and freedom. Therefore, when parliaments do not talk about colonial matters, what is omitted is not a mere trifle. Labra's reasonable proposal to the Spanish *Cortes* was quite exceptional, if only for its constitutional commitment, and was not less reasonable than the financial law that was being discussed for overseas territories; yet, neither received a great deal of interest.[51]

Being separate from the parliamentary logic and lacking freedom and autonomous powers, the colonial constitution seemed to mirror the metropolitan constitution:

> it ought not to be forgotten that colonial law, by nature, cannot be created on the same grounds and with the same criteria as metropolitan law. It refers to populations which are less civilized than European ones, and for whom a kind of government similar to the one we had in ancient times is more suitable; vice versa, it cannot adopt the principles of modern constitutionalism.[52]

The view that Western law, the pride of our civilization and the enemy of old despotisms, proved to be the most effective means to subdue non-European cultures in the European interest, has been endorsed by the most authoritative historiography concerned with the American experience,[53] but its harsh judgements may be easily extended also to African territories. The metropolitan regime of freedom did not seem compatible with the more rigid colonial domination and, for this reason, old solutions – which our modern jurists, such as Santi Romano, confidently ascribe to the Ancient Regime – were adopted.

There undoubtedly were some exceptions. Adolfo González Posada, speaking in French to an international audience, said:

> It is impossible to ignore a matter which has obviously been overlooked by colonizers, conquerors and adventurers, which the moralist however – every historian, just like every critic, is or should also be a moralist – must take into account, just like the sociologist, though under different perspectives. The point is to know what right entitles a given people (deeming itself to be more civilized) to invade, through immigration or a political collective action, the territory of the people or peoples it wishes to colonize.

"Can a man and, above all, can a state exterminate a people at its own discretion?" At last, we find the underpinning question nobody is bold enough to ask; a decisive issue whose simple formulation is sufficient to question the partitioning of African land and peoples, which had been easily agreed upon *unter den Linden*. Unlike his European colleagues, who were more involved in the modern colonial adventure, Adolfo Posada's lucid freedom of mind resulted from his unique[54] capacity of both *krausista* and Spaniard:

I believe that a colony, even when it is originally nothing but a commercial enterprise or the expression of an adventurous spirit, necessarily ends up being either an action of extermination or of regeneration, or moral and legal elevation, of natives; I also believe that, not only for humanitarian but also for sociological and political reasons, colonization must satisfy the ethical needs humanity cannot neglect by being truly concerned with the fate of natives, attracting them thereto and elevating them, thus uniting the colonizing element and the dominating element in a sole ethnographic formation.[55]

Posada *dixit*. His thoughts (expressed at a seminar held in Oviedo for law students and shortly after published, in a magazine keen on examining the colonies' situation[56] when Spain lost the Antilles and Philippines), represent the soundest legal reasoning on colonial matters that an embittered late nineteenth-century Spain was able to produce.[57] The amalgamation of races, imposed by Europe and seriously threatening to extinguish different cultures, undoubtedly appears today as a despicable suggestion, though it would not be fair to apply our politically correct criteria to Posada. Posada, at least, was bold enough to turn the taken-for-granted, and generally not discussed, issue of colonial domination into a real problem.

Moreover, Posada rightly resorted to law to understand the relationship between the "civilized" and the "uncivilized": on a legal level, it is evident that "between this and that man there can *never* be such a huge difference so as to imply that one is a *mere means* for the other (which is why slavery is so absurd)". Let us continue examining Adolfo Posada's thoughts. By recognizing the dignity of people who are culturally different, his suggestions (collected in an overlooked essay which responded to a contemporary anticolonialist pamphlet[58] using legal means), also acknowledged the "European talent".[59] "The constitutive traits of civilization must be detected. These are peoples working in backward material conditions; undoubtedly ... they are meek, simple, amicable, sincere and welcoming. Civilization usually brings about the most disgraceful and shameful vices".[60] Quite an unquestionable remark. Yet, the law Posada grounded his reasoning on belongs to our European tradition; it is a law marked by cultural meanings and functional to a political project producing both winners and losers. "Isn't the uncivilized and wild people a real constituted state legally deserving respect? Isn't the isolated savage a subject of law, isn't he a human being? Do the declarations of human rights, even without the abstract value ascribed thereto by the French constituent assembly (according to Rousseau), expressly exclude the races we deem to be inferior?"[61]

Therefore, with respect to the *savages*, a given *political law* – i.e. that created by Europe for Africa through the Treaty of Congo – which protected, safeguarded, but ultimately subdued individuals, is questioned:

the human being endowed with reason must, first of all, respect the rational aims of his fellow creatures. He *cannot*, or rather, he *must* not destroy them, they ought to be considered for what they are, as human beings deserving respect; secondly, in his relationship with the savage, the more civilized being is also the more legally obliged, since legal obligations are directly proportionate to the subject's rational capacity. In the light of this, savages' rights are preserved, and the civilized man is in such a position as to interact with them *even when the savages are in conflict therewith*.[62]

4 LOCATIO-CONDUCTIO ET IURA AETHIOPUM

Even when the savages are in conflict (italics by Posada). His words contain a cautious, though clearly new, reference to the laws of the Indies – to the old reasoning, by Vitoria, Suárez, and alike, which justified the American conquest in the name of an Aristotle-inspired sort of sociability which turned the protection of *commercium* among men into a more than sufficient reason to dominate savages. The reader will certainly recall the reasoning: everybody is entitled to go anywhere and cannot exclude from the land (which belongs to all) any peaceful stranger who does not disturb anyone and does not give rise to suspicions (*perigrinari cuivis quocumque fas est, nefas vero hospitem pacatum neque laedentem, neque suspectum communi solo excludere*[63]). Things change when the exercise of such a social interaction, which is so characteristically human, is rendered difficult: it is then lawful to invade the savages' territories (*licet ergo, licet sine ulla dubitatione barbarorum fines penetrare, idque si renuant nulla vel accepta vel merito expectata iniuria, iniqui sunt*[64]). It is not by any chance that, when the *ius publicum europaeum* started circulating along the boulevards of Berlin, the Spanish Dominican Francisco de Vitoria began his brilliant career as the founding father of international law.[65]

Going from Berlin to Vitoria (and always in the light of our analysis of Guinea), we have entered a world of virtual realities, i.e. of thoughts contaminated by the cultural filter.[66] Bypassing all sense of limitation, a new form of anthropology, which did even appeal to the shared idea of the superiority of the white race, was established as a scientific discipline.[67] A number of European writers, musicians, and painters dealt with exotic matters in their famous writings, works, or paintings, thus both spreading trivial images and relenting tensions endemic to the metropolitan conscience through "cultural practices that distance and 'aesthetize' their object".[68] And these were neither forms of knowledge extraneous to law nor artistic passions which did not affect jurists. Therefore, a new *comparative law doctrine*, together with a modern Roman law discipline denying jurisprudence without being after interpolations, were now easily mixed with other social sciences, including anthropology.[69] All such disciplines shared the same hidden beliefs and prejudices. Even the guild of legal historians gave its embarrassing contribution to colonialism: given its recognized competence in primitive customs and its familiarity with the description of backward political regimes, "the study of law's comparative history offers colonization its most considerable services".[70]

Furthermore, there are a number of mouldy Latin texts which then began to be re-examined through new editions and studies after having been long neglected during the Enlightenment.[71] The "confessional" way of considering such texts left little doubt as to the legitimacy of European expansion, and thousands of venerable pages created and reproduced images of barbarism which were particularly vivid also in the colonial period. The Indians subdued by Hernán Cortés and whom Bartolomé de las Casas tried to save, the blacks of Albert Schweizer or of Governor Barrera all matched the same model, i.e. the cliché which pitilessly depicted non-European populations as being, *inter alia*, indolent, infantile, drunk, coward, mistrustful, superstitious, emotional, and so on.[72] Jurists were well aware of such factors:

> the African black race displays its typical traits in Central and Eastern Africa, in Sudan, in Senegambia and in Guinea: an elongated and compressed skull, narrow at the temples; flat nostrils, non vertical though leaning teeth, thus lifting the upper lip; short neck, wide and cylindrical chest; slightly curved feet; black, short and wool-like hair. Such anatomical traits are accompanied by given moral characteristics: an underdeveloped mind [...] and a great susceptibility. The black being, if left on his own, is hardly able to abandon tribal lifestyles through civilization.[73]

Under such a perspective, it mattered little whether the West was interested in exploring this or that side of the Atlantic and whether its domination was recent or centuries old: experts could always rely on historical accounts of colonization – these being a fundamental chapter of all writings on colonial law – which linked Stanley, Gallieni, or Cecil Rhodes with Columbus and even with ancient Romans.[74]

Such remarks ought not to be misunderstood. To stress the continuity of a given line of thought – the European racial and cultural superiority – is not to disown the multiple differences between the conquest of the United States and the exploitation of Africa. Suffice it to recall one significant difference: towards the end of the nineteenth century, the Western mythical idea of progress – superior political structures, modern sciences and medicine, productive economies, technological innovations[75] – had (almost) completely replaced the missionary vocation of the past. Progress now moved together with a new *universal public law* consecrating "civilization" as a "modern political idea", which was just as fundamental as the old revolutionary key words of equality and freedom, and was capable, if necessary, of subverting them:

> progress must not be denied to anyone, whether he be white or black. All individuals must be allowed to compete with the most noble and intelligent, and must be allowed to rival in their efforts for the public good and for humanity. However, the limit of what is rational ought not to be overstepped. Politicians, blinded by false equality, have forgotten that real differences are nonetheless very important. The state official cannot disown psychological factors linked with the hereditary transmission of given qualities, good or bad, neither can he ignore the impact of race on individual aptitudes.[76]

The above ideas are indeed very different; yet, our textual history also detects *some* common traits: starting with Acosta, there emerged an empirical and compared – in other words, *modern* – ethnography which connects the late sixteenth century to the late nineteenth century.[77] The Western conception of labour – a biblical curse and a legitimate title for appropriation, but also a necessary concurrence of forces for the exploitation of African resources – also includes an unlimited trust in its civilizing function, which seems to remain unaltered throughout centuries, and which makes the Jesuit missionaries of the past seem not that different from modern colonial governors. And what may be said (in 1588) for the American Indians ("these savage nations, mainly the peoples of Ethiopia and of the Western Indies must be educated like the Jews [...] they will refrain from any idleness and excess of passion through a reasonable amount of work and must be compelled to abide by their duty by striking them with fear"[78]) may be valid also for Guinea in 1907: "much must be done on the island of Fernando Póo to submit the *bubis*, and one of the conditions required to dominate them, to make them work and to know the number of people living on the island is to set up police postings".[79]

Only 10 years had lapsed since the Treaty of Berlin; yet, the colonial *social question* was already a leading concern of the main European centre for colonial studies.[80] Quite obviously, the cultural filters of the anthropological adventure came into play: faced with the untamed idleness ascribed to the blacks and already manifested by the Indians, the

European strategy – regardless of whether it was devised by José de Acosta or Angel Barrera – consisted in imposing a working regime which civilized one group of people in order to enrich another, and did not hesitate to use pre-Enlightenment criminal law, a means to ensure productivity and discipline.[81] The culture of colonialism established a particular connection between Europe and Africa whereby the whites brought progress and the blacks paid for it by offering their labour forces: "civilized and learned cultures have the duty to bring civil life to human beings living in primitive and wild conditions, and to turn them into useful and productive men; they also have the duty to discover and exploit the richness of virgin territories inhabited by the latter, thus rendering a service to Humanity and Progress and conferring great part of such richness to the civilizing nation".[82] The lack of Africans' consent as to their progress and work did not appear to be a problem. In a similar context, the rigid defence of mandatory labour, often prescribed by law and always used in colonial regimes, ended up by claiming to indicate European esteem for traditional cultures: "colonizers have simply used a local customary formula corresponding to the local conception of work".[83] What was ignored, however, was that aversion to work or bad performance was the natives' natural mechanism of resistance against the foreign dominator.[84]

It was the early twentieth century in the Guinea Gulf; yet, the principles conceived for the Indies at the end of the sixteenth century still seemed to hold ground. At a time when there used to be a European "common" law with a universal vocation, the American Indians were seen, if not directly as animals, in any event as miserable, rough, and inferior people; they had a particular *status* in a world of privileges and were classified in the lowest and most defenceless ranks of the social system. Being victims of their infantile condition, they did not even enjoy the familiar autonomy which was granted to the poorest or the "rough" people.[85] Three centuries later, another "common" law, i.e. the colonial law of Berlin, was applied in the African continent. The archaic categories of "roughness" and misery were no longer used, and nobody viewed the Church as a civilizing and protecting institution. Yet, the idea of Africans' "under age" status was upheld by civil codes and used by the colonial legislators to subdue the blacks in the name of their wildness: "savages may be easily assimilated to minors or to individuals unable to make correct judgements"; they are all disabled and under guardianship.[86] In the name of protection, which no African had ever asked for, Europe expropriated individual wills: it compensated *more suo* Africans' declared incapacity by compelling them to work.

In such a perspective, which saw natives as metropolitan children or as mentally insane, public international law recycled private law concepts and extended the latter's protective measures – protectorate, mandate or trust – to all exotic populations lacking a defined public apparatus: peoples thus paid for their political infancy through their dependence on Western remote motherlands.

Colonial subjects were forced into their proper classification: "the intellectual faculties of our black Africans are on average limited, this rendering their autonomy difficult not only in the political world but also in the private domain"; the expression of their allegedly disturbed will had to be entrusted to special officials and patronages.[87] What mechanisms could guarantee greater submission? Blacks are like children, with the terrible difference that time does not lapse for them: once Africans were put indefinitely under guardianship, tropical medicine, grounded on statistical reasoning, and physical anthropology, conceiving of sexual development itself as the ultimate limit of intellectual maturity, were able to determine the mental age of Guinea's *bubis* as that of a 12-year-old child.[88]

The issue of "work" lies at "the very heart of the colonial problem".[89] There certainly were European workers in the African continent who were subject to special norms for the whites;[90] yet, after the Berlin conference, there arose a widespread opposition to their presence in Africa, for both hygienic reasons related to the harshness of tropical weather and for stronger reasons connected with the dignity of the white race: "Guinea is not a colony for the immigration of labour. The white worker cannot live with the daily wage given to the black, his working rate is not similar to the latter's, the dignity of his race does not allow him to bow before the blacks, and he cannot perform a hard job without his health being damaged".[91] The white workers' poor biological fitness to tropical weather was even welcomed as a potential safeguard for races deemed to be inferior; yet, virtual domination was what actually took place: as a matter of fact, immigration legislation of the time did not even contemplate the possibility of emigrating to Africa to work.[92]

Once again, not Spain alone was concerned with the above problems. When the International Institute of Brussels became aware of the changes taking place in the exotic dominions of old European powers (i.e. when the States which were once objects of colonial domination began entering the League of Nations), it began devoting its collective efforts to the *Régime et l'Organisation du Travail des Indigènes dans les Colonies Tropicales*.[93] Guinea, once again, allows us to examine a common principle of labour under colonial "common" law, whose enactment varied according to the circumstances of each single country.[94] In Spain-dominated equatorial Africa the persistent "labour problem", i.e. the shortage of workers in the plantations of Fernando Póo, seriously jeopardized the fate of such a small territory, that had few capitals, sufficient foreign penetration, and very few resources; however, the colony's economic history – the discontinuous grants of land, the risks of cocoa's monocultivation, the duty barrier in the Peninsula, the difficult "importation" of workers from the Kru coast, from Sierra Leone or Biafra – ought not to conceal the fact that such difficulties were local manifestations of much wider phenomena endemic to the culture of imperialism itself.

5 DE THEOBROMATE COLLIGENDO MORE GUINEANO

Now we have come to 1906, Spain still lacked specific legislation on labour agreements, though the "Temporary Regulation on Native Labour in the Spanish territories of the Gulf of Guinea" was then implemented in Spain's tropical territories.[95] Being the key element of the exploitation plan carried out in accordance with the colonial government through the 1904 organic statute, such a Regulation was a low-profile metropolitan law with a strong local imprint, its content being entirely due to the Royal Commissioner Diego Saavedra, a Governor who was particularly sensitive to landowners' needs.[96] The Spanish Regulation drew inspiration from the Portuguese legislation which followed the Treaty of Berlin[97] and aimed at guaranteeing sufficient labour on the island; although it did not attain its immediate aim, it paved the way for a good number of minor legislations, made "of decrees, orders, bans and instructions, whose good intentions are frustrated by the congenital slackness of the people they are addressed to".[98]

The decrees issued by Barrera in 1911 are an example, *inter alia*, of such detailed governmental provisions driven by "good intentions". Ever since then, the African constitution was marked by a similar form of legislation, "since the legislator better understands the subjects of law and fully grasps the problems of colonial sociology";[99] yet, it is precisely through such a modest way of introducing local provisions that the common principle of hard labour was introduced in Guinea. Such a principle did not apply to the *bubis*; according to the 1906 Labour Regulation, "all residents of the island of Fernando Póo with no property, job, legal and acknowledged occupation, or not domiciled in the social Registries kept by local Councils for this purpose, will be subject to the guardianship of the *Curaduría* and will be obliged to work, both under contract with private beings and for the state. This rule does not apply to the *bubis*, though agreements therewith are not forbidden as long as they are accepted by the former" (Article 24).

In order to account for such an exception, let us refer back to the general and straightforward principle: Africans "will be subject to guardianship and will be obliged to work". Such a precept entails much more than two mere propositions linked by a copulative conjunction. The blacks' *savage* nature, coupled with the whites' obligation to civilize savages, legitimated the former's submission to the latter. Ergo, in European legal terms, the subjection of colonial populations depended on a guardianship bond, which protected the savages by civilizing them and civilized them by imbuing them with a work-based productive culture: in other words, the obligation to work imposed on the Guineans is the result of their being minors under guardianship.

In the light of the above, the logic behind the Regulation is clear. The circumstance that such a norm refers to native labour, and that labour is the main theme of its provisions (Article 24–76), is due to the fact that the 1906 Regulation hinges upon a protective institution, the so-called colonial *curaduría* (Article 1–23; see also Article 77–79), which represents Spain itself in its capacity of guardian of the savage-disabled. Indian precedents – an example against nations suspicious of the moral stature of Spain – were not forgotten, yet the terminology and mechanisms used came now from "common" colonial law.[100] This led to the double aim of "protection" and "work" – "to protect" natives in order to subdue them to work – which was typical of Spanish guardians: "such officials' duties are to avoid and, where necessary, to punish violence committed by Europeans on natives, to control agreements between the former and the latter, in particular salaried labour agreement, which are the most open to abuse, as well as other similar agreements".[101] As was the rule in European constitutions for Africa, the line between assisted contractual wills and violent impositions of labour agreements simply did not exist: the armed forces of the protective institution were able to ensure the reasonable behaviour of its most recalcitrant protected individuals.[102]

Could the *bubis* still be legally exempt from work, even though in practice they were under guardianship? Did not the Spanish Authorities' detailed decrees re-establish the inexorable logic of the constitution, subverted for the time being by a non-subsequent norm? The presence in Fernando Póo of foreign labour, which was decisive at the beginning of the century and which was related to the conception of islanders as physically and morally weak beings and thus not very useful to landowners, certainly played a significant role in the original exception: "a rickety and degenerated race ... quite a repulsive lot ... with an under-developed physical constitution",[103] "the disgraceful *bubis* of the coast are an inferior race, a race degenerated by alcohol abuse, supporting the whites with the only aim of gaining some benefits"[104] and coming up to a fast extinction.[105] Such remarks are undoubtedly terrible in themselves but a closer examination is required. Besides oppressive conditions and rough ethnographic evaluations, the issues of "protection" and "work" are fundamental in understanding the lack of legally established rights in the Black Continent.

Let us now leave for a while the legal profile of such non-existent rights. Let us examine the magazines which we briefly mentioned above in order to understand colonial legislation. Matters are so clear, and the network of representations rotating around the Guinean harvesting of cocoa is so obvious, that any example, just like the following one, may be used in this respect. It was in 1921, in the presence of the new District Delegate, D. Emilio G. Laygorri, the city of San Carlos was happily celebrating the King's name day. "Quite nicely, during the celebrations, nearly all the district *bubis* came to pay homage to their beloved King in the person of his friendly representative. All united by the same ideal, colonial people rivalled in expressing their patriotism ... then, as it happens in families sharing the same feeling, their interest aroused their honour".[106] We shall later deal with some picturesque aspects of such patriotic celebrations, but, for the time being, we wish to stress an ordinary word used by the reporter of such friendly events. Being whites and blacks united in their vivid love for the Spanish monarchy, the inhabitants of San Carlos are, in colonial eyes, a close family, indeed, a *family*.

The family rhetoric thus provides the framework within which colonial norms could be set. Let us now examine the situation in 1921. On 31 December, Governor Barrera docked at Santa Isabel. He was returning from Spain and was warmly welcomed by local people.[107] "The Local Council has erected a beautiful arabesque arch at the gates of the city with an inscription bearing the words: 'Most Excellent Mr. D. Angel Barrera: to his adopted Son, the grateful people'. The inscription underlines the intelligent contribution of the Public Works Officer D. Francisco Bermejo. In the arch erected by the Company *Daughters of Africa*, the simplicity and typical style of the country stand out, along with the following affectionate inscription: 'To father Barrera, the daughters of Africa': national colours were the main trait of the lively work".

Should we despise the repeated use of the above metaphor? All individuals' mother was the distant Spanish homeland, which the Governor had just visited. He was born there in 1863, precisely in Burgos, *caput Castellae*, though he had now been adopted by Santa Isabel, a young colonial capital. The Governor, who was the lawful son of Fernando Póo, was himself a progenitor. The so-called *Daughters of Africa*, who saluted the arrival of the Governor, were also daughters of Barrera: they used the same appellation as for their fathers, i.e. *papá* (daddy). This was a common usage: during the same celebration, some *batukos*, tribal chiefs of the *bubis*, submissively kissed the Governor's hands and bent down at "the feet of their idol, *Papá Barrera*". Such pieces of news came from the colony, but they rapidly reached the homeland.[108]

The historian must take these repulsive anecdotes seriously and grasp their juridical meaning.[109] The family metaphor, which was so recurrent in colonial language, was not a mere rhetorical contrivance used by European consciences to underline both the West's racial superiority and its commitment to the political domination of Asia or Africa. Owing to a discourse which sublimated any kind of inequality, not only was any potential debate on the rights and freedoms of non-European races avoided; the family picture also eliminated the conceptual incoherence of jurists who were compelled to use principles for Africa that were completely opposite to the ones used for European countries. The proclamation of the so-called universal political principles, continuously thwarted on grounds of race, social organization, or development, effectively complemented, by resorting to the "family" image, the state's means of dominance, i.e. its protectorate on native peoples or the protection of its single members. It "ought not to be forgotten" – says Santi Romano – "that colonial law cannot, by nature, be set up on the same basis and with the same criteria as metropolitan law. It refers to peoples who are less civilized than the European ones, for whom a kind of government similar to the one we had in ancient times is more suitable; vice versa, it cannot adopt the principles of modern constitutionalism".

A precise content to the above Italian jurist's general consideration can now be ascribed. In more ancient times, even in Europe, the family was the leading structure of social life.[110] Within the domestic setting, which became the model for republics, there was a paternal power (precisely an *economic* one) with a discipline of its own, just as closed to justice as it was open to religion. Being exempted from any legal control, the family chief's decisions could not be questioned. The father's task was to educate, correct, and complete the reduced capacities of his children and wife. Biological links were not decisive in legitimating submission to paternal authority: familiar bonds compelled non-European men and women, like domestic servants, slaves, or sons in custody, to abide by their white masters' authority. The family itself was the most important agency of criminal policy and was responsible if this first circuit of punishment failed. Through discipline, economy, and religion, the family embodied the paradigm of the despotic government, which had been harshly criticized by enlightened intellectuals with the aim of creating a different world. Let us just quote the following words by Marquis Beccaria:

> such ruinous and authorized injustices were approved even by the most learned men and carried out by the freest republics, which deemed society to be a union of families rather than a union of men. Let us imagine a hundred thousand men, [or] i.e. twenty thousand families, each of the latter being made of five members, including the chief representing it: if the association is created for families, there will be twenty thousand men and eighty thousand slaves; if the association is made of men, there will be a hundred thousand citizens and no slave [...] Such conflicts between family rules and the republic's fundamental rules give rise to another set of contradictions between domestic and public morals and also bring about a perpetual conflict in the soul of each individual. The former inspires submission and fear, the latter courage and freedom; one restricts charitable acts to a small number of people with no spontaneous choice, the other extends them to all human classes.

"This shows how limited most legislators' points of view were". Such words need not be further analyzed, since their mere quotation allows us to grasp the political (or antipolitical, if you like) spirit embedded in the old domestic setting.[111] Such considerations do not distract us from our main concern, i.e. colonial work. The family entails both working under submission and disciplinary powers not subject to law: hence, it is by examining the dogmatic meaning of familial metaphors that we can truly appreciate the central role of work in colonial constitutions.[112] At the time and place which were object of the Treaty of Congo, the above ideology legitimated the exertion of a very old patriarchal power, and familial bonds were used to submit equally (no matter whether labour was private or public) prudent domestic servants, efficient officials, and exploited workmen. We shall not deal either with the conceptual changes which affected labour agreements when Europe took hold of Africa,[113] or with the labour relationships effective in the colonizing countries.[114] What is important, and thus particularly illustrative on colonial work, is that our forefathers believed that work was to be technically conceived of not as a civil law obligation, but rather as a chance of collaborating with capital, which hence found its meaning within the institutions of family law.[115]

We can therefore understand the meaning of those "amorous" figures which occur from time to time in our texts. Suffice it to think about the plural use, in any European language of the late nineteenth century, of the innocent word *colonia*: this Latin word, through its underlying meanings of abandonment and dependence, could equally be applied to industrial factories, forsaken pupils, or prisoners, all these being potentially redeemable through a good measure of work.[116] Being viewed both as a child before the law, as a being to be civilized, and as a worker, the African had both an infantile condition as well as a worker's status, which ultimately led to his double submission: even the most humble white man, exempt from any kind of protection, was always better than the most proud *bantu* labourer. The European governor was both the natives' father and master. Colonial policy turned into a labour issue and colonial law was but a set of instruments used to force the black to produce to the white's benefit.

6 SI VIS PACEM, PARA BELLUM

Behind the "disabled" beings' backs, Guinean whites devised a number of strategies arousing rivalry among tribes – *divide ut regnes*, as it was said[117] – and aimed at instilling the need for money in the blacks' minds through artificial consumption habits: the mark of civilization, which coincided with the adoption of clothes, had more to do with money and wages rather than with the development of delicate, moral, or decent feelings.[118]

> Quite recently, luckily, thanks to the Colonial Department [of the Ministry of State], which has fought off the suggestions coming from scrupulous souls and female hearts [...], a new direction has been given to colonial politics, this being called 'of attraction'; ever since the most illustrious Governor, Don Luis Ramos Izquierdo, implemented a plan of military action for the effective occupation of Fernando's island, thus establishing military postings, calling the *botucos* to its attention and obliging them through force to account for their failure to comply with orders, establishing the obligation to work, curbing the use of alcohol and using other means typical of governments [...] ever since then, the impact of our sovereignty on the colony has been sensibly increasing, and the rural situation has been notably improved since the number of labourers has been timely suited to the number of plantations.[119]

This was the kind of story told (with the greatest sang-froid) about Guinea. Thus: "si vis pacem, para bellum". Such an expression – first employed by E. d'Almonte when speaking to an audience of geographers about the "inhabitants of Spanish Guinea, viewed in their status of Spanish subjects"[120] – united the new Spanish approach towards natives with both the public expression of colonial interests and colonial military organization: despite their differences, these stances were all connected – not only in terms of simultaneity – within the final aim of compelling such "Spanish subjects" to hard labour. In the Guinean press, however, the voice of the old but still forceful Labra, a Member of Parliament, occasionally resounded; speaking to the *Cortes*, to whomever was still interested in listening to him, he argued that

> a Colony is not an *estate*, a garrison, a place for arms, a religious *mission* or a monastery [...] A colony is a civil society, governed by normal laws, identical to the Metropolis in its basic features, in its unity of law and civil freedom, whose progress must be guaranteed by individual expansion and safety, by the readiness and competence of Administration, by the progressive consecration of the autonomist principle with respect to local culture and means, and by metropolitan Public Powers' attention to the Colony's needs and requirements and to the universal progresses of Political Economy and International Law.[121]

Such an ideal model, however, did not prevent Spain from losing its beloved Cuba and was contradicted, as never before, by Guinean institutions and facts. Moreover, without expressly mentioning the colonized and by implicitly referring to the different situation of the lost Antilles, Labra's references "to the Colony's needs" implied, when referred to Guinea and despite his likely intentions, the dangerous universal public law principle whereby all extraordinary actions by the state are legitimate: the state is thus seen as "such a particular subject that, if its preservation and existence require individual rights and existing laws to be breached, its extraordinary acts are justified in the light of the country's needs ... 'Salus populi suprema lex esto'".[122]

"Exceptional law is applied only when there is an exceptional situation, and it can never constitute a new kind of ordinary law."[123] Yet, in Africa, where every exception was the rule, such timid warnings were not followed. The Guinean *Boletìn* provides an example in this respect. Without paying much attention to the role of the trustee, who is a mediator in the contractual ambit, the new provisions on individual labour (1907) were completed in 1908 by setting up the Colonial Guard, this being arranged by the Governor responsible for the *bubis*' mobilization, i.e. Sir Don Luis Ramos-Izquierdo. Thanks to the Guard, Spanish domination could be extended to tropical peoples and territories, and labour could be imposed through violence: from the very beginning, the cult of work and love for the King and the Spanish Homeland – one along with the other – were the Guard's key concerns.[124]

Just when Barrera was about to commence his long governing experience, a bloody strife, i.e. the rebellion of the Balachá (often mentioned in decrees and provisions) was the reason for the enactment of harsh military measures to be applied to the recruitment of labourers.

Such violent events were stirred by the 1910 decree on individual labour, whose terms ("to attract *bubi* inhabitants to the hardship of labour and thus civilize them within the social order") were very similar to the ones we have already seen.[125] During the "facts of San Carlos", which took place in an area where the presence of *claretianos* was particularly strong, the *bubis* fought against hard labour; the press preferred to disguise such events as fights among natives to conquer power in local tribes, which supposedly led to the killing of an innocent (white) chief of the Guard; the death of the rebellious tribe chief, which supposedly happened as a result of fortuitous gun shots, and the destruction of his houses were described as a "weakness of Spain ... towards them [the black]". Quite luckily, the united forces of guards and colonizers (Anglo-Saxon and Catalan names abound in the expedition, for example "Dn. Maximiliano C. Jones, Dn. Juan Bravo, Dn. José Bronn y los Srs. Faura, Baide, Roig, Macmen, Ramón, Vila, Clark y Lues") were able to tame, after several days of confusion, the modest rebellion.[126]

"The mountain has given birth to a mouse", as will be said;[127] the *bubis'* war was extensively dealt with by the *Boletìn* in the following months. "The problem of labourers may be resolved through sheer willingness, patience and energy, ensuring by all possible means that the *bubis* work; I believe it necessary, for such a purpose, to set up police postings".[128] Given Governor Barrera's extensive intervention on the conditions of the territories, his determination in applying the colonial constitution was quite foreseeable, so much so that the 1911 decree on *bubis*, rather than being the continuation of the plan started by Luis Ramos-Izquierdo, became the legal expression of the Governor's personal belief: the colony could be governed only through patriotism, through an iron hand and by obliging the natives to work.[129]

In the absence of political rights and civil participation, only a number of spiritual values was in force in Guinea, namely those embodied by the King of Spain. In this respect, let us examine what was reported about Santa Isabel in 1921.

Echoes of the Celebrations for the King. In the previous issue, we did not have a chance to describe, for want of space, the fantastic Civil-Military Parade which took place on occasion of the celebrations held for our August Sovereign's name-day; we will now complete the description by providing our indulgent readers with a general illustration of the symbolism and allegories of the artistic carriages that, through two endless lines of natives carrying Venetian lanterns, paraded through the town's main streets. The first of these beautiful carriages, pulled by seven vampires and guided by a Cupid, represented our Homeland, tightly embracing our prestigious Army and our heroic War Navy, and folding men's labour, which is a source of honesty and wellbeing, in its arms. The noble and beautiful figure of our August Sovereign which nicely stood out on a big drum, adorned with frills of the national flag, placed between the images of a castle and a lion, completed and topped the whole carriage, which was both fantastic and artistic. The second carriage was less allegoric, though equally artistic, and represented the Command of the Colonial Guard in such an artistic and accurate way that it was like filigree. On the 25th day, at half past four p.m., a lively, contended and interesting football match took place in the field near the telegraph. There was a team of European gentlemen and another of natives; the former, which was indeed very clever, won the match. Our most sincere congratulations.[130]

Such patriotic games among youngsters (i.e. among colonized African natives), illustrated by ineffable graphic evidence,[131] bring back our attention to the conceptions we have dealt with above and which may apply also with respect to the deployment of the Guard and the *bubis'* obligation to work. The happy Guinean tribes (of course native subjects, as demanded by the colonial constitution[132]) conferred liveliness on the celebrations whilst also guaranteeing safety to the European organizers. Yet, there were other reasons behind the black guards' escort of the royal carriage parade: a coach pulled by vampires [!] which united, under a rough image of Alfonso XIII, oil-painted on a drum [!!], the images of the Motherland, of the Army and Navy, which are undoubtedly Spanish images, embraced to the image of Labour (in truth only African labour). "Members of the Colonial Guard". For instance, the "authorized native chiefs" Cayetano Cien Duros, Antonio Asombra Cánovas y Manuel Mochila Morral, who received medals (though not a pension) thanks to their "merits in military operations carried out between August 5 and 12 to punish the Ysen tribe (District of Bata) for its rebellious behaviour against Colonial Authorities",[133] and all colonial guards "are entrusted with the task of defending such feelings of love for the Motherland, willingness to work and obedience among natives inhabiting the areas for which they are responsible".[134]

Love for Spain and work in Africa. Even without such an explicit textual support, it is not difficult to grasp the meanings of the rough Hispano-Guinean iconography. The hard labour imposed by the armed forces of a faraway motherland was the result of the same European culture, supposedly a "source of honesty and well-being", received willy-nilly by the *bubis* of Fernando Póo. Lacking rights and legal capacity, bound to work only on the grounds of being "Spanish subjects", all natives were sons of the King (represented in his walk around Guinea), and were also vicarious sons of the real representative, of the Rear Admiral and of the Governor.[135] Love, respect, and services were owed to their royal father Alfonso XIII. His illustrious proxy, *papá* Barrera, instilled such precepts through a number of celebrations, paid by himself,[136] and at the same time demanded obedience to such precepts through orders and decrees, thus enriching colonial landowners.[137] Since Barrera's corrective powers were exerted with respect to "sons" deemed to be *minors*, such powers were unlimited: through the support of local canon law, such an exertion benefited ("I curtly do them justice, leaving sentences and allocutions aside ... I punish them ... with respect to the two things that they value the most: their money and body"[138]) local landowners. The reason behind Spain's presence in Guinea was a patriotic obligation to work. Under such an economic and not simply etymological perspective, governmental provisions on labourers went well beyond the harvesting of cocoa and thus made up the African constitution itself.

7 PRAESTANTIA LINGUAE LATINAE

The colonial constitution is the colonial occurrence itself. "Upon commencing the harvest of cocoa, it is customary for the Governor to publish a provision whereby all natives who are neither landowners nor have any means to live on or any acknowledged occupation, are compelled to register to work as farm labourers. Such a decree is an effective labour regulation, whereby the rights and obligations of masters and labourers are defined; the elderly and minors are exempt from such an obligation, just like women, although contracts may be made with the latter as long as they voluntarily offer their services". Given that, according to the temporary Regulation of 1906, the hard labour of *bubis* is prohibited, local circumstances require labour law to force the latter to make agreements with landowners. Although the organic Regulation of 1904 provides Governors with the instruments needed to suit law to the colony's local needs,[139] the measures enacted by Barrera and its immediate predecessors (such as the *Real Orden* ratifying them) need not even to appeal to such a regime to legally justify the denial of the blacks' contractual will.

Some antiliberal conceptions typical of the rule of law resounded in colonial provisions and were easily implemented in Africa: the 1906 Regulation and the 1904 organic statute consecrated freedom, which, however disappeared (thanks to the providential intervention of the "Government's authority") when peaceful citizens turned into "disturbing elements".[140] Such antiliberal arguments drew inspiration from the "legendary decree of the Roman Senate: Videant Cónsules, ut ne [!] quid detrimenti Respublica capiat".

The Latin maxim leads us to our conclusive remarks. It is 1912. A Royal Order for the Guinea Gulf was enacted in Madrid and signed in San Sebastián.[141] On such a historical occasion, at such geographical latitudes, it may be argued that the Roman Senate and People were only a dim recollection in a crumpled school book. The legal reasoning of the Spanish legislators, entrusted with the embarrassing task of suppressing those civil rights which they had recently granted, resorted to addressing the *bubis* in some mysterious words from a dead language.

Such a language, however, was actually not so "dead" in this case. Let us just recall what follows. "The Senate has established that the Consul Lucio Opimio shall take all required measures to ensure the republic does not suffer any damage".[142] "The Senatus Consultum has decided that Consuls C. Marius and L. Valerius shall summon the tribunes of the people and the praetors, whom they consider to be necessary, in order to preserve the power".[143] Further examples are not needed.[144]

Videant consules. Such two words were first pronounced in a precise moment in time, they were repeated throughout a long literary tradition, and were finally preserved in the libraries containing great texts by eminent learned men. Twenty centuries after having been first pronounced and written, these ancient words on the *extra ordinem* defence of the Roman Republic were exhumed to compel natives of Spanish Equatorial Guinea to work. Ancient expressions were used to support extraordinary powers; classical Latin expressions were incorporated in the "Royal Order" enacted for Guinea and justified the antijuridical measures enacted by the Governor. From Spain to Africa, it seems that some principles of the colonial constitution could be expressed only in Latin.

The Latin language is something more than a constitutive element of our deepest culture and is more than a solid support of law. It is a hypostasis of culture and an expression of dominance. Throughout the centuries, a Latin upbringing has drawn a line between the European male child's family life, under the dominance of the mother and of maternal languages, and the social life of the white adult who, together with other individuals in an exclusively male world, united the social category of the economically successful man with the Latin language. Different educational practices of body punishment hinged upon the teaching of some texts, which were learned through blood: physical pain was wanted, rather than a mere threat, which stimulated memory and tamed individual will; a school of vigorous behaviour and a doctrine of virility were upheld. Moreover, were not the Latin protagonists of violent battles – the destruction of Carthage, the bloody fight between Opimio, and Caio Gracco, Cicero's attacks at the traitor Catilina – (told over and over again in texts teaching Latin), real heroes, demigods, or supermen? Being agonistic and male, being an instrument of initiation to the secrets of a long tradition reserved only to state representatives, Latin represented the *transition rite practised* by European cultures.[145]

This ideology was not perceived by its victims; nonetheless, the white warrior leaving Berlin to conquer Africa appealed to twenty centuries of Latin as if this were a very useful weapon. As a matter of fact, before the beginning of the African adventure, to speak Latin was tantamount to possess knowledge: it was necessary to the liturgy whereby God was worshipped, to gaining access to the dominant culture and to the beginning of any professional activity. When the African adventure was embarked upon, the ancient language was but a subject matter of *philology*, the Western world being dominated by vulgar idioms. The new turn of events, however, led Europeans to claim that "in a nation with a Latin race such as Spain, which possesses a rich and harmonious idiom, with an incredible number of words and sayings of Latin origin, in a nation proud of its classical traditions ... the weakened interest in Latin studies cannot be taken light-heartedly; not only is such a study the foundation and principle required to know and correctly use the Castilian language ... but it is also the only means to have access to the treasures of the Past".[146] But despite such thinking, a new culture, which was not grounded on the cult of martial virtues but rather on the proclamation of rights, started viewing Latin as a mere slang used by a decadent priestly class: "it is about time that public teaching satisfied the needs of modern life and had as its main aim the upbringing of Enlightened citizens rather than Latin rectors".[147]

With the Restoration, Latin in Spain once again began affecting education. Attention was paid to Cicero and to his first *Catilinaria*, to the solemn maxim which places the preservation of the *Respublica* above all other considerations: such a maxim was taught, *inter alia*, to a young citizen of Burgos, the future Governor of Guinea, and to other adolescents, who later became councillors of the Ministry of State.[148] Not surprisingly, however, other neo-Latin and neo-Germanic languages were taught in Africa. In Guinea, the state official subscribing labour mobilization was also responsible for subscribing the teaching programme to be applied to colonial public schools: "Castilian Grammar and Spelling Principles" were taught, attention was paid to "Notions on the harvesting of coffee, cocoa, cotton, vanilla and other products typical of such intertropical countries"; Latin was not mentioned at all.[149] Once again, the colonized's will was blatantly ignored: "we want to have more than what we have today. That is, our children want to be taught to read and write, to carry out a job. In this manner, our children will be able to earn a living under the Spanish flag. Today, instead of learning what is needed, children are taught to climb up bamboos, to fish and do other things which we are not lacking in".[150] Any theoretical formation or any more elevated form of access to Western culture were kept at the margins of the colonial constitution: "teaching to natives must refrain from being too book-based, too 'intellectualistic' ... Teaching is aimed at both educating and instructing natives ... For this purpose, school programmes and timetables must devote ample room to the *leçons des choses* and to the manual and professional training of pupils".[151]

Leçons de choses, when *civilization* was at stake. Such an aim was attained, for many generations, by the Spanish Motherland in Guinea. "Are we Spanish?" – the teacher used to ask – "We are Spanish by the grace of God". "Why are we Spanish?" – he insisted – "We are Spanish" – answered the boys – "because we were lucky to be born in a country called Spain".[152] A "flourishing and peaceful future" was envisaged in tropical lands, whose richness and well-being were guaranteed by Spain and the Latin language.

8 CONCLUSIONS

Let us now conclude our study. The reading of some exotic texts, which are so eloquent on the fate of the liberal rule of law in the African continent, rather than illustrating the terribly weak foundations of the institutions brought about by the decolonizations of the 1960s and 1970s,[153] provide us with a very clear picture – pitiless in its clarity – of precisely that political form as it exists in Europe. After all, only a Western analysis from outside Europe, once its picturesque orientalisms have been spotted, can thoroughly study our local culture.

The first element of such an analysis brings us to the "age" of modernity. The history of the rule of law as a form of state, i.e. the history of modern legal and political culture in general, presents an aggregate of both old and new facts, ideas and projects, marked by deletions as well as continuities: lower chambers resulting from an ever-enlarging electoral body and coexisting with upper chambers where nobility maintains (hardly disguised) secular privileges; monarchies striving to share sovereignty with national subjects; the flaunted triumph of public transparency in the political and legal world together with the peculiar preservation of the *arcana imperii*: in other words, the persistence of the *ancien régime*, as in the well known title of Arno J. Mayer's work.[154] This persistence becomes overwhelming (as it is expressed, e.g., by Santi

Romano's honest contributions) whenever the European state turns into a colonial metropolis. The dramatic adventures of crowned heads in the African continent – such as the geographical curiosity and the economic interests of Leopold, King of Belgium[155] – is not only a terrible example of "persistence" but also a metaphor of a very old politics incompatible with pure rules of law.

The second thought that strikes the observer of the African reflection of the European state refers to space, this being simply meant as the element that affects – and circumscribes in legal terms – any legal system. Let us put it more simply: the recently underlined paradox between tradition and modernity is reflected in the tension within European law between universalism and localism. Under this perspective, the age of imperialism appears also as the age of a *science* of law, i.e. of the supposedly universal meaning of dogmas and categories which undoubtedly contrast (govern, coexist, fight) with *national* legal definitions. In some cases, the specificity of legislation is in line with the universality of law (and thus the aspirations surface that support modern comparative law); in any event, colonial law provides in my view a very interesting subject for the analysis of the circulation of different models and experiences within an institutional area created, strictly speaking, by the succession of *international* treaties.[156]

Thirdly, the latter adjective allows us to underline the existence of a very wide scope of action of the rule of law even where its legal reference, which is conceptually inevitable, does not appear at all. We owe the public law jurist Allegretti the historiographic merit of stressing how liberal foreign politics remained tied to the terrible logic of the "reason of state"; while the passage from the *ancien régime* to the new modern order deeply affected the distribution of political competences among constitutional organs, it left the goals and the spirit of the state's international action unaltered.[157] This door (it is up to the reader to say whether open or closed), which is the only way to the African experience, conceals either very ancient institutions (such as slavery or forced labour in colonies) or overwhelming "family" logics (such as the protectorate of peoples and the "condition of minority" of non-European races).

The history that follows is well-known. The old colonial powers, after the First World War (a colossal conflict which witnessed the fall of many crowned heads), conceived of a new kind of state, where new institutions – democracy and rights[158] – resolved (as best as they could) the dilemma of power. Such a state triumphed in Europe, for the time being, precisely when colonialism in Africa was coming to an end: it might be wondered, however, whether this laid the best foundations for political autonomy in the African continent, the latter being wrapped up in the quasi-legal (or not legal at all) net of the old rule of law (as demonstrated by the example of Guinea, daughter of a Spanish motherland jealous of its "parental" *power*).

NOTES

1. The relative documents, including the *Boletín* issues, are to be found in *Archivo General de la Administratción* (Alcalá de Henares, Madrid), Sección Africa, leg. G-2.
2. See B. Roig, "El trabajo a destajo en Fernando Póo", *La Voz de Fernando Póo*, 27 (15 July 1911), pp. 7–8; 28 (1 August 1911), pp. 8–9; 29 (15 August 1911), pp. 6–8; 31 (15 September 1911), pp. 6–8; 33 (15 October 1911), pp. 9–11. Cf. S. Muguerza, "La cuestión obrera", *La Voz de Fernando Póo*, 46 (1 May 1912), pp. 4–5; 47 (15 May 1912), pp. 4–5; 48 (1 June 1912), pp. 5–7.
3. E. López Perea, *Las posesiones españolas del Golfo de Guinea y datos comerciales del Africa Occidental*, Madrid, 1906.
4. C. Fernández (C.M.F.), *Misiones y misioneros en la Guinea española. Historia documentada de sus primeros azarosos días (1883–1912)*, Madrid: Editorial Co.Cul, 1962. See also (Misioneros Claretianos), *Cien años de evangelización en Guinea Ecuatorial (1883–1983)*, Barcelona: Claret, 1983; T.L. Pujadas, *La iglesia en la Guinea Ecuatorial*, I–II, Barcelona: Claret, 1983.
5. Cf. "La prensa de Fernando Póo", in *La Voz de Fernando Póo*, 25 (15 June 1911), pp. 3–7, in particular p. 5. We must also add the *Boletín de la Cámara Oficial Agrícola de Fernando Póo* (1 March 1907 to 31 October 1910), as well as other publications concerned with Africa and dealing with Morocco and partly with Guinea. See *Africa. Revista política y comercial consagrada á la defensa de los intereses españoles en Marruecos, Costa del Sahara y Golfo de Guinea*, long-lived magazine of Barcelona (1906–1936).
6. A.M. Junco, *Leyes coloniales*, Madrid (RJvadeneyra), 1945; S. Llompart Aulet, *Legislación del trabajo de los Territorios españoles del Golfo de Guinea*, Madrid, 1946. See also F. Martos Avila, *Indice legislativo de Guinea*, Madrid: Instituto de Estudios Políticos, 1944, a useful way of access to the local *Boletín*.
7. See A. Carrasco González, "El proyecto de venta de Fernando Póo y Annobón a Gran Bretaña en 1841", *Estudios Africanos*, 10 (1996), pp. 47–63.
8. Judging by their early efforts: see J.B. González, "Expedición Argelejo: primer intento colonizador de España en Africa ecuatorial", *Revista de Historia Militar*, 32 (1988), pp. 73–109; Up and until the last ones: see M. Iradier, *Africa. Viajes y trabajos de la Asociación Eúskara La Exploradora* [1887], I: *Primer viaje. Exploración del país del Muni* [1875–1877], II: *Segundo viaje. Adquisición del país del Muni* [1884], Madrid: Miraguano-Polifemo (Biblioteca de Viajeros Hispánicos), 1994.
9. M. Liniger-Goumer, *La Guinée équatoriale. Un pays méconu*, Paris: Ed. l'Harmattan, 1979; by the same author, *Small Is Not Always Beautiful. The Story of Equatorial Guinea*, London: C. Hurst, 1989. See E. Borrajo Viñas, Chief State Captain, *Demarcación de la Guinea española. Conferencia dada en la Real Sociedad Geográfica*, Madrid: Talleres del depósito de la Guerra, 1903, for a wider picture.

10. Luis Ramos-Izquierdo y Vivar, former Deputy Governor of the District of Bata and former Governor General, *Descripción geográfica, y gobierno, administración y colonización de las Colonias españolas del Golfo de Guinea*, Madrid: Imprenta de Felipe Peña, 1912, published on Santa Isabel some significant data on the population of Fernando Póo: 190 whites (170 Spaniards) and 1,500 blacks (200 foreigners) (p. 26), with an estimated Muni population of (p. 43) 130 whites (90 Spaniards) and 89,320 blacks (350 coming from Senegal and Camerun); following the author's classification, there were primitive *natives* (81,000), with a medium degree of civilization (4,449) and civilized (3,521)). Great Elobey, inhabited by 230 blacks, has no white population (p. 57), whereas in Annobón there are seven Spaniards and 1,200 blacks (p. 60). According to the 1923 census of the white population in Fernando Póo there were 526 Spaniards (out of 650 men) and 261 foreigners (118 Portuguese and 66 Germans), and 61 in the continental part of the colony (with 26 foreigners); in Elobey, Corisco and Annobón only 39 (plus six foreigners). However, in 1942 in Muni there were only 955 white inhabitants, while on the main island they amounted to 1,579.
11. See J.M. Cordero Torres, *Tratado elemental de derecho colonial español*, Madrid: Editora Nacional, 1941, p. 40.
12. Ibid., pp. 80 ff.
13. Royal Decree of 11 July 1904, Estatuto orgánico. In the *Archivo General de la Administración*, Alcalá de Henares, Madrid, Africa, box G-560, there is an important collection of Portuguese colonial provisions (1901–1903), which are undoubtedly related to the decree.
14. Ibid.
15. See in general M. Fioravanti, "Lo Stato di diritto come forma di Stato. Notazioni preliminari sulla tradizione europeo-continentale", in R. Gherardi and G. Gozzi (eds), *Saperi della borghesia e storia dei concetti fra Otto e Novecento*, Bologna: il Mulino, 1995, pp. 161–77.
16. See R.D. of 30 July 1902, which created an Advisory Committee on the Spanish territories in Western Africa. Its members (art. 2) were mostly former ministers (Maura, Castellanos, García Sancho, Ugarte) and former undersecretaries (Alvarado), together with a few colonial managers of the time (the State Undersecretary Pérez-Caballero, the chief of the Colonial Department Bosch, and the Governor Ibarra). Parliament (Bergamín, Huelín, Labra), the Royal Geographic Society (Fernández Duro, Beltrán), and the similar Royal Commission for Western Africa (Ossorio, López Vilches) were quite represented.
17. By means of the R.O. of 25 November 1911, upon the Minister of War's proposal, the Governor of Guinea was awarded the honour of General of Brigade.
18. See Law 2 April 1845, ed. by T. Ramón Fernández and J.A. Santamaría, *Legislación administrativa española del siglo XIX*, Madrid: Instituto de Estudios Administrativos, 1977, ref. no. 120, pp. 574–5.
19. The issue of law in the Indies was a frequent matter in Hispano-Guinean legislation, especially with respect to natives' lands: see Real Decreto of 26 November 1880, art. 8, 1st; Real Decreto of 17 February 1888, art. 7. In the notable Real Decreto of 11 July 1904, which establishes the statute on lands in the colony, the 1680 "Recopilación" appears only in the law's list of reasons, as a sort of national glorious antecedent of the "universally accepted principle of modern law, in accordance with its most recent provisions and authorizations" whereby the land belongs to the

State, it is not granted to single beings, which means that the lands of natives – "an unquestionable right that cannot be denied thereto" – are subject to the limits imposed by the Governor (arts. 11–12).

20. See Real Decreto of 13 December 1858, art. 5 (award of discretionary powers to the Governor); Real Decreto of 12 November 1868 (art. 4, in similar terms). The Real Decreto of 26 November 1880, regulating the position of the Governor in art. 2, generically refers "to the functions, both ordinary and extraordinary, which the laws in force give to the high Authority of Overseas", literally repeated by the following Real Decreto of 17 February 1888 (art. 1).
21. L. de Arrazola (ed.), *Enciclopedia española de Derecho y Administración, ó Nuevo Teatro Universal de la Legislación de España é Indias*, X, Madrid: Imprenta de la Revista de Legislación y Jurisprudencia, 1858, see "colonia", pp. 5–26, in particular pp. 23–4.
22. R.M. de Labra, "La justicia en Ultramar", *La Escuela del Derecho*, 3 (1863), pp. 209–32, p. 217.
23. See J. Lalinde Abadía, *La administración en el siglo XIX puertorriqueño. (Pervivencia de la variante indiana del decisionismo castellano en Puerto Rico)*, Sevilla, Escuela de Estudios Hispanoamericanos, 1980, in particular pp. 125 ff. on the "Administrative System".
24. See Freire, "Al Sr. Ministro de Estado", *La Voz de Fernando Póo*, 26, (1 July 1911.
25. Art. 14 of the Real Decreto establishes that "the local councils will be made up of a Government Delegate as a president and two assistants, whether or not native, appointed every three years by the Council of Authorities"; the same article seems to acknowledge the residual role of natives with respect to the "municipal functions (of the peoples) compatible with the cultural level of their members"; in any event, this was a temporary formulation, until "conditions similar to Santa Isabel" were created (art. 14). Such false expressions of municipal life clearly represent the imposition of cohabitation models in the sole interests of Spain: "governmental authorities will promote, by using the means that caution will dictate and in accordance with the directives of the Ministry of State, the grouping of natives in villages and the following setting up of local Councils" (art. 22).
26. The Real Orden of 27 July 1905 extended art. 23 of the 1904 Real Decreto to other authorities not mentioned here. Four years later (Real Orden of 8 October 1909) it was stressed that the judicial competences of governmental delegates had not to reduce those of the first hearing Court of Santa Isabel. As for the civil recording of religious marriages between natives, a decree by the Governor (4 October 1915) transferred the competence therefore from the municipal Judge to the military commanders of the garrison. See also "Una memoria", Cap. II, *La Voz de Fernando Póo*, 16 (1 February 1911), pp. 6–8.
27. J. Muñoz y Núñez de Prado, "Organización de la justicia en Guinea", *Revista de los tribunales y de legislación universal*, 65 (1931), pp. 123–4, as "El ministerio fiscal en Guinea", ibid., pp. 204–5; also, by the same author, "El régimen judicial de nuestras posesiones en Africa occidental. Contestación concisa a una pregunta del programa de oposiciones a la judicatura", ibid., 67 (1933), p. 571. It was an endemic problem: A. Frik, "Funcionarios coloniales en Fernando Póo", *Africa*, IV (2nd epoch), November–December 1910, pp. 13–14, in particular p. 14, "in some instances, the same person had both the functions of Secretary of Government, of first hearing Court, of Administrator of Rural Farms and of Notary";

L. Ramos-Izquierdo, *Descripción geográfica del Golfo de Guinea*, pp. 325–6: "sometimes an illiterate becomes a first hearing judge, while sometimes the same individual first is a secretary then a Prosecutor and even a Judge by means of internal appointments". E.V. Ynfante, *Cubanos en Fernando Póo; horrores de la dominación española*, Habana: El Figaro, 1898, pp. 53 ff., describes, at the end of the nineteenth century, a "justice of the *cadi*" entirely corrupted with respect to, e.g., the local administration of Post Offices.

28. For a legal analysis, see P. Cruz Villalón, *El estado de sitio y la Constitución. La constitucionalziación de la protección extraordinaria del Estado (1789–1878)*, Madrid: Centro de Estudios Constitucionales, 1980, especially pp. 429 ff. on the original art. 17 of the Constitution.
29. In fact: "In the territories of the Guinea Gulf, the rights granted to Spaniards by the Monarchy's Constitution will be valid, and their exercise will be in accordance with such a decree and with the complementary provisions needed to adapt its norms, as those of the general Codes, to the status of such territories" (art. 27).
30. See art. 7: "The General Governor's provisions may be revoked or reformed by the supreme Government, *ex officio* or through a separate instance, when the matter so allows, or when they are deemed to be contrary to the laws, regulations and provisions in force, or when they are unsuitable to the government or proper administration of the Spanish territories in the Guinea Gulf".
31. See the introduction by P. Guillaume, *Le monde colonial. XIXe–XXe siècle*, Paris: Armand Colin, 1974, in particular pp. 129 ff. on "colonial administration".
32. See G. Crotti de Costiglione, *Les représentants des colonies au Parlement*, Paris (Thèse droit), 1908; V. Dupuich, *Le régime législatif des colonies*, Paris (Thèse droit), 1912. A very useful work is *Les Lois Organiques des Colonies. Documents officiels précédés de notices historiques*, I–III, Bruxelles: Institut Colonial International, 1906.
33. J. Maldonado Macanaz, *Arte de la colonización*, Madrid: Impr. M. Tello, 1875, pp. 224–5. Above all, it refers to H. Merivale, *Lectures on Colonization and Colonies*, London: Longman, 1861.
34. J. Maldonado Macanaz, *Arte de la colonizacion*, pp. 257–8.
35. See G.R. España, "Tratado de derecho administrativo colonial. I. Organización administrativa", *Revista de Legislación*, Madrid, 1894, without specific information on Guinea other than the annexed Real Decreto of 17 February 1888 (pp. 319–29).
36. S. Romano, *Corso di diritto coloniale.* I *Parte generale*, Roma: Athenaeum, 1918, pp. 32 ff. See C. Grilli, "Gli esperimenti coloniali nell'Africa neolatina", *Rivista Internazionale di Scienze sociali e discipline ausiliare*, 62 (1913), pp. 433–62; 63 (1913), pp. 30–64, 145–73, 449–77; 64 (1914), pp. 29–42, 74–194, 309–32, and the following issues too.
37. The Royal Decree of 18 July 1913 was quite important, in that it granted the Ministry of State the competence which he had contended with the Navy, upon request by the Hispano-African Society of Credit and Development. It was argued (on the basis of art. 89 of the Constitution) that "the Spanish territories in Western Africa are a colony grounded on special provisions and laws for its government and administration in the hands of the Ministry of State ... the laws enacted, or to be enacted, by the Peninsula are not applicable, unless the Government provides for their application by making any changes it deems appropriate". Such a decision represented a precedent for the Royal Order of 2 June 1922. See in general Francisco Martos Avila, *Indice legislativo*, "Prólogo", pp. vii–xviii.

38. See J.M. Cordero Torres, *Tratado de derecho colonial*, p. 278: "Since Spain is not (and neither has it ever been) a racist colonial Power, it is difficult to deal with the problem of half-breeds. This, in fact, is practically unconceivable even without the need for an official ban, not on the grounds of racial prejudices, but rather for the natives' state of degeneration and backwardness". However, such a ban will be contained in the Decree of 30 September 1944 against mixed marriages: J.M. de la Torre, "La tragedia de Guinea", *Tiempo de Historia*, 36 (1977), pp. 120–1, in particular p. 120.
39. S. Romano, *Corso di diritto coloniale*, pp. 42 ff. See A. Delvaux, *Les Protectorats de la France en Afrique*, Dijon (Thèse droit, Paris), 1903.
40. Apart from the case of L. Ramos-Izquierdo, *Descripción geográfica del Golfo de Guinea*, we can add, without leaving Guinea, A. Barrera y Luyando, *Lo que son y lo que deben ser las posesiones españolas del Golfo de Guinea*, Madrid: Imprenta Eduardo Arias, 1907, conference at the Real Sociedad Geográfica (20 June 1907). See, in general, E. Hernández Sandoica, "La ciencia geográfica y el colonialismo español en torno a 1880", *Revista de la Universidad Complutense*, 28 (1979), pp. 183–99; J.M. Llorente Pinto, "Colonialismo y geografía en España en el último cuarto del siglo XIX. Auge y descrédito de la geografía colonial", *Eria*, 15 (1988), pp. 51–76; and, lastly, A. Gollewska and Neil Smith (eds), *Geography and Empire*, Oxford: Blackwell, 1994.
41. S. Romano, *Corso di diritto coloniale*, pp. 139 ff.
42. J.G. Bluntschli, *Derecho público universal*, I–II, Madrid: Góngora, 1917, II, p. 228.
43. See *Lois Organiques des Colonies*, I, pp. 11 ff. The authority is Ch.J. Tarring, *Law Relating to the Colonies*, London: Stevens and Haynes, 1913.
44. J. Gingast, *De l'oeuvre et du rôle des gouverneurs coloniaux*, Rennes: Impr. Rennaise (Thèse droit), 1902, pp. 124 ff. ("le gouverneur a des attributions générales comme représentant à la fois l'intérêt métropolitain et l'intérêt de la colonie; il a des attributions législatives et d'autres relatives à l'administration de la justice; il a des pouvoirs militaires; il est, en outre, dépositaire de tous les droits que doit avoir le premier mandataire du gouvernement pour le mantien de l'ordre et de la sécurité publique dans la colonie").
45. S. Romano, *Corso di diritto coloniale*, p. 159, on the issue of the French "senatus consultum" of 3 May 1854 under the constitutional laws of the Third Republic; cf. A. Bienvenu, "Le législateur colonial", *Revue du droit public et de la science politique en France et a l'etranger*, 36 (1929), pp. 224–42. See also A. Bonnefoy-Sibour, *Le Pouvoir législatif aux colonies. Essai historique sur le Droit de légiferer en matière coloniale*, Dijon: Imp. Régionale (Thèse droit, Montpellier), 1908, p. 296: "In the colonies of exploitation or, quite simply, in the new colonies the power to make laws must exclusively belong to the Governor".
46. The King enacted the law by decree, assisted by a *Conseil Colonial* with non-binding powers, which was, in its majority, extraneous to Parliament; the latter maintained a decisive role only in budget matters. The Governor of Congo might thus enact orders, subject to the *Conseil*'s ratification, for urgent reasons, although governmental authorities used to continuously intervene on a normative level through more or less abusive "executive decrees". See P. Dufrénoy, *Précis de Droit Colonial*, Bruxelles: E. Bruylant, 1946, pp. 25 ff.
47. See O. Köbner, "Les organes de législation pour les colonies allemandes", in *Lois Organiques des Colonies*, III, pp. 333–53. According to the *Schutzgebietsgesetz* of 25 July to 10 September 1900 (included in this work, pp. 355 ff.) the Emperor makes

laws through orders, whereas very few subjects are reserved to the Diet; with respect to natives, such a legislative imperial power has no limits, though it refers to the *Reich*'s wide regulating powers which, by proxy, Governors regularly exert. See R. Lobstein, *Essai sur la législation coloniale de l'Allemagne*, Paris (Thèse droit, Poitiers), 1902; A. Chéradame, *De la condition juridique des colonies allemandes*, Paris (Thèse droit), 1905. Nowadays, not only within the German context, it is acknowledged that this is "an unexplored juridical ambit"; cf. U. Wolter (in collaboration with P. Kaller), "Deutsches Kolonialrecht – ein wenig erforschtes Rechtsgebiet, dargestellt anhand des Arbeitsrechts der Eingeborenen", *Zeitschrift für Neuere Rechtsgeschichte*, 17 (1995), pp. 201–44, in particular pp. 214 ff. on colonial law.

48. The *Ordinamento della Colonia Eritrea*, Law of 24 May 1903 (through the following administrative regulation of 22 September 1905) is unquestionably one of the clearest expressions of what I mean by colonial constitution. Further texts in *Lois Organiques des Colonies*, III, pp. 399 ff. See also G. Marller, *Le Droit colonial italien*, Nancy (Thèse droit), 1909; T. Scovazzi, *Assab, Massaua, Uccialli, Adua. Gli strumenti giuridici del primo colonialismo italiano*, Torino: Giappichelli, 1996.
49. A. de Magalhâes, *Estudos coloniaes. I. Legislaçâo colonial. Seu espirito, sua formaçâo e seus defeitos*, Coimbra: F. França Amado, 1907, p. 107.
50. In R.M. de Labra, *Nuestras colonias de Africa. Fernando Póo y la Guinea española en 1898*, Madrid: Tipografía de Alfredo Alonso, 1898, p. 25; a parliamentary intervention of 8 June 1898 is quoted. However, in his opening speech of the Second Africanist Congress held in the Hall of the Chamber of Commerce, Industrial and Agricultural, of Saragoza, on 26–31 October 1908, upon initiative of the Agencies for the Hispano-Moroccan Trade (Barcelona: Imprenta "España en Africa", 1908, pp. 30–8, in particular pp. 30–1), Labra pronounced himself "against such an aberration, against such a constitutional breach", referring to the "many provisions" being enacted by governments "without any parliamentary intervention".
51. See *La Voz de Fernando Póo*, 14 (1 January 1911), p. 15.
52. S. Romano, *Corso di diritto coloniale*, p. 167.
53. R.A. Williams, Jr., *The American Indian in Western Legal Thought. The Discourses of Conquest*, New York/Oxford: Oxford University Press, 1990, p.6: "Law, regarded by the West as its most respected and cherished instrument of civilization, was also the West's most vital and effective instrument of empire during its genocidal conquest and colonization of non-Western peoples of the New World, the American Indians".
54. A. Posada, *Breve historia del krausismo español* [1925], Oviedo: Universidad-Servicio de Publicaciones, 1981. See F.J. Laporta, *Adolfo Posada: Política y Sociología en la crisis del liberalismo español*, Madrid: Edicusa, 1974.
55. A. Posada, "Le régimen colonial de l'Espagne. Les origines et le développement historique", *Revue de Droit Public*, 10 (1898), pp. 385–418; 11 (1899), pp. 33–71. The excerpt corresponds to the first part, pp. 389–91.
56. See A. Girault, "Chronique coloniale", *Revue de Droit Public*, 10 (1898), pp. 451–89, where reference is made to the resurgence of the "contrainte par corps" in French India "à l'égard des indigènes seulement", after it was abolished in the metropolitan territories in 1867 by means of provisions which would be extended to the colonies in 1891. It is said that, in relation to Madagascar, "l'œuvre de la pacification méthodique de l'île, habilement conduite par le général Gallieni, avance progressivement", even though there is an increasing shortage of labour: "le mal a deux causes,

le petit nombre des indigènes et leur hésitation à travailler pour les Français". This is exactly our problem.

57. See S. Romano, *Corso di diritto coloniale*, bibliography at pp. 16–18, with this sole reference to Spain.
58. E. Cimbali, *Popoli barbari e popoli civili. Osservazioni sulla politica coloniale*, Roma: Ferdinando Strambi, 1887. Posada's interlocutor was one of the few experts on international matters – perhaps he was one of those who arose greater controversial interest – and fought against colonialism, until he began supporting Fascism.
59. A. Posada, "Los salvajes y el Derecho político", *La Nueva Ciencia Jurídica. Antropología, sociología*, 1 (1892), pp. 193–9, in particular p. 197. The importance at the time of the "absurd" institution of slavery, despite Posada's contributions, cannot be dealt with here: J. Goudal, "La lutte international contre l'esclavage", *Revue générale de Droit International Publique*, 35 (1928), pp. 591–625.
60. A. Posada, "Los salvajes", p. 197.
61. Ibid., p. 195. See also A. Posada, "Animal Societies and Primitive Societies", in A. Kocourek and J.H. Wigmore (eds), *Evolution in Law*, III. *Formative Influences of Legal Development*, Boston: Little, Brown and Co., 1918, pp. 267–87.
62. A. Posada, "Los salvajes", pp. 197–98. See in general K. Braun, *Die Kolonisations-Bestrebungen der modernen europäischen Völker und Staaten*, Berlin, 1886; G. de Courcel, *L'influence de la Conférence de Berlin de 1885 sur le Droit Colonial International*, Paris: Les Éditions Internationales (Thèse droit), 1935.
63. J. de Acosta, *De procuranda Indorum salute* [1588], ed. by L. Pereña *et al.*, Madrid: Consejo Superior de Investigaciones Científicas (*Corpus Hispanorum de Pace*, XXIII), 1984, II, XIII.1, pp. 340–43. On Acosta's activity and thoughts, see A. Pagden, *La caida del hombre natural* [1982], Madrid: Alianza, 1988, p. 216 for this grounding (the only acceptable one, according to Acosta) of sociability.
64. Ibid., II, XIII. 3, p. 344. It is an orthodox thought, later exhumed to be used by Fascist Abyssinia: A. Messineo, S.J., "L'annessione territoriale nella tradizione cattolica", *La Civiltà Cattolica*, 87 (1936), 1, pp. 190–202, 291–303.
65. R.A. Williams, Jr., *The American Indian in Western Legal Thought*, pp. 96 ff.
66. R. Preiswerk and D. Perrot, *Ethnocentrisme et Histoire*, Paris: Anthropos, 1975; P.A. Taguieff, *La force du préjugé. Essai sur le racisme et ses doubles*, Paris: La Découverte, 1988.
67. J. Copans, *Anthropologie et Impérialisme*, Paris: Maspéro, 1975; G.W. Stocking, Jr., *Victorian Anthropology*, New York: Free Press, 1987, in particular pp. 81 ff. on "The Benevolent Colonial Despot as Etnographer" (referring to Sir George Grey); H. Kuklick, *The Savage Within. The Social History of British Anthropology, 1885–1945*, Cambridge: Cambridge University Press, 1991, with a specific chapter on "The colonial exchange", pp. 182 ff.
68. E.S. Said, *Cultura e imperialismo*, Barcelona: Anagrama, 1996, p. 213, with a brilliant chapter on Verdi's *Aida* (on Egypt and its Canal).
69. L. Capogrossi Colognesi, *Modelli di Stato e di famiglia nella storiografia dell'800*, Roma: La Sapienza Editrice, 1994.
70. É. Jobbé-Duval, "L'histoire comparé du droit et l'expansion coloniale de la France" (contribution of July 27, 1900 at the "Congrès d'histoire comparée, section d'histoire du droit et des institutions"), *Annales internationales d'histoire*, Macon, 1902, (3)–32, p. 6 of the excerpt: ("la science de l'histoire comparée du droit peut d'ailleurs rendre à la colonisation les services les plus considérables").

71. See E. de Hinojosa, "Francisco de Vitoria y sus escritos jurídicos" [1889], in E. de Hinojosa, *Obras*, III. *Estudios de síntesis*, Madrid: Instituto Nacional de Estudios Jurídicos, 1974, pp. 375–425.
72. N. Thomas, *Colonialism's Culture. Anthropology, Travel and Government*, Cambridge: Polity Press, 1994, following the classical study by E.W. Said on orientalism. For the importance of the cliché with respect to Guinea, cf. C. Crespo Gil-Delgado, Conde de Castillo-Fiel, *Notas para un estudio antropológico y etnológico del bubi de Fernando Póo*, Madrid: Instituto de Estudios Africanos (CSIC), 1949, pp. 78 ff. on "psychological traits".
73. J. Maldonado Macanaz, *Arte de la colonización*, p. 104.
74. The main authority in this respect is, quite undoubtedly, P. Leroy-Beaulieu, *De la Colonisation chez les peuples modernes*, I–II [1874], Paris: Guillaumin, 1902. See also C. Sumner Lobingier, "Colonial Administration", in E.R.A. Saligman and A. Johnson (eds), *Encyclopaedia of the Social Sciences*, III (1930), New York: Macmillan, repr. 1963, pp. 641–6.
75. With respect to the most unfamiliar matters of such a complex process, see M. Adas, *Machines as the Measure of Men. Science, Technology and Ideologies of Western Dominance*, Ithaca (NY): Cornell University Press, 1989; M. Vaughan, *Curing their Ills. Colonial Power and African Illness*, Cambridge: Polity Press, 1991.
76. J.G. Bluntschli, *Derecho público universal*, II, pp. 141–2. See also J. Fisch, "Zivilisation, Kultur", in O. Brunner *et al.* (eds), *Geschichtliche Grundbegriffe*, VII, Stuttgart: Klett-Cotta, 1992, pp. 679–774 (p. 745 on Berlin).
77. A. Pagden, *La caída del hombre natural*, pp. 261 ff.
78. J. de Acosta, *De procuranda Indorum salute*, I, VII.4, trans. at p. 147. See also ibid., III, IX, pp. 442 ff. ("An propter revocandos ab otio barbaros tributa graviora imperanda sint"), III, XVII, pp. 506 ff. ("De servitio personali indorum").
79. A. Barrera, *Lo que son y lo que deben ser*, p. 17.
80. See *La Main-d'oeuvre aux Colonies. Documents officiels*, I–III, Bruxelles: Institut Colonial International, 1895–1898.
81. U. Wolter, "Deutsches Kolonialrecht", pp. 231 ff., supported by G. Walz, *Die Entwicklung der Strafrechtspflege in Kamerun unter deutscher Herrschaft* 1894–1914, Freiburh: Schvarz, 1981. Failures in performing one's job, generally punished by the whip, correspond to the following cliché: *Ungehorsam, Faulheit, fortgesetzte Faulheit, Trunkheit im Dienst, Widersetzlichkeit im Dienst, Zuspätkommen und Nachlässigkeit im Dienst, unbegründetes Verlassen der Arbeit*, etc.
82. L. Ramos-Izquierdo, *Descripción geográfica del Golfo de Guinea*, p. 69.
83. R. Mercier, *Le travail obligatoire dans les Colonies Africaines*, Paris: Émile Larose (Thèse droit), 1933, p. 235; it thus follows (ibid.): "Indolent, enserré dans les liens d'une vie collective, où une place infime est laissé à l'initiative individuelle, l'indigène ne travaillait, le plus souvent, que sur les injonctions précises du chef ou du marabout. Sous le régime du travail obligatoire, il continue de travailler dans les conditions où il avait l'habitude de travailler".
84. Cf. E.S. Said, *Cultura e imperialismo*, pp. 393 ff.; Said disputes S.H. Alatas, *The Mith of the Lazy Native*, London: Cass, 1977.
85. The main texts are in P. Castañeda Delgado, "La condición miserable del indio y sus privilegios", *Anuario de Estudios Americanos*, 28 (1971), pp. 245–335; the best interpretation is by B. Clavero, *Derecho indígena y cultura constitucional en América*, México: Siglo XXI, 1994, in particular pp. 11 ff. on the "*status* of ethnic groups".

86. J. Maldonado Macanaz, *Arte de la colonización*, p. 214.
87. Patronato de Indígenas de los Territorios españoles del Golfo de Guinea (Delegación de Asuntos indígenas del distrito insular), *Patronato de Indígenas. Datos para su historia. Antecedentes y memoria de 1954*, Madrid: Hijo de R. Oviedo, 1955, p. 7.
88. C. Crespo, *Estudio antropológico y etnológico del bubi*, pp. 79 ff. Even though the author seems to be sceptical about the studies in question (i.e. V.B. González *et al.*, *Capacidad mental del negro. Los métodos de Binet-Botertag y de Yerkes, para determinar la edad y coeficiente mental aplicados al negro*, Madrid, 1944), by following tests realized by Europeans, Crespo argues that the mental development of the *bubi* does not go beyond puberty, since sex "absorbs all its faculties".
89. R. Mercier, *Le travail obligatoire*, p. 8. See also J. Ots Capdequí, W.C. MacLeod, and S.H. Roberts, "Native Policy", in *Encyclopaedia of the Social Sciences*, XI (1933), pp. 252–83.
90. See R. Pommier, *Les contrats coloniaux de louage de services*, Paris: Librairie Arthur Rousseau, 1932.
91. See F. del Río Joan, *Africa Occidental Española (Sahara y Guinea)*, Madrid: Imprenta de la "Revista Técnica de Infantería y Caballería", 1915, p. 179; see also A. Barrera, *Lo que son y lo que deben ser*, p. 45: "in exploitation territories as these ones [the territories of the Guinea Gulf] ... it is absurd to look for labour in the metropolis, since this, without an adequate and costly preparation is tantamount to leading whites to misery and death".
92. See law 21 December 1907 and the Real Decreto of 30 April 1908, "Reglamento provisional de la Ley de Emigración", art. 1, 5, ed. by A. Martín Valverde, y otros, *La legislación social en la historia de España. De la revolución liberal a 1936*, Madrid: Congreso de los Diputados, 1987, ref. 96, pp. 238–42; ref. 97, pp. 243–48.
93. Bruxelles: Établissements Généraux d'Imprimerie, 1929. In 1950, and maybe even before then, there was a significant change in the official name of the Belgian centre, which was turned into a brand new "Institut International des Sciences Politiques et Sociales Appliquées aux Pays de Civilisations différentes". *The status quo* agreed at the Conference of Congo was coming to an end.
94. G. Sanz Casas, "Los finqueros y el uso del trabajo forzado en la agricultura colonial de la isla de Fernando Poo", *Arxiu d'Etnografia de Cataluyna*, 3 (1984), pp. 121–36.
95. Royal Order 6 August 1906. The text with the following reforms is S. Llompart, *Legislación del trabajo*, pp. 23–38.
96. See A. Barrera, *Lo que son y lo que deben ser*, pp. 18–19; R. Beltrán y Rózpide, *La expansión europea en Africa (1907–1909)*, Madrid: Imprenta del Patronato de Huérfanos de Administración Militar, 1910, pp. 76 ff. on the "problem of labourers".
97. "Os indígenas das províncias ultramarinas [tema] obrigaçâo, moral e legal, de procurar adquirir pelo trabalho os meios que lhes falten, de subsistir e de melhorar a própria condiçâo social": art. 1 of the *Regolamento* on labour of 1899 (D. November 9). See J.M. Silva Cunha, *O trabalho indígena*, Lisboa: Agência geral do Ultramar, 1955, pp. 151 ff. The "príncipio de coerçâo", which established a system of "trabalho compelido" under the threat of "trabalho correccional" (arts. 33–34), was a direct effect of the economic exploitation consecrated in 1885; the liberal postulate underpinning the previous *Regolamento* of 1878 was relinquished. The 1899 regime was altered, without changing its coercive basis, through the new decrees of 1911 and 1914. However its principles were derogated from by the enactment of the "Código de Trabalho dos Indígenas das Colónias Portuguesas de Africa" (Decreto 16.199, of 6 December 1928), i.e. with the ratification of the International Convention condemning slavery (25 September 1926).

98. S. Llompart, *Legislación del trabajo*, p. 10.
99. J.M. Cordero Torres, *Tratado de derecho colonial*, p. 176. See also p. 185: the law on native labour "stems from local fragmentary provisions first collected in 1907 [!] and from the fact that, through the aggregation of customary rules, a real Labour Code has been created".
100. On the Indies, C. Bayle, S.J., *El protector de indios*, Sevilla: Editorial Católica Española, 1945 ("Anuario de Estudios Americanos", 2 (1945), pp. 1 ff.); M. Norma Olivares, "Construcción jurídica del régimen tutelar del indio", *Revista del Instituto de Historia del Derecho Ricardo Levene*, 18 (1967), pp. 105–26; C.R. Cutter, *The 'Protector de Indios' in Colonial New Mexico, 1659–1821*, Albuquerque (N.M.): The University of New Mexico, 1992. On Portuguese colonial law, cf. J.M. da Silva Cunha, *O trabalho indígena*, and E. d'Almonte, "El régimen del trabajo indígena en las colonias portuguesas de Africa", *Revista de Geografía Colonial y Mercantil*, 7 (1910), pp. 484–8, doubting the extension of the described system to Spain. On Guinea, J.M. Cordero Torres, *Tratado de derecho colonial*, pp. 173 ff.
101. J. Maldonado Macanaz, *Arte de la colonización*, p. 214.
102. Decree of the Governor General of 16 July 1912, Reglamento de la policía de la Curaduría Colonial: the main tasks of the force, defined in art. 1, are: "(1) to find and detain labourers under contract who have escaped from farms; (2) to collect idlers and tramps without a legally recognized occupation or job".
103. L. Ramos-Izquierdo, *Descripción geográfica del Golfo de Guinea*, pp. 32–4 on "Usages, customs, political and social organization of the *búbi* race inhabiting the island of Fernando Póo". See also M. Góngora Echenique, *Angel Barrera y las posesiones españolas del Golfo de Guinea*, Madrid: Imprenta San Bernardo, 1923, p. 22, with the image of the dissolute, coward and drunk *bubi*.
104. See E.V. Ynfante, *Cubanos en Fernando Póo*, p. 61: "you can't expect ... hard work" of *bubees* (author's anglicism).
105. C. Crespo, *Estudio antropológico y etnológico del bubi*, pp. 35 ff.
106. C. Mangado (C.M.F.), "De San Carlos. Fiestas de S.M. el Rey", *La Guinea Española*, 491, 10 February 1921, pp. 46–7; the patroness of San Carlos, the main *claretianos*' missionary centre, was Moreneta: see ibid., 497, 10 May 1921, pp. 142–3.
107. "El Exmo. Sr. D. Angel Barrera", ibid., 512, 10 January 1922, pp. 10–11.
108. M. Góngora, *Angel Barrera*, p. 35, with the quotations from the Madrilenian "ABC" (February 1922).
109. Failing the headword "Kolonien" in the great collection of the *Geschichtliche Grundbegriffe*, we can only refer to W. Konze, "Rasse", ibid., V (1984), pp. 135–78. See also J. Fisch, D. Groh, and R. Walther, "Imperialismus", ibid., III (1982), pp. 171–236.
110. The conceptual history we are dealing with arose precisely from this context: O. Brunner, "La 'casa grande' y la 'Oeconomica' de la vieja Europa", in *Nuevos caminos de la historia social y constitucional* [1968], Buenos Aires: Alfa, 1976, pp. 87–123. The most developed history of institutions equally starts from such a setting, of which some examples are here given: A.M. Hespanha, "Justiça e administraçâo entre o Antico Regime e a Revoluçâo", in P. Grossi, y otros, *Hispania. Entre derechos propios y derechos nacionales*, Milano: Giuffrè, 1990, I, pp. 135–204; B. Clavero, "Beati dictum: derecho de linaje, economía de familia y cultura de orden", *Anuario de Historia del Derecho Español*, 63–64 (1993–1994), pp. 7–148;

L. Mannori, "Per una 'preistoria' della funzione amministrativa. Cultura giuridica e attività dei pubblici apparati nell'età del tardo diritto comune", *Quaderni fiorentini per la storia del pensiero giuridico moderno*, 19 (1990), pp. 323–504.

111. C. Beccaria, *Dei delitti e delle pene* (1764), ed. by F. Venturi, Torino: Einaudi, 1965, p. xxvi: "Dello spirito di famiglia", pp. 56–9.
112. Reference must also be made to U. Wolter, "Deutsches Kolonialrecht", since the author, despite ignoring the above interrelations, examines the texts of colonial law precisely "anhand des Arbeitsrechts der Eingeborenen".
113. See U. Wolter, "Deutsches Kolonialrecht", pp. 237 ff. on "Das Recht der gewerblichen Arbeiter", with bibliography. See also J. Rückert, "Libero e sociale: concezioni del contratto di lavoro fra Otto e Novecento in Germania", in R. Gherardi and G. Gozzi (eds), *I concetti fondamentali delle scienze sociali e dello Stato in Italia e Germania tra Otto e Novecento*, Bologna: il Mulino, 1992, pp. 269–389.
114. See also U. Wolter, "Deutsches Kolonialrecht", pp. 239 ff. on "das Gesinderecht" of the old Prussian code where, it is rightly held when referring to the "Züchtigungsbefugnis der Dienstherrschaft", the German regulation should be placed. However, the master's wide corrective powers should have suggested Wolter to be more cautious in asserting the voluntary nature ("die Idee des freien Vertragsschlusses") of colonial work.
115. See J. Rückert, "Libero e sociale", p. 272, who refers to the Bluntschli of *Deutsches Privatrecht* to argue that labour law was going to be conceived "as 'special law' or as private law mixed with family law, i.e. as private law which was not pure rather mixed, 'morally heteronomous'".
116. L. Moutón y Ocampo (dir.), *Enciclopedia Jurídica Española*, VII, Barcelona: Francisco Seix, about 1914, headword "Colonia", pp. 129–60; "Colonias escolares", pp. 160–64; "Colonias penitenciarias" (P. Dorado), pp. 164–80; "Colonias industriales" and "Colonias obreras", p. 164.
117. E. d'Almonte, *Los naturales de la Guinea española considerados bajo el aspecto de su condición de súbditos españoles*, Madrid: Imprenta del Patronato de Huérfanos de la Administración Militar, 1910, p. 18.
118. So reports the text (without title) by Angel Traval y Roset ("Vicepresident of the Committe of the Rural Chamber of Fernando Póo in Barcelona and former president of the Local Council of Santa Isabel") at the *Segundo Congreso Africanista*, pp. lxxiv–lxxviii; A. Pérez ("of the Committe of the Rural Chamber of Fernando Póo in Barcelona"), "Problema obrero", ibid., pp. lvi–lxxiii. See also E. Borrajo Viñas, *Demarcación de la Guinea española*, p. 35.
119. A. Traval, "Un merecidísimo aplauso", *Africa*, 4 (1910), p. 11.
120. E. d'Almonte, *Los naturales*, p. 26.
121. Rafael María de Labra's speech at the Senate took place on occasion of the 1911 Plan for Guinea (session of 17 December), and was reported in "La Voz de Fernando Póo", 17 (15 February 1911), p. 3. The speech concerned the "despicable ban enacted by the temporary Governor ... on last 15 June, and the work of *bubis*". The quoted sentence is found in the autonomous edition of the speech, Madrid: Sindicato de la Publicidad, 1910, pp. 7–8.
122. J.G. Bluntschli, *Derecho público universal*, I, p. 311. These are, quite obviously, Cicero's words (Cicero, *De legibus*, 3, 8: "The good of the people is the supreme law").

123. J.G. Bluntschli, op. cit., I, p. 314.
124. See the General Order of 16 March 1908 on the Colonial Guard, art. 2: "In each garrison, where the flag is daily hoisted with the established honours, a portrait of our august King (may God protect him) will be hanged, and inscriptions bearing maxims such as the following ones will be hanged on other walls: *Spain is the Sovereign of our Territories, The mission of the Colonial Guard is always to defend our Motherland and our August Sovereign don Alfonso XIII, Work ennobles men, Agriculture is a source of wealth*, etc."; and art. 3: "If service so allows, the Commanders of the posting will devote two hours of their time to teach their troop to speak Spanish and will instil in its members feelings of love for the Motherland and the King, and will tell them about the advantages brought about by working, so that, when returning to their peoples and tribes and once the service is over, the latter will be the first to divulge the benefits received from the Spanish Motherland to their people, thus explaining what civilization entails". In L. Ramos-Izquierdo, *Descripción geográfica del Golfo de Guinea*, pp. 295 ff.
125. Decree of 15 June 1910, in S. Llompart, *Legislación del trabajo*, pp. 53–5.
126. See "Guinea española. I. El trabajo de los indígenas. II. Los sucesos de San Carlos", *Revista de Geografía Colonial y Mercantil*, 7 (1910), pp. 384–9; and the news published in *La Guinea Española* ("La Misión católica y los sucesos de Balachá", August 1910), as main source; see also "La rebelión de Balachá", *La Voz de Fernando Póo*, 10 (1 November 1910), p. 100; and "De Fernando Póo. Sobre la colisión de Julio", ibid., 15 (15 January 1911), pp. 1–2; see also A. Traval, "Un merecidísimo aplauso". Yet, the best version summing up (years later) all the previous ones, is by C. Crespo, *Estudio antropológico y etnológico del bubi*, pp. 182–4 on the "bubi war". The historian also examines documents taken from the "Archivo General de la Administración" (Alcalá de Henares, Madrid), Sección Africa, caja G-7, exp. 2 on the "Sucesos de Balachá (San Carlos), 1911".
127. E. d'Almonte, *Los naturales*, p. 39.
128. A. Barrera, *Lo que son y lo que deben ser*, pp. 38 ff.
129. Barrera's quotation is part of a conference dated 20 June 1907, i.e. before the first provision enacted on the *bubis* work (30 August 1907). Barrera and Ramos-Izquierdo expressed a common opinion, though it was the former who had the doubtful honour of certifying the non-application of the Labour Regulation of 1906.
130. See "La Guinea Española", 491, 10 February 1921, p. 47.
131. See "Fiestas que se acostumbra á celebrar en Sta. Isabel. Carroza presentada por una factoría española", *La Voz de Fernando Póo*, 49 (15 June 1912), p. 7; "Ultimos festejos en Sta. Isabel. Carroza presentada por la Guardia Colonial", ibid., p. 11. The cover picture dates back to a period which is closer to the quotation reported in the text, and it is by *La Guinea Española*, 545 (25 May 1923), where the carriage of the Rural Chamber of Fernando Póo is shown: its building and figure are represented within the same image, with the writing "Hurrah for the King" below and the official coat of arms on one side.
132. See in general G. Pasquier, *L'organisation des troupes indigènes en Afrique Occidentale*, Paris (Thèse Droit), 1912. More specifically, E. d'Almonte, *Los naturales*, pp. 29 ff. on "Los elementos de fuerza más adecuados á las condiciones de la Guinea española"; G. Granados, "Proyecto de Organización Militar para los territorios españoles del Golfo de Guinea", in Cuarto Congreso Africanista celebrado en el Salón de Actos del Ateneo Científico-Literario-Artístico de Madrid, en los

días 12, 14, 15, 16 y 17 de Diciembre de 1910, por iniciativa de los Centros Comerciales Hispano-Marroquíes, Barcelona: Imprenta. *España en Africa*, 1910, xix–xxviii, also collected in *La Voz de Fernando Póo*, 16, 1 February 1911, pp. 8–11.

133. Real Orden of 26 Juanuary 1914, "Boletín Oficial de los Territorios Españoles del Golfo de Guinea", 15 March 1914, p. 45. The following figures were also awarded with medals: the tenant of the Guardia Civil, assigned to the colonies, Joaquín Moreno Sáez, the "European sergent" Angel Vals Capilla and natives (without a pension, though at least they could keep their African names) Momo Limba Musa, Yemis Dongo Batarga, Kame, Somo y Dokoko.

134. See the General Order of 16 March 1908 on the Colonial Guard.

135. The long period of colonial government included, for promotional purposes, many years of embarking war ships, as told by the *Claretian* fathers: "Nuestra colonia", *La Guinea Española*, 495, 10 April 1921, pp. 107–8.

136. M. Góngora, *Angel Barrera*, p. 106.

137. For this reason Barrera, an energic repressor of dissents, was a highly celebrated figure by the harsh press of landowners. See "Nuevo gobernador", *Boletín del Comité de defensa Agrícola de Fernando Póo*, 7 (15 September 1910), p. 56; A. Traval, "Un merecidísimo aplauso". See also C.A., "Los pobrecitos indígenas. Una política atractiva"; e Mandín, "Sublevaciones en el Muni", *La Voz de Fernando Póo*, 22, 1 May 1911, pp. 7–9, articles taken from the Barcelona newspaper *El Noticiero Universal* (April 25) and *La Vanguardia* (April 23).

138. This will be the rule from the very start (V.B.A., "Cómo trataría V. al indígenea?", *Boletín de la Cámara Agrícola de Fernando Póo*, III, 5 (31 May 1909), 59–61 where the quotation is taken from) till the end of the period in question (Ruiaz, "Nuestra agricultura", *La Guinea Española*, 509 (25 November 1921), pp. 5–6). See Father Armengol Coll, *Segunda memoria de las Misiones de Fernando Póo y sus dependencias*, Madrid: Imprenta Ibérica, 1911, pp. 226 ff. on "Moral means" for colonization; by the same author, *El misionero en el Golfo de Guinea*, ibid., 1912, pp. 74 ff on "Trato con los indígenas que no han estado en los Colegios". See also *Polisinodiales o legislación supletoria del Vicariato Apostólico de Fernando Póo*, Barcelona: Casals, 1925, especially pp. 39 ff. It should be recalled that *Claretians* were not keen on going to Guinea ever since Father A. Puiggrós murdered a girl *bubi* in the mission of Cabo Sanjuán (1894): see an interesting version in C. Fernández, *Misiones y misioneros en la Guinea española*, pp. 695 ff.

139. They may suspend the metropolitan legislation, giving account thereof to the Ministry of State (art. 4, 2 of this Decree), or even adopt extraordinary measures to preserve internal peace (art. 3). The task of "assigning individual labour" (art. 4, 11) may be also recalled, this being subject to a hearing of the "Committee of the Authorities" in this case and in the former one (art. 12, 1, and 5).

140. Report of the Colonial Department of the Ministry of State, 6 July 1912, *infra* document no. 3: "this paragraph [the 2nd of art. 24 of the 1906 Regulation], just like the provision of art. 32 of the organic Royal Decree of the Colony, undoubtedly refer to the freedom of each individual to work or not to work, as he thinks proper. Yet, when he is asked to use such individual freedom to make *collective agreements* which, for their imposing character, disturb the peace, prosperity and life of a State, or part thereof, [the provisions in questions] do not allow the governmental authority to fold its arms or abide by the provisions for peaceful citizens; these, when

ceasing to be so and turning into disturbing elements, lose their rights and always justify the Authority's extreme and dictatorial decisions".

141. Real Orden of 2 August 1912.
142. "Decrevit quondam senatus, ut L. Opimius consul videret, ne quid res publica detrimenti caperet" (Cicero, *In Catilinam*, I, 4); "Senatus decrevit darent operam consules, ne quid res publica detrimenti caperet" (Sallustius, *De coniuratione Catilinae*, XXIX, 2) [The Senate established that the consuls shall act to ensure that the republic does not suffer any damage].
143. "Fit Senatus consultum, ut C. Marius L. Valerius consules adhiberent tribunos plebis et praetores quos eis videretur operamque darent, ut imperium populi Romani maiestasque conservaretur" (Cicero, *Pro Rabiro perduellionis reo*, XX).
144. See in general S. Mendner, "Videant consules", *Philologus. Zeitschrift für klassische Philologie*, 110 (1966), pp. 258–67.
145. W.J. Ong, "Latin Language Study as a Renaissance Puberty Rite" [1959], in Id., *Rhetoric, Romance, and Technology. Studies in the Interaction of Expression and Culture*, Ithaca/London: Cornell University Press, 1971, pp. 113–41. By the same author, *Fighting for Life. Contest, Sexuality and Consciousness* [1981], Amherst (MA): University of Massachusetts Press, 1989.
146. Preamble to the Educating Plan of 1866, in F. Sanz Franco, "Las lenguas clásicas y los planes de estudios españoles", *Estudios Clásicos*, 15 (1971), pp. 242–3.
147. Preamble to the Plan of 1868, ibid., pp. 244–5.
148. Ibid., education scheme at pp. 236–9, 245 ff on the Plan of 1894. On the presence of Cicero in schools see M. Marín Peña, "Sobre la elección de textos latinos en la enseñanza media", in *Didáctica de las lenguas clásicas*, 1. *Estudios monográficos*, Madrid: Dirección General de Enseñanza Media, 1966, pp. 77–86.
149. Ban of 28 February 1907, ibid., pp. 186–8. See art. 2: "The teaching programme in force in all schools of the territories is the following: Literature and writing. Castilian grammar and spelling principles. Christian doctrine. The four arithmetic operations. The system of weights, measures and coins. Outline of Spanish history and geography. Industrial and trade notions. Notions on the harvesting of coffee, cocoa, cotton, vanilla and other products typical of such intertropical countries". See in general O. Negrín Fajardo, *Historia de la educación en Guinea. El modelo educativo colonial español*, Madrid: UNED, 1993.
150. L. Ramos-Izquierdo, *Descripción geográfica del Golfo de Guinea*, p. 84. It is a complaint on education, advanced to the Governor of Uganda, Andrés Grigengi and Buando, chief of Corisco.
151. O. Louwers, "Rapport général", in Institut Colonial International, *L'enseignement aux Indigènes. Native Education*, Bruxelles: Etablissements généraux d'imprimerie, 1931, pp. 4–75, in particular p. 45.
152. J.M. de la Torre, "La tragedia de Guinea", p. 120.
153. See in particular C. Young, *The African Colonial State in Comparative Perspective*, New Haven/London: Yale University Press, 1994, pp. 244 ff. ("Imperial Legacy and State Traditions").
154. A.J. Mayer, *La persistencia del Antiguo Régimen. Europa hasta la Gran Guerra* [1981], Madrid: Alianza Editorial, 1984.
155. A. Hochschild, *King Leopolds's Ghost. A Story of Greed, Terror, and Heroism in Colonial Africa*, Boston/New York: Houghton Mifflin, 1998.

156. See in general A. Padoa-Schioppa (ed.), *La comparazione giuridica tra Ottocento e Novecento*, Milano: Istituto Lombardo, 2001; For doctrines of international law, see S. Mannoni, *Potenza e ragione. La scienza del diritto internazionale nella crisi dell'equilibrio europeo* (*1870–1914*), Milano: Giuffrè, 1999, pp. 103 ff. ("Colonialism and civilization").
157. Cf. U. Allegretti, *Profilo di storia costituzionale italiana*, with its illustrative subtitle: *Individualismo e assolutismo nello stato liberale*, Bologna: il Mulino, 1989, pp. 120 ff. on "the *non-legality* of liberal foreign policy".
158. See in this respect the notable contribution by G. Gozzi, *Democrazia e diritti. Germania: dallo Stato di diritto alla democrazia costituzionale*, Roma-Bari: Laterza, 1999.

PART V

THE RULE OF LAW IN ISLAM

CHAPTER 15

IS CONSTITUTIONALISM COMPATIBLE WITH ISLAM?

Raja Bahlul

1 INTRODUCTION

The object of this chapter is to discuss the meaning that "constitutionalism" has (or may come to have) in the context of Arab-Islamic political thought. Other terms which have sometimes been used as equivalents of "constitutionalism" in Western languages include "rule of law", *Rechtsstaat*, and *état de droit*. Some of these terms have natural-sounding equivalents in Arabic: thus *dawlat al-qanun* will do very nicely for *Rechtsstaat*, and *hukm al-qanun* for *rule of law*. "Constitutionalism", however, has no readily identifiable Arabic equivalent.

In Western political thought, terms such as "constitutionalism" and "rule of law" have come to express richer and more complex meanings than are suggested by etymology or mere juxtaposition of words. This is usually the mark of terms and concepts that have come to play a pivotal role in the theory of the subject matter in which the term is used. Such terms invariably carry a greater semantic burden than is suggested by their linguistic derivation or by the sum of their parts.

The same cannot be said for the equivalent terms used in Arab-Islamic political writings. But this need not mean that Arab-Islamic political thought does not know what constitutionalism means, or that it is conceptually unequipped to deal with the issues that constitutionalism addresses. On the contrary, a concern with ruling in accordance with the law, the people's right to oppose unjust rule, liberties which rulers are not permitted to infringe, have existed in Arab-Islamic political thought since the earliest times.

There is much to be said for discussing the meaning and role constitutionalism has in Arab-Islamic political thought. Firstly, a discussion of this type can help us make sense of (or at least thematize) some of the concerns that are being expressed by Arab and Islamic political thinkers. Secondly, the concept of "constitutionalism" has come to be regarded as extremely important, as far as Western political thought is concerned.

P. Costa and D. Zolo (eds.), The Rule of Law: History, Theory and Criticism, 515–542.

This invites us to wonder about its universality, since concepts that are truly fundamental should not be (are not normally) of mere local relevance. Thus discussing the meaning and possibility of "constitutionalism" in Arab-Islamic thought may function as a partial test for the universality of this concept.

In Section 2, I shall first go over the meaning of "constitutionalism", as the term is used in contemporary Western political thought. Then I shall go on to raise the question of whether we have any reasons to think that the concept of "constitutionalism" (as the term is used in Western political writings) has any meaning as far as Arab-Islamic political thought is concerned.

In Section 3 I shall proceed to discuss the foundations of constitutionalism in Arab-Islamic political thought. As we will find, this constitutionalism can be said to rest upon "theistic" foundations since they bear primary reference to divine law and revelation. But the theism manifested by Islamic thought is not homogeneous. It is possible to distinguish between two varieties of theism. The Ash'arite variety has a voluntarist outlook, which is almost devoid of rational elements. The Mu'tazilite, on the other hand, follows an objectivist line of thought, and is well known for its rationalism. Both outlooks can be used to establish foundations for constitutionalism in Islamic thought.

In Sections 4 and 5 I discuss the scope of Islamic constitutionalism by looking at the topics and themes relevant to it, and which have been touched upon by Islamic writers. Section 4 will deal with the different individual rights and the protection that Islamic laws may be expected to offer (according to the Ash'arite or Mu'tazilite readings of Islamic law). These rights will be compared with international schemes of human rights. Section 5 will examine the meaning and possibility of a doctrine of "the separation of powers" based on Islamic premises, stopping to consider the views of some "Islamic democrats" on this topic, which has only recently become an object of interest in Islamic political thought.

In the concluding section I shall try to close some of the remaining gaps in the Islamic discussion on constitutionalism. It will be suggested that critics of the Islamic conception of democracy and constitutionalism often base their criticism on the assumption that belief in secularism is required for the possibility of these institutions. This assumption can be questioned, and in fact has been questioned by some Islamic writers. I will therefore conclude that the current Islamic conceptions of democracy and constitutionalism need reconsideration.

2 THE MEANING OF CONSTITUTIONALISM

Unlike some other concepts which play an important role in contemporary Western political thought (e.g. *democracy*), the concept of *constitutionalism* is not "essentially contested".[1] However, difficult questions continue to be raised about the *consequences* of constitutionalism for the functioning of democracy, and the extent to which constitutionalism can be seen as imposing restrictions on liberty of ordinary citizens, government officials, even of future generations. However, this debate takes place within a framework of broad agreement on what constitutionalism basically means.

According to Jon Elster, "constitutionalism refers to limitations imposed on majority decisions; more specifically, to limitations that are in some sense self-imposed".[2] Dario Castiglione, on the other hand, defines constitutionalism arguing that "it comprises those theories which offer a series of principled arguments for the limitation of political power in general, and of government's sway over citizens in particular".[3]

Some writers prefer to understand constitutionalism by reference to the nature of *constitutions*, as the term invites us to do. Thus C.R. Sunstein introduces the meaning of constitutionalism by reference to *constitutions*, which "operate as constraints on the governing ability of majorities".[4] In the same vein, Elster attributes to constitutions two functions: "they protect individual rights, and they pose an obstacle to certain political changes which would have been carried out had the majority had its way".[5]

No matter where one chooses to begin, the basic idea that appears to underlie constitutionalism is that there should be checks and limitations – and means for checking – on the political power of those who are in a position to abuse it, if they were to have their way. Of course, in order to have an effect on the way political power is managed, checks and limitations have to be proclaimed, or otherwise impressed upon society. In modern times, this has come to be accomplished increasingly by means of written constitutions, which seek not only to "protect" the people from the state, but also to regulate the operation of the state so that the power of the state is "internally controlled". For these reasons, I shall discuss Islamic views on constitutionalism in terms of the following characterization proposed by Jan-Erik Lane:

> Two ideas are basic to constitutionalism: 1) the limitation of the state versus society in the form of respect for a set of human rights covering not only civic rights but also political and economic rights; 2) the implementation of separation of powers within the state.[6]

These two ideas are not unconnected. According to Lane, the former functions as an "external principle" which restricts state power with respect to civil society, while the latter functions as an "internal principle" which ensures that nobody (either as an organ or as a person) in the state completely prevails over the others.[7]

As we have seen, there are no exact equivalents within Islamic intellectual history for concepts such as *separation of powers, human rights*, and *civil society*. This makes it easy to understand why some students of Islamic thought may feel unsympathetic about looking for the grounds for constitutionalism in Islam. They see it as yet another attempt to subject Islamic thought to the categories and concepts of Western thought.

Of course, the charges of "hegemonic Western discourse" have to be met and rebutted (if possible) on their own grounds. However, in general, there are no *a priori* reasons to expect Islamic political ideas to be utterly dissimilar to those which have been expressed in Western political thought. On the contrary, there are reasons for expecting similarities and points of correspondence between these two intellectual traditions. These reasons hinge on two powerful considerations.

Firstly, both cultural traditions have been shaped by the operation of monotheistic faiths that can be considered to be "sisters" in more than one sense. Judaism, Christianity, and Islam belong to the same Near Eastern spiritual tradition. They speak the same religious language, even when they disagree on points of doctrine. Secondly, both cultural traditions have absorbed a large dose of Greek thought, which has survived (in different forms and to different degrees) right up to the present day.

These two reasons should constitute a strong enough basis for seeking similarities and areas of correspondence. Islamic thought has always been closer to Western thought than to Eastern intellectual traditions. This can be asserted on the sheer strength of historical influences and intellectual contents, regardless of one's position in the "hegemonic Western discourse" debate, as abstractly understood.

Still, these factors alone cannot allay our doubts about the meaningfulness of the concept of constitutionalism in the context of Arab-Islamic political thought. However, a rapid overview of the discussions that have taken place among Islamic thinkers (and others) about the notion of "divine sovereignty", as well as the causes which underlie demands for the application of the *Shari'a* (Islamic law), should prove the viability of the idea of seeking to understand constitutionalism in Islamic terms.

Consider the notion of "divine sovereignty", which is popular among many Islamic thinkers and young intellectuals. How should we understand their proclamation *al-hakimiyyatu li-Allah*, which may be roughly rendered as "sovereignty (rulership) belongs to God"? Bernard Lewis maintains that "the Islamic state was in principle a theocracy, not in the Western sense of a state ruled by the Church and the clergy [...] but *in the more literal sense of a polity ruled by God* ...".[8]

Lewis' explanation paves the way for viewing the Islamic polity as a *despotic* state, for God is hardly the sort of ruler who could be held to account for His actions, or who would need to consult with any of His subjects. However, the Tunisian Islamic thinker Rachid al-Ghannouchi offers a more plausible explanation of "divine sovereignty", with the additional virtue of relating this notion to our current concern with constitutionalism. According to Ghannouchi,

> Those who proclaim that sovereignty belongs to God do not mean to suggest that God rules over the affairs of the Muslim community directly, or through the clergy. For there is no clergy in Islam, and God cannot be perceived directly, nor does He dwell in a human being or an institution which can speak for Him. What the slogan "sovereignty belongs to God" means is *rule of law* (*hukm al-qanun*), government by the people.[9]

The idea that Islamic calls for "divine sovereignty" and the application of the *Shari'a* should be understood as nods towards constitutionalism (or an Islamic version thereof) is not an instance of wishful thinking on the part of those inclined to view Islam sympathetically. The idea has not been lost on the more astute Arab secularists, such as Amzi Bisharah, who claims that in times when social consciousness takes a religious form, calls for the application of *Shari'a* may express a democratic tendency, or at least an opposition to despotism, simply because *Shari'a* rule implies restrictions on the exercise of political power over and above the mere will of rulers.[10]

Remarks by Ghannouchi, Bisharah, and others[11] indicate that it may be possible to find elements of constitutionalism in Islam. These elements can be expressed by means of modern terms, such as "rule of law" (as opposed to the "rule of men").

Of course, constitutionalism does not reduce to the simple idea of legality, or to the mere imposition of restrictions on the power of earthly rulers. For these ideas, noble as they may be, can be undermined by other elements implicit in the tradition, which could make the claim to constitutionalism rather pointless. This will be dealt with in due course. The most suitable starting point is inquiring about the place of the law in Islam. Such an inquiry will hopefully provide us with some insights about the Islamic constitution, and the constitutionalism which it implies.

3 FOUNDATIONS OF ISLAMIC CONSTITUTIONALISM

Constitutionalism refers to the concept of *law*, inasmuch as it requires that the conduct of different organs of state vis-à-vis the citizen, as well as between each other, be regulated by *laws* or *rules* (which may or may not be written down). For this reason it is convenient to begin our inquiry into the possible foundations of constitutionalism in Islamic thought by finding out what Islamic law really is, and by determining the place it holds in society. It is here that we would hope to discover the foundations of constitutionalism, or a certain version thereof, in Islam.

A statement by Mawdudi, an influential Islamic theorist of modern times, indicates that Islamic thinking does not draw a line between the laws which govern the system of nature (considered as mere physical reality) and the laws which govern (or ought to govern) human affairs in society. To the Muslim thinker *all* laws, ultimately considered, are *God's laws*. In a statement which is reminiscent of Aquinas's distinction between eternal law and divine, *revealed* law,[12] Mawdudi says:

> From the moment of their conception to the very last day of their lives, human beings are completely subjected to God's natural law, unable to break it, or to go against it. Those who believe in divine revelation must also believe that God rules over the voluntary part of our lives as well as the involuntary part, and the universe in its entirety.[13]

If we put aside the laws which govern the motions of the planets and other parts of physical reality as irrelevant to our purposes, we are left with those portions of God's law which are collectively referred to as *Shari'a*. The *Shari'a*, as understood by many Islamic thinkers, is all-encompassing, taking into purview all acts that human beings are capable of in society. In Mawdudi's words:

> [*Shari'a*] judgments of good and evil extend to all parts of our lives. They cover religious acts and duties, as well as actions undertaken by individuals which reflect their way of life, morals, customs, manners of eating, drinking, attire, speech, and family affairs. They cover social relations, financial, economic and administrative matters, rights and duties of citizenship, organs of government, war and peace, and relations with foreign powers. [...] There is no part of our lives where the *Shari'a* does not distinguish between good and evil.[14]

Presumably, it is in the rich and varied field of *Shari'a* that we would expect to find elements of an *Islamic constitution*, as well as of a *constitutionalism* to be defined in reference to it. This is a legitimate expectation, which is supported by the fact that Islamic thinkers often view the *Shari'a* as a constitution of sorts. Hasan Turabi, for example, thinks that "*Shari'a* is the higher law, just like the constitution, except that it is a detailed constitution".[15] Mawdudi himself believes that the "unwritten

Islamic constitution" already exists, and that it is only awaiting efforts to codify it on the basis of its original sources, which are identical with the sources as the *Shari'a*.[16]

In the next two sections of this chapter I shall discuss the various constitutionalist themes that can be found in Islamic thought, but first we must examine the basis of the obligatory character which laws have in the Islamic view of law. If we are to arrive at an Islamic view of constitutionalism, we must not only determine the type and number of laws considered to be relevant to constitutionalism as it is understood in the West, but we must also inquire into the rationale which underlies these laws. For, this will give us an insight into the normative character of the laws, the attribute which is needed to provide a situation of *obligation* towards the law, as opposed to *coercion*.

There are essentially two schools of Islamic thought which deal with the question of sources of moral obligation.[17] We do not speak here of moral obligation in general, but of the moral obligation to obey the laws, and to engage in practices which touch upon different aspects of our life, both private and public. These may range all the way from the duty to help a needy wayfarer to the obligation to obey those who are in authority over us.

The first and by far the most enduring and influential of these two schools of thought is the Ash'arite school. This has existed (at least as a tendency) since the early days of Islamic theology, to judge from the letter which al-Hasan al-Basri (d. 728) wrote in rebuttal of certain conceptions of divine justice and human responsibility that tend to go with this view.[18] There is probably nothing which is more suggestive of the spirit which animates the Ash'arite view of morality than the definition which it offers of basic moral notions such as *good*, *evil*, and *justice*. Consider what Ash'ari (d. 935) says about the actions which God is capable of doing. According to the Islamic (as well as the Judeo-Christian) tradition, God is omnipotent. Does this mean that there is nothing which God cannot, in a moral sense, do? According to Ash'ari:

> God is entitled to do everything which He does. This is proven by the fact that He is the overpowering Master; there is nothing which has power over Him, no prohibiter, no commander, ... nothing which sets limits to His power, or draws a boundary around His actions. This being so, it follows that nothing which God may do can be considered to be evil. For to do evil is simply to go beyond what has been assigned to one as a boundary, to do that which one is not entitled to do.[19]

What makes this passage of critical importance is its possible relevance to the question of whether God is to be conceived of as behaving like a "constitutional monarch", or as a despot who is subject to nothing but the dictates of his will. There are reasons to believe that this will have negative implications for the resulting view of constitutionalism, even if "constitutionalism", in its primary application, is not an attribute of individual agents such as God(s) or monarchs.

The Ash'arites, on the whole, do not seem to view God as a "constitutional" being. Foremost among the laws which God would have to observe, if indeed there were any at all, would be laws such as: *the innocent shall not be punished*, or, perhaps, *the well-doers shall be rewarded.* But this is not the case, according to the famous theologian Ghazali (d. 1111), who followed in the footsteps of Ash'ari. According to Ghazali:

God ... can hurt and torture creatures, despite their having committed no previous wrong. He can also refrain from rewarding them in the Hereafter. For God is entitled to do as He wishes in His dominion (*mulk*). ... To do injustice is simply to undertake actions in a dominion which is ruled over by another, without first obtaining permission from the master. This is, of course, impossible in the case of God, for there is no dominion which does not belong to Him. Hence there is no dominion where He can act unjustly.[20]

This passage may sound highly implausible, but in order to understand it we have to consider the reasons which may have led early Islamic theologians to this conclusion. It is difficult for theologians who take divine omnipotence seriously to accept the idea that God is *subject* to anything, even if it is something intangible, such as the law. One should consider the position of the early Muslim theologians who began to reflect on these philosophical matters in the centuries following the Islamic conquest of the ancient centres of civilization. Filled with a sense of piety and wonder of the divine power, many of them must have found it extremely hard to come to terms with the idea of a limited God, a God whose scope of willing and doing was in anyway restricted.

In some ways, the Ash'arist view resembles legal positivism, albeit as a *theistic* variant thereof. Like positive law, God's law is to be understood with reference to the *agent* who *enacts* it as law. Furthermore (according to the Ash'arites), the obligatory character of God's law is not to be explained with reference to the *content* of the law. Nor does it depend on our understanding as *rational* creatures of what the law actually means. Rather, its obligatory nature must be explained in terms of the relationship which stands between those who are *subject*s of the law, and the agent who is recognized as a legitimate source of law.[21]

In the case of Ash'ari's theistic positivism, the agent who enacts the law and proclaims it as such is none other than God Himself. The relationship between the lawgiver and those who are subject to the law is one of power. God is the master of the universe, and we are part of his dominion, subject to His sanctions. We are not in a position to question His commands or His prohibitions. Good and evil, obligatory and forbidden, as well as all other moral attributes of actions must be defined by reference to God's commands.

Positivism, whether it is of the more familiar natural variety, or the supra-mundane variety which we have attributed to the Ash'arite school, runs into many difficulties. With respect to both varieties we have to ask: "Why does the choice made by the lawgiver have a normative nature, which means that it is binding and therefore ought to be accepted?"[22] It is hard to imagine that an answer to this question would be forthcoming without reference to the *meaning* of the law, and the position which we take towards it as rational, interested creatures.

Of course, the Ash'arite theologian may well object that we are raising an impious question, one which should not be raised in the first place. But this is not a convincing reply, even for those who firmly stand on Islamic grounds. For not only does God explain his commands and prohibitions in many places in the Qur'an, but the Ash'arite interpretation of the meaning of the basic moral terms actually stands to make no sense of many verses in the Qur'an. As Hourani says:

> The repeated commands of God to do what is right would be empty of force and insipid, if they meant only "commands to do what He commands". It is even harder to make sense of statements that God is always just to His servants if all that "just" means is "commanded by God". The only possible move at this point would be resorting to transcendence of meaning in reference to God – always the refuge of the baffled theologian.[23]

Whatever the philosophical difficulties faced by Ash'arism, this does not mean that it is impossible to make a case for constitutionalism on Ash'arite grounds. What it means is that the constitutionalism in question is likely to be *literal* (out of respect for the letter of the scripture, which is, after all, God's word), *rigid* (so as not to risk legislating against God's commands) and *non-rationalistic*.[24] In these respects Ash'arism differs from Mu'tazilism. The latter can arguably be said to support a more rationalistic, less conservative, and more enlightened type of constitutionalism, as can be seen from its moral philosophy.

The Mu'tazilites, as R.M. Frank characterize their view, hold that "all men of sound mind know in an immediate and irreducible intuition that certain actions ... are morally obligatory ... and that certain actions are morally bad".[25] Ethical predicates such as "good" and "evil" can be attributed to actions in an objective manner, that is to say, in a manner which is determined by the qualities of the actions themselves, and not by the attitude of the beholder of the action, be that a human being or God Himself.

The following passage from the late Mu'tazilite thinker, al-Qadi 'Abd al-Jabbar (d. 1025?), illustrates this approach to morality. 'Abd al-Jabbar maintains that knowledge of good (when this knowledge actually exists) is sufficient to determine moral obligation. He explicitly denies that good and evil are to be defined in terms of what is commanded or prohibited by revelation. These points are made with the help of the example of purely devotional duties (such as the duty to perform prayers in a certain manner, at certain times during the day) which are known only by revelation.

Revelation only tell us about the character of those aspects of acts whose evil or goodness we should recognize if only we could know them by reason; for if we had known by reason that prayer is of great benefit to us ... we should have known its obligatory character [also] by reason. Therefore we say that revelation does not necessitate (la yujib) the evil or goodness of anything. It only uncovers the character of the act by way of indication, just as reason does, and distinguishes between the command of the Exalted and that of another being by His wisdom, Who never commands what it is evil to command.26

The intellectual orientation of the Mu'tazilite approach to morality promises to deliver a different type of constitutionalism to the Ash'arite type. To begin with, the Mu'tazilite view of the law is far less heteronymous than that of the Ash'arites. According to the latter, the law consists of a number of divine dictates which neither emanate from human reason, nor can be questioned by it. God, moreover, assumes the role of the absolute ruler whose power is utterly unrestrained, but whose judgment defines what is good and bad, what is legal and what is illegal. The Mu'tazilite God, on the other hand, seems very different. To the extent that He abides by moral laws which are valid independently of the attitude of the beholder (or knower) He can be viewed as a "constitutional monarch", one who is not above the law in every respect.

The Mu'tazilites did not only believe in the rationality and objectivity of morality and of the laws which must be justified accordingly, they also characteristically espoused the doctrine of the creation of the Qur'an, which is God's *speech*. This doctrine, which is bound to sound peculiar to modern ears, engendered much debate during the Mu'tazilite period of Islamic intellectual history. Since this debate, at least in part, can be viewed as a debate about constitutionalism and the limits of authority, it may be useful to briefly review the position adopted by the Mu'tazilites.

By the time the issue of the creation of the Qur'an erupted on the Islamic intellectual scene during the second century of Abbasid rule (750–1258), political views were polarized between what W. Montgomery

Watt calls a "constitutionalist bloc" and an "autocratic bloc". The constitutionalist bloc comprised, among others, the nascent body of *'ulema*, and others who were united in the belief that "the Islamic community's way of life was constituted by the supernatural revelation contained in the Qur'an and the Traditions [of the Prophet]".[27]

To suggest that the Qur'an was created did not only mean that the Qur'an might be less than divine but it must also have meant that the caliph (who headed the "autocratic bloc") had a free hand when it came to interpreting the scriptures and enacting the laws. It was also to take away from the authority of the class of the *'ulema*, who enjoyed a popular following among ordinary people, and whose status and authority in the community partly emanated from their special connection to the scripture as students and interpreters. In a way, opposition to the doctrine of the creation of the Qur'an meant opposition to despotism, or unchecked power. According to Watt's estimate:

> The general conception of the caliphate was at stake – not which particular family or person was to rule, but what kind of ruler one was to look for. Must the caliph be a person with a 'divine right' to rule, and so the primary fount of all law in the state? Or was he merely a man subject to the divine law contained in the Qur'an and the Sunnah of the Prophet?[28]

The Mu'tazilites sided with the autocratic party, and their fate was sealed when official support for the doctrine of the creation of the Qur'an stopped during the reign of al-Mutawakil (d. 861). This need not be a reflection on their moral doctrine. For there can be no doubt that the Mu'tazilite alliance with the powers that be was not a logical consequence of their doctrine. Rather, it represents the temptation which enlightened elites throughout Islamic history have always had: unable to put their faith in the ability of the people to rule themselves with good laws, they tended to put their trust in the wise, enlightened ruler who possessed total power. The rule of such a ruler would prove no more lawless or unconstitutional than the rule of Plato's philosopher-king. But it would not be "democratic", either.

In fact, it may be helpful (if this is not altogether too anachronistic) to view the difference between the Ash'arite and Mu'tazilite outlooks in the light of the distinction which Elster makes between two "sides" of constitutionalism. According to Elster, one side of constitutionalism can be summed up as "rules vs. discretion".[29] The meaning of this is clarified by reference to the "war" which constitutionalism wages against the executive power in order to prevent rulers from obtaining too much *discretionary* power in their conduct of government. By insisting on laws and rules, constitutionalism takes decisions out of the realm of private, individual judgment, even when this latter aims at nothing but the common good. Ash'arist foundations for Islamic constitutionalism may be viewed as taking aim at the discretionary powers which rulers may otherwise be inclined to exercise. By holding the *Shari'a* over their heads as the divine constitution which cannot be overturned, rulers would be kept in check.

The other side of constitutionalism, according to Elster, may be summed up as "rules vs. passion". Under this aspect constitutionalism is seen as fighting a war not against the executive, but against the legislative power. The idea here is to ensure good government by somewhat insulating the political process from the "whims" and "passions" of transient and possibly irresponsible majorities which can threaten to encroach on the legislative branch of government. Viewed in this light, constitutionalism dwells in the halls of the Constitutional Court (the Supreme Court of the United States), which is authorized to review legislation and check it for constitutionality.[30]

Of course, it cannot be said that the Ash'arites represented the democratic party, nor can it be said that the Mu'tazilites anticipated the idea of a separate judicial power. Such thinking would be anachronistic, and, what is more, there are no facts to support it. Still, to the extent that Ash'arites had popular following and represented opposition to despotic rule, one could be excused for momentarily blurring the distinction between populism and democracy. On the other hand, it cannot be denied that the Mu'tazilites, in many ways, represented the "voice of reason", enlightenment, and progressivism, which modern constitutionalists sometimes look for in the Constitutional Court. The Mu'tazilites stood against a certain type of conservatism (traditionalism), which could cause stagnation, if it were to have its way. Indeed, one cannot take the Mu'tazilites to have represented that side of constitutionalism which guards against the "passion" of the masses. However, it is plausible to view their constitutionalism as guarding against the inertia, traditionalism, and weak rationality of the masses.

To sum up our discussion so far, we have seen how the idea of government in accordance with the "law" is an essential part of Islamic political thought. The *Shari'a* is simply God's *law* and it is undeniably at the heart of the Islamic faith. But the *Shari'a* can be approached either in a conservative-literal manner (which is the method used by the Ash'arites), or in a liberal-rational manner (which is what the Mu'tazilites chose to do). Both approaches to the *Shari'a* can yield constitutionalism.

We must now explore the themes, elements, and concepts that can be brought together under the rubric of constitutionalism in an Islamic sense. What we need to ask is: what is constitutional in the Islamic *Shari'a*? What potential does it hold for further development of constitutionalist ideas?

4 THE SCOPE OF ISLAMIC CONSTITUTIONALISM: THE QUESTION OF RIGHTS

In the following section we shall keep to Lane's idea of constitutionalism, as explained Section 2. The same idea is succinctly expressed in Article 16 of The Declaration of the Rights of Man and the Citizen (1789): "A society in which rights are not secured nor the separation of powers established is a society without a constitution".[31] We shall first tackle the question of rights, which is easier than the question about the different branches of government, and the relationship between them. What rights do individuals have in Islam? How does the Islamic scheme of individual (and human) rights compare to other schemes?

It is commonplace to say that Islam is not the same thing to all who profess to believe in it, or practise it. This is true in many ways, but the question of rights stands out as a subject of which drastically different interpretations are possible. It is useful to think of the range of possible interpretations in terms of the old rivalry between the Ash'arites and the Mu'tazilites. It is true that contemporary adversaries do not see themselves as historical continuations of that old rivalry, but there is no doubt that many of the concerns, rationales, even conflicting interests which caused that ancient split are still operative now, and are likely to continue in the future.

As one might expect, Ash'arite-minded thinkers tend be literal and traditional, and take a more defensive stance towards modernity, including the question of human rights. Mu'tazilite-minded thinkers, on the other hand, tend to be more progressive and daring in the interpretations and innovations they propose.

To see how rights are dealt with on the Ash'arite model, consider the writings of Mawdudi, an Islamic thinker of considerable fame and influence. In his *al-Khilafah wa al-Mulk* (*Caliphate and Kingship*) he enumerates no fewer than 13 rights that citizens hold against their government. They include the right to life, dignity, privacy, property, due process, equality before the law, freedom of belief, freedom to assemble, and freedom from religious persecution. The majority of the rights which he mentions are supported by reference to Qur'anic verses.[32]

When viewed abstractly, some of the individual rights which Mawdudi dwells on are remarkably similar to the rights mentioned in the Universal Declaration of Human Rights. In the light of Mawdudi's other writings, however, we find reasons to reconsider, specially insofar as women and non-Muslims are concerned. In his *Tadwin al-Dustoor al-Islami* (*Codification of the Islamic Constitution*), rights of women are severely abridged. For example, they are not allowed to be members of the "Consultative Council" (*majlis al-shura*), on the strength of a Prophetic tradition which says: "Never will a people who are led by a woman prosper".[33] Similarly, in his *al-Qanun al-Islami wa Turuq Tanfithih* (*Islamic Law and Methods of its Application*), non-Muslims do not enjoy the same political rights as Muslims, even if the denial is couched in terms of the idea that the Islamic polity is, by definition, non-secular, so that it cannot ignore religion in the apportionment of political rights without self-contradiction.[34]

The same conservative spirit seems to be operative also in many of the Islamic human rights schemes that have been made public. The documents in question tend to be guarded, on account of their being addressed also to non-Muslim audiences. Still, many inconsistencies, obfuscations, and equivocations are to be found in several places, specially in the areas of freedom of thought, the treatment of non-Muslims, and women's rights. For example, whereas the English version of Article XXa of the Universal Islamic Declaration of Human Rights says that a husband owes his wife means of support "in the event of divorce", the Arabic version of the same article uses the phrase "if he divorces her". What the English version passes over in silence is, of course, the troublesome problem of "the unconditional right to divorce", which *Shari'a* has always given to men exclusively. In addition, the Arabic version invokes the notion of *qiwamah* (authority which men have over women), something which the English version omits altogether.

This is not the place to discuss Islamic human rights schemes, nor the circumstances, pressures, and compromises which gave rise to them. Suffice it to say that many concepts are not understood in the same way by conservative Islamists and secular human rights advocates. To the Ash'arite-minded thinker, "the law" simply means (or *ought to mean*) the Law of *Shari'a*. Thus when he welcomes the modern-sounding notion of "equality before the law" he is in fact welcoming the not-so-modern notion of "equality before *Shari'a*". As Ann Mayer says:

> They took the position that equality before the law meant that all Muslims should be treated equally under *Shari'a* and that all non-Muslims should also be treated equally under *Shari'a* – not that Muslims and non-Muslims should be treated alike, or accorded the same rights under the law.[35]

This should not, however, blind us to the wide variety of rights and instruments of protections which *Shari'a* affords – even when it is conservatively understood. In addition to the rights listed above, the social and economic rights ought to be mentioned. Individuals can press against the state and society as a whole on the basis of fairly unequivocal verses in the Qur'an ("[may those be saved] whose wealth is a right known for the beggar and outcast", Q. LXX, 25). Individuals have rights not only during times of peace, but also during times of war and instability – such as the right of asylum, which *Shari'a* extend to unbelievers ("And if any one of the idolaters seeks of thee protection, grant him protection till he hears the words of God, then do thou convey him to his place of security", Q. IX, 6).

Significantly, individuals have also political rights, such as the right to oppose an unjust ruler, on the strength of the Prophetic tradition which says: "There is no obedience to a creature in sin against the Creator". The Universal Islamic Declaration of Human Rights goes so far as to make democracy (at least in theory) a human right. According to Article XI of the Declaration "The process of free consultation (*shura*) is the basis of the administrative relationship between government and the people. People also have the right to choose and remove their rulers in accordance with this principle".

Despite all these positive provisions, the scheme of individual rights and protections which Ash'arite-minded thinkers offer leaves many things to be desired, at least from the perspective of those who want Islamic human rights to conform fully to international standards. Such is the attitude of the contemporary Islamic thinker Abdullahi an-Na'im, whose approach to ethics, and whose daring views on how to interpret *Shari'a* are reminiscent of Mu'tazilism. Naturally, an-Na'im accepts all the non-controversial provisions *Shari'a* has to offer but he pushes reform further, aiming to bring Islamic legislation up to the mark of full correspondence with international human rights provisions.

Not only is Abdullahi an-Na'im a rationalist thinker when it comes to ethical theory, but he is also a historically minded thinker. Following his teacher Mahmoud Taha, he distinguishes between two stages of Islam. During the first Meccan stage, when Islam was still a weak and persecuted religion, Islam presented itself as a simple spiritual message which recognized the dignity and humanity of all persons, without reference to gender or religious belief. During the second Medinan stage, however, the victorious Islam formed a polity which needed to be governed in specific ways, appropriate to the prevailing historical conditions. According to an-Na'im:

Unless the basis of modern Islamic law is shifted away from those texts of the Qur'an and Sunnah of the Medina stage, which constituted the foundations of the constructions of *Shari'a*, there is no way of avoiding drastic and serious violation of human rights. There is no way to abolish slavery as a legal institution and no way to eliminate all forms and shades of discrimination against women and non-Muslims as long as we remain bound by the framework of *Shari'a*.[36]

An-Na'im, in effect, proposes a new *Shari'a*, based on the earlier Islamic message, which he elsewhere described as "the eternal and fundamental message of Islam".[37] To give an impression of the content of his essentially ethical-humanistic message, consider the following verses from an early Meccan *sura* (VI, 150–151):

Say: Come, I will recite what your Lord has forbidden you: that you associate not anything with Him, and to be good to your parents, and not to slay you children because of poverty; We will provide you and them; and that you approach not any indecency outward or inward, and that you slay not the soul God has forbidden, except by right. That then He has charged you; haply you will understand. And that you approach not the property of the orphan, save in the fairer manner, until he is of age. And fill up the measure and the balance with justice. We charge not any soul save to its capacity. And when you speak, be just, even if it should be to near kinsman. And fulfil God's covenant. That He has charged you; haply will remember.[38]

An-Na'im relies on a "principle of reciprocity", by which we are enjoined not to deny others rights which we believe we are entitled to. This principle underlies the universality of human rights, and is to be found in all the major religious traditions, including Islam:

There is a common normative principle shared by all the major cultural traditions which, if construed in an enlightened manner, is capable of sustaining universal standards of human rights. That is the principle that one should treat other people as he or she wishes to be treated by them. This golden rule, referred to as the principle of reciprocity, is shared by all the major religions traditions of the world. Moreover, the moral and logical force of this simple proposition can easily be appreciated by all human beings of whatever cultural tradition or philosophical persuasion.[39]

Arguing in this manner, an-Na'im invokes the ethical-humanistic Meccan texts, and looks for contextual explanations of the Medinan texts which enable him to put them aside as being inappropriate to modern conditions. In this way an-Na'im arrives at a "reformed" *Shari'a* which bans slavery, recognizes equality of men and women, and grants full citizenship rights to all citizens, regardless of religious affiliation.

To summarize, we can say that the *Shari'a* offers a rich and varied field for human rights to be grounded in. Depending on how *Shari'a* is interpreted, there may be limitations, serious omissions, and shortcomings which our modern ethical sensibilities cannot accept. However, neither the Islamic *Shari'a* nor any other religious tradition should be judged too harshly. After all, we would never have been able to entertain the vision of one humanity, whose members are equal in worth and dignity, endowed with inalienable human rights, regardless of gender, race, or social position, had we not "stood on the shoulders" of prophets who were the first to announce the equality of all humans in the sight of God, their Creator.

5 THE SCOPE OF ISLAMIC CONSTITUTIONALISM: THE SEPARATION OF POWERS

We now turn to the question of the internal workings of government from the point of view of the *Shari'a*. The first thing to notice here is that *Shari'a* (as it has been understood and practised until very recently) does not offer a doctrine of the "separation of powers". This should come as no surprise, for the Western doctrine of the separation of powers itself has recent origins. Moreover, the Islamic traditional *Shari'a* did not conceive of distinct governmental powers to be separated from each other, in the first place.

Of course, there is no reason why contemporary *Shari'a* thinkers cannot take up the challenge to elaborate a position with respect to the separation of the different branches of government. However, before looking at the prospects for accomplishing this task, and the possible picture that can emerge from it, it may be useful to take into account Mawardi's (d. 1031) political theory. In some ways, his theory represents the "political sphere", as conceived of by traditional *Shari'a*.

Mawardi considers (or, at least, seems to consider) the caliphate to be an elective office. Mawardi notes that there is some disagreement about the number of the "electors", with some saying the electors are "the generality" throughout the land, some saying five, and others saying "at least one". Moreover, "investment by the nomination of a predecessor is permissible and correct". This is based on the precedent of Abu Bakr (the first caliph) who nominated 'Umar for the caliphate.[40] Beyond mentioning the qualifications which the electors should have, such as probity, knowledge, and prudence, Mawardi does not say how the electors are to be chosen. Given the important role which the electors can play, this is no a minor omission.

Allegiance to the caliph is not an absolute, unconditional duty of the subjects. In fact, there are two circumstances under which the caliph may be legitimately disqualified: lack of justice, and physical disability.

"An incumbent so disqualified must step down and may not be reinstated upon regaining probity without new appointment".[41] However, Mawardi does not deal with the question of who declares, and by what procedure, that the ruler has become illegitimate (in the event of his lack of justice or otherwise). According to Bernard Lewis, this is "the crucial question which a modern constitutional lawyer would put".[42]

Lewis's remark draws attention to another question: what sort of constitution, if any, should a *Shari'a*-based regime have? In recent decades, modern Islamic thinkers have begun to discuss this question, after they absorbed the lesson that a modern Islamic state, like other modern states, requires separate branches of government (executive, legislative, and judiciary), as well as different types of law (constitutional, criminal, administrative, public, etc.)

Concern with the structure and inner workings of government has reached a considerable degree of maturity in the theories and proposals of the Islamic thinkers who have seriously grappled with the question of democracy or popular government. Among such thinkers, Ghannouchi, Turabi, Mawdudi, and M. Khatami are probably the best-known.

Despite his conservatism, Mawdudi offers a clear treatment of the questions at hand. In his *Tadwin al-Dustoor al-Islami* (*Codification of the Islamic Constitution*) he recognizes an existing but "unwritten" Islamic constitution, and in his *al-Qanun al-Islami* (*Islamic Law*) he explains the various types of law (constitutional and other) which Islamic lawmakers need to design.

Along with other Islamic thinkers, Mawdudi paves the way for a discussion of the meaning and role of the parliament ("legislative assembly") in the Islamic regime, because he takes the decisive step of espousing popular government, where people can freely elect their representatives. Some pious remarks which serve as a preface to these passages need not detain us here; they include a reminder that "sovereignty" is retained by "God alone"[43] while the people as a whole act as "vice-regents":

> The Qur'an has established that the caliphate [...] is not a right that inheres in a certain individual, or family or class. It is a right which belongs to all those who recognize divine sovereignty, and who believe in the supremacy of divine law. [...] This feature makes the Islamic caliphate democratic, in contrast to caesarism, papism, or theocracy, as known in the West. It must also be recognized that the system which is called democracy in the West is not one that allows the people to be sovereign. Our [Islamic] democratic system, which we call the 'caliphate', allows the people to be vice-regents of God, while reserving the sovereignty to God alone.[44]

Mawdudi is not alone in his espousal of the democratic method of government. Similar positions have been taken by both Turabi and Ghannouchi. Having recognized the people's right to elect the caliph, it is not a great additional step to recognize the people's right to elect "representatives" with the task of voicing people's concerns, and watching over the executive power, which is represented by the caliph and his officers.

With two organs of government at hand, the question of the relationship between them immediately arises. Adapting an ancient term to modern usage, Mawdudi often refers to members of the parliament as "those who lose and bind" (*ahl al-hal wa al-'aqd*). He raises the question of what position they have, whether they serve as mere consultants to the caliph, or whether the caliph is "bound" by their decisions. His answer is that "we have no choice but to make the executive power subject to the majority decision of the legislative council".[45]

The question of whether or not the executive power should be subject to the authority of the parliament (or to the legislative council) is not the most interesting that the Islamic debate on constitutionalism gave rise to. Most "Islamic democrats", if they may be referred to in this manner, answered the question in the affirmative, and then they proceeded to discuss another, more serious and (to our mind) interesting matter: the question of *the limits of the legislative power*.

With this question we finally reach a point on which modern Western constitutionalists and Islamic constitutionalists see eye to eye. In both cases there is a concern with the possibility that the legislative power may pass wrong or unjust laws.

We have already cited Elster's presentation of constitutionalism fighting a "two-front war": against the executive branch of government, which is liable to ask for much discretion in the interest of efficiency, and against the legislative branch, which may give rise to oppressive or foolish majorities. Islamic constitutionalists (and democrats) greatest fear is that the legislative branch may legislate measures inconsistent with the *Shari'a*. For this reason many of them reject the idea of an "unqualified popular sovereignty" out of hand. This can be illustrated by referring to the writings of Ghannouchi and Turabi. According to the former:

> In the Qur'an it is stated: 'O believers, obey God, and obey the Messenger and those in authority over you'. (Q. IV, 59). [This verse] clearly indicates the centre of supreme authority in the lives of Muslims ... After this comes the power which the people exercise. The legitimate scope for this power does not violate divine law which is found in the Qur'an and the Traditions of the Messenger.[46]

Turabi, on the other hand, says:

Naturally, there is no place in Islam for a popular government which is separated from the Faith. ... Democracy in Islam does not mean absolute popular power, but rather popular power in accordance with *Shari'a*.[47]

Very often, Arab secularists who see themselves as supporters of democracy do not realize the need for placing constitutional restrictions on the power of the legislative assembly. They fail to distinguish between *democracy*, pure and simple (which can degenerate into populism or anarchy), and *constitutional democracy*, which (presumably) has inherent protections against such deformations. To them the qualifications which Ghannouchi and Turabi would impose on the power of the legislative branch are a violation of democracy and they cite these as evidence of the spuriousness of the Islamic claim to democracy.

We shall not discuss here the various concepts of democracy in relation to secularism (more about this issue will be found in the final section of this chapter). We will focus instead on the significance of the restrictions which Islamic democrats intend to place on the power of the legislative branch of government.

It is fairly obvious that an agency is needed in order to review the laws that the Parliament can propose and approve. The most natural way to conceptualize this function is in terms of a third branch of government, a *judicial branch*, including a Constitutional Court charged with the task of reviewing legislation. It is here that critics begin to see threats to the very concept of democracy. It is also here that Islamic constitutionalism has to step carefully, if it is to succeed in avoiding this charge.

It is instructive to look at the way these matters are dealt with in the constitution of the Islamic Republic of Iran.[48] This constitution probably represents the first attempt that has ever been made to write a detailed constitution from an Islamic point of view. Here are some of the relevant articles:

All civil, penal, financial, administrative, cultural, military, political laws and regulations, as well as other laws or regulations, should be based on Islamic principles. This principle will in general prevail over all of the principles of the constitution, and other laws and regulations as well. Any judgment in regard to this will be made by the clerical members of the Council of Guardians (Article 4).

The Islamic Consultative Assembly cannot enact laws contrary to the *usul* (fundamentals) and *ahkam* (judgments) of the official religion of the country or to the Constitution. It is the duty of the Guardian Council to determine whether a violation has occurred in accordance with Article 96 (Article 72).

The determination of compatibility of the legislation passed by the Islamic Consultative Assembly with the laws of Islam rests with the majority vote of the *fuqaha'* of the Guardian Council; and the determination of its compatibility with the Constitution rests with the majority of all the members of the Guardian Council (Article 96).

The Guardian Council is not a popularly elected body. The clerical members, who are six in number, are appointed by the religious leader, while the remaining six are nominated by head of the Judicial Power, who is appointed by the religious leader. This moves Mayer to say: "In consequence, not even constitutional rights guarantees can have force, should the clerics ... decide that those guarantees are not based on Islamic principles".[49]

At this stage Islamic constitutionalists face problems which, in all fairness, are not radically different from the ones being discussed by contemporary Western thinkers. For if Islamic thinkers were to make the Constitutional Court – or the "guardian council", or any agency that is entrusted with the task of deciding on constitutional matters – completely subject to the will of the legislative branch, this would tilt the balance of power towards the legislative, with the risk of oppressive, unenlightened, or wayward majority rule. On the other hand, if the "guardian council" is made completely independent of the popular will, this risks robbing democracy, which is "government by the people", of its very meaning.

There are no easy, obvious, or perfect solutions to these problems, which are discussed at length by Mawdudi in *Tadwin al-Dustoor al-Islami*. It is worth following his train of thought on this matter, because it is representative of the ideals which move many Islamic thinkers. He begins by reflecting on the Islamic "golden age", i.e. the period of the "the rightly-guided caliphs" (*al-khulafa'u al-rashidun*). In those times the caliph could be the head of three different offices: the caliphate, the judges, and *ahl al-hal wa al-'aqd*. Mawdudi seems to think of these as Islamic prototypes of the modern branches of government. This positing of a "golden age" rests on the assumption that the men who lived back then were men of a special type: the caliphs were "rightly-guided" (by God, of course), and "those who bind and lose" were no ordinary politicians insofar they were wise, truthful, trustworthy, well-qualified, and distinguished by their work for Islam.

Mawdudi finds no precedent, during the period of the rightly-guided caliphs, of the judges overruling judgments made by *ahl al-hal wa al-'aqd*. The reason for this, according to Mawdudi, is that members of the latter group (headed by the caliph) were men of great insight. They were simply incapable of producing legislation that contravened the Qur'an or Prophetic practice.[50] During this period, also, the advice of *ahl al-hal wa al-'aqd* to the caliph was not always binding. The first caliph waged war against the apostates (*al-murtaddin*) despite advice to the contrary. The caliph was perceptive enough, and his companions had faith in his good judgment, so that all things went well.[51]

Mawdudi recognizes that the golden age of Islamic "civic virtue" is forever gone, and that different times require different methods. However, this remains clearly his ideal. Short of attaining it, he suggests to resort to plebiscites in cases of irresolvable conflict between the legislative and the executive branches of government.[52] "Public opinion", led and articulated by *ahl al-hal wa al-'aqd*, carries considerable weight for Mawdudi. *Ahl al-hal wa al-'aqd*, who play a vital role in the public affairs of the polity, are distinguished primarily by their standing with the people in the community. They are held in esteem not as a consequence of their wealth or inherited position, but on account of their courage, wisdom, dedication to Islam, and public service to the community.

Mawdudi's position offers valuable insight into the basic concerns that Islamic constitutionalism tries to address. On the one hand, Islamic constitutionalism is concerned that neither the executive, nor the legislative branch of government act in ways that contravene *Shari'a*. Yet there is a reluctance to place all authority in the hands of one person, or agency, as the willingness to "devolve" decisive power to the community (led by *ahl al-hal wa al-'aqd*, who possess Islamic "civic virtue") clearly shows.

CONCLUDING REMARKS: NO PLACE FOR SECULARISM

The objective of these final remarks is to tie some loose ends, and deal with some unanswered questions. Constitutionalism, democracy, and the separation of powers are closely connected, both conceptually and in practice. In the West they have arisen in the context of secularism, which (as some have argued) is a condition presupposed by all three. Since most Islamic thinkers firmly reject secularism, the question often arises of how one can speak of Islam, constitutionalism, and democracy in the same breath.

How can an Islamic regime be democratic, if it is not secular? Democracy requires giving citizens equal political rights, but to think of the possibility of a head of an Islamic state to be Christian, Jewish, or atheist strains credulity. Islam is therefore incompatible with democracy. Constitutionalism, on the other hand, requires democracy, for it is hard to think how individual rights could be protected, and government kept in check, if the political regime is not democratic. Thus, if constitutionalism presupposes democracy and democracy presupposes secularism, constitutionalism, too, presupposes secularism. Yet Islam rejects secularism. It follows that Islam is incompatible with both democracy and constitutionalism.

Obviously, secularism lies at the heart of the problem here. Unless a way is found to put secularism aside as being only contingently related to democracy and constitutionalism, there may be no way to combine Islam with either of these forms. Let us look at how some contemporary Islamic democrats propose to deal with these problems.

Simply stated, the basic logical move which some contemporary Islamic democrats propose is to view democracy as a "doctrine of procedure", a mere method for dispensing, sharing, and managing political power. This outlook has been classically expressed by Joseph Schumpeter in these words:

> Democracy is a political *method*, that is to say, a certain type of institutional arrangement for arriving at political – legislative and administrative – decisions, and hence incapable of being an end in itself, irrespective of what decisions it will produce under given historical conditions.[53]

According to Schumpeter's definition, democracy is neutral between ends and values which may prevail in a given society. According to Ghannouchi, who also takes democracy to be a "doctrine of procedure":

> It is possible for the mechanisms of democracy ... to operate in different cultural milieus. ... Secularism, nationalism, ... and the deification of man ... are not inevitable consequences of democracy, inasmuch as this latter resolves itself into popular sovereignty, equality between citizens, ... and recognition of the majority's right to rule. There is nothing in these procedures which necessarily conflicts with Islamic values.[54]

The conceptually innovative move of Ghannouchi and others, such as Khatami,[55] lies in their claim that democracy *as such* is only contingently related to the abhorred doctrine of secularism. Democracy means popular sovereignty, political equality, representative government, and majority rule. None of these things spell secularism. Hence there is no call (from an Islamic point of view) for rejecting democracy.

Ghannouchi welcomes free elections, believing that an Islamic society will want to live in an Islamic way. His has an equally welcoming attitude toward political pluralism, party competition, parliamentary debates, and other aspects of democratic practice. This is because he imagines that all the competition, opposition and debate will take place within limits set by a *national consensus on an Islamic constitution*. If and when this consensus comes into being, some groups of people may well stand outside it, unable to agree on the basic assumptions and values which are to govern the social structure. Ghannouchi does not call for suppressing these groups. His wager is that "civil society will see to it that such groups will remain marginal, [so] there will be no need to resort to state power [in order to 'contain' them]".[56]

That pluralism and opposition (so characteristic of democratic practice, as it is customarily understood) take place within the framework of a basic constitutional consensus is not an original insight on the part of Islamic writers examining the presuppositions of democracy. Many Western political writers recognize this. According to Esposito and Voll:

> In standard modern Western political thought, acceptable opposition in a democratic system is closely tied to the concept of a constitutional government, in which there is an underlying, fundamental consensus on the 'rules of the game' of politics. Opposition is the legitimate disagreement with particular policies of specific leaders within the mutually accepted framework of the principles of an underlying constitution that is either written or based on long-established practice.[57]

Islamic thinkers could heartily agree with this. In their case, however, the constitution derives from the basic principles of the faith. This is all too evident in the case of Turabi, who clearly understands the logic of "government and loyal opposition", as practised in Western democracy:

> Such a consensus on the foundations, ... in whose light specific policies may be debated, is a condition for the stability of all democratic systems. This is how Western democracies have achieved their stability: the people, through a process of cultural and political development, have eventually reached a consensus on the foundations, and have succeeded in isolating the matters which are subject to consultation and parliamentary debate. [Thus] when we look at partisan debates in Western democratic countries we find that the debates take place within an established [constitutional] framework. For example, the difference between Labour and the Conservatives in Britain is very limited, and so is the difference between the Republican and Democratic Parties in America.[58]

This is, therefore, the Islamic "take" on democracy. Islamic democrats propose to free democracy from secularism, to adopt the former, and leave the other one behind. This proposal also goes a long way toward solving (or alleviating) the perceived conflict between Islam and constitutionalism.

Standing on Islamic ground, an Islamic democrat may follow the path taken by An-Na'im, which is to accept all international legal instruments that have to do with human rights. Such an Islamic democrat can expect much criticism from many Islamic quarters, to the effect that conformity to all international human rights legislation is bound to dilute Islam beyond recognition, and that acceptance of these bills is just a polite way of rejecting Islam altogether.

It is also possible for Islamic democrats to insist on a more specific conception of rights, while rejecting secularism on the strength of independent philosophical arguments. Many philosophers have argued, and continue to argue, that the universality of human rights is a fiction. According to Rorty, for example, there are no universal "foundations" for human rights – not An-Na'im's rule of reciprocity, not Kant's categorical imperative, nor Plato's rationality. It is all a matter of social facts: "nothing relevant to moral choice separates human beings from animals, except historically contingent facts of the world, cultural facts".[59] This view of morality is shared by Michael Walzer, who claims that:

> We cannot say what is due to this person or that one until we know how these people relate to one another through the things they make and distribute. ... A given society is just if its substantive life is lived in a certain way – that is, in a way faithful to the shared understandings of the members. ... Every substantive account of distributive justice is a local account.[60]

As far as some Islamic thinkers are concerned, secularism (and other modern values such as rationalism, utilitarianism, belief in science) is a philosophy, one among many others. It is a philosophy which says that religion is not the right way to employ in the ordering of society. Islam is another type of philosophy. Each has its view of human life, rights, and obligations.

If rights and duties are (to some degree, at least) socially and culturally specific, if we are not in possession of universally acceptable arguments for all the rights and protections which human beings are entitled to, then it stands to reason to think that constitutionalism is (or can be) realized differently in different societies, each according to its conception of rights and obligations. This should leave room for a certain brand of constitutionalism – call it "Islamic constitutionalism" – which in some ways differs from, and in other ways resembles constitutionalism in its Western form.

NOTES

1. In Gallie's sense, a term is "essentially contested" when there are disputes about the *use* of the term – disputes "which, although not resolvable by arguments of any kind, are nevertheless sustained by perfectly respectable arguments and evidence" (W.B. Gallie, *Philosophy and the Historical Understanding*, London: Chatto & Windus, 1964, p. 14).
2. J. Elster, "Introduction", in J. Elster and R. Slagstad (eds), *Constitutionalism and Democracy: Studies in Rationality and Social Change*, Cambridge: Cambridge University Press, 1988, p. 2.

3. D. Castiglione, "The political theory of the constitution", in R. Bellamy and D. Castiglione (eds), *Constitutionalism in Transformation*, London: Blackwell, 1996, p. 5.
4. C. Sunstein, "Constitutions and democracies: an epilogue", in J. Elster and R. Slagstad (eds), op. cit., p. 327.
5. J. Elster, op. cit., p. 3.
6. J.E. Lane, *Constitutions and Political Theory*, Manchester: Manchester University Press, 1996, p. 25.
7. Ibid.
8. B. Lewis, "Islam and liberal democracy", *Atlantic Monthly*, 27 (1993), pp. 89–98, quoted in S.M. Lipset, "The social requisites of democracy revisited", *American Sociological Review*, 59 (1994), p. 6., italics added.
9. R. Ghannouchi, *Muqarabat fi al-'Ilmaniyya wa al-Mujatama' al-Madani* (*Conceptions of Secularity and Civil Society*), London: al-Markaz al-Magharibi lil-buhuth wa al-tarjamah, 1999, p. 155, italics added.
10. A. Bisharah, "Madkhal li-Mu'alajat al-Demoqratiyya wa-Anmat at-Tadayyun" ("Democracy and Religious Forms"), in B. Ghalyun *et al.* (eds), *Hawla al-Khiyar al-Demoqrati* (*The Democratic Alternative*), Ramallah: Muwatin, 1993, p. 83.
11. T. al-Bishri, *Al-Wad'u al-Qanuni baina al-Shari'a al-Islamiyya wa al-Qanun al-Wad'i* (*The legal situation with regard to Islamic Shari'a and positive law*), Cairo: Dar al-Shuruq, 1996, p. 121. Cf. Nazih Ayubi's remark that "[the Islamists] are thus after a kind of 'nomocracy', not the reign of any group in particular (democracy, aristocracy or, for that matter, theocracy)" (N. Ayubi, *Political Islam: Religion and Politics in the Arab World*, London: Routledge, 1991, p. 218).
12. A. Pegis (ed.), *The Basic Works of St. Thomas Aquinas*, New York: Random House, 1944, vol. 2, pp. 748–57.
13. Mawdudi, *Al-Qanun al-Islami wa Turuq Tanfithih* (*The Islamic Law and the Methods of its Application*), Beirut: Mu'assat al-Risalah, 1975, p. 18.
14. Ibid., p. 24.
15. H. Turabi, *Qadaya al-Hurriyyah wa al-Wihdah wa al-Shura wa al-Dimoqratiyyah* (*Problems of Liberty, Unity, Consultation and Democracy*), Jedda: al-Dar al-Su'udiyyah lil-Nashr, 1987, p. 25.
16. Mawdudi, *Tadwin al-Dustoor al-Islami* ("The Codification of the Islamic Constitution"), Beirut: Mu'assat al-Risalah, 1975, p. 11.
17. Cf. R.M. Frank, "Moral obligation in classical Muslim theology", *Religious Ethics*, 11 (1983), pp. 204–23.
18. H. Ritter, "Studien zur Geschichte der Islamischen Frömmigkeit", *Der Islam*, 21 (1935).
19. Ash'ari, *Kitab al-Luma' fi al-Raddi 'ala Ahl al-Zaigh wa al-Bida'* (*The Theology of al-Ash'ari*), Cairo: Matba'at Misr, 1955, p. 117.
20. Ghazali, *Ihyz' 'Ulum al-Din* (*Reviving the Sciences of Religion*), Beirut: Dar al-fikr, 1975, p. 3.
21. For a discussion of the meaning and role of positive law in relation to natural law see S. Cotta, "Positive law and natural law", *Review of Metaphysics*, 37 (1983), pp. 265–85, According to Cotta, the "positivity" of positive law has to do with the fact that it is "*factually* enacted" (ibid., p. 267). Compare this with what Schacht says about the Islamic law: "It follows from the heteronymous and irrational side of Islamic law that its rules are valid by virtue of their *mere existence* and not by virtue

of their rationality" (J. Schacht, *An Introduction to Islamic Law*, Oxford: Clarendon Press, 1964, p. 203, italics added). I take *factuality* and *mere existence* to be nearly synonymous in the present context.

22. S. Cotta, op. cit., p. 276.
23. G.F. Hourani, "Divine justice and human reason in Mu'tazilite ethical theology", in R. Hovannisian (ed.), *Ethics in Islam*, Malibu (CA): Undena Publications, 1985, p. 81.
24. Schacht prefers to speak of the "irrationality" of Islamic law (see note 21 above.), but I think "non-rationality" will serve the purpose better. That which does not belong to reason need not, therefore, be *opposed* to reason, which is what the term "irrationality" suggests.
25. R.M. Frank, op. cit., p. 205.
26. Abd al-Jabbar, *Al-Mughni*, (ed.) by A.F. al-Ahawani, Cairo: al-Mu'asasa al-Misriyah li-ta'lif wa al-tarjamah, 1962, vol. 6, sect. 1, p. 64. I follow Hourani's translation, in G.F. Hourani, "The rationalist ethics of'Abd al-Jabbar", in S.M. Stern *et al.* (eds), *Islamic Philosophy and the Classical Tradition*, Oxford: Bruno Cassirer, 1972, p. 111.
27. W. Montgomery Watt, "The political attitudes on the Mu'tazilah", *Journal of the Royal Asiatic Society*, (1963), p. 44.
28. Ibid., p. 48.
29. J. Elster, op. cit., p. 6.
30. Ibid., pp. 6, 7.
31. S.E. Finer (ed.), *Five Constitutions: Contrasts and Comparisons*, New York: Penguin Books, 1979, p. 271.
32. Mawdudi, *Al-Khilafah wa al-Mulk* (*Caliphate and Kingship*), Kuwait: Dar al-Qalam, 1987, pp. 27–31.
33. Mawdudi, *Tadwin al-Dustoor al-Islami*, p. 65.
34. Mawdudi, *Al-Qanun al-Islami wa Turuq Tanfithih*, p. 47.
35. A.E. Mayer, *Islam and Human Rights: Tradition and Politics*, Boulder (CO): Westview, 1991, p. 98.
36. A.A. an-Na'im, *Toward an Islamic Reformation: Civil Liberties, Human Rights, and International Law*, Syracuse (NY): Syracuse University Press, 1990, p. 179.
37. Ibid., p. 52.
38. I have used Arberry's translation in A.J. Arberry, *The Koran Interpreted*, London: Oxford University Press, 1964, p. 140.
39. A.A. an-Na'im, op. cit., p. 163. It is not obvious that the principle of reciprocity, or the golden rule, as explained by An-Na'im, is sufficient as a basis for universal morality. It does indeed deliver the correct judgement in the case of the sadist who does not wish to be tortured, or the robber who wishes not to be robbed. But the sadistic-masochist survives the test of reciprocity; so does the robber who self-consistently refuses to condemn robbery, no matter who is affected by it. Yet (presumably) sadism and robbery are unethical.
40. Mawardi, *The Ordinances of Government* (*Al-Ahkam al-sultaniyya wa al-wilayat al-diniyyah*), tr. W.H. Wahba, Reading: Garnet, 1996, p. 9.
41. Ibid., p. 17.
42. B. Lewis, *The Political Language of Islam*, Chicago: The University of Chicago Press, 1988, p. 94.
43. Using different types of argument, secularists and Islamic conservatives often reach the same conclusion, namely that Islam is incompatible with democracy. In their

arguments both parties use the premise that divine sovereignty and popular sovereignty are incompatible. This premise is far from obvious. In fact, it can be argued that it is false. Cf. R. Bahlul, "Democracy without secularism?", in J. Bunzl (ed.), *Islam, Judaism, and the Political Role of Religions in the Middle East*, Florida: University Press of Florida, 2004; Id., "People vs. God: The logic of 'divine sovereignty' in Islamic democratic discourse", *Islam and Muslim-Christian Relations*, 11 (2000), 3, pp. 287–97.

44. Mawdudi, *Al-Qanun al-Islami*, p. 25.
45. Ibid., p. 38.
46. R. Ghannouchi, *al-Hurriyat al-'Ammah fi al-Dawlah al-Islamiyya* (*Public Liberties within the Islamic State*), Beirut: Markaz Dirasat al-Wihdah al-Arabiyyah, 1993, p. 119.
47. H. Turabi, op. cit., pp. 63–4, 67.
48. A. Blaustein and G. Flanz (eds), *Constitutions of the World*, Dobbs Ferry (NY): Oceana, 1986.
49. A.E. Mayer, op. cit., p. 37.
50. Mawdudi, *Tadwin al-Dustoor al-Islami*, p. 35.
51. Ibid., p. 37.
52. Ibid., p. 38.
53. J.A. Schumpeter, *Capitalism, Socialism and Democracy*, London: Allen & Unwin, 1954, p. 242.
54. R. Ghannouchi, *al-Hurriyat al-'Ammah fi al-Dawlah al-Islamiyya*, p. 88.
55. M. Khatami, *Mutala'at fi al-Din wal-Islam wal-'Asr* (*Writings on Religion, Islam and Times*), Beirut: Dar al-Jadid, 1998, p. 103.
56. R. Ghannouchi, *al-Hurriyat al-'Ammah fi al-Dawlah al-Islamiyya*, p. 295.
57. J.L. Esposito and J. Voll, *Islam and Democracy*, Oxford: Oxford University Press, 1996, p. 36.
58. H. Turabi, op. cit., p. 68.
59. R. Rorty, "Human rights, rationality and sentimentality", in id., *Truth and Progress*, Cambridge: Cambridge University Press, 1994, p. 170.
60. M. Walzer, *Spheres of Justice*, Oxford: Blackwell, 1983, pp. 312–14.

CHAPTER 16

THE RULE OF MORALLY CONSTRAINED LAW: THE CASE OF CONTEMPORARY EGYPT

Baudouin Dupret

1 INTRODUCTION

This chapter will deal with the limitations that the current Egyptian judicial context may place on law by invoking morality.

The Western traditional legal-philosophical belief in the social and non-metaphysical nature of norms has allowed for their understanding as positive data. On such groundings, moral norms and legal norms have been distinguished; modern law has been built upon, *inter alia*, such a fundamental principle. Austin, for instance, deems law to be distinct from other norms since the former is a command expressed by a de facto legitimate authority with punishing powers. Such a theory aims at affirming law's predictability and replacing the hold of transcendence. Herbert Hart, the leading figure of "soft positivism", claims that legal rules may, though not necessarily, reflect or respond to moral requirements.[1] He argues against any necessary relationship between law and morality. Hart's conception is strongly criticized by Ronald Dworkin,[2] because it allegedly fails to appreciate that law is much more than a mere system of rules; rather, it is the combination of rules and principles. He believes that there exist general and fundamental judicial maxims, not official rules, which nonetheless guide judges in their decisions. Such principles are not univocal and are open to different interpretations, so that their weight and appropriateness need to be assessed in every individual situation.

Dworkin allows morality to be introduced into the legal system as one of its major components. However, such a perspective is incomplete. In fact, he believes that judges act as if each case had its own correct solution in which principles are framing rules; yet, no suggestion is advanced as to how such principles are constituted, mobilized, and characterized. A more pragmatic approach is thus needed.

The sociological suggestion that individuals assimilate and express norms through their automatic and unconscious conduct does not account for the way people interpret the world and recognize what is familiar and acceptable.[3] Pragmatic theory, instead, assumes that norms,

P. Costa and D. Zolo (eds.), The Rule of Law: History, Theory and Criticism, 543–561.

especially moral norms, are a public phenomenon whose meaning is socially constructed. Their meaning is socially attributed in situ so that their object is granted a typical, uniform, and interchangeable dimension.[4] Hence, the moral order is what is deemed to be true and fair in a given context. Practice creates norms, not vice versa. Moral norms are unquestionable in that they are socially known and foreseeable. They express what people are deemed to know and contain pious allusions to presumed, deep, pre-existing moral commonalties, mirroring the normative version of reality open to public acceptance.[5] This is guaranteed through the interplay of institutional settings and languages such as law.

Law and morality are not totally independent of one another but intricately connected. Law must express what, in non-codified terms, is morally acceptable. In this respect, a number of notions, such as public order or policy, custom, good moral behaviour, the inner nature of things, together with legal standards, and interplay in the judge's performance of his duties. It will be argued in this chapter that Islamic normativity (the *Shari'a*) is an example of such moral notions and standards.

The moral order, being postulated rather than deduced, ascribes a determining role to a given norm which hence cannot be questioned. This essay aims at showing the ways in which Egyptian law is constrained in the name of morality. I will first describe how the new legal and judicial system was established through the codification and transfer of legal technologies, as a result of which the *Shari'a* was fragmented into both positive legal norms and emphatic moral principles. Secondly, I will show how moral principles are invoked in order to restrictively implement law and narrow its open texture. I will show how morality, including the *Shari'a*, becomes a major means to share power and reshape the public sphere. In conclusion, I will argue that although morality has a heteronomous legal nature – in that law finds the means to solve hard cases outside of itself – it is the legal profession which interprets the content of moral principles; in other words, the legal profession ultimately defines and implements morality.

This chapter does not address the relationship between law and morality within the general Islamic world for several reasons. Firstly, the existence of an Islamic world as such is seriously doubted. My approach is anticulturalist: the Egyptian case is neither an exception nor a paradigm of the Islamic way of dealing with the rule of law and with the relationship between law and morality. There is a persistent trend in referring the study of societies in which Islam is present as a religion to a specific area rather than to a number of disciplines. Such an approach merely indicates a given priority in dealing with the issue at hand: if one wishes to avoid the trap of "geographic" specialization, it is imperative to re-establish the priority of science over local particularities, since there is not (neither can there be) a local science. Certain aspects of the present dynamics of Arab-Muslim societies may be described without necessarily resorting to specific references. The universality of cognitive frameworks available to the researcher corresponds to the universality of cognitive frameworks available to its protagonists.[6]

Secondly, since the *Shari'a* is morality, the issue as to the application of the rule of law in Egypt is difficult, not because it is located within an Arab or an Islamic context but rather because the Egyptian context particularly feels the strain between law and morality. It must be underlined that such a strain is not per se specific to Egypt. Egyptian law is, in fact, generally grounded on "modern law" and in particular on the family of civil law, and thus merely reflects some of the latter's specific tensions, among which those resulting from the (denied though real) relationship between law and morality, which is examined also by Western thinkers and sociologists. The Egyptian situation exemplifies the awkward relationship between law and morality, which deeply constrains the application of the rule of law. The Egyptian case is thus worth examining, not because it mirrors an Islamic conception of the rule of law but because it (quasi-pathologically) shows that the rule of law is largely determined by a complex cluster of relations between the legal and the moral dimensions of norms.

Before describing the way morality constrains law in contemporary Egypt, I will briefly illustrate some of the major changes undergone by the country's legal and judicial system over the last two centuries. This will help in setting both the formal separation of law and morality, and the evolution of the *Shari'a* (i.e. Islamic law) within their historical framework.

2 LEGAL TRANSFERS AND THE IMPLOSION OF SHARI'A IN EGYPT

If it is true, as argued, e.g. by Nathan Brown that contemporary Egyptian law cannot be considered a mere instrument of imperialist domination and the role of Egyptian elites must not be overlooked when examining how the legal system was created in order to set up the state and successively liberate it from imperial domination,[7] it is equally true that the current legal system is mainly the product of a transfer. The consequences of such a process need to be evaluated. The main legal changes that have occurred during the last two centuries first need to be described. Then, three questions ought to be raised: why did Egyptian elites turn to French law? To what extent were the legal standards and postulates of imported French law brought into Egyptian law? Did this process transform Islamic law?

The French legal system was imported into Egypt in 1876 (through the setting up of mixed courts with codes of their own) and later in 1883 (through the setting up of national courts with codes of their own). Lord Cromer, the British Resident in Egypt, argued that such codes were not sufficiently Egyptian. These were the result of a long process dating back to the late eighteenth century.[8] Throughout the nineteenth century, the many Ottoman governors, viceroys, and *khedives* strove to give the legal and judicial system a "modern", i.e. mainly Western imprint.[9] In less than a century, the *qadi*'s jurisdiction – which was complemented by the executive's coercive enforcement of the law – was gradually turned "into a much more complex and sophisticated type of justice, administered by a full-fledged judiciary".[10] It was later replaced by a French-modelled court system. In the early days of the process, justice and administration were merged. Since the foundation of the major pillars of administration was at stake, there arose conciliar bodies. Successively, the need for specialization began to be felt, so that bodies specialized in enforcing law were established. Meanwhile, the initially bureaucratic procedure before the new councils was turned into a procedure resembling a trial.[11] There arose many judicial institutions, such as the High Court (*majlis al-ahkam*), and later on, due to the constraints of international trade and Western imperialism, special courts for merchants (*majalis al-tujjar*), adopting French law and resorting to French lawyers. From the late 1870s onward, both mixed courts (*mahakim mukhtalita*) and national courts (*mahakim ahliyya*) operated, together with religious courts (*mahakim shar'iyya*) for matters pertaining to individuals' personal status. However, the latter courts were progressively deprived of their jurisdiction and were encompassed in 1956 within a unified national court system. In line with the French separation between civil and administrative law, the Council of State (*majlis al-dawla*) was set up in 1946. In 1969, the Supreme Court (*al-mahkama al-'ulya*) was established, this being competent for constitutional matters, and was replaced in 1979 by the Supreme Constitutional Court (SCC) (*al-mahkama al-dusturiyya al-'ulya*).

Moreover, during the nineteenth century, Egypt underwent a huge codification process. Decrees and laws had been regulating criminal matters since 1829. Such decrees and laws formed a collection, the so-called

Qanun al-Muntakhabat, whose articles were at times the clumsy translation of the 1810 French Criminal Code. A new Criminal Code (*al-Qanunnameh al-Sultani*) was enacted in 1852, whose first three chapters were largely identical to the 1851 Ottoman Criminal Code.[12] The Criminal Code supported the discretionary power given by the *Shari'a* to the state to punish sinful and undesirable behaviour, which stops short of strict Islamic provisions and procedures (*ta'zir*). In any event, French law massively permeated Ottoman criminal law in the new 1858 Criminal Code; this happened also in Egypt through the enactment of the mixed and national codes of 1876 and 1883. Other codifications followed the lead of criminal legislation. In the Ottoman Empire, five main French-modelled codes were adopted: the Commercial Code of 1850 (amended in 1861), the Code of Maritime Trade of 1863, the Code of Commercial Procedure of 1863, and the Codes of Civil Procedure and of Criminal Procedure of 1879.[13] Quite similarly, the new Egyptian codes of 1876 and 1883, drafted by French and Italian lawyers, largely drew upon French models. In civil matters, the Ottoman empire adopted a Civil Code, the *Mecelle*, between 1869 and 1882, which attempted to combine Islamic law with the Napoleon Code. Egypt, instead, directly imported French codes, despite Qadri Pasha's attempt (in his *Murshid al-Hayran*) to codify a kind of Islamic law similar to the *Mecelle*. It was only through the 1948 Civil Code drafted by the prominent lawyer 'Abd al-Razzaq al-Sanhuri that an attempt was made, similar to that of the *Mecelle*, to establish codified civil law grounded on Islamic legal principles.

Chibli Mallat argues that the reception of the above civil law system was facilitated by two underlying trends:

> firstly, the comparative ease with which nineteenth- and twentieth-century standards could be reached by adopting French-like comprehensive codes, especially when compared with the slow judicial creation of common law. Like Japan under the Meiji, there was the need for clear, simple, and comprehensive codes regulating the most common legal transactions, and Napoleonic Codes offered the adequate solution in this respect. Secondly, the reception of the French system was facilitated by the nineteenth-century codification of Islamic law in important parts of the Middle East under the Ottoman rule.[14]

It was an attempt exactly similar (though its final shape was totally different) to the 1940s Sanhuri attempt. However, the above explanation is not sufficient. Apart from the usefulness of French law in opposing colonialism and in imposing a centralized control on the country, the process was prompted by the asymmetric relationship between Egypt and a colonial power such as France, which demanded the adoption of French law as a unilateral obligation. Moreover, as in Christianity,[15] the whole process was facilitated by the similarity between civil and Islamic law, both in terms of their structure and language.[16] Finally, the process was made possible only through a huge transformation – which Armando Salvatore defines as the "implosion"[17] – of the *Shari'a*, which was confined in legal matters to the role of a mere identity postulate of indigenous law: a legal postulate allowing a group to preserve in law what it considers to be its cultural identity.[18]

Before further examining the last point, we need to evaluate whether the transfer of the French legal system into the Egyptian one affected the system's fundamental postulates and standards. Undoubtedly, contemporary law in Egypt is indeed Egyptian. The question is whether French law has been completely "indigenized", and whether the current legal system corresponds to the former local system disguised as a French one.[19] The answer is that contemporary Egyptian law has a civil-law formal structure. In other words, Egyptian law (legislation and case law) adopts the complex set of postulates and standards operating in any civil law country, among which are: the worship of statute law, the unity of legislation, and the possibility of inferring the legislator's intention from texts and preliminary works; the system's pyramidal structure; the rationality and coherence of the legislature (which "always speaks to say something meaningful"); the clarity of the legal language; the syllogistic application of law to facts; the values of security, stability, and order; the principles of public order or policy; of good moral character; of the good family man (*bon père de famille*), etc.[20]

Going back to Salvatore's so-called implosion of the *Shari'a*, the radical transformation that the *Shari'a* has experienced over the last two centuries ought to be underlined. The *Shari'a* might be properly translated into "Islamic normativeness",[21] and includes both moral and legal norms. According to Salvatore, the dual nature of the *Shari'a* is to be set within the tension between the Egyptian autonomous and differentiated legal system and the completely opposite inspiration of Islamic reform (*islah*).[22] At the end of the nineteenth century, the rise of an Egyptian public sphere was accompanied by further legal codification and by the emergence of a legal and constitutional movement. It is in this context that the paradoxical experience of the *Shari'a* began, in that it was both differentiated from law and judicial institutions and used to legitimate the normative and, in due course, legal system. Hence, the implosion of the *Shari'a* stands for the transformation of its positive, systemic, and institutional efficiency – typical of the period before the modern state – into its supposedly authentic, normative, and civilizing nature.[23]

According to Rudolph Peters, the adoption of French law led to the marginalization and then almost complete neglect of the *Shari'a*; however, during the second half of the nineteenth century, once the Egyptian state apparatus was better organized, *Shari'a* justice was better set up through clearer legislation, the regulation of the *mufti* function, and the creation of procedures controlling the *qadi*'s decisions.[24] It might nonetheless be argued that the transformation or the rise of the public sphere, entailing the transformation or the rise of the state apparatus, and of ways to legally regulate its relationships with citizens, did not lead to the neglect of the *Shari'a* but rather to its implosion. In other words, the *Shari'a* experienced an internal split that marginalized its positive legal dimension and inflated its metanormative moral dimension.

Bearing in mind both the legal system's many postulates and standards, and the implosion of the *Shari'a*, Egyptian legal and judicial practice ought to be examined in order to appreciate the relationship between law and morality, including the *Shari'a*.

3 THE EMPIRE OF MORALLY CONSTRAINED LAW

Egyptian jurisprudence acknowledges the difference between law and morality. As to the former's definition, it largely follows Austin's command theory. For instance, Hassan Gemei defines law as the set of rules governing individuals' behaviour within society, whose breach leads to punishments imposed by competent authorities.[25] Gemei argues that legal rules are not alone in regulating and stabilizing social relationships, since they are assisted by the rules of courtesy, customs, traditions, morality, and religion. As for moral rules, these are principles and teachings considered by most people to be binding behavioural rules aimed at achieving high ideals.[26] Some traits of such rules are also shared by legal rules: both sets of rules change over time and in different places, they aim at organizing society, they have a binding nature and are connected with punishment. However, they are different in four respects. Firstly, their scope: whereas morality includes personal and social customs, law considers only the external aspect of behaviours arising from human relationships, not the intentions which are unassociated with physical actions;[27] secondly, the kind of punishment applicable: whereas the punishment associated with the breach of moral rules is remorse, social denunciation, and disdain, the punishment for breaching legal rules is the physical deprivation of freedom, imprisonment, hard labour etc., and is imposed by public authorities;[28] thirdly, the purpose: whereas moral rules seek to achieve human perfection, legal rules seek to achieve social stability and order;[29] fourthly, the form: legal rules most often appear in a clear and specific form, whereas moral rules are not so clearly stated, since they relate to internal feelings, which may differ from one person to another.[30]

Turning to religious rules, Gemei underlines that they have much in common with legal rules, though the former's sphere is much broader, and the punishment connected with their breach is imposed in the Other World, i.e. in life after death.[31] Quite obviously, the line Gemei draws between moral and religious rules is very subtle. However, Gemei also adds that the differentiation between legal and religious rules cannot be applied to the Islamic *Shari'a*,[32] since Islam is a comprehensive faith that encompasses also law. Hence, the scope of the *Shari'a* is broader than that of law. According to Gemei, the Islamic *Shari'a* is the source of legislation from which the legal rules must be drawn in Islamic states;[33] moreover, the Islamic *Shari'a* was ordained as divine law to govern Islamic societies, to form Moslems' thinking, and to govern human relations. Revealed by Allah, the *Shari'a* guides society to the highest ideals and seeks to achieve wisdom for which God has created man on earth.[34] Despite his refusal to distinguish between law and the *Shari'a*, Gemei's argument is similar to that made when considering moral and religious rules, although law's scope, nature, punishments, and purposes are different from morality, it nonetheless follows (or should follow) such higher and ideal principles. In other words, although claiming a special status for the *Shari'a*, Gemei – an excellent representative of Egyptian jurisprudence – makes a twofold contention: Islamic rules are today very similar to moral rules. Law, through its specific technical tools, pursues objectives which do not generally run against those of morality and religion.

Moreover, it must be observed that during the last three decades, there has been an increasing trend to call for the application of the *Shari'a*. We need not be concerned with the historical reasons behind such a trend, ranging from the political arena to the judiciary; though we need to examine its meaning in terms of the relationship between law and morality. In other words, we need to assess how the legal profession conceives of the relationship between state law and the *Shari'a*, and how courts ground their decisions by appealing to the *Shari'a*. Such decisions reflect the constraining effect that morality, including religious morality, exerts on legal theory and practice.

Legal practitioners hold different conceptions of Islam and of its role in Egyptian law. In general, they stress the duality of Egyptian legal sources, though they also underline the comprehensive nature of the

Shari'a: "The *Shari'a* is the basis on which statute law rests".[35] To a certain extent, this means that the *Shari'a* transcends law: "There is a huge difference between a legislative document and the *Shari'a*. The *Shari'a* is not a legislative document, but a life program".[36] This might also mean that positive law and the *Shari'a* are not related: "Positive laws do not run against Islam, no more than they are in line with it. ... I believe that Islam cannot and will never be reduced to laws".[37] Thus, in general terms, the only problematic issue is the source, rather than the content, of provisions whose compatibility is indeed widely acknowledged by legal practitioners: "The interpretation of texts and their application should refer to Islam. If this referential framework were found today, ninety percent of our problems would be solved".[38] The idea of a "referential framework" reflects a form of cultural normality, i.e. an authentic tradition deemed by society to be the only legitimate one: "If people feel that it is their law and religion, they will comply with it".[39] Quite obviously, the reference to tradition can be analysed only within the framework of a (re)-construction process. Within this process, actors have expectations as to what they believe to be socially acceptable and desirable. Their self-perception, which narrowly determines their behaviour and the content of their actions, stems from their perceptions and evaluations of the social realm: they attribute a set of idealized norms to society.

In any event, the interaction with the political realm remains crucial in assessing the approach of the legal practitioners who were interviewed. The idea of solidarity without consensus[40] can surely be used in this case. It remains to be seen what causes disagreements as to the implications and content of a framework of reference, i.e. the Islamic legal repertoire, which is the shared reference point of legal practitioners. The only plausible explanation is of a political nature: what is at stake is power and the use of the *Shari'a* in this context. Suffice it to compare the following remarks: "I am personally convinced that this type of legal conflict [between *Shari'a* principles and positive law] entails the state's downfall, which neither the SCC nor any reasonable individual can allow";[41] "If Egyptians were given the opportunity to choose their leaders, they would certainly choose the *Shari'a*";[42] "Some people think that everything is constraining, even some customs. I don't think this trend, called '*salafite*', can serve as a basis for modern society. However, the adoption of the *Shari'a* as a legal referential framework may favor the renewal of rules pertaining to daily transactions";[43] "In Egypt, the *Shari'a* can be readily applied".[44] One of the key elements of the issue may indeed lie here. Advocating the implementation of the *Shari'a* may reflect a wish to turn what is socially accepted and desirable (or supposed to be so) into a set of prescriptive and proscriptive rules. If this happened, a structural inversion would take place: a "cultural order" conveyed and manipulated by the norm would give way to a "legal order" influencing culture and setting its legitimate norms. Such a transitional process would probably strengthen the norm itself. However, such a process is possible only if the initial normative repertoire can be given a regulatory nature. Moreover, such a condition is not sufficient, since it must be accompanied by political circumstances favouring the inclusion of such regulatory features into the normative repertoire.[45]

We shall now consider cases in which morality, including (though not exclusively) religious morality, has played an important role. There are many such cases in present-day Egypt. Some would even consider it a judicial pathology. We shall be focusing on the judiciary and referring to three cases which illustrate the constraining impact of morality on the implementation of law. Each case exemplifies a specific aspect of such a contingent relationship: the procedural constraints and common-sense typifications affecting the legal understanding of facts; the articulation of morality, religion, and politics; the power of the normality argument. Moreover, all such cases demonstrate the political dimension of the combination.

The first case is known as the Maadi girl case. In January 1985, five young men kidnapped under the threat of violence a 17-year-old girl together with her boyfriend, took them in an isolated place, where two of the men raped her. They were then compelled to move to another place. A sixth young man allowed them to stay in the garage he was living in, where they all but the sixth man, raped her. They also robbed the couple of their watches and jewelry. They released the victims in the neighbourhood. The victims brought a charge against their assailants, who were soon arrested and were found whilst still possessing the knife that they had used to threaten the couple and their small booty. The case was extensively dealt with by the media and was followed by a short trial which condemned the five main assailants to the death penalty on the charges of abduction, rape, and robbery, and condemned the sixth man to a 7-year imprisonment for his active involvement in the crime. The Mufti of the Republic confirmed the death penalties and the sentences were executed.

The case is interesting in many respects, in strictly pragmatic terms, it is noteworthy for the construction of morality within judicial settings, and in general terms, for the political effects of non-political cases. Under a pragmatic perspective, the definitions given by the Egyptian

Court of Cassation (*mahkamat al-naqd*) to the victim's sexual physical parts (*mi'yar al-'awra*), whose violation was condemned, are worth recalling: "the offender lays the (female) victim on the ground and breaks her hymen with his finger"; "the offender pinches the woman's bottom"; "the offender grasps the victim's breast"; "the offender pinches the (female) victim's thigh", etc. According to such a criterion, courts do not view the kissing of a girl on the cheek or the kissing of a boy on the neck, or biting rather than kissing, a violation of her/his modesty.[46] Moreover, the approach adopted by the magistrates in dealing with the case ought to be underlined. The procedural approach to the case, i.e. the way in which magistrates formulate rules they refer to, is what distinguishes professional from lay people. In other words, their framing of the case makes its facts relevant in legal terms, i.e. it legally qualifies them and allows for the relevant criminal conviction. Moreover, the way the public prosecutor "tells his tale" is a sort of "hyper-accusation" which anticipates the use thereof by the court.[47] Finally, one can observe the many strategies to assess or to escape the stigmatizing nature of the accusations: the public prosecutor strives to demonstrate the intentional nature of the offenders' crimes, whereas the offenders seek alternative descriptions of the facts which may dissociate them from the potentially damaging implications of the magistrate's wording; alternatively, they seek to underplay their involvement in the facts so as to avoid liability. In this respect, the offenders stress either the collective nature of the crime, or the victim's near-consensual behaviour, or the importance of circumstances. Offenders do not challenge the morality at stake; rather, they argue their compliance with such a morality but seek to provide an alternative picture of their participation in the crime and of its moral implications for their own morality.[48]

Under another perspective, this case, though not apparently political, became political for its consequences. It was extensively and publicly dealt with: paradigmatic conceptions of female modesty, sexuality, sexual control, and the repression of violations were largely unfolded (much more than they were debated). This clearly shows how moral issues are (made) public. Sexual relations are totally emptied of their intimacy and feeling, and are turned into a public legal question revolving around their only legitimate definition, i.e. marriage, and their counter-definition, i.e. rape and non-marital relationships. The public nature of cases connected with morality is thus easily made political, with all public authorities commenting thereon. For instance, in another rape case, that of the "Ataba girl", President Mubarak accepted a bill amending the existing law on rape, with the consequence that the law was actually amended and that the penalty was strengthened. An Islamic yearly publication commenting on the same case explicitly related the decrease of social security to an increasing focus on political security. Endorsing the trend expressed by the Muslim Brotherhood, it also stated that the new law was in contradiction with the Islamic *Shari'a*, since it failed to deal with the question of honour and to inflict punishment for consensual sexual intercourse.[49]

The second case is about female circumcision. In July 1996, the Egyptian Minister of Health enacted Decree 261/1996, whereby female circumcision, whether in hospitals or public and private clinics, was forbidden (except in cases of illness); it also established penalties for non-physicians performing the operation. The Decree was contested before the Cairo Administrative Court by a group of people led by a prominent Islamic figure, Shaykh Yusif al-Badri, it was argued that the Decree was void since it violated Islamic law principles which, according to Article 2 of the Constitution, are "the main source of legislation". In their opinion, female circumcision was a legitimate practice, and governors could not impose restrictions limiting what the *Shari'a* allowed, obliged, or recommended. The Administrative Court accepted the plaintiffs' claim; yet, the Minister of Health appealed to the Supreme Administrative Court, which in turn quashed the previous ruling. Firstly, the Supreme Administrative Court stated that where an administrative decree is challenged before administrative courts, whoever is legally involved in the case is interested in pursuing a legal action. Consequently, whoever believes in Islam and claims that the correct opinion on female circumcision is dictated by his faith has a personal interest in bringing an action. Secondly, and along the lines of the SCC, the Court held that failing a definite provision of the *Shari'a* governing a particular matter, the legislature was entitled to act independently and in line with the particular context of the case. Since there is currently no consensus among Islamic scholars regarding female circumcision, a clear and definite provision cannot be inferred therefrom; hence, the legislature must interpret general Islamic principles in the light of contemporary social conditions. Thirdly, according to the Supreme Administrative Court, any intrusion with personal and physical integrity requires to be legitimated, and this is not the case of female circumcision, except in the very few cases in which it is medically justified.[50]

The case raises important questions as to the relationship between morality and law, and between morality and politics. Female circumcision is the archetype of what, under the Islamic *Shari'a*, pertains to the realm of morality; morality includes what is not compulsory, though allowed (*mubah*) or recommended (*mandub*) by some traditions. However, given the differentiation between law and morality, the issue is not what the *Shari'a* considers good, neutral, or bad, but rather what the state decides so as to extend its control over people. As a matter of fact, legal authorities have started to interfere with issues that were previously outside their scope of intervention, e.g. sexuality and sexual control. In other words, they have started to legislate on intimacy. The Egyptian legislature and judiciary have enacted laws and passed judgments forbidding any kind of violation of physical integrity, except for healing purposes. Thus, the differentiation between law and morality leads to the *Shari'a* being confined to the ambit of morality, so that it is merely one among many other moralities available (although it is, quite probably, the most important). By challenging the Egyptian government's attempt to ban female circumcision, the plaintiffs attempted to reintroduce religion as a set of moral principles upon which law ought to be grounded. No private interest was at stake in this case, but a claim to define what principles are of paramount importance in the definition of law. The Court did acknowledge that law was set within the framework of Islamic principles, though it provided a different understanding of the latter's meaning. However, this does not imply that legislation and religious law have once again merged, but rather that religion is a moral reference point. Through the legal and judicial process, the principles of the *Shari'a* have been given the status of the main moral source of legislation.

The above case also sheds light on the relationship between morality, law, and politics. Contesting before an administrative court a Decree prohibiting female circumcision was a means to raise a public debate on a specific issue, thus presenting and defending a specific conception of society's general order. Female circumcision is raised to the "status" of a cause upon which the general interest is mobilized to the benefit of the public good (at least a certain conception of the public good), beyond the interests of any single individual.[51] The issue of female circumcision allows for the "public staging" of arguments opposing it and becomes a "cause" to promote more general interests. The case, which thus becomes a public legal affair, is used to support claims as to the Islamic nature of the Egyptian state and its institutions, and to the definition of such an Islamic nature. As stated by Claverie, this is a model of "critical demonstration":[52] certain actors – by using the many institutional resources at their disposal – can twist the substantial definition of the referential framework adopted by authorities, whilst still formally remaining within such a framework. In the case of female circumcision, power and the powerful are not at stake; rather, law and the judicial arena are used to enjoy such power whilst remaining within the institutional framework, though also attempting to define the major principles upon which power is built.

The third case relates to the privatization of the Egyptian public sector. It is, by nature, a political case, since it deals directly with the nature of the regime. During a period of economic reforms, the Egyptian government enacted a number of commercial and economic laws, without however changing the constitutional principles that state the country's socialist nature. The Egyptian SCC was thus asked to deal with the tensions between a market economy and a "socialist" Constitution. By its ruling of 1 February 1997, the Court held that Law 203/1991 on the privatization of public enterprises was not contrary to the Constitution. In this case, the plaintiff, a former public sector employee, claimed that the privatization of public enterprises violated the Constitution's economic principles. According to the Court, however, the Constitution does not provide for a specific economic system; hence, constitutional provisions are to be interpreted in the light of their general aim, i.e. development and economic growth, these depending on private investments. The only function of public investment is to pave the way for private investment, a goal, therefore, which is in line with the privatization of public enterprises. On such groundings, the plaintiff's claim was dismissed.[53]

The case clearly deals with moral principles. It raises the following questions: is privatization a good and fair economic policy? To what extent are liberal principles desirable? What is the "benefit" to be attained? The case is expressed in legal terms and might be seen as a test of Dworkin's theory of law as integrity. However, what is most interesting is the way the SCC interprets principles and provisions so as to make moral what would otherwise have appeared unfair. It shows how far interpretation can go so as to twist a normative provision and adapt it to new moral and political purposes. In other words, it stresses the judiciary's (in this case the SCC's) primary role in conferring a legal existence upon moral principles through the interpretation of legal criteria. In this case, it was held that constitutional principles were to be interpreted in the light of their ultimate goal, i.e. the political and economic liberation of the country and of its citizens. It follows that the state must fulfil its duties in terms of the country's defence, security, justice, health, education, and environment, although it is exempted from further duties. Hence, the constitutional notion of socialist development is not strictly defined: the Constitution is a progressive document to be interpreted in an evolutionary way. According to the Court, constitutional texts must not be construed as if they provided a definite and perpetual solution to ever-changing economic issues; the meaning of the Constitution must be in line with the spirit of the time. This is what was once called the normality argument: the statistical and ethical meanings of the norm were conflated so as to give normative weight to the description of allegedly statistical facts. By appealing to the spirit of the time, judges claim the Constitution to be in line with their perception of Egyptian economic and political normality. It is assumed that such principles (such as the new goals society pursues) are widely shared because they are objectively grounded, the complementary role of the private sector, its efficiency and dynamism are presented by the SCC's judges as unquestionable. They belong to the realm of normalcy, in that they are morally desirable and shared, and hence legally binding.

4 CONCLUSIONS

Moral principles affect law considerably and this holds true also in Egypt. The problem is to understand on which grounds such principles operate. Legal positivism firmly establishes law's autonomous nature, i.e. its being determined by human beings. Hence, its original source, be it divine or human, does not matter in practice. However, such a theory is wrong in that it circumscribes law to the legal system's primary (substantial) and secondary (procedural) rules. It fails to consider the important principles that both the legislature and the judiciary refer to and, by so doing, encompass within law's framework. Dworkin's theory is equally questionable. He, in fact, believes that the moral principles judges refer to are embedded, as from the beginning, within a coherent legal system; yet, it might be argued that it is the jurist or legal practitioner who makes such principles legal. Under this perspective, focus must be placed on the legal profession's performance of its activities. Through such activities, general and vague principles are substantiated. In other words, a close look at law in action allows us to understand that the lawyer deals with moral constraints not by acknowledging the different nature of morality but rather by turning some of its principles into legal rules. For instance, in the Maadi case, moral conceptions of sexual physical parts were given a legal definition by the judges of the Court of Cassation. Similarly, in the female circumcision case, although the judges of the Council of State did not deny the legal relevance of the *Shari'a*, they ordered the latter's principles and selected which among these principles could be considered as law. In the privatization case, the SCC's judges turned the liberal conception of development and economic growth into a binding legal rule, thus allowing for the privatization of the public sector. Such a "legalization" of moral principles is best carried out by asserting the latter's "normal" nature; the shift from the norm's alleged statistical dimension to its binding and authoritatively imposed dimension is thus made feasible.

The rule of law is a principle enshrined in the Egyptian constitution. Article 64 provides that "the sovereignty of law (*siyadat al-qanun*) is at the root of the state's power". Indeed, the state's compliance with the rule of law is one of the major claims advanced by the Egyptian political opposition. At the same time, the country's legislature nowadays enacts a huge number of legislative texts, and its courts are swamped with civil and criminal disputes, meaning that Egyptian people are somehow convinced that courts effectively apply Egyptian law. Quite likely, this shows the paradoxical nature of the rule of law: its respect may be deemed to protect individuals against the state's arbitrariness, though it may also be used to build "a stronger, more effective, more centralized and more intrusive state".[54] This is exemplified by the relationship between law and morality. On the one hand, to resort to moral principles allows individuals to challenge the state's authority; on the other hand, however, it also enables the judiciary to construct a legal and officially sanctioned interpretation of such principles.

In other words, morality constrains law, though it is the lawyers who make morality legal. By so doing, the allegedly heteronomous status of morality is turned into a positive and legal one. The rule of law is thus strengthened, given that people and the state must abide by legally and judicially defined rules. However, this is a "rule of lawyers' law"; hence, it raises the issue as to the latter's power to exercise a legislative function without being democratically empowered to do so. This is the so-called and well known problem of government by judges (*gouvernement des juges*). What is more, in the Egyptian political context, the problem is wider, since no institution can truly claim democratic legitimacy. To focus on the judiciary's government dodges the issues of political debate, of its legislative outcome, and of the exercise of power. In the Egyptian context, where politically sensitive issues are monopolized by the executive by creating a dichotomy opposing not law to morality but rather ordinary law to exceptional law, the problem is no longer simply that of the rule of morally constrained law. Rather, the problem is also about the rule of hierarchical law, whereby cases are treated differently according to their political nature. The rule of law is thus turned into the rule of the ruler.

NOTES

1. H.L.A. Hart, *The Concept of Law*, Oxford: Oxford University Press, 1961, p. 224.
2. R. Dworkin, *A Matter of Principle*, Oxford: Oxford University Press, 1985.
3. A. Coulon, *Harold Garfinkel, présentation*, in K.M. Van Meter (ed.) *La Sociologie*, Paris: Larousse, 1994, p. 648.
4. R. Watson, "Ethnomethodology, Consciousness and Self", *Journal of Consciousness Studies*, 5 (1998) 2, p. 215.
5. S.F. Moore, "Introduction: Moralizing States and the Ethnography of the Present", in S.F. Moore (ed.), *Moralizing States and the Ethnography of the Present*, Arlington (VA): American Anthropological Association, 1993, pp. 1–2.
6. B. Dupret and J.N. Ferrié, "For intérieur et ordre public: ou comment la problématique de l'Aufklärung peut permettre de décrire un débat égyptien", in G. Boëtsch, B. Dupret and J.N. Ferrié (eds), *Droits et sociétés dans le monde arabe. Perspectives socio-anthropologiques*, Aix-en-Provence: Presses de l'Université d'Aix-Marseille, 1997; Eng. tr. "The Inner Self and Public Order: About a Recent Egyptian Affair", in A. Salvatore (ed.), *Muslim Traditions and Modern Techniques of Power*, Yearbook of the Sociology of Islam, vol. 3, 2000.
7. N.J. Brown, "Law and Imperialism: Egypt in Comparative Perspective", *Law & Society Review*, 29 (1995), 1, pp. 103–25.
8. J. Goldberg, "Réception du droit français sous les Britanniques en Égypte: un paradoxe?", *Egypte-Monde arabe*, (1998), 34, pp. 67–79.
9. E. Hill, "Al-Sanhuri and Islamic Law", *Cairo Papers in Social Science*, 10 (1987), 1; D. Reid, *Lawyers and Politics in the Arab World*, Minneapolis-Chicago: Bibliotheca Islamica, 1981; F. Ziadeh, *Lawyers, the Rule of Law and Liberalism in Modern Egypt*, Stanford (CA): Hoover Institution, 1968; B. Botiveau, "L'adaptation d'un modèle français d'enseignement du droit au Proche-Orient", in M. Flory and J.R. Henry, *L'enseignement du droit musulman*, Marseille: Ed. du Cnrs, 1989, pp. 229–52.
10. R. Peters, "Administrators and Magistrates: The Development of a Secular Justice in Egypt, 1842–1871", *Die Welt des Islams*, 1999.
11. Ibid.
12. R. Peters, "Sharia and the State: Criminal Law in Nineteenth-Century Egypt", in C. van Dijk and A.H. de Groot (eds), *State and Islam*, Leiden: Cnws, 1995.
13. J. Lafon, "L'Empire ottoman et les codes occidentaux", *Droits*, 26 (1997), pp. 51–69.
14. C. Mallat, "Islamic law, droit positif and codification: reflections on longue durée", in Id., *Plurality of Norms and State Power from 18th to 20th Century*, Vienna: Vienna Workshop, 1997.
15. P. Legendre, *L'amour du censeur. Essai sur l'ordre dogmatique*, Paris: Seuil, 1974.
16. B. Dupret, "'Vent d'est, vent d'ouest': l'Occident du droit égyptien", *Egypte-Monde arabe*, (1997), 30–1, pp. 93–112; B. Dupret, *Au nom de quel droit. Répertoires juridiques et référence religieuse dans la société égyptienne musulmane contemporaine*, Paris: Maison des sciences de l'homme, 2000.
17. A. Salvatore, "La sharî'a moderne en quête de droit: raison transcendante, métanorme publique et système juridique", *Droit et Société*, 39 (1998), pp. 293–316.
18. M. Chiba, "The Identity Postulate of Indigenous Law and its Function in Legal Transplantation", in P. Sack and E. Minchin (eds), *Legal Pluralism. Proceedings of*

the Canberra Law Workshop VII, Canberra: Law Department, Research School of Social Sciences, Australian National University, 1986.

19. B. Botiveau, *Loi islamique et droit dans les sociétés arabes. Mutations des systèmes juridiques du Moyen-Orient*, Paris: Karthala-Iremam, 1993.
20. B. Dupret, "'Vent d'est, vent d'ouest': l'Occident du droit égyptien", passim.
21. B. Johansen, *Contingency in a Sacred Law. Legal and Ethical Norms in the Muslim Fiqh*, Leiden-Boston-Köln: Brill, 1998, p. 39.
22. A. Salvatore, op. cit., passim.
23. Ibid.
24. R. Peters, "Sharia and the State: Criminal Law in Nineteenth-Century Egypt", passim.
25. H. Gemei, *Introduction to Law: Theory of Law, Theory of Right*, Cairo: Cairo University, 1997, p. 6.
26. Ibid., p. 15.
27. Ibid., p. 16.
28. Ibid., p. 17.
29. Ibid.
30. Ibid.
31. Ibid., p. 18.
32. Ibid.
33. Ibid., p. 27.
34. Ibid., p. 28.
35. Interview with MD, lawyer, October 1994.
36. Interview with NH, lawyer, January 1994.
37. Ibid.
38. Interview with AW, lawyer and former magistrate, June 1994.
39. Ibid.
40. D. Kertzer, *Rituals, Politics and Power*, New Haven (CT): Yale University Press, 1988; J.N. Ferrié, "Les paradoxes de la réislamisation en Égypte", *Maghreb Machrek* (1996), 151, pp. 3–5.
41. Interview with NH, lawyer, January 1994.
42. Ibid.
43. Interview with BI, magistrate, November 1993.
44. Interview with MZ, *ulema*, January 1994.
45. B. Dupret, *Au nom de quel droit*, passim; B. Dupret, "A Return to the Shari'a? Egyptian Judges and Referring to Islam", in F. Burgat (ed.), *Islam and Re-islamization*, forthcoming.
46. N. Hasan, Majallat al-qânûn wa l-iqtisâd - huqûq al-insân, (*Law of the protection of decency*), unpublished paper.
47. M. Komter, *Dilemmas in the Courtroom. A Study of Trials of Violent Crime in the Netherlands*, Mahwah (NJ): Lawrence Erlbaum Associates, 1998 p. 168.
48. For lengthy excerpts and comments on the case, see B. Dupret, "La typification des atteinte aux bonnes mœurs: approche praxéologique d'une affaire égyptienne", *International Journal for the Semiotics of Law/Revue Internationale de Sémiotique Juridique*, 11 (1998), 33, pp. 303–22; B. Dupret, "Repères pour une praxéologie de l'activité juridique: le traitement judiciaire de la moralité à partir d'un exemple égyptien", *Egypte-Monde arabe*, 34 (1998), pp. 115–39.

49. Cfr. Markaz al-Dirâsât al-hadâriyya (*The Nation in One Year. An Arab Political and Economic Report*), Cairo, 1993; B. Dupret, "L'Annuaire de l'Umma et la question sécuritaire", *Egypte-Monde arabe*, 17 (1994), pp. 157–84.
50. K. Bälz, "Human Rights, The Rule of Law and the Construction of Tradition: The Egyptian Supreme Administrative Court and Female Circumcision", *Egypte-Monde arabe*, (1998), 34, pp. 141–53; B. Dupret, "Justice and Sexual Morality: Female Circumcision and Sex Change Operations Before Egyptian Courts", *Islamic Law and Society*, forthcoming.
51. E. Claverie, "Procès, Affaire, Cause. Voltaire et l'innovation critique", *Politics*, 26 (1994), p. 82.
52. Ibid., p. 85.
53. K. Bälz, "Marktwirtschaft unter einer sozialistischen Verfassung? Verfassungsrechtliche Aspekte der Privatisierung von Staatsunternehmen in Ägypten" (VerfGH, Urteil 7/16 vom 1.2.1997), *Zeitschrift für ausländisches öffentliches Recht und Völkerrecht*, 58 (1998), 3, pp. 703–11; B. Dupret, "L'interprétation libérale d'une Constitution socialiste: La Haute Cour constitutionnelle égyptienne et la privatisation du secteur public", in D. El-Khawaga and E. Kienle (eds), *Political Structures and Logics of Actions in the Face of Economic Liberalization*, forthcoming.
54. N.J. Brown, op. cit., p. 237.

PART VI

THE RULE OF LAW AND ORIENTAL CULTURES

CHAPTER 17

"ASIAN VALUES" AND THE RULE OF LAW

Alice Ehr-Soon Tay

1 ASIAN VALUES?

The creation of a nation and the search for a country's identity are not experiences peculiar only to modern history. The lessons of such experiences are rarely learnt; the illusions they nurture are often quickly shattered; the dreams they foster give way to new suffering. Some well known satiric verses of Daniel Defoe remind us of the risks run by nation-builders and identity-seekers.[1] The less poetic words of a nineteenth-century quip convey the same idea: a nation is a group of persons united by a common error about their ancestry and a common dislike of their neighbours.

Since the end of the Second World War, several new and independent states have emerged as a result of Asian decolonization. Although originally applicable to Europe, the two observations above might equally well be addressed to Asian states which, over the last decades, have sought a national identity and a cultural uniqueness of their own.

So what is "new" about Asian identity-seeking and the creation of Asian nations after their independence? Different contexts have witnessed their rise and have shaped their development. Such contexts ought to be examined in order both to understand how "Asian values" are a specific trait of contemporary Asian societies and to define their content and their connection with the rule of law.

Before identifying such contexts, it is important to stress that "Asia" and "Asian" do not constitute a single evaluative concept; neither do they delineate a single geographical space, a specific historical spiritual manifestation, a racial community, economic unity, or region; quite similarly, "the West" is not an intelligible concept depicting a cultural, political, economic, and historical unity. "Asia" stretches from Japan through China to Indonesia, the Philippines, the South Asian subcontinent and reaches the Middle East. "Asia" embraces all the major "native" religions of the world, and it also includes a number of "adopted" ones. Quite obviously, it is not culturally, economically, and politically homogeneous; rather, it is complexly and interestingly heterogeneous.

P. Costa and D. Zolo (eds.), The Rule of Law: History, Theory and Criticism, 565–586.

Throughout ancient and modern times, Asian cultures have come in contact, crossed and mixed, economies and politics have changed and adapted, and national boundaries have been drawn and redrawn all over "Asia". As Yash Ghai of the University of Hong Kong has clearly put it:

> All the world's major religions are represented in Asia and are, in one place or another, State religions (or enjoy a comparable status: Christianity in the Philippines, Islam in Malaysia, Hinduism in Nepal, and Buddhism in Sri Lanka and Thailand). Political ideologies, like socialism, democracy or feudalism, animate Asian peoples and governments. Besides religious differences, other factors have produced rich cultural diversities. Cultures, moreover, are not static, so that many accounts dealing with Asian culture are probably true only when referred to specific moments in time. Nor are the economic circumstances of all Asian countries similar. Japan, Singapore and Hong Kong are among the world's most prosperous countries, while there is grinding poverty in Bangladesh, India and the Philippines. The economic and political systems in Asia likewise are remarkably diverse.[2]

Precisely because "Asia" and "Asian" are too broad and loose concepts, the "Asian values" discussed below will be merely illustrative examples depicting specific interests, ways of thinking, and concerns. Most importantly, they will be placed within the broad context of a Chinese culture exemplifying "Confucian values".

2 THE HISTORICAL AND POLITICAL CONTEXTS

Let us now turn to the contexts in which we find "Asian values" and in which the rule of law is applied.

2.1 The historical role of western legal and political institutions in Asia

Most theories of "Asian values" assume that "Western" and "Asian" political institutions and ideologies, cultures and values are separate and not historically related. Such an assumption is not the result of ignorance but rather of the wish to overlook inconvenient evidence.

Between the late nineteenth century and the early twentieth century, all Asian countries had "Western" systems of law and government. These had been either colonially imposed – such as in India and the former East Indies (now Indonesia), the Philippines, contemporary Malaysia, Singapore, Hong Kong, Vietnam, Cambodia, and Laos; or had been voluntarily adopted – Japan, Korea, Formosa/Taiwan, and Nationalist China; or had been adopted by osmosis, as in Thailand, by a number of nineteenth century Thai kings.

Western legal and political cultures were introduced in different ways: the common law and the British parliamentary system were introduced by the British; civil and Roman–Dutch law and administration were introduced by the Dutch, the French, the Portuguese, and the Spanish; and, as late as the second half of the twentieth century, Soviet-socialist systems were brought by Marxism-communism. A variety of cultural *milieux* thus emerged in "Asia", encompassing law and political administration on the one hand, and arts, culture, and educational processes on the other. Although consciously running the risk of being stereotypical or "essentialist", I would argue that the main cultural feature of former British colonies was "pragmatism", whereas "cultural elitism" was typical of former French colonies, "administrative authoritarianism" of Dutch colonies, and "social hierarchy" of Spanish colonies. Such features, in a subtle though decisive manner, marked each society: the values and approach of the British District Officer Lee Kuan Yew, the former Singaporean Prime Minister, could never have been nurtured in French bureaucratic Cambodia; nor could the French-educated and French-espoused King Sihanouk have lived through his long paternalistic reign in Indonesia's feudal militarism; nor could the Nehru-Gandhi dynasty have reigned and survived electoral rejection and electoral return – nor could democracy have been restored in the Philippines – in any non-common law country.

Be that as it may, "Western" political and legal institutions were planted, took root and continued to flourish in all parts of Asia – save for a limited period in China and Vietnam after their "liberation" – thus moulding the new States' institutions. They also limited potential radical changes. Thus, as pointed out by John Hazard, the doyen of Soviet legal scholarship, in the heyday of Soviet ideological expansion in Africa and Latin America, only one of the sovietized states had been a common law country: the trial and error method typical of the common law judicial process had inculcated a profound habit of piecemeal adjustment rather than the urge for a revolutionary overhaul! Among the civil or common law countries that maintained Western institutions after their liberation or independence, two exceptions stand out, i.e. Vietnam and the People's Republic of China, which became and still are communist countries. Yet, under a central and crucial perspective, such countries are exceptions proving the rule: by adopting a (socialist) market economy, both Vietnam and China have returned within the civil law group of countries, enacting civil codes based on East German models and establishing a European-continental criminal process. China's history is indeed more complex: up and until very recent times, the civil law system, which strove to be implanted between the 1920s and 1930s, had no chances of taking roots on the mainland or, after 1949, in Taiwan. Nowadays, through the Open Door Policy and Economic Reform, China has once again adopted the continental European codified legal model whilst retaining various features of its soviet-socialist predecessors, these being themselves grounded on civil law.

This holds true also for Asian political structures. The English parliamentary system, bipartisan or multiparty government, democratic elections, the rule of law, the separation of powers, were all preserved, adopted or adapted by newly independent and industrialized Asian countries, with the addition of a number of constitutional monarchies – Thailand, Cambodia, Malaysia – and two absolute monarchies – Brunei and Bhutan.

Therefore, to treat "democracy" and the rule of law as uncommon or as new concepts in Asian states, having no roots therein would amount to adopting a prejudiced or ignorant approach. Until independence, "local" or "native" aspirants to political leadership were easily eliminated by colonial leaders or found no opportunities to implement their democratic aspirations and exercise their talents in democratic governance: they were relegated to low and middle level public civil posts or, if they were too forceful, they were sent to detention centres under "emergency" or public security regulations. Yet, as minor administrators and low civil servants, they did undergo some apprenticeship in law-abiding colonial administrations, whose value should not be underestimated. The leadership of trade unions in all British colonies was totally native or local, mostly Indian. In schools for native pupils, most teachers were local teachers, especially Indian, trained either locally or in the colonial "motherland" on the basis of imperial syllabuses, and ultimately examined by British, Dutch, or French university authorities. Demands for freedom, equality, democracy, and independence were first advanced within such a *milieu* of trade unionists and teachers, journalists and intellectuals; similarly, most radical political leaders emerged therefrom.

2.2 The rejection or modification of inherited western infrastructures

The starting point for newly independent Asian states seeking a national identity of their own was indeed "Western". The degree of rejection or modification of such a model varied enormously, this hinging in part on the length and nature of the colonial domination, on the circumstances leading to independence and on the background and character of local leadership at the time: the longer the period of colonial domination, the more entrenched the "Western" models; the more difficult the struggle for independence and the more brutal and self-centred the colonial rule, the sharper the rejection of colonial structures; the less impressive the local historical myths and memory, the smoother the way for democratic processes.

For instance, in spite of its highly complex cultural, racial, religious, and social divisions, India, which had experienced some 300 years of British rule and law, retained after its independence all the fundamental principles of the British parliamentary system, which could not be eroded either by a written constitution or by the institution of a presidency. Its democratic character was vindicated when the increasingly autocratic and personal rule by the Prime Minister Indira Gandhi was amazingly halted by popular vote, although it was subsequently reinstated by another popular vote. After all, the essence of democracy is that it is up to the people to decide which government they want. I indeed welcomed the rejection of Ms Gandhi and the Congress Party at a time when Asian authoritarianism was a real risk, and military and martial law regimes proliferated everywhere. In the Philippines, the deposition of Mr Marcos was achieved by a democratic and popular vote, supported by "People's Power"; similarly, it was through a popular vote that the State of Law and Order Revolutionary Council (SLORC)[3] military regime was rejected by the people of Myanmar. Nowadays, India claims, quite rightly, to be the largest democracy in the world. Its first "native" leaders were British-educated at the London School of Economics and Politics as well as at Oxford and Cambridge. Its past and present leaders include lawyers, political scientists, and theorists. Its Supreme Court stands out for its support of liberal democratic rights and for the protection of the deprived and downtrodden, of outcasts and low castes, women and children.

Similar considerations are to be made for Singapore and Malaysia. Having been subject to only half of the 300 years of British Indian rule and having been "awarded", i.e. not had to fight for, their independence, neither state made many amendments to the multiparty and British parliamentary system of the departing British rulers.

It cannot be ignored that, since then, Singapore has experienced some 30 years of a de facto one-party government. Collective representation (Group Representative Constituencies) has only been recently introduced to give voice to "ethnic minorities" and functional/interest groups (Non Constituency Members of Parliament); until such a change, the democratic character of the electoral process was maintained by ensuring that in principle (though unlikely in fact), the People's Action Party – which has occupied almost all parliamentary seats for 30 years, though it has recently lost ground – could be "voted out". All "visible" manifestations of the common law are nowadays respected: for instance, should a political opponent be particularly troublesome, Mr Lee and his ministers do not need to resort to arbitrary arrest or detention under emergency or public security powers; quite simply, instead, they appeal to the laws on defamation or to regulatory rules. It is true that Mr Lee has yet not lost any of the 19 actions for defamation brought so far against troublesome opponents. Yet, although Mr Lee might be accused of having invented a new definition of vexatious litigation, he certainly cannot be accused of having avoided the judicial process. Singapore, just like most common law jurisdictions, has been overtaken by statute law and has thus become a legislative state. Common law has practically ceased to develop – its true and full development would open the government to unpredictability, now deemed thereby to be uncongenial. Legislation itself may distort the true function of the common law and jeopardize the rule of law, though it is nonetheless enacted within a democratic and rule-of-law based framework.[4]

Given its historical importance within the Muslim world and the role of its traditional rulers as religious heads, Malaysia has added a federal structure and a constitutional monarchy to the British parliamentary model; more precisely, it has ten "monarchs" – the nine sultans of its nine states, together with a super-king elected and thereby representing the Federal monarchy – whose functions are analogous to those performed by the Queen of England. The Malaysian monarchy is also characterized by a Conference of Rulers determining all matters pertaining to the Islamic religion, as well as the privileges and immunities of its nine kings (Agongs) and super-king (Yang Di Pertuan Agong). Like Singapore and India, its judiciary is constitutionally independent. Unlike in India, though like in Singapore, the independence of the Malaysian judiciary was attacked by its Prime Minister in the 1980s, and its public standing was reduced; this created outrage in the democratic world. The Anwar Ibrahim trial of 1999 confirmed the subjugation of the judiciary to an oppressive executive. The latter's comprehensive story cannot be recounted here, though it has been largely documented.[5] Suffice it to say that the Malaysian judiciary has been successfully cowed. The 1999 trial and conviction of Anwar Ibrahim, former Deputy Prime Minister, has proved that the administration of justice in Malaysia is far from being fearless and unprejudiced.

After their independence, Vietnam, China, and North Korea opted for communism. Before this occurrence, all three states had been influenced by Chinese culture and civil law juridical systems. These States, including North Korea in a very primitive form, have recently reverted to the civil law system, together with the endorsement of a regulated market economy and the rule of law. However, the former two states have also embarked upon programmes of economic reform (Vietnam) and a multisectorial or socialist market economy (China) that require the creation, reform, or restructuring of the legal system. Throughout such a process, both countries have acknowledged that their modern legal systems are essentially civil law based, although most commercial/financial legislation draws upon Anglo-American and international models.

Burma/Myanmar and Indonesia – for different reasons – were directly or indirectly subject to military control.[6] Many scholarly studies attribute the lengthy period of military rule after Burma's independence to its early Hindu history, this entailing the innate rejection of human equality, the glorification of the warrior cult depicted in Hindu epics, the primacy of strong leaders and the ensuing passivity of rural populations.[7] Similar cultural features have also been related to the brutality of the Pol Pot era.[8]

As regards Indonesia, its apparent democracy was overladen with a form of principled paternalism which replaced the harsh Dutch administrative paternalism, thus introducing a "Guided Democracy" in the new (1959), though now old, order. After electing the government and President, the "Guided Democracy" was supposed to "liberate" the people's spirit in accordance with what was established by their leader. Thus, on 1 June 1945, before national independence was officially declared, the former President Sukarno argued that independence was essential if individuals were to be free:

> If every Indonesian out of the country's 70 million people is to be mentally free before political independence is achieved, we will not gain independence until Doomsday. On the contrary, it is within an independent Indonesia that we will liberate our people and their hearts.

Even after the country's independence, such a call for the people's liberation epitomized the recognition of the latter's sovereignty, their human rights, and obligations. A constitutional order was thus to be established, in which the state would help people achieve their ideals, and governmental power would protect human rights. In other words, the rule of law was to be established! Yet, Indonesia soon became the Asian authoritarian/military state par excellence. Why and how did this happen?[9]

The above provides a scenario of the legal and political structures and values which Asian states drew upon after their independence. In the light of the above, it cannot be argued that such states' recent histories and experiences were unfavourable to democracy and the rule of law. It follows that the reason behind their deviance from the latter is to be found elsewhere.

2.3 *The internationalization and ideologization of fundamental precepts of human dignity and human rights*

The era of Asian nation-building and identity-seeking first began with the establishment of the United Nations and continued through the collapse of communism in Eastern Europe and the Soviet Union. During this period, politics and economics were internationalized and culture was Americanized; moreover, human beings were ideologized as the end, rather than the means, of all social endeavours.

For Asian peoples, just as for Africans, the above processes led to the international support of their demands for sovereignty first, and then for nationhood. Once independence was achieved, it was then necessary to start "living again". There were huge problems in this respect: the need to feed chronically poor and hungry people, population growth, the need to repair devastation brought by the Japanese invasion and occupation, development of their economies (which had been run by colonial rulers and entrepreneurs to their own advantage), the undertaking of responsibilities once managed by colonial rulers, building cohesive societies that merged different migrant communities that did not perceive themselves as part of a single people, but rather as distinct and separate, sharing no common rights and responsibilities. All such problems were to be tackled by the mainly young radicals who had demanded and obtained freedom and independence.

The "right to development" proclaimed by the United Nations initially implied nothing more than the right to receive assistance. The United Nations General Assembly defined development as

> A comprehensive economic, social, cultural and political process that aims at the constant improvement of the wellbeing of the entire population and of all individuals on the basis of their active, free and meaningful participation in development and in the fair distribution of the benefits resulting therefrom (41st Session, November 1986).

It is argued that, for people struggling for bare subsistence, for those engaged in building industries and setting up schools, in feeding and clothing, in providing shelter and in defending hundreds of millions of people, the right to development does not leave room for civil and political rights. In the meanwhile, aid donors – the World Bank, IMF, etc. – demand the protection of human fundamental rights and threaten to withhold their support if countries default on the this protection

The internationalization of human rights ideology, combined with the end of the Cold War, has allowed Western energies to be released and to focus on the Asian world. In this respect, there is wide evidence of arbitrary arrests, prolonged detentions, ill-treatment, brutality, and torture practised on Asians or individuals with other nationalities, for religious, intellectual, or political reasons; there is also wide evidence of censorship and control of the media, manipulation of and constraints upon the judiciary, etc. In other words, increasing evidence proves the unsatisfactory protection of human rights in Asia.

Asian States are required to recognize their citizens' civil and political rights, as well as their social, cultural, and economic rights. According to Western thinking, the universality of human rights means that the latter entail universal standards to be respected by all nations, these being above local laws and not being open to limitations. The inclusion of human rights within customary international law means that no nation can avoid an obligation to protect such rights and that all countries are potentially subject to charges of abuse. The effect of international criticism and outrage, together with the role of the United Nations, cannot be underestimated. In this respect, the story of Cambodia's path to democracy is exemplary[10]

Mohamed Mahathir clearly underlined the connection between the above two factors in 1994:

> Much later the Cold War ended and the Soviet Union collapsed leaving a unipolar world. All pretence at non-interference in the affairs of independent nations was dropped. A new international order was enunciated in which the powerful countries claim a right to impose their system of government, their free market and their concept of human rights on every country.[11]

2.4 *The Asian miracle and Asian leadership*

No Asian state remained unaffected by the Second World War. Indeed, all states suffered extensive damage to their economies and environment. Yet, they all began their reconstruction processes in the following 10–15 years and, within 20 years, they all experienced strong economic growth. Asian nations were swiftly turned from simple agrarian and resource-supplying economies to industrialized or industrializing states, and then to technologically skilled nations. The so-called "Asian miracle" occurred. The "Asian Tigers" or "Dragons" began to emerge. Current living standards in Hong Kong, Singapore, Japan, and Taiwan, are ranked within the top ten of all world economies. Throughout Asia, the percentage of poor people has been halved and even quartered. The twenty-first century has been announced as the Asian and Pacific century.

In East Asia itself, Malay *kampongs* and Chinese market gardens have been replaced by supermarkets and shopping malls; crafts shops and artisan corners, coffee and wine houses, have been given way to residential skyscrapers; intensive labour factories have been transformed into sleek industrial areas and even into high-skill technological centres. McDonalds competes with *satay* and noodle hawkers and stalls. Bangkok streets are congested with business and private cars, international transport trucks, tour coaches, and other visible expressions of globalized economies and prosperity.

Asia has reached the end of the twentieth century as an economic success. Economic success has brought about new ways of life. As foreseen by Mr Lee Kuan Yew in 1995:

> Singapore's life-styles and its political world have been heavily influenced by the West. I believe Western influence amounts to 60 per cent, with Asian values' influence amounting to 40 per cent. In 20 years' time, this ratio will shift, since East Asia will gradually produce its own mass products and coin its own political vocabulary. The influence of the West on our life-styles, foods, fashion, politics and media, will drop to 40 per cent and Asian influence will increase to 60 per cent.[12]

The above forecast is backed by evidence provided by Tommy Koh Tiong Bee, Singapore's well known and well respected diplomat with a 20-year experience of New York and Washington:

> Barring a major catastrophe, the World Bank and International Monetary Fund (IMF) are optimistic about East Asia's future. They have predicted that East Asia' combined GDP should continue to increase by 5–6 per cent per annum, on average, over the next few decades. The growth rate would be even higher, at 7 per cent, if Japan were excluded.
>
> The increase will amount to US$13 trillion (in 1990 prices) over the next two decades (by 2015) or an increase that is roughly twice the current size of North American. Even if North America and Europe were to see sustained growth at moderate rates, East Asia's GDP should be almost as large as the combined GDP of North America and Europe three decades from now (2025).[13]

On the political and ideological front, the Asian claim to equal status has been asserted by new Asian nations by resorting to the tools and weapons learnt from their colonial masters.

Suffice it to recall that, in the 1950s, young Asian men and women streamed to the United Kingdom to attend London School of Economics (LSE) Fabian and Labour lectures on law and politics, to study Locke, Hobbes and Hume, Burke, Marx and Lenin. They learnt whatever they could, absorbed and brought it home with them. They thus returned to their countries being dissatisfied therewith and willing to change their status from subjects to citizens, from low civil servants to popular leaders. In their twenties or thirties, such young and inexperienced people took the reins of government in their hands and promised freedom, equality, and independence. In 20–30 years, they brought about the people's prosperity and security, human pride and dignity in politics, science, and commerce. Quite paradoxically, these are the leaders, now in their sixties and seventies, to whom "the West" currently preaches democracy and human rights and demands their accountability! As Anwar Ibrahim said: "Where were they when we were fighting for our freedom, when we were struggling for our survival?"

This is the historical and political framework of the rise and function of "Asian values". Let us now turn to the latter's claims.

3 THE CRITICISM OF THE NOTION OF "ASIAN VALUES"

The term "Asian values" was first coined by the former Prime Minister (now Senior Minister) of Singapore, Mr Lee Kuan Yew. Over the years, the term has been adopted by the Prime Minister of Malaysia, Dr Mahathir, and by other Asian political leaders, including leaders of Japan and Korea and, most recently, by the Chief Executive of the Hong Kong Special Administrative Region, Mr Tung Chee Wah. As employed by Mr Lee and by Japanese, Korean and Hong Kong leaders, it is often synonymous with "Confucian values".

According to such leaders, the term stands for a system of values, primary among which is economic development, which is to be followed by better living standards; hence, civil and political rights could legitimately be postponed until economic development is achieved; indeed, their denial is necessary to ensure economic progress and its ensuing benefits.Together with the economic justification, the model of a bureaucratic–authoritarian government is also advanced, this being empowered to regulate and deeply control its citizens in the manner deemed appropriate in order to achieve social goals.

Another function performed by arguments on "Asian values" is to prevent scrutiny of human rights practices in China, Singapore, Malaysia, and Vietnam by viewing criticisms as "interferences with the internal affairs" of sovereign states. Advocates of "Asian values" thus reject, on the grounds of cultural relativity, the universality of human rights, that is rights belonging to all human beings as members of the human species.

According to current theories of "Asian values", the latter encompass certain allegedly Confucian virtues: primacy of collective interests of the community over those of the individual to ensure social harmony; respect for the elderly; an interest in order and stability, in the family, nation and community; the value of frugality, parsimony and hard work; self-sacrifice in the name of the family; denial of present gratification for long-term benefits; commitment to education. Tommy Koh Tiong Bee updates such "East Asian values" by adding ten further values: the rejection of "Western" individualism; the importance of a strong family; an emphasis on education; the virtues of saving and frugality; the value of hard work and teamwork; the importance of a social contract between the people and the state; the importance of a morally wholesome environment; and the belief that freedom is not an absolute right.[14]

According to Mr Lee, such "Asian values" have allowed for the Asian miracle. They have brought about Singapore's law and order and have enabled it to avoid Western societies' urban chaos, anarchy, and violence. Such an assumption is grounded on the belief in "Asian democracy", which has legitimated the rigid regulation of social and economic life and which has led to Singapore's soft or bureaucratic authoritarianism.

Critics of Mr Lee's conception of "Asian values" underline the problem connected with their application to Asia through their juxtaposition to "Western" values. The following objections are advanced:

3.1. "Asia" is not a monolithic culture, in that it has enormous cultural and geographical diversities. "Asia" is not a single and cohesive cultural unity, though it might also share universalistic values. "Confucianism" may underpin only some Asian cultures. In cultural matters, there are no plausible Cartesian reference points. It is precisely Asia's cultural diversity that renders Asian states so rich, colourful, interesting, and enduring, so resourceful, resilient, and capable.

3.2. All alleged "Asian values", no matter how "Confucian" they are, can be found in all cultures in varying degrees and at all historical times.

3.3. Confucianism does leave room for the individual. In focusing on the "national economic interest" which the collectivity of "Asian" societies must serve, a number of secondary Confucian doctrines are highlighted, the core of which is individuals' moral growth; this, in turn, leads to the community's moral elevation which paves the way for a benevolent and caring state. Confucius expresses this precept in a number of ways: the citizen, for instance, is said to be more important than the family/community, and the family/community in turn is more important than the ruler.

3.4. It is wrong to assert that Asia has never endorsed human rights or democracy; moreover, it is equally incorrect to assert that Asia does not need the latter. As stated by the President of the Republic of Korea, Mr Kim Dae-Jung, at a time when he was a dissident journalist, any argument advocating respect for cultural differences is extremely offensive when it is used to justify authoritarian governments in Asian states.[15] To claim that Asians do not understand human rights severely offends the many people who have struggled for and achieved democratic reforms, often in extremely difficult and dangerous circumstances.[16] As was said in Mr Kim's *Asia's Destiny*,[17] Asia has a rich heritage of democracy-oriented philosophies and traditions, and has made great strides towards democratization; its conditions are such as to develop democracy even beyond the Western level. Asia should waste no time in firmly establishing democracy and strengthening human rights. The biggest obstacle is not its cultural heritage, but rather the resistance of authoritarian rules and their apologists. Democracy, rather than culture, is necessarily Asia's destiny. Mr Kim is not alone in his belief: Aung San Suu Kyi, in her *Freedom from Fear*[18] argues that there is nothing new in Third World governments seeking to justify and perpetuate their authoritarian rule by denouncing liberal democratic principles as alien. They implicitly claim the right to decide what does or does not conform to indigenous cultural norms.

3.5. The circumstance that democracy and human rights are "based on Western values" does not imply their inappropriateness in shaping Asian constitutional systems. Ideas and concepts do not cease to be universal simply because they are developed in a specific part of the world.[19] H.P. Lee, of Monash University, warns that trumpeting of Asian values has obfuscated the debate over them and that attempts to highlight an East–West dichotomy in the analysis of democracy and human rights miss a vital point, i.e. that certain values are not characterized by Eastern–Western natures or origins but by their universality.[20] Thus, in spite of such differences, a number of universal values on which each democracy must be based can be identified. Whilst there are many models of democracy, there is a clear core of values or a bottom line to be observed in the search for democracy and freedom.[21]

In a recent interview with Mr Chris Patten, the last governor of colonial Hong Kong, Mr Lee retreated slightly by arguing that "Asian values" were no more than a label or catch-phrase. There is no comprehensive system of single values applicable across all Asian countries; rather, there are common principles, such as family responsibilities and kinship. Although such principles may be deemed universal, they have developed in different manners. Confucianism, which is commonly identified with all Asian countries, comprises different lines of thought; although core values, such as the importance of one's family and its associated responsibilities, are indeed "Asian", other values placed under such a philosophy may also be applicable elsewhere.[22]

3.6. If "Asian values" created the Asian miracle, to which values would Mr Lee and his followers attribute the Asian financial crisis? The best argument is that good "Asian values" supported the Asian miracle, whereas bad "Asian values" brought about the Asian crisis. Bad Asian values allegedly include the feudal tradition of exacting dues, rulers' high living standards in the midst of the people's absolute poverty, unquestioning obedience, favouritism and nepotism, the authority's power to grant or withhold favours, rights and privileges, corruption, extortion, extravagant gifts, bribery. In the light of the East's economic decline and of great disparities between rich and poor people, the contention that democracy is necessary for development, in any meaningful sense of the word, is a stronger claim than that of authoritarianism. In any event, as pointed out by Amartya Sen,[23] there is little evidence that authoritarianism and the suppression of political and civil rights are really useful in encouraging economic development.

4 SOME CONNECTED CONCEPTS

I shall now examine some of the concepts connected with "Asian values":

4.1 Confucianism

Those who claim the primacy of collective over individual interests in the name of Confucianism should take into account the omnipresent tension between family and state interests throughout China's history, as well as the real degree of collectivism and pluralism of values which have always existed within "Confucian" societies. The Japanese, Korean, Vietnamese, Taiwanese, and Chinese societies, all descending from Confucian cultures, have all followed different routes in their formation and cultural growth. Advocates of Asian authoritarianism should be reminded of the latter's real and potential capacity to allow the exploitation of its subjects in the interest of a single individual, i.e. the leader, as well as in the alleged interests of a "collectivity" or community. Chinese women know that suicide is their only effective, and socially accepted, means of protesting against their inhuman treatment for failing to satisfy their family – for example by failing to give birth to a heir – or for incurring the wrath of a mother-in-law by gaining her son's love. The fate of Hindu brides failing to deliver the promised dowry and thus being subject to countless brutalities and humiliations is no less cruel.

Confucianism is not so much about the assertion of society's interests through order and discipline as it is about the interconnection of human actions through time and space; hence, individual actions bear consequences for the individual himself and for others. The indirect and not immediate consequences of one's actions fall upon the one's family and descendants. Individuals' awareness of the consequences of their actions leads to specific preconditions for order and to specific demands of personal discipline within social life. It is unquestionable that this is a benefit in itself and has positive consequences. Yet to equate Confucianism with an authoritarianism aimed at keeping at bay disturbing or inconvenient diversities or at promoting uniformity in order to avoid potentially conflicting pluralisms means to undermine such a philosophy. It means distorting its social ethics, which stress the development of human capacities resulting from individual moral choice and commitment. Confucianism does not demand blind faith and unquestioning loyalty; rather, it is concerned about human decisions and their power to affect others, being individuals guided by their family's long-term interests.

Confucianism does allow for authorities to be criticized. Yet, although scholars' duty to ensure governors' proper behaviour through criticism is noble, it is also very dangerous. The irascible scholar Hai Rui was said to have bought his own coffin before proceeding to criticize the emperor. Hence, Confucian contradictions are most revealing: education and public services are highly esteemed, though the government is not to be trusted. Therefore, the family has an unparalleled importance, and the latter's demands and needs take precedence over one's service to the state or even to the emperor.

Why has Confucianism been misunderstood? How have its precepts been overturned? C.O. Khong juxtaposes "high Confucianism's abstract concepts" to "popular Confucianism", this being a "vague amalgam of residual ethical beliefs".[24] High Confucianism, which propounds non-materialist ethics, apparently discourages entrepreneurial activity and new ideas, whereas popular Confucianism, grounded on the realistic need to care for and maintain one's family, encourages such activities.

Khong identifies two Confucian strands. The first "supports the existing social order as a result of its fear of chaos and instability", while the second "stresses the idea that people have fate in their own hands and are able to improve their future".[25] The latter idea cannot be imposed from above but rather must rise from below. Hence, order is preserved by the individual, who cannot but take into account his relations with others (relations between ruler and ruled, father and son, elder brother and younger brother, husband and wife, and friends). Such relationships – which, with one exception, are not hierarchical – do not lead in themselves to authoritarianism. The duties and responsibilities imposed upon each party to the relationship do not create or depend on rights. The superiors' obligation to ensure the welfare of their subordinates can itself lead to democracy, in that the latter may propose and participate in different ways of performing their obligations. What is relevant, however, is the weak role, or even the absence, of procedures regulating access to and control of power. Amartya Sen[26] reminds us that, where there is a conflict between the family and State, Confucius claims the former's priority.[27]

4.2 Rhetoric versus practice

In some respects, Asia is ready to embrace the rhetoric of democracy and its ensuing rights. The Bangkok Declaration is exemplary in this respect. At the same time, however, many Asian countries have constitutions that endorse democratic but are not democratic in their actual practice. It has been argued that Asian governments would conveniently opt for arbitrariness.[28] Yet, the demand for the rule of law and for democracy is a powerful one that, throughout history (including in recent Asian experiences), governments have had to take into account. The claim that the people of South East Asia do not believe it important to have a liberal democratic state or to protect a wide range of rights can be easily refuted by simply recalling repeated and sustained demonstrations of the contrary. Quite similarly, the claim that many Asians believe too many freedoms and not enough individual responsibility will result in ineffective government and social decay is to be rejected. As observed by Aung San Suu Kyi, not all individuals are brave enough to take up the fight; yet, their silence should not be mistaken for acquiescence, and the masses usually follow the minority if this is successful.[29]

4.3 Civil and political rights versus social, economic and cultural rights

The material well-being that rapid technological and economic development has brought and, despite their financial crisis, is still bringing to East Asian countries paves the way for wide individual and communal choices, both cultural and political. To claim that economic prosperity can be obtained only by relinquishing human freedom is ridiculous and outrageous. In an age of technological and scientific advancement, where knowledge is spread and skills are shared, current generations need not be sacrificed for the advancement of future generations and for the future prosperity of East Asia. East Asia does not need – and neither should it be allowed – to experience European socialism and fascism, which subjected many generations to horrendous cruelties and brutalities for the alleged greater good of future generations.[30]

Moreover, violations of human rights do not always take the shape of killing or torturing single beings. In East Timor, Irian Jaya, Burma, Tibet, Xinjiang, Zaire, Rwanda, Kosovo, etc., such violations have taken the shape of the killing and brutalization of entire communities and races, of the destruction of whole cultures and the uprooting of religions. In such cases, when is the single sacrifice made for the protection of the collective culture? For what future order, stability, discipline, and prosperity are individuals being sacrificed? For what purposes, then, are the so-called Asian values being elevated, or rather justified? For what future to come?

4.4 *The erosion of Asia's "uniqueness"*

Asia's "uniqueness" lies, at best, in its undeniable geographical divide from the "West" and in the continental enormity of its regions and subregions, as well as in the wealth of its histories, religions, ideologies, forms of government and politics, cultures, peoples and languages, economies, and lifestyles. The notion of Asia's "uniqueness" is at times used to claim a cohesion and commonality that, in fact, has never existed. Similarly, Asia is not "unique" in its diverse colonial experiences, repressions, and recent instability. As a matter of fact, the latter are also experienced by the United States, the United Kingdom, Africa, Europe, Latin America, and indeed by the whole world. The "uniqueness" of "Asian values" (provided it ever existed), is being fast eroded by technology and science, i.e. precisely by the means of Asia's economic success, by communication and imitation (not just of the West by the East, but also of the East by the West), by social sciences and their conceptualizations and analyses, by an increasing acceptance of the commonality of human races and peoples, by aspirations, beliefs, and sensitivities. Hence, it is now believed that murder is murder everywhere, that pain and suffering are equally felt by all individuals, that hunger and starvation kill in the same way, that a specific race or people may suffer more continuously through its history than other peoples though it cannot claim, either positively or negatively, to be the sole people to have had such an experience. Such a perception has been declared by the 1948 United Nations Universal Declaration of Human Rights, which underlined the universality and indivisibility of human rights. To acknowledge human rights is to declare that there are no subhuman beings.[31]

4.5 *"Asian values" or Asian power structures?*

Mr Wiryono, Indonesia's Ambassador in Australia, revealed an ill-kept secret when asserting that "the debate on the concept of human rights [...] is not so much about the east or the west [...] but [...] about the alternative between the principle of individual liberty and the principle of a strong law and authority", the latter being perceived thereby as necessary to ensure stability.[32] Such an argument is endorsed by Girling[33] who suggests an alternative to the distinction between the East and the West. He argues that, in modern Asia, the role of institutionalized power structures replaces that of values as the foundation of social cohesion. Where there are authoritarian and strong centralized power structures, in the hands of either a single person or of forces such as the military, human rights are given less importance: as Girling has said, values and powers are inversely related.[34] It may be argued that such power structures embody "bad" Asian values – nepotistic capitalism, corruption, secrecy or non-transparency, unaccountability.[35]

Authoritarian regimes are indeed "better" in so far as they achieve their immediate goals much more rapidly and effectively than other regimes; yet, there is little evidence definitely proving that economic development and success are more easily attained by authoritarianism through the suppression of political and civil rights. Nor is there evidence as to the capacity of such regimes to sustain development and maintain their rule in the long term. It may be said that many Singaporeans and other Asians accept some of the above Asian values; yet, it may be wondered whether such values are applied to relations with the state so as to enable the latter to direct citizens in manners suitable to its purposes. The fact that given aspects of Asian or Chinese-based societies allow for their easy manipulation adds further dangers. Francis Fukuyama, by doubting the alleged propensity of Confucian societies to discipline, says: "one is led to suspect that the emphasis on political authoritarianism is less a reflection of those societies' self-discipline – as outsiders are led to believe – than their rather low level of spontaneous citizenry and of the corresponding fear of coming apart in the absence of coercive political authority".[36]

Fukuyama claims that the fact that Confucian societies are based on strong family ties leads to a general mistrust of what is beyond the family ambit, and to a little sense of citizenship or community. There is not a cultural basis for the acceptance of political authority. Given such a weakness, there is therefore a greater need for strong political control. Thus Fukuyama contrasts Chinese societies with so-called group-oriented societies, such as Japan, where group organizations beyond the family ambit and community-wide norms and values are more readily accepted.

4.6 The cultural relativity argument

All claims as to the inapplicability of universal human rights to Asia as a result of its "unique" values endorse the cultural relativist argument. According to the latter, social actions can be understood and evaluated only according to the specific criteria adopted by a given culture seeking to understand and evaluate such actions. Hence, given that there are no identical societies, no criteria of any given society can be successfully transposed or can transcend cultural boundaries.

The (People's Republic) Chinese view of cultural relativism is well known, though still worth recalling. As officially stated by the Deputy Foreign Minister, Mr Liu Huaqiu, on the occasion of the 1993 Vienna World Conference on Human Rights:

> The concept of human rights is a product of historical development. It is closely associated with specific social, political and economic conditions and the specific history, culture and values of a particular country. Different historical development stages have different human rights requirements. Thus, one should not and cannot think the human rights standards and models of certain countries as the only proper ones and demand all other countries to comply with them. For the vast number of developing countries, to respect and protect human rights is first and foremost to ensure the full realisation of the rights to subsistence and development.

The Bangkok Declaration (made on the occasion of the Asian Regional Meeting of the World Conference on Human Rights), did not take a firm stand in this respect: though it accepted universality, it also emphasized cultural circumstances; it acknowledged that "while human rights are universal in nature, they must be considered within the context of a dynamic and evolving process of international norm setting, bearing in mind the significance of national and regional particularities and various historical, cultural and religious backgrounds".[37]

Cultural pluralists and universalists claim that cultural relativism is ethnocentric: human rights transcend time, culture, ideology, and value systems. Human rights are not contingent upon beliefs, time, institutions, cultures; rather, they are inalienable rights belonging to all human beings. The Western emphasis on personal autonomy does not necessarily entail the denial of Asians' personal autonomy. Rather, what varies is the centrality of such a value within each society at any particular moment in time. The respect, courtesy or reverence customarily accorded to the elderly and to leaders similarly varies; differences may be so extensive and bear such consequential effects that one may be forgiven for not clearly appreciating the nature of such values. Yet, such differences do have relevant implications: when compared with other values and ideologies, a given value may acquire given effects not to be found within the same value elsewhere: for instance, the Confucian duty of respect, together with the five relationships and the ensuing ancestral worship, does not allow for corresponding and reciprocal rights.[38] Obligations deriving from relationships must be satisfied independently of whether they are deserved or not by those to whom they are due. The absence of a corresponding or reciprocal right of the ruled, the son, the wife or the younger brother to the duties of the ruler, the father, husband or elder brother is logically and empirically justified by the fact that duties are perceived as owed to community members rather than single human beings. The ultimate claim is that such duties – with or without reciprocal rights – have never been perceived or have never operated as controls upon authorities, be they the family or the state.

4.7 Human rights as a western ideology

Given that the nineteenth-century liberalism that gave birth to the modern ideology of human rights was the result of Western thinking, it has been argued that it mirrors Western values that are not appropriate to the Eastern world: this is indeed the argument of cultural relativism. Yet, the circumstance that human rights are Western outputs does not imply that human rights reflect only Western values. As argued by Ms Margaret Ng, the human rights ideology was an articulation of a universally valid ideal which then became a reality.[39] The Western origin of the ideal of human rights thus does not imply the latter's intrinsic Western character.

4.8 Human rights and economic development

According to most East Asian leaders, the issue at hand is as much about economic priorities as it is about the treatment of subjects, people, and peoples. By placing the family, the community, society, and nation before the individual, "Asian values" give pre-eminence to economic development over civil and political rights. It is believed that economic development will result in better living conditions; the denial or postponement of civil and political rights – freedoms of movement, speech, dissent, association, and so on – will help in maintaining the social order and the political stability necessary for economic progress and its ensuing benefits. Yet, "necessary for what and for whom?".

Let us conclude with a hopeful comment. In 1992, Asia-Pacific Non-Governmental Organizations, in preparation for the World Conference on Human Rights, issued a statement which thus referred to the universality of human rights:

> Universal human rights standards are rooted in many cultures. We affirm the basis of universality of human rights which afford protection to all of humanity, including special groups such as women, children, minorities and indigenous peoples, workers, refugees and displaced persons, the disabled and the elderly. While advocating cultural pluralism, those cultural practices which derogate from universally accepted human rights, including women's rights, must not be tolerated. As human rights are of universal concern and are universal in value, the advocacy of human rights cannot be considered to be an encroachment upon national sovereignty.

NOTES

1. "Thus from a Mixture of all kinds began/That Heterogeneous Thing, an Englishman/ ... This Nauseous Brood directly did contain/The well-extracted Blood of Englishmen" (D. Defoe, *The True-Born Englishman and Other Writings*, London: Penguin, 1997).
2. Y. Ghai, "Asian perspectives on human rights", *Hong Kong Law Journal*, 23 (1993), p. 342. In 1993 Hong Kong was still an independent state.
3. In 1990, the military regime called for a multiparty general election which saw the National League for Democracy (NLD), together with the support of smaller political parties sharing its platform, winning 78% of the popular vote. However, the military regime failed to handover power as promised. It has remained in control ever since.
4. See Tan Yock Lin, "Legal change and commercial law in Singapore", in A. Tay (ed.), *East Asia: Human Rights, Nation-Building, Trade*, Baden-Baden: Nomos, 1999, pp. 27–69.
5. Cf., for example, R.H. Hickling, "The Malaysian Judiciary in crisis", *Public Law*, 20 (1989); F.A. Trindade, "The removal of the Malaysian Judges", *Law Quarterly Review*, 106 (1989), p. 51; H.P. Lee, "A fragile Bastion under siege: the 1988 Convulsion in the Malaysian Judiciary", *Melbourne University Law Review*, 17 (1990), p. 386.
6. In 1998, Soeharto's 32-year-rule ended; his Vice President Habibie came into power, who in turn was defeated by the 1999 general election and replaced by Abdurrahman Wahid.
7. See L. Fernando, "The Burmese road to development and human rights", in A. Tay (ed.), *East Asia: Human Rights, Nation-Building, Trade*, pp. 282–332.
8. L. Fernando, "Khmer Socialism, human rights and the UN intervention", ibid., pp. 441–97.
9. See A.B. Nasution, "Democracy's struggle in Indonesia", in L. Palmier (ed.), *State and Law in Eastern Asia*, Aldershot: Dartmouth Publishing, 1996, pp. 23–69.
10. See L. Fernando, "Khmer socialism, human rights and UN intervention", pp. 441–97.
11. Speech by Dr Mohamed Mahathir at the International Conference on *Rethinking Human Rights*, Kuala Lumpur, 6 December 1994.
12. Speech by the Senior Minister Mr Lee Kuan Yew at Tanjong Pagar and Tiong Bahru Lunar New Year Get-Together, 5 February 1995.
13. T.T.B. Koh, *The United States and East Asia: Conflict and Co-operation*, Singapore: Times Academic Press, 1995, pp. 2–3.
14. Ibid., p. 5.
15. Speech delivered upon receiving an honorary degree from the University of Sydney, reported in "Democracy champion backs our Asia role", *The Australian*, 3 September 1996, p. 2.
16. Department of Foreign Affairs and Trade, *Australia in East Asia and the Asian Pacific: Beyond the Looking Glass*, official statement, 20 March 1995, p. 14.
17. Kim Dae-Jung, "Asia's destiny", *The Weekend Australian*, 31 December 1994.
18. A.S.S. Kyi, *Freedom from Fear and Other Writings*, ed. by M. Aris, London: Penguin, 1995.
19. M. Ng, "Why Asia needs democracy: a view from Hong Kong", in L. Diamond and M.F. Plattner (eds), *Democracy in East Asia*, Baltimore: John Hopkins Press, 1998,

p. 5; A. Sen, "Human rights and Asian values: what Lee Kuan Yew and Li Peng don't understand about Asia", *The New Republic*, 217 (1997), 2–3, p. 33.

20. H.P. Lee, "Constitutional values in turbulent Asia", *Monash University Law Review*, 23 (1997), 2, p. 306.
21. Cf. H. de Jonge, *Democracy and Economic Development in the Asia-Pacific Region*, quoted in H.P. Lee, op. cit., p. 376, note 3.
22. *The Straits Times*, 28 September 1998, p. 2.
23. A. Sen, op. cit., passim.
24. C.O. Khong, *Asian Values: The Debate Revisited*, paper delivered at the 'Asian Values' and Democracy in Asia Conference, 28 March 1997, Hamamatsu, Shizuoka, Japan, p. 4; see http://www.unu.edu/hp /unupress/asian-value.html
25. Ibid., p. 17.
26. A. Sen, op. cit., p. 5.
27. In the imperial Codes of Punishment and Administration officials were expected to relinquish their positions on the death of their parents so as to observe familial ceremonies and duties; even an inconvenienced Emperor could only but express admiration and respect for such filial piety.
28. L. Palmier, "Conclusion: conditions for the rule of law", in L. Palmier (ed.), *State and Law in Eastern Asia*.
29. Chee Soon Juan, *To be Free*, Clayton (Aus.): Monash Asia Institute, 1998, p. 294.
30. See A. Tay, "A policy for human rights in the Asia Pacific", in B. Galligan and C. Sampford (eds), *Rethinking Human Rights*, Sidney (Aus.): The Federation Press, 1997, p. 87.
31. See A. Tay, "Introduction", in A. Tay (ed.), *East Asia: Human Rights, Nation-Building, Trade*, pp. 16–17.
32. See *Doing Human Rights in Asia Background Briefing*, Radio National, 24 July 1997, http://www.abc.net.au/talks/bbing/stories/s10583.html.
33. J. Girling, "Lessons of Cambodia", in J. Girling (ed.), *Human Rights in the Asia-Pacific Region*, Canberra (Aus.): Australian National University Press, 1991, p. 28.
34. Ibid., p. 31.
35. D.E. Sanger, "The darker side of Asian values", *The Straits Times*, 2 December 1997.
36. F. Fukuyama, "Confucianism and democracy", *Journal of Democracy*, 6 (1995), 2, p. 28, cited in T. Inoguchi and E. Newman, *Introduction: Asian Values and Democracy*, paper delivered at the *'Asian Values' and Democracy in Asia* Conference, p. 4.
37. Declaration of the Ministers and Representatives of Asian States, 29 March–2 April 1993, in *Our Voice, Bangkok NGOs Declaration on Human Rights*, Bangkok: Asian Cultural Forum on Development, 1993.
38. Ibid.
39. M. Ng, op. cit., passim.

CHAPTER 18

THE RULE OF LAW AND INDIAN SOCIETY: FROM COLONIALISM TO POST-COLONIALISM

Ananta Kumar Giri

> The Western contemporary legal system mirrors an egalitarian and individualistic society. It centres around individuals and epitomizes the latter's understanding of the social order. The Indian traditional legal system replaces the notion of legality with that of *authority*. The precepts of the *smruti* are "authority" since they are deemed to express the law. ... Yet, they have no binding power in themselves. ... Society is thus organized on its own model.
>
> Robert Lingat[1]

> Whatever might have been the emphasis of traditional Indian culture, both equality and the individual are central concerns in Indian contemporary constitutional and legal systems; it is impossible to understand what is happening in India today without taking into account the Constitution, law, and politics.
>
> André Beteille[2]

> In Indian epics, just like in many pagan countries, it is believed that nobody is entirely perfect, not even gods. Neither is anybody entirely evil; we are all flawed though we also have redeeming capacities. [According to Radhabinod Pal, the only dissenting judge of the International Court judging the Japanese war crimes] justice should not be invoked only for the prolongation of vindictive retaliation.
>
> Ashis Nandy[3]

1 THE *DHARMA* AND THE RULE OF LAW IN CLASSICAL INDIAN TRADITIONS

When compared with modern Western cultures, classical Indian traditions show a very different conception of both rules and law. While the constraining power of legality is central to Western cultures, in Indian classical traditions the moral authority is at the heart of the rule of law.[4] Indian traditional law is not characterized by positive law and legality but rather by moral authority and duty, i.e. by the so-called *dharma*. Not only does the *dharma* encompass eternal rules preserving the world, but it also imposes a number of duties upon individuals. According to classical Indian traditions, the rule of law, implied in the notion of *dharma*, is part of a transcendental arrangement. God, or the Creator, is the ultimate source of law. In this respect, the *dharma* connects the transcendental

P. Costa and D. Zolo (eds.), The Rule of Law: History, Theory and Criticism, 587–614.

realm with the earthly world and with society. The *dharma* purports to create a better world where individuals and societies can attain divine self-realization. As underlined by Robert Lingat, the law expressed by the *sastras* (sacred texts) does not arise from human will. The rules of conduct and the duties which it enunciates are preconditions for the realizations of the social order in line with what intended by the Creator. As argued by Lingat, such rules existed well before they were first formally expressed.[5] In classical India, rules are thought of as having a divine origin, whereas Western traditional law is conceived of as stemming from individuals' conscious deliberation within society. Although law in classical India is of divine origin, custom is concrete and part of reality. Unlike law, custom is a purely human development in the sense that it develops at the level of the human groups involved. Yet, unlike Roman jurisprudence, in the classical Indian tradition, the origin of custom was not solely attributable to human and social deliberation; its origin eludes human memory, which confers upon it an almost sacred character and gives it a force which it neither had nor has in Western civilizations.[6]

In classical India, legal and governmental institutions are subordinated to an ideal spiritual authority. In empirical terms, such a specific understanding of the rule of law does not allow for all individuals' respectful treatment and equality, though, in ideational terms, the subordination of political power to the spiritual authority provides a framework for all individuals' ideal participation.[7] Deviation from such an ideal conceptualization leads to disorder, anarchy or the so-called *arajakata*. In other words, anarchy is caused by people deviating from the *dharma*, i.e. righteous conduct. In this respect, anarchy does not stand for an external power vacuum within society, i.e. the interregnum between the death and the succession of kings, but rather for the specific situation when the weak are oppressed and exploited at the hands of the strong.[8] *Arajakata* indicates the condition when the so-called *matsya nyaya*, or the law of the fish, prevails, in that the strong swallow the weak without either their conscience being affected or without being subject to social punishment. Classical Indian traditions normatively conceive both order and anarchy, particularly in the traditions and practice of the *Vedas* and the *Upanishads*. In his recent and provoking work, *Beyond Ego's Domain: Being and Order in the Vedas*, the pre-eminent Indian political theorist Ramashroy Roy argues that deviation from the *dharma*, causing anarchy or *arajakata*, can be brought about by greed and by the tendency ingrained in every individual to acquire for himself as many worldly goods as possible to the detriment of others.[9]

Under the Vedic perspective, in line with Platonic thinking, the establishment of public order is to go hand in hand with the establishment of order in the individual's self, which, in turn, requires individuals to overcome greed, passion and egotism, and nurture feelings of altruism and interest in the public good. Such a process involves attuning one's soul to the self's divine ground by relinquishing passion. Such a relinquishment is necessary because when passions seize control of the individual's life, his soul is afflicted with disorder.[10] Yet, to go beyond individual passions and refrain from controlling others' lives – which, as the modern theorist Teressa Brennan states, constitutes the core of social evil – cannot be attained by merely participating in the polis.[11] The shortcomings of one's personal character cannot be rectified by the public realm. Individuals need to be conceptualized as citizens not only of the *polis* but rather also of the community of good and of Kant's "kingdom of ends"; this, in turn, requires individuals to abide by the *dharma*, and willingly to accept a life dedicated to the cultivation of the *dharma*. According to Roy, without the discipline of the *dharma*, *matsya nyaya* becomes a harsh reality and public order is endangered.[12] Order is guaranteed by following the *dharma* in both one's private and public life; deviation therefrom leads to lawlessness, anarchy (*arajakata*), and social disorder.

Given that, within a respectable society, order entails an appropriate coordination of individuals' lives and societies, it requires suitable self-preparation. Classical Indian traditions concerned with order and with the rule of law stress both the centrality of appropriate self-preparation and the limits of external legislation in establishing order. Curbing and controlling unruly passions depend not so much on external regulations and sanctions as on generating a psychic force which promotes individual salvation and social concord; this occurs through the development of the sense of sociality that sustains the individual's commitment to the *dharma*. According to classical Indian traditions, the rule of law is addressed to individuals who are unable, by themselves, to develop order in their psyche, and need the constant persuasion of *nomos* and the sanctions of law.

Hence, the rule of law in Indian traditions is centred around the *dharma* or the path of duty or righteous conduct. Yet, the rule of the *dharma* is not merely confined to the psychic realm and to the efforts made to overcome passion and be appropriately and psychically motivated. In fact, the rule of the *dharma* also needs an appropriate social and institutional arrangement. The interaction between the social order – which embodies the principles constituting the rule of the *dharma* – and its members is characterized by "reciprocal responsiveness". On the one hand, it requires the individual consciously and actively to uphold its integrity; on the other hand, it requires the social order to safeguard individual integrity and dignity.[13] The aim of such "reciprocal responsiveness" is to render individual and society compatible not only at an external level, but also at a deeper level. This is emphasized by both Sri Aurobindo and Coomaraswamy, two great contemporary savants of Indian tradition and thinking. According to Sri Aurobindo,

> since the proper relationship between the soul and the Supreme (while it is in the Universe) is neither to assert egoistically its separate being nor to blot itself out in the Indefinable, but rather to realize its unity with the Divine and the world and unite them within the individual, the proper relationship between the individual and the collectivity is neither to pursue egoistically his own material or mental progress or spiritual salvation without regard to his fellows, nor to suppress or maim his proper development for the sake of the community; but rather to sum up in himself all his best and fullest possibilities and spread them out through thought, action and all other means, so that the whole race may come closer to the attainment of its supreme personalities.[14]

According to Coomaraswamy, the individual is thus no longer enslaved by his own desires, and finds an infallible guide and mentor in the *dharma* or Indwelling Spirit. "Self-government" or *swaraj*, which depends upon self-control (*atmasamyama*), is thus central to politics and self-realization.[15]

Within the ambit of self-rule or self-governance, rule, and power are qualitatively different from the rule of law in the public domain. While the latter is only allowed to adopt a controlling, regulative and domineering method, self-rule cannot solely adopt the power model, this being meant as control and domination or as the Nietzchean and Weberian idea of carrying out one's will against the will of others; self-rule, instead, entails a newly transmuted and transfigured understanding of rule and power. In other words, power within self-rule calls for a new relationship with one's self, i.e. a relationship of persuasion and dialogue; such a dialogical self-rule may contribute to the realization of dialogical democracy within the public domain.[16]

In classical Indian traditions, it is believed that the king, as the executive of political power, is subordinate to the priest, the *purohita*, the Brahman. Ananda Coomaraswamy regards this principle as epitomizing the subordination of temporal power to spiritual authority. Such a principle is in contrast with the conventional understanding of classical Indian rulers as oriental despots. Coomaraswamy argues that the kingship envisaged by Indian traditional doctrines is thus as far removed as it can possibly be from our understanding of absolute monarchy or individualism. Even the supposedly Machiavellian *Arthasastra* believes that only a ruler who is subject to rule himself can rule others for a long time.[17] The rulers' need for self-rule is akin to what Plutarch recommends to Western ancient governors in his *To an Uneducated Ruler*: "One will not be able to rule if one is not oneself ruled. Now, who can govern the ruler? Law, of course; this must not, however, be understood as written law, but rather as reason, the *logos*, which is within the ruler's soul and must never abandon him".[18]

It follows that, according to traditional thinking, the core of the rule of law is self-rule. This is nowadays particularly important when dealing with the limits of law as a foundation of individual good life and when tackling the apathy of legal minimalism. However, the central problem of the traditional conception of law and ideal participation – self-formation and a public order following the path of the *dharma* – is that institutions in traditional Indian society were unable to match such an ideal model. *Manusmriti*, or the Laws of Manu, an important source of law in traditional Indian society, supported distinctions of caste and gender: in ancient India, the Brahmans were considered to be the superior class. As such, they had both in law and in fact privileges and prerogatives denied to other sections of Hindu society.[19]

There were two sources of law in classical India: written law, called *smritis* (such as *Manu Smriti*), and custom. The *sastras*, or sacred texts, were sources of written law, whereas customs were unwritten laws. Nonetheless, the *sastra* inevitably incorporated numerous customs since it was itself the result of systematized customs.[20] Furthermore, since the *sastra* was based on usage, especially in its practical (*vyavaharic*) chapters, usage could be referred to so as to explain written law, and the *sastras* offered an umbrella under which various judicial forms could find shelter.[21] The relationship between *sastric* written laws and unwritten customs was complex. There were many instances when customs were in contrast with written laws, and rulers and judges had to accept custom as a ground of valid law. Both the *sastras* and customs were presented as constant and eternal, though in fact they were both open to change. However, both were not codified and were variously construed. In the West, law is nowadays generally though of as fixed law, not liable to be differently interpreted; hence, Zygmunt Bauman regards law as characteristic of modernity and interpretativeness as characteristic of postmodernity.[22] Yet in classical Indian tradition, interpretativeness was indeed at the heart of the rule of law: this is particularly explicable in the light of the Indian sensitivity to contexts, which is in striking contrast with the context-transcendent character of modern law.[23]

Although the *sastras* and customs were sources of law, actual law was that applied by judicial courts. The king was the highest appellate court, though judges were guaranteed a certain degree of autonomy. Indian traditional law, which was modified over time, remained valid for many centuries and its fundamental structures were not affected by the period of Muslim' rule in India. As Lingat points out, the system the invaders imported was fundamentally similar to that of the Hindus. In both cases, law's authority rested not on the will of those who were governed by it but rather on divine revelation: on the one hand on *The Koran* and the *Sunna*, and on the other hand on the *Vedas* and *smriti*. Islamic law was applied only to believers, while Hindus continued to be ruled by the *dharmasastras*. Under both Hindu and Islamic laws, interpretation was equally important and custom held a significant (if not the same) role, even though in principle it could not contradict a revealed text.[24] Quite differently, however, Indian law and society were deeply affected by British colonialism. Though the initial period was a period of reciprocal observation, during which the ruling British refrained from imposing their rules on India, indigenous law was soon replaced by modern law. Such a "colonial encounter" deeply affected the Indian rule of law and society; in fact, the foundations of modern law laid during colonialism still continue to influence and determine the relationship between law and society in contemporary India.

2 THE RULE OF LAW AND THE COLONIAL ENCOUNTER

The onset of the British rule in India was a major watershed in Indian society and history. The East India Company, which had ruled parts of India in the eighteenth century, introduced autonomous judicial and political forms of administration in its territories. As the historical anthropologist Bernard Cohn reports, in the second half of the eighteenth century, the East India Company had to create a state through which it could administer its rapidly expanding territories acquired by conquest or accession. The invention of such a state was without precedent in British constitutional history. As a matter of fact, the British colonies in North America and the Caribbean had, from their inception, a form of governance that was largely an extension of British basic political and legal institutions.[25] In India, instead, the British had to create a separate system of political and juridical administration. At first, the early British rulers were not keen on introducing English rules in India since they preferred not to interfere with the functioning of Indian society. At the same time, the British felt the need to create new instrumental laws which would be in tune with the Indian ethos. In this respect, India was also used as a "testing ground" for experimenting with new models of rule and governance emerging in Great Britain, such as the ones proposed by utilitarians. As Erik Stokes holds in his instructive historical study, *English Utilitarians and India*, the British mind found incomprehensible a society based on unwritten customs and on government by personal discretion; it accepted only one sure method of marking off public from private rights – the introduction of a system of legality under which rights were defined by a body of formal law equally binding upon the state as upon its subjects.[26]

Two important considerations underpinned the introduction of law in India during the early days of colonialism, i.e. the need to create laws on property and to create procedural rules. In the latter respect, there were two prevailing lines of thought: on the one hand, it was believed that the new rules should be based on the existing Indian rules; on the other hand, it was thought that the native rules were too chaotic, so that they needed to be formalized and codified. Hence, on the one hand, Warren Hastings, appointed as the first Governor General of Bengal in 1772, together with scholars of the early British Raj in India – known as Orientalists – respected native Indian traditions and thus wished the new rules to be in tune with the *dharmasastras*; on the other hand, people such as Thomas Macaulay and James Mill were influenced by the prevailing utilitarian ideology and thus advocated formal rules in line with English law.

Following a act of parliament, Warren Hastings was instructed by the Board of Directors to place the governance of Bengal on a stable footing. Hastings had had some experience of Muslim rule in Bengal and did not believe Indian rules to be despotic. Rather, Hastings argued that Indian knowledge and experience, embodied in the varied textual traditions of Hindus and Muslims, were relevant for developing British administrative institutions. He encouraged a group of young servants of the East India Company to study Indian "classical" languages – Sanskrit, Persian, and Arabic – as part of a scholarly and pragmatic project aimed at creating a body of knowledge that could be utilized in the effective control of India. The aim was to help the British define what was Indian, and to create a system of rules that would be congruent with what supposedly were indigenous institutions. Yet, this system of rules was to be run by Englishmen and had to take into account British ideas of justice and proper discipline, form of deference and demeanour marking the relations between rulers and ruled.[27]

Sir William Jones (1746–1794), a classical scholar who had studied Persian and Arabic at Oxford, greatly helped Hastings in the above task. Jones and his colleagues believed that a fixed body of Indian laws was to be found in Hindu and Muslim texts. Just like Hastings, William Jones rejected the idea that India's civic constitution was despotic, and believed that there had been Indian legislators and lawgivers in the past – among whom Manu (the creator of the famous and important *Manusmriti*) was not only the oldest but also the holiest.[28] Following Jones's dedicated work on the *dharmasastras*, his successor H.T. Colebrook published *The Digest of Hindu Law on Contracts and Succession* in Calcutta in 1798. The Digest codified given Hindu laws, which were thus made unalterable, unlike other "flexible" Hindu laws. In the administration of justice, the courts initially turned to scriptures for domestic and social norms, and rested heavily on the interpretation of *pundits* (traditional Hindu scholars) for Hindu law. These interpretations reflected a Brahminical view of society, which regarded Hindu law in terms of immutable religious principles. During the early years of colonialism, this canonical Hindu law expanded its authority across large areas of society that it had not covered before or which, for a very long period, had possessed their own more localized and non-scriptural customs. According to David Washbrook, the rise of Hindu law was one of the many developments that made the nineteenth century a "Brahmin century", in contrast with the twentieth century, which was an "anti-Brahmin century".[29] During early colonialism, the British were enthusiastic "patrons of the *sastras*"[30] and believed that original or ancient texts were the most authentic. However, within such an Orientalist understanding of India and its law, the dynamic interaction between textual law and non-textual custom, which had gradually evolved in pre-British India, was hypostatized.[31]

The search for a formal code of procedural rules followed the introduction of more secure rules on private property. Cornwalis, the Governor General of Bengal who succeeded Hastings, introduced the *zamindari* system, the so-called Permanent Settlement, in 1793. The Permanent Settlement offered landownership to the *zamindars* or landlords in exchange for a fixed yearly payment to the government. Such a fixed fee ensured a regular revenue to colonial rulers. The introduction of private property was perceived as the fundamental means for ordering Indian agrarian society and for the establishment of an ideologically coherent and functionally systematic basis for revenue collection.[32] If the *zamindars* failed to pay the fixed yearly payment, their estate was sold by auction. Yet, Henry Munro, the Governor General of the South-eastern Presidency of Madras, disagreed with such a system, and thus introduced the *ryotwari* system, whereby landownership was conferred upon single tenants or *ryots* rather than on great landlords. This established a direct relationship between the colonial state and farmers; according to

Munro, his system was much more in line with the ethos of traditional Indian society. His criticism of the Permanent Settlement is instructive: "We have, in our anxiety to make everything as English as possible in a country which resembles England in nothing, attempted to create at once throughout extensive provinces a kind of landed property which had never existed in them".[33] Munro grounded the system of land revenues on the traditional criterion adopted by good Indian rulers, whereby the state's share of produce should not exceed one-third.[34] Like William Jones, Munro was keen on native institutions; he thus wanted to restore the jurisdiction of the *panchayats*, i.e. customary tribunals composed of village elders, and to invest the village headman with limited powers in petty civil and criminal cases, thus appointing new grades of Indian "native judges" with greatly extended jurisdiction, and limiting the rights of people from the lower courts.

Under British colonial rule, the rule of law and property law developed together, though the conferral of permanent property rights on great landlords under the Permanent Settlement devastated rather than developed the Indian countryside. Far from defining and protecting existing rights, Cornwalis had thrown the land system into confusion by vesting an almost absolute property right in the great *zamindars* and leaving all subordinate interests undefined. The mass of litigation arising out of the Permanent Settlement was dealt with by a judicial organization that was wholly inadequate, both in its scope and arrangement. Furthermore, the length and cost of the judicial process had become so huge as to be tantamount to a virtual denial of justice and to "destructive anarchy".[35] As the historical anthropologist Nicholas Dirks wrote,

> the permanent settlement provides one of the clearest examples of the British reification of their concept of old regime, within the framework of a new "progressive" system governed by the overarching principles of order and revenue. Boundaries became fixed, relationships became bureaucratically codified. The fixity of the revenue demand was both a metaphor of such changes and the fundamental cornerstone of the new regime. To maintain both the revenue demand and local social order, Kings – and Kingdoms – were subordinated to the institutional structures of the new colonial legal system.[36]

It ought to be recalled that pre-colonial land ownership was very far from the British notion of fixed and permanent ownership. In pre-colonial India, there were different kinds of ownership, including communal ownership; moreover, in the eighteenth century, in parts of India (such as Tamil Nadu), between 50% and 60% of all cultivable land was conveyed under the category of *inam* (tax-exempt) land. Unlike their colonial masters, kings did not rule by administrating land whose chief value was connected with the revenue it produced, but rather by making donations thereof.[37] The British, having a very different view of property rights, did not understand such an arrangement and, when attempting to establish who owned the land, grounded their assumptions on opposition, rather than complementarity; they thought the landowner was to be either the cultivator or the king, and thus created many classificatory problems in this respect.[38]

As regards the rule of law, traditional law was gradually altered during colonialism and, later on, during post-independent India. We ought to recall that, when Sir William Jones and his colleagues produced the Digest of Hindu laws, such codified laws were themselves already different from their pre-colonial conceptualization and elaboration. As argued by Archana Parashar, even though judges applied the rules of Hindu and Islamic laws, they interpreted them according to their own understanding and training. Moreover, procedural and evidential rules were alien to Hindus or Islamic laws and, when applied to the latter, they radically transformed them.[39] The British sought to formalize and systematize law in colonial Indian society. As a matter of fact, in pre-British India, there were innumerable overlapping local jurisdictions and many groups enjoyed different degrees of autonomy in administering law. The relation between the highest and most authoritative levels of the legal system and the "lowest" levels was not that of subordination within a bureaucratic hierarchy. Instead of being systematically imposed on lower courts, "higher" law was filtered downwards (and occasionally even upwards) through different ideas and techniques.[40] The British, instead, formalized the judicial hierarchy and sought to make it centralized and systematic.

Thomas Macaulay, a member of the 1835 Law Commission, played a crucial role in such codification and formalization. Macaulay's most important and lasting contribution to Indian law was the establishment of the Indian Criminal Code. In 1835, Macaulay instructed the Law Commission to create an exhaustive criminal code for the whole Indian Empire; it was not to be a digest of existing laws but rather was to include all desirable reforms.[41] Macaulay refused to ground the new criminal code on the existing Indian criminal law system; in this respect, he provided significant evidence allegedly proving the despotic and chaotic nature of the existing Indian criminal codes. At the time, not only were Hindus and Muslims governed by different civil codes and personal laws but also by different criminal codes. Macaulay indeed realized that the establishment of a uniform civil code would be difficult as it would touch upon the jurisdiction of the Hindu and Islamic religions. Hence, he restricted his efforts to the creation of a uniform criminal code. Yet, in 1835, the Muslim criminal law which the British had inherited and claimed to administer, had been so overlaid by Regulation Law that it was unrecognizable.[42] Not surprisingly, as early as in 1832, the British had discontinued the practice of *fatwa* prescribed by Muslim personal law.

The draft of the 1835 Criminal Code took more than 20 years and was enacted in 1860 as India's general criminal law. In its specific formulation, Macaulay was influenced by British utilitarians (especially by Jeremy Bentham) whose search for firm rules was also driven by authoritarian purposes. James Mill, who was directly involved in the administration of India, argued that India desperately needed a common code, and that this could be achieved only by an "absolute government",[43] and not by popular government. As a matter of fact, it was precisely such an authoritarian conception which led Mills to favour the establishment of a Law Commission with as few constitutive members as possible. In this respect, law-making became an elitist process ad was not meant to be part of what Habermas would later call a public discursive formation of will.[44] More than 150 years after the establishment of the first Law Commission of India, such an elitist law-making process is still the rule: as claimed by Upendra Baxi with respect to the contemporary scene, law-making remains more or less the exclusive prerogative of a small cross-section of elites. This necessarily affects both the quality of the law enacted and its social communication, diffusion, acceptance, and effectiveness.[45]

After the Sepoy Mutiny of 1857 – the first Indian War of Independence, during which Hindus and Muslims fought against the colonial rule of the East India Company – India came under the direct rule of the British Crown in 1858. In 1864, the judicial system was radically reformed, and Hindu and Muslim law officers were removed from various Indian courts. The codification of law and the consolidation of the procedural system was further intensified in the quarter of the century following India's takeover by the British Crown. While the law applied in the courts before 1860 had been extremely varied, by 1882 there was a virtually complete codification of all fields of commercial, criminal, and procedural law, with the sole exception of Hindus and Muslims' personal laws. While Hindu and Muslim laws had previously applied to a variety of matters, they were now circumscribed to personal law matters (family law, inheritance, succession, caste, religious endowments). Moreover, the new codes did not represent a fusion with indigenous law;[46] rather, they radically transformed it. The procedural administration of law was shifted from informal tribunals to governmental courts curtailing and transforming the applicability of indigenous law.[47]

The transformation of the rule of law that such a "colonial encounter" brought about represented, in Henry Maine's words, a differential historical shift "from status to contract". Yet, according to a number of critical students of Indian history and society, the rule of law in the colonial period tightly fixed individual and collective boundaries. This is exemplified by the reification of villages, castes and tribes that took place during British colonialism. Richard Smith, for instance, maintained that

> when new territories were brought under the British rule, the village community as an administrative unit was idealized as a "petty commonwealth" or "a little republic". The "caste", on the other hand, was a different concept, with different potential official uses. Being a source of knowledge of Indian society rather than an administrative unit, its great virtue was that it embraced the whole of India and all sections of Indian society. Although it could not ground the extraction of revenues, it was important for a circumscribed construction of Indian society.[48]

In the reification of castes, which marked the "rule by reports", the individual was deprived of the universality of his social roles within the "village community" and clothed with a specific Indian garment, i.e. the "caste". Thus, although the Government had established a direct link with each individual, the latter's rights depended on his status within society. It might be said that, within the rule of law, the shift from contract to status had come full circle.

The above newly formulated codes and laws were applied in a complex manner. Arjun Appadurai presents an ethnohistorical description of such a complex functioning of the rule of law with respect to the administration of temples.[49] In pre-colonial India, kings alone, not legislators, were the administrators of temples, there being no law of endowment in this respect. When the rule of law was formalized by colonialism, temples began to be administered on the English "charitable trust" model. However, the English model of the trust, whereby endowed property was transferred to (and vested in) a trustee in the interests of the beneficiaries, was clearly not applicable to the Hindu temple, where property was clearly vested in the idol and was only managed on its behalf by the trustee.[50] Quite likely, it was because of such ambiguities that religious endowments were explicitly exempted from the scope of the 1882 Indian Trusts Act. Nevertheless, given the lack of a systematic alternative, the English trust model continued to be applied by way of analogy, thus guiding the judgments of Anglo-Indian courts.[51] In this respect, Appadurai's contribution is significant in that it illustrates the impact of the colonial rule of law on the administration of Indian temples; Appadurai reports that the judicial activity of English courts in Madras between 1878 and 1925 had two far reaching effects on the Sri Partasarati Svami Temple (of Triplicane, Madras): firstly, the notion of a *Tenkalai* community (the community of temple worshippers) was elaborated, refined and codified; at the same time, and paradoxically, various subgroups and individuals within the *Tenkalai* community were encouraged to emphasize the heterogeneity of their interests and to formulate their *special* rights in a mutually antagonistic way, thus rendering authority in the temple even more fragile than it had previously been. The judicial effort to classify, define, and demarcate the concept of the "Tenkalai" community generated more tensions than those it resolved. The "schemes" for the governance of the temple, the judgements and precedents created by the courts provided more opportunities for litigants to reflexively refine their self-conceptions and political aspirations. The legal texts encouraged the multiplication of ideas of the past as well as of models for the future.[52]

It should be noted that, during British colonialism, India was not entirely under the direct rule of the British, in that there were two kinds of "Indian territory", i.e. British India and princely India. The latter, amounting to a third of the Indian subcontinent, was ruled by native princes and was relatively autonomous. In princely states, progressive legislation was at times introduced, especially in the fields of family and personal law. During colonialism, in fact, Hindus and Muslims were governed by their respective personal laws; although such laws were gender-biased and discriminatory towards women, British rulers preferred not to interfere therewith. Rulers of princely states, instead, attempted to redress such discriminatory personal laws. For example, the princely state of Baroda was the first state to introduce legislation on divorce. Similar progressive legislation was enacted in the princely state of Mysore; as specified by the social historian Janaki Nair,

Mysore introduced and took several measures to implement an Infant Marriage Prevention Act as early as in 1894, avoiding the bitter debates over the Age of Consent Act that took place in British India. Moreover, a bill granting rights to women under Hindu Law, which extended property rights, granted maintenance, adoption and related rights, became law with relatively little opposition in 1933, four years before a merely partial bill was passed by the Central Legislature.[53]

In Bernard Cohn's examination of the British attempts to establish a formal rule of law in India in the period between Warren Hasting's attempts in 1772 and the last quarter of the nineteenth century, it is argued that the publication of authoritative decisions in English completely turned "Hindu law" into a form of English case law. Upon examining a book on Hindu law, we are nowadays confronted with a huge number of citations referring to precedents (as in all Anglo-Saxon legal systems), law-making being left to the judiciary's skills and experience. Hence, Warren Hastings and Sir William Jones's early attempt to detect the "ancient Indian constitution" was transformed into what they had fiercely opposed, i.e. English law becoming the law of India.[54]

3 POST-COLONIAL EXPERIMENTS

The legal system set up during the British rule in India was maintained also after India's independence. Within the Constituent Assembly, which discussed the concept and text of a new Indian Constitution for 2 years (1947–1949), no concerted effort was made to create indigenous law based on the *dharmasastras*[55] or to revive local customary law. M.K. Gandhi, the leader of the Indian struggle for freedom, was a great critic of Western lifestyles, including the legal system. Gandhi supported the village, rather than the individual, as the administrator of justice; yet, Gandhians' attempt to form a polity based on village autonomy and self-sufficiency was rejected by the Assembly, which opted for a federal and parliamentary republic with a centralized bureaucratic administration. As noted by Marc Galanter with respect to the creation of constitutional law in post-colonial independent India, the only concession to the Gandhians was a directive principle favouring village *panchayats* as local self-government units. The existing legal system was left unaltered; new powers were granted to the judiciary and its independence was enhanced by elaborate guarantees.[56] Yet, while the village *panchayats* were initially acknowledged as a unit of local administration by the state directive principle, since 1992, in conformity with the 72nd and 73rd Amendments to the Constitution, it has become constitutionally mandatory to hold regular elections of the *panchayats* and to share power with their representatives.

The introduction of the new Indian Constitution was a decisive moment in Indian history. The Indian Constitution provided an alternative to the *dharmasastras* as the foundation of the rule of law. The normative dissonance introduced by the Constitution within traditional Indian society is well described by André Beteille, the pre-eminent sociologist of India; according to Beteille, the traditional Hindu society is a harmonic system where inequality exists and is perceived to be legitimate, whereas the Constitution introduces a diachronic system where inequality exists though it is no longer legitimate.[57] The Constitution guarantees secularism and promises socio-economic equality and dignity to all citizens. Ever since its enactment, the Constitution has been seen as a document potentially bringing greater democracy. The rule of law enshrined in the Indian Constitution not only upholds the legal system's autonomy but also supports law as an instrument for social transformation and for a fair social order. Jawaharlal Nehru, India's first Prime Minister, particularly urged the use of law and the Constitution for socio-economic reforms. Most programmes for socio-economic change were entrusted to the Directive Principle of the State Policy. As argued by Rajeev Dhavan, a careful commentator on these issues, this led to the creation of a positivistic welfare state, which required enormous legal powers to carry out India's social and economic transformation. Law had to be functionally geared towards achieving politically ordained social changes.[58] During the process leading to the Constitution, there was broad social and political consensus as to the idea that the only way India could dispense substantive *socio-economic* justice was through not just planned development but an effective transformation of Indian society;[59] and law was to be an instrument of such a transformation.

The use of the Constitution as a means to ensure socio-economic justice still inspires contemporary debates. Quite recently, the creation of public interest litigation (PIL) allowed India's Supreme Court to revitalize the judiciary as an instrument of governance. PIL entitles concerned claimants – citizens and other voluntary organizations – to raise issues to be immediately addressed before the Supreme Court or the High Courts on behalf of the concerned parties. Sangeeta Ahuja, who has thoroughly examined this development, observes that PIL was first envisaged in the late 1970s as a way of ensuring justice and resolving public important issues, and was addressed to those lacking the knowledge or resources needed to bring an action. Many early PIL cases dealt with prisoners' conditions and instances where fundamental rights were abused. Justice P.N. Bhagwati, a former Chief Justice of India's Supreme Court, who played an important role in instituting the PIL, argues that PIL is brought before the Court not for the purpose of enforcing the right of one single individual against another, as is the case of ordinary litigation; rather, it is intended to promote and vindicate the public interest, this requiring the redress of violations of constitutional and legal rights suffered by a large number of poor or ignorant people, or by individuals in socially or economically backward conditions[60] In the last two decades, the Supreme Court of India has dealt with PIL in diverse contexts, such as the environment and environmental pollution, corruption, and human rights abuses.

It is now worth pondering on the Supreme Court of India, this being the highest institution of the Indian rule of law. Ever since its setting up, the Supreme Court of India has embodied two different approaches, i.e. a conservative and a radical approach. In the founding years of the Constitution, Prime Minister Nehru expressed dissatisfaction with the stances of a number of Supreme Court judges, since they gave more primacy to property rights than to equality in judicially interpreting the Constitution. Nehru, in fact, was keen on abolishing *zamindari* or landlordships, and the Supreme Court's preeminence given to property created notable stumbling blocks in this respect. Nowadays, the Supreme Court still embodies the above-mentioned orientations. In some cases, the Supreme Court has approved radical legislative measures, e.g. the 1990 Governmental notification implementing the Mandal Commission's recommendations on reserving jobs to economically and socially underprivileged classes. Up and until then, places within education and employment had been reserved only to the most underprivileged and oppressed castes and tribes, known as the Scheduled Castes and Tribes; the legislation enacted by the new Government extended such reservations to other economically and socially underprivileged castes. Though, during the early years of post-independent India, the judiciary was thought of as a governmental institution, it was later gradually perceived as belonging to the Government's constitutional polarity, and it is nowadays regarded as an institution of governance in its own right.[61] The functioning of PIL in the last 20 years mirrors the development of the judiciary as an autonomous entity. The Supreme Court has occasionally taken some bold though controversial decisions, such as the shutting down of polluting industries in the capital city, Delhi. In independent India, the judiciary has been responsible both in structural and "value-oriented" terms. As it has been argued, since democratic structures are essentially majority structures, decisions should not only be democratically accountable in structural terms but also be "value accountable", so that the ends of justice are fairly met.[62]

As seen above, the British statute-based legal system initially collided with the Indian value-based traditional legal system. Yet, in contemporary Indian legal institutions, the value-based legal system has not been totally replaced by statute-based law. Though the Constitution has replaced the *dharmasastra*, judges continue to adopt a *dharmasastric* approach to the Constitution in as much as they stress the inviolable basic structure of the Constitution, this being grounded on democracy and secularism. As Rajeev Dhavan points out, even if Indian law is now statute-based and is thoroughly "Western", Indian judges are still keen on adopting a *dharmasastric* approach to Anglophone laws. This might explain their affinity with widely stated doctrines of judicial review, including the famous basic structure doctrine, which powerfully supports constitutionalism in unprecedented ways. According to some observers of the Indian juridical scene, such as Chris Fuller, the way Indian judges work is largely similar to that of traditional *pundits*, i.e. the interpreters of sacred texts. According to Fuller, the certainty of modern law is an ideal, since precedents (like legislation) are always subject to judicial interpretation. This was known long before Dworkin stressed the role of interpretation in the legal process. Once the flexibility of modern law is acknowledged, the contrast between modern and traditional law becomes only a matter of degree, just like the difference between modern judicial reasoning and classical Hindu religious interpretation.[63]

The introduction of a uniform civil code is part of the directive principles of the state policy established by the Constitution. As we have seen, during colonialism, Hindus, Muslims, and Christians had their own different personal laws. In practice, however, the personal laws of Hindus and Muslims were subject to Brahminization and Islamization processes, in that colonial administrators ascertained and established such personal laws on the basis of their scriptural texts.[64] After India's independence and the enactment of the Constitution, Hindu personal laws were greatly modified. In 1955–1956, the Indian Parliament passed a series of acts, collectively known as the Hindu Code, as a result of which Hindu law was radically transformed: Hindu social arrangements were, for the first time, placed entirely within the ambit of legislative regulation; hence, the *sastric* tradition was almost entirely dispensed with.[65] Furthermore, the code established Parliament as a central legislative body for Hindus in family and social matters.[66] However, according to students of critical family law reform in India, such as Archana Parashar, the reform of Hindu personal law did not bring about full and substantive gender equality: although reforms made to Hindu law were initially designed to give women more legal rights, complete legal equality for women was never really pursued. Furthermore, by viewing sex equality and uniformity in Hindu law as desirable goals, political leaders used law reform as an instrument of political development rather than as a means to ensure legal equality as such.[67]

Nowadays, Muslims and Christians continue to have their own ancient personal laws, although the government has recently sought to introduce new laws making it easier for Christian women to obtain a divorce. Dieter Conrad, who has long studied the constitutional problem of personal law in India, claims that there is a wide area within the Indian legal system where constitutional rules do not apply, or rather are not applied by either the legislature or the judiciary. The area is not just one of the many faceted ramifications of law and social life, but rather it concerns the core of the individual's position as a human being within society. The crucial issue is the condition of women who, in all personal laws, though in varying degrees, are subject to discriminatory treatment[68] For example, under Muslim personal law, polygamy is permitted to men though not to women, and even after the Hindu Code of 1955, Hindu daughters continue to be excluded from coparcenary by the law of the *mitakhara* joint family.[69]

The existence of such discriminating personal laws requires Indian law and society to further deepen and universalize the rule of law. However, the setting up of a uniform civil code, which is supposedly meant to ensure the above universalization, has to come to terms with the fact that large groups of citizens regard their personal laws as an essential part of their religion. According to the Supreme Court, such a factor needs to be taken into account in determining the scope of permissible legislation.[70]

The case of Shah Bano, a repudiated Muslim woman, dramatically epitomizes the difficulties connected with the formulation of a uniform civil code. Shah Bano, a poor Muslim woman, applied to the Court for maintenance from her former husband; in 1985, the Supreme Court of India upheld the decision of the High Court, which ordered the husband to pay maintenance to Shah Bano. Yet, the Muslim Personal Law Board contested the Supreme Court judgment, claiming the decision grossly interfered with Muslim personal laws; very rapidly, conservative political and religious forces, allegedly representing minorities' religious interests, exerted political pressure on the Government. Under the leadership of the Prime Minister Rajiv Gandhi, the Government, instead of exploiting this opportunity to foster a debate for reform, introduced a new legislation which nullified the decision of the Supreme Court, thus denying justice to Muslim women. Such a case illustrates the triumph of conservative male Muslim religious and political leaders, who pretend to represent the entire Muslim population. Such leaders oppose a uniform civil code on the grounds that it would interfere with their religious personal laws. Yet, religious leaders ought to reinterpret religious laws in the light of contemporary challenges. It might be wondered whether freedom of religion can be used to suppress the constitutionally guaranteed right to equality of all individuals, especially women. The key issue centres around the conflict between the rights of minorities and the rights of women of minority communities.[71] The representatives of religious minorities do not give voice to suppressed groups within their communities. In this context, a variety of solutions are advanced. According to radical critics, such as Parashar, personal law should be abolished.[72] Other thinkers, however, such as Dieter Conrad, suggest introducing "individual choice" in matters governed by personal law, just as it happens under the 1954 Special Marriage Act, or through the optional clause in the 1937 Muslim Personal Law (Shariat) Application Act. According to Conrad, the individual's choice would ensure that personal law is not enforced as an ascriptive status on grounds of religious affiliation alone. Quite paradoxically, peculiarities of the hierarchical law could be more easily justified if they were accepted through the individual's choice.[73]

4 CRITICAL REFLECTIONS ON THE RULE OF LAW IN CONTEMPORARY INDIAN SOCIETY

The sociologist André Beteille is a keen and critical commentator on the rule of law in Indian society. According to Beteille, Indian activists, scholars, and citizens have not paid enough attention to the need to scrupulously follow rules and procedures in what he calls the populist interpretation and mobilization of democracy.[74] Beteille, who has a constitutionalist and procedural understanding of democracy, believes that the Indian society's general tendency is for regulation by persons rather than by rules.[75] By following Irawati Karve's view – whereby Indian civilization has been shaped by a principle of accretion, which has allowed for the continuous accumulation of rules without the elimination of old ones – Beteille argues that when new rules are enacted in India, old ones are not necessarily discarded; hence, new rules coexist with obsolete, anachronistic and inconsistent rules. In India, administration through impersonal rules hinders systematization, since this would require the continuous elimination of old and anachronistic rules.[76]

Beteille's contention that India can be hardly subject to the rule of law is corroborated by other critical commentators, such as Satish Saberwal and Upendra Baxi. According to the former, Indian society is not historically inclined to abide by general rules: under Manu's codes, for instance, punishment depends on the culprit's caste status.[77] According to Upendra Baxi, Indian political elites and upper middle classes have not internalized the value of legalism. Baxi's thinking, dating back to 20 years ago, still holds true today: a large number of Indians feel that following rules is not only unjustified but counterproductive.[78] Corruption and governmental lawlessness, its violation of laws and human rights, and its failure to implement its statutory obligations further challenge the Indian establishment of the rule of law.[79]

Beteille underlines the distinction between the Directive Principles of the State Policy and constitutional Fundamental Rights: all Fundamental Rights, including equality, are enforceable by the courts. On the contrary, the Directive Principles of the State Policy are not judicially enforceable though they have a great social and political value.[80] However, over the years, the primacy of Fundamental Rights has been relativized to give importance to social justice and egalitarian policies. Soon after the new Constitution was enacted, two major instruments of the egalitarian policy, i.e. the agrarian reform on the one hand and benign quotas on the other, were confronted with Fundamental Rights. The latter, therefore, were adjusted by the First Amendment of the

Constitution so as to accommodate policies designed to reduce disparities among classes and castes.[81] Equality as a right has thus given way to equality as a policy. Beteille is particularly critical of introducing reservations in terms of education and job opportunities benefiting socially and economically backward castes, since he believes that this makes a mockery of individuals' equality, especially their equality of opportunity.

Yet, while Beteille laments the dilution of legal equality into a mere policy brought about by populist mobilizations, given thinkers, such as Upendra Baxi, praise the transformation of constitutional provisions into concrete measures for the attainment of individuals' socio-economic rights. As a matter of fact, Baxi stresses the way in which existing legal institutions create hurdles for the realization of constitutional emancipatory and normative provisions. Baxi believes that the Constitution and law have a generally strong redistributive thrust; yet, the Indian legal system's major institutions tend to maintain and even worsen the *status quo*. Legal institutions generally decelerate and even prevent the inherent dynamism of constitutional aspirations for a just social order.[82] According to a number of critical students of law and society, such as Rajeev Dhavan, the constitutional promises for a just social order are themselves "half-hearted"; Dhavan argues that there has never been any great dissonance between Nehru's developmental plan for the Indian people and the British positivist legal theory transmitted to the courts of independent India. The fact that the Constituent Assembly included a judicially enforceable Bill of Rights into the Constitution did not prejudice the positivist credentials of Indian law. The fundamental rights guaranteed to citizens were in fact perceived as "legal rights" granted by a special statute: each right had some limitations and was interpreted like any other legal provision.[83]

Baxi goes even further by underlining the continuance of the colonial model grounded on law's reactive, rather than proactive, mobilization.[84] He also stresses the problem of access to the rule of law: the State's legal system, which is highly pervasive in urban areas, is hardly present in rural areas. The low visibility of the State's legal system and its slender presence render official law, together with its values and processes, inaccessible and even irrelevant to people.[85] Moreover, exorbitant court fees discourage people from taking legal action. A number of efforts have been made over the years to make law more accessible: 40 years ago, *Nyaya Panchayats* were established to redress the balance, yet these did not make much headway.[86] Even the new *Panchayat Raj System* has not brought significant changes in the attainment of local justice.

India is currently ruled by a coalition of parties constituting the so-called National Democratic Alliance, whose leading figure is the Bharatiya

Janata Party, actively supporting the agenda of Hindu fundamentalists. The recent upheavals of Indian political and social systems have led to the demise of a one-party-dominance in India's political world, which in turn has led to a central political instability. Suffice it to say that, in the last 5 years alone, there have been three general elections for the Indian Parliament – in 1996, 1998, and 1999. After the last general election, the ruling coalition established a Constitutional Review Committee entrusted with the task of reviewing the Constitution. The review is meant to examine salient issues in the area of governance, above all federalist reforms – these pertaining to the relation between the central power and the States, which is still characterized by the unfair sharing of economic resources and political power – the attainment of present and future political stability and the Union of Governments in an era of fragmented coalitions.[87] While the review commission is likely to examine the conversion of given Directive Principles into Fundamental Rights (especially the right to primary education), the Indian people's widespread and contemporary fear is that the review of the Constitution is a surreptitious attempt on the part of the ruling party to dismantle basic Indian constitutional structures, such as secularism and parliamentary democracy. Upendra Baxi argues that a review commission is not needed since the Constitution itself allows for changes through constitutional amendments. Yet, while the Constitution allows for changes *within* it, it does not allow for changes *thereof*: changes *of* the Constitution are not allowed by current Indian constitutionalism, which denies the legitimacy of its subversion.[88]

The need to be vigilant about any constitutional subversion is also strongly upheld by the President of the Indian Republic, K.R. Narayanan. He was born into a poor isolated family in Kerala; even access to his primary school was difficult. He is now the President of the Republic of India, and his "journey" from an isolated hamlet in Kerala to the office of the President of the Republic symbolizes the social transformation that has taken place in post-independent India. The Indian Constitution has played an inspiring role in such a transformation. Narayanan has often prompted Indian parties favouring changes to the Constitution to ponder on whether they have failed the Constitution or whether the Constitution has failed them. In his speech to the nation on the eve of the Golden Jubilee for the enactment of the Indian Constitution on 25 January 2001, he stated that the constitutional social commitments could not be ignored. His words were specifically addressed to Indian parties wishing to subvert the emancipatory promises of the Constitution. According to Narayanan, democracy has flourished during the last 50 years under the flexible and spacious provisions of the Constitution. India is nowadays acknowledged as a great democracy – indeed the greatest democracy in the world – and the Indian Constitution embodies people's political, social, and economic rights.[89]

5 THE RULE OF LAW AND THE CALL FOR SELF-TRANSFORMATION

In this essay, we have covered a long historical period of more than 5,000 years, and have dealt with the way Indian society has conceived the rule of law throughout its history. We have examined the rule of law in classical Indian traditions and its functioning under the Constitution of independent India. The contemporary Indian Constitution seeks to create a more equal and just rule of law than the one guaranteed by traditional authorities, such as *Manusmriti*. The Constitution aims at eliminating humiliations inherent in traditional castes and patriarchy, thus creating new grounds for the realization of human dignity. The current attainment of both formal and substantive equality can foster a life of *dharma* or of righteous conduct within individuals' self and within society. In the first section of this essay, we underlined how self-rule is central to the realization of the individual and collective order. Yet, self-rule needs to be facilitated by the existence of a proper social, institutional, and legal order that guarantees legal equality to all individuals, irrespectively of their class, caste, religion, and gender. Hence, modern law can create appropriate sociological conditions for the realization of a life of *dharma*.

Yet, although modern law is necessary, it is not sufficient for the realization of self-rule and of social order. In this respect, modern theories of law, both in contemporary India and in the West, can draw inspiration from Indian traditions on self-development and self-transformation. It is self-transformation that allows us to "go beyond" the discourse on the rule of law, on one's self and society, and reach a new level of analysis; Indian spiritual traditions represent a challenge which continuously prompt us to incorporate such a further level in our legal routines. As argued by J.D.M. Derrett, the unbroken tradition of Hindu legal doctrine underlines that Hindu law is concerned with eternity and morality in their broadest meanings, thus not circumscribed to material and contingent considerations.[90] Sasheej Hegde argues that rules and laws in Indian traditions endorse a morality of subjectivation, going beyond the scope of power. There is indeed an imperative/prescriptive dimension of the rule of law in Indian tradition, though this cannot be imposed upon groups and institutions as an extrinsic constraint, and cannot be made merely instrumental to its exercise; the principle of universalization that such a dimension might help in attaining must be met by a clarification from a *moral* point of view.[91] The epithets "legal" and "moral" are deemed to be roughly coeval and, in Indian traditions, they are conceived of as complementary modes of guiding power.[92] The transformational impact of morality on the rule of law – being morality meant as much more than simply abiding by social norms – entails the possibility of acting righteously in accordance with one's conscience, and thus has an epochal significance. As claimed by Veena Das, sacred texts (including the *dharmasastras*), rather than prescribing specific behaviour, describe codes of conduct deemed to be exemplary or desirable. If such a conception is characterized as purely *Brahmanic*, the opportunity of treating it as an important conceptual resource is missed.[93]

Within modern Western traditions, the various conceptualizations of the rule of law were first propounded with an emancipatory stance; yet, as early as the mid nineteenth century, Western law as emancipation had already been overridden by the notion of law as regulation. The contemporary crisis of the rule of law, both in India and in the West, witnesses the collapse of emancipation which is reduced to regulation; hence, the emancipatory dimension of the rule of law needs to be reassessed and revitalized.[94] This calls for both incorporating the old models of emancipation – which entailed fighting against external oppressive forces – and for conceiving and realizing emancipation from social oppression, together with its ensuing empowerment; this must be accompanied by the relinquishing of egotistic passions and the desire to control other people, and by the wish to contribute to a participatory and transformational creation of society as an area of spiritual freedom and shared intersubjectivity.[95] In order to elaborate such a new emancipatory dimension, grounded on self-development, self-transcendence, and self-transformation, a new understanding of individuals and society is needed.

Santos claims that the collapse of emancipation into regulation represents the exhaustion of the paradigm of modernity: a narrow view of ourselves tends to encourage a narrower view of others.[96] Santos believes that the new emerging paradigm of law entails a triple transformation, whereby power becomes shared authority, despotic law becomes democratic law, and knowledge as regulation becomes knowledge as emancipation.[97] In order to achieve such a triple transformation, a new subjectivity is required, i.e. a subjectivity constituted by the *topos* of a prudent knowledge for a decent life.[98] According to Santos, law's rising subjectivity lives "on the frontier"; to live on the frontier is to live in abeyance, in an empty space, in a time between times.[99] To live in an empty space and time requires us to appreciate the dialectic between time and eternity, tradition and modernity; in this respect, Indian socio-spiritual and traditional openness to emptiness as an integral dimension of space, time, one's self and society may help us in bringing emancipation to the heart of the rule of law.

Law's rising subjectivity requires new ethics, in which a priori rules and regulations alone are not enough in ensuring prudential judgments on dilemmas in legal, ethical, and moral contexts, or in living a just and responsible life.[100] Responsibility as an unconditional obligation ought to be brought within the scope of the rule of law, so that it is subject to compensation and punishment.[101] A responsible life requires prudential judgments which, in turn, demand our conscience's continuous guidance. Yet, in modern Western legal and political traditions, exemplified by the works of Kant, Rawls and Habermas, conscience shares the features of social legality internalized as pure morality. On the contrary, in order to bring conscience to the heart of law, we need to understand that conscience is not just a product of society. Rather, it is conscience that makes the individual understand that other individuals' lives are as important as his own.[102] An ontologically responsive interpretation of conscience for a fair rule of law is thus crucial, and the Indian *dharma* approach may help us in this respect.

In his critical reflection on Indian law and society, André Beteille argues that individual rights do not have the same depth and firmness in India and the same anchorage in its social structure as they have in the United States.[103] Yet, such a relativization of Indian individual rights may allow us to devise a more balanced relationship between individual and collective rights. Modern Western legal cultures have traditionally granted unquestioned primacy to individual rights; nonetheless, through the social and theoretical revolution of postmodernism and multiculturalism, Western legal systems have slowly recognized and instituted collective rights. Yet, a proper balance between individual and collective rights is still nowadays a great challenge; Western experiments in this respect can draw inspiration from Indian attempts, in which policies of compensatory discrimination have sought to strive a balance between individual and collective rights.[104] The traditional and modern Indian attempt to establish a creative relationship between individuals and society is still incomplete. However, it has always striven to relativize the egoistic primacy of collective or individual rights, of society or individuals, by introducing a transcendental dimension into governmental and legal routines. Indian spiritual traditions have always emphasized that society is not merely a contract. Such an insight is nowadays immensely helpful in rethinking and reconstituting law and society.

NOTES

1. R. Lingat, *The Classical Law of India*, Delhi: Thompson Press, 1973, p. 258.
2. A. Beteille, *Society and Politics in India*, Delhi: Oxford University Press, 1997, p. 218.
3. A. Nandy, "The other within: the strange case of Radhabinod Pal's judgment of culpability", in A. Nandy (ed.), *The Savage Freud*, Delhi: Oxford University Press, 1995, p. 53.
4. R. Lingat, op. cit., passim.
5. Ibid., p. 176.
6. Ibid., p. 177.
7. Ibid., p. 259.
8. R. Roy, *Beyond Ego's Domain: Being and Order in the Vedas*, Delhi: Shipra, 1999, p. 8.
9. Ibid., p. 2.
10. Ibid., p. 221.
11. T. Brennan, *History After Lacan*, London: Routledge, 1993.
12. R. Roy, op. cit., p. 5.
13. See A.K. Giri, "Rethinking systems as frames of coordination: dialogical intersubjectivity and the creativity of action", *Man and Development*, May 2000.
14. S. Aurobindo, *The Synthesis of Yoga*, Pondicherry: Sri Aurobindo Ashram, 1948, p. 17.
15. A.K. Coomaraswamy, *Spiritual Authority and Temporal Power in the Indian Theory of Government*, Delhi: Munshiram Manoharlal, 1978, pp. 84–5.
16. F. Dallmayr, *What is Swaraj? Lessons from Gandhi*, Notre Dame (IN): University of Notre Dame, 1997, manuscript.
17. A.K. Coomaraswamy, op. cit., p. 86.
18. Quoted in M. Foucault, *Care of the Self*, New York: Pantheon, 1986, p. 88.
19. J.W. Spellman, *Political Theory of Ancient India: A Study of Kingship from the Earliest Times to Roughly A.D. 300*, Oxford: Clarendon Press, 1964, p. 111.
20. J.D.M. Derrett, *Religion, Law and State in India*, London: Faber & Faber, 1968, p. 158.
21. Ibid., p. 160.
22. Z. Bauman, *Legislators and Interpreters: On Modernity, Postmodernity and the Intellectuals*, Cambridge: Polity Press, 1987.
23. A.K. Ramanujan, "Is there an Indian way of thinking? An informal essay", *Contributions to Indian Sociology*, 23 (1989), pp. 41–58.
24. R. Lingat, op. cit., p. 261.
25. B. Cohn, *Colonialism and Its Forms of Knowledge*, Delhi: Oxford University Press, 1997, p. 57.
26. E. Stokes, *The English Utilitarians and India*, Delhi: Oxford University Press, 1982, p. 82.

27. B. Cohn, op. cit., p. 61.
28. Ibid., p. 72.
29. D. Washbrook, "Law, state and agrarian society in colonial India", *Modern Asian Studies*, 15 (1981), 3, p. 653.
30. J.D.M. Derrett, op. cit., passim.
31. J. Nair, *Women and Law in Colonial India: A Social History*, Delhi: Kali for Women, 1996, p. 21.
32. N.B. Dirks, "From little king to landlord: property, law and the gift under the Madras permanent settlement", *Comparative Studies in Society and History*, 28 (1986), 2, pp. 307–33.
33. Quoted in N.B. Dirks, op. cit., p. 318.
34. E. Stokes, op. cit., 1982, p. 84.
35. Ibid., p. 141.
36. N.B. Dirks, op. cit., p. 330.
37. Ibid., p. 312.
38. Ibid., p. 311.
39. A. Parashar, *Women and Family Law Reform in India: Uniform Civil Code and Gender Equality*, Delhi: Sage, 1992, p. 72.
40. M. Galanter, *Law and Society in Modern India*, Delhi: Oxford University Press, 1989, p. 16.
41. E. Stokes, op. cit., p. 222.
42. Ibid., p. 223.
43. Ibid., p. 219.
44. J. Habermas, *Between Facts and Norms: Contributions Towards a Discourse Theory of Law and Democracy*, Cambridge: Polity Press, 1996.
45. U. Baxi, *The Crisis of the Indian Legal System*, Delhi: Vikas, 1982, p. 45.
46. M. Galanter, op. cit., p. 18.
47. Ibid., pp. 18–19.
48. R.S. Smith, "Rule-by-records and rule-by-reports: complimentary aspects of the British Imperial rule of law", *Contributions to Indian Sociology*, 19 (1985), 1, p. 172.
49. A. Appadurai, *Worship and Conflict Under Colonial Rule: A South Indian Case*, Delhi: Orient Longman, 1983.
50. Ibid., p. 173.
51. Ibid., p. 174.
52. Ibid., pp. 178–9.
53. J. Nair, op. cit., p. 42.
54. B. Cohn, op. cit., p. 75.
55. G. Austin, *Working a Democratic Constitution: The Indian Experience*, Delhi: Oxford University Press, 1999.
56. M. Galanter, op. cit., p. 40.
57. Quoted in U. Baxi, op. cit., p. 339.
58. R. Dhavan, "Judges and Indian democracy: the lesser evil?", in F.R. Frankel *et al.* (eds), *Transforming India: Social and Political Dynamics of Democracy*, Delhi: Oxford University Press, 2000, p. 322.
59. Ibid., p. 321.
60. S. Ahuja, *People, Law and Justice: A Casebook of Public Interest Litigation*, Delhi: Orient Longman, 1997, pp. 1–2.
61. R. Dhavan, op. cit., passim.
62. Ibid., p. 337.

63. C. Fuller, "Hinduism and scriptural authority in modern Indian law", *Comparative Studies in Society and History*, 30 (1988), pp. 246–7. Fuller further writes: "Hindu scriptural discourse is not and never has been monolithic ... and it does perennially generate reinterpretations of itself" (p. 241). Fuller quotes Lingat: "The role of interpretation amounts to this: it offers society the means whereby it can rediscover itself." (ibid.).
64. A. Parashar, op. cit., p. 66.
65. M. Galanter, op. cit., p. 29.
66. Ibid., p. 30.
67. A. Parashar, op. cit., p. 76.
68. D. Conrad, "Rule of law and constitutional problems of personal laws in India", in S. Saberwal and H. Sievers (eds), *Rules, Laws, Constitutions*, Delhi: Sage, 1998, p. 227.
69. In traditional Indian society the rights of most Hindu women were governed by the *mitakshara* and *dayabhaga* legal systems. The *mitakshara* conferred coparcenary rights upon birth on sons, but the *dayabhaga* system ensured no such birth right. Thus the chances for a woman "inheriting property under the *dayabhaga* were slightly better". The Hindu Code of 1955 did not bring any change as to property inheritance rights of Hindu women living under the *mitakshara* legal system; cf. J. Nair, op. cit., pp. 196–7.
70. Ibid., p. 229.
71. A. Parashar, 1992, p. 229.
72. Ibid., p. 258.
73. D. Conrad, op. cit., p. 230.
74. A. Beteille, "Citizenship, state and civil society", *Economic and Political Weekly*, 4 September 1999.
75. A. Beteille, "Experience of governance: a sociological view", in R.K. Darr (ed.), *Governance and the IAS*, Delhi: Tata McGraw-Hill, 1999, p. 200.
76. Ibid., p. 228.
77. S. Saberwal, "Introduction: why do we need rules and laws?", in S. Saberwal and H. Sievers (eds), *Rules, Laws, Constitutions*, p. 16.
78. U. Baxi, op. cit., p. 7.
79. Ibid., p. 28.
80. A. Beteille, *Society and Politics in India: Essays in a Comparative Perspective*, Delhi: Oxford University Press, 1997, p. 192.
81. Ibid., p. 202.
82. U. Baxi, op. cit., p. 30.
83. R. Dhavan, op. cit., p. 32.
84. U. Baxi, op. cit., p. 47.
85. Ibid., p. 345.
86. U. Baxi, op. cit., passim; M. Galanter, op. cit., passim.
87. U. Baxi, "*Karv seva* of the Indian constitution? Reflections on proposals for review of the Indian constitution", *Economic and Political Weekly*, 11 March 2000, p. 892.
88. Ibid., p. 891.
89. President K.R. Narayanan's speech to the Nation, Delhi, 25 January 2001.
90. J.D.M. Derrett, op. cit., p. 101.
91. S. Hegde, "Rules and laws in Indian traditions: a reconstructive appropriation", in S. Saberwal and H. Sievers (eds), *Rules, Laws, Constitutions*, p. 116.
92. Ibid., p. 99.
93. Quoted in S. Hegde, op. cit., p. 102.

94. B. Santos, *Toward a New Common Sense: Law, Science and Politics in the Paradigmatic Transition*, London: Routledge, 1995.
95. A.K. Giri, "Moral consciousness and communicative action: from discourse ethics to spiritual transformation", *History of the Human Sciences*, 1998; E. Laclau, "Beyond emancipation", in J.N. Pieterse (ed.), *Emancipations, Modern and Postmodern*, London: Sage, 1992.
96. B. Santos, op. cit., p. xi.
97. Ibid., p. 482.
98. Ibid., p. 489.
99. B. Santos, op. cit., p. 491.
100. A.K. Giri and P. Quarles van Ufford, *Reconstituting Development as a Shared Responsibility: Ethics, Aesthetics and a Creative Shaping of Human Possibilities*, Madras: Madras Institute of Development Studies, Working Paper, 2000.
101. P. Ricoeur, *The Just*, Chicago: The University of Chicago Press, 2000, p. 12.
102. Ibid., p. 152.
103. A. Beteille, op. cit., p. 198.
104. Marc Galanter writes: "Compensatory discrimination offers a way to leaven our formalism without entirely abandoning its comforts. The Indian example is instructive: India has managed to pursue a commitment to substantive justice without allowing that commitment to dissolve competing commitments to formal equality that make law viable in a diverse society with limited consensus. The Indian experience displays a principled eclecticism that avoids suppressing the altruistic fraternal impulse that animates compensatory policies, but that also avoids being enslaved by it. From afar it reflects to us a tempered legalism – one which we find more congenial in practice than theory" (M. Galanter, op. cit., p. 567).

CHAPTER 19

THE CHINESE LEGAL TRADITION AND THE EUROPEAN VIEW OF THE RULE OF LAW

Wu Shu-Chen

The great differences existing between the legal tradition in China and the spirit of the rule of law as understood in Europe are the result of two utterly different traditions in social life and national culture.[1] Nevertheless China's legal tradition[2] has some apparent likenesses to the European spirit of the rule of law. Differences in human culture cannot only be accounted for in terms of geography and history. Whether consciously or not, humans tend to take a common road to development. China's legal tradition first embarked upon modernization in 1840, the date which marks the beginning of the modern period, steering away from a course which was heading towards disaster. The twentieth century unravelled between two major legal landmarks that allowed the development of legal activities. The first was the Constitutional Reform of 1898,[3] just before the beginning of the century, while the strategy of "Running the Country According to Law" was formally established just before the close of the century, in 1997.[4]

1 ON CHINESE LEGAL TRADITION

The Chinese legal tradition is not only an object of study for legal experts and legal historians. The field represents a living cultural factor of great impact in the legal life of modern China.

1.1 What is a legal tradition?

My understanding of the legal tradition differs somewhat from the views of other legal experts. This tradition can be subdivided into two aspects. Firstly, there are the *value bases*, governing the practice of legal activity and expressing the theory of law, as well as the philosophy and ethics that inform it. All these factors are inseparable from a country's or a nation's historical and cultural experience; they come into being gradually, as the result of a very long process. They are passed on from generation to generation, without much change, in relative stability. The second aspect comprises legal activities in themselves, i.e. the working methods

P. Costa and D. Zolo (eds.), The Rule of Law: History, Theory and Criticism, 615–632.

of the legislation and the administration of justice as, for instance, the formal law, the case law, and that legal area which combines the formal law and the case law. On the one hand, therefore, we must take into account the sets of values (*value bases*) that inform a country or nation, thereby dominating its legal practices. On the other hand, we have the socialized working forms which allow these value bases to be enacted through the process of legislation and the administration of justice. A country's or a nation's legal tradition consists in the combination of these two fundamental aspects.[5]

My definition of a legal tradition is influenced by the theory of the *genealogy of law*, although I do not intend to accept this theory wholesale, and will suggest some revisions. Before attempting a classification of the legal traditions of the world on a macro-level, rigorous criteria must be defined in order to avoid using double or more standards all at once. If, therefore, we divide the legal traditions of the world by *value bases*, we end up with two main groups: the Western legal tradition of *individualism* and the Eastern legal tradition of *collectivism*. A classification by legal *types* (legislation, the administration of justice, and basic working methods), on the other hand, yields three different groups: *written law* (the genealogy of law in the European continent), *case law* (the Anglo-American genealogy of law), and *mixed law* (the Chinese genealogy of law). The two major genealogies of law in the west have similar *value bases*, but differ in terms of *type*. If we compare, for example, the typology of the former Soviet law to that of the written law of the European Continent, we do not find significant differences concerning the *type* of law, though the two systems clearly rest upon different sets of *value bases*. Soviet law obviously differs from the two major Western genealogies, though it resembles them in *type*. Generally speaking, a country's or a nation's legal tradition consists in the way its *value basis* and legal *type* are reflected in its legal practice.

1.2 The two essential factors of the Chinese legal tradition

The Chinese legal tradition emerges from practical legal activities which have been ongoing for thousands of years. It still plays an important role in today's social life. It has collectivism as a *value basis*, and it features a *mixed method* in terms of *type*.

1.2.1 Collectivism as a value basis. The Chinese legal tradition is based upon collectivism, which is made up of the *patriarchal clan system* on the one hand and *centralized nationalism* on the other. This tradition is quite opposite to Western individualism. *Rite* is central to the patriarchal clan system, which rests upon the right of the male venerable elder. This right embodies the moral conception and principle of the patriarchal clan; it hinges on sets of relationships such as *kind father–dutiful son* and *male with high position–female with low position*. The social value of the *rite* lies in regulating a series of individual obligations in order to keep the peace within the clan. For thousands of years people's activities and thinking were restricted by the *rite*.

Centralized nationalism, on the other hand, embodies and reflects the spirit and workings of the bureaucratic state regime and its centralized, autocratic monarchy, as well as the laws drawn up and enforced by the regime. The laws stipulated a series of obligations for the subjects and envisaged cruel penalties for those who dared to violate them; their main function was maintaining the stability of the autocratic state. The *rite* (of the patriarchal clan) and the *law* (of the autocratic state) thus combined to restrict individual freedom. You would be hard pressed to find such terms as *rights of the individual* and *freedom* in the cultural dictionaries of ancient China.

1.2.2 Mixed law as a legal type. In Chinese feudal society, every generation of a dynasty attached great importance to compiling a written code to determine the administration of justice. Under special historical circumstances the judges at different levels were allowed to create the laws and apply them according to the practice of judicial precedent. These special cases mostly occurred following the overthrow of an old dynasty, before the new rulers had had enough time to compile a new written code. With the pace of the social life speeding up, the old written code would inevitably be found wanting and out of date. The new dynasty had to update the old legal code by introducing a new legal orthodoxy. The judicial precedents were compiled into volumes and classified into categories for the use of judges. Some principles from these judicial precedents might in time come to be absorbed into legislation and form a new part of the written code. Thus, ancient China can be said to have had *mixed law* as a *type*. Xun Zi, one of the Confucian representatives at the end of the Period of the Warring States, fathered this type of legal practice, i.e. the practice of judging by the existing written law, or by the most suitable legal precedent should written law be found to be lacking.[6]

To recapitulate, we have established above that the Chinese legal tradition features *collectivism* as a *value basis* and *mixed law* as a *type*.

1.3 The historical development of the Chinese legal tradition

The Chinese legal tradition has a long historical evolution, undergoing three main stages of development:

1.3.1 The "rule by rite" and "case law" period. The ancient periods of Xi-Zhou (from the eleventh century BC to 771 BC) and Chun-Qiu (from 770 BC to 476 BC) were governed in the spirit of *rule by rite* and *case law*. The principle of *rite* governed all aspects of social life in this era. The aristocratic system of government was the reflection of the patriarchal clan system on a state level.

Aristocrats at all levels in their estate enjoyed independent political, economic, military, and legal rights. These rights were hereditary. The law was imbued with the spirit of *rite*, "strictly punishing", for example, "those who do not show filial obedience to their elders",[7] and ensuring that "the party with a lower position in the family hierarchy would be found guilty, if the reasons for proceedings taken by both sides were same".[8]

The post of judge was also hereditary; younger generations of judges decided cases in the way of their fathers. Not only was this "the done thing"; it was an actual moral and practical requirement of "filial piety".[9] In the long run, this practice resulted in a tradition of compliance with whatever had gone on before. The outcome of a trial or a legal case had to comply with the *rite*, there being no written code to refer to. The *rite* remained standard practice for centuries, coming to be considered to be the *inexhaustible source of law*. The aristocratic system and the practice of case law favoured the figure of the ruler as *individual*. The good government of an estate or a case being judged correctly largely depended on the subjective, *individual* qualities and mettle of the person wielding authority. Here are the social reasons for the prominence of *rule by the individual* in ancient China.[10]

1.3.2 The "ruling by the law" and "written law" period. The period of the Warring States (475–221 BC) and the Qin Dynasty (221–206 BC) constitute an era of *ruling by the law* and *written law*. At this time, landlords and common people wrenched state power from aristocrats and feudal princes. They tried to unify the country through the annexation of territory by military conquest. They founded the centralized autocratic monarchy as a political system. The will of the monarch thus came to be reflected in the form of the law. This is known as the *ruling by the law* or *governing the state by law* period. The Legalists, a school of thought from the Chun-Qiu and the Warring States Periods, were the theorists of *Ruling by the law*. The individual had to obey the state and the law unconditionally, lest he or she incur severe punishment. The state was no longer ruled by the blood lineage of the patriarchal clan, but relied on institutions of regional administration.

During this period, the written law proliferated, so that it came to regulate all aspects of society.[11] Judges were not allowed to invoke precedent or to rely on their personal judgement; they had to strictly comply with the provisions of the written law, which had supreme authority. Anybody who disagreed with a law after its enactment was subjected to severe punishment.[12]

1.3.3 The "Combination of rite law and mixed law" period. From the period of the Western Han Dynasty to the end of Qing Dynasty (202 BC–AD 1912), China saw a period combining a *rite law* with *mixed law*. The main characteristic of this 2000-year-long feudal era was the close combination of autocratic monarchy as a political system with the patriarchal clan as a social system, against the background of an agricultural system of self-sufficient farming. The law in this phase became the tool with which the monarch expressed his will and intentions, and the means by which he controlled the colossal bureaucratic machine – needless to say, the law became immensely important.

The law in the Chinese feudal period can be seen as an *officials' law*, the law by which the monarch could manage his officials and cadres, whilst in the realm of social life the natural economy promoted the restoration and development of the patriarchal clan. The *rite*, which had never ceased to play an essential role as a custom and tradition among the people, regained prominence. The objective conditions allowed *ruling by the law* to combine with *rule by rite*. These two systems played their social roles without hindering one another, operating in separate spheres. *Ruling by the law* maintained the central autocratic monarchy's political system, whilst *rule by rite* maintained the social basis of the system – the society of the patriarchal clan.

Although judges were expected to try cases according to written law where this touched upon social life, the written law's impact on the land was limited, for several reasons. Firstly, by virtue of its inbuilt characteristics, the written law was severely hampered by long procedures which made it hard to see cases through to their completion. Furthermore, its irrevocable character made it unsuitable to many occurrences in the daily administration of social life. Secondly, the scope of the written code was not wide enough to cover all of the issues that came to the attention of judges throughout the land; besides, it was plagued by flaws and defects. Last, but not least, China's vast area meant that the greatly varying customs and conditions encompassed by its jurisdiction often made the legal code inadequate, inapplicable, or otherwise wanting in particular local situations. Thus, the written code's position of pre-eminence came to be relativized during the actual trials. At particular historical junctions judges created or made use of precedents in order to remedy or circumvent shortfalls in the written law. Once again, the *rite* came to play a crucial role as source of law. *Episodes* and *examples* from previous dynasties were compiled into volumes and classified by contents, and put away to be drawn upon as the need arose. Eventually they came to play a dominant role.[13]

1.3.4 Social causes for the Chinese legal tradition. The basic characteristics of ancient Chinese society are expressed in the term *three-in-one*, which refers to the close combination of the three elements which composed it: agricultural production within a natural economy, the social structure of the patriarchal clan, and an autocratic monarchy ruling over centralized state. China's cultural heartland lies in the area around the middle and lower reaches of the Yellow River known as the Central Plains; this area was inhabited by farming populations. The closure and stability of agricultural life promoted the development of the patriarchal clan. The *rite* took shape in this environment. More dynamic traditions such as those of the *advocate of meritorious service*, the *advocate of law*, and *centralization*, however, came first into being among the nomadic peoples of the Northwest of China, and were fostered by social needs arising from these people's means and mode of production.

The *ruling by the law* and *written law* periods were times of social transformation and war and led to an opposition between the *rite* and *the law*. When society finally became stable, however, a new formation, consciously or unconsciously, came about. Thus, the centralized autocratic monarchy flaunted its adherence to standard of *ruling by the law* but allowed the values of the patriarchal clan, which constituted the basic cell of Chinese society, to thrive in the local environment. The rural world was often remote and out of the reach of the arm of the state, and continued to be governed by *rite*. In this way, *ruling by the law* and *rule by rite* had parallel existences, tacitly supporting each other. Ancient Chinese society developed very slowly, never experiencing fundamental qualitative changes. The *three-in-one* structure was strong enough to resist and suppress the development of a commercial economy and of a strong urban society in the towns. Enlightened thinkers at the end of Ming Dynasty and in the early Qing Dynasty sensed the calling of the new century, but this change did not come as scheduled, after all. Only after the Opium War of 1840 did advanced Chinese open their eyes to the world outside of China, as they were faced a national disaster.

2 CRISIS IN THE CHINESE LEGAL TRADITION: THE IMPORTATION OF EUROPEAN LEGAL AND POLITICAL THOUGHT

Modern capitalist legal and political thought is not a natural product in China. These notions came by boat like "imported goods" and "foreign imports" from the West. They were accompanied by warships and shelling from foreign powers. The brave and wise Chinese resisted the foreign invaders with broadsword and pike in one hand, and books in the other, so as to learn the political means of survival from foreign civilizations. The motif of national struggle against foreign invasion is interwoven with that of the political reform movement that followed in the footsteps of the invading powers, in the fabric of modern Chinese social history.

2.1 The crisis in the Chinese legal tradition: the Opium War of 1840 and consular jurisdiction

The Opium War of 1820 resulted in the defeat of the Qing Dynasty government. China signed an infamous treaty of national betrayal and humiliation with Great Britain in 1843. The treaty provided a legitimate basis for the establishment of a consular jurisdiction by the foreign power on Chinese soil.[14] The other powers rapidly followed suit by signing similar treaties with the Qing government.

Under the terms of the treaty, foreigners committing a crime in China were not to be tried by the local authorities but were to be handed over to the foreign consulate for punishment. Britain cited China's "uncivilized" law and the savagery of its penal system among the reasons for this measure, but promised in the treaty that it would abandon its consular jurisdiction as China reformed its laws and prison acts.[15]

The feudal dynasty which had regarded itself and China for thousands of years as "the superior state in the world" was deeply injured by these provisions, in several ways.

Firstly, the imperial court had been the highest authority in China for thousands of years. Its laws had had to be implemented without exception throughout the land. The establishment of consular jurisdiction directly undermined the highest authority of the feudal court, and amounted to a major loss of face. Secondly, due to the proliferation of the activities of foreign missionaries in China a great number of Chinese started going to church. The number of Chinese converts increased steadily. Conflicts between members of these congregations and locals became commonplace. What is more, the Christians often benefited from the protection of foreign consulates, which challenged local authority, even, sometimes overriding it. The social chaos which came to be known as the Church Case ensued. This further disturbed the precarious social order of the dynasty.[16] Thirdly, the Qing government had no actual administration in the leased territories, which, as a result of this, became breeding grounds for revolutionary activity against the imperial court. Requests to extradite revolutionaries were often refused; many carried out their activities unhampered. The Shanghai case of June 1903[17] is a case in point, and threatened the power of the Qing Dynasty directly.

Getting rid of consular jurisdiction was the Qing Dynasty's most ardent wish, but it simply did not have the force to achieve this under the circumstances The dynasty therefore opted to play another game and set about reforming the Chinese legal system, so as to fulfil the foreigners' conditions, hoping that they would in turn keep their promises and abandon their consular jurisdiction.

This thinking, in retrospect, seems quite naive, for consular jurisdiction was not in itself a legal question but a matter of state sovereignty hinging on force. The opinion that held sway among the highest officials and the learned men of the time, however, was that if the old legal system were reformed, the foreigners would pack up and go, or at least give up their consular jurisdiction. Consequently, at the end of the Qing Dynasty was dominated by a legal reform movement, which threatened to put an end to the thousands of years of Chinese legal tradition.

2.2 European political and legal thought as foreign imports: democratic and liberal thought in a different context

After the Opium War of 1840, China spiralled into a deepening national crisis. Some moderate patriots began to pay close attention to Western civilization and its ideas. Lin Zexu,[18] the first man to open his eyes to the rest of the world, wrote *Sizhouzhi*.[19] Wei Yuan[20] wrote *Hai Guo Tu Zhi* arguing that it was worth learning from the development of foreign countries.[21] Neither of them had ever been abroad, and their books were written from secondary sources.

These cultural cases, however, moved a string of Chinese officials and men of learning to go abroad. They visited Europe and Japan to study their cultures. They described the legal and political systems that they encountered in their diaries, impressions, and travel notes, and they pondered upon the theory, local conditions, and customs of Western countries and Japan. All of these works have been collected in the *Going to the World Series*.[22] Many students left China, too, mostly heading for Japan. Some of the scholars who visited Western countries set about a fundamental work of translation; Yan Fu[23] remains to this day the most influential. The Western classics which he translated and published included *Evolution and Ethics, and Other Essays* by the biologist Thomas Henry Huxley, *An Inquiry into the Nature of the Wealth of Nations* by Adam Smith, *The Principles of Sociology* by Spencer, *On Liberty* by John Stuart Mill, *A History of Politics* by Edward Jenks, *L'Esprit des Lois* by Charles-Louis de Montesquieu, among others.[24] These Chinese versions played an important role in spreading Western political and legal thought in China.

The long-standing history and cultural tradition of China were so set in their ways that absorbing cultural influences from abroad could only come about as a matter of volition; it was not an organic process. The history of this process shows that ways of thought cannot be simply transplanted from one place to another. When systems of Western political and legal thought such as democracy, constitutionalism, and liberalism were introduced into China, interesting new phenomena determined by local conditions and interpretations came into being.

Democracy, constitutionalism, liberalism, and individualism developed in the West out of an historical culture closely connected to the culture of capitalism, which had little or nothing to do with China's society and traditions. When these ideological "foreign goods" entered China, therefore, they could not keep their original aspect, but became the object of selection, transformation, and processing on the part of their recipients in China. Yan Fu has written that Western countries "took freedom as the framework, and democracy as the tool".[25] Democracy, constitutionalism, and the theory of liberalism are integral to Western thinking. Not all of these ideas, however, were equally well received in China. The Chinese attached more importance to democracy and constitutionalism than to the doctrine of liberalism and individualism. They believed that democracy and constitutionalism lay at the foundations of Western power and were the secret of its success. Japan's recent reforms seemed to support this belief within an Asian context. The progressive personalities who were bent on saving the nation from extinction made great efforts to build a political framework for democracy and constitutionalism, hoping to overturn the unhappy fate of backwardness which left China at the mercy of the Great Powers. These men did not have the time to build a system of thought that would tally exactly with their role models of democracy and constitutionalism, nor could they dispose of the necessary preconditions. As a result, liberalism and individualism were tacitly ignored. These notions came to be propagated in China half a century after the introduction of democratic and constitutionalist ideas.[26]

There are many reasons for this interesting social phenomenon; the powerful inertia of Chinese traditional culture counts as foremost among them. Though democracy and constitutionalism came from foreign countries, they were perceived as consonant with those aspects of the Chinese tradition which were "based on the people". Some even went as far as to argue that democracy and constitutionalism had been introduced into Europe from ancient China, whilst bourgeois constitutionalists used the doctrine of Confucius and Mencius to preach Western democracy and constitutionalism. Western liberalism was, however, so different from the Chinese traditional conception that there were almost no grounds to mediate between the two. This is why liberalism met with indifference and even an instinctive resistance from the traditional national psychology. Moreover the Chinese bourgeoisie, which was potentially the deadly enemy of feudalism, was in no fit state to assert itself. Due to its economic and political weakness and to the limitations imposed by the Chinese system of estates, it had not developed a mature class consciousness, neither in terms of politics nor in terms of ideology. The bourgeoisie lacked the courage and strength that a clean break with feudal forces and culture would have required. They hoped to barter their acceptance of the feudal heritage with an equal share in society, or at least with peaceful coexistence. This conservatism may go some way to explain the Chinese bourgeoisie's reluctance to adopt liberalism. But, the bourgeoisie was not impermeable to the influx of Western political and legal thinking. It is worthy of note, however, that these ideas mostly came to China via Japan, and that Japan's experience, for reasons tied to national history, culture, as well as political reality, focused on the constitution whilst ignoring its liberal and individualist implications. The Japanese example therefore reiterated the omission of liberalism by the above-mentioned Chinese intellectuals, further delaying its impact on China.

We have looked at reasons for the delay with which individualism and liberalism came to influence Chinese thought, and have noted that these notions are conspicuously absent from the Chinese tradition; they can only be glimpsed among the most enlightened and democratic policies advocated by some Confucian thinkers and administrators. Furthermore, the cultural isolation of China was such that, at first, these terms could scarcely be translated into Chinese. As we have seen, China's domestic troubles and foreign invasions led progressive intellectuals to focus on European democratic politics and to criticize feudalism and the autocratic political system through the lens of the experience of Japan, which had already taken liberalism out of the equation. Japan's unexpected military victory over Russia and China was perceived as a consequence of the Meiji Reform. In this way a democratic political system came to be seen as a panacea which would build up the might and wealth of the Chinese people. This single-minded pursuit of the democratic goal made progressive thinkers forego a deeper research into the liberalism and individualism that lay at the core of European democratic politics. These concepts remained foreign to them, and were mentioned only in passing. The failure of progressive intellectuals to insist on the actual overthrow of the autocratic monarchy betrays their weakness. They preached the establishment of a constitutional monarchy instead, which entailed summoning parliament, formulating a constitution, and carrying out the separation of the three powers, on the condition that the emperor should stay. In the final analysis, European political thought was perceived as an invaluable *method* for governing the country, not as a *belief*.

The call for a set of fundamental human rights to preserve human dignity, personal property and safety, as well as to ensure freedom and equality, was to come half a century later; it was not immediately recognized as part and parcel of "democracy". Even as mere concepts, however, human rights did play a key role in sweeping away traditional ideas. The liberal idea of "human rights" lent democracy weight on a theoretical level. The influx and dissemination of Western democracy and constitutionalism, the ideas represented by liberalism and legal science awakened the powerful, sleeping Chinese lion. The lion stretched its limbs, raised its head, and opened its eyes to the world, as it began to think about its next step forward.

2.3 The democratic ideal and the constitutional reform of the Hundred Days: the turbulent year of 1898

The Wuxu Constitutional Reform still stands as the great attempt made by Chinese progressives who tried to follow the example of the modern powers in order to save China from extinction. Represented by Kang Youwei[27] and Liang Qichao,[28] the bourgeois reformists were imbued with the spirit of national salvation; they carefully set about designing a blueprint for a constitutional monarchy based on the example of Western countries. They advocated the establishment of parliament and a national conference, and wanted to see honest and fair-minded people with the courage to criticize authority installed in a position of power. National policies should be discussed by the monarch and the people. They also wanted a constitution to stipulate the rights and obligations of the monarch, officials, and the people. The constitution was to be the highest code for all people in the country. They also wanted to establish a system featuring a tripartite balance of forces: parliament was to legislate, the magistracy to deal with issues of justice, the government with administration. All of these would be under the monarch.

The constitutional reform was to take place with radical intellectuals submitting their memoranda to Emperor Guang Xu,[29] who alone had the power to promulgate them. The feudal diehards being in a position of strength and the national bourgeoisie being weak, however, the new politics survived no more than 100 days or so. When the forces of reaction inevitably clamped down on the movement, the six reformists who had inspired the movement for constitutional reform met their deaths like heroes.[30]

Although sincere in its aspirations, the reform movement was bound to fail, as it depended on a reform "from top to bottom", which ultimately had to be enacted by the emperor. The Hundred Days' Constitutional Reform, however, remains a landmark event in the modern history of China, its failure notwithstanding. The Chinese bourgeoisie in fact succeeded in spreading democratic and constitutionalist ideas widely, and this had a significant effect on future generations. The political and legal theory of the Western bourgeoisie could now take root in the soil of China.

2.4 The dawn of liberalism and legal reform at the end of the Qing Dynasty: the 1902–1911 revisions and their historical significance

As we have seen, the constitutional reform of 1898 was quashed. China was beset with internal and external difficulties. At the beginning of the twentieth century, the Qing Dynasty faced the aggression of the Eight Allied Powers[31] and the revolutionary movement under the leadership of Sun Yat-sen.[32] In order to save the tottering regime Cixi, the Empress Dowager,[33] issued a decree to implement "new policies" and to establish a "constitution". Reforming the law was a main concern of these policies. The revisions of 1902–1911 mark the beginning of the transition from 2000 years of feudal law to modern times. Needless to say, a fierce debate about the guidelines that these revisions ought to follow broke out.

The Party of *Rite* insisted that reforms should be undertaken on the grounds of the patriarchal *rite* intrinsic to the Chinese tradition, while the Legal Theory Party insisted on Western liberal guidelines based on an individualist theory of law. The former still considered China to be quite different from the west. As we have seen, the social structure of China had patriarchal clans as its basic unit, and the Party of *Rite* argued that the stability of the state and society rested on the stability of the clan. Feudal rights and the primacy of patriarchy should be maintained. Individualism meant that sons would turn against their fathers, invoking "legitimate defence", should the fathers blame them and beat them. The world would be turned upside down, and China would be plunged into chaos. The Legal Theory Party identified the equality and liberalism of Western powers as the sources of their strength. In order to stand on its own two feet and catch up with the rest of the world, China had to break the back of the ancient patriarchal system and devise a new one based on individualist law.[34]

The Legal Theory Party characteristically ended the debate with a compromise which resulted in democracy and constitutionalism playing a far greater role than liberalism in modern China. Nevertheless, the revision of the law swept away for good the traditional spirit of feudal law. These reforms constitute a great new start, and codified the spirit of Western law into actual legal articles. Important principles such as the observance of legality in criminal cases, transparency in trial and judgement, a system of advocacy with the right to a defence and the equality of all before the law were established and codified. Furthermore, the important distinction between the law and procedural law was introduced, with an independent code and added special regulations. The foundations of modern Chinese law were aligned more closely to the tradition of continental Europe. This is why the modernization of Chinese law is sometimes said to be synonymous with the "Europeanization of Chinese law". Legal science circles in China, however, only began to study and absorb the results of the British legal tradition as late as the 1980s, around the time that *The Oxford Companion to Law* was translated and published.[35]

3 CONTRASTS BETWEEN ANCIENT CHINESE THEORIES OF LAW AND MODERN EUROPEAN LAW[36]

3.1 The theory of ancient Chinese law: ruling by the law under the centralized system of government

During the period of the Warring States, the Legalists, a school of thought representing the burgeoning landlord class, formulated a "theory of law" whereby the country should be ruled according to the law. According to a key work by the Legalists, *Guan Zi* [*On Law*], "a society may be called the Great Order – which is the perfect state for a country – only when everybody in this society, from the monarch himself, through civil or military officials, the nobles, to the common people, abides by the laws".

The theory of *ruling by the law* presented by the Legalists had to be implemented with the support of the centralized political system. However, it was the monarch who had constructed the system of centralized autocratic government on the ruins of the outdated patriarchal clan system. As he had formulated the system of law, the paradox of two authorities that are by definition contradictory inevitably arose: the law demanded that everybody be subject to it, as did the authority of the Monarch. As Liang Qichao, a famous thinker of modern China, put it, if the theory of *ruling by the law* could ever be put into practice, it could only be done by the powerful backing of constitutionalism.[37] An ancient Chinese fable illustrates the logical absurdity and the paralysing antinomy presented by this version of *ruling by the law*. A merchant was selling a spear and a shield in the market. He declared his spear to be the sharpest in the world, and that it could pierce any shield. At the same time he boasted that his shield was the most solid in the world and that it could not be pierced by any spear. The people confuted him with a very simple question: "What happens if you use your spear against your shield?"

According to the Legalists' logic, everybody except the monarch must comply with the law. This practically amounted to this form of the rule of law being subject to the centralized political system.

3.2 The essential difference between ancient Chinese law and modern European law

The differences between ancient Chinese and modern European law are obvious. Firstly, the former belongs to Eastern culture, while the latter reflects Western culture. Secondly, the former is ancient, while the other is a product of modernity. Thirdly, the former is associated with the centralized autocratic system, while the latter is associated with the democratic system. The causes of such differences can be construed from different historical cultures and economic systems. Ancient Chinese law embodies collectivism and autocracy as *value bases*, whilst European modern law incarnates liberalism and individualism.

3.3 The superficial similarity of ancient Chinese law and modern european law

The law played an overwhelming role in social life and in the practice of *ruling by the law* in ancient China, especially during the Qin Dynasty, when it was implemented to the utmost. The authority of the law was accepted by society. A law tolerated no criticism after it was promulgated, and any official who added or took away one word from the law without authorization stood to be penalized. The authorities were ruthless with those who broke the law and committed crimes, and blind to wealth and rank. The functions of government agencies were regulated by the relevant laws and were subject to rigid supervision. Officials had to handle cases and arbitrate in strict conformity with the legal provisions. No personal judgement was to be involved, and no previous cases were to be cited. Owing to the meticulousness of the system of law, and to its "literal" application, the state machinery could function smoothly in a country as large and populous as China.

Liang Qichao has argued that the fundamental spirit of the Legalists was to ensure the holiness of the law and to prohibit the government from operating beyond its scope. These stances are consonant with the spirit of modern constitutional monarchy; indeed, they are identical.[38] Yan Buke points out that this spirit determined the necessity of the existence of the system of social estates, of statute law and of a body of professionals. The practice of *ruling by the law* under the Legalists' theory envisages a kind of rationalized administration under the guidance of such a spirit. The Legalists contributed important elaborations to the technical meaning of social order, power, regulation, and obligation, and to the composition of the administrative system and its operating mechanism.[39]

4 CONCLUDING REMARKS: BY WHAT STANDARDS CAN WE MEASURE THE ACHIEVEMENTS OF THE LEGAL CULTURE OF HUMAN BEINGS?

Geography makes for very real differences on the legal culture of human beings, as do the economic life and the historical and cultural traditions of countries and peoples. The task of a comparative jurist is to find out, by research, the causes behind such differences, and to try to make forecasts about the future. The Chinese legal tradition is the result of a natural evolution under a distinctive environment. Its history reveals one aspect of the legal experience of human beings, and we can find elements that reflect the common character of human culture even within its specificity. The mixed law that appeared in China alone, combining written law and case law, is a case in point. The rapid development of international exchanges entails the proliferation of the legal practices of a country or a nation, and the legal tradition must necessarily adapt. The trend towards a common development of legal practices on a global scale is bound to become more marked. The Chinese legal tradition in the future will no doubt participate in this common trend.

NOTES

1. In ancient China, many works were edited as collections of papers. Usually the papers did not contain the name of the author and the pages were not numbered. Moreover, most Chinese ancient works were edited in unknown times. Since there was no press in ancient China, works were copied by hand. Thus, when referring to

the content, Chinese scholars only indicated the name of the work and the name of the paper. In modern China, some scholars re-edited these ancient works and wrote modern Chinese introductions. For better referring to Chinese ancient works and papers, I have maintained their Chinese names while providing their English translations. Furthermore, I cite the introduction, relevant to the referred ancient works, published in modern times. Note that all the Chinese names in my essay have the surname in the first position and the given name in the second position, following the Chinese tradition.

2. For example, in the third century BC the legalists advocated handling affairs according to law, and proposed that the monarch, the officials, the nobles, the common people, the rich and the poor should abide by law with no exception. In the Tang Dynasty, there were severe legal norms to punish an official's illegal behaviour. Cf. Guan Zhong, *Guan Zi* [*On Law*]; the ancient Chinese editor of this work, who was known as Guan Zhong, is not the author of the bulk of the essays included in it; cf. Shi Yishen, *A Present Introduction to Guan Zi*, Beijing: Zhong-Guo-Shu-Dian Press, 1988, p. 336.
3. In June 1898 Emperor Guang Xu of Qing Dynasty adopted a constitutional monarchy and the tripartite system of powers, which was proposed by progressive exponents such as Kang Youwei and Liang Qichao. In September 1898, due to the strong opposition of the conservative forces, the reform failed.
4. The 15th National Congress of the Communist Party of China, held in September 1997, formulated the general policy of "governing the country according to law and transforming China into a country with strengthened socialist legal system". This is one of the key reforms in the realm of the superstructure during the transformation of the economic base from planned economy into market economy. This reform in essence refuses the practices of the past, according to which everything should depend on policies, political cadres, and the masses. It claims that the political, economic, and cultural life in China should entirely be brought into the orbit of the legal system. The large-scale legislating practices during the last 20 years, from 1978 to 1997, have created the necessary conditions for the implementation of such a general policy. The judiciary reform which was realized in recent years will further guarantee that implementation.
5. Wu Shu-chen, *The Traditional Legal Culture in China*, Beijing: Beijing University Press, 1994, pp. 35–41.
6. Xun Kuang, *Xun Zi – Wang Zhi*. Cf. Zhang Shitong, *A Preliminary Introduction of Xun Zi*, Shanghai: Shanghai People's Press, 1977, p. 77.
7. *ShangShu – Jiugao*. This political work was edited by an ancient, unknown scholar; cf. Wang Shishun, *Introduction to ShangShu*, Sichuan: Sichuan People's Press, 1982, p. 164.
8. Zuo Qiuming, *ZuoZhuang – Min Gong Yuan Nian*; cf. Yang Bojun, *An Introduction to Chun-Qiu ZuoZhuang*, Beijing: Zhong-Hua-Shu-Ju Press, 1981, p. 255.
9. A son is allowed to follow his own ideals when his father is alive. However, after the father passed away, his behaviour must be followed as a model. If the son follows and maintains his father's principles, he could be regarded as a worthy progeny (Confucius, *LunYu – Xue Er*). Cf. Yang Bojun, *An Introduction to Chun-Qiu ZuoZhuang*, Beijing: Zhong-Hua-Shu-Ju Press, 1980, p. 2.
10. The character of the ruler is the key element in the administration of a country. A good man in power results in a country's flourishing, but a bad man in power

bring declining fortune to the country (*LiJi – Zhong Yong*); cf. Chen Hao, *An Introduction to LiJi*, Shanghai: Shanghai Ancient Works Press, 1987, p. 290.

11. Each side of social life had its corresponding laws and decrees (Sima Qian, *ShiJi – Qin Shi Huang Ben Ji*); cf. *ShiJi*, Beijing: Zhong-Hua-Shu-Ju Press, 1972, p. 223.
12. Guan Zhong, *Guan Zi*.
13. Wu Shu-chen, *The Traditional Legal Culture in China*, pp. 413–27.
14. According to art. 13 of the *General Regulation under which the British Trade is to be Conducted at the Five Post at Canton, Amoy, Foochow, Ningpo and Shanghai* (8 October 1843), if a Chinese man was accused of a crime and had to be prosecuted, he should be tried by Chinese authorities, while in the case of a British man, he should be tried by an official of the British Consulate; cf. Wang Tieya, *The Collection of Old Treaties between China and Foreign Countries*, Beijing: San-Lian-Shu-Dian Press, 1957.
15. According to art. 12 of the *Commercial Treaty between China and Britain* (August 1903), the Chinese government should modify its national legal system assuming as a model the legislation of the Western countries. The British government declared to be inclined to assist the Chinese government in the course of the reform and to be ready to renounce to the consular jurisdiction just after the accomplishment of the reform of Chinese legal system and in particular the judicial structures and procedures. Cf. *Guang Xu Chao Dong Hua Lu*, ed. by Chao Dong (a scholar belonging to the Qing Dynasty), Beijing: Zhong-Hua-Shu-Ju Press, 1958.
16. Zhang Li and Liu Jiantang, *The History of Chinese Religious Cases*, Sichuan: Sichuan Social Science Press, 1987.
17. In Shanghai Public Concession some revolutionary militants were the publishers of a newspaper, *The Soviet Newspaper*, and other books advocating revolution. A Ministry of the Concession decided their imprisonment. The government of Qing Dynasty strongly claimed their extradition but without any success.
18. Lin Zexu (1785–1850) was an official of Qing Dynasty. As an imperial envoy, he ordered the destruction of more than one million kilograms of opium in Guang Zhou city. He recommended the study of the advanced technologies of the enemies in order to subdue them.
19. Lin Zexu, *Si Zhou Zhi*. Cf. Xiong Yuezhi, *The History of Democratic Thoughts in Modern China*, Shanghai: Shanghai People's Press, 1986, p. 72.
20. Wei Yuan (1794–1857), an official of Qing Dynasty, maintained political opinions similar to those of Lin Zexu.
21. Wei Yuan, *Hai Guo Tu Zhi*. Cf. Xiong Yuezhi, *The History of Democratic Thoughts in Modern China*, p. 73.
22. In January 1985, the Yue-Lu-Shu-She Press published the first volume of the series *Going through the World*, collecting in ten books notes and diaries written by officials, diplomatic envoys, and scholars who had visited Europe, the United States, and Japan before 1912; cf. *Series of Going to the World*, vol. 1, Hunan: Yue-Lu-Shu-She Press, 1985.
23. Yan Fu (1854–1921), famous enlightenment thinker, studied at Greenwich Navy College in Great Britain. He advocated political reforms according to Western models, and the practice of constitutional monarchy.
24. Yan Fu, *Yan Yi Ming Zhu Cong Kan*, Beijing: Shang-Wu-Yin-Shu-Guan Press, 1931.
25. Yan Fu, *Yan Fu Ji – Yuan Qiang*, Beijing: Zhong-Hua-Shu-Ju Press, 1986, p. 11.

26. Xiong Yuezhi, *The Democratic Thought. History of Modern China*, Shanghai: Shanghai People's Press, 1986, pp. 20, 15.
27. Kang Youwei (1858–1927), leader of modern Chinese bourgeois reformism, took part in the constitutional reform of 1898. After the failure of the reform he was incriminated and fled abroad.
28. Liang Qichao (1873–1929), another leader of modern Chinese bourgeois reformism, in 1898 cooperated with Kang Youwei in constitutional reform. After the failure of the reform he took refuge in Japan.
29. Emperor Guang Xu (1871–1908), member of the Qing Dynasty, was on the throne from 1875 to 1908. On 11 June 1898, he declared his propensity to political reforms. In 21 September 1898, he was put under house arrest during the coup d'etat organized by Empress dowager Ci Xi.
30. On September 1898, the "Six Gentlemen" – Tan Sitong, Kang Guangren, Liu Guangdi, Lin Xu, Yang Rui, and Yang Shengxiu – were put to death.
31. The allied forces of eight countries (Great Britain, the United States, Germany, France, Russia, Japan, Italy, and Austria) occupied Beijing on 14 August 1900. They committed robberies and massacres. The government of Qing Dynasty was obliged by the eight victorious countries to sign humiliating treaties.
32. Sun Zhongshan (1866–1925), the forerunner of the Chinese revolution and the founder of the KuoMinTang party, proclaimed the Three People's Principles: nationalism, democracy, and people's welfare.
33. Ci Xi (1835–1908), Empress-Dowager at the end of the Qing Dynasty, was the most powerful representative of the conservative forces.
34. Wu Shu-chen, *The Traditional Legal Culture in China*, chap. 8, sect. 2.
35. D.M. Walker, *Oxford Companion Dictionary to Law*, New York: Oxford University Press, 1958.
36. From my point of view, I look on the word "contrast" as a method or angle for research, which may be most suited to the following two cases: (1) objects *a* and *b* start off at two different points. After undergoing different tracks, they arrive at the same terminal point *c*; (2) objects *a* and *b* are originally at the same point *c*. After going through different tracks, they arrive at different terminal points *a* and *b*. In the case when objects *a* and *b* share no common starting point and no common terminal point but run abreast, contrast is also suitable. It is necessary to avoid only enumerating facts in a superficial way. It is also my point that the objective of contrast is not only to find the difference between different objects, but also to reveal the historical causes of the difference, and to discover the laws governing the development of history. Genuine contrast by no means implies the judgement that one object is superior, while the other is inferior. However, it is hard to compare objectively, because people are always living within a certain cultural frame, and are always accustomed to making judgements using their own cultural values.
37. Liang Qichao, *Political Thought History of Earlier Qing Dynasty*, Beijing: Zhong-Hua-Shu-Ju Press, 1936, p. 149.
38. Ibid., p. 147.
39. Yan Buke, The *History of the Development of Literati and Officialdom Politics*, Beijing: Beijing University Press, 1996, p. 171.

CHAPTER 20

MODERN CONSTITUTIONALISM IN CHINA

Lin Feng

1 INTRODUCTION

The origin of the concept of "constitution" is generally believed to date back to ancient Greece.[1] The word "constitution" (Xian) existed also in ancient Chinese literature,[2] though it only referred to the country's national code or ordinary legislation.[3] Its meaning, therefore, was quite different from contemporary understanding of "constitution" as the highest law of a nation or state. Such a modern understanding of "constitution" has been adopted in contemporary China since the late Qing Dynasty, when the concept of constitutionalism was first introduced into China.[4] This chapter will examine China's constitutional development.

2 CHINA'S CONSTITUTIONAL DEVELOPMENT BEFORE 1949

Constitutionalism in modern China dates back to the late nineteenth century, when it was felt that a written constitution could save the collapsing Qing Dynasty.[5] The idea of the necessity and importance of a constitution started to gain ground. The establishment of a monarchical constitutional structure was suggested. The Qing Government outlined the general principles of its proposed constitution in 1908.[6] Three years later, the last Qing Government enacted China's first written constitution.[7] Yet, the Qing Dynasty and its written constitution shortly came to an end when the National Party established its interim government of the Republic of China in Nanjing on 1 January 1912.

On 11 March, Sun Yat-sen, the interim President, promulgated the Interim Constitution, which had been approved by the Senate. The Interim Constitution differed dramatically from the constitution of the Qing Government, in that it established, for the first time in history, that the sovereignty of the Republic of China belonged to all citizens. It also incorporated popular participation (through elections), democratic freedom, and the doctrine of separation of powers.[8] Soon after the constitution's enactment, there started a period of fighting among warlords

P. Costa and D. Zolo (eds.), The Rule of Law: History, Theory and Criticism, 633–646.

for the conquest of political leadership, which led to the abolition of the Interim Constitution; it gave way to the warlords' ambition for totalitarian control. Each warlord who came into power enacted his own constitution.[9] In 1931, the National Party regained power and enacted another constitution that recognized both the leading status of the National Party and Jiang Jieshi as President. According to this constitution, the government was subordinated to the National Party. It remained in force until 1946, when the National Congress enacted the Constitution of the Republic of China.[10] The latter, however, remained valid on Mainland China only for 3 years, since the National Party was defeated in 1949 by the Communist Party and left for Taiwan.

3 CHINESE CONSTITUTIONAL DEVELOPMENT UNDER COMMUNIST PARTY LEADERSHIP

In the 1930s, i.e. even before taking control of the whole of Mainland China,[11] the Chinese Communist Party started enacting constitutional documents in order to facilitate its administration. Such constitutional documents provided the basis for the enactment of the Common Programme, i.e. the Interim Constitution of the People's Republic of China (hereinafter "the PRC"), this being established when the Communist Party took full control of China in 1949.[12] Since 1949 and until today, the PRC has adopted one interim constitution and four formal constitutions. The Interim Constitution, i.e. the so-called Common Programme, was enacted in 1949 by the new national Chinese People's Political Consultative Conference (hereinafter as "the CPPCC").[13] The four formal constitutions were enacted by the National People's Congress (NPC) in 1954, 1975, 1978, and 1982.

3.1 The 1949 "Common Programme"

Beginning from 1948, the Chinese Communist Party called upon a large number of Chinese people, including democratic parties, people's organizations, and democratic advocates without any political affiliation, to attend the national CPPCC so as to set up a Chinese united democratic government.[14] The CPPCC held its first meeting on 21 September 1949. On this occasion, Mao Zedong stated that the meeting represented all Chinese people's will and was aimed at their unity.[15] He announced that Chinese people, amounting to one-fourth of the world population, would now have a decisive role.[16] After thorough discussions, the meeting adopted the Common Programme of the CPPCC on 29 September 1949. In line with Marxism, the Common Programme was not deemed to be a constitutional document, since the CPPCC was not the State's supreme power organ, i.e. the NPC, and therefore was not allowed to enact a constitutional document. Yet, in practice, the Common Programme did perform the functions typical of a constitution and thus was a de facto interim constitution.

The Common Programme was made of one preamble, seven chapters, and 60 articles. As an interim constitution, it proclaimed the creation and legitimacy of the PRC and laid down the state's basic policies and tasks, together with the people's fundamental rights and obligations.[17] It established that the PRC acknowledged the people's democratic dictatorship,[18] to be exerted through the people's congresses and governments at various levels.[19] Given that the Common Programme mainly set the State's tasks for that specific stage of its development,[20] it was more an action plan rather than a Western-style constitutional document.

It is not surprising that the Common Programme was clearly marked by its contingent historical circumstances. Firstly, for example, the subjects entitled to exercise state power were the people, i.e. a political concept, rather than the citizens, i.e. a civil concept.[21] The former concept has indeed a narrower scope than the latter. The reason behind such an approach was that the Chinese Communist Party had just come into power and was still trying to consolidate its control of society. Secondly, both the people's congress and its government were authorized to exercise state power. The Common Programme did not feel the need to clearly define the powers of the people's congress and the people's government respectively, together with the relationship between these two organs.[22] Thirdly, the Common Programme did not incorporate socialism, since national capitalism still played an important role in society.

The composition of the first CPPCC might be regarded as very democratic, since out of its 180 members, 120 were not members of the Chinese Communist Party. Moreover, 17 out of 28 members of the CPPCC's Standing Committee were not members of the Chinese Communist Party.[23] Hence, the CPPCC's composition was quite representative and the Chinese Communist Party was not the majority. In practice, however, the Chinese Communist Party was confident it could control the CPPCC as a result of the allocation of the quota of CPPCC members: one-third to the Communist Party, one-third to those who supported the Communist Party, and one-third to those whose position was still unclear.[24] Hence, the Communist Party was confident it could obtain a two-thirds majority in any vote.

3.2 The 1954 Constitution

Shortly after the founding of the PRC, Mao Zedong visited the former Soviet Union. During his visit, Stalin urged him to hold an NPC and to enact a constitution.[25] This suggestion was accepted by Mao and China, since it was believed that both the former Soviet Union and China endorsed the same regime, i.e. the international communist regime; moreover, it was felt that the former Soviet Union was "the big brother" of socialist countries.[26] Apart from the Soviet Union's impact, the enactment of the 1954 Constitution was due to a further and more important practical reason. As a matter of fact, after several years during which the Chinese Communist Party had consolidated its power, it now had to choose whether to endorse capitalism or socialism.[27] At the time, even though land had been allocated to peasants, national capitalists still controlled cities' industries and commerce. Two lines of thought contested within the Communist Party. Some members argued that stability was very important and that, consequently, the Common Programme approach was to be left unaltered. This meant that it was more natural for the PRC to develop capitalism.[28] Yet, the majority of the Party's leaders questioned the adoption of capitalism, which would imply a shift from the people's democratic dictatorship, under the leadership of the working class, to capitalist dictatorship.[29] In the light of such circumstances, the Chinese Communist Party opted for socialism. Quite likely, the communist concepts of the State and law had a strong impact upon such a decision. According to Marxism, human development may be divided into six stages: primitive communism, slavery, feudalism, capitalism, socialism, and communism.[30] A socialist society is more advanced than a capitalist society. Since China had the choice of endorsing a more advanced society, i.e. a socialist society, by bypassing the capitalist one, it would have been unforgivable for the Chinese Communist Party to choose a path leading to a less advanced stage of human development.[31]

On such groundings, the Chinese Communist Party enacted a formal constitution for the administration of the PRC. The drafting committee of the constitution held its first meeting on 24 March 1954, and accepted the draft constitution proposed by the Chinese Communist Party's Central Committee.[32] More than 8,000 people actively participated in the research and discussion of the draft constitution. Moreover, more than 150 million citizens nationwide participated in such a discussion and 1,180,420 opinions and proposals were put forward.[33] After the incorporation of some of the above opinions and proposals, the Central People's Governmental Committee (the predecessor of the State Council) adopted the amended draft constitution and submitted it to the first NPC for its consideration, which adopted it on 20 September 1954.[34]

The 1954 Constitution was based upon the Common Programme, though it developed it even further. It comprised one preamble, four chapters, and 106 articles. It "normalized" the social and political order under the governance of the Chinese Communist Party. One of the main functions of China's first constitution was to legitimize the socialist transformation, though the constitution was later highly praised not only for the direction towards which it led the nation, but also for its democratic drafting process. It confirmed the tasks of the state during its transition towards socialism, and established the people's congress system.[35]

The 1954 Constitution was deeply affected by the Soviet model. Its structure, general principles, the state's apparatus, and citizen's fundamental rights and obligations were very similar to the relevant provisions of the former Soviet Union's constitution of 1936.[36] Although the constitution was positively viewed, its enactment was soon interrupted by a series of political movements which started in 1956.[37]

3.3 The 1975 Constitution

From 1956 to 1976, there was a total lack of respect for law and the constitution. In 1975, when such an unprecedented period of political disaster was drawing to an end, the PRC enacted its second constitution. The 1975 Constitution was a big step backwards with respect to the 1954 Constitution, and clearly reflected the historical circumstances of the time. The aim of the 1975 Constitution was to consolidate the alleged "achievements" of the Cultural Revolution.[38] It contained only 30 articles. The chapter on the constitution's general principles was made of 15 articles, whereas the chapter on citizens' basic rights and obligations only had four articles. Only one article concerned the judiciary, one regarded ethnic minorities living in autonomous regions, two articles dealt with the State Council, and three with the NPC.[39]

The 1975 Constitution clearly demonstrated how a constitutional document could be used to negate and eliminate constitutionalism.[40]

3.4 The 1978 Constitution

Three years later, and following another dramatic political movement in 1976 (when the "Gang of Four" was removed from the political arena), a new constitution was adopted on 5 March 1978 with the aim of bringing the state back to its normal track, thus repudiating its immediate predecessor. The 1978 Constitution was made of a preamble, four chapters, and 60 articles. However, it was clearly still influenced by the Cultural

Revolution, especially in its emphasis on class struggles.[41] The 1978 Constitution failed to address many issues, such as the role of private economy, the stability and authority of constitutional amendments, and so on.[42] It was amended twice, in 1979 and in 1980. The 1979 amendment aimed at strengthening local governments, whereas the 1980 amendment aimed at attaining political stability by removing the right "to freely speak out and give voice to opinions, to hold great debates and write big-character posters".[43] Western scholars believed that the removal of such rights was carried out to suppress the democratic movement led by Wei Jinsheng and others at the end of August 1978.[44] Yet, most Chinese constitutional scholars claimed it was mainly aimed at preventing the recurrence of events similar to the Cultural Revolution. Moreover, it was held that such articles were redundant in that freedom of expression was guaranteed by the 1978 Constitution itself.[45]

3.5 The 1982 Constitution

The 1982 Constitution is regarded as China's best constitution. It is made of a preamble, four chapters, and 138 articles. The preamble highlights the country's four cardinal principles,[46] the state's basic tasks during the new historical period, the relevant national policies, and the supremacy of the constitution.[47] It officially confirms the primacy of the constitution and the fact that other legislation ought to be grounded thereon. No laws or administrative rules and regulations may contravene the constitution.[48] It has been argued that such a legal hierarchy guarantees the Chinese legal system's integrity.[49] However, there may arise tensions between the constitution's authority and the NPC's supremacy, which is further complicated by the confirmed leadership of the Chinese Communist Party.

The 1982 Constitution was amended on three occasions, respectively in 1988, 1993, and 1999. The 1988 amendments added a new paragraph to Article 11 of the 1982 Constitution, this establishing that "The State allows private economy to exist and develop within the limits prescribed by law. Private economy integrates socialist public economy. The State protects the lawful rights and interests of the private sector of economy, and exercises its guidance, supervision and control over it".[50] The fourth paragraph of Article 10 of the 1982 Constitution was also amended, so that "No organization or individual may appropriate, buy, sell or otherwise be engaged in the transfer of land by unlawful means. The right to use land may be transferred according to law".[51] The incorporation of such provisions, mainly concerned with the economic system, formally legitimized the private economy as well as the transfer of land rights.

Such amendments clearly epitomized the Chinese economy's opening up to the market and the relinquishment of socialist dogmas in the name of pragmatism.

The 1993 amendments included nine articles,[52] mainly aimed at setting up a Chinese-inspired form of socialism.[53] The constitution was also revised in a number of articles in order to keep abreast with economic development trends. Out of these nine articles, six concerned different aspects of the so-called socialist market economy with Chinese characteristics,[54] two dealt with politics (re-emphasizing the leading status of the Chinese Communist Party[55]), and one regarded the state's basic tasks.[56]

Six amendments were made to the constitution in 1999[57] with the aim of incorporating therein specific decisions made by the 15th National Congress of the Chinese Communist Party.[58] Out of the six amendments, three were concerned with the establishment of the market economy with Chinese characteristics, granting the private economy the same status as that of the state-owned public economy and legitimizing other means of allocation.[59] One amendment concerned the state's basic tasks and also incorporated Deng Xiaoping's theory into the constitution's preamble.[60] One amendment established the country's governance according to law,[61] which thus formally committed the Chinese Communist Party to adopt the rule of law within the PRC. The last amendment turned counter-revolutionary crimes into offences against national security, in line with the latest changes in Chinese criminal law.[62] Once again, the 1999 constitutional amendments simply confirmed and legitimized the PRC's already-existing practices.

4 COMMENTS

The above discussion leads us to the following comments. Firstly, the 1982 Constitution is explicitly grounded on Marxism–Leninism and on Mao Zedong's thinking.[63] Such an express constitutional reference means that the constitution is bound to mirror Marxist constitutional theories on the state and law. According to Marxism, economy is the basis, and law is the superstructure, the former's nature determining the latter's. China's modern constitutional history clearly demonstrates that China's constitutional practice is fully consistent with Marxism. Its constitution is largely devoted to the economic system.[64] Since the Chinese economy often undergoes a number of fundamental reforms, the constitution occasionally and unavoidably represents an obstacle, and therefore needs to be from time to time amended. Quite often, unauthorized economic activities are carried out even before the relevant amendments are made.[65] For this reason, a number of scholars have suggested the idea of a benign constitutional violation (*liang xing wei xian*) and have argued that, such a violation being unavoidable, it should also be tolerated.[66] Yet, such an approach has been strongly criticized by other Chinese constitutional scholars.[67]

Secondly, the 1982 Constitution still reflects a class approach. According to the orthodox Marxist approach, the constitution is nothing but the representation of the ruling class's will. Although class struggle has given way to economic development, it does not necessarily follow that the constitution or law are not class-oriented.[68] Nowadays, the class approach is clearly matched by the affirmation of the Chinese Communist Party's leadership, this representing the working class, which is also China's ruling class. Such a leadership has been reconfirmed by the 1999 constitutional amendments.

Thirdly, ever since China's 1949 constitutional development, China has endorsed an instrumentalist conception of the constitution.[69] While, in the past, the constitution was used as an instrument for political struggle, as from the 1980s it has been used for the country's economic development. Hence, the constitution has been turned from an instrument for class struggle to an indispensable instrument for economic development. Whether or not the specific provisions of the constitution are complied with is largely dependent on how well such provisions serve the government's aims. Such an instrumentalist approach is evidenced by the frequency of constitutional amendments.

China's pragmatic and instrumental approach towards the constitution has both negatively and positively affected social development. Indeed, given that China is still undergoing a transitional period from a planned economy to a market economy, the need to frequently change laws is particularly strong. Yet, the constitution is the prime legislation: it should be as certain as possible and should only be rarely amended. In order to guarantee its certainty, its preamble could be removed, this simply being an overview of China's historical development and an ideological statement. Moreover, the relevant provisions on the economic system could be annulled, since the system itself is still undergoing significant changes. Alternatively, the preamble of the constitution could be seen as a set of programmatic and non-enforceable provisions; in this case, only its provisions on the economic system would need to be removed. If China really wishes to develop a lasting and respectable constitutional order, it may have to give up its instrumental approach and adopt the rule of law principle, of which the 1999 amendments are a first endorsement.

5 A COMPARISON WITH US CONSTITUTIONAL DEVELOPMENT

Although a detailed comparison with the constitutional development of the different world jurisdictions is beyond the scope of this short chapter, it is believed that a brief comparison between Chinese and US constitutional development, the latter having the oldest written constitution, will contribute to a better understanding of Chinese constitutional development and its future. The following differences can be identified.

Firstly, the background against which the constitutions were enacted is different. The US constitution was enacted after 6 years of warfare with Britain and after a further 6 years of political uncertainty under its Confederation.[70] Hence, the constitution's main task was to forge a sense of nationhood and to foster the American people's trust in the durability of the federal republic.[71] In China, instead, its first constitutional document was aimed at saving the collapsing Qing Dynasty; Communist China's very first constitutional document, i.e. the Common Programme, was enacted shortly after the Chinese Communist Party had defeated the National Party and taken control of the whole of mainland China; therefore, its purpose in enacting the Interim Constitution was to ensure the leading status of the Chinese Communist Party.

Secondly, the fundamental aims behind the enactment of the Chinese and US constitutions were entirely different. The founders of the US constitution aimed at striking a proper balance between liberty and authority through the setting up of a political system, allowing for democracy and popular participation, both at the State level and in the lower legislature.[72] The American people's liberties are constitutionally protected by: (1) the division of power among groups with different interests, so that each state organ controls and counterbalances other organs and (2) a strong consensus and commitment to respect fundamental liberties on behalf of civil society which, albeit external to government, is nonetheless fundamental for the latter's support.[73] In contemporary China, the constitution has been often used as an instrument to consolidate the Communist Party's war achievements and its leading position. A proper balance between authority and people's liberties is lacking in all the Communist Party's five constitutional documents. Although protection of liberties is indeed mentioned, it is far from matching the description that was given thereof by Justice Oliver Wendell Holmes of the US Supreme Court about half a century ago: "If there is any principle of the constitution that more imperatively calls for attachment than any other, it is the principle of free thought; not free thought for those who agree with us but freedom for the thought we hate".[74] Since such a principle is not endorsed by the Chinese Communist Party in constitutional documents, it follows that freedom to differ from the Chinese Communist Party is not allowed.

Thirdly, even though both the US and Chinese constitutions are "rigid" constitutions, their degree of inflexibility is different. In the United States, the constitution may be amended only by two-thirds of the House and Senate and by three-fourths of the States; hence, a bipartisan agreement is required and both parties need to support the amendment.[75] History has proven that the US political party system, depicted by James Madison as "a natural offspring of freedom",[76] renders constitutional amendments very difficult. All four Chinese constitutions are theoretically rigid though, as seen above, they have frequently been replaced by new constitutions or have been constitutionally amended. The reason behind such a circumstance is that the Chinese constitution has failed to sufficiently and constitutionally guarantee freedom. Hence, its "natural offspring", i.e. a mature political party system, has not developed; the Chinese Communist Party has always exercised absolute control over the country and, most importantly, also over the supreme organ of state power, i.e. the NPC, which is entitled to enact and amend the constitution.

Fourthly, the US and Chinese different constitutional aims result in different constitutional contexts. The US constitution is primarily divided into two parts: one concerning the government's constitutional structure, the other dealing with the protection of people's liberties. The Chinese constitution contains more substantial provisions than the US one. For instance, it contains provisions on the economic system, which leads to it being frequently amended. It also contains provisions restricting people's liberties. Yet, it is clear that any change in Chinese constitutional contexts must necessarily be matched by changes in the understanding of the constitution's role and purposes.

Fifthly, the control on the constitution's enforcement is different. In the United States, any issue relating to constitutionality is reviewed by the courts and ultimately by the Supreme Court. In China, the NPC and its Standing Committee, i.e., the Legislature, are theoretically entitled to control the enforcement of the constitution. In practice, however, the constitution is not taken seriously: no single case concerning constitutionality has ever been examined by the NPC or its Standing Committee. In order for the constitution to be taken seriously and to be treated as China's supreme law, a proper and effective mechanism for constitutional review should be established. It would indeed contribute to the development of China's constitutionalism.

The above comparison has shown that there is ample room for further improvement in China's future constitutional development. The US constitutional model has been a comparatively successful one, from which China can learn significant lessons. However, it ought to be recalled that the US model is not perfect: as has been argued, the US constitutional structure is affected by severe problems, such as an executive and legislature divided on partisan lines and the lack of a mechanism for the resolution of a governmental crisis, which may lead the country to a notable institutional *impasse*.[77]

NOTES

1. Aristotle, *Politics*, book 4, chap. 1, in S. Everson (ed.), *The Politics and the Constitution of Athens*, Cambridge: Cambridge University Press, 1996, pp. 91–118; cf. also Wang Shijie and Qian DuanSheng, *Bijiao Xianfa* [*Comparative Constitutional Law*], Beijing: China University of Politics and Law, 1997, pp. 14–15.
2. For a detailed discussion of the word "Xian" [Constitution], cf. Qian Daqun, "Xian Yi Nue Kao" ["A Brief Research on the Meaning of 'Xian'"], in *Nanjin Daxue XueBao* [*Academic Journal of Nanjing University*], 2 (1984). Cf. also Zhang Qingfu, "The nature of constitution", in Li Buyun (ed.), *Comparative Study of Constitution*, Beijing: Law Publishing House, 1998, pp. 8–10.
3. Xu Chongde, *Zhongguo Xianfa* [*Chinese Constitutional Law*], Beijing: People's University Press, 1996, p. 20.
4. Ibid., p. 21.
5. See Wang Yongxiang, *Zhongguo Xiandai Xianzheng Yundong Shi* [*The History of Constitutionalism in Modern China*], Beijing: People's Press, 1996, p. 3; cf. also Xu Chongde, op. cit., pp. 5–6.
6. The proposal was not constitutional itself and therefore had no legal effect. It consisted of two parts: one concerning the sovereign's authority (14 articles) and the other concerning citizens' rights and duties (9 articles). It was modelled on the Japanese Constitution. For details, cf. Yin Xiaohu, *Jindai Zhongguo Xianzheng Shi* [*The History of Modern Constitutionalism in China*], Shanghai: Shanghai People's Press, 1997, p. 54.
7. It had 19 articles and was modelled on the United Kingdom Sovereign Charter. It imposed certain restrictions on the authority of the Emperor and expanded Parliament's power. Yet, it also removed the section devoted to citizens' rights and duties. For details, cf. Yin Xiaohu, op. cit., pp. 96–104.
8. Ibid., pp. 128–38.
9. For a detailed discussion of such constitutions, cf. Yin Xiaohu, op. cit., pp. 138–219.
10. In 1932, the National Party decided to organize a national congress to enact a formal constitution. A constitutional drafting committee was set up in 1933. For a detailed discussion, cf. Yin Xiaohu, op. cit., pp. 230–58.
11. See Yin Xiaohu, op. cit., pp. 259–74.
12. See Wen Zhengbang, *Gongheguo Xianzheng Licheng* [*The History of Constitutionalism in the People's Republic of China*], Zhenzhou: Henan People's Press, 1994, pp. 1–17.

13. Cf. Xu Chongde, op. cit., pp. 97–110.
14. Cf. Wen Zhengbang, op. cit., pp. 2–3.
15. Ibid., p. 22.
16. Mao Zedong, *Maozedong Xuanji* [*Collection of Mao's Works*], Beijing: People's Press, 1996, vol. 5, pp. 3, 5, 6, 8.
17. See the preamble and chap. 1 of the 1949 Common Programme.
18. See the preamble and art. 1 of the 1949 Common Programme.
19. See art. 12 of the 1949 Common Programme.
20. See chaps. 1, 4, and 5 of the 1949 Common Programme.
21. The Chinese word for "people" is Ren Min, and for "citizen" is Gong Min. The former refers to those who support the leadership of the Communist Party, whereas the latter refers to all individuals with a Chinese nationality. For details, cf. Xu Congde, op. cit., p. 399.
22. See the Common Programme, art. 12, collected in *Zhonghua Renmin Gongheguo Falu Fagui Quanshu* [*Collection of the Laws and Regulations of the People's Republic of China*], Beijing: China Democracy and Legal System Press, 1994, vol. 1, p. 2.
23. Cf. Wen Zhenbang, op. cit., pp. 11–12.
24. Ibid., p. 12.
25. Ibid., p. 18.
26. Ibid., pp. 18–22.
27. Ibid., pp. 23–7.
28. Ibid., p. 25.
29. Ibid.
30. See Albert HY Chen, *An Introduction to the Legal System of the People's Republic of China*, Singapore: Butterworths Asia, 1992, chaps. 2 and 3.
31. Cf. Wen Zhengbang, op. cit., p. 25.
32. The draft constitution was proposed by the Communist Party, as it is always the case in the People's Republic of China. This is quite an extraordinary circumstance according to modern standards, given that nowadays such drafts are commonly proposed by an authorized state organ rather than by a party institution.
33. Cf. Wen Zhengbang, op. cit., pp. 27–30.
34. At the same meeting several national laws were adopted, among which the Organic Law of the National People's Congress of the People's Republic of China, the Organic Law of the State Council of the People's Republic of China, the Organic Law of the People's Procurator of the People's Republic of China, and the Organic Law of the Local People's Congresses and Local People's Committees of the People's Republic of China.
35. See the preamble to and art. 2 of the 1954 Constitution of the People's Republic of China, collected in *Zhonghua Renmin Gongheguo Falu Fagui Quanshu* [*Collection of Laws and Regulations of the People's Republic of China*], Beijing: China Democracy and Legal System Press, 1994, vol. 1, p. 5. Cf. also Han Dayuan (ed.), *Xinzhongguo Xianfa Fazhanshi* [*The Historical Constitutional Development of the PRC*], Shijiazhuang: Hebei People's Press, 2000, pp. 36–95.
36. Cf. Wen Zhengbang, op. cit., p. 55.
37. Ibid., chaps. 4 and 5, pp. 58–94.
38. It is explicitly stated as one of the six principles contained in the notice issued by the Communist Party's Central Committee concerning the discussion of the bill of the 1975 Constitution; cf. Han Dayuan, op. cit., pp. 108–11.

39. Cf. Wen Zhengbang, op. cit., chap. 6, pp. 95–119.
40. Ibid.
41. Ibid., chap. 7, pp. 120–42. See paras. 4 and 5 of the preamble to the 1978 Constitution.
42. Ibid., chap. 7, pp. 120–42.
43. They are the so-called four great rights. Chinese and Western scholars attach different importance to such rights. For details, cf. Albert Hy Chen, op. cit., p. 44; and Wen Zhengbang, op. cit., chap. 8, pp. 143–62.
44. Cf. Albert Hy Chen, op. cit., p. 44.
45. Cf. Wen Zhengbang, op. cit., chap. 8, pp. 143–62.
46. The four cardinal principles are the leadership of the Communist Party, the guidance of Marxism–Leninism and Mao Zedong's thoughts, the endorsement of the people's democratic dictatorship and socialism. See the preamble to the 1982 Constitution of the People's Republic of China, collected in *Zhonghua Renmin Gongheguo Falu Fagui Quanshu* [*Collection of Laws and Regulations of the People's Republic of China*], Beijing: China Democracy and Legal System Press, 1994, vol. 1, pp. 20–1.
47. See chap. 1 and the last paragraph of the preamble to the 1982 Constitution.
48. See the last paragraph of the preamble and art. 5(2) of the 1982 Constitution.
49. Cf. Wen Zhengbang, op. cit., pp. 215–16.
50. See art. 1 of the Constitutional Amendments.
51. See art. 2 of the Constitutional Amendments.
52. They are arts. 3–11 of the Constitutional Amendments.
53. Cf. Han Dayuan, op. cit., pp. 230–35.
54. See arts. 5–10 of the Constitutional Amendments.
55. See arts. 4 and 11 of the Constitutional Amendments.
56. See art. 3 of the Constitutional Amendments.
57. They constitute arts. 12–17 of the Constitutional Amendments.
58. Cf. Han Dayuan, op. cit., pp. 235–59.
59. See arts. 14–16 of the Constitutional Amendments.
60. See art. 12 of the Constitutional Amendments.
61. See art. 13 of the Constitutional Amendments.
62. See art. 17 of the Constitutional Amendments.
63. See the 1982 Constitution, *Preamble*.
64. See the 1982 Constitution, arts. 6–8.
65. For example, the right to use land became transferable in Shenzhen even before the 1988 Constitutional Amendments.
66. Cf. Hao Tiechuan, "Lun Liangxin Weixian" ["Analysis of Beneficial Violation of Constitution"], *Faxue Yanjiu* [*Legal Studies*], 18 (1996), 4, pp. 89–91.
67. Cf. Tong Zhiwei, "Liangxin Weixian Buyi Kending – Dui Hao Tiecuan Tongzhi Youguan Zhuzhang de Butong Kanfa" ["Benign Violation of Constitution should not be Accepted – A Different View from the Views of Hao Tiachuan"], *Faxue Yanjiu* [*Legal Studies*], 18 (1996), pp. 19–22; cf. also Tong Zhi Wei, "Xiafa Sheshi Linghuoxing de Dixian-Zai yu Hao Tiechuan Tongzhi Shangque" ["The Bottomline of Flexible Implementation of the Constitution – Another Dialogue with Hao Tiechuan"], *Fa Xue* [*Legal Science*], 5 (1997), pp. 15–17.
68. Cf. the Group on Politics of the Research Office of the General Office of the Standing Committee of the National People's Congress, *Zhongguo Xianfa Jingshe* [*Detailed Annotation of Chinese Constitution*], Beijing: Zhongguo Minzhu Fazhi

[Democracy and Legal System Press], 1996, pp. 84–5. Cf. also Xu Chongde, op. cit., pp. 24–6.
69. Cf. Yu Xingzhong, "Legal pragmatism in the People's Republic of China", *Journal of Chinese Law*, 1989, pp. 40–2.
70. See R. Garson, "The Intellectual Reference of the American Constitution", in R. Maidment and J. Zvesper (eds), *Reflections on the Constitution: the American Constitution after Two Hundred Years*, Manchester/New York: Manchester University Press, 1989, p. 3.
71. Ibid., passim.
72. Ibid., pp. 1–13.
73. Cf. W.B. Mead, *The United States Constitution: Personalities, Principles, and Issues*, Columbia (SC): University of South Carolina Press, 1987, pp. 5–6.
74. See *US v. Schwimmer*, 1929.
75. Cf. D.S. Lutz, *The Origins of American Constitutionalism*, Baton Rouge (LA)/London: Louisiana State University Press, 1988, p. 177.
76. Cf. J.L. Sundquist, "Is the US Constitution adequate for the twenty-first century?", in R.C. Simmons, *The United States Constitution: The First 200 Years*, Manchester: Manchester University Press, 1989, p. 175.
77. Ibid., p. 183.

CHAPTER 21

HUMAN RIGHTS AND THE RULE OF LAW IN CONTEMPORARY CHINA

Wang Zhenmin and Li Zhenghui

1 THE HISTORICAL LESSON OF THE CULTURAL REVOLUTION

It has been roughly estimated that the direct economic loss suffered by China as a result of its 10-year Cultural Revolution amounted to RMB 500 billion yuan. The loss caused by the 1958 Great Leap Forward amounted to 120 billion yuan. However, China's overall investment in building infrastructures from 1949 to 1979 was equal only to RMB 600 billion yuan.[1] In 1976, at the end of the Cultural Revolution, China's national economy was about to collapse. It is by no means possible to calculate the ensuing irremediable devastation caused, *inter alia*, to China's education, science, and culture.

Once the Cultural Revolution came to an end, China reviewed such a disastrous experience and longed for peace and order. What had exactly caused this nationwide and long-term political turbulence which had brought about such immense losses? In 1978, the Communist Party of China held its 3rd Plenary Session of the 11th Central Committee. The Session analysed the causes of the Cultural Revolution and advanced measures aimed at avoiding the recurrence of similar tragedies. For such a purpose, the Session reappraised the issue of democracy and examined the Chinese legal system; it concluded: "Democracy must be substantial for proper centralization to be carried out. ... In the past, we have striven for centralization failing democracy. ... There is too little democracy."[2] Hence, the Session concluded that the main cause of the 10-year political turbulence had been the long-term absence of political democracy, and that "the practice whereby what one single person says counts" had brought about such a tragedy. It was realized that long-term peace, stability, and economic development could not be achieved without democracy. It was indeed acknowledged that, after the founding of the Popular Republic of China, much had been done to promote democracy, and the foundations of a socialist democracy had been laid. Why, then, had the Cultural Revolution nonetheless occurred?

P. Costa and D. Zolo (eds.), The Rule of Law: History, Theory and Criticism, 647–670.

Numerous historical experiences have proven that democracy alone is not sufficient: failing suitable protection thereof, democracy, let alone a country, cannot be preserved. In order for democracy to develop, fundamental and deeply rooted democratic institutions are needed, and ought to be conscientiously preserved and supported by the people, particularly by all government officials. More importantly, the stability, continuity, and strong vitality of such institutions ought to be guaranteed without them being open to changes *ad libitum*. Express laws and democratic institutions must ensure that governmental agencies exercise their power with the aim of better protecting citizens' rights and freedom. Law's primacy ought to be established, this standing for the primacy of the people's will. China's laws per se reflect democracy. They are enacted by the Chinese legislature pursuant to democratic procedures, and are suited to China's social development and its people's will. In this respect, the above Session pointed out: "To guarantee popular democracy, it is necessary to strengthen the socialist legal system and institutionalize and legalize the democratic system so as to ensure the stability, continuity and maximum authority thereof and of its laws."[3]

Contemporary Chinese history shows that democracy cannot be guaranteed failing laws and institutions' strong safeguard. To strive for democracy without ensuring the rule of law inevitably leads to "absolute democracy" or to the Cultural Revolution's kind of "democracy", which purportedly removed all kinds of authority, though in practice it brought tyranny, autocracy, and disaster rather than the free development of human beings. If democracy implies the people's government, the rule of law can protect such a condition. Therefore, popular democracy is necessarily intertwined with the rule of law. By strictly enforcing the rule of law, a country and its people can carry out their activities in a guided and standardized way: people exercise their democratic rights within law, thus avoiding legal anarchism and legal nihilism; moreover, the rule of law substantially and legally protects such rights, since public authorities are subject to controls not allowing them to impinge upon individual rights, these being open to change only by law. Indeed, although many complex social and historical factors caused the Cultural Revolution, it is undeniable that legal nihilism played a fundamental role in this respect. Moreover, the legal system itself must be grounded on democracy: democracy is the basis of the rule of law and, in turn, the latter protects the former. In this respect, the above-mentioned Session suggested the guiding principle of "promoting socialist democracy and strengthening the socialist legal system": not only did this represent a historic turning point in China's setting up of democracy and of the legal system, but it also marked China's rejection of legal nihilism in favour of the rule of law, thus reflecting a qualitative advance in the Communist Party's understanding of the legal system.

Yet, it may be said that the principle advanced by the Session focused only on the need to change the unruly status quo and to establish the "rule by law", without dealing with the full implications of the "rule of law". Under the rule of law, the exercise of power by governmental organs is subject to legal restrictions and supervision. Moreover, the people are to be the subject, rather than the object, of the rule of law; democracy is to permeate the entire legislative process, ensuring the representation of the people's will and interests; the Constitution and laws must enjoy the supreme authority. Moreover, whilst the Communist Party's leadership role is acknowledged, the Party nevertheless has to carry out its activities within the scope of law; citizens' freedoms and rights are strictly protected by the Constitution and law; all citizens and legal subjects are equal before the law. Democracy needs to be protected by legal institutions, and the legal system itself has to reflect the spirit of democracy. Under this perspective, the rule of law stands for the institutionalization and legalization of the people's will. The people's primacy cannot be realized unless their will is expressed by law, and the rule of law is not attained unless it embodies the people's will. The rule of law in China is not satisfied if it fails to both promote democracy and strengthen the legal system.

2 THE 1982 CONSTITUTION

In 1982, after the Communist Party's 12th National Congress, the 5th Session of the 5th National People's Congress radically amended the 1978 Constitution. The new Constitution laid out China's fundamental political and economic system, the country's primary tasks, its judicial system, and citizens' fundamental rights. Such provisions laid the legal foundation for China's reform and development. Indeed, such a Constitution has been regarded by the Chinese legal world as the best one ever since the founding of new China. Under the basic principles and framework of the new Constitution, the Chinese legal system thus reaches a new level of development.

Ever since its foundation in 1949, the Popular Republic of China has always been engaged in developing a legal system with the aim of protecting human rights. Especially since 1978, and following the Cultural Revolution which had despised and destroyed human rights, China's legislature has enacted numerous laws, regulations, and resolutions aimed at providing legal grounding – mainly centred around the Constitution – for the protection of human rights. The 1982 Constitution encompasses a number of provisions based on the declarations of human rights contained in the country's former three constitutions.[4] Not only does it have more provisions in this respect, but it is also more detailed and effective in acknowledging people's political, economic, socio-cultural rights and freedom. For instance, in terms of protection of children's rights, Article 49 of the Constitution is very detailed, in that it provides that "[p]arents have the duty to bring up and educate their children under age, and children who have come of age have the duty to support and assist their parents. ... Ill-treatment of old people, women and children is prohibited."

Furthermore, the 1982 Constitution contains important structural changes. In the previous constitutions, the chapter on "Citizens' Fundamental Rights and Duties" always followed the chapter on "The Structure of the State"; such a structure implied the primacy of the State's power over citizens' fundamental rights. By placing fundamental rights in Chapter 2, immediately after the Constitution's "General Principles", the 1982 Constitution underlines that citizens' rights are closely connected with the political and social system and are the continuation of the "General Principles" from which they should not to be separated. This arrangement is in line with other countries' constitutions, which place fundamental rights before the government's structure and powers. Moreover, it clearly mirrors China's different approach towards citizens' fundamental rights.

3 THE DEVELOPMENT OF HUMAN RIGHTS

Within the framework of the 1982 Constitution, and with the aim of satisfying the needs of the rising commodity economy, several civil and economic laws were rapidly enacted in the period in question. The first comprehensive civil legislation, i.e. the "General Principles of Civil Law", was promulgated in 1986. Although it was not sufficiently detailed, it provided the fundamental functioning rules of the commodity economy.[5]

In 1987, the Communist Party's 13th National Congress advanced a long-term reform of the political arena with the aim of establishing a highly democratic socialist political system and a sound legal system. China's understanding of the rule of law was thus further renewed. Apart from the Constitution, numerous laws and regulations were enacted in this period with the aim of effectively and legally protecting human rights. A sound framework for the judicial protection of human rights was also gradually set up. According to law, the judiciary is now entrusted with the task of protecting citizens' fundamental rights and freedoms and any other legitimate right and interest thereof, of protecting public property as well as property privately and lawfully owned by citizens, of preserving social order, of safeguarding the regular development of China's modernization, and of punishing offenders. The judiciary's prime role in protecting human rights is thus asserted.

In performing their activities, it is established that China's public security organs and judicial departments must strictly respect the following principles:

1. All citizens are equal before the law. The lawful rights and interests of any given citizen are to be protected by law, and any unlawful or criminal behaviour must be subject to law's scrutiny.
2. China's public security organs and judicial institutions must deal with cases on the basis of facts, and follow law as their guiding criterion.
3. In accordance with law, people's courts must exercise judicial power and people's procuratorates[6] must enforce law; both organs must act in an independent manner. They are both subject only to law and are free from interferences by administrative organs, social organizations, and individuals. In criminal proceedings, people's courts, people's procuratorates, and public security organs must divide their responsibilities, coordinate their efforts, and supervise each other to ensure law's correct and effective enforcement. They must solely perform their assigned tasks, and cannot replace each other. People's procuratorates must supervise the activities performed by public security organs, courts, prisons, detention centres, and organs in charge of reform through labour and make sure that such activities conform to law.

The above judicial principles are expressly stipulated in the Chinese Constitution and in its laws, and guarantee the protection of human rights throughout judicial proceedings. Moreover, in order to fully protect human rights, Chinese laws incorporate explicit and strict provisions specifically governing the tasks of public security and judicial organs as well as the carrying out of judicial procedures. The following are some major provisions in this respect.

1. *Custody and arrest*. No citizen may be arrested except with the approval of either a people's procuratorate or a people's court, and arrests must be made by a public security organ. The unauthorized detention or deprivation or restriction of citizens' freedom, as well as their unlawful search, is prohibited. China's criminal procedural law provides for specific time limits of criminal cases.

2. *Search and collection of evidence.* The 1982 Constitution provides that the unlawful search of citizens is prohibited; citizens' private domicile is inviolable, and the unlawful search of, or entry into, a citizen's private domicile is forbidden. China's criminal procedural law stipulates that search by public security organs must strictly abide by law. It is a principle, as well as the discipline of public security and judicial organs, that no confessions can be extorted by torture, and all violations in this respect are to be investigated.
3. *Prosecution and trial.* The trials carried out in people's courts are open to the public, unless they involve state secrets, personal privacy, or crimes committed by minors. People's courts publicly pass judgment in all cases, whether publicly tried or not. People's courts must gather full evidence according to the procedures established by law. The accused is entitled to provide a defence. Pursuant to the Criminal Procedural Law, in addition to such a right, the criminal suspect or the accused may entrust lawyers, relatives, or other citizens to be his or her advocates. People's courts, strictly abiding by the Constitution and by Criminal Procedural Law, must ensure the effective protection of the criminal suspect or the right to defence of the accused throughout the judicial proceedings. The criminal suspect and the accused have the right to appeal and the right to advance petitions.
4. *The judgment passed by a people's court.* According to law, a party refusing to accept the judgment or order passed by a people's court of first instance is entitled to appeal to the court of second instance. A party may advance a petition to a people's court or a people's procuratorate questioning the legality of a given judgment or order. Appeal, in itself, does not result in harsher punishment. China's Criminal Code encompasses specific provisions on juvenile crimes and criminal liabilities. People's procuratorates must strictly supervise litigations and trials so as to ensure they conform to law. As in several other countries in the world, the death penalty is applicable in China, though it is subject to rigorous restrictions. The circumstance that a death sentence may be imposed whilst suspending its execution for 2 years allows for the system to strictly control the application of such punishment.
5. *Prison work and prisoners' rights.* Chinese prisons and organs in charge of reform through labour must deal with convicted criminals in strict accordance with the law. Prisons or other executing organs may refuse to take criminals into their custody if the respective legal documents are absent or not valid. The detaining organs must notify the prisoners' families of the detention within 3 days of its commencement. Under

certain circumstances, prisoners are allowed to serve their sentence in the area where they are domiciled, so as to allow their families and original working units to assist them in their reform. In China, prisoners' rights are protected by law. According to Chinese law, prisoners have the right to vote unless deprived thereof by law. They have the right to petition, defence, inviolability of their own person and lawful property, complaint and report, together with other citizens' rights allowed by law. People's procuratorates control the guarantee of prisoners' lawful rights and interests. By order of a people's court, a criminal may have his or her punishment commuted or may be released on parole if he or she shows true repentance or performs meritorious service while serving the sentence.

6. *Prisoners' labour*. Prisoners must work if they are able to do so; the working time cannot exceed 8 hours a day. Prisoners are entitled to rest on holidays, and to enjoy the compensatory treatment granted to workers engaged in similar activities in state-owned enterprises. The products produced by prisoners' labour are mainly used to satisfy the prison's needs, and only a small percentage thereof reaches the domestic market. No prisoners' products can be exported.
7. *Reform through labour and the rights of people under reform*. Reform through labour is an administrative penalty rather than a judicial one. Special Committees in charge of reform through labour are set up by governments of large and medium-sized cities of all provinces, autonomous regions, and municipalities, and are under the direct control of the central government. People's procuratorates have supervising powers in this ambit. People subject to such a penalty are over 16 years of age, and have committed offences endangering social order in large and medium-sized cities and have refused to redress their errors despite repeated warnings; alternatively, they have committed minor offences whose circumstances are not serious enough to call for criminal punishment. In line with the relevant laws and regulations, the Committee must decide the length of the reform, ranging from 1 to 3 years.[7] Individuals refusing such decisions may petition to the Committee or file a suit with a people's court in line with Administrative Procedural Law. People under reform through labour enjoy extensive citizens' rights guaranteed by the Constitution and legislation, though they must abide by reforming measures which may restrict their rights.

At this specific stage of its historical development, China has actively participated in international human rights institutions. As a founding member of the United Nations and as a permanent member of its

Security Council, China acknowledges the aim and principles of the United Nations Charter on the protection and development of human rights; moreover, since 1979, it has sent its delegates to United Nations Human Rights Committee meetings. China substantially contributes to the development of human rights in the world, as is widely acknowledged by developing countries.

4 THE WHITE PAPER ON HUMAN RIGHTS

Before 1988, the expression "human rights" was quite unpopular; up and until then, human rights had been a "forbidden topic" in China. During the 10-year Cultural Revolution and the following decade, they were regarded as "the patent of the bourgeoisie". Only general "citizens' rights" were mentioned. After the Tian An Men Incident in 1989, China was harshly criticized by the international world for its lack of protection of human rights. In truth, the noble issue of human rights was severely distorted by the Cold War and by "Cold War thinking", which made human rights seem a matter of ideological imposition, implying double standards in the diplomatic struggle that had marked the previous 40 years.

The issue of human rights was first tackled in the course of a small-scale symposium on human rights held by the Communist Party, in line with the Chinese leadership's directives. After Jiang Zemin's instructions regarding the need to conduct research on human rights so as to respond to Western countries' criticism, in 1991 the Chinese government radically changed its stance in this respect. The once "forbidden topic" of human rights was thus widely discussed in many meetings held by research institutions.[8]

China's State Council published an unprecedented "White Paper" on *The Situation of Human Rights in China*, which officially tackled the issue of human rights. In the 1990s, human rights were fiercely debated by the Chinese academic world. Human rights were gradually seen as universal rather than exclusively pertaining to a given class of people, and the protection of human rights was finally regarded as the hallmark of civilized and developed societies.

5 THE CONSTITUTIONAL INCORPORATION OF THE RULE OF LAW

In promoting human rights, not only does China nowadays attach importance to social development and to the legal, institutional, and material protection of human rights, but it is also engaged in conducting research on human rights and increasing popular awareness thereof. The

Chinese academic world is very active in this respect, including professional researchers, scholars, and experts coming from institutions of higher learning and research. A number of nationwide academic associations, such as the China Society of Human Rights, have emerged, together with several institutions devoted to research on human rights founded by higher learning centres.[9] What is more, institutions specialized in the human rights of specific groups, such as women, children, and the disabled, have also been set up.

The Chinese government, together with given relevant foundations, supports and funds research programmes on human rights. The resulting academic works and articles have significantly contributed to the creation of human rights policies, whilst also promoting citizens' awareness of human rights and fostering social development. Furthermore, the Chinese academic world has translated and published numerous foreign works on human rights and has gathered extensive and systematic material thereon.

With the aim of increasing people's awareness of the issue at hand, the Information Office of China's State Council has recently published a number of White Papers, such as *The Situation of Human Rights in China*, *The Sovereignty over Tibet and the Situation of Human Rights*, *The Chinese Situation of Reforming Criminals*, and *The Situation of Women in China*. Chinese governmental agencies, social organizations, research institutions, the media, and publishing institutions have extensively divulged and discussed the above documents.

Individuals' awareness of human rights goes hand in hand with the country's legal enactments. Whenever laws regarding human rights are enacted and promulgated, educational activities are conducted in order to promote citizens' awareness of their rights. A course on human rights is nowadays part of national education and professional training programmes. Lectures and courses on human rights are held at many universities and training institutions. Citizens' exertion and enjoyment of human rights are fostered.[10] The Communist Party's Central Committee recently held a number of law lectures informing the central leadership of these matters, and this generated strong repercussions throughout the country.

When China formally recognized the market economy, following the former leader Deng Xiaoping's momentous visit to the South of China in 1992, the legal system underwent a period of fundamental change and transition.[11] It was understood that the market economy had to be grounded on a sound legal system, and that laws enacted on the basis of a centrally planned economy should be either amended or abolished; in other words, the legal framework was to be suited to the market economy. Hence, China's legislation was rapidly and radically altered.[12]

The development of the market economy fosters the development of China's democracy and legal system, and provides fundamental grounds for the rule of law. Through reforms and radical changes, the development of the market economy, as well as of economic activities and relationships among different interest groups, become increasingly complex. The rule of law has thus been endorsed by the country, the former being needed to preserve the order required for the development of the market economy, to solve problems connected with the country's economic social advancement, and to facilitate a coordinated economic and social development.

For this purpose, the Communist Party's 15th National Congress, for the first time in the party's history, expressly and entirely endorsed the rule of law as its basic guiding principle, ascribing thereto a place of its own within the scope of political reforms. The Congress also suggested setting up a comprehensive legal framework with Chinese characteristics by 2010. Such a proposal marked a new leap forward in the Communist Party's understanding of law, and a significant new milestone in the development of the country's democracy and legal system.[13] As a matter of fact, it represented the shift from a "rule by law" to the "rule of law", and thus the rule of law acquired a strategic rather than a mere technical value.

Throughout its 20-year legal development, China has deepened its understanding of the primacy of the rule of law. Law is effective not only in combating "evil forces", but also in promoting justice, enhancing efficiency, and creating economic benefits. The rule of law can facilitate economic and social development, as well as spiritual civilization. In international economic and commercial transactions, the quality of the legal environment is a key factor for investors, since a sound legal system cannot but encourage investments. Law is the primary and ultimate "legitimate" means for solving social problems and disputes. Failing adequate legal means, individuals cannot obtain redress of their complaints, and solutions may be provided only through violence or illegal means. In such circumstances, society relapses into anarchy and chaos, thus running the risk of reliving the Cultural Revolution experience. Therefore, law stands for hope, confidence, and security, as well as optimism towards one's country, government, and society. History has taught us dramatic lessons concerning what happens when people are mistrustful of their country and law, and are doubtful of the latter's fairness.[14] Violence begins when justice ends.

Hence, by officially establishing the "rule of law", the Communist Party's 15th National Congress significantly affected China's twenty-first-century development. The Constitution was also amended during the 2nd Session of the 9th National People's Congress in March 1999 so as to incorporate the fundamental principle of the rule of law. Hence, ever since then, the rule of law has been acknowledged as a constitutional principle.[15] For the first time in its history, on occasion of its 15th National Congress, the Communist Party declared an intention to "to respect and protect human rights". This confirmed the system's fundamental interest in developing a rule of law strongly upholding democracy and human rights.

The development of the market economy has increased citizens' awareness of both their economic independence and of their rights. The once merely theoretical rights are now legal means citizens can resort to so as to protect their own interests. The exercise and protection of individual rights through legal means urges the government to seriously acknowledge such rights. Hence, the amelioration of China's legal system has been accompanied by that of its laws, now upholding citizen's constitutional rights and ensuring their judicial enforceability. Both domestic and international experiences demonstrate that human rights need to be protected by judicial power and procedures. The country's systematic legal framework has thus been altered to legally protect citizens' rights together with every aspect of their social life.[16] For instance, in February 1995, the electoral legislation and other relevant laws were revised so as to ensure the exercise of democratic rights by people and their delegates. In November 1998, the new Organic Law of Villagers' Committees was adopted to provide effective legal protection and further the democratic development of rural areas.

In March 1997, a new Criminal Code was adopted, which added 260 articles to the original code.[17] The revised Criminal Code endorses the principles of *nulla poena sine lege*, of the "equal protection by law" and of "punishment fitting the crime". In addition, the "crimes of counter-revolution" to be found in the old criminal laws, which were political and ideological in nature, are replaced by "crimes endangering national security". Acts that used to be labelled counter-revolutionary crimes, though in truth they were no more than common offences, are thus finally placed under their proper heading.

The conduct of administrative and law enforcement agencies is nowadays regulated in order to prevent the infringement of citizens' lawful rights. The Administrative Litigation Law, in force from 1 October 1990, is particularly effective in this respect. It establishes that "if a citizen, a legal person or any other organization believes that its lawful rights and interests have been infringed by a specific act by an administrative organ or personnel, it is entitled to bring an action before a people's court". The State Council has also issued the Regulations on Administrative Reconsideration as an auxiliary regulation to the Law. Pursuant to such a Law, it is established that public organizations must support citizens bringing lawsuits and must protect their right of action. Public organizations may be entrusted to act as agents *ad litem*. With the aim of promoting such actions, the Supreme Court has held that judicial expenses may be postponed, reduced, or even exempted.[18]

Moreover, according to the State Indemnity Law (May 1994), if a governmental agency (or its personnel) unlawfully encroaches upon a citizen or organization's legitimate rights and interests and thus causes a loss, the damaged party is entitled to claim the State's indemnity. People's courts at intermediate and upper levels have set up special indemnity committees to hear such cases. Furthermore, the Law on Administrative Punishments (March 1996) governs administrative sanctions by government agencies. People's procuratorates are particularly careful in investigating and dealing with criminal cases involving the Communist Party, the government, judicial agencies, and departments responsible for economic management.

As regards the protection of prisoners' rights, China has enacted and executed the 1994 Prison Law. Out of the latter's 78 articles, more than 20 are directly concerned with the protection of prisoners' rights. The Law provides that "prisoners' human dignity shall not be humiliated, and their personal safety, lawful property, and their right to defence, petition, complaint and accusation as well as other rights which have not been deprived of or restricted by law shall not be breached". The Law also adds a number of rights, such as the right not to be subject to corporal punishment and ill-treatment, the right to petition, exchange correspondence, meet relatives, receive education, rest, and receive income through their labour.

Throughout judicial proceedings, confessions cannot be extorted by compulsion or torture, which is expressly dealt with by a number of laws. In 1988, China subscribed to the International Convention against Torture and Other Cruel, Inhuman or Degrading Treatment or Punishment. Delegates of people's procuratorates supervise prisons and detention houses in order to ensure detainees are not tortured or ill-treated.

In order to standardize police practices in protecting human rights, the Police Law (enacted and enforced in February 1995) provides that the police must ensure people's safety, and must promptly act to help citizens whose property is endangered; the police are strictly prohibited from unlawfully depriving citizens of their freedom and are subject to social supervision in the exercise of their functions; citizens have the right to report to relevant authorities any unlawful conduct by the police. The ratio between Chinese police and population is 7.4:10,000, which is lower than the Western standard of more than 20:10,000.[19]

The Procuratorate Law and Judge Law (enacted in February 1995 and validated in July 1995) establishes that procuratorates or judges independently exercise their procuratorial and judicial power and must not be subject to interference by any administrative organ, public organization, or individual; they must consider all the facts of the case whilst taking law as their guiding criterion; they must act fairly, with integrity and uprightness. Such principles, which had already been upheld in the past, are now standardized and specified to ensure their effective enforcement.

China has also significantly revised its 1979 Criminal Procedural Law so as to improve criminal judicial procedures and incorporate provisions protecting human rights. The presumption of innocence and the adversarial system have thus been introduced. Lawyers are endowed with sufficient rights to represent their clients. Chinese lawyers are nowadays growing in both number and quality and indeed play an important role in safeguarding citizens' rights and interests. In the past, lawyers were deemed to be governmental, rather than private, workers. According to China's Law on Lawyers (1996), lawyers are now "legal practitioners who have obtained the legal authorization to provide legal services to society". The Law also establishes the necessary requisites for legal practice and business, together with lawyers' rights and duties.[20] Legal aid has been established, and indeed has been playing an increasingly important role in improving judicial mechanisms and safeguarding citizens' rights.[21]

In October 1997 and October 1998, the Chinese government signed respectively the International Covenant on Economic, Social and Cultural Rights and the International Covenant on Civil and Political Rights. China is currently ratifying such covenants in line with the provisions of its Constitution and laws.[22] China's signing of the International Covenant on Civil and Political Rights demonstrates its increasing involvement in international human rights issues and discussions. It also enhances the prestige and influence of the Covenant, this being now endorsed by a country with a population of 1.2 billion people. China's involvement promotes the universal realization of all civil and political rights recognized by the Covenant and thus expresses China's contribution to the realization of the United Nation's principle of respecting human rights; it also proves China's determination to identify common international norms governing this matter. This may help in changing the international mistrust towards China's protection of human rights.

6 CONTEMPORARY TRENDS

Through China's deep reforms and changes, its political, economic, and cultural framework has been altered to better protect human rights. As regards China's endorsement of the above two International Covenants on human rights, the Chinese government and many Chinese scholars believe that the Covenants' core provisions are in line with China's current Constitution and laws. However, there are a number of differences between domestic Chinese law and the said Covenants. For instance, Chinese norms establishing the death penalty also for economic crimes are inconsistent with Article 6 of the Covenant on Civil and Political Rights. Moreover, "reform through labour" is a unique Chinese means of punishment regulated by administrative provisions; yet, such a practice is not in line with Article 8, clause 3, of the Covenant. Should China intend to retain this measure, it would need to clearly establish that such a practice is applied by judicial organs pursuant to regular proceedings. Furthermore, both Article 3 of the Covenant and Chinese law explicitly prohibit torture; however, it is well known that the Chinese police often abuse their power. Article 93 of China's Criminal Procedural Law establishes that "the criminal suspect shall truthfully answer the investigatory personnel's questions". Such a provision may be used by ill-trained police as justifying their abuses. Furthermore, the provision is inconsistent with Article 14, clauses 2 and 3, of the Covenant. Article 14, clause 1, provides that courts are to be qualified, independent, and impartial. Yet, nowadays, given Chinese judges still lack legal training, Chinese courts are dependent on local congresses and governments in terms of judicial personnel, as well as financial and material support.

The non-discrimination principle enshrined in Article 2 of the Covenant on Civil and Political Rights is the key principle on human rights. As China's domiciliary control system has become gradually more flexible, the difference between agricultural and urban households is not so great as it used to be 20 or 30 years ago. However, there are still differences between rural areas and cities, and also between big cities and small ones, which result in unequal and discriminatory practices, in terms of education, employment, marriage, and social conditions. It is unlikely that such a situation will rapidly and substantially change in less-developed areas with huge populations. Where necessary, China could make reservations with respect to a number of articles in the Covenant on the grounds of its enormous population and of its specific economic situation. It should be added that even developed countries have made a number of reservations in signing the Covenant.

Article 12, clause 2, of the above-mentioned Covenant establishes the freedom of migration. China's Constitution omits such a constitutional right in the light of the long-existing differences between its urban and rural areas in terms of economic development and lifestyles. The freedom of migration and of choosing one's own residence or own work have not been adequately protected as a result of the shortage of housing, of public facilities and job opportunities. However, the grain allocation system, which underpins the denial of individual freedom of migration, has abolished the domiciliary control system. As a matter of fact, large labour forces are now increasingly moving to urban areas. Such social changes have created the conditions necessary for the realization of the freedom of migration. It follows that China will soon be compelled to incorporate such a right into its domestic law.[23]

Although China's laws and fundamental policies are basically consistent with the Covenant, China's protection of human rights still remains unsatisfactory. It is undeniable that considerable time is needed to solve such an issue. The differences between Chinese law and the Covenant, in terms of both their scope and contents, have several causes. Legislation and judicial measures could help to eliminate some differences. Moreover, China could make some reservations with respect to given provisions of the Covenant justified by its specific economic and cultural situation. However, it ought to be recalled that the Covenant's provisions themselves are yet to be thoroughly and effectively implemented within China's Constitution.

The Chinese Constitution establishes citizens' rights; yet, only the freedom of thought, person, communication, and residence are explicitly and constitutionally enunciated, and can be directly resorted to. Other rights such as the right to equality, election, gathering and association, personal dignity, criticism and suggestion, petition and accusation, work and rest, education, welfare, research and creation, and gender equality are stipulated by way of principle, and their implementation is guaranteed by other specific detailed laws and regulations. The constitutional amendments which have been approved up till now have not dealt with citizens' fundamental rights, despite these being vital in grounding citizens' respect for, and trust in, the constitution. Proposals have been put forward to draft provisions concerning fundamental citizens' rights drawing upon foreign experiences.

China is gradually fostering the protection of fundamental human rights through legislation and by reforming its economic and political structures. The gap between the Chinese and the international level of protection of such rights is gradually decreasing. Certain Western countries criticize the human rights situation in developing countries by assuming a "supervisory stance". Such an approach may be open to criticism for a number of reasons, including the "Cold War psychology", or the lack of knowledge with respect to the protection of human rights in specific countries such as China. Moreover, it should be recalled that even developed Western countries still experience human rights problems, and not all provisions of the human rights Covenants are fully and continuously implemented by them. For instance, although Britain signed the Covenant on Civil and Political Rights a number of years ago and its Parliament soon ratified it, the Covenant has not yet become directly enforceable. According to the United States Federal Constitution, international conventions and federal laws are equally effective. However, by dividing international conventions into self-executing and non-self-executing ones and by categorizing international human rights covenants as non-self-executing, the latter cannot be directly applied. Hence, human rights problems do not pertain solely to China.

China has signed 17 international human rights conventions. The Chinese people are bound to enjoy their human rights increasingly and more extensively in the future since the country, just like most countries in the world, is currently strengthening such rights.

7 DIFFERENT HUMAN RIGHTS THEORIES

We conclude our essay by suggesting a comparison between the different human rights theories that are supported by developed and developing countries.

Right to subsistence. Whereas this right is generally and negatively perceived by the Western world, it is greatly emphasized by developing countries, which deem it to be the most fundamental human right with realistic and universal significance. It follows that the international community should safeguard such a right.[24]

Right to development. Western countries have generally accepted the "right to development", though they are strikingly at variance with developing countries' understanding of the right in terms of its content, status, role, relationship with other human rights, and grounding. Developing countries believe it is a basic human right with a very wide-ranging content; its core is about economic and social development, and is inseparable from other human rights since it materially protects them; they also believe that its realization hinges upon national self-determination, on the transformation of an irrational and unfair international economic order and on the removal of obstacles hindering development.

Right to equality. Developing countries believe that the right to equality primarily entails the rejection of all forms of discrimination, particularly racial and sex discrimination, and that equality of economic, social, and cultural rights is as important as political equality; the right of collective equality is also stressed, particularly racial equality, sex equality, and the equality of native populations; finally, large-scale violations of human rights are to be eliminated in order to guarantee such a right.

Right to national self-determination. Developing countries believe that national self-determination is a fundamental human right as well as a principle of international law. Yet, the right is applicable only to colonies, not to independent nations.

The relationship between sovereignty and human rights. The human rights problem essentially pertains to a country's internal affairs. Through the recent increasing attention on human rights and the adoption of international laws thereon, the relationship between human rights and sovereignty has become a significant concern for China.[25] The majority of Chinese scholars believe that sovereignty and human rights are interrelated and complementary to each other. No straightforward arguments can be advanced to demonstrate which of the two is superior. In certain countries, sovereignty is the prerequisite for human rights; however, even where full sovereignty is guaranteed, people do not necessarily enjoy human rights. Hence, laws are always needed to protect them. Human rights pertain to a country's domestic affairs, and the international community should be entitled to intervention on behalf of human rights without this constituting interference with the internal affairs of a country. This conclusion is in line with the provisions of the United Nations Charter and customary international law, and is supported by cases of violations of human rights.

Standards of human rights. Developing countries hold that human rights must be respected in line with the "international standards" set forth in international human rights conventions (including the Universal Declaration of Human Rights), rather than the standards of any given country or group of countries or regions. The principles to be followed in the protection of human rights are universality, non-selectivity, objectivity, and fairness.

China acknowledges the need for a common understanding of human rights, this being required for the subsistence and development of human beings; it also accepts that such an understanding may, through international instruments, become the prevailing standard of human rights commonly recognized and protected by signatory states. However, differences are bound to emerge with respect to the social needs and interests of individuals living in different countries with different economic and cultural development standards. It is quite natural, therefore, for the values, legislation, and realization of human rights to differ.

The universality of human rights must be assessed together with the specific situations of different countries. The value, ideal, and objective of human rights are indeed universal. All people enjoy all human rights, and this is the main aim to be achieved. However, in realistic terms, no country in the world has fully attained such an ideal. The universality of human rights has two implications. Firstly, it entails the universality of the holders of human rights, so that all people are to enjoy such rights as human beings, regardless of their race, colour, sex, language, religion, political view, nationality, social status, property, education, and capability; the universality of human rights also refers to the universality of holders of collective human rights, so that every nation or country holds the latter kind of rights.[26]

Secondly, the universality of human rights implies the universality of the latter's principles and contents. The universality of human rights can only be realized through human rights practices in different regions and countries. Human rights are peculiar in that they refer to specific social characteristics and values, as well as to different ways of realizing them. Due to countries' differences in terms of their history, culture, values, religious background, development level, and social systems, it is natural that the understanding of human rights, together with the problems faced thereby, are different across the world. Therefore, countries' programmes for promoting and protecting human rights and the means for doing this are bound to differ. The relationship between the universality of human rights and their peculiarity indicates that the internationally recognized universality of human rights must be interpreted in line with each country's different conditions. Once the universality of human rights is recognized, the government and people of each country are entitled to choose their programmes and ways of implementing such rights, thus adopting different regulations according to their national situation. In other words, on the one hand, each country must strive to respect and realize the universality of human rights; on the other hand, the peculiarity of practices adopted by different regions and countries must be fully respected. Developing countries include three-quarters of the world's population: their demands and suggestions on human rights must therefore be seriously taken into account; similarly, their practices and experiences, based on their own specific situations, ought to be respected.

It follows that all matters pertaining to human rights need to be treated in a comprehensive and balanced manner. Human rights include civil and political rights, on the one hand, and economic, social, and cultural rights, i.e. individual and collective human rights, on the other. Civil and political rights, together with economic, social, and cultural rights are two inseparable components of the human rights system. The former mirror and politically protect citizens' personal dignity and human rights. The latter represent the fundamental conditions for the enjoyment of citizens' social, economic, and cultural rights. Human rights may be individual or collective. The holders of individual human rights are individuals, whereas the holders of collective human rights are social groups, nations, and states. Collective human rights are the prerequisites and the necessary protection for the full realization of individual human rights. The interrelationship between such categories of rights is due to the fact that individuals cannot live isolated from other people and society. International human rights instruments must be read in a comprehensive and overall manner. Hence, equal importance must be attached to civil and political rights on the one hand, and economic, social, and cultural rights on the other, and both kinds of rights must be promoted in a comprehensive and balanced way. In the light of historical experiences, the international community should pay more attention to economic, social, and cultural rights, these affecting the subsistence and development of developing countries; by so doing, human rights will be dealt with in a non-discriminatory and non-selective manner.

The rights to subsistence and development are primary human rights. The right to subsistence refers to everyone's right to enjoy free and equal living conditions, including both the political conditions for the non-violation of individual life and the social conditions for the maintenance of basic living standards. Such a right pertains to each human being and to the whole of mankind. The right to development may be effectively used by developing countries to defend their interests against neo-colonialism's depredation, polarization, and exploitation. China is a developing country; it has the biggest world population and only 7% of the cultivable land in the world. Hence, given China's national situation, priority must be attached to the rights to subsistence and development, since these are required for the development of human rights and for the overall interest of the Chinese people.

Human rights entail rights and obligations. There are no rights without corresponding obligations and vice versa. On such grounding, China rejects the Western idea of the supremacy of human rights. Every individual is entitled to require other individuals, the state, and society to respect his or her human rights, though at the same time every individual is obliged to respect other individuals' human rights, together with the interests of the state and society. The Chinese constitution provides that, in exercising their freedom and rights, citizens cannot infringe upon the interests of the state, society, or collectivity, or upon other citizens' lawful freedom and rights. In other words, China stresses the integration between rights and obligations, for this is the only way to ensure the former's realization.[27]

Significant importance is attached to creating the necessary social and economic conditions for the realization of human rights. Stability is deemed to be a prerequisite for the realization of human rights: democracy, freedom, and human rights can be achieved only through social advancement, stability, and economic development.[28] As regards the relationship between human rights and development, East and Southeast Asian countries advocate the principle of "good government". Such regions stress the importance of governmental authority, and regard social development and prosperity as their main objective. In China, it is believed that "human rights in developing countries are guaranteed if the policies and practices adopted are beneficial to economic and social development, and ensure proper living conditions and people's well-being."[29] The realization of human rights is inseparable from world peace and development, which are the two main concerns of the contemporary world. Universal human rights cannot be achieved in the absence of a peaceful and stable international environment, as well as of a fair and rational international economic order.

The protection of human rights in a given country cannot be judged independently of its history and national conditions. Human rights are historically ingrained, and are subject to countries' historical, social, economic, and cultural conditions.[30] Therefore, the observation and evaluation of human rights conditions in a given country cannot be made by simplistically comparing them with the conditions in force in other countries or regions.

China upholds the aims and principles of the United Nations Charter, and believes that only dialogue and cooperation can correctly promote the development of international human rights. The Charter establishes that the main strategy to promote human rights is through international cooperation. The international community's protection and promotion of human rights must occur through dialogue and cooperation, by seeking a common ground whilst preserving countries' differences, and by enhancing mutual understanding rather than by imposing sanctions, let alone the exercise of military force, and by opposing hegemony.[31]

China's view on human rights may be summarized as follows. Firstly, human rights in China refer to the rights of vast masses of people. This is the major starting point for the Chinese government's understanding and protection of human rights. Secondly, China's view on human rights is in conformity with the basic standards expressed by international instruments on human rights. China recognizes and abides by the universality of human rights and regards the protection thereof as one of its key aims for the preservation of democracy and the legal system. The country has subscribed to 15 international human rights conventions and signed the above-mentioned two Covenants; moreover, it has taken an active part in drafting and enacting United Nations human rights instruments. Such actions mirror China's respect for the international human rights cause. Thirdly, China's understanding of human rights reflects its national conditions and its political, historical, and cultural traditions. Yet, it also draws upon international conceptions of human rights.

8 POSTSCRIPT. THE DEVELOPMENT OF HUMAN RIGHTS IN CHINA 2000–2005[32]

As China enters the twenty-first century, human rights theoretical research and human rights implementation have made considerable progress. In 2000, the 3rd Session of the 9th National People's Congress passed the *Law on Legislation of the People's Republic of China*. This law regulated the legislative activities in China and safeguarded basic human rights through the standardization of legislative activities. For instance, Article 8 of this law stipulates that only the National People's Congress and its Standing Committee can enact laws concerning the deprivation of the political rights of citizens, the restriction of personal freedom through compulsory measures and penalties, and the expropriation of non-state assets. Other governmental organs including the State Council do not have the power to make regulations restricting the citizens' rights in these aspects.

Article 90 of this Law is the first and foremost statute in Chinese political and legal history to provide for constitutional review procedures. It allows every citizen or social organization to make a request to the Standing Committee of the National People's Congress for a constitutional review of any regulations which are allegedly in contravention of the Constitution. Five years of experience has shown that this article has started off China's constitutional review mechanism and has brought about a great leap forward in the protection of human rights in China.

In 2001, China revised the Regulation on the Administration of Publication and the Provisions on the Administration of Publication of Audio and Video Products, in order to further protect the legal rights of information, speech, and publication of the citizens. For instance, the Regulation on the Administration of Publication stipulated that "the citizens may, in accordance with this regulation, publicize their views and wills concerning the state affairs, economic and cultural affairs, and social affairs in publications, and also freely deliver the fruits of their scientific researches, cultural and artistic creations and other cultural activities".[33]

That was the year of the famous case *Qi Yuling v. Chen Xiaoqi*, which concerned the dispute over infringement of constitutional right to education and was regarded as the "first case of constitutional (judicial) review" in China. The Supreme Court for the first time cited the articles of the Constitution in its decision, in which it was emphasized that the court should protect the basic constitutional rights of citizens by judicial means. Scholars have made thorough discussions in relation to the methods of redress available against infringement of the basic human rights of citizens, especially in the area of judicial review.

On 29 August 2002, the Standing Committee of the National People's Congress promulgated the Decision on Approving the Optional Protocol to the Convention on the Rights of the Child on the Sale of Children, Child Prostitution and Child Pornography. Also in this year, cases relating to human rights constantly attracted considerable attention, with issues mainly focusing on the rights of equality, privacy, and peace in residence. The most important cases with the human rights aspects in this year included *Jiangtao v. Chengdu Branch of Industrial and Commercial Bank of China*, concerning discrimination in height, and the *Zhang couple in Yanan city of Shanxi province v. the police* concerning the infringement of right to watch sexual movies at home.

In March 2003, the incident of Sun Zhigang, a university student who died while in police custody in Guangzhou, resulted in an intense debate. Scholars in Beijing for the first time "tested" the "constitutional law review procedures" provided by the Law on Legislation of the People's Republic of China (2000), requesting the Standing Committee of the National People's Congress to abolish the "Measures for the Taking or Repatriation of Vagrants and Beggars without Assured Living Sources in Cities" enacted by the State Council in 1982 which infringed upon basic human rights and the Chinese Constitution. "The Defendant", the State Council, responded quickly by abolishing these measures and replacing them with the "Measures for the Administration of Relief for Vagrants and Beggars without Assured Living Sources in Cities", which complied with the spirit of human rights and with the needs and opinions of the community. This is regarded as the landmark case in the history of the development of human rights and the rule of law in China.

In March 2004, the 2nd Session of the National People's Congress approved a revision of the constitution, and for the first time added "the state respect and protection of human rights" to the fundamental law of the country, in order to turn the principle of respecting and protecting human rights from a Party and Administration policy to a constitutional principle, and to establish further the prominent status of the protection of human rights in the legal system and state development strategies. This revision of the constitution also included the protection of private property. These acts had significant implications.

In 2005, the Law of the People's Republic of China on the Protection of Women's Rights and Interests was revised to provide an even better protection to women's rights. The State Copyright Bureau and the Ministry of Information Industry have enacted and released the Measures for the Administrative Protection of Internet Copyright to provide the legal basis for citizens' rights to freedom of information, speech, and publication on the Internet.

In June 2005, the Ministry of Foreign Affairs of China and the European Union co-held a China–European Union Human Rights Meeting in Beijing, focusing on the issues of freedom of expression and the death penalty. This is the 13th human rights meeting between China and the European Union within 8 years.

NOTES

1. Jin Chuming *et al.*, *Studies on the 'Cultural Revolution'*, Beijing: PLR Press, 1985, pp. 103–4.
2. The Communist Party of China Central Committee, *Selected Important Party Documents Since 1978*, vol. 1, Beijing: Central Documents Press, 1997, p. 26.
3. Ibid., pp. 26–7.
4. The first formal Constitution was adopted in 1954 after the 1949 foundation of new China. It was replaced by the 1975 Constitution, which is thought of as the worst constitution by Chinese legal scholars. In 1978, after the Cultural Revolution, such a Constitution was revised. The 1978 version was fundamentally amended in 1982 in the light of the country's development.
5. In this period, the official description of China's economic system was that of a "socialist commodity economy". The concept of "market economy" had not yet been accepted.
6. Procuratorates correspond to public prosecutors. Apart from the criminal prosecution of offenders, their responsibilities are much broader than those of Attorneys General in common law countries. They also generally supervise any government organ, including judicial courts.
7. State Council Information Office, *White Paper on Human Rights in China.*
8. Guo Danhui and TaoWei, "How the forbidden zone of human rights in China was broken?", *Legal Science* (1999), 5.
9. State Council Information Office, *White Paper on Human Rights in China.*

10. State Council Information Office, *The Progress of the Cause of Human Rights in China*, December 1995.
11. The Communist Party of China Central Committee, *Selected Important Party Documents Since 1978*, vol. 2, Beijing: Central Documents Press, 1997, p. 180.
12. From 1979 to April 1999 the National People's Congress and its Standing Committee adopted 351 laws, and decisions on other relevant laws; the State Council enacted over 800 administrative regulations; peoples' congresses and their standing committees at the local level enacted more than 6000 local regulations; see *People's Daily*, 14 March 1998.
13. The Communist Party of China Central Committee, *Selected Important Party Documents Since 1978*, vol. 2, Beijing: Central Documents Press, 1997, p. 436.
14. Wang Zhenmin, "News media and the judiciary", *Legal Daily*, 9 September 1999.
15. Wang Zhenmin, "The recent Constitutional Amendments in China", Paper presented at the Fifth World Congress of the International Association of Constitutional Law (12–16 July 1999, Rotterdam, The Netherlands).
16. State Council Information Office, *The Progress of the Cause of Human Rights in China*, December 1995.
17. The original Criminal Code was passed in 1979. The new one has 452 articles and is China's longest law up to date.
18. State Council Information Office, *The Progress of the Cause of Human Rights in China*, December 1995.
19. Ibid.
20. *Lawyers' Newspaper*, 13 December 1997.
21. State Council Information Office, *The Progress of the Cause of Human Rights in China*, December 1995.
22. According to the Chinese Constitution, the Standing Committee of the National People's Congress is responsible for deciding on the ratification or abrogation of treaties and important agreements concluded with foreign states. Therefore, having been signed by the Chinese Government, the two international Covenants are to be discussed by China's top legislative organs for their final approval and enforcement in China. The question as to how they might be internally applied in China remains unsolved.
23. "Seminar on constitutional amendments and the constitutional development in 21st century", *Studies on Law and Commerce* (1999), 3.
24. Li Peng, "Interview with journalists from Xinhua News Agency", *People's Daily*, 20 May 1991.
25. State Council Information Office, *White Paper on Human Rights in China*.
26. Li Ruihuan, "China's foreign policy and modernization", *People's Daily*, 19 May 1994.
27. Jiang Zemin, "Interview with American journalists", *People's Daily*, 19 May 1994.
28. Jiang Zemin, "Interview with American journalists", *Guangming Daily*, 2 November 1991.
29. Liu Huaqiu, "Speech at the World Congress on Human Rights", *Guangming Daily*, 17 June 1993.
30. Li Ruihuan, op. cit.
31. Ibid.
32. Xiang Fei collected materials for this part. Claudia Ng translated the Chinese version into English.
33. "Progress in China's Human Rights Cause in 2003", at http://www.china.org.cn/ch-book/20040330/index.htm.

SELECT BIBLIOGRAPHY

Francesco Paolo Vertova

Since the issue of the rule of law involves virtually all aspects of legal, philosophical, and political theoretical thought, a thematic subdivision of a bibliography on such a vast topic cannot, but be somewhat arbitrary. I decided to take the title of this volume as the basis for classification, at least partly, and to divide the works into three categories: the history, the theory, and the future of the rule of law.

In the first group I have gathered some works that recommend themselves to gain a deeper insight into such issues as the historical relationship between different conceptions or versions of the rule of law (German *Rechtsstaat*, English and American rule of law, and French *État de droit*), the debate on the rule of law, and rights in German constitutional history and public law theory between the nineteenth and the twentieth centuries, the fortune of Albert Venn Dicey in English legal thought and his reception by continental European thought, the colonial model of the rule of law.

In the second group I have selected some works that are especially relevant for such issues as Kelsen's and Schmitt's accounts on the constitution and the rule of law, legal certainty, the relationship between the constitution, rights and popular sovereignty, the relationship between the rule of law and the primacy of legislative power, the principle of legality and the subordination of the legislative to the respect of individuals' rights, the constitutional definition and acknowledgement of the latter, the foundation and universality of rights. As well as the link or the opposition between the rule of law and democracy, on one side, and the welfare stare on the other, and Hayek's critique of the primacy of legislation in the continental European conception of the rule of law in favour of the spontaneous order of the English rule of law. Moreover, I have collected in this section some works concerning the critique of the rule of law from the perspective of women's difference, and the study of the historical and theoretical connection between the rule of law and the republican tradition in political thought.

Finally, in the third group I have put together some works that are especially relevant for a number of open issues (or factors of crisis) concerning the rule of law at the beginning of the third millennium: economic globalization, the rule of law and world order, the erosion of the national rule of law and the development of international law, the rule of law and the institutions of the European Union, the possibility of applying – and to what extent – the principles of the rule of law to the interstate relationships, the new international judicial bodies, the link between the rule of law, the "government of law" and the "government of judges", hence the issue of legal culture and judges' education and training.

1 HISTORY OF THE RULE OF LAW

Babington, A., *The Rule of Law in Britain from the Roman Occupation to the Present Day*, Chichester: Barry Rose, 1978.

Bacot, G., *Carré de Malberg et l'origine de la distinction entre souveraineté du peuple et souveraineté nationale*, Paris: CNRS, 1985.

Bähr, O. von, *Der Rechtsstaat* [1864], Aalen: Scientia, 1961.

Barret-Kriegel, B., *L'état et les esclaves*, Paris: Payot, 1989.

Battaglia, F., "Ancora sullo 'Stato di diritto'", *Rivista internazionale di filosofia del diritto*, 25 (1948).

Bodda, P., *Lo Stato di diritto*, Milano: Giuffrè, 1935.

Bongiovanni, G., *Reine Rechtslehre e dottrina giuridica dello Stato. H. Kelsen e la costituzione austriaca del 1920*, Milano: Giuffrè, 1998.

Burdeau, F., *Histoire du droit administratif*, Paris: Presses Universitaires de France, 1995.

Caristia, C., "Venture e avventure di una formula: 'Rechtsstaat'", *Rivista di diritto pubblico*, I (1934).

Cassese, S., "Albert Venn Dicey e il diritto amministrativo", *Quaderni fiorentini per la storia del pensiero giuridico moderno*, 19 (1990).

Cassese, S., "La ricezione di Dicey in Italia e in Francia. Contributo allo studio del mito dell'amministrazione senza diritto amministrativo", *Materiali per una storia della cultura giuridica*, 25 (1995), 1.

Clavero, B., *Derecho indígena y cultura constitucional en América*, México: Siglo XXI, 1994.

Clavero, B., "Imperio de la ley y rule of law: léxico jurídico y tópica constitucional", *Quaderni fiorentini per la storia del pensiero giuridico moderno*, 25 (1996).

Cordero Torres, J.M., *Tratado elemental de derecho colonial español*, Madrid: Editora Nacional, 1941.

Cosgrove, R.A., *The Rule of Law: Albert Venn Dicey, Victorian Jurist*, London: Macmillan, 1980.

Costa, P., *Lo Stato immaginario. Metafore e paradigmi nella cultura giuridica italiana fra Ottocento e Novecento*, Milano: Giuffrè, 1986.

Costa, P., *Civitas. Storia della cittadinanza in Europa*, vols. 1–4, Roma-Bari: Laterza, 1999–2001.

Duguit, L., *Traité de droit constitutionnel*, Paris: E. De Boccard, 1927.

Fioravanti, M., *Appunti di storia delle costituzioni moderne*, I: *Le libertà: presupposti culturali e modelli storici*, Torino: Giappichelli, 1991.

Fioravanti, M., *Costituzione*, Bologna: il Mulino, 1999.
Fioravanti, M., "Costituzione e Stato di diritto", in *La scienza del diritto pubblico. Dottrine dello Stato e della costituzione tra Otto e Novecento*, Milano: Giuffrè, 2001.
Ford, T.H., *Albert Venn Dicey*, Chichester: Barry Rose, 1985.
Gerber, C.F.W. von, *Grundzüge des deutschen Staatsrechts* [1865], Hildesheim/Zürich/New York: Olms-Weidmann, 1998.
Gozzi, G., *Democrazia e diritti. Germania: dallo Stato di diritto alla democrazia costituzionale*, Roma-Bari: Laterza, 1999.
Gozzi, G. and Gherardi, R. (eds), *Saperi della borghesia e storia dei concetti fra Otto e Novecento*, Bologna: il Mulino, 1995.
Hauriou, M., *Précis de droit constitutionnel*, Paris: Sirey, 1929.
Hearn, W.E., *The Government of England. Its Structure and its Development*, London: Longmans, 1866.
Hobson, C.F., *The Great Chief Justice. John Marshall and the Rule of Law*, Lawrence (KS): Kansas University Press, 1996.
Jellinek, G., *Die rechtliche Natur der Staatsverträge*, Wien: Hölder, 1880.
Jellinek, G., *System der subjektiven öffentlichen Rechts* [1892], Tübingen: Mohr, 1905.
Jellinek, G., *Allgemeine Staatslehre*, Berlin: Häring, 1905.
Jhering, R. von, *Der Zweck im Recht*, Leipzig: Breitkopf und Härtel, 1923.
Jouannet, E., *Emer de Vattel et l'émergence doctrinale du droit international classique*, Paris: Pédone, 1998.
Kahn, P.W., *The Reign of Law. Marbury v. Madison and the Construction of America*, New Haven (CT): Yale University Press, 1997.
Koellreutter, O., "Der nationale Rechtsstaat", *Deutsche Juristen-Zeitung*, 38 (1933).
Koellreutter, O., *Grundriss der allgemeinen Staatslehre*, Tübingen: Mohr, 1933.
Laband, P., *Das Staatsrecht des deutschen Reiches* [1876], Aalen: Scientia, 1964.
Lambert, E., *Le gouvernement des juges et la lutte contre la législation sociale aux Etats-Unis*, Paris: Giard, 1921.
Lanchester, F. and Staff, I. (eds), *Lo Stato di diritto democratico dopo il fascismo ed il nazionalsocialismo*, Milano/Baden-Baden: Giuffrè/Nomos Verlag, 1999.
Mann, K. and Roberts, R. (eds), *Law in Colonial Africa*, London: Heinemann, 1991.
Mannoni, S., *Potenza e ragione. La scienza del diritto internazionale nella crisi dell'equilibrio europeo (1870–1914)*, Milano: Giuffrè, 1999.
McIlwain, C.H., *Constitutionalism and the Changing World*, London: Cambridge University Press, 1939.
McIlwain, C.H., *Constitutionalism: Ancient and Modern*, Ithaca (NY): Cornell University Press, 1947.
Merkl, A., "Idee und Gestalt der politischen Freheit", in *Demokratie und Rechtsstaat. Festgabe zum 60. Geburtstag von Zaccaria Giacometti*, Zürich: Polygraphischer Verlag A.G., 1953.
Merkl, A., *Il duplice volto del diritto*, Milano: Giuffrè, 1987.
Mohl, R. von, *Die Polizeiwissenschaft nach den Grundsätzen des Rechtsstaates*, vols. 1–3, Laupp, Tübingen, 1832–34.
Panunzio, S., *Lo Stato di diritto*, Città di Castello: Il Solco, 1921.
Pocock, J.G.A., *The Ancient Constitution and the Feudal Law. English Historical Thought in the Seventeenth Century*, Cambridge: Cambridge University Press, 1987.
Radbruch, G., *Der Geist des englischen Rechts*, Göttingen: Vanderhoeck & Ruprecht, 1946.

Rait, R.S. (ed.), *Memorials of Albert Venn Dicey*, London: Macmillan, 1925.
Raynaud, P., "Des droits de l'homme a l'état de droit. Les droits de l'homme et leurs garanties chez les théoriciens français classiques du droit public", *Droits*, 2 (1985).
Redor, M.-J., *De l'État légal à l'État de droit. L'évolution des conceptions de la doctrine publiciste française 1879–1914*, Paris: Economica, 1992.
Romano, S., *Corso di diritto coloniale*, Roma: Athenaeum, 1918.
Sandoz, E. (ed.), *The Roots of Liberty*, Columbia (MO)/London: Missouri University Press, 1992.
Sordi, B., *Tra Weimar e Vienna. Amministrazione pubblica e teoria giuridica nel primo dopoguerra*, Milano: Giuffrè, 1987.
Sordi, B., "Un diritto amministrativo per le democrazie degli anni Venti. La 'Verwaltung' nella riflessione della 'Wiener Rechtstheoretische Schule'", in G. Gozzi and P. Schiera (eds), *Crisi istituzionale e teoria dello Stato in Germania dopo la Prima guerra mondiale*, Bologna: il Mulino, 1987.
Stahl, F.J., *Die Philosophie des Rechts* [1878], Hildesheim: Olms, 1963.
Stein, L. von, "Rechtsstaat und Verwaltungsrechtspflege", *Zeitschrift für das privat- und öffentlichen Recht der Gegenwart*, 6 (1879).
Stolleis, M., "Rechtsstaat", in A. Erler and E. Kaufmann (eds), *Handwörterbuch zur deutscher Rechtsgeschichte*, IV, Berlin: Schmidt, 1990.
Stolleis, M., *Geschichte des öffentlichen Rechts in Deutschland*, München: Beck, 1992–1999.
Thoma, R., *Rechtsstaatsidee und Verwaltungsrechtswissenschaft*, in "Jahrbuch des öffentlichen Rechts der Gegenwart", 4 (1910).
Verdu, P.L., *La lucha por el Estado de derecho*, Bologna: Real Colegio de España, 1975.
Villey, M., *La formation de la pensée juridique moderne*, Paris: Montchrestien, 1975.
Wade, E.C.S., "Introduction", in A.V. Dicey, *Introduction to the Study of the Law of the Constitution*, London: Macmillan, 1960.
Williams, R.A. Jr., *The American Indian in Western Legal Thought. The Discourses of Conquest*, Oxford: Oxford University Press, 1990.
Ziadeh, F., *Lawyers, the Rule of Law and Liberalism in Modern Egypt*, Stanford (CA): Hoover Institution, 1968.
Zimmern, A.E., *The League of Nations and the Rule of Law, 1918–1935*, New York: Russell & Russell, 1969.

2 THEORIES OF THE RULE OF LAW

Ackerman, B., *We the People*, I: *Foundations*, Cambridge (MA): Harvard University Press, 1991.
Ackerman, B., *We the People*. II: *Transformations*, Cambridge (MA): Harvard University Press, 1998.
Agresto, J., *The Supreme Court and Constitutional Democracy*, Ithaca (NY): Cornell University Press, 1984.
Allan, J., "Bills of Rights and Judicial Power. A Liberal's Quandary", *Oxford Journal of Legal Studies*, 16 (1996), 2.
Allan, T.R.S., "Dworkin and Dicey: The Rule of Law as Integrity", *Oxford Journal of Legal Studies*, 8 (1988), 2.
Allan, T.R.S., *Law, Liberty, and Justice*, Oxford: Oxford University Press, 1995.

Allen, C.K., *Law in the Making*, Oxford: Clarendon Press, 1964.

Allen, F.A., *The Habits of Legality*, Oxford: Oxford University Press, 1996.

Amato, S., "Lo Stato di diritto: l'immagine e l'allegoria", *Rivista internazionale di filosofia del diritto*, 68 (1991).

Arthurs, H.W., "Rethinking Administrative Law: A Slightly Dicey Business", *Osgoode Hall Law Journal*, 17 (1979), 1.

Arthurs, H.W., *Without the Law*, Toronto: Toronto University Press, 1985.

Baccelli, L., *Il particolarismo dei diritti. Poteri degli individui e paradossi dell'individualismo*, Roma: Carocci, 1999.

Barbalet, J.M., *Citizenship*, Milton Keynes: Open University Press, 1988.

Barbera, A. (ed.), *Le basi filosofiche del costituzionalismo*, Roma-Bari: Laterza, 1997.

Bankowski, Z., *Ambiguities of the Rule of Law*, in H. Jung, H. Müller-Dietz, and U. Neumann (eds), *Recht und Moral*, Baden-Baden: Nomos, 1991.

Barnett, R.E., *The Structure of Liberty*, Oxford: Clarendon Press, 1998.

Bellamy, R.P. (ed.), *Constitutionalism, Democracy and Sovereignty. American and European Perspectives*, Aldershot: Avebury, 1996.

Bellamy, R.P., *Liberalism and Pluralism. Towards a Politics of Compromise*, London: Routledge, 1999.

Bellamy, R.P. and Castiglione, D. (eds), *Constitutionalism in Transformation*, Oxford: Blackwell, 1996.

Berlin, I., *Four Essays on Liberty*, Oxford: Oxford University Press, 1969.

Bobbio, N., *Il futuro della democrazia*, Torino: Einaudi, 1984.

Bobbio, N., *L'età dei diritti*, Torino: Einaudi, 1992.

Böckenförde, E.-W., "Entstehung und Wandel des Rechtsstaatsbegriffs", in *Staat, Gesellschaft, Freiheit. Studien zur Staatstheorie und zum Verfassungsrecht*, Frankfurt a.M.: Suhrkamp, 1976.

Böckenförde, E.-W., *Staat, Verfassung, Demokratie*, Frankfurt a.M.: Suhrkamp, 1991.

Carrino, A., *Ideologia e coscienza. Critical Legal Studies*, Napoli: Esi, 1992.

Carrino, A., "Roberto Unger e i 'Critical Legal Studies': scetticismo e diritto", in G. Zanetti (ed.), *Filosofi del diritto contemporanei*, Milano: Cortina, 1999.

Chevallier, J., *L'État de droit*, Paris: Montchrestien, 1999.

Coleman, J., "On the Relationship between Law and Morality", *Ratio Juris*, 2 (1989), 1.

Craig, P.P., *Public Law and Democracy in the United Kingdom and the United States of America*, Oxford: Clarendon Press, 1990.

Craig, P.P., "Formal and substantive conceptions of the rule of law", *Diritto pubblico*, 1 (1995), 1.

De Q. Walker, G., *The Rule of Law*, Melbourne: Melbourne University Press, 1989.

Dicey, A.V., *Lectures on the Relation between Law and Public Opinion in England during the Nineteenth Century*, London: Macmillan, 1914.

Dicey, A.V., *Introduction to the Study of the Law of the Constitution*, Indianapolis (IN): Liberty Fund, 1982.

Dogliani, M., *Introduzione al diritto costituzionale*, Bologna: il Mulino, 1994.

Dworkin, R.M., *Taking Rights Seriously*, London: Duckworth, 1977.

Dworkin, R.M., *A Matter of Principle*, Cambridge (MA): Harvard University Press, 1985.

Dworkin, R.M., *Law's Empire*, Cambridge (MA): Harvard University Press, 1986.

Dworkin, R.M., "Constitutionalism and Democracy", *European Journal of Philosophy*, 3 (1995).

Dworkin, R.M., *Freedom's Law. The Moral Reading of the American Constitution*, Cambridge (MA): Harvard University Press, 1996.

Dyzenhaus, D., *Hard Cases in Wicked Legal Systems: South Africa Law in the Perspective of Legal Philosophy*, Oxford: Clarendon Press, 1991.

Dyzenhaus, D., *Legality and Legitimacy*, Oxford: Clarendon Press, 1997.

Dyzenhaus, D. (ed.), *Recrafting the Rule of Law*, Oxford: Hart Publishing, 1999.

Elkin, S.L. and Soltan, K.E., *A New Constitutionalism*, Chicago: Chicago University Press, 1993.

Elster, J. and Slagstad, R. (eds), *Constitutionalism and Democracy: Studies in Rationality and Social Change*, Cambridge: Cambridge University Press, 1988.

Ely, J., *Democracy and Distrust: A Theory of Judicial Review*, Cambridge (MA): Harvard University Press, 1980.

Facchi, A., "Il pensiero femminista sul diritto: un percorso da Carol Gilligan a Tove Stang Dahl", in G. Zanetti (ed.), *Filosofi del diritto contemporanei*, Milano: Cortina, 1999.

Fassò, G., "Stato di diritto e Stato di giustizia", in R. Orecchia (ed.), *Atti del VI Congresso nazionale di filosofia del diritto*, I, Milano: Giuffrè, 1963.

Favoreu, L., "De la démocratie à l'État de droit", *Le Débat*, 64 (1991).

Ferrajoli, L., *La sovranità nel mondo moderno. Nascita e crisi dello Stato nazionale*, Milano: Anabasi, 1995.

Ferrajoli, L., *Diritto e ragione. Teoria del garantismo penale* [1989], Roma-Bari: Laterza, 2000.

Ferrajoli, L., *Diritti fondamentali*, organizado por E. Vitale, Roma-Bari: Laterza, 2001.

Fine, B., *Democracy and the Rule of Law*, London: Pluto Press, 1984.

Finnis, J., *Natural Law and Natural Rights*, Oxford: Clarendon, 1980.

Finnis, J.M., "Law as Coordination", *Ratio Juris*, 2 (1989), 1.

Forsthoff, E., *Rechtsstaat im Wandel*, Stuttgart: Kohlhammer, 1964.

Forsthoff, E. (ed.), *Rechtsstaatlichkeit und Sozialstaatlichkeit. Aufsätze und Essays*, Darmstadt: Wissenschaftliche Buchgesellschaft, 1968.

Friedman, R.B., "Oakeshott on the Authority of Law", *Ratio Juris*, 2 (1989), 1.

Friedrich, C.J., *Constitutional Government and Democracy*, Boston (MA): Ginn & Co., 1950.

Fuller, L.L., *The Morality of Law*, New Haven (CT): Yale University Press, 1969.

Fuller, T., "Friedrich Hayek's Moral Science", *Ratio Juris*, 2 (1989), 1.

Galli, C., *Genealogia della politica. Carl Schmitt e la crisi del pensiero politico moderno*, Bologna: il Mulino, 1996.

Geuna, M., "La tradizione repubblicana e i suoi interpreti: famiglie teoriche e discontinuità concettuali", *Filosofia politica*, 12 (1998), 1.

Goodhart, A.L., "The Rule of Law and Absolute Sovereignty", *University of Pennsylvania Law Review*, 106 (1958), 7.

Gozzi, G. (ed.), *Democrazia, diritti, costituzione*, Bologna: il Mulino, 1997.

Graziosi, M., "Infirmitas sexus. La donna nell'immaginario penalistico", *Democrazia e diritto*, 33 (1993), 2.

Griffin, S.M., *American Constitutionalism*, Princeton (NJ): Princeton University Press, 1996.

Grimm, D., "Reformalisierung des Rechtsstaats als Demokratiepostulat?" *JuS*, 10 (1980).

Grimm, D., *Die Zukunft der Verfassung*, Frankfurt a.M.: Suhrkamp, 1991.

Guastini, R., "Diritto mite, diritto incerto", *Materiali per una storia della cultura giuridica*, 2 (1996).

Gutmann, A. and Thompson, D., *Democracy and Disagreement*, Cambridge (MA): Harvard University Press, 1996.

Habermas, J., *Faktizität und Geltung*, Frankfurt a.M.: Suhrkamp, 1992.
Habermas, J., *Die Einbeziehung des Anderen*, Frankfurt a.M.: Suhrkamp, 1999.
Habermas, J., "Stato di diritto e democrazia: nesso paradossale di principi contraddittori?" *Teoria politica*, 16 (2000), 3.
Harden, I. and Lewis, N., *The Noble Lie*, London: Hutchinson, 1986.
Hase, F., Ladeur, K.-H. and Ridder, H., "Nochmals: Reformalisierung des Rechtsstaats als Demokratiepostulat?" *JuS*, 11 (1981).
Hayek, F.A., *The Constitution of Liberty*, London: Routledge & Kegan Paul, 1960.
Hayek, F.A., *Law, Legislation and Liberty*, London: Routledge, 1973–1979.
Heller, H., *Gesammelte Schriften*, II, *Recht, Staat, Macht*, Leiden: Sijthoff, 1971.
Heller, H., *Stato di diritto o dittatura? e altri scritti*, Napoli: Editoriale Scientifica, 1998.
Hofmann, H., "Geschichtlichkeit und Universalitätsanspruch des Rechtsstaats", *Archiv für Rechts- und Sozialphilosophie*, Beiheft 65, Stuttgart: Franz Steiner, 1996.
Horwitz, M.J., "The Rule of Law: An Unqualified Human Good?" *The Yale Law Journal*, 86 (1977).
Horwitz, M.J., "Why is Anglo-American Jurisprudence Unhistorical?" *Oxford Journal of Legal Studies*, 17 (1997).
Hughes, J.C., *The Federal Courts, Politics, and the Rule of Law*, New York: HarperCollins, 1995.
Hutchinson, A.C. and Monahan, P. (eds), *The Rule of Law. Ideal or Ideology*, Toronto: Carswell, 1987.
Jennings, I., *The British Constitution*, Cambridge: Cambridge University Press, 1966.
Jennings, I., *The Law and the Constitution*, London: London University Press, 1967.
Jowell, J.L., *Law and Bureaucracy*, New York: Dunellen, 1975.
Jowell, J.L. and Oliver, D. (eds), *The Changing Constitution*, Oxford: Clarendon Press, 1994.
Kägi, W., "Rechtsstaat und Demokratie", in *Demokratie und Rechtsstaat. Festgabe zum 60. Geburtstag von Zaccaria Giacometti*, Zürich: Polygraphischer Verlag A.G., 1953.
Kant, I., *Scritti politici e di filosofia della storia e del diritto*, organizado por N. Bobbio, L. Firpo, V. Mathieu, Torino: Utet, 1956.
Kaufmann, E., *Critica della filosofia neokantiana del diritto*, organizado por A. Carrino, Napoli: Esi, 1992.
Kelsen, H., *Das Problem der Souveränität und die Theorie des Völkerrechts. Beitrag zu einer Reinen Rechtslehre*, Tübingen: Mohr, 1920.
Kelsen, H., "Das Verhältnis von Staat und Recht im Lichte der Erkenntniskritik", *Zeitschrift für öffentliches Recht*, 2 (1921).
Kelsen, H., "Die Lehre von der drei Gewalten oder Funktionen des Staates", *Archiv für Rechts- und Wirtschaftsphilosophie*, 17 (1923–1924).
Kelsen, H., *Vom Wesen und Wert der Demokratie*, Tübingen: Mohr, 1929.
Kelsen, H., *General Theory of Law and State*, Cambridge: Harvard University Press, 1945.
Kelsen, H., *Hauptprobleme der Staatsrechtslehre* [1911], Aalen: Scientia, 1960.
Kelsen, H., *La giustizia costituzionale*, organizado por G. Geraci, Milano: Giuffrè, 1981.
Kelsen, H., *Dio e Stato. La giurisprudenza come scienza dello spirito*, organizado por A. Carrino, Napoli: Esi, 1988.
Kennedy, D., *A Critique of Adjudication*, Cambridge (MA): Harvard University Press, 1998.
Kirchheimer, O., *Social democracy and the rule of law*, London: Allen & Unwin, 1987.
Kunig, P., *Das Rechtsstaatsprinzip*, Tübingen: Mohr Siebeck, 1986.
La Torre, M., *Disavventure del diritto soggettivo. Una vicenda teorica*, Milano: Giuffrè, 1996.

Lawson, F.H., "Dicey Revisited", *Political Studies*, 7 (1959), 2.

Leiser, B.M., *Values in Conflict*, New York: Macmillan, 1981.

Leoni, B., *Freedom and the Law*, Indianapolis (IN): Liberty Fund, 1991.

Leoni, B., *Le pretese ed i poteri: le radici individuali del potere e della politica*, M. Stoppino (ed.), Milano: Società Aperta, 1997.

Letwin, S.R., "Morality and Law", *Ratio Juris*, 2 (1989), 1.

Lombardi, L., *Saggio sul diritto giurisprudenziale*, Milano: Giuffrè, 1975.

Lopez de Oñate, F., *La certezza del diritto*, Milano: Giuffrè, 1968.

Lord Hewart of Bury, *The New Despotism*, London: Ernest Benn, 1945.

Luhmann, N., "Gesellschaftliche und politische Bedingungen des Rechtsstaates", in id., *Politische Planung*, Opladen: Westdeutscher Verlag, 1971.

MacCormick, D.N., "Der Rechtsstaat und die rule of law", *Juristen Zeitung*, 39 (1984).

MacCormick, D.N., "Spontaneous Order and the Rule of Law: Some Problems", *Ratio Juris*, 2 (1989), 1.

Marsh, N.S., "The Rule of Law as a Supra national Concept", in A.G. Guest (ed.), *Oxford Essays in Jurisprudence*, Oxford: Oxford University Press, 1961.

Mathews, A.S., *Freedom, State Security and the Rule of Law*, London: Sweet & Maxwell, 1988.

Matteucci, N., *Organizzazione del potere e libertà*, Torino: Utet, 1976.

Matteucci, N., *Positivismo giuridico e costituzionalismo*, Bologna: il Mulino, 1996.

McAuslan, P. and McEldowney, J.F., *Law, Legitimacy and the Constitution. Essays Marking the Centenary of Dicey's Law of the Constitution*, London: Sweet & Maxwell, 1985.

Michelman, F.I., "Law's Republic", *The Yale Law Journal*, 97 (1988), 8.

Montanari, B. (ed.), *Stato di diritto e trasformazione della politica*, Torino: Giappichelli, 1992.

Müller, C. and Staff, I. (eds), *Der soziale Rechtsstaat*, Baden-Baden: Nomos, 1984.

Münch, I. von, "Rechtsstaat versus Gerechtigkeit?" *Der Staat*, 33 (1994), 2.

Neumann, F., *Die Herrschaft des Gesetzes*, Frankfurt a.M.: Suhrkamp, 1980.

Neumann, F., *The Rule of Law. Political Theory and the Legal System in Modern Society* (1935), Leamington: Berg, 1986.

Noske, H. (ed.), *Der Rechtsstaat am Ende? Analyse, Standpunkte, Perspektiven*, München: Olzog, 1995.

Oakeshott, M., "The Rule of Law", in *On History and Other Essays*, Oxford: Blackwell, 1983.

Palombella, G., "I limiti del diritto mite", *Democrazia e diritto* (1994), 4.

Palombella, G., *Costituzione e sovranità. Il senso della democrazia costituzionale*, Bari: Dedalo, 1997.

Paulson, S.L., "Teorie giuridiche e Rule of Law", in P. Comanducci and R. Guastini (eds), *Analisi e diritto 1992*, Torino: Giappichelli, 1992.

Pettit, P., *Republicanism. A Theory of Freedom and Government*, Oxford: Clarendon Press, 1997.

Pocock, J.G.A., *The Machiavellian Moment: Florentine Political Thought and the Atlantic Republican Tradition*, Princeton (NJ): Princeton University Press, 1975.

Portinaro, P.P., *Il realismo politico*, Roma-Bari: Laterza, 1999.

Posner, R.A., *Economic Analysis of Law*, Boston (MA): Little, Brown, 1992.

Preterossi, G., *Carl Schmitt e la tradizione moderna*, Roma-Bari: Laterza, 1996.

Preuβ, U.K., *Zum Begriff der Verfassung*, Frankfurt a.M.: Fischer, 1994.

Rawls, J., *Political Liberalism*, Cambridge (MA): Harvard University Press, 1993.

Raz, J., "The Rule of Law and Its Virtue", in *The Authority of Law. Essays on Law and Morality*, Oxford: Clarendon Press, 1979.
Raz, J., "The Politics of the Rule of Law", *Ratio Juris*, 3 (1990), 3.
Reynolds, Noel B., "Grounding the Rule of Law", *Ratio Juris*, 2 (1989), 1.
Reynolds, Noel B., "Law as Convention", *Ratio Juris*, 2 (1989), 1.
Rorty, R., "Human Rights, Rationality, and Sentimentality", in S. Shute and S. Hurley (eds), *On Human Rights. Oxford Amnesty Lectures*, New York: Basic Books, 1993.
Rosenfeld, M. and Arato, A. (eds), *Habermas on Law and Democracy*, Berkeley (CA): California University Press, 1998.
Ross, A., *On Law and Justice*, London: Steven & Sons, 1958.
Rusconi, G.E., "Quale 'democrazia costituzionale'? La Corte federale nella politica tedesca e il problema della costituzione europea", *Rivista italiana di scienza politica*, 27 (1997), 2.
Santoro, E., *Autonomia individuale, libertà e diritti. Una critica dell'antropologia liberale*, Pisa: Ets, 1999.
Santoro, E., Common law *e costituzione nell'Inghilterra moderna. Introduzione al pensiero di Albert Venn Dicey*, Torino: Giappichelli, 1999.
Scalia, A., "The Rule of Law as a Law of Rules", *Harvard Law School*, 56 (1989), 4.
Scheuerman, W.E., *Between the Norm and the Exception*, Cambridge (MA): Mit Press, 1994.
Scheuerman, W.E. (ed.), *The Rule of Law under Siege*, Berkeley (CA): California University Press, 1996.
Schmidt-Assmann, E., "Der Rechtsstaat", in J. Isensee and P. Kirchhof (eds), *Handbuch des Staatsrechts*, Heidelberg: Müller, 1995.
Schmitt, C., "Der bürgerliche Rechtsstaat", *Die Schildgenossen* (1928), 2.
Schmitt, C., *Verfassungslehre*, Berlin: Duncker & Humblot, 1928.
Schmitt, C., *Der Hüter der Verfassung*, Berlin: Duncker & Humblot, 1931.
Schmitt, C., "Nationalsozialismus und Rechtsstaat", *Juristische Wochenschrift*, 63 (1934).
Schmitt, C., "Der Rechtsstaat", in H. Frank (ed.), *Nationalsozialistisches Handbuch für Recht und Gesetzgebung*, München: NSDAP, 1935.
Schmitt, C., "Was bedeutet der Streit um den 'Rechtsstaat'?" [1935], in G. Maschke (ed.), *Staat, Großraum, Nomos. Arbeiten aus den Jahren 1916–1969*, Berlin: Duncker & Humblot, 1995.
Shapiro, I. (ed.), *The Rule of Law (Nomos 36)*, New York: New York University Press, 1994.
Skinner, Q., *Liberty before Liberalism*, Cambridge: Cambridge University Press, 1998.
Sobota, K., *Das Prinzip Rechtsstaat. Verfassungs- und verwaltungsrechtliche Aspekte*, Tübingen: Mohr Siebeck, 1997.
Sugarman, D., "The Legal Boundaries of Liberty: Dicey, Liberalism and Legal Science", *Modern Law Review*, 46 (1983).
Sunstein, C.R., *The Partial Constitution*, Cambridge (MA): Harvard University Press, 1993.
Sunstein, C.R., *Legal Reasoning and Political Conflict*, Oxford: Oxford University Press, 1996.
Tohidipur, M. (ed.), *Der bürgerliche Rechtsstaat*, Frankfurt a.M.: Suhrkamp, 1978.
Tremblay, L., *The Rule of Law, Justice, and Interpretation*, Montréal: McGill-Queens University Press, 1997.
Treves, R., "Stato di diritto e Stato totalitario", in *Studi in onore di G.M. De Francesco*, 2, Milano: Giuffrè, 1957.
Treves, R., "Considerazioni sullo Stato di diritto", in *Studi in onore di E. Crosa*, Milano: Giuffrè, 1960.

Troper, M., "Le concept d'État de droit", *Droits*, 15 (1992).
Unger, R.M., *Law in Modern Society*, New York: The Free Press, 1976.
Unger, R.M., "The Critical Legal Studies Movement", *Harvard Law Review*, 3 (1983).
Waldron, J., "The Rule of Law in Contemporary Liberal Theory", *Ratio Juris*, 2 (1989), 1.
Waldron, J., "The Rule of Law", in *The Law*, London/New York: Routledge, 1990.
Weber, M., *Wirtschaft und Gesellschaft*, Tübingen: Mohr, 1922.
Wolff, R.P. (ed.), *The Rule of Law*, New York: Simon & Schuster, 1971.
Zagrebelsky, G., *Il diritto mite*, Torino: Einaudi, 1992.
Zagrebelsky, G., Portinaro, P.P., and Luther, J. (eds), *Il futuro della Costituzione*, Torino: Einaudi, 1996.
Zolo, D., *Il principato democratico*, Milano: Feltrinelli, 1992, Eng. tr. *Democracy and Complexity*, Cambridge: Polity Press, 1992.

3 THE FUTURE OF THE RULE OF LAW

Abu-Sahlieh, A. and Sami, A., *Les Musulmans face aux droits de l'homme: religion, droit, politique*, Bochum: Winkler, 1994.
Alpa, G., *L'arte di giudicare*, Roma-Bari: Laterza, 1996.
an-Na'im, A.A., *Toward an Islamic Reformation: Civil Liberties, Human Rights, and International Law*, Syracuse (NY): Syracuse University Press, 1990.
Ayubi, N., *Political Islam: Religion and Politics in the Arab World*, London: Routledge, 1991.
Baxi, U., *The Crisis of the Indian Legal System*, Delhi: Vikas, 1982.
Bellamy, R.P., Bufacchi, V. and Castiglione, D. (eds), *Democracy and Constitutional Culture in the Union of Europe*, London: Lothian Foundation Press, 1995.
Brown, N.J., *The Rule of Law in the Arab World*, Cambridge: Cambridge University Press, 1997.
Bruti Liberati, E., Ceretti, A. and Giasanti, A. (eds), *Governo dei giudici. La magistratura tra diritto e politica*, Milano: Feltrinelli, 1996.
Butler, W.E., *Perestroika and the Rule of Law*, London: Tauris, 1991.
Conrad, D., *Rule of Law and Constitutional Problems of Personal Laws in India*, in S. Saberwal and H. Sievers (eds), *Rules, Laws, Constitutions*, Delhi: Sage Publications, 1998.
Dell'Aquila, E., *Il diritto cinese*, Padova: Cedam, 1981.
Ferrarese, M.R., *Le istituzioni della globalizzazione. Diritto e diritti nella società transnazionale*, Bologna: il Mulino, 2000.
Finn, J.E., *Constitutions in Crisis*, New York: Oxford University Press, 1991.
Fitzpatrick, P. (ed.), *Nationalism, Racism and the Rule of Law*, Aldershot: Dartmouth, 1995.
Franck, T.M., *Political Questions/Judicial Answers. Does the Rule of Law Apply to Foreign Affairs?* Princeton (NJ): Princeton University Press, 1992.
Gallino, L., *Globalizzazione e disuguaglianze*, Roma-Bari: Laterza, 2000.
Garapon, A., *Le gardien des promesses. Justice et démocratie*, Paris: Odile Jacob, 1996.
Gozzi, G. (ed.), *Islam e democrazia*, Bologna: il Mulino, 1998.
Held, D., *Democracy and the Global Order: From the Modern State to Cosmopolitan Governance*, Cambridge: Polity Press, 1995.
Hirst, P. and Thompson, G., *Globalisation in Question: The International Economy and the Possibilities of Governance*, Cambridge: Polity Press, 1996.
Holden, B. (ed.), *Global Democracy. Key Debates*, London: Routledge, 2000.

Keith, R.C., *China's Struggle for the Rule of Law*, London: Macmillan, 1994.
Kochler, H. (ed.), *Democracy and the International Rule of Law*, Wien/New York: Springer, 1995.
Lawyers Committee for Human Rights, *Beset by Contradictions. Islamization, Legal Reform and Human Rights in Sudan*, New York: Lawyers Committee for Human Rights, 1996.
Mayer, A.E., *Islam and Human Rights: Tradition and Politics*, Boulder (CO): Westview, 1991.
McAdams, A.J. (ed.), *Transitional Justice and the Rule of Law in New Democracies*, Notre Dame: Notre Dame University Press, 1997.
Moore, J.N., *Crisis in the Gulf. Enforcing the Rule of Law*, New York: Oceana, 1992.
Moravcsik, A., "Preferences and Power in the European Community: A Liberal Intergovernmentalist Approach", *Journal of Common Market Studies*, 31 (1993).
Palmier, L. (ed.), *State and Law in Eastern Asia*, Aldershot: Dartmouth, 1996.
Pizzorno, A., *Il potere dei giudici. Stato democratico e controllo di virtù*, Roma-Bari: Laterza, 1998.
Pritchard, S. (ed.), *Indigenous Peoples, United Nations and Human Rights*, London: Zed Books, 1998.
Rodotà, S., *Tecnologie e diritti*, Bologna: il Mulino, 1995.
Salvatore, A., "La sharî'a moderne en quête de droit: raison transcendante, métanorme publique et système juridique", *Droit et société*, 39 (1998).
Schmale, W. (ed.), *Human Rights and Cultural Diversity: Europe, Islamic World, Africa, China*, Goldbach: Keip, 1993.
Tate, N. and Vallinder, T. (eds), *The Global Expansion of Judicial Power*, New York: New York University Press, 1995.
Teubner, G. (ed.), *Global Law without a State*, Aldershot: Dartmouth, 1996.
Varga, C., *Transition to the Rule of Law*, Budapest: Akaprint, 1995.
Zolo, D., *Cosmopolis. La prospettiva del governo mondiale*, Milano: Feltrinelli, 1995, Eng. tr. *Cosmopolis*, Cambridge: Polity Press, 1997.
Zolo, D., *I signori della pace. Una critica del globalismo giuridico*, Roma: Carocci, 1998.
Zolo, D., *Chi dice umanità. Guerra, diritto e ordine globale*, Torino: Einaudi, 2000, Eng. tr. *Invoking Humanity*, London/New York: Continuum International, 2002.

LIST OF AUTHORS

Luca Baccelli (Lucca, 1960) is Professor of Philosophy and Sociology of Law at the Legal Faculty of the University of Pisa (Italy). His publications include *Praxis e poiesis nella filosofia politica moderna*, Milano: Angeli, 1991; *Il particolarismo dei diritti*, Roma: Carocci, 1999; *Critica del repubblicanesimo*, Roma-Bari: Laterza, 2003.

Raja Bahlul (Abwein, Palestine, 1951) is Professor of Philosophy at Birzeit University, Birzeit (Palestine), and the United Arab Emirates University (UAE). He is member of the Arab Philosophical Society. His recent publications include *From Jihad to Peaceful Co-existence*, Birzeit: Ialiis Publications, 2003; "Democracy without Secularism?", in J. Bunzl (ed.), *Islam, Judaism, and the Political Role of Religions in the Middle East*, Florida: University Press of Florida, 2004.

Giorgio Bongiovanni (Mantova, 1956) is Professor of Philosophy of Law at the Legal Faculty of the University of Bologna. He is Associate editor of *Ratio Juris*. His recent publications include *Reine Rechtslehre e dottrina giuridica dello Stato. Hans Kelsen e la Costituzione austriaca del 1920*, Milano: Giuffrè, 1998; *Teorie 'costituzionalistiche' del diritto*, Bologna: Clueb, 2000.

Brunella Casalini (Orbetello, 1963) is Researcher in Political Philosophy at the Political Sciences Faculty of the University of Florence. Her publications include *Antropologia, filosofia e politica in John Dewey*, Napoli: Morano, 1995; "American Citizenship Between Past and Future", in R. Bellamy *et al.* (eds), *Lineages of European Citizenship*, Houndmills/New York: Palgrave, 2004; *I rischi del 'materno'. Pensiero politico femminista e critica del patriarcalismo tra Sette e Ottocento*, Pisa: Plus, 2004.

Bartolomé Clavero (Madrid, 1947) is Professor of History of Law at the University of Sevilla (Spain). He is coordinator of the interuniversity research team on Historia Cultural e Institucional del Constitucionalismo en España. His publications include *La grâce du don*, Paris: Albin Michel, 1996; *Tomás y Valiente: una biografía intelectual*, Milano:

Giuffrè, 1996; *Happy Constitution. Cultura y lengua constitucionales*, Madrid: Tecnos, 1997; *Ama llunku, Abya Yala. Constituyencia indígena y código ladino por América*, Madrid: Centro de Estudios Políticos y Constitucionales, 2000.

Pietro Costa (Firenze, 1945) is Professor of History of Law at the Legal Faculty of the University of Florence. He is member of the editorial board of *Quaderni fiorentini per la storia del pensiero giuridico moderno* and the scientific council of *Diritto pubblico*. His numerous publications include *Il progetto giuridico*, Milano: Giuffrè, 1974; *Lo Stato immaginario*, Milano: Giuffrè, 1986; "La cittadinanza: un tentativo di ricostruzione 'archeologica'", in D. Zolo (ed.), *La cittadinanza*, Roma-Bari: Laterza, 1994; *Civitas. Storia della cittadinanza in Europa*, vol. 4, Roma-Bari: Laterza, 1999–2001.

Baudouin Dupret (Jerusalem, 1965) is Researcher at the French "Centre National de la Recherche Scientifique" and currently based at the Institut Français du Proche-Orient, Damascus (Syria). His publications include *Au nom de quel droit*, Paris: Maison des sciences de l'homme, 2000; (ed.), *Egypt and Its Laws*, The Hague: Kluwer Law International, 2001; (ed.), *Standing Trial: Law and the Person in the Modern Middle-East*, London: I.B. Tauris, 2004.

Alice Ehr-Soon Tay (Singapore) was Challis Professor of Jurisprudence at the University of Sydney, and since 1998 President of the Human Rights and Equal Opportunities Commission of Australia. She was also solicitor at the Australian Supreme Court, and Ministry of Justice. Her publications include *Law and Social Control* (ed. in cooperation), London: Arnold, 1980; *Konstitutionalismus versus Legalismus* (ed. in cooperation), Stuttgart: Steiner Verlag, 1991.

Luigi Ferrajoli (Firenze, 1940) is Professor of Philosophy of Law at the University of Rome Three. From 1967 to 1975 he was a magistrate and a member of "Magistratura Democratica". His numerous publications include *Diritto e ragione. Teoria del garantismo penale*, Roma-Bari: Laterza, 1989; *La sovranità nel mondo moderno*, Roma-Bari: Laterza, 1997; *La cultura giuridica nell'Italia del Novecento*, Roma-Bari: Laterza, 1999; *Diritti fondamentali*, Roma-Bari: Laterza, 2001.

Ananta Kumar Giri (Jamalpur, India, 1965) is teacher at the Madras Institute of Development Studies, Chennai (India). His publications include *Conversations and Transformations: Towards a New Ethics of Self and Society*, Lanham (MD): Lexington Books, 2001; *Building in the*

Margins of Shacks: The Vision and Projects of Habitat for Humanity, New Delhi: Orient Longman, 2001.

Gustavo Gozzi (Ferrara, 1947) is Professor of History of Political Thought within the course in Civilisations of East Europe and the Mediterranean Area at the University of Bologna. His recent publications include *Democrazia e diritti. Germania: dallo Stato di diritto alla democrazia costituzionale*, Roma-Bari: Laterza, 1999; (ed.) *Tradizioni culturali, sistemi giuridici e diritti umani nell'area del Mediterraneo*, Bologna: il Mulino, 2003; (ed.) *Guerre e minoranze*, Bologna: il Mulino 2004.

Alain Laquièze (Nice, 1965) was *Maître de Conférences* in Public Law at the Université Panthéon-Assas, Paris II. At present he is Professor of Public Law at the University of Angers (France) and *Chargé de mission* for the social and human sciences at the French Ministère de la Recherche. His publications include *Les origines du régime parlementaire sous la Restauration et la Monarchie de Juillet (1814–1848)*, Paris: Presses Universitaires de France, 2002.

Li Zhenghui (Tianjin, China, 1973) is lawyer at the law firm of Wilmer Cutler Pickering Hale and Dorr LLP, in Washington (USA). He obtained his law degree from Tsinghua University School of Law of Beijing (China) and LL.M. from the University of Michigan. His publications include *On Rule of Law and Spiritual Civilization*, Beijing: China Press of Legal Systems, 1997; "From Nihilism in Law to Rule of Law" (in cooperation), *Tsinghua University Journal of Social Sciences* (1998), 4.

Lin Feng (Shanghai, China, 1965) is Associate Professor of Law at the Law School of the City University of Hong Kong, where he is also Associate Director of the Centre for the Chinese Law and Comparative Law. He was Visiting Scholar at the University of Aix-Marseille, France. His publications include *Constitutional Law in China*, Hong Kong: Sweet & Maxwell Asia, 2000; "Impact of the Basic Law upon Judicial Review in Hong Kong", *Jurists' Review* (2001), 4 [in Chinese].

Anna Loretoni (Narni, 1960) is Researcher at the Scuola Superiore di Studi Universitari e di Perfezionamento Sant'Anna, of Pisa (Italy). Her publications include *Pace e progresso in Kant*, Napoli: Esi, 1996; *Interviste sull'Europa. Integrazione e identità nella globalizzazione*, Roma: Carocci, 2001; *The Emerging European Union: Identity, Citizenship, Rights*, Pisa: Ets, 2004.

Carlos Petit (Sevilla, 1955) is Professor of History of Law at the Universidad de Huelva (Spain). His publications include *Discurso sobre* *el discurso. Oralidad y escritura en la cultura jurídica de la España liberal*, Huelva: Universidad de Huelva, 2000; *Pasiones del jurista. Amor, memoria, melancolía, imaginación*, Madrid: Centro de Estudios Constitucionales, 1997.

Maria Chiara Pievatolo (Firenze, 1963) is Professor of Political Philosophy at the University of Pisa (Italy). She is editor of the *Bollettino telematico di filosofia politica*. Her recent publications include *La giustizia degli invisibili. L'identificazione del soggetto morale a ripartire da Kant*, Roma: Carocci, 1999; *I padroni del discorso. Platone e la libertà della conoscenza*, Pisa: Plus, 2003.

Pier Paolo Portinaro (Torino, 1953) is Professor of Political Philosophy at the University of Torino. He taught Political Science at the University of Breiburg and Sociology at the University of Mainz. His numerous publications include *Interesse nazionale e interesse globale*, Milano: Angeli, 1996; *Stato*, Bologna: il Mulino, 1999; *Il realismo politico*, Roma-Bari: Laterza, 1999; (ed.) *I concetti del male*, Torino: Einaudi, 2002.

Emilio Santoro (Parma, 1963) is Professor of Philosophy and Sociology of Law at the University of Florence. He was Visiting Fellow at the School of Economic and Social Studies of the University of East Anglia. He is the director of *L'altro diritto*, Centre for documentation on prison, deviancy and marginality. His publications include Common law *e costituzione nell'Inghilterra moderna*, Torino: Giappichelli, 1999; *Autonomy, Freedom and Rights*, Dordrecht: Kluwer, 2003; *Carcere e società liberale*, Torino: Giappichelli, 2004; *Estado de direito e interpretação*, Porto Alegre: Editoria Libraria do Advogado, 2005.

Francesco Paolo Vertova (Firenze, 1963) obtained the title of Research Doctor in Political Philosophy at the University of Pisa (Italy). He was Visiting Fellow at the School of Economic and Social Studies of the University of East Anglia. He is member of the editorial board and webmaster of *Jura Gentium*, Center for Philosophy of International Law and Global Politics. His publications include "Liberalismo e neutralità in Ronald Dworkin", *Iride* (1991), 3, p. 6; "Cittadinanza liberale, identità collettive e diritti sociali", in D. Zolo (ed.), *La cittadinanza*, Roma-Bari: Laterza, 1999.

Wang Zhenmin (Henan, China, 1966) is Professor and Vice Dean of the Law School of Tsinghua University in Beijing (China). He is the Vice President of Beijing Constitutional Law Association. He was Visiting Scholar at Melbourne University, the University of Aix-Marseille and

Harvard University. His publications include *The Foundations of Chinese Law*, Beijing: Tsinghua University Press, 2000 (in cooperation); *The Central-Hong Kong and Macau SARs Relationship and Rule of Law in China*, Beijing: Tsinghua University Press, 2002; *Constitutional Review in China*, Beijing: China University of Political Science and Law Press, 2004.

Wu Shuchen (Beijing, China, 1949) is Professor at the Legal School of Beijiing University and, since 1997, Senior Judge and Vice-President of the Second Intermediate People's Court of Beijing. In 1999 he was Visiting Scholar at the University of Waseda (Japan). His publications include *The Traditional Culture of Law in China*, Beijing: Press of Beijing University, 1994 [in Chinese]; *The Collection of Wu Shuchen's Publications on Law*, Beijing: Press of Chinese University of Political Science and Law, 2003 [in Chinese].

Danilo Zolo (Rijeka, Croatia, 1936) is Professor of Philosophy of Law at the University of Florence. He has been Visiting Fellow at Boston University, the University of Cambridge, Harvard University and the University of Princeton. In 1993 he was Jemolo Fellow at Nuffield College, Oxford. He delivered courses of lectures at universities of Argentina, Brazil, and Mexico. His publications in English include *Reflexive Epistemology*, Dordrecht-Boston: Kluwer, 1989; *Democracy and Complexity*, Cambridge: Polity Press, 1992; *Cosmopolis: Prospects for World Government*, Cambridge: Polity Press, 1997; *Invoking Humanity: War, Law and Global Order*, London/New York: Continuum International, 2001; *Globalization: An Overview,* Essex, European consortium for Political Research, 2007.

INDEX

[*]This index contains the names of authors cited in the text and also those briefly discussed or frequently cited in the notes.

Abd al-Jabbar al-Qadi, 524
Abd al-Razzaq al-Sanhuri, 547
Abendroth W., 148, 259
Abu Bakr, 531
Ackerman B., 60, 213, 221–224, 227–228, 235, 406, 420
Adams J., 205–207
Ahuja Sangeeta, 601
al-Badri Shaykh Yusif, 554
al-Basri Hasan, 521
Alexy R., 66
Alfonso XIII, 467, 492
al-Ghannouchi R., 519, 532–534, 537–538, 540, 542
Allegretti U., 497, 512
Allen C.K., 60, 176, 178, 197
al-Mutawakil, 525
Alpa G., 148–149, 197, 352, 386
Amar, 225
an-Na'im A.A., 529, 530
Anwar Ibrahim, 570, 575
Appadurai A., 598
Appleby J., 230
Arendt H., 205
Aretin von J.C.F., 139, 242–243, 256
Aristotle, 75–76, 139, 205, 350, 390–393, 412–413, 415, 643
Arthur J., 233–234
Aung San Suu Kyi, 577, 580
Austin J., 40, 102, 104, 161, 170–172, 187, 192, 194–195, 197, 326, 332, 543
Avenarius R., 112

Bähr von O., 6, 94–95, 140, 186, 246–247, 255, 257–258, 355
Baratta A., 58–59, 148, 197
Barbalet J., 37–8, 69
Barbera A., 259
Barendt E., 194
Barile P., 66
Barrera y Luyando A., 467, 469, 482
Barret-Kriegel B., 74
Battaglia F., 128
Bäumlin R., 259
Bauman Z., 591
Baxi U., 597, 605–607, 612–613, 680
Beccaria C., 190–191, 508
Beck U., 52, 68, 70, 368
Bee T.K.T., 574–575
Benoist C., 269
Bentham J., 323–333, 351, 597
Berlin I., 64, 414
Bermejo F., 486
Bernatzik E., 300, 316
Berthélemy H., 272, 288
Beseler G., 244, 257
Beteille A., 600, 605–606, 611, 613–614

Bhagwati P.N., 601
Bickel A., 222, 235
Bisharah A., 519, 540
Blackstone W., 9, 60, 82, 154, 164, 177, 190–191, 197–198
Bluntschli J.K., 245, 257
Bobbio N., 4, 19, 32, 37–39, 48, 52–53, 57–58, 62–63, 65–67, 69–71, 146–147, 317, 350, 400–401
Böckenförde E.-W., 59, 62, 66, 139, 253, 259, 360, 365–366, 368–369, 384
Bodin J., 76–77, 262
Bonald de L., 262
Bossuet J.B., 262
Bourdieu P., 48, 69
Bracton H., 60
Bradley, judge, 379
Bradwell M., 379
Brennan T., 589, 611
Brown N.J., 545
Bryce J., 105–106, 111, 148
Bull H., 42, 67
Burdeau G., 276, 286
Burgh J., 205
Burke E., 60, 83, 159, 204, 429

Calamandrei P., 130, 147
Caravita B., 318–319
Carbonnier J., 290
Carré de Malberg R., 13, 15, 34, 61, 62, 109–111, 118, 142, 265–266, 271, 287–289
Carrino A., 61, 66, 142–144, 675, 677
Carrol L., 178
Cassese A., 66, 367
Cassese S., 59, 141, 672
Cassirer E., 143
Castiglione D., 65, 517, 540
Chen A.H., 65, 644–645
Chevallier J., 61, 138, 281, 286–290
Ci Xi, 632
Claverie E., 555, 561
Cohen J., 65
Cohn B., 592, 611–612
Coke E., 9, 17, 60, 82, 105, 153, 158, 176, 178, 189, 193, 196, 197, 231
Colebrook H.T., 594
Condorcet J.A.N., 84, 139
Confucius, 576, 580, 624, 630
Conrad D., 603–604, 613, 680
Constant B., 6, 87–88, 140, 264, 287
Coomaraswamy A.K., 590, 611
Cordero Torres J.M., 67, 499, 502, 507, 672
Cornwalis W., 594–595
Cortés H., 480
Costa P., 58–61, 63, 73, 138, 146, 186, 422
Craig P.P., 58, 61, 65, 138, 142, 149, 192
Crespo C., 505–507, 509

Dahlmann F.C., 244
Dahrendorf R., 4, 32, 57, 351
Das V., 609
de Acosta J., 482, 504–505
De Foe D., 565, 585
De Q., Walker G., 169, 194
De Staël Madame de, 87
Deng Xiaoping, 639, 655
Dezalay Y., 369
Dhavan R., 601–602, 606, 612–613
Dicey A.V., 5, 7–10, 13, 17, 40, 46, 57, 59, 60, 62–64, 67, 102–109, 115, 133, 135, 141–142, 153, 161–199, 239–240, 254, 366, 408
Dirks N., 595, 612
Disraeli B., 160
Dogliani M., 59, 61–62, 318, 437, 675
Duez P., 269–270, 287–288
Duguit L., 111, 118, 142, 267–268, 273, 287–289, 672

Durkheim E., 274
Dworkin R.M., 4, 56–57, 70, 213, 216–221, 227–228, 234, 237

Eisenmann C.,269, 279
Elster J., 517, 525–526, 533, 539–540, 676
Ely J., 60, 231, 235
Esmein A., 267–268, 274–275
Esposito J.L., 63, 538

Falk R., 42, 67
Fassò G., 65, 148, 426, 437
Favoreu L., 278–279, 289–290
Feinberg J., 400, 418
Ferguson A., 28, 386, 397–398, 417, 429
Fernando L., 585
Ferrajoli L., 34, 57–58, 62–64, 66–70, 138, 323, 365
Ferrarese M.R., 69, 71, 351, 420, 680
Filangieri G., 88, 140
Finnis J., 138, 420
Fioravanti M., 60–62, 69, 138, 140–141, 143, 148–149, 253, 314–316, 318, 366, 437, 439, 499
Forsthoff E., 61, 132, 146, 148, 256, 366
Foucault M., 611
Franklin B., 204, 223
Fukuyama F., 582, 586
Fuller C., 602, 613

Galanter M., 600, 612–614
Galli C., 58, 63, 64, 145
Gallieni J.-S., 480, 503
Gallino L., 68, 369, 680
Gandhi I., 569
Gandhi M.K., 600, 611
Gandhi R., 604
Garzoni F., 5, 58
Gemei H., 549, 550, 560
Gentile G., 128, 147
Gény F., 269
Gerber von C.F., 95–97, 99, 101, 141, 247–250, 258, 261, 315
Geuna M., 231, 414
Ghai Y., 566, 585
Ghannouchi, 519, 532–534, 537, 538, 540, 542
Ghazali, 522, 540
Giannotti, D., 392
Gierke von O., 94, 96, 97, 101, 108, 141, 289
Giorgio III, 66, 293, 683
Giovanni Paolo II, 47, 128
Girault A., 503
Girling J., 582, 586
Gladstone W.E., 160
Glendon M.A., 216, 234
Gneist von R., 6, 258, 314, 355
Goodman N., 199
Gordon J., 205
Graziosi M., 63, 386
Grimm D., 252, 256–259, 319, 352, 384, 408, 420
Guang Xu, Emperor, 626, 630–632
Guastini R., 64, 366
Guicciardini F., 391–392, 394–395, 415
Guizot F.-P.-G., 87, 263
Gurvitch G., 276
Gutmann A., 220, 234–235

Häberle P., 362, 365, 369
Habermas J., 4, 32, 42, 57, 65, 67–68, 220, 234, 361, 369, 374–375, 385, 399, 400, 402–403, 405, 413, 417–420, 597, 610, 612
Hai Rui, 579
Hale M., 82, 176–180, 183–184, 197, 685
Hamilton A., 10, 232
Harrington J., 391, 393–394, 398, 413–414
Hart H.L.A., 417–418, 543, 559
Harvie C., 159–160, 191
Hastings W., 593–594, 599

Hauriou M., 117–119, 144–145, 267–271, 287–88
Hay D., 153–157, 190
Hayek F., von, 24, 45, 64, 68, 133, 136, 148, 169, 194, 202, 364, 369, 408, 421, 427–439, 671
Hazard J., 567
Hearn W.E., 7, 59, 191–192
Hegde S., 608, 613
Hegel G.W.F., 125, 147, 365
Held D., 67
Held J., 257
Heller H., 120–123, 132, 134, 145, 148
Hello C.-G., 264, 287
Hesse K., 240, 252–253, 259
Hirst P., 68, 395
Hitler A., 126
Hobbes T., 78, 82, 172, 231, 325–328, 350–351, 393, 401, 574
Höffe O., 69, 362, 367, 369, 420
Hofmann H., 139, 238, 253, 366
Holmes S., 66–67, 226, 235, 418
Honneth A., 385, 402, 418
Hourani G., 523, 541
Howe A., 376, 385
Huber M., 254, 256–257, 316
Humboldt W., 6, 11, 91
Hume D., 42, 429, 574
Hutcheson F., 82
Huxley T.H., 623

Jefferson T., 10, 84, 205–210, 221, 230–232
Jellinek G., 11, 12, 40, 60–62, 67, 98–101, 108–109, 112, 135, 141, 186, 247–250, 258, 261, 266, 273, 296–297, 299, 303, 315–316, 318
Jenks E., 623
Jennings I., 142, 175, 180, 194–195, 197, 254
Jèze G., 273, 288
Jhering R., von, 11, 56, 61, 70, 98–101, 110, 141, 146, 186, 261
Jiang Jieshi, 634
Jiang Zemin, 654, 670
Jones W., 593, 594, 596, 599

Kägi W., 250, 259, 316
Kahn P., 60, 232
Kang Youwei, 625, 630, 632
Kant I., 139, 241, 248, 253, 255, 390–391, 412–413, 434, 539, 589, 610, 677
Karve I., 605
Kaufmann E., 58, 117, 138, 144, 254–255
Kelsen H., 34, 47, 53, 69, 111–116, 118, 122, 135, 142–144, 186, 189, 269, 314–319, 333, 349–351, 357, 366, 367
Kennedy D., 217, 234, 377, 385
Kern F., 355
Khatami, 532, 537, 542
Khong C.O., 579, 586
Kim Dae Jung, 576, 585
Koellreutter O., 124–125, 127, 145–146
Koh Tiong Bee T., 574–575
Kruman M.W., 229
Kunig P., 58, 365

Laband P., 96–97, 141, 247–249, 258, 261, 273, 286, 297–298, 315
Laboulaye E., 264, 287
Labra de R.M., 476–477, 490, 499–500, 503, 508
Lane J.-E., 517, 527, 540
Lange H., 5, 58
La Torre M., 141, 418, 502, 511
Laygorri E.G., 486
Le Bret C., 262, 286
Lee Kuan Yew, 567, 574–575, 585–586
Leoni B., 24, 45, 59–60, 64, 68, 133, 136, 148, 408–410, 420–421, 426–427, 429, 435–439, 678

Leopold, King of Belgium, 472, 476, 497, 511
Lewis B., 519, 532, 540–541
Liang Qichao, 625, 628–630, 632
Lin Zexu, 622, 631
Lingat R., 588, 592, 611, 613
Liu Huaqiu, 583, 670
Locke J., 12, 61, 78, 81, 84, 169, 185, 204–205, 209, 230–231, 238, 248, 253, 350, 416, 574
Lolme De J.-L., 104
Lopez de Oñate F., 130, 147
López Perea E., 469, 498
Losano M.G., 65, 141
Luciani M., 317–318
Luhmann N., 24, 61–64, 68, 356, 362, 366, 369, 438
Luigi XV, 4, 34, 58, 66, 68, 70, 365, 400

Mably G., Bonnot de, 88
Macaulay T., 593, 596–597
MacCormick D.N., 57, 60, 62, 138–139, 198, 237–238, 253, 417, 678
Mach E., 112
Machiavelli N., 387, 389, 414–416, 420
Madison J., 10–11, 60, 202, 204, 207–209, 225, 230, 232, 332, 642
Mahathir M., 573, 575, 585
Mahmoud Taha, 529
Mallat C., 547, 559
Manfredi C.P., 236
Manu, 591, 594
Mao Zedong, 634, 636, 639, 644–645
Marcos F., 569
Maritain J., 131
Mariz Maia L., 70
Marshall J., 11, 84, 202, 208, 230, 232
Marshall T.H., 25, 38, 45–46, 64
Marx K., 28, 64, 574
Matteucci N., 58, 68, 365–366, 678
Mawardi, 531–532, 541
Mawdudi, 520, 527–528, 532–533, 535–536, 540–542
Mayer A.E., 528, 535, 541–542, 681
Mayer A.J., 496, 511
Mayer D.N., 231
Mayer O., 11, 61, 140, 258, 298
McKibbin R., 160, 191
McKinnon C., 376, 385
Mencius, 624
Merkl A., 114, 144, 298, 305, 313–315, 317, 319
Michelman F.I., 56, 70–71, 235, 400, 403–404, 406–407, 418–420
Michoud L., 272–276, 288–289
Mill J.S., 165, 193, 593, 597, 623
Minow M., 373–374, 377, 385
Mohl von R., 6, 61, 90, 92–93, 101, 140, 237, 242, 253, 255–256, 258, 261, 286, 355
Moller Okin S., 379, 385
Mommsen T., 244, 257
Montesquieu de C.-L., 6, 26, 78, 136, 185–189, 198, 202, 238, 355, 623
Moreau J.N., 262
Morgenthau H., 41, 67
Mounier E., 131
Mubarak H., 553
Munro H., 594–595
Mussolini B., 333

Nair J., 599, 612–613
Nandy A., 611
Narayanan K.R., 607, 613
Nehru J., 567, 600–601, 606
Neumann F., 122, 138, 145, 238–239, 254, 365, 369
Ng M., 584–586
Noske H., 139

O'Donnell L., 472
Oakeshott M., 202
Olivier-Martin F., 286
Orlando V.E., 7, 59, 109, 135, 141, 147

Paine T., 10, 84, 160, 206
Paley W., 429
Palombella G., 234–235, 439
Panunzio S., 5, 58, 127–128, 146
Parashar A., 596, 603–604, 612–613
Patten C., 577
Peel R., 160
Perry M., 234
Peters R., 549, 559–560
Pettit Ph., 205–206, 231, 405, 413–414, 419
Picard E., 284, 290
Pitch T., 63, 376, 385–386
Pizzorno A., 69, 359, 368
Placidus J.W., 87, 255
Platone, 686
Plutarch, 591
Pocock J.G.A., 60, 229–231, 391–393, 398, 412–414, 417
Pol Pot, 571
Portalis J.-E.-M., 54
Posada Gonzales A., 477–479
Posner R.A., 60, 70, 418, 678
Postema G.J., 176, 177, 197
Primus R.A., 230, 231
Puchta G.F., 12
Pufendorf S., 326

Qadri, Pasha, 547

Radbruch G., 148, 197, 253, 673
Ramos Izquierdo L., 469, 489–491, 499, 501–502, 505, 507, 509, 511
Ramsey A., 204
Rawls J., 52, 66, 361, 369, 420, 610, 678
Raynaud P., 140, 142, 235, 674
Raz J., 58, 65, 138, 417
Rhodes C., 480
Rials S., 286, 291
Richelieu A.-J., 262
Robespierre M., 80, 91, 139
Rodotà S., 368–369, 386, 681
Rodriguez Sampedro F., 470, 472
Romano S., 67, 141, 477, 487, 497, 501–504, 674
Roosevelt F.D., 223, 419
Rorty R., 420, 539, 542, 679
Rosmini A., 89, 140
Ross A., 70, 417
Rotteck von C., 241–243, 255, 256
Roy, R., 611
Royer-Collard P.L., 263
Rückert J., 508
Rusconi G.E., 368, 679

Saavedra D., 484
Said E.S., 504–505
Saint-Just L.-A.-L., 80
Salas D., 283, 290
Salvatore A., 548, 559–560, 681
Sartori G., 47, 69, 148, 404
Saberwal S., 605, 613, 680
Savigny von F., 12, 16, 332
Scalia A., 31, 58, 65, 213–216, 221, 233, 234, 679
Scelle G., 276
Schacht J., 540, 541
Schmitt C., 5, 6, 12–13, 16, 21, 54, 58, 61–63, 67, 70, 120, 124–127, 132–133, 143, 145–146, 148, 313–314, 356, 366–367, 676–679
Schmittener F., 242, 256
Schumpeter J.A., 32, 404, 537, 542
Schweizer A., 58, 315, 480
Sen A., 420, 586
Sidney A., 204–205, 231, 586
Sieyès E.J., 14, 23, 79, 81, 86, 263
Sihanouk re, 567
Skinner Q., 393, 397, 414, 416–417, 479
Smart C., 63, 382, 386
Smith A., 429, 623, 689
Smith R.M., 231, 232
Smith R.S., 612
Sobota K., 58, 365, 366, 679
Sordi B., 140, 143, 148, 314–317, 674

Spencer H., 623
Spinoza B., 20
Sri Aurobindo, 590, 611
Stahl F.J., 6, 90, 91–95, 125, 129, 135, 140, 241, 254–255, 259, 261, 286, 674
Stalin I.V., 636
Stammler R., 117
Stein von L., 237, 247, 253, 258, 674
Stokes E., 593, 611–612
Stolleis M., 58, 138–141, 145, 247, 255–256, 258, 365, 674
Stuart Mill J., 165, 264, 623
Suárez F., 479
Sukarno A., 571
Sun Yat-sen, 623, 626
Sunstein C.R., 60, 66, 225–227, 234–235, 407, 418, 420, 517, 540, 679

Tay A., 585, 586
Taylor C., 375, 413
Teitgen P.-H., 278
Tezner F., 299–300, 314, 316
Thoma R., 259, 298, 315, 674
Thomasius C., 326
Thompson C.B., 231–232
Thompson D., 235, 676
Thompson E.P., 155, 190, 191
Tocqueville de A., 10, 87, 195, 269, 287
Trenchard J., 205
Treves R., 147
Tribe L., 232, 233
Troper M., 61, 138, 144, 149, 281, 286, 290–291
Tucker J., 429
Tully J., 397, 416–417
Tung Chee Wah, 575
Turabi H., 520, 532–534, 538, 540, 542

Unger R.M., 61, 66, 70, 213, 233

Vaihinger H., 112
Vattel de E., 41, 457, 466
Verdross A., 114
Villey M., 62, 365
Vitoria de F., 479, 505
Victoria Eugenia, Queen, 467
Voll J., 538, 542
Volpicelli A., 128, 147

Wacquant L.J.D., 48, 66, 69
Waldron J., 58, 60, 224, 235, 417, 439
Walz G.A., 124–125, 146, 505
Washbrook D., 594, 612
Watt W.M., 525, 541
Weber M., 256, 404, 590
Wei Jinsheng, 638
Wei Yuan, 622, 631, 638
Weiler J.H.H., 70, 351
Welcker C., 139, 241, 253, 255–256
Wendell Holmes O., 58, 65, 233, 641
Williams R.A., 466, 503–504
Wiryono, 581
Wolgast E.H., 374, 385, 418
Wolter U., 503, 505, 508
Wood G., 229, 230, 234

Xun Zi, 617, 630

Yan Buke, 629, 632
Yan Fu, 623, 631
Young I.M., 381, 385–386
Yuezhi Xiong, 631–632

Zachariä H.A., 256
Zagrebelsky G., 62, 65–66, 69, 149, 229, 318, 352, 369, 384, 386, 420
Zanetti G., 61, 63, 259, 385
Zhengbang Wen, 643–645
Zoepfl H., 243, 256

Law and Philosophy Library

1. E. Bulygin, J.-L. Gardies and I. Niiniluoto (eds.): *Man, Law and Modern Forms of Life.* With an Introduction by M.D. Bayles. 1985 ISBN 90-277-1869-5
2. W. Sadurski: *Giving Desert Its Due.* Social Justice and Legal Theory. 1985 ISBN 90-277-1941-1
3. N. MacCormick and O.Weinberger: *An Institutional Theory of Law.* New Approaches to Legal Positivism. 1986 ISBN 90-277-2079-7
4. A. Aarnio: *The Rational as Reasonable.* A Treatise on Legal Justification. 1987 ISBN 90-277-2276-5
5. M.D. Bayles: *Principles of Law.* A Normative Analysis. 1987 ISBN 90-277-2412-1; Pb: 90-277-2413-X
6. A. Soeteman: *Logic in Law.* Remarks on Logic and Rationality in Normative Reasoning, Especially in Law. 1989 ISBN 0-7923-0042-4
7. C.T. Sistare: *Responsibility and Criminal Liability.* 1989 ISBN 0-7923-0396-2
8. A. Peczenik: *On Law and Reason.* 1989 ISBN 0-7923-0444-6
9. W. Sadurski: *Moral Pluralism and Legal Neutrality.* 1990 ISBN 0-7923-0565-5
10. M.D. Bayles: *Procedural Justice.* Allocating to Individuals. 1990 ISBN 0-7923-0567-1
11. P. Nerhot (ed.): *Law, Interpretation and Reality.* Essays in Epistemology, Hermeneutics and Jurisprudence. 1990 ISBN 0-7923-0593-0
12. A.W. Norrie: *Law, Ideology and Punishment.* Retrieval and Critique of the Liberal Ideal of Criminal Justice. 1991 ISBN 0-7923-1013-6
13. P. Nerhot (ed.): *Legal Knowledge and Analogy.* Fragments of Legal Epistemology, Hermeneutics and Linguistics. 1991 ISBN 0-7923-1065-9
14. O. Weinberger: *Law, Institution and Legal Politics.* Fundamental Problems of Legal Theory and Social Philosophy. 1991 ISBN 0-7923-1143-4
15. J. Wróblewski: *The Judicial Application of Law.* Edited by Z. Bańkowski and N. MacCormick. 1992 ISBN 0-7923-1569-3
16. T. Wilhelmsson: *Critical Studies in Private Law.* A Treatise on Need-Rational Principles in Modern Law. 1992 ISBN 0-7923-1659-2
17. M.D. Bayles: *Hart's Legal Philosophy.* An Examination. 1992 ISBN 0-7923-1981-8
18. D.W.P. Ruiter: *Institutional Legal Facts.* Legal Powers and their Effects. 1993 ISBN 0-7923-2441-2
19. J. Schonsheck: *On Criminalization.* An Essay in the Philosophy of the Criminal Law. 1994 ISBN 0-7923-2663-6
20. R.P. Malloy and J. Evensky (eds.): *Adam Smith and the Philosophy of Law and Economics.* 1994 ISBN 0-7923-2796-9
21. Z. Bańkowski, I. White and U. Hahn (eds.): *Informatics and the Foundations of Legal Reasoning.* 1995 ISBN 0-7923-3455-8
22. E. Lagerspetz: *The Opposite Mirrors.* An Essay on the Conventionalist Theory of Institutions. 1995 ISBN 0-7923-3325-X

Law and Philosophy Library

23. M. van Hees: *Rights and Decisions.* Formal Models of Law and Liberalism. 1995 ISBN 0-7923-3754-9
24. B. Anderson: *"Discovery" in Legal Decision-Making.* 1996 ISBN 0-7923-3981-9
25. S. Urbina: *Reason, Democracy, Society.* A Study on the Basis of Legal Thinking. 1996 ISBN 0-7923-4262-3
26. E. Attwooll: *The Tapestry of the Law.* Scotland, Legal Culture and Legal Theory. 1997 ISBN 0-7923-4310-7
27. J.C. Hage: *Reasoning with Rules.* An Essay on Legal Reasoning and Its Underlying Logic. 1997 ISBN 0-7923-4325-5
28. R.A. Hillman: *The Richness of Contract Law.* An Analysis and Critique of Contemporary Theories of Contract Law. 1997 ISBN 0-7923-4336-0; 0-7923-5063-4 (Pb)
29. C. Wellman: *An Approach to Rights.* Studies in the Philosophy of Law and Morals. 1997 ISBN 0-7923-4467-7
30. B. van Roermund: *Law, Narrative and Reality.* An Essay in Intercepting Politics. 1997 ISBN 0-7923-4621-1
31. I. Ward: *Kantianism, Postmodernism and Critical Legal Thought.* 1997 ISBN 0-7923-4745-5
32. H. Prakken: *Logical Tools for Modelling Legal Argument.* A Study of Defeasible Reasoning in Law. 1997 ISBN 0-7923-4776-5
33. T. May: *Autonomy, Authority and Moral Responsibility.* 1998 ISBN 0-7923-4851-6
34. M. Atienza and J.R. Manero: *A Theory of Legal Sentences.* 1998 ISBN 0-7923-4856-7
35. E.A. Christodoulidis: *Law and Reflexive Politics.* 1998 ISBN 0-7923-4954-7
36. L.M.M. Royakkers: *Extending Deontic Logic for the Formalisation of Legal Rules.* 1998 ISBN 0-7923-4982-2
37. J.J. Moreso: *Legal Indeterminacy and Constitutional Interpretation.* 1998 ISBN 0-7923-5156-8
38. W. Sadurski: *Freedom of Speech and Its Limits.* 1999 ISBN 0-7923-5523-7
39. J. Wolenski (ed.): *Kazimierz Opalek Selected Papers in Legal Philosophy.* 1999 ISBN 0-7923-5732-9
40. H.P. Visser 't Hooft: *Justice to Future Generations and the Environment.* 1999 ISBN 0-7923-5756-6
41. L.J. Wintgens (ed.): *The Law in Philosophical Perspectives.* My Philosophy of Law. 1999 ISBN 0-7923-5796-5
42. A.R. Lodder: *DiaLaw.* On Legal Justification and Dialogical Models of Argumentation. 1999 ISBN 0-7923-5830-9
43. C. Redondo: *Reasons for Action and the Law.* 1999 ISBN 0-7923-5912-7
44. M. Friedman, L. May, K. Parsons and J. Stiff (eds.): *Rights and Reason.* Essays in Honor of Carl Wellman. 2000 ISBN 0-7923-6198-9
45. G.C. Christie: *The Notion of an Ideal Audience in Legal Argument.* 2000 ISBN 0-7923-6283-7

Law and Philosophy Library

46. R.S. Summers: *Essays in Legal Theory.* 2000 ISBN 0-7923-6367-1
47. M. van Hees: *Legal Reductionism and Freedom.* 2000 ISBN 0-7923-6491-0
48. R. Gargarella: *The Scepter of Reason.* Public Discussion and Political Radicalism in the Origins of Constitutionalism. 2000 ISBN 0-7923-6508-9
49. M. Iglesias Vila: *Facing Judicial Discretion.* Legal Knowledge and Right Answers Revisited. 2001 ISBN 0-7923-6778-2
50. M. Kiikeri: *Comparative Legal Reasoning and European Law.* 2001 ISBN 0-7923-6884-3
51. A.J. Menéndez: *Justifying Taxes.* Some Elements for a General Theory of Democratic Tax Law. 2001 ISBN 0-7923-7052-X
52. W.E. Conklin: *The Invisible Origins of Legal Positivism.* A Re-Reading of a Tradition. 2001 ISBN 0-7923-7101-1
53. Z. Bańkowski: *Living Lawfully.* Love in Law and Law in Love. 2001 ISBN 0-7923-7180-1
54. A.N. Shytov: *Conscience and Love in Making Judicial Decisions.* 2001 ISBN 1-4020-0168-1
55. D.W.P. Ruiter: *Legal Institutions.* 2001 ISBN 1-4020-0186-X

Volumes 56–63 were published by Kluwer Law International.

---

56. G. den Hartogh: *Mutual Expectations.* A Conventionalist Theory of Law. 2002 ISBN 90-411-1796-2
57. W.L. Robison (ed.): *The Legal Essays of Michael Bayles.* 2002 ISBN 90-411-1835-7
58. U. Bindreiter: *Why Grundnorm?* A Treatise on the Implications of Kelsen's Doctrine. 2002 ISBN 90-411-1867-5
59. S. Urbina: *Legal Method and the Rule of Law.* 2002 ISBN 90-411-1870-5
60. M. Baurmann: *The Market of Virtue.* Morality and Commitment in a Liberal Society. 2002 ISBN 90-411-1874-8
61. G. Zanetti: *Political Friendship and the Good Life.* Two Liberal Arguments against Perfectionism. 2002 ISBN 90-411-1881-0
62. W. Sadurski (ed.): *Constitutional Justice, East and West.* 2002 ISBN 90-411-1883-7
63. S. Taekema: *The Concept of Ideals in Legal Theory.* 2003 ISBN 90-411-1971-X
64. J. Raitio: *The Principle of Legal Certainty in EC Law.* 2003 ISBN 1-4020-1217-9
65. E. Santoro: *Autonomy, Freedom and Rights.* A Critique of Liberal Subjectivity. 2003 ISBN 1-4020-1404-X
66. S. Eng: *Analysis of Dislagreement – with particular reference to Law and Legal Theory.* 2003 ISBN 1-4020-1490-2
67. D. González Lagier: *The Paradoxes of Action.* (Human Action, Law and Philosophy). 2003 ISBN Hb-1-4020-1661-1
68. R. Zimmerling: *Influence and Power.* Variations on a Messy Theme. 2004 ISBN Hb-1-4020-2986-1

Law and Philosophy Library

69. A. Stranieri and J. Zeleznikow (eds.): *Knowledge Discovery from Legal Databases.* 2005 ISBN 1-4020-3036-3
70. J. Hage: *Studies in Legal Logic.* 2005 ISBN 1-4020-3517-9
71. C. Wellman: *Medical Law and Moral Rights.* 2005 ISBN 1-4020-3751-1
72. T. Meisels: *Territorial Rights.* 2005 ISBN 1-4020-3822-4
73. G.W. Rainbolt: *The Concept of Rights.* 2005 ISBN 1-4020-3976-X
74. O. Ezra: *Moral Dilemmas in Real Life.* Current Issues in Applied Ethics. 2006 ISBN 1-4020-4103-9
75. N.T. Casals: *Group Rights as Human Rights.* A Liberal Approach to Multiculturalism. 2006 ISBN 1-4020-4208-6
76. C. Michelon Jr.: *Being Apart from Reasons.* The Role of Reasons in Public and Private Moral Decision-Making. 2006 ISBN 1-4020-4282-5
77. A.J. Menendez and E.O. Eriksen (eds): Arguing Fundamental Rights. 2006 ISBN 1-4020-4918-8
78. J. Stelmach and B. Brozek: Methods of Legal Reasoning. 2006 ISBN 1-4020-4936-6
79. M. La Torre: *Constitutionalism and Legal Reasoning*. A New Paradigm for the Concept of Law. 2007 ISBN 978-1-4020-5594-2
80. P. Costa and D. Zolo (eds.): *The Rule of Law*. History, Theory and Criticism. 2007 ISBN 978-1-4020-5744-1

Breinigsville, PA USA
30 November 2009

228223BV00009B/25/A

9 781402 057441